THE BLACKWELL HANDBOOK OF ENTREPRENEURSHIP

Handbooks in Management

Forthcoming

Edwin Locke
The Blackwell Handbook of Organizational Behavior

Edwin Locke
The Blackwell Handbook of Strategy

Michael Hitt, Edward Freeman and Jeffrey Harrison
The Blackwell Handbook of Strategy

Martin Gannon and Karen Newman
The Blackwell Handbook of Cross-cultural Management

Robert E. Cole, Barrie G. Dale and Noriaki Kano
The Blackwell Handbook of Total Quality Management

THE BLACKWELL HANDBOOK OF ENTREPRENEURSHIP

Edited by

DONALD L. SEXTON
Nova Southeastern University And
Kauffman Center for Entrepreneurial Leadership

HANS LANDSTRÖM
Halmstad University and
Bodö Graduate School Of Business

in conjunction with

The School of Business and Entrepreneurship at
Nova Southeastern University

Copyright © Blackwell Publishers Ltd 2000

Editorial apparatus and arrangement copyright © Donald L. Sexton and Hans Landström 2000

First published 2000

2 4 6 8 10 9 7 5 3 1

Blackwell Publishers Ltd
108 Cowley Road
Oxford OX4 1JF
UK

Blackwell Publishers Inc.
350 Main Street
Malden, MA 02148
USA

British Library Cataloguing in Publication Data

A CIP catalogue record for this book is available from the British Library.

Library of Congress Cataloging-in-Publication Data has been applied for

ISBN 0-631-21573-5 (hbk)

Typeset in 10 on 12 pt Baskerville by Ace Filmsetting Ltd, Frome, Somerset
Printed in Great Britain by MPG Books Ltd, Bodmin, Cornwall

This book is printed on acid-free paper.

Contents

List of Figures

List of Tables

Contributors, Sponsors and Editors

CONTRIBUTORS

Howard Aldrich is the Kenan Professor of Sociology, the Director of the Industrial Relations Curriculum and an Adjunct Professor of Business at the University of North Carolina at Chapel Hill.

Raphael Amit is the Peter Wall Distinguished Professor of Business and Director of the W. Maurice Young Entrepreneurship and Venture Capital Research Centre at the University of British Columbia.

J.B. (Ben) Arbaugh is an Associate Professor of Business Administration at the University of Wisconsin at Oskosh.

David Audretsch holds the Ameritech Chair of Economic Development and is the Director of the Institute for Development Strategies at Indiana University.

Erkko Autio is an Associate Professor of Entrepreneurship at the Helsinki University of Technology and a Visiting Research Fellow at London Business School.

James Brander is the Asia–Pacific Professor of International Business and Public Policy at the University of British Columbia.

Sue Birley is the Director of Research and a Professor of Entrepreneurship at the Imperial College.

S. Michael Camp is the Director of the National Center for Entrepreneurship Research at the Ewing Marion Kauffman Foundation.

Arnold Cooper is the Louis A. Weil, Jr. Professor of Management at Purdue University and the 1997 recipient of the International Award for Entrepreneurship and Small Business Research.

Per Davidsson is a Professor in Entrepreneurship at Jonkoping International Business School, Sweden.

Dennis De is a Professor at Reutlingen University and a former Senior Researcher at the Institut fur Mittelstandsforchung, Bonn, Germany.

William Dennis, Jr. is a Senior Research Fellow and Research Director at the National Federation of Independent Business Education Foundation in Washington, DC.

Rik Donckels is a Professor of Economics at the Catholic University Brussels, Belgium.

Timothy Folta is an Assistant Professor of Management at Purdue University.

Selcuk Gulhan is a graduate student in European Public Administration at Erasmus University, Rotterdam.

Richard Harrison is a Professor of Management Studies and Director of the Center for Entrepreneurship at the University of Aberdeen, Scotland. He also holds the Chair in Strategy and Organizational Development at the University of Ulster, Northern Ireland.

Michael Hitt holds the Paul M. and Rosalie Robertson Chair in Business Administration at Texas A and M University. He is a Past President of the Academy of Management and has been selected to receive an Honorary Doctorate from the Universidad Carlos III de Madrid.

Robert van der Horst is the manager of the International Department at the EIM Small Business Research and Consultancy, Zoetermeer, The Netherlands.

Frank Hoy is Dean of the College of Business Administration at the University of Texas at El Paso and holds UTEP's endowed Chair for the Study of Trade in the Americas.

R. Duane Ireland holds the Curtis Hankamer Chair in Entrepreneurship and is the Director of Entrepreneurial Studies at Baylor University.

Bengt Johannisson is a Professor of Entrepreneurship and Business Development at Lund University and Vaxjo University in Sweden. With Hans Landström he founded the Scandinavian Institute for Research in Entrepreneurship (SIRE).

Sophie Manigart is a Professor of Corporate Finance and co-program director of the financial MBA program at the University of Ghent in Belgium.

Colin Mason is a Professor of Economic Geography at the University of Southampton, UK.

Josef Mugler is a Professor and Head of the Department of Small Business Management at Vienna University of Economics and Business Administration, Austria.

Andre Nijsen is the Manager of the Department of Labor Market and Income at the EIM Small Business Research and Consultancy, Zoetermeer, The Netherlands.

David Purdy is the Deputy Director of the International Franchise Research Centre at the University of Westminster, London, UK.

Harry Sapienza is an Associate Professor of Management at the University of South Carolina and a Visiting Professor at London Business School.

John Stanworth is a Professor and Director of the International Franchise Research Center at the University of Westminster, London, UK.

Simon Stockley is a Doctoral Candidate in the Management School at the Imperial College of Science, Technology and Medicine, London.

David Storey is a Professor and Director of the Small and Medium Sized Entrepreneurship Center at the University of Warwick, UK and the 1998 recipient of the International Award for Entrepreneurship and Small Business Research.

Mark Weaver is a Professor of Management, Director of the Small Business Institute, and Coordinator of the Entrepreneurship and Small Company Management Program at the University of Alabama.

Johan Wiklund is a Research Fellow at Jonkoping International Business School, Sweden.

Christoph Zott is an Assistant Professor in Entrepreneurship at INSEAD.

ABOUT THE SPONSOR

Nova Southeastern University is a nonprofit, fully accredited, co-education institution founded in 1964 as Nova University. In 1994 Nova University merged with Southeastern University of Health Sciences to form Nova Southeastern University. Nova Southeastern is the largest private, independent institution of higher education in southeastern United States and one of the twenty largest private institutions nationally.

The School of Business and Entrepreneurship offers masters and doctoral degrees in business administration, international business, public administration plus a number of other business related areas. Programs are offered under flexible program scheduling and in different formats to meet the needs of its students.

The goal of the masters division is to produce managers who can cope successfully with the rapidly changing circumstances of today's business world.

The doctoral division offers candidates an opportunity to pursue studies in an environment that promotes the application of advanced studies to the problems of business, industry, education and government.

About the Editors

Hans Landström is a Professor of Entrepreneurship and Small Business Management at Halmstad University in Sweden. He also holds a chair in Entrepreneurship at Bodo Graduate School of Business in Norway.

He co-founded the Scandinavian Institute for Research in Entrepreneurship (SIRE) with Bengt Johannisson and serves as the research coordinator.

Dr. Landström received his doctorate in Industrial Economics from the Lund Institute of Technology in Sweden. He has taught graduate and undergraduate courses in entrepreneurship, innovation management, organization theory and financial management. His research interests include the formal and informal venture capital market and the development of young technology-based firms.

Dr. Landström is the Chairman of the Research Committee and President Elect of the European Council for Small Business. His recent book, *Entrepreneurship and Small Business Research in Europe*, coedited with Hermann Frank and José Veciana was published in 1997.

Donald L. Sexton is an Adjunct Professor in the School of Business and Entrepreneurship at Nova Southeastern University and a Scholar in Residence at the Ewing Marion Kauffman Foundation.

He received his Ph.D. in Business Administration from the Ohio State University. Dr. Sexton has taught graduate and undergraduate courses in entrepreneurship and strategic management. He held the Caruth Chair in Entrepreneurship at Baylor University and the William H. Davis Chair in entrepreneurship at the Ohio State University. While at Baylor, he established the Center for Entrepreneurship in 1984, the undergraduate major in entrepreneurship in 1980.

Prior to his academic career he worked for a number of years in the engineering field and turned around four firms from losses to profitable operations.

He retired from academe in 1994 and accepted a position with the Ewing Marion Kauffman Foundation where he established and served as Director of the National Center for Entrepreneurship.

The Blackwell Handbook of Entrepreneurship is the fifth state-of-the-art and the first international book which he has coedited. The first state-of-the-art book was published in 1981.

Foreword

The continuing expansion of global linkages in the 1990s is creating a new dimension for studies of entrepreneurship. As the field of entrepreneurship grows significantly more sophisticated in countries throughout the world, we have seen the corresponding development of research frameworks, within which scholars are constantly pushing the boundaries of knowledge. This publication, *The Blackwell Handbook of Entrepreneurship*, results from the fifth conference in the series, representing the best contemporary work of international scholars, showcasing research from many countries both within domestic settings and across borders. It is clear that in the coming decade, international entrepreneurship will develop as an important division of the expanding entrepreneurship field.

At the macroeconomic level, government policies toward new business creation vary tremendously across nations. Government trade policies and, in turn, industrial policies are increasingly controlled by World Trade Organization (WTO) agreements, as well as by regional trade agreements – witness the North American Free Trade Agreement (NAFTA) and European Union (EU) agreements. As controls on trade are lifted or weakened, so the potential for foreign direct investment increases, with firms seeking continuous competitive advantage, on the wider world stage.

The level of activity in international linkages is growing exponentially, as business moves more and more to a geocentric view of the world. This is a major global development, which is supported by technological and communications revolutions, reducing time barriers to communications and decreasing the costs of developing international business.

International joint ventures and strategic alliances have been a necessary path for international expansion in many regions and countries, which have strong trade controls and high levels of perceived risk, such as China, India, Africa and Latin America. Increasingly we see entrepreneurial expansion occurring through mergers and acquisitions as a response to the threat of global competition and as a strategically proactive decision.

Entrepreneurship research follows this tremendously increasing trend in entrepreneurial activity, led by small and medium-sized firms. Access to technology, the lessening of governmental restrictions to investment, access to capital financing and finally the breakdown of barriers for firms in transitioning economies all contribute to tremendous change and growth in economic activity. By building on solid foundations of academic work, this publication takes us farther along the path to understanding a complex, global market and the players who define entrepreneurship and competitiveness.

Nova Southeastern University is proud to have been host to the 1999 International State of the Art in Entrepreneurship Conference. The School of Business and Entrepreneurship actively supports academic research and practice in International Entrepreneurship, in conjunction with our mission of increasing international programs, in the United States and at campuses around the world.

Dr. Randolph Pohlman, Dean
School of Business and
Entrepreneurship
Nova Southeastern University

Dr. Ruth Clarke, Director
Masters in International
Business Administration
Program
Nova Southeastern University

Acknowledgements

The state of the art in entrepreneurship research is a moving target that changes positions frequently. Entrepreneurs face a similar situation when they identify an opportunity and gather the resources to pursue it.

The concept for this book began when a longtime friend and colleague, William Dennis, Jr., suggested an opportunity to combine forces to conduct an international state-of-the-art conference in entrepreneurship research and share the findings with others interested in entrepreneurship throughout the world.

Both editors accepted the challenge with vigor and began the process of identifying the most important topics. Senior researchers throughout Europe, Canada and the United States were asked to identify current research needs and identify researchers most knowledgeable about the suggested research areas.

When entrepreneurs identify an opportunity, their next step is to identify and acquire commitments for funding the project. Randolph Pohlman, Dean of the School of Business and Entrepreneurship at Nova Southeastern University, enthusiastically supported pursuing the opportunity by providing not only funding for the conference but also capable support staff.

Catriona King, Commissioning Editor at Blackwell Publishers, was also an early supporter of the project by signing this book on the basis of the concept, the topics and the contributors in the book proposal. She, like Randy Pohlman, saw the conference and the book as an opportunity for filling a need to assess the current international state-of-the-art in entrepreneurship, given the massive changes in the economic and political situations in Europe and the globalization of the marketplace.

Dean Pohlman also assigned Tamara Terry as the local arrangement chair for the conference. Her commitment to a conference that would allow the participants to have a memorable experience resulted in numerous hours involving arrangements for rooms, travel schedules, food and all the other special requests. Tammy worked diligently and succeeded in making the conference truly a memorable experience for all participants. Others on the staff and faculty that supported and participated in the conference were Dr. Ruth Clarke, Director of the Masters in International Business Administration

Program; Dr. Ron Needleman, Director of Doctoral Research and Professor of Economics; Dr. Ed Pierce, Professor of Finance and Strategy; and Dr. Robert Berg, Professor of International Business.

The program was also enhanced by the presentation by A.J. Scribante, the Honorable Lynda Scribante and H. Wayne Huizenga who shared their experiences in building and selling successful organizations.

As the project moved from a conference to a book, we especially thank our editor, Dave Prout, for making the manuscript more readable and consistent for Blackwell. Besides Catriona King, our Commissioning Editor, we would also like to thank the other members of the Blackwell team: Bridget Jennings, Publishing Assistant; Joanna Pyke, Editorial Controller; Rhonda Pearce, Production Controller; and Sarah Redford, Marketing Manager.

Our entrepreneurial partners, Susanne Erlandsson and Carol Sexton, not only shared their time with us during this project but also provided support in the correspondence with the contributors and the moral support, so we could complete the project.

Finally, each of us wishes to thank our coeditor for making this, our first joint venture, an exciting and rewarding effort.

Donald L. Sexton   Hans Landström

Introduction

The worlds of the entrepreneur and entrepreneurship researchers are changing dramatically. The changes are due to the rapidly converging intersection of the entrepreneurial revolution of the 1980s in the United States with the free market revolution in Europe. This has resulted in a globalization of the marketplace, and with it, new opportunities for growth, new competitive structures and new ways of doing business.

In the world of academic research the intersection of the two revolutions in conjunction with major technological changes in communications has resulted in new opportunities for international research, joint research projects and a sharing of research findings. This has provided a new impetus to entrepreneurship research that has no national boundaries.

Significant and rapid changes, combined with new opportunities can be both exciting and difficult. Many European countries are still struggling with the economic, social and political problems associated with a free market economy. The revolution will not be short and even though the impetus is there, some things change slowly.

These changes are reflected in this, the fifth state-of-the-art and the first international state-of-the-art in entrepreneurship research book.

The primary objective of our continuing research into entrepreneurship has been to effectively communicate to faculty, student, researchers, entrepreneurs and public policy makers new developments which will increase the understanding of the phenomenon called "entrepreneurship." By doing so we hope to encourage entrepreneurial efforts worldwide to create jobs, improve the economic well-being of all social strata and promote public policy that will encourage these efforts.

HISTORICAL CONCEPTS OF ENTREPRENEURSHIP

Entrepreneurship research as we currently know it and entrepreneurship education are relatively recent phenomena, dating only to the middle 1970s and early 1980s. However, the concept of entrepreneurship had much earlier beginnings.

Entrepreneurship in an economic context, appeared in the writings of Richard Contillon (1680–1734) as the act of purchasing products, repackaging them and then marketing the products at an unpredictable and uncertain price. Hence the emphasis on risk and uncertainty. In the early 1800s Jean Baptiste Say (1767–1832) saw the entrepreneur as a "broker" who produced and sold a product. He, too, saw the process as one of taking a risk. In the 1920 era, Frank Knight (1885–1972) made a distinction between risk and uncertainty and took the view that the skill of the entrepreneur was in the ability to handle the uncertainty that exists in society (Knight 1916, 1921). Joseph Schumpeter (1883–1950) took the approach that the economic system of supply and demand was in equilibrium and that the entrepreneur tended to break the equilibrium by introducing innovations into the system in the form of new products, new methods of production or new markets. Schumpeter called the process "creative destruction." (Schumpeter 1911, 1926, 1934).

Subsequent to Schumpeter, two separate schools of thought have emerged. The Research Center in Entrepreneurial History at Harvard University, founded in 1948, has suggested that entrepreneurship is associated with changes in the economic system, the creation of organizations for the commercialization of innovations and the task of the entrepreneur is to create profits. A different approach was developed by Frederick van Hayek (1906–1972) and Ludwig von Mises (1881–1973). Mises observed that people are alert to opportunities in the marketplace and Hayek suggested that only a few people are aware of unexploited market profit opportunities.

More recently Israel Kirsner, theorized that the economy was imbalanced and the entrepreneur was a person who identified these imbalances and exploited them (Kirsner 1973, 1982). This tends to bring the process towards equilibrium. He further notes that entrepreneurs also stimulate market demand through persuasion via advertising, thus creating additional disequilibrium in the market. Hence, the entrepreneur is not only one who sees and exploits opportunities, but also creates other opportunities and exploits them.

ENTREPRENEURSHIP RESEARCH

Entrepreneurship as an academic field began in the late 1970s and exploded in the 1980s as courses, centers, and chairs were developed and funded. The first of the state-of-the-art in entrepreneurship research conferences was held in 1980 and the book that resulted from the conference, *The Encyclopedia of Entrepreneurship*, was published in 1982 (Kent et al. 1982).

Research streams in entrepreneurship have ranged from a focus on the characteristics of the individual and on the behavioral process of starting the business to the individual's freedom of choice when deciding to start a business (Shaver and Scott 1991). In essence, this line of behavioral science has addressed the questions of who is the entrepreneur? And why does the entrepreneur act in an attempt to understand the entrepreneur as an individual (Stevenson and Jarillo, 1990).

Subsequently, authors have redirected the focus of research from the individual and focused on the process as suggested by Carsrud et al. (1986), Churchill and Lewis (1986), Wortman (1986), Bygrave and Hofer (1991).

In addition, entrepreneurship research has broadened further and has attracted researchers form a number of different disciplines. It can now be regarded as a multidisciplinary field of research. Herron et al. (1992) suggests that each discipline seems to have its own view of entrepreneurship and these views are relatively uninfluenced by other disciplines' ways of looking at entrepreneurship. As a result, the field appears to be more undisciplinary rather interdisciplinary.

As the world changes, so does the expression of entrepreneurship. The current approach is to address the boundaries for entrepreneurship, the uniqueness about it that cannot be understood within the framework of existing scientific disciplines and the contribution of entrepreneurship research. These issues lie at the core of entrepreneurship research.

The recent changes in the world economy, as a result of the intersection of the entrepreneurial and the free market revolutions, have resulted in an increased emphasis on entrepreneurship research to enhance the knowledge of students, academics, practitioners and public policy makers.

This book, like the previous state-of-the-art books, addresses the current state of entrepreneurship research on the topical areas deemed by the top researchers in the field to be those in which additional research is of a critical nature for the advancement of the field.

As the world has changed, the emphasis on topics of primary concern to the field has also changed as reflected by the writings in this book. The chapters fall into five categories: 1, Setting the Stage for International Research in Entrepreneruship; 2, Government Impacts on Entrepreneurship; 3, Financing Growth; 4, Achieving Growth: Internal and External Approaches; 5, Research Issues in Entrepreneurship. With a strong emphasis on international entrepreneurship, the impact of public policy on entrepreneurial ventures, financing and growth, the authors hope that the field will become united and that all constituents, including the authors themselves, will benefit from the international approach to entrepreneurship.

SETTING THE STAGE FOR INTERNATIONAL RESEARCH IN ENTREPRENEURSHIP

The chapters in this part cover the topics of national differences in entrepreneurship research, challenges in the study of growth, the intersections of research in strategic management and entrepreneurship, and a discussion of public policy research in the United States.

Aldrich compares and contrasts research methodologies, government support and funding in Europe and North America and suggests that the increase in the number of international journals, visiting professorships and joint research will allow us to learn from each other and enhance our understanding of the field. Davidsson and Wiklund take a critical view of research in the area of growth. They suggest that the general view of growth is too simplistic, that measurements are inconsistent and that theoretical developments are not usually considered. Hitt and Ireland feel that the areas of strategic management and entrepreneurship are changing and growing closer together. They suggest that development in both areas could be enhanced by consideration of developments in the other field and by joint research efforts. Dennis, emphasizing the importance of research in public policy contends that research has been too little, too late, conducted by people outside the area, and funded by organizations that have a vested interest in the output.

GOVERNMENT IMPACTS ON ENTREPRENEURSHIP

The change from a controlled economy to a free market economy has resulted in significant changes in the economic, social and political climate and a major restructing effort is underway. This will not be a speedy or a smooth transition. In addition, not all countries in transition started at the same level or the same time. As a result some countries have changed more rapidly than others. While the change to a free market economy has been significant, the changes in public policy and regulations have been even greater. The problem for most firms now is the extensive burden of administrative costs associated with regulatory compliance and the lack of responsiveness by the public servants to the concerns and needs of the entrepreneurs.

The chapters in this section cover the areas of small and medium size enterprises (SME) policy, regulatory policies, the evaluation of policies, entrepreneurship in Germany and the climate for entrepreneurship in the countries in transition.

De assesses small and medium size enterprises policies throughout Europe and the burden of two levels of policy and regulation that occur within the member states and the European Union (EU). Audretsch examines the special case of Germany with an examination of the significant growth after the unification, the downsizing by the large firms in order to compete in the global marketplace and the recent recognition and stimulation of programs to facilitate growth in new and existing smaller firms. Van der Horst reports on the impact of regulatory policies throughout Europe and the administrative costs that SMEs incur in complying with regulatory and reporting requirements. Mugler addresses the problems and progress of the move from a controlled to a free market economy. He notes that progress is occurring at different rates, resulting from the different starting points and political environments. Storey examines the evaluation, or lack thereof, of programs designed to meet on often-unspecified objective within an unspecified period of time. He recommends a program for accomplishment of specified objectives at a specified time.

FINANCING GROWTH

When the planned growth rate exceeds the availability of the resources owned or controlled, the ability to grow is dependent upon the availability of funding from external sources. When the amount of funding required exceeds that which can be obtained from family, friends or other individuals, entrepreneurs typically turn to banks for debt financing or venture capitalists for a combination of debt and equity funds.

In this section, the chapters cover financing in general, informal sources of venture financing (IVC), and formal venture capital (VC) sources in the UK and in Canada, the impact of venture capital on firm growth and a theoretical approach to understanding the venture capital market.

Donckels provides a comparative analysis of the availability or financing and the requirements for obtaining it throughout Europe. Mason and Harrison address the issues involved with the availability of informal venture capital and the problems associated with locating these "business angels."

Manigart and Sapienza review the impact of venture capital on economic growth and focus on new insights gained in the 1990s in North America and Europe.

Amit, Brander and Zott describe venture capital in Canada and present data on the number, type, and amount of VC investments. They also develop a theory of VC investments based on a large, longitudinal database thought to be the largest and most complete database of VC investments.

Achieving Growth: Internal and External Approaches

It is erroneous to assume that all growth occurs in the same way. Entrepreneurs have a number of different approaches to achieving growth. Some are internal and some are external involving various arrangements with other organizations or other firms. In this section the chapters cover a broad range of topics ranging from how the firm handles the transitions that must be managed to achieve growth, the impact of the entrepreneurial team and networking, the impact of location, to strategic alliances and franchising. In addition there are other approaches that were not included due to a lack of impact or a need for additional research.

Birley and Stockley begin this section with an analysis of the entrepreneurial team on the firm's growth. They recognize that businesses do not grow on the basis of the entrepreneur as a "lone ranger" but on the combined efforts of a team of individuals with special knowledge in key areas of a growth firm. Arbaugh and Camp review research on the management of transitions as a firm grows. They find a paucity of research on this topic that affects all growing firms. Perhaps the lack of research is reflected by the fact that firms do not undergo a single transition but find that transitions occur in all aspects at different times. Autio reviews growth of technology based firms and suggests that the introduction of a new technology brings growth not only to the firm that developed the technology but to those firms that utilize the technology in their operations. Cooper and Folta ask the question "what are the benefits of locating the firm within close proximity to other firms in the same industry?" Clusters of high-tech firms have developed in numerous areas throughout the world. Yet studies of why the clusters are formed and why the cluster is selected over another remain to be addressed. Johannisson suggests that the initiation of a new venture is the result of the accumulation of resources that are owned by the entrepreneur in combination with the social network developed by the entrepreneur that provide consultation, advice and access to other people and can benefit the initiation and growth of the new business. Weaver discusses alliances between two or more firms that range from the friendly transference of ideas to formal arrangements to shared manufacturing and distribution systems. These alliances have become especially important as firms move into international alliances in order to compete in the global market. Finally Hoy, Stanworth and Purdy examine another type of strategic alliance called franchising. They suggest that the access to partners and the growth rate inherent in this type of an alliance merit consideration. They also suggest that the failure rate of franchises is roughly the same as it is for independent businesses.

The purpose of this book is to examine the current state-of-the-art in international entrepreneurship research in areas identified as critical to the growth of the field. Research questions and issues along with potential research and methodology are suggested.

The book will have served its purpose if researchers, after reading it, embark in a number of studies that will help propel academics and entrepreneurs on a growth direction that will thrust them into the new century.

References

Bygrave, W. and Hofer, C. 1991. Theorizing about Entrepreneurship. *Entrepreneurship Theory and Practice* 15(2) 13–22.

Carsrud, A., Olm, K. and Eddy, G., 1986. Entrepreneurship: Research in Quest of a Paradigm. In D. Sexton and R. Smilor (eds.), *The Art and Science of Entrepreneurship*. Cambridge, Ballinger, 367–78.

Cantillion, R. 1775. (published posthumously) *Essai Sur la Nature du Commerce en General.*

Churchilll, N. and Lewis, V. 1986. Entrepreneurship Research: Directions and Methods. In D. Sexton and R. Smilor (eds.), *The Art and Science of Entrepreneurship Research*. Cambridge, Ballinger, 339–65.

Herron, L., Sapienza, H. and Smith-Cook, D. 1992. Entrepreneurship Theory from an Interdisciplinary Perspective. *Entrepreneurship: Theory and Practice* 16(3) 5–11.

Kent, C., Sexton, D. and Vesper, K. 1982. *The Encyclopedia of Entrepreneurship*. Englewood Cliffs, Prentice-Hall.

Kirsner, I. 1973. *Competition and Entrepreneurship*. Chicago, University of Chicago.

Kirsner, I. 1982. The Theory of Entrepreneurship in Economic Growth. In C. Kent, D. Sexton and K. Vesper (eds.), *Encyclopedia of Entrepreneurship*. Englewood Cliffs, Prentice-Hall, 272–6.

Knight, F. 1916, 1921. *Risk, Uncertainty and Profit*. New York, Harper & Row.

Say, J. 1814. *Tracte d'economie politique.*

Say, J. 1816. *Cours complet d'economie politique pratique.*

Schumpeter, J. 1911, 1926, 1934. *Theorie der wirtschaftlichen Entwicklung (Theory of Economic Development: An Inquiry into Profits, Capital, Credit, Interest and the Business Cycle)*, trans. Redovers Opie. Cambridge, Harvard University.

Sexton, D., and Smilor, R. (eds.). 1986. *The Art and Science of Entrepreneurship*. Cambridge, Ballinger. 273–331.

Shaver, K. and Scott, L. 1991. Person, Process, Choice: The Psychology of New Venture Creation. *Entrepreneurship Theory and Practice* 16(2) 23–45.

Stevenson, H. and Jarillo, J. 1990. A Paradigm of Entrepreneurship: Entrepreneurial Management. *Strategic Management Journal* 11, 17–27.

Wortman, M. 1986. A Unified Framework, Research Typologies, and Research Prospectuses for the Interface between Entrepreneurship and Small Business. In D. Sexton and R. Smilor (eds.), *The Art and Science of Entrepreneurship*. Cambridge, Ballinger, 367–78.

Part I

Setting the Stage for International Research in Entrepreneurship

From 1988 to 1992, when all east European countries gained their "formal" autonomy from the former statist system, their main task has been to overcome their centrally planned system and adopt the market economy. This period is often referred to as a free market economy revolution. The free market revolution, combined with the entrepreneurial revolution in the United States, has resulted in a shift to a global / international marketplace.

Entrepreneurship scholars and researchers, in response to a globalized economy, have renewed their interest in the field and have begun more cooperative research projects and a sharing of research methods and concepts.

This first part of the book provides a broad overview of the chapters that follow to set the stage for the book, namely, the international state of the art in entrepreneurship research.

The chapters in this part include: "Learning Together: National Differences in Entrepreneurship Research" by Aldrich, who compares research methods, concepts, funding and dissemination in North America and Europe. Davidsson examines the problems associated with research on growth considered by many to be the distinguishing factor of entrepreneurship in chapter 2, "Conceptual and Empirical Challenges in the Study of Firm Growth." Hitt and Ireland examine the similarities between research in strategic management and entrepreneurship in chapter 3, "The Intersection of Entrepreneurship and Strategic Management Research." Finally, Dennis examines the state of public policy research in chapter 4, "Research Mimicking Policy: Entrepreneurship / Small Business Policy Research in the United States."

This broad overview will set the stage for the remaining parts and chapters, which have been developed to examine further the state of the art in entrepreneurship research. By identifying the current state of research and identifying those issues that need further research, it is hoped that future researchers will advance the body of knowledge of the field.

In his assessment of the current state of international research in entrepreneurship, Aldrich concludes the following:

- Entrepreneurship research, while improving, is still of limited topical concerns and value to entrepreneurs.
- Research on entrepreneurship has developed in partial isolation between Europe and North America.
- Researchers on both sides of the Atlantic have a strong normative and prescriptive orientation. European researchers focus on fieldwork while North American researchers prefer survey methods.
- Entrepreneurship as a research field includes scholars of many different disciplines and each view entrepreneurship from their own academic perspective.

Davidsson and Wiklund, examining the research on growth, suggest:

- Existing studies of firm growth are far from generating a useful theory of growth.
- Traditional assumptions about growth firms are too simplistic.
- Little congruence exists among currently used growth measures.
- Growth research, in many cases, does not explicitly state the theory, the level of obstruction is low, the empirical work is unimpressive, and the data collection is cross-sectional.

Hitt and Ireland, comparing research in strategic management and entrepreneurship, suggest that each area can be expanded considering the following:

- Examine the research findings in the other area for possible extrapolation.
- Both areas are expanding and growing closer together.
- Entrepreneurship research still needs developed theories, models and methods.
- Researchers in both areas should collaborate more frequently and intensively to examine topics of mutual interest.

Public policy and its intended regulations and reporting requirements is often considered as the bane of entrepreneurs. Dennis suggest that the entrepreneurship researcher could help alleviate this problem with a proactive approach. He notes:

- US entrepreneurial and small business policy is a de facto competition policy designed to provide ground rules for all firms (competitors) and provide privileges for none.

- ◆ Research on entrepreneurship/small business policy is inadequate and focused on broad policy questions rather than impacts.
- ◆ Most research is conducted by nonacademics or academics outside of business schools and funded by disparate sources.
- ◆ With a few notable exceptions, entrepreneurship/small business policy research has done little to affect policy.

Although entrepreneurship as a concept was developed in the late seventeenth century by a number of different economists, it has only recently become a field of academic research and endeavor. Have we really only begun to understand the phenomenon, or does the thought of Henri Bergson apply? Namely, "To exist is to change, to change is to mature, to mature is to go on creating oneself endlessly."

1

Learning Together: National Differences in Entrepreneurship Research

HOWARD ALDRICH

CROSS-NATIONAL DIFFERENCES: AN OLD DEBATE
CROSS-NATIONAL RESEARCH: SIMILARITIES AND DIFFERENCES
EVOLVING TRENDS
CONCLUSIONS

In the period since the publication of the *Encyclopedia of Entrepreneurship* (Kent et al. 1982) three related titles have appeared that continue to summarize the state of the art. As a participant in those efforts, as well as the current one, I have witnessed a continuing debate over the sophistication of research methods in entrepreneurship. Although change has proceeded unevenly, substantial progress has been made on many fronts. Nonetheless, in a recent volume, *Entrepreneurship 2000* (Sexton and Smilor 1997), Baker and I concluded: "Judging from normal science standards, entrepreneurship research is still in a very early stage. If no single powerful paradigm exists, then there is even less evidence for multiple coherent points of view . . . Entrepreneurship research is improving but still of limited topical concern and value to practicing entrepreneurs" (Aldrich and Baker 1997: 398).

Curiously missing in these earlier volumes was any substantial assessment of the state of the art in regions other than North America. This omission was surprising given that international participation in conferences and journals has increased substantially over the years. For example, overseas scholars are now regular participants at the Babson College Entrepreneurship Conferences, and at least eight journals on entrepreneurship or small business are published in Europe (Huse and Landström 1997). Thus, I am pleased that North American scholars are turning their attention to research beyond their borders and that European scholars are making explicit comparisons to the work of North American researchers (Landström and Huse 1996).

Consideration of international entrepreneurship research raises major issues for our field. Can we preserve valuable diversity in research methods while at the same time learning from one another? Are there distinct national styles? If there are distinctive differences, are they being wiped out by pressures toward convergence? Or are barriers to convergence so high that they are sustaining diversity? I recognize that I write as a North American and thus cannot truly stand outside the issues I review. Nonetheless, with the help of criticism from non-North American friends and colleagues on early drafts, I hope I have achieved a somewhat balanced view.

In this chapter I first review the debate about cross-national differences that has raged in the organization theory field since the late 1970s. Many of the issues raised in that debate have striking parallels in the debates over research methods in entrepreneurship. Next, I examine four similarities in entrepreneurship research carried out in North America and Europe.

The first similarity is that research on entrepreneurship and research on organizations developed in partial isolation from one another in both regions. Thus, researchers in each region replicated many of the same disputes that occurred earlier in organization theory.

Second, North American and European researchers have also been united by a strong normative and prescriptive orientation underlying their research. Accordingly, they have kept in close touch with practitioners and policymakers.

Third, entrepreneurship research in both regions has focused more on description than hypothesis testing, although forces of diffusion and borrowing are now raising the salience of causal model building in the field.

Fourth, researchers in both regions have focused mainly on established organizations, rather than on founding processes among start-ups. The four similarities between the regions have been strengthened by a strong set of forces promoting diffusion and borrowing among researchers.

I next review three differences that characterize the field. First, in contrast with their European colleagues, North American scholars have traditionally assumed that their findings are universal as opposed to being nation-specific. Second, European researchers have relied more on qualitative fieldwork methods than on the survey research designs favored by North Americans. Finally, the level of government and foundation support for entrepreneurship research is substantially larger in Europe than in North America.

After surveying similarities and differences in the final section of this chapter, I consider some forces that might narrow international differences. I argue that vitality in the field of entrepreneurship studies depends upon maintaining diversity in research approaches. We have much to learn from one another, and many channels have opened through which we can carry on fruitful conversations about research and methods.

CROSS-NATIONAL DIFFERENCES: AN OLD DEBATE

We can learn a great deal about the issues involved in international comparisons by examining debates in a parallel field: organization theory. Since the 1960s, North American and European scholars have alternatively clashed and cooperated in trying to sort out their differences and similarities. Organization theory has contributed a great deal to the entrepreneurship field. For example, concepts such as competence-destroying and competence-enhancing innovation have come from organization theory, as well as principles of organizational learning and organizational knowledge. Thus, I think it is useful to review the issues raised in organization theory with an eye to what they may tell us about entrepreneurship research.

Historical precedents

One of the first scholars to take up the question of North American versus European approaches was Kassem (1976). He painted a stark contrast between the two continents, exploring differences along several dimensions. Americans, he thought, focused on narrowly based micro-issues, whereas Europeans were more concerned with macro-level issues, such as the societal context of organizational actions. On the ideological front, Americans built their models based on assumptions of harmony and consensus, while Europeans were more interested in conflict and power. Perhaps most important for us, Kassem saw Americans as much more concerned about methods and techniques than Europeans, who were more oriented toward theory.

In the mid-1980s, Donaldson (1985) expressed concern that the critical approach taken by European organization theorists was damaging the foundation of organization theory. Aldrich (1988) countered with an analysis showing that the critical theorists who worried Donaldson actually had little impact on work published in American journals. Hinings (1988), while agreeing that North Americans had ignored the critics, argued that British scholars shared much in common with their continental colleagues. In the early 1990s, Lammers (1990) painted a more complex picture of national differences. In contrast to Kassem's assessment of a substantial divergence between North American and European theorizing and research, Lammers emphasized intra-European differences. While acknowledging American supremacy – partly because of the dominance of English as an international language, as well as the preeminence of the top American journals – he resisted the notion of a united European way.

By the mid-1990s, Üsdiken and Pasadeos (1995) were convinced that the past several decades had been characterized by an oscillation between convergence and divergence. They saw the 1970s as a period of convergence around open systems and contingency theories and pointed to the birth of competing approaches in North America that attracted attention in Europe. They saw the 1980s as a period of divergence during which national differences – suppressed during the 1970s – once again became salient. Not content with an impressionist survey of similarities and differences, Üsdiken and Pasadeos examined citation practices of North American and European scholars in two leading organization journals. They concluded that the flow of international influence was decidedly asymmetric, from North America to Europe.

Üsdiken and Pasadeos (1995: 519) concluded that a new kind of divergence was occurring in the 1990s between North American and European scholars. They argued that their results showed "certain approaches and styles are predominantly European," although intraregional variation existed. Historical differences in dominant traditions and differing institutional contexts of scholarly work had led to increasing cross-national divergence. In North America, organization studies had moved from sociology and psychology departments into business schools, marked by an increased positivist orientation toward research. In particular, the institutional reward structure in the United States, especially modes of graduate training and an emphasis on publishing in journals, pushed scholars toward narrow empirical projects. Collin et al.'s (1996) study of articles published in four US and four European journals in 1993 confirmed many of Üsdiken and Pasadeos' assertions.

In Europe, reaction against the growing dominance of North American paradigms heightened the salience of traditions such as a "stronger philosophical orientation, a legacy of critical approaches, and a history more sensitive to class and national differences" (Üsdiken and Pasadeos 1995: 521). In some nations, academic work was organized more like the humanities in the United States, following an apprenticeship model. However, the model was changing in other nations because they were modifying their graduate training programs along American lines, such as in Norway. These programs included more attention to quantitative methods and an emphasis on hypothesis testing.

In contrast to Üsdiken and Pasadeos, Koza and Thoenig (1995) noted substantial cross-national differences but nonetheless emphasized forces of convergence between European and North American organization scholars. They began by documenting significant differences in theoretical orientation, problems chosen for study, and methods of research. Indeed, they described the situation as like "two ships passing in the night." Historically, European researchers emphasized qualitative case studies that were grounded in interpretive discussions. Koza and Thoenig characterized North American researchers as traditionally interested in building and testing causal propositions deduced from formal theories. Collin et al.'s (1996) results for journal articles supported their argument, with US authors much more likely to report hypothesis tests than European authors. From a European perspective, American researchers often devoted a great deal of time to trivial pursuits, rather than socially significant questions.

Despite these extreme caricatures of seemingly disconnected endeavors, Koza and Thoenig (1995: 3) asserted that, over the previous decade, common themes had emerged on the two continents. To what did they attribute the apparent convergence? Close examination of their argument reveals only two possible pressures toward convergence: the increased importance of professional associations oriented toward international activities and the growing importance of international English-language journals. Such journals promoted a common standard of evaluation and professional prestige. Otherwise, their description of research in Europe and North America conformed to the picture painted by Kassem (1976) two decades earlier. They argued that national loyalty and interest dominate European intellectual life, national academic systems and job markets are quite distinct, and "global intellectual debates" are the goal at scientific meetings in Europe but not North America.

Koza and Thoenig ended their review with the observation that each side has ignored substantial diversity within the other. From the American side, European diversity is difficult to perceive because Americans typically do not read languages other than English and follow only work published in the journals to which they subscribe. From the European side, American diversity is difficult to perceive because of the highly specialized and fragmented American academic community. Research streams other than "normal science" are often not apparent to outsiders. Europeans, for example, might be surprised to learn that a "critical theory" interest group has formed within the Academy of Management, with hundreds of followers.

Lessons for entrepreneurship researchers

To the extent that organization studies and entrepreneurship research share the same intellectual roots and participate in the same academic reward systems, the picture I have painted above applies to both. Entrepreneurship researchers are a small community within the much larger academic and professional universe and thus cannot escape the influence of such partisan debates. If the larger reward system favors a particular style of research, then entrepreneurship researchers may find it difficult to resist. Indeed, if we ignore the historical context within which national differences have developed, we risk perpetuating the same misunderstandings that have characterized the controversy between organization theorists.

I take two lessons away from this review. First, dispassionate observers must admit that substantial diversity exists between and within the North American and European research communities (Huse and Landström 1997). No single monolithic approach dominates either. Groups doing similar research can be found in all nations. However, they are building on a tradition of differences. Second, international diffusion mechanisms have spread information about differences and similarities throughout the global research community. Researchers are no longer working in as much isolation as a generation ago. Exchanges of papers, visiting scholars, travel to international meetings, and other mechanisms are forcing us to confront our differences. I turn now to an examination of the entrepreneurship research community.

CROSS-NATIONAL RESEARCH: SIMILARITIES AND DIFFERENCES

Based on my reading of the literature, participation in conferences, discussions with entrepreneurship researchers and clinical observations, I have drawn up a list of similarities and differences. More general surveys of the entrepreneurship field are available elsewhere, such as Cooper et al.'s (1997) review of North American developments. I begin with consideration of the similarities across nations, pointing out the parallels between North America and Europe. Although many forces toward convergence are evident, strong differences still exist, as I point out in a subsequent section.

Similarities

I address four similarities across nations:

1 On both continents, research on entrepreneurship and organizations has developed in partial isolation from one another, resulting in entrepreneurship researchers duplicating some of the same disputes that earlier characterized organization theory.
2 Strong normative and prescriptive orientation underlies entrepreneurship research in North America and Europe.
3 Entrepreneurship research historically focused more on description than hypothesis testing, although signs of change are apparent.
4 In both regions, researchers have focused mainly on established organizations, rather than the founding process.

Let's now consider each of these four similarities in turn.

In each region, entrepreneurship research initially developed somewhat independently of the organization theory, organizational behavior and strategy literature. Because it developed out of a different institutional context than fields more firmly rooted in disciplinary homes, entrepreneurship research in both regions was characterized by more overt conflict over research methods and standards than other fields. This line of development left entrepreneurship scholars in both regions searching for basic theory. In North America, they turned to psychology, sociology, business strategy and marketing, whereas European scholars turned to a more eclectic mix of disciplines (Cooper et al. 1997; Landström and Huse 1996). In this respect entrepreneurship research resembles organization theory, a field that went through a paradigm crisis in the 1970s (Aldrich 1992a).

Almost all of the current professional associations in North America and Europe devoted to entrepreneurship (as opposed to "small business") were created since the late 1980s. The Entrepreneurship Division of the Academy of Management did not form until 1987, although it began in 1974 as an interest group within the Division of Business Policy and Planning. In Europe, the RENT (Research in ENTrepreneurship) Conference was created in 1987. Until these new organizations were formed, entrepreneurship researchers had no collective action organizations comparable to those enjoyed by their colleagues in organization theory.

What effect did the separation between organization theory and entrepreneurship theory have on the field? From the beginning of systematic reflections on entrepreneurship research's fate, commentators have lamented the absence of a unified theory of entrepreneurship. They have also recommended borrowing methods from more advanced fields (Paulin et al. 1982; Peterson and Horvath 1982). Although some observers were more forgiving of entrepreneurship research design shortcomings (Perryman 1982), others were extremely critical (Carsrud et al. 1986). Implicitly, almost all had in mind a standard set by studies in organization theory and management studies, finding entrepreneurship research did not measure up.

Wortman (1986) even included the phrase "a unified framework" in the title of his paper, apparently in the belief that such a framework could be found in the home disciplines of entrepreneurship studies. Wortman seemed to favor psychological roots for the field, whereas Churchill and Lewis (1986) saw business policy and marketing as more natural affiliates. Carsrud et al. (1986) proposed a unified research paradigm that would include psychological, organizational and environmental variables. Aldrich (1990) argued for a more sociological focus, using ecological models, building on several papers that had appeared in the first comprehensive review volume covering entrepreneurship research (Kent et al. 1982). Reynolds and White (1997) made a similar argument, focusing on community and societal level explanations of entrepreneurship.

A survey of research in Europe documented the incredibly eclectic borrowing of disciplinary ideas by entrepreneurship researchers (Landström et al. 1997). Implicitly, it also painted a picture of confusion and disagreement over how to use such ideas. Similarly, based on their analysis of European entrepreneurship journals, Landström and Huse (1996: 11) concluded that it was "difficult to identify any core literature within the field, which means that researchers may fail to take note of what has been published previously and to build upon it in a cumulative way." A series of global conferences organized by Birley and MacMillan (1992) generated empirical papers that also documented the diverse and multidisciplinary perspectives of entrepreneurship researchers. In its annual reports (e.g., ENSR 1996), the European Observatory for Small and Medium-Sized Enterprises has been careful not to impose a unified theoretical framework on the statistics it reports, although an implicit economic model of business growth underlies many of the chapters.

In Europe since the late 1980s, many new venues for national and international collaboration have formed. Some national organizations now link scholars interested in small business and entrepreneurship, with the small business foundation having been laid some time ago. Indeed, Landström and Huse (1996) detected a trend toward greater connections between a traditional small business orientation and a more recent entrepreneurship orientation among European researchers. In Sweden, the Foundation for Small Business Research (Forum för Smaaföretagsforskning), which was started in 1994, and the Scandinavian Institute for Research in Entrepreneurship (SIRE) are small network organizations. The Nordic Conference on Small Business Management meets every two years, with the first meeting held in 1980 in Växjö. The conference is mainly on small business, reflecting the nature of research in Scandinavia. The Nordic Conference on Business Studies began in 1971 but did not add an entrepreneurship track until much later. In Germany, Professor Heinz Klandt of the European Business School in Dortmund has begun organizing conferences on entrepreneurship research. In December 1997, Klandt (1997) organized a first conference on business start-ups

The European Council for Small Business (ECSB), the European equivalent of the United States Association for Small Business and Entrepreneurship (USASBE), was founded in 1989 and links small business researchers in Europe. It is connected to the International Council for Small Business (ICSB). The RENT conference, the largest European conference on entrepreneurship, meets on an annual basis. The conference usually includes about seventy papers, lasts for two days and has a conference for doctoral students. In theory, all European nations are involved. However, national representation depends on where the conference is held. The ECSB initiated the European Doctoral Programme in Entrepreneurship and Small Business Management in 1990, a multiuniversity consortium for educating graduate students. Recently, the Universitat Autonoma de Barcelona in Spain and Växjö University in Sweden have jointly operated the program. Nonetheless, the "number of such courses is quite limited in many countries" (Huse and Landström 1997: 7).

Regardless of the proposals offered by advocates of one point of view or another, entrepreneurship researchers in North America and Europe struggled for years to find a theoretical identity. Since the late 1980s, a tentative theoretical identity has begun to emerge. For example, Landström and Johannisson (1998) argued that doctoral theses on entrepreneurship in Sweden now reflect a strong theoretical basis in organization theory. A turning point for many North American researchers occurred in the early 1980s, when their emphasis shifted from a focus on small businesses to a greater concern for business growth. A similar shift also occurred in Europe, around the same time. Let's now turn to an examination of the institutional contexts within which entrepreneurship researchers have worked.

A strong prescriptive and policy orientation has guided research in North America and Europe. Many scholars have noted that entrepreneurship research is strongly value-laden and that cross-national differences often turn up in discussions of entrepreneurship (e.g., Peterson and

Horvath 1982; Peterson was working in Canada at that time, and Horvath had worked in Sweden). Ironically, one of the charges often leveled by North American scholars against European organizational research has been that is it more normative than explanatory (Koza and Thoenig 1995). In this respect, entrepreneurship research in North American shares more in common with European entrepreneurship research than with other American business-oriented research.

In North America and Europe, some researchers have argued that it is more important to tackle important questions than to be concerned with methodological purity (Hoy 1997). Current social, economic and political considerations should govern what issues are chosen for study. Changing conditions, not abstract methodological concerns, should drive research practices. Many entrepreneurship research projects are energized by the belief that entrepreneurial firms generate a high proportion of job growth in industrial societies and are a powerful engine for economic innovation (Low and MacMillan 1988). Many nations within the European Union, as well as the EU itself, have begun research projects based on these assumptions.

At the 1985 state-of-the-art conference on entrepreneurship (Sexton and Smilor 1986), Churchill and Lewis (1986) noted a conflict in entrepreneurship research between scholars who wanted to pursue science for its own sake and others who were more interested in applying their knowledge to the broader problems of society. A heavily practice-oriented discipline labors under difficulties that theory-oriented disciplines avoid. First, a practice-oriented field takes a great deal from the disciplines but may return very little to them. Second, a focus on practice may contribute little toward generic knowledge of entrepreneurship and also fail to provide a basis upon which theoretical understanding can be built (Wortman 1986). Mone and McKinley (1993) argued that a practitioner orientation places a positive value on topicality, uniqueness and usefulness rather than adherence to a strict code of research practice. They feared that rewards for topicality and uniqueness could create feedback loops that destroyed researchers' commitment to normal science norms.

Entrepreneurship researchers have countered such charges by noting that practice-oriented studies can provide feedback from which researchers can assess the accuracy of their models. Of course, this claim depends upon a tight coupling between the researchers who apply theories and those who test and refine them. Because of its historical roots in small business-oriented programs, many of which were heavily devoted to outreach efforts, the linkage between application and theory testing in entrepreneurship research has been weak.

The practice orientation of entrepreneurship research in North America has led to significant amounts of funding by entrepreneurs for academic chairs. Many of the chairs are funded with endowments of two million dollars or more. Although not all of the endowment funding is used for research, such chairs have nonetheless had a significant impact on the field. For example, the Kauffman Foundation recently committed significant funds to Babson College, the University of Chicago and Stanford University. Funds from these commitments may substantially increase the linkage between application and theory testing.

Entrepreneurship research has been more descriptive than theory-driven in North America and Europe. Hypothesis testing and the building of causal models are downplayed. The tension between description and explanation has been a theme running through all previous commentaries on entrepreneurship research methods. At the first state-of-the-art conference (Kent et al. 1982), Paulin et al. (1982) noted that the entrepreneurship literature contained quite a few informal, anecdotal schemes developed from nonsystematic research designs. At that same conference, however, Perryman (1982) argued against asking any more of researchers, and he asserted that it was premature to move much beyond rich description. At the second state-of-the-art conference (Sexton and Smilor 1986), Wortman (1986) lamented the lack of sophisticated hypothesis testing in the studies he reviewed. Indeed, he felt the field had been overwhelmed by exploratory and purely descriptive studies. Churchill and Lewis (1986) were more forgiving, agreeing with Perryman that the field was still evolving. By contrast, Carsrud et al. (1986) felt that it was time for a change. They claimed that researchers were spending an excessive amount of time on descriptive statistics concerning particular groups, as well as too much time on case studies.

At the last state-of-the-art conference, Ted Baker and I examined whether entrepreneurship researchers had moved away from descriptive statistics and toward more use of statistical tests in their research. Baker and I found that Babson conference presentations were more likely to be based on identifiable populations than in the past, but the great majority of investigators were still using samples of convenience (Aldrich and Baker 1997). About half of the empirical entrepreneurship articles published between 1991 and 1995 included some sort of hypothesis test. By contrast, over four-fifths of the empirical papers in the top organization studies journals were based on tests of formal hypotheses. In their comparison of papers published in 1994, Landström and Huse (1996: 14) concluded that in contrast with North American research, "More European studies are based on anecdotal data, and the studies are usually descriptive in character." However, the regions did not differ significantly in the proportion of papers devoted to explanatory research.

In my assessment of statistical methods at the third state-of-the-art conference (Sexton and Kasarda 1992), I noted that entrepreneurship researchers in North America continued to rely heavily on simple descriptive statistics (Aldrich 1992b). However, I detected a trend toward the greater use of significance tests and models assessing the strength of associations between variables. That trend continued into the mid-1990s (Aldrich and Baker 1997). Simple percentages, raw numbers, or no numbers at all dropped from 53 percent at the 1986 Babson conference to 28 percent in 1994. In entrepreneurship journals, use of methods that explored the form of associations between variables increased from 28 percent from 1985 to 1990 to 34 percent from 1991 to 1995. However, when compared with the statistical methods used in the top organization and management journals, the sophistication gap was still enormous.

Several developments make it increasingly likely that North American and European developments on the theory-testing versus descriptive-reporting front will be closely linked in the future. First, various graduate training programs in Europe are increasingly using international journals as a standard for research design and analysis. Second, several international collaborative research efforts have joined North American and European investigators on the same teams. Third, strong champions of improved doctoral training in entrepreneurship research have bolstered intensive programs at the Academy of Management, the Babson conference, the Global Entrepreneurship Conference and other venues. The British Academy of Management has a program for doctoral students but not specifically for entrepreneurship students. Colleagues in Germany and Italy tell me that they do not yet have a training program for entrepreneurship scholars. Professor Gianni Lorenzoni, at the University of Bologna, sends students abroad to learn state-of-the-art research techniques.

Few studies of actual foundings have been carried out in Europe or North America. Instead, most research has studied established organizations. Much of this research uses survey research methods. One curious feature of the entrepreneurship literature in North American and Europe is that few researchers actually study organizations going through the start-up process. Given the difficulty of finding organizations in the process of being formed, almost all research-ers study successful foundings (Aldrich et al. 1989; Reynolds and White 1997). Moreover, most samples of organizations included in entrepreneurship journals contain firms well beyond infancy. Indeed, it is not uncommon to find "entrepreneurship" articles on samples of organizations whose average age is 10 or 15 years.

At any given time, we observe only a surviving fraction of a much larger pool of start-ups begun but abandoned by nascent entrepreneurs (Katz and Gartner 1988). Failure to appreciate the level of turnover and turbulence in business populations has blinded mainstream organization theorists to the organizational simmerings just below the sur-face in modern societies. Most new organizations are quite small and short-lived, but their emergence augments the bubbling cauldron of organizational soup so vividly described by Kaufman (1985). Without them, organization studies would have no subject matter. Nonetheless, entrepreneurship researchers have not been paying much attention to studies of the founding process. Signs of change are apparent, however, as researchers call for more attention to the issue (Frank and Lueger 1997).

Differences

I address three differences across nations:

1 The extent to which scholars build their research models on the assumption that their findings are universal as opposed to nation-specific.
2 The degree to which researchers rely on qualitative fieldwork methods as opposed to other research designs.
3 The sizeable difference in the level of government and foundation support for entrepreneurship research between the regions.

North American scholars tend to assume their models are universal, whereas European scholars assume theirs are nation-specific. A curious trend characterizes entrepreneurship research around the world. New nations are included in our studies each year, but only a small fraction of these studies involve explicit cross-national comparisons. One consequence of the neglect of truly comparative research designs is that North American researchers continue to report their results as if national context did not matter. By contrast, with the blossoming of the European Union, European scholars are becomingly increasingly aware that national context is critical. Articles based on US samples, for example, almost never contain any qualifying phrases in their conclusions about limits to generalization. Euro-pean scholars are faced with a different problem, that of deciding what contrasts to emphasize, given the "large differences between regions and countries" (Huse and Landström 1997: 9).

Beginning with the first state-of-the-art conference, calls have been heard for more cross-national research. Although North Americans are still the predominant authors of papers at state-of-the-art conferences, international authorship at Babson conference meetings has steadily increased. With Babson holding its meetings overseas every few years and Birley and MacMillan (1992) sponsoring the Global Entrepreneurship Conferences, entrepreneurship research has taken on a strong international flavor. A steady increase has occurred in the proportion of English-language papers and articles reporting on research in nations other than the United States and Canada.

For Babson, articles based on non-US samples grew from 33 percent in 1986 to 43 percent in 1994. For the major entrepreneurship journals, non-US studies grew from 18 percent in 1985–90 to 40 percent in 1991–5. Against this record of internationalization, the mainstream organization theory journals stand out as decidedly parochial. Only about one in five of the articles in *Administrative Science Quarterly* and *Academy of Management Journal* were based on non-US samples.

Despite this dramatic increase, the lack of truly comparative designs has allowed North American scholars to preserve their universalistic assumptions. Only about 16 percent of the Babson papers and 14 percent of the entrepreneurship journal articles involved more than one nation. Thus, regardless of increased international participation in entrepreneurship conferences and research carried out by North Americans in other nations, cross-national comparisons are still infrequent. Without similar measures from comparable samples in different nations, American scholars seem reluctant to part with their assumptions.

European researchers have a much stronger fieldwork orientation than American researchers. Ethnographic observations allow researchers to uncover the meaning of patterns in social processes and to detect subtle processes that may not be reported in interviews or in surveys. Unlike mailed surveys or archival records, ethnographic methods allow researchers to pursue intriguing lines of thought they had not considered before entering a field site. Themes in the anthropological ethnographic literature mesh very well with the concerns of entrepreneurship researchers, including the process of accumulating knowledge and gaining access to resources. It is extremely time-consuming, requiring significant investments in training and subsequent work in the field.

European social scientists have a long tradition of anthropological fieldwork, with many classic texts produced by reports from the field (e.g., Nadel 1957). In organization studies, European sociologists have produced key works from intensive field-based observations (e.g., Crozier 1964). The tradition continues today in ethnographies such as Botti's (1995) study of a Japanese firm in Italy and Pettigrew's (1979) research on an English public school. Czarniawska's (1997) advocacy of fieldwork as a way to uncover important organizational processes was based on her fieldwork in Swedish bureaucracies and other kinds of organizations.

In North America, several researchers in organization theory have carried on the tradition of systematic ethnographies of the kind advocated by Goffman (1974) and others. Van Maanen (1976) studied the socialization of police recruits, and his student Kunda (1992) examined the organizational culture of a high-technology firm. Jackall (1988) described conflict and intrigue among middle managers at large industrial firms in the United States, and Kanter (1977) portrayed homosocial reproduction among the middle managers at a large industrial firm in the northeastern United States. Ethnographic research is particularly valued among organizational culture researchers (e.g., Frost et al. 1991).

Only a handful of entrepreneurship researchers in North America have undertaken similar efforts (e.g., Stewart 1998). At the third state-of-the-art conference, I found only thirteen true field studies (Aldrich 1992b). At the fourth conference, only six true field studies were found, with two from the Babson conference and four in *Journal of Business Venturing* (Aldrich and Baker 1997). At every state-of-the-art conference, calls have been heard for more ethnographic research. Despite such appeals, the number of studies has steadily fallen. The lack of such studies cannot be attributed to ignorance, given that methods for carrying it out are well documented. Sage, for example, publishes a series of short books that report results of ethnographic research and methods for how to conduct such work.

Understanding why European researchers show more interest in fieldwork than North Americans requires that I clarify the meaning of the term itself. "Fieldwork" has at least two different meanings. First, it describes a very specific set of structured activities engaged in by participant or nonparticipant observers who have been trained in systematic observation and record-keeping. Second, it is used as a general term for qualitative analysis involving unstructured interviewing and casual observation.

As used by classical anthropological researchers, the term refers to long-term, systematic observation of social situations (Kleinman and Copp 1992; Stewart 1998). Usually an observer compiles extensive field notes that can subsequently be analyzed through quantitative techniques. Simple techniques may involve merely counting the occurrences of key events, whereas complex techniques may involve the creation of elaborate sociograms (Boissevain and Mitchell 1973). Some sociologists doing ethnographic studies have spent a year or more at their field site (Kleinman 1996). Few fieldworkers in Europe or North America today practice the kind of disciplined observation for which classical ethnographers are known.

European researchers often use the term "fieldwork" and "qualitative analysis" as synonyms, not separating out the process used to collect data from the methods used to interpret it. In their studies, fieldwork refers to a more unstructured set of activities than those used by classical ethnographers. Fieldwork may include unstructured interviewing, walking around the organization, observing interaction between employees and customers and studying organizational documents. Typically, it does not include coding of observational data for possible quantitative analysis, as in Mintzberg's (1973) field study of managers.

Many European scholars make use of the unstructured variety of fieldwork. At Linköping and Umeå, Holmquist and Sundin (1990) are working on an entrepreneurship project that focuses on gender issues. Together with their students, they are collecting data in the field through visits and unstructured interviews. They have also used data from surveys and government archives (Sundin 1996). In Austria, Frank and Lueger (1993) used fieldwork to study the transformation of a cooperative business. In France, Fayolle and Livian (1995: 210) studied the entrepreneurial behavior of French engineers with a "qualitative field study using semi-directed interviews lasting, on average, three hours."

Arguments over the relative merits of qualitative fieldwork versus more quantitative research divide entrepreneurship researchers in much the same way as they have split the management studies community. Advocates of more fieldwork studies argue that quantitative researchers rush to premature judgments because they have not taken the time to get to know their subjects. For example, Huse and Landström (1997: 9) argued that qualitative studies are used in Europe to generate concepts and models that lead to a deeper understanding of problems. Detractors say that qualitative research is descriptive, rather than theory-driven, and hampers the accumulation of well-grounded empirical generalizations. Fieldwork advocates counter that ethnographies can be carried out as rigorously as other kinds of research and that detractors are focusing only on poorly done work.

Given the diversity of research methods now found in Europe, we can no longer draw a sharp contrast between quantitative North American research and qualitative European research. However, we can say that a much larger proportion of European than North American researchers uses fieldwork and other qualitative methods. The critical issue is whether new and improved methods, drawing on advances in computer software programs, such as Ethnograph and Nudist, will raise the overall level of qualitative research in the entrepreneurship research community.

European governments have funded many more research initiatives than North American governments. Government support for entrepreneurship research in North America has never been very strong, and scholars have mostly depended on private foundations and small grants at the university level. Most of the funding has been for small business research, rather than on start-ups or high-growth firms. As a consequence, entrepreneurship research in North America has been operated very much like a cottage industry, with small-scale craft production limiting the scope and quality of research undertaken. By contrast, European governments have supported independent institutes and research initiatives – mainly in Northern Europe – that have permitted larger studies and longer time frames.

In the United States, a recent example illustrates the scope of the problem facing researchers. The Small Business Data Base was developed and then abandoned by the Small Business Administration. Throughout the 1980s and early 1990s, the SBA maintained the SBDB by purchasing data from Dun and Bradstreet, which collected business data for its credit reporting activities. Because Dun and Bradstreet's database was never intended for research purposes, a great deal of manipulation was required to construct data files that were useful for analytic purposes, such as in Birch's (1979, 1987) studies. In the early 1990s, the SBA began working on a new longitudinal database, developed from data collected by the Census Bureau, to measure business foundings and disbandings. Unfortunately, in the mid-1990s the SBA's effort was abandoned because of funding constraints and a decision to strengthen the Census Bureau's activities. Until other databases are perfected, investigators will have to rely on government data originally collected for administrative and regulatory purposes, rather than for organizational research.

In general, the United States government has funded policy-oriented and public intervention activities only at a very low and inconsistent level. In Canada, recent initiatives have enjoyed more success. An excellent example was the Canadian Entrepreneurship Research Alliance (ERA), chaired by Rafael Amit of the University of British Columbia. ERA was a multiyear, multimillion dollar operation involving five subprojects at different universities across Canada. Some were based on intensive field study, some on surveys and government data and still others on laboratory experiments. In the United States, private initiatives, such as the National Federation of Independent Businesses' database and the Kauffman Foundation's acquisition of the Dun and Bradstreet financial statement database, have partially replaced government-funded databases.

In sharp contrast to the United States, government support in Europe for entrepreneurship research has been much more forthcoming. The structural economic crises of the 1970s prompted European governments to reconsider their traditional emphasis on economic development through large firms. New policies were created to improve the situation of entrepreneurs and small businesses (Huse and Landström 1997: 4–5). In England, the Economic and Social Science Research Council began supporting research on small firms (Aldrich et al. 1983), and the Department of Employment funded projects on new firm formation and growth (Keeble et al. 1993). In Norway, government support allowed Lars Kolvereid, at Bodô Graduate School of Business, to field a major study of nascent entrepreneurs. In Sweden, Per Davidsson's research on nascent entrepreneurs was made possible by government funding, supplemented by funds from the Wallenberg Foundation. The Swedish Ministry of Industry is a major source of funding, either directly or through the Swedish National Board for Industrial and Technical Development.

The most striking European innovation in entrepreneurship research has no parallel in North America: the European Observatory for SMEs, coordinated by the EIM Small Business Research and Consultancy in the Netherlands. The pan-European alliance, called the European Network for SME Research (ENSR) was established in 1992 by the Directorate-General XXIII of the Commission of the European Communities. This EU project was founded to produce an independent annual report on small and medium-sized enterprises and the craft trades. Originally covering only the twelve member states of the EU, the report has gradually expanded to include nineteen nations. Although problems of differing national data collection systems have made exact comparisons somewhat difficult, the reports still provide a rich overview of business trends on the European continent (ENSR 1996).

Judged by the availability of government funding and support for data collection on entrepreneurship, North America lags far behind Europe. With its greater reliance on private donors and corporate sponsorship, the entrepreneurship research community in North America has been forced to collect data on small and limited samples of firms. Although the situation is improving through initiatives such as the Entrepreneurship Research Consortium and the Kauffman Foundation's growing support for entrepreneurship research and database development, North American scholars suffer from an information deficit, compared with European researchers.

EVOLVING TRENDS?

What are the prospects for the future? Will North American and European research become more similar, or will their differences persist?

Diffusion and isomorphism

Many forces are at work that promise to bring European and North American researchers closer together. I will treat them under the general rubric of diffusion and isomorphism, focusing on mechanisms through which scholars learn about research methods and results in other nations. Forces promoting diffusion and copying include journals, books, conferences, cross-national working groups and the international exchange of scholars. Ratnatunga and Romano (1997), for example, noted the powerful influence of a handful of top journals from 1986 to 1992.

Before considering the vehicles through which diffusion and borrowing occur, I examine the copying rules by which imitation might occur. Miner et al. (forthcoming) argued that organizations may choose to imitate others by following three different copying rules: frequency, trait and outcome-based. We can use the same framework to examine the behavior of researchers.

Frequency-based rules exist when scholars decide to imitate the most frequently used practice. For example, a frequency-based rule would be "Most articles in the *Journal of Business Venturing* use survey research methods and so will I." If followed blindly, this rule would lead to the total domination of one practice over others. Trait-based rules exist when scholars copy a practice because of *who* is using it, regardless of how many other people use it. For example, a trait-based rule would be "Imitate practices used at the Harvard Graduate School of Business." This rule gives more weight to prestigious and well-connected exemplars.

Outcome-based rules exist when scholars copy a practice because they perceive it is successful, regardless of how many other people use it or who is using it. For example, an outcome-based rule would be "Human capital models always seem to get published, so I'll use human capital variables in my research design." This rule gives more weight to institutional processes that lead to some practices being defined as "successful" and others not and thus is subject to the vagaries of bandwagon effects, fads and fashions (Abrahamson 1991).

Journals, books and conferences provide opportunities for the application of all three copying rules. In the field of entrepreneurship, the formation of a new journal in 1985 (*Journal of Business Venturing*) and the renaming of two existing ones (*Entrepreneurship and Regional Development* and *Entrepreneurship: Theory and Practice*) in 1988 facilitated the international diffusion of information about research standards and designs. Currently, there are twenty-one journals on entrepreneurship or small business, with at least ten published outside the United States, though American-based journals dominate the field (Cooper et al. 1997). The *International Small Business Journal* serves a distribution function, but it covers mostly small business rather than entrepreneurship. New journals continue to form, particularly in Europe, with two based in the United Kingdom created in the past several years. The *International Journal of Entrepreneurial Behaviour and Research* was started around 1995 and is only available on the Web. A new journal entitled *Venture Capital*, edited by Colin Mason and Richard Harrison, was started in 1998.

How might such journals homogenize practices across Europe and North America? Consider the power of journals as exemplars and their ability to institutionalize norms of professionalism in the field. For example, Watkins (1995) found that conference papers on entrepreneurship and small business in Great Britain between 1980 and 1992 were increasingly likely to cite articles in refereed journals. In 1998, the *Journal of Business Venturing* announced a special issue in honor of Mike Scott on "qualitative methods in entrepreneurship research," edited by Sue Birley and Bill Gartner. They explicitly called for submissions using ethnography, grounded theory, case studies and phenomenological methods. As noted earlier, the number of ethnographic studies in North America has been so small that a frequency-based copying rule would shortly mean their demise. However, an endorsement by a major international journal provides both trait and outcome-based justification for having another look at the practice.

Edited book series can also raise the visibility of practices within a national context and provide a focal point for the research community. For example, in Germany in 1998, Dieter Bögenhold began coediting (with Michael Fritsch, an economist, and Jürgen Schmude, a geographer) a new book series in the field of entrepreneurship. For several years, Birley and MacMillan published the results of their Global Entrepreneurship Conference in edited books. In addition, yearly reports by the SBA on the State of Small Business and periodic reports by the National Federation of Independent Businesses provide information that circulates widely in the entrepreneurship research community.

Conferences, cross-national working groups and the international exchange of scholars also promote the spread of alternative models of research practice. For example, Dieter Bögenhold is co-chair of the Working Group on SMEs and Labour Market Research (Arbeitskreis sozialwissenschaftliche Arbeitsmarktforschung) established in 1978. From Finland, Antti Haahti organized a research group from nine countries on small and medium-sized enterprises (Haahti et al. 1998). Earlier I mentioned the efforts of Heinz Klandt in organizing entrepreneurship meetings in Germany. Also in Europe, a number of conferences on small businesses have been meeting for quite some time, as mentioned earlier, such as the Nordic Conference on Small Business Management and the European Council for Small Business. The RENT Conference is explicitly devoted to entrepreneurship research that links all of Europe.

The flow of information across continents has been more one-sided than the flow across nations within Europe (Collin et al. 1996). In the past, scholars in Europe adopted concepts and methods from their US colleagues and applied them to local entrepreneurial studies. Few formed collaborative relationships or research teams with US scholars that would permit both groups to conduct research on a truly comparative basis. In their study of five entrepreneurship journals in 1994, Landström and Huse (1996: 8) found few papers coauthored by North American and European scholars. However, cross-national collaboration is beginning to blossom. I have mentioned a number of initiatives that involve cross-national collaboration, and more are forming every year.

Retention and inertia

Will the various copying rules mean that eventually a single dominant set of research practices will characterize North America and Europe? I do not think so. At one time, observers could have pointed to historical differences between the two continents as a reason for continued differentiation. Today, however, strong research subcommunities perpetuate and sustain diverse research styles *within* North America and Europe. In addition, the various intellectual homes for entrepreneurship research – universities in North America versus independent institutes in Europe – will keep differences alive.

One factor that will slow any move toward convergence, moreover, is the continuing contrast between North America and Europe in political solutions to problems such as unemployment. North American politicians still favor market solutions, whereas European politicians favor various forms of government intervention. Even though EU nations are funding many entrepreneurship initiatives with the explicit hope that job creation will result, other features of the European political scene limit the likelihood of any Silicon Valley kind of renaissance. For example, venture capital research in the United States is a vibrant area mainly because that industry is a vital part of business growth in several sectors. By contrast, such research is lagging in Europe because of its less hospitable institutional context for venture finance and risky investments.

CONCLUSIONS

Historically, research on entrepreneurship and research on organizations developed in partial isolation from one another in North America and Europe. Consequently, entrepreneurship researchers in each region repeated many of the same disputes that earlier characterized organization theory. Curiously enough, however, the international community of entrepreneurship researchers has been quicker to recognize points of agreement than the organization theory community. Perhaps one reason is the strong set of forces promoting diffusion and borrowing among entrepreneurship researchers in the different regions. Another similarity underlying entrepreneurship research in North America and Europe has been a strong normative and prescriptive orientation. This orientation has kept each research community much more in touch with practitioners and policymakers than other fields of business studies.

A third point of commonality has been that entrepreneurship research in both regions historically focused more on description than hypothesis testing, although signs of change are apparent. Again, forces of diffusion and borrowing have somewhat narrowed the gap between advocates of building causal models and others. Finally, in both regions, researchers have focused mainly on established organizations, rather than the founding process. New research initiatives such as the Entrepreneurship Research Council (ERC), focusing on nascent entrepreneurs, may redress this imbalance.

I also noted three points of difference across nations. First, North American scholars have traditionally built their research models on the assumption that their findings are universal as opposed to nation-specific. By contrast, European researchers appear to have made national differences a much more important part of their arguments. They are more likely to compare industries, regions or countries than their North American colleagues. Second, the regions are still somewhat separated in the degree to which researchers rely on qualitative fieldwork methods as opposed to other research designs. Finally, the level of government and foundation support for entrepreneurship research is larger in Europe than in North America. In this regard, North American researchers have much to learn about funding from their European colleagues.

Researchers on both sides of the Atlantic have a stake in maintaining diversity in the field of entrepreneurship studies. As Landström and Huse (1996: 19) remarked, "US and European scholars within the field have much to learn from each other." For example, North American research tends to be grounded more firmly in basic theories and models than European research, whereas European researchers appear more open to a variety of methodological approaches than North American researchers. As several readers of early drafts reminded me, science depends on open and ongoing conversations about research and methods. Were the current dialogue between international researchers to collapse into a monologue, we would all suffer. Dogmatic claims of superiority by one approach have no place in our field.

NOTE

I owe a debt of gratitude to many readers of early drafts and others who answered my questions about developments in their countries: Sue Birley, Dieter Bögenhold, Per Davidsson, Bill Gartner, Daniel Hjorth, Stefan Kwiatkowski, Hans Landström, Jerry Katz, Paul Reynolds, Olav Spilling and Luca Solari.

REFERENCES

Abrahamson, E. 1991. Managerial Fads and Fashions: The Diffusion and Rejection of Innovations. *Academy of Management Review* 16(3): 586–612.

Aldrich, H.E. 1988. Paradigm Wars: Donaldson versus the Critics of Organization Theory. *Organization Studies* 9(1): 19–25.

Aldrich, H.E. 1990. Using an Ecological Perspective to Study Organizational Founding Rates. *Entrepreneurship: Theory and Practice* 14(3): 7–24.

Aldrich, H.E. 1992a. Paradigm Incommensurability: Three Perspectives on Organizations. In M.I. Reed and M.D. Hughes (eds.), *Rethinking Organization: New Directions in Organizational Theory and Analysis*. Newbury Park, CA: Sage, pp. 17–45.

Aldrich, H.E. 1992b. Methods in Our Madness? Trends in Entrepreneurship Research. In D.L. Sexton and J.D. Kasarda (eds.), *The State of the Art of Entrepreneurship*. Boston: PWS-Kent Publishing, pp. 191–213.

Aldrich, H.E. and Baker, T. 1997. Blinded by the Cites? Has There Been Progress in Entrepreneurship Research? In D.L. Sexton and R.W. Smilor (eds.), *Entrepreneurship: 2000*. Chicago: Upstart, pp. 377–400.

Aldrich, H.E., Cater, J., Jones, T. and McEvoy, D. 1983. From Periphery to Peripheral: The South Asian Petite Bourgeoisie in England. In I.H. Simpson and R. Simpson (eds.), *Research in the Sociology of Work*, vol. 2. Greenwich, CN: JAI Press, pp. 1–32.

Aldrich, H.E., Kalleberg, A.L., Marsden, P.V. and Cassell, J. 1989. In Pursuit of Evidence: Strategies for Locating New Businesses. *Journal of Business Venturing* 4 (November): 367–86.

Birch, D.L. 1979. *The Job Generation Process*. Cambridge, MA: MIT Program on Neighborhood and Regional Change.

Birch, D.L. 1987. *Job Creation in America: How Our Smallest Companies Put the Most People to Work*. New York: Free Press.

Birley, S. and MacMillan, I.C. (eds.), 1992. *International Perspectives on Entrepreneurship Research*. Amsterdam: Elsevier.

Boissevain, J. and Mitchell, J.C. (eds.) 1973. *Network Analysis: Studies in Human Interaction*. The Hague: Mouton.

Botti, H.F. 1995. Misunderstandings: A Japanese Transplant in Italy Strives for Lean Production. *Organization* 2(1): 55–86.

Carsrud, A.L., Olm, K.W. and Eddy, G.E. 1986. Entrepreneurship: Research in Quest of a

Paradigm. In D.L. Sexton and R. Smilor (eds.), *The Art and Science of Entrepreneurship*. Cambridge, MA: Ballinger, pp. 367–78.

Churchill, N. and Lewis, V.L. 1986. Entrepreneurship Research: Directions and Methods. In D.L. Sexton and R. Smilor (eds.), *The Art and Science of Entrepreneurship*. Cambridge, MA: Ballinger, pp. 333–65.

Collin, S.O., Johansson, U., Svensson, K. and Ulvenblad, P.O. 1996. Market Segmentation in Scientific Publications: Research Patterns in American vs. European Management Journals. *British Journal of Management* 7: 141–54.

Cooper, A.C., Hornaday, J.A. and Vesper, K.H. 1997. The Field of Entrepreneurship over Time. In P.D. Reynolds et al. (eds.), *Frontiers of Entrepreneurship Research 1997*. Babson Park, MA: Babson College Center for Entrepreneurial Studies, pp. xi–xvii.

Crozier, M. 1964. *The Bureaucratic Phenomenon*. Chicago: University of Chicago Press.

Czarniawska, B. 1997. *Narrating the Organization: Dramas of Institutional Identity*. Chicago: University of Chicago.

Donaldson, L. 1985. *In Defence of Organization Theory: A Reply to the Critics*. Cambridge: Cambridge University.

European Network for SME Research (ENSR). 1996. *The European Observatory for SMEs: Fourth Annual Report*. Zoetermeer, The Netherlands: European Observatory for SME Research and EIM Small Business Research and Consultancy.

Fayolle, A. and Livian, Y.F. 1995. Entrepreneurial Behavior of French Engineers. In S. Birley and I.C. MacMillan (eds.), *International Entrepreneurship*. London: Routledge, pp. 201–28.

Frank, H. and Lueger, M. 1993. Transformationen kooperativen Handelns: Von der Gründung eines selbstverwalteten Betriebes zum erfolgreichen kooperative geführten Unternehmen (The Transformation of Cooperative Activity: From the Start-up of a Self-Administered Business to the Successfully Managed Firm). *Zeitschrift für Soziologie* 22(1): 49–64.

Frank, H. and Lueger, M. 1997. Reconstructing Development Processes: Conceptual Basis and Empirical Analysis of Setting Up a Business. *International Studies of Management & Organization* 27(3): 34–63.

Frost, P.J., Moore, L.F., Louis, M.R., Lundberg, C.C. and Martin, J. 1991. *Reframing Organizational Culture*. Newbury Park, CA: Sage.

Goffman, Erving. 1974. *Frame Analysis*. Cambridge, MA: Harvard University Press.

Haahti, A., Hall, G. and Donckels, R. (eds.). 1998. *The Internationalization of SMEs: The Interstratos Project*. London: Routledge.

Hinings, R. 1988. Defending Organization Theory: A British View from North America. *Organization Studies* 9(1): 2–7.

Holmquist, C. and Sundin, E. 1990. What's Special about Highly Educated Women Entrepreneurs? *Entrepreneurship and Regional Development* 2: 181–93.

Hoy, F. 1997. Relevance in Entrepreneurship Research. In D.L. Sexton and R.W. Smilor (eds.), *Entrepreneurship 2000*. Chicago: Upstart, pp. 361–75.

Huse, M. and Landström, H. 1997. European Entrepreneurship and Small Business Research: Methodological Openness and Contextual Differences. *International Studies of Management and Organization* 27(3): 3–12.

Jackall, R. 1988. *Moral Mazes: The World of Corporate Managers*. New York: Oxford.

Kanter, Rosabeth Moss. 1977. *Men and Women of the Corporation*. New York: Basic Books.

Kassem, M.S. 1976. Introduction: European versus American Organization Theories. In G. Hofstede and M.S. Kassem (eds.), *European Contributions to Organization Theory*. Amsterdam: Van Gorcum, pp. 1–17.

Katz, J. and Gartner, W.B. 1988. Properties of Emerging Organizations. *Academy of Management Review* 13 (July): 429–41.

Kaufman, H. 1985. *Time, Chance, and Organizations*. Chatham, NJ: Chatham House.

Keeble, D., Walker, S. and Robson, M. 1993. *New Firm Formation and Small Business Growth in the United Kingdom: Spatial and Temporal Variations and Determinants.* Department of Geography and Small Business Research Centre, University of Cambridge, England.

Kent, C.A., Sexton, D. and Vesper, K. (eds.), 1982. *Encyclopedia of Entrepreneurship.* Englewood Cliffs, NJ: Prentice-Hall.

Klandt, H. 1997. Conference on Entrepreneurship.
http//:www.g-forum.de

Kleinman, S. 1996. *Opposing Ambitions.* Chicago: University of Chicago Press.

Kleinman, S. and Copp, M. 1992. *Emotions and Field Work.* Newbury Park, CA: Sage.

Koza, M.P. and Thoenig, J.C. 1995. Organization Theory at the Crossroads: Some Reflections on European and United States Approaches to Organizational Research. *Organization Science* 6(1): 1–8.

Kunda, G. 1992. *Engineering Culture: Control and Commitment in a High Tech Corporation.* Philadelphia: Temple University Press.

Lammers, C.J. 1990. Sociology of Organizations Around the Globe: Similarities and Differences Between American, British, French, German, and Dutch Brands. *Organization Studies* 11(2): 179–205.

Landström, H. and Huse, M. 1996. *Trends in European Entrepreneurship and Small-Business Research: A Comparison between Europe and the US.* Working Paper 1993:3, Scandinavian Institute for Research in Entrepreneurship.

Landström, H. and Johannisson, B. 1998. *Theoretical Foundations in Swedish Entrepreneurship and Small Business Research.* SIRE Working Paper 1. Halmstead University, Sweden.

Landström, H., Frank, H. and Veciana, J.M. (eds.). 1997. *Entrepreneurship and Small Business Research in Europe: An ECSB Survey.* Aldershot, England: Avebury.

Low, M. and MacMillan, I.C. 1988. Entrepreneurship: Past Research and Future Challenges. *Journal of Management* 14(2): 139–61.

Miner, A.S., Raghavan, S.V. and Haunschild, P.S. Forthcoming. The Influence of Interorganizational Imitation Modes on Population Level Learning. In J.A.C. Baum and B. McKelvey (eds.), *Variations in Organization Science: In Honor of Donald T. Campbell.* Newbury Park, CA: Sage.

Minztberg, H. 1973. *The Nature of Managerial Work.* New York: Harper & Row.

Mone, M.A. and McKinley, W.A. 1993. The Uniqueness Value and Its Consequences for Organization Studies. *Journal of Management Inquiry* 2(3): 284–96.

Nadel, S.F. 1957. *The Theory of Social Structure.* Glencoe, IL, Free Press.

Paulin, W.L., Coffey, R.E. and Spaulding, M.E. 1982. Entrepreneurship Research: Methods and Directions. In C.A. Kent, D.L. Sexton and K. Vesper (eds.), *Encyclopedia of Entrepreneurship.* Englewood Cliffs, NJ: Prentice-Hall, pp. 353–73.

Perryman, M.R. 1982. Commentary on Research in the Field of Entrepreneurship. In C.A. Kent, D.L. Sexton and K. Vesper (eds.), *Encyclopedia of Entrepreneurship.* Englewood Cliffs, NJ: Prentice-Hall, pp. 377–8.

Peterson, R. and Horvath, D. 1982. Commentary on Research in the Field of Entrepreneurship. In C.A. Kent, D.L. Sexton, and K. Vesper (eds.), *Encyclopedia of Entrepreneurship.* Englewood Cliffs, NJ: Prentice-Hall, pp. 374–6.

Pettigrew, Andrew. 1979. On Studying Organizational Culture. *Administrative Science Quarterly* 24(4): 570–81.

Ratnatunga, J. and Romano, C. 1997. A "Citation Classics" Analysis of Articles in Contemporary Small Enterprise Research. *Journal of Business Venturing* 12(3): 197–212.

Reynolds, P.D. and White, S.B. 1997. *The Entrepreneurial Process: Economic Growth, Men, Women, and Minorities.* Westport, CN: Quorum Books.

Sexton, D.L. and Smilor, R. W. (eds.). 1986. *The Art and Science of Entrepreneurship.* Cambridge, MA: Ballinger.

Sexton, D.L. and Kasarda, J.D. (eds.). 1992. *The State of the Art of Entrepreneurship*. Boston, MA: PWS-Kent.

Sexton, D.L. and Smilor, R.W. (eds.). 1997. *Entrepreneurship 2000*. Chicago: Upstart.

Stewart, A. 1998. *The Ethnographer's Method*. Thousand Oaks, CA: Sage Publications.

Sundin, E. 1996. Entrepreneurship – Female Liberation or Male Encroachment? Department of Technology and Social Change, Linköping University, Sweden. Paper presented at the 41st ISCB World Conference, June 20–3.

Üsdiken, B. and Pasadeos, Y. 1995. Organizational Analysis in North America and Europe: A Comparison of Co-citation Networks. *Organization Studies* 16(3): 503–26.

Van Maanen, J. 1976. Breaking In: Socialization to Work. In R. Dubin (ed.), *Handbook of Work, Organization, and Society*. Chicago: Rand McNally, pp. 67–130.

Watkins, D. 1995. Changes in the Nature of UK Small Business Research, 1980–1990. Part Two: Changes in the Nature of the Output. *Small Business and Enterprise Development* 2(1): 59–66.

Wortman, M.S. Jr. 1986. A Unified Framework, Research Typologies, and Research Prospectuses for the Interface between Entrepreneurship and Small Business. In D.L. Sexton and R.W. Smilor (eds.), *The Art and Science of Entrepreneurship*. Cambridge, MA: Ballinger, pp. 272–332.

2

Conceptual and Empirical Challenges in the Study of Firm Growth

PER DAVIDSSON AND JOHAN WIKLUND

THE NEED FOR LONGITUDINAL RESEARCH ON FIRM GROWTH
WHAT IS GROWING?
FIRM GROWTH THEORY
DIFFERENTIAL KNOWLEDGE USER INTERESTS
OPERATIONALIZING GROWTH
CONCLUSIONS

When the first author reviewed the literature on small firm growth in the mid-1980s for his dissertation, he noted that surprisingly few studies had focused on that specific problem (Davidsson 1989a, 1989b). Today, this is no longer true. In recent years ever more comprehensive lists of studies have been compiled and reviewed. Storey (1997) compiled results from more than twenty-five studies. Delmar (1997) scrutinized the operationalizations of growth in fifty-five studies. The second author of this chapter recently reviewed and classified close to seventy studies for his dissertation (Wiklund 1998), while Ardishvili et al. (1998) included in their classification a full 105 published and unpublished studies focusing on new venture growth. However, rather than presenting a set of solid generalizations on the causes and effects of growth, these reviewers all tend to come up with relatively critical accounts concerning both theoretical and methodological shortcomings (Storey 1997: 5, 125; Cooper 1995: 120; Delmar 1997: 205, 212; Wiklund 1998: 6–7, 19; Ardishvili et al. 1998: 1).

Besides the above evaluations of research specifically on growth, we have also observed that longitudinal designs are generally lacking in entrepreneurship research (Cooper 1995: 112; Wiklund 1998: 7). In addition, Aldrich and Baker (1997: 389) and Sexton (1997: 407) also identified the lack of longitudinal studies in entrepreneurship research as a major impediment.

Despite the shortcomings pointed out by the critics, knowledge about what facilitates and hinders growth is still scattered and limited today. The same is true for insights into the process of firm growth. Apparently, the large number of empirical studies has not had a high yield of generalizable knowledge. This suggests that researchers who set out to contribute meaningfully to this line of empirical research have a number of challenges to deal with. On the basis of the above criticisms, we would suggest that some of the more important challenges are the following:

- to develop a satisfactory basic research design
- to apply a well-founded conceptualization of growth, which in turn requires a well thought-out conceptualization of the firm
- to adequately match this conceptualization with the purpose of the study, the theories used and the operationalization of growth.

In the next section we argue that growth studies need to be longitudinal and why this is so. We then turn to the conceptualization of the firm as the unit of analysis in growth studies, which turns out to be a really difficult problem. After that we discuss theoretical perspectives and how these match with different conceptualizations of the firm. Finally, we turn to operationalization issues – the choice of growth indicators, specific ways to model growth trajectories and the distinction between organic and acquired growth. Throughout, we also discuss how these issues relate to different purposes, i.e., whose knowledge interests does a study try to satisfy?

THE NEED FOR LONGITUDINAL RESEARCH ON FIRM GROWTH

Growth is a process that needs to be studied over time. To date, studies that use data from several points in time have usually been based on secondary data. Such studies may serve the purpose of testing simple theoretical propositions or estimating empirical relationships like the influence of firm age and size on growth (cf. Evans 1987). They sometimes suffice for richer demographic profiles of growth firms or to propose the existence of different types of growth firms (Davidsson and Delmar 1997; Delmar and Davidsson 1998). Since they typically comprise only a minimum of variables, secondary data sets cannot, however, be used for testing or developing conceptually richer theories.

Case studies are sometimes longitudinal not only in the sense that the firm's history is investigated but also in the sense that the firm's development is followed in real time (Brytting 1991). While such studies are valuable for developing hypotheses and for suggesting interpretations of the results obtained in surveys, they will never suffice for making generalizations about relationships among variables.

Most studies on firm growth are survey-based. Survey data are more or less the only alternative if we want to have data on attitudes, perceptions, strategies and resources from a large number of cases. The problem is that, with a few exceptions (e.g., Cooper 1995; Wiklund 1998), the studies are cross-sectional. This leaves the researcher with several less-than-satisfactory alternatives.

The first is to use historical growth as the dependent variable in causal analysis. This method measures a growth process that started some time ago and that ends at the time of data collection. Explanatory variables are collected at the same time and measure the present situation of the firm. In other words, explanatory variables collected today are used to predict a past process, which breaks with the principle that the cause must precede the effect. The researcher may justify this by assuming that the explanatory variables do not change during the period over which growth is studied. This is reasonable only when variables such as sex, age and ethnicity are used for explaining growth. The other possible justification is that past growth predicts future growth. That is, the growth measure calculated from the past should be seen as a forecast of future growth, and the regression equation predicts this future growth. Unfortunately, Storey (1997) and others show that this is not a plausible assumption. In addition, failures are typically not included in surveys. Therefore, when past growth is used as the dependent variable, factors that increase the probability of *both* success and failure will be misinterpreted as "success factors." Firm development needs to be studied in real time to avoid this error.

The second less-than-satisfactory solution is to study growth willingness rather than actual growth (Davidsson 1989b; Wiklund et al. 1997). While less problematic from a causality point of view, this introduces the question of attitude-behavior consistency (Foxall 1984). We are left not knowing whether growth willingness is a strong predictor of subsequent growth.

The problems are essentially the same for analyses that focus on the consequences of growth rather than its antecedents. Only with longitudinal data can really satisfactory analyses for theory testing and development be undertaken. The challenge for future research is to generate funds and develop data collection procedures that make the building of such data sets possible.

WHAT IS GROWING?

A minimum requirement for knowledge development is that we know what we want to study. This implies a need for a clear conceptualization of the micro unit of the analysis. The embarrassing fact is that researchers in the field, ourselves included, have not been clear about the concept of "the firm." A likely reason why this has not been much considered is that most empirical research has been cross-sectional. Theorists, in their turn, have perhaps not done enough empirical research to see the conceptual problems. When growth is studied empirically and longitudinally, they become apparent.

Let's consider entrepreneur X. In the late 1970s, he stumbled into becoming a part-time small business owner-manager as a result of writing some accounting software for his wife's business. Others with similar needs showed an interest, and before long X was running a high-growth firm developing and selling software for business applications. The operations continued to grow by related diversification: consulting, information technology education programs, software development for nonbusiness applications and so on. Some of this developed organically while other parts were acquired. After a successful decade the firm had some 150 employees and ran activities in several places. Legally, however, they were all in the same limited liability company.

Now the firm encountered severe difficulties for the first time. In order to regain some of the spirit of the young and small firm, entrepreneur X decided to break the firm into smaller, more independent units. He could do this in three different ways (but had to choose one):

1 Form a number of wholly owned but semi-independent, separate legal units that represented the different lines of business under a holding company, which would retain a few central functions.

2 Like (1) but with more complete separate companies, the holding company essentially being only the owner of the brand name and functioning as the group's internal bank.

3 Like (2) but with transfer of majority ownership to the top management in the new units, entrepreneur X only keeping a minority stake via the holding company.

In all three options, one new company would represent the group's original core business: software development for business applications.

What is the firm in this story? How much has it grown? In what sense is the resulting company group the same entity as the original part-time business? Do we want it to be regarded as the same entity? If so, does that apply regardless of which options entrepreneur X chooses? Is it just the software development company that should be counted or all business activities that are still under X's ownership control? These questions are not easy, but they need reasonable answers if we are to study firm growth as a process over time.

At a given point in time, it is relatively easy to define or describe what a particular firm is. Important aspects of this description could be what it offers to the market and what assets it controls. Its legal form, its ownership and its established relationships may be other important dimensions. The paradox is that if we try to follow the unit thus defined over time in order to study its growth, the definition will no longer hold. Over time, the firm is likely to change its activities, its assets, its ownership and its legal form, and if something has grown, it is *not* the firm as originally defined.

The heart of the problem is that firms are *not* like biological individuals. There is no question that the pony-size five-year-old Great Dane is the same entity as the little newborn puppy it once was. Not so with firms. Metaphorically speaking, a duckling may actually become a swan in the world of firms. The fact that firms are not individuals is a fundamental challenge to any attempt to study business growth at the firm level. An analogy to quantum physics and Heisenberg's uncertainty principle may serve to summarize our point: you cannot simultaneously determine the firm's identity and study its growth.

As shown in table 2.1, microlevel changes that make the concept of firm problematic are not delimited to cases like entrepreneur X. They are the rule rather than the exception. These data are based on a Swedish data set comprising all commercial, nongovernment firms that were in existence during the entire November 1987 to November 1996 period, and which had an end size of at least twenty employees. Here firm means the legal enterprise. Different enterprises that are wholly owned by the same company group appear as separate cases. Constellations of surviving establishments that appear under one company code the first year, and another company code the second year are regarded as representing the same surviving firm. Table 2.1 only shows the dynamics that relate directly to the problem of what unit should be regarded as the firm.

The results show that roughly 400 firms annually are probably acquired, as indicated by changes (b) and (f). Are those firms still the same after they were acquired? What if activities that already employed ten people in the acquiring company group are inte-

TABLE 2.1 Category changes over time in 8,562 surviving (1987–1996) Swedish firms with 20 or more employees in 1996

Year	1988	1989	1990	1991	1992	1993	1994	1995	1996	Entire period
Change governance										
(a) indep.→parent	171	192	140	191	102	122	140	112	115	1,238
(b) indep.→daughter	244	238	216	222	237	215	293	290	196	1,964
(c) daughter→indep.	123	88	123	445	158	205	143	220	228	1,559
(d) parent→indep.	80	47	56	119	88	87	61	92	113	718
(e) daughter→parent	44	44	65	78	46	44	57	48	57	462
(f) parent→daughter	100	121	131	131	77	83	152	155	92	1,005
Change abroad										
(g) started majority-owned activity abroad (from some to none)	91	27	51	95	48	64	159	140	121	754
(h) terminated majority-owned activity abroad (from none to some)	18	16	40	27	15	63	53	26	112	356
Any type of change (a) through (h)	858	766	803	1275	755	853	1033	1049	988	4,779 (55.8%)

Entries do not sum up horizontally because some firms undergo the same type of change several times, and not vertically because some firms undergo several different changes.

grated with the acquired firm while activities in the latter employing five people are dissolved, has the latter then grown? Some 200 to 300 firms annually are likely to represent spinoffs or buyouts (c and e). Were they really firms before they were spun off? If so, are they still the same firms as before? Roughly 150 firms annually change from independent to parent company (a). This probably represents either acquisition of an existing firm or reorganization of a business that was previously run as a single company to becoming a company group. When the growth of these cases is assessed, should not both the parent and the daughters be included in the second year? Similar problems with the growth computation apply to firms, which start or terminate activities abroad (g and h).

Over a ten-year period a majority (4,779 out of 8,562 companies) undergo changes that make it questionable whether they still are the same firm; hence, the basis for a growth computation is ambiguous. While ten years is a long time, it is clear from these data that also analyses with a three or five-year time frame would also be highly problematic in these respects.

Despite all these problems, we hold that firm growth can and should be studied. The above examples clearly illustrate that our interpretation of the growth of the firm depends on our definition of what the firm is, and that this definition has to be made *before* any meaningful discussion of growth can take place. Our alternative to viewing the firm as an unspecified, taken-for-granted entity would be to utilize one or more of the three units of analyses below. Imagine how different our analyses and interpretations in the above examples would have been, depending on which alternative was chosen:

- All business activities controlled by *an individual* or group of individuals. The entrepreneur or the entrepreneurial team would be the unit to follow over time. The individual(s) may choose to expand a specific existing legal unit or place the growth in a new independent firm or a subsidiary. Existing activities may be expanded, or new unrelated activities may be added as a result of innovation or acquisition. Thus, the types and number of activities and governance structures controlled by the individual(s) may change over time.
- A particular *business activity* or a related set of business activities. Here, the unit of analysis would be a particular product or product line, or perhaps entire business concepts as in business format franchising. These activities may, over time, be in different governance structures and controlled by different individuals. They may represent only part of the total operations of a legal entity or, in other cases, all operations of an entire company group.
- A *governance structure*, which is a decision-making unit, coherently administered and controlled. This unit of analysis could (but does not necessarily) coincide with a specific legal or statistical unit that can be found in data registers. In a multi-establishment company group, the unit of analysis could be an establishment, a company or the entire group. The ownership of a given governance structure may shift over time, and so may its business activities.

Much research to date has implicitly assumed a complete overlap between these three units of analysis. When an individual starts and runs one single organization, which expands organically, not diversifying its activities, this is true. In every other route of expansion, these units of analysis will differ from each other. Depending on which unit of analysis the researcher chooses, interpretations and conclusions will differ. The longer the time span over which growth is studied, the more likely is the assumption of complete overlap to be wrong – an important fact, so far largely overlooked.

FIRM GROWTH THEORY

In order to be able to use appropriate units of analysis – and the theories connected with them – one must start with a conceptualization of the firm. In their review of different theories of the firm, Seth and Thomas (1994) identify four different theoretical firm conceptualizations. The firm as:

- a "production function" in neoclassical economics,
- a "strategic player" in new industrial organization economics,
- a "nexus of contracts" in agency theory, or
- a "governance structure" in transaction cost economics.

Unfortunately, none of these conceptualizations was created for the specific purpose of analyzing firm growth. That is, they do not provide us with an answer to the question, What is the unit of our analysis whose size development we want to study over time?

The shortcomings of approaches with a theoretical firm as point of departure may explain why firm growth researchers have taken a different tack. It is more common to utilize some of the theories grounded in real-world firm conceptualizations, called "empirical firm" theories by Seth and Thomas (1994: 168). However, as the above examples and our review in the introduction have illustrated, these conceptualizations are rarely clear or explicit. Nevertheless, conceptualizations of firms and theoretical perspectives in previous empirical research into firm growth can be inferred.

Ardishvili et al. (1998) classified empirical growth studies as either factors of growth studies or growth process studies. The former deal with seeking *explanations* as to why firms grow, i.e., antecedents of growth are sought and growth is treated as dependent variable. The latter are concerned with the changes that take place in an organization as a *consequence* of growth. Growth is the starting point, the cause.

Firm growth studies can be categorized in more detail based on their underlying assumptions. With a focus on general assumptions, concepts and relationships among concepts, we identified four theoretical perspectives that fall into either of the factor or process categories:

- the resources-based perspective
- the motivation perspective
- the strategic adaptation perspective
- the configuration perspective (Wiklund 1998).

Three of these are linked to factor studies and one to process studies. As we will later show, each of these theoretical perspectives correspond in a natural way to the previously introduced units of analysis, namely, individual(s), activity or governance structure.

In *the resource-based perspective*, the focus is on the firm as a bundle of resources and the activities it can perform based on these resources. Thus, it is most appropriate for growth studies within the resource-based perspective to use the business activity or related set of business activities as the unit of analysis. Growth in this case would refer to the expansion of related business activities, made possible by the unique combination and/or deployment of resources. This is not to say that this theoretical perspective is entirely incompatible with other units of analysis. Both enterprising individuals and governance structures are associated with certain resources, some of which are so general (e.g., financial resources or highly educated staff) that they are of relevance for a wide range of business activities. Therefore, the individual(s) and the governance structure are secondary alternatives for unit of analysis when growth is to be studied from a resource-based perspective.

With its focus on power distribution, structural complexity and control mechanisms, the conceptualization of the firm in *the strategic adaptation perspective* relates to the governance structure unit of analysis. Thus, growth studies applying strategic adaptation as the theoretical perspective would benefit from using the governance structure as their unit of analysis. A secondary alternative is the activity because different strategies can be applied for different strategic business units that encounter different environmental threats. The strategic adaptation perspective is clearly not designed for the individual unit of analysis. For example, from an enterprising individual's perspective, selling off or closing down entire activities or governance structures may be rational strategic options, which still leads to growth of the individual's total business activities. This is not the kind of strategic option visible or relevant from "within" an activity or a governance structure.

In *the motivation perspective* of firm growth, as in all psychological studies, the focus is on individuals and their actions. Hence, motivational studies of firm growth use the individual(s) as the unit of analysis. To investigate the relationship between an individual's motivation and firm growth, the individual's entire business activities need to be followed. This perspective reveals what particular activities under the individual's control expand or not as a result of his or her level of motivation. The same is true for the specific make-up of the governance structure(s) within which the expansion takes place. Therefore, following one legal unit under the individual's control may lead to erroneous results. However, the motivation of key individuals has a place also in studies using the activity or the governance structure as the unit of analysis.

While the three previously mentioned theoretical perspectives are concerned with factors of growth, *the configuration perspective* deals with the growth process. This perspective focuses on how managerial problems appear and can be dealt with during a firm's growth through (presumed) typical stages of development. This conforms to using the governance structure as the unit of analysis, which focuses on a particular decision-making unit coherently administered and controlled. Product life-cycle theory (e.g., Day 1981) can be regarded as a variation on this theme, more adapted to using the activity as the unit of analysis. Configuration theories are clearly not consistent with using the individual unit of analysis. On the contrary, several adherents address the possibility (sometimes presented as a necessity) of replacing the founder in order to achieve successful further growth of the firm.

DIFFERENTIAL KNOWLEDGE USER INTERESTS

The three possible units of analysis identified above and their suitability within the four theoretical perspectives prevalent in growth studies are summarized in table 2.2. Our analysis suggests that different units of analysis are "optimal" for different theories. Further, while the governance structure, and possibly also the activity, as unit of analysis seems to have some compatibility with each theoretical perspective, current formulations of strategic adaptation and configuration perspectives seem ill-adapted for using the

TABLE 2.2 Different units of analysis and ranking of their suitability within different theoretical perspectives

Resource based	Motivation	Strategic adaptation	Configuration

1 Activity
2 Individual
  or governance
  structure
	1 Individual
	2 Activity or governance
	  structure
		1 Governance
		  structure
		2 Activity
		3 Individual
			1 Governance
			  structure
			2 Activity

Within each theoretical perspective, 1 denotes the most suitable unit of analysis, 2 the second most suitable and so on.

individual's entire business activities as the unit of analysis. As we shall see, however, the individual as unit of analysis has other advantages.

Although each of the theoretical perspectives reviewed provides us with valuable insights into the growth of the firm, they address different specific issues. To get a fuller understanding for the antecedents of growth as well as the growth process, it may be beneficial to integrate some or all the theoretical perspectives in a model. Such a model integrating the theoretical perspectives has been suggested by Wiklund (1998). However, when such integrative models are applied to empirical research, different conceptualizations of the firm and different units of analysis may have to be used in parallel.

Keeping track of the development of different units of analysis when they no longer overlap 100 percent would be cumbersome in longitudinal survey studies and virtually impossible in longitudinal studies utilizing secondary data. To some extent, the researcher will have to compromise in the conceptualization of the firm and the unit of analysis. However, it is important that these compromises are made consciously, that the most appropriate methods with relation to the theories are applied and that the specific empirical issues are investigated. Table 2.2 can serve as an aid when doing such compromises. The alternative, which would be to disregard the fact that the unit of analysis affects empirical results and that different units of analysis are more appropriate for certain theoretical perspectives, is not an acceptable solution. Empirical complexity is a challenge that must be accepted and not disregarded. If not, results and conclusions may be seriously flawed.

The relative merits of these units of analysis are also contingent on the fundamental question *why* we want to study growth. In table 2.3, we try to assess the relevance of the different units of analysis to three groups of potential users of research-based knowledge on firm growth: owners, managers and policymakers.

TABLE 2.3 Different units of analysis and their relevance for different user groups

	Individual(s)	*Activity*	*Governance structure*
Owners	Very high relevance	High relevance	Some relevance
Managers	Some relevance	High relevance	Very high relevance
Policymakers	High relevance	Very high relevance	Some relevance

From an owner's point of view, the totality of her or his business activities is the main interest. Within that totality, what particular activities grow or not is also relevant. Since the organizational framework is also part of the totality, the growth of a particular governance structure is also of some relevance to owners.

A manager is typically the manager of a governance structure, and the causes and consequences of growth of that unit is therefore the main interest. It is also highly relevant to managers what factors contribute to the growth of particular business activities under their control. The growth of individuals' entire business operations is of secondary interest for managers.

Policymakers may show a keen interest in high-growth firms, but we hold that this interest is misdirected if focused on the growth of governance structures. Policymakers' positive interest in high-growth firms is, or should be, concerned instead with the growth of activities. It is the emergence and growth of new activities that add value and create genuinely new jobs.

Reading the table column-wise, activity-based growth analysis seems to be of high interest to all three parties. The other two units of analysis are more likely to lead in wrong directions for certain purposes.

This analysis also provides us with an interesting possibility to clarify the differential foci of the overlapping interests of entrepreneurship research, management research and economics. The management discipline is fundamentally about the micro level in the economy. Its core concerns primarily the performance of established business organizations and what managers can do to influence performance. The fate of the individuals involved is secondary, as is the question whether success of the firm also contributes to the economy at large or merely is part of a zero-sum game on the macro level.

Economics is fundamentally about the macro level. The performance of the economy at large is in focus. The micro level analysis is there only to give an atomistic rationale for macro level phenomena. Even for those who theorize about (romanticize?) the entrepreneur (e.g., Schumpeter 1934), the ultimate interest is always with the macro level effects (Kirzner 1983).

Entrepreneurship research concerns itself both with micro and macro levels. It takes a clear voluntaristic stance, based on the assumption that individual initiative is a crucial force in the economy at large. It takes a genuine interest in the characteristics and behavior of the individuals who take such initiatives. At the same time, entrepreneurship research takes an interest in value creation on the societal level. On this macro level the main interest in growth studies from an entrepreneurship point of view is the growth of activities. What new activities contribute to the gross domestic product (GDP) and job creation comes to the fore, not primarily what particular individuals are behind it and certainly not the growth of governance structures that may represent mere reshuffling of existing activities or even unsound concentration tendencies.

For these reasons, entrepreneurship researchers may want to consider more explicitly favoring the individual(s) or the activity(ies) as the unit of analysis. The study of *entrepreneurial management* is a different story. The boundary where entrepreneurship and management disciplines overlap may be where the governance structure is the most appropriate unit of analysis.

From a more pragmatic research stance, it is also possible to assess how easy or difficult the units of analysis are to work with empirically, as summarized in table 2.4. Obtaining a random sample of enterprising individuals is difficult, and there is certainly no directory of entrepreneurial teams available to the researcher before data collection. If companies are sampled with the intention to study owner-managers, those running several businesses will be oversampled. However, for the purposes of theory construction and testing, the resulting deviations from population representativeness need not always be damaging.

One of the great advantages of using the individual(s) as a unit of analysis is that, once identified, collecting data from them and following them over time is relatively easy. Teams may be more problematic as members come and go and the distinctions among team member, network or employee may be diffuse. The major problem over time,

TABLE 2.4 Different units of analysis and their ease of use in empirical research

	Individual(s)	Activity	Governance structure
Sampling	Difficult	Very difficult	Easy, but can be deceptive
Initial data collection	Easy	Easy to difficult	Relatively easy
Longitudinal data collection	Relatively easy	Increasingly difficult (especially in surveys)	Increasingly difficult if done properly

however, is dealing with retirement: When is the unit dead, and when should it be kept? Keeping it means compromising the unit of analysis, but dropping such cases means excluding a phenomenon that may be central to many growth processes. And if kept, is it sensible to use the old owner's dispositions and attitudes as explanatory variables in a growth analysis? The answer is not self-evident (Schein 1983; Wiklund 1998).

Activities may be the most difficult units for researchers to study at arm's length. No satisfactory sampling frame can be created beforehand. The sampling unit would therefore probably have to be something like individuals, establishments or companies, all of which may perform several separate activities. Initial data collection may sometimes be easy, if the total operations are limited and of low complexity. Over time the sampling units will likely add new activities, ranging from those very closely related to those completely unrelated. It would then be hard to determine what is and what is not part of the focal activity. Sometimes the studied activity would no longer be associated with the original sampling unit.

However, studying the growth of specific activities is highly relevant. Growth often stems from specific activities related to individual innovations. A focus on activities has the potential for studying growth regardless of individuals or organizational context, both of which may change. What at arm's length may look like an individual start-up failing after a few years may in fact be an innovation transferred to another organization where it is wildly successful. Only activity-based growth analysis can handle that sort of phenomenon properly. In the case of the Ericsson group, the activities related to cellular phones (which are spread over a number of different companies) have grown tremendously while other parts of the company have shrunk almost as dramatically. Using the entire governance structure as a unit of analysis apparently gives the wrong impression for many purposes. Although activity-based growth studies are important, because of the problems of sampling and data collection, the growth of activities may best be studied with a case approach.

The governance structure, approximated by the legal company or the company group, is by far the easiest to sample. In most countries relatively complete registers can be found for such entities. This is also what is so deceptive. In the example of entrepreneur X above, the exact same activities may be placed within different governance solutions. Once identified, initial (or cross-sectional) data collection from the unit is relatively easy. However, an issue that comes more to the fore here than with the individual is whether one key informant can adequately represent the firm.

The problems of following the sampled governance structure over time have been illustrated already in table 2.1. Clearly, a serious effort to study firm-governance structure growth over time requires procedures for dealing with a range of qualitative changes that the originally sampled unit may go through.

OPERATIONALIZING GROWTH

Suitable indicators of growth

Hoy et al. (1992) stress that a consensus has been reached among academics that sales growth is the best growth measure. It reflects both short and long-term changes in the firm and is easily obtainable. Furthermore, these authors, as well as Barkham et al. (1996), maintain that sales growth is the most common performance indicator among entrepreneurs themselves.

The growth process as such provides further arguments for advocating sales growth. A growth process is likely to be driven by increased demand for the firm's products or services. That is, sales increase first and thus allow the acquisition of additional resources, such as employees or machinery (Flamholtz 1986). It seems unlikely that growth in other dimensions could take place without increasing sales. It is also possible to increase sales without acquiring additional resources or employing additional staff, for example, by outsourcing the increased business volumes. In this case, only sales would increase. Thus, sales growth has high generality.

On the other hand, there is a widespread interest in the creation of new employment. This makes employment growth another important aspect to capture. In a process of rationalization, employees can be replaced with capital investments. In other words, to some extent an inverse relationship exists between capital investment and employment growth. As a consequence, assets are another important aspect of growth. Measuring growth in terms of assets is often considered problematic in the service sector (Weinzimmer et al. 1998), but this appears to be mainly an accounting problem. While intangible assets may indeed expand in a growing service firm, this is not reflected in the firm's balance sheet. Thus, the problem of studying growing assets in service industries is related to difficulty in data collection rather than lack of relevance.

In the selection of appropriate indicators, theoretical considerations are as necessary as those of an empirical nature (Weinzimmer et al. 1998). The suitability of utilizing any of these three aspects of growth is contingent on the unit of analysis. The relationship between suitable growth indicators and the unit of analysis is shown in table 2.5. For a

TABLE 2.5 The relationship between unit of analysis and suitable growth indicators

	Individual(s)	*Activity*	*Governance structure*
Sales	High suitability	High suitability	High suitability
Employment	Low suitability	Limited suitability	High suitability
Assets	High suitability	Limited suitability	High suitability

growth-oriented entrepreneur, the firm is a vehicle to the accumulation of wealth. This implies that when the individual is the unit of analysis, the growth of assets may come to the fore. Since entrepreneurs tend to use sales growth as a performance indicator, this dimension is equally interesting when the individual is the unit of analysis. The growth in terms of employment may however be of secondary relevance in this case. Employment growth is almost never a goal in itself (Wiklund 1998).

When governance structures are studied, managerial problems related to organizational complexity are of particular interest. Organizational complexity is most likely linked to the size and growth of the firm with respect to all three indicators, namely, employment, sales and assets growth. The need to transform a governance structure from entrepreneurial to professional management, for example, will depend on factors such as the number of departments and the number of staff within each department (employment), the number and size of orders (sales), and also the amount of equipment (assets). This calls for the use of all three indicators in these types of studies.

The growth of activities, finally, can be captured mainly in the expansion of sales. Activities have the clearest connection to the market and their growth reflects an increased demand for the products and services provided to the market. While assets and employment may be valuable inputs to any activity, sales reflect the output of activities. The output volume of activities will depend upon other factors in addition to assets and employment, such as the organization's managerial capabilities.

Others have pointed out that multiple indicators of growth give richer information and may therefore be better than single indicators (Birley and Westhead 1990; Weinzimmer et al. 1998; Wiklund 1998). Provided that proper analytical techniques are applied, the present authors support this viewpoint. However, this section attempts to illustrate that not all indicators are equally valid for all purposes and that additional *theoretical* considerations should be taken into account in the selection of proper indicators. It is when the governance structure is the unit of analysis and the strategic adaptation and/or the configuration theoretical approach is applied that the call for multiple measures is most relevant.

Relative and absolute growth

There are two basic approaches to measuring growth: absolute or relative. Measures of absolute growth examine the actual difference in firm size from one observation to another. Growth rates refer to relative changes in size; that is, size changes are related to the initial size of the firm, typically by dividing the absolute growth by the initial size of the firm. Both approaches are associated with the problem of the effect of initial size on firm growth. Initial firm size typically has a positive association with absolute growth but a negative one with relative growth (Delmar 1997; Storey 1997; Weinzimmer et al. 1998)

The fact that size affects growth is conceptually problematic. This is apparent if the size changes of a cohort of firms started a particular year is studied during some later period of time. The vast majority of firms start very small. Over time, the firms that grow more become larger than those that grow less. If both larger and smaller firms exhibit the same amount of absolute growth during a later time period, the larger firms will get a lower growth rate. But overall, they have grown faster, so they are "punished" for having achieved a larger size to use as a denominator. Thus, any results concerning the possible influence of size on growth should be interpreted with great care because choices made by the researcher affect results. Not only relative/absolute measures but also the time between start-up and first observation, the growth of the firms up to this point and the length of the studied time period will all influence results.

A wiser decision is to use initial size as a methodological control variable. However, it is probable that many other commonly used antecedents of growth are influenced by size. Thus, the use of initial size as a control variable does not solve the size/growth relationship in a totally satisfactory way. Our recommended solution is to utilize both absolute and relative measures in parallel.

Some researchers have tried to surpass the inherent problems of absolute and relative growth measures by calculating compound measures containing elements of both types (Birch 1987). Although possibly technically superior, such measures are conceptually empty, since it is impossible to state what dimensions they determine (neither dollars nor percent).

Modeling growth rates with two size observations

In most studies, growth is calculated from the present size compared with an earlier size, i.e., from two points in time. When such a calculation is performed, the researcher is actually assuming a particular growth pattern during the time interval between the measurements. Therefore, we will investigate the growth patterns implicitly assumed by three different growth calculations and assess their appropriateness.

The most prevalent measure, according to Delmar (1997) and Weinzimmer et al. (1998), has the following mathematical expression:

$$g = (S_{t1} - S_{t0})/S_{t0} \qquad (2.1)$$

Where g refers to the *total* growth rate during the whole period, S_{t0} refers to the size at the start of the period and S_{t1} refers to the size at the end of the period.

Equation (2.1) models growth as a quantum size leap at some time during the period studied, i.e., all sales (or employees or assets) are added at one time. Mathematically, this is explained by the fact that previous size is used in the denominator, i.e., any new sales or employees are added to the firm at the size it had at the beginning of the period. This model is likely to lead to two types of problems. First, it is not probable that all growth takes place as a quantum leap at one particular point in time, particularly when longer time frames are studied. Second, the model is very sensitive to the initial size of the firm. This measure therefore has a bias in favor of firms that *initially* had a smaller size. As a result, initial firm size may appear among the strongest explanatory variables for firm growth.

In other contexts, economists frequently use Gibrat's law, which assumes that the growth rate of a firm is constant. Mathematically, the expression is:

$$S_{t1} = S_{t0}(1 + g)^{t1-t0} \qquad (2.2)$$

Where g refers to the *annual* growth rate.

According to this model, an equivalent *relative share* of new sales or employees is added each year, as with retained compound interest in a bank account. This model is less sensitive to the initial size of the firm, which is advantageous since it reduces the magnitude of the size/growth relationship. The initial size effect is smaller in this case because growth is assumed to be spread over all the years of the period. However, it appears unlikely that a constant growth rate (i.e., a growth curve with an exponential shape) would be exhaustive over longer time frames, particularly for firms exhibiting rapid growth.

A third model assumes that an equivalent *amount* of new sales or employees is added each year. As far as we are aware, this model has so far only been used by Wiklund (1998). When an equal amount is added each year, the mathematical expression becomes:

$$g = 1/N \sum_{n=1}^{n=N} (S_{tn+1} - S_{tn})/S_{tn} \tag{2.3}$$

Where $S_{tn} = S_{t1} + S_{tn}(n-1)/N$, and g is the *annual* growth rate. N refers to the total number of years studied, n refers to any given year. S_{tn} refers to the size at year n, and $S_{t,N}$ is the size at the end of the period.

This model is similar to the first equation, the major difference being that the denominator changes every year. Thus, this model is less sensitive to the initial size of the firm and does not assume one large quantum size leap during the period but rather smaller, annual changes.

Regardless of which model we use, we make certain assumptions of the growth curve of the firm and reach different empirical results regarding growth rates. From both a conceptual and empirical standpoint, the first model, which is the most common, seems to be the *least* appropriate. A constant growth rate, implying exponential growth, would be exhaustive over longer time frames and seems unlikely. But the linear third model, which assumes that an equal size change takes place each year, appears to have a lot of merit.

Modeling growth rates with more than two size observations

Access to more than two size observations opens opportunities for more elaborate models. In a recent review, only three out of thirty-five reviewed studies included more than two observations (Weinzimmer et al. 1998). These authors discuss two different approaches to the analysis of longitudinal data: fitting a regression line or calculating the average of annual size changes. Fine-grained fluctuations can be taken into account in both these models. The authors advocate the use of the regression line since the effects of outliers can be dampened. However, while better than the two-point models, this model has some weaknesses. It is difficult to utilize multiple indicators of growth, and the model assumes constant growth. A promising alternative is the growth modeling of longitudinal data using latent variables developed by Muthén (1997; Muthén and Curran 1997). While this modeling technique has, to our knowledge, not yet been applied to the study of firm growth, it seems to have a clear merit. First, size is a latent variable and any number and type of manifest indicators may be utilized (e.g., sales, assets, and employment). Second, different growth patterns and growth rates can be modeled during different time intervals of the study. Third, the approach accounts for individual differences between firms as well as similarities among groups of firms.

Organic and total growth

A firm could grow organically through the expansion of current activities or by acquiring those already existing. It is likely that the processes underlying these different types of growth are fundamentally different, as are the implications for the economy at large. If these two types of growth mechanisms are not separated, results can be confounded, leading to misinterpretations of findings.

Davidsson and Delmar (1997, which uses the same database as in table 2.1 above), is one of the few studies separating organic from acquired growth. Their results show that the difference in interpretation can be quite dramatic depending on which growth criterion is used. They defined firms as high-growth if they were among the top 10 percent in terms of annual absolute employment growth. Among firms younger than 10 years, 58 to 96 percent of total growth was organic. Among older firms, only 16 percent was organic. When the analysis was performed across size classes, the difference was even more dramatic. In the smallest size class (0 to 9 employees), 93 percent of total growth was organic, whereas the largest high-growth firms (2,500+ employees) actually shrunk in organic terms.

This example illustrates the differences in empirical results. Theoretical considerations are necessary in order to determine whether organic or total growth is more interesting to the researcher. From an entrepreneurship perspective, concerned with the creation of value and combination of resources, organic growth is most interesting. From a management perspective, on the other hand, the total resources and activities are of greater interest regardless of how they became part of the firm.

CONCLUSIONS

We have argued that despite the increasing number of empirical studies addressing firm growth, not much of a common body of well-founded knowledge about the causes, effects or processes of growth exists. Arguing that gaining such knowledge through empirical research is a much more difficult task than it might at first seem, we hold that future research on firm growth has to address the following challenges:

- to develop a satisfactory basic research design
- to apply a well-founded conceptualization of growth, which in turn requires a well thought-out conceptualization of the firm
- to adequately match this conceptualization with the purpose of the study, the theories used and the operationalization of growth.

With respect to the first point, our message was straightforward: growth is a process, and therefore designs must be longitudinal. We then noted that when growth is studied over time, the conceptualization of the firm becomes problematic. The root of this problem is that the firm is not like a biological individual; the firm can change and transform itself in an indeterminate number of ways. We discussed three alternative micro-level units of analysis: (1) an individual's or group of individuals' entire business activities, (2) a certain business activity or set of related business activities or (3) a governance structure (often an establishment, a registered legal company or a company group).

We argued that the governance structure, which is the prevalent choice in empirical work, is subject to methodological pitfalls, especially in longitudinal studies. Furthermore, from an entrepreneurship research point of view, the growth of governance structures, which may merely represent ownership shifts of established and not necessarily growing activities, should not be the main interest. The totality of individual entrepreneurs' contributions or the growth of new business activities are alternatives more in line with the core interest of entrepreneurship as academic discipline.

The choice of unit of analysis is also a matter of what theoretical perspective is applied. We argued that the strategic adaptation and the configuration perspectives were most in line with using the governance structure conceptualization of the firm. The motivation perspective clearly points at using the individual as the unit of analysis, while the resource-based perspective goes well with using the activity as the unit of analysis. Combining several theoretical perspectives may be beneficial in many ways, but the researcher should be aware that this might require different conceptualizations of a firm, some of which may be erroneous.

We have also discussed many aspects of operationalization of growth. We agree with others that sales turnover may be the most universal growth indicator. Sales alone is not, however, satisfactory for all purposes. Again, it is a matter of matching with the conceptualization of the firm, the theoretical perspective and the purpose of the study.

Our principal answer to the question whether an absolute or a relative growth measure should be used was to recommend that the analysis be performed with both types of growth measures in parallel. This may help the researcher avoid drawing erroneous conclusions about the effect of initial size and explanatory variables that are correlated with size. We noted that the most common formula for modeling growth – end size minus start size divided by start size – has several disadvantages. A better formula models a fixed amount of absolute growth annually, which implies a growth rate that decreases with increasing size and age. If the study has more than two data points, additional alternatives are available. Finally, we argued that from an entrepreneurship research point of view, organic growth is more relevant than total growth. Empirical evidence suggests that this choice can have a major impact on the results.

Conducting empirical research on firm growth is indeed no easy task. Hopefully the disclosure of the pitfalls and problems associated with such research has not discouraged others to continue their efforts. It is our solid belief that research on firm growth is possible, valuable and necessary. Firm growth is a key to economic development and to the creation of wealth and employment. Thus, increased understanding of this phenomenon is of utmost importance. Reviews of the research in the field so far have been critical in several respects. We have presented what we feel are the most important challenges for future research and guidelines to how these challenges can be met. If they are seriously addressed in empirical research, future literature reviews are likely to be more enthusiastic than previous ones. If not, progress will be limited.

REFERENCES

Aldrich, H. and Baker, T. 1997. Blinded by the cites? Has there been progress in the entrepreneurship field? In D.L. Sexton and R.W. Smilor (eds.), *Entrepreneurship 2000*. Chicago: Upstart.

Ardishvili, A., Cardozo, S., Harmon, S. and Vadakath, S. 1998. Towards a theory of new venture growth. Paper presented at the 1998 Babson Entrepreneurship Research Conference, Ghent, Belgium, May 21–3.

Barkham, R., Gudgin, G., Hart, M. and Hanvey, E. 1996. *The Determinants of Small Firm Growth*. Gateshead, Tyne and Wear, UK: Athenaeum.

Birch, D.L. 1987. *Job Creation in America: How Our Smallest Companies Put the Most People to Work*. New York: Free Press.

Birley, S. and Westhead, P. 1990. Growth and performance contrasts between "types" of small firms. *Strategic Management Journal* 2: 535–57.

Brytting, T. 1991. Organizing in the small growing firm – a grounded theory approach. Stockholm: Stockholm School of Economics (dissertation).

Cooper, A.C. 1995. Challenges in predicting new venture performance. In I. Bull, H. Thomas and G. Willard (eds.), *Entrepreneurship: Perspectives on Theory Building*. London: Elsevier Science.

Davidsson, P. 1989a. Continued entrepreneurship and small firm growth. Stockholm: Stockholm School of Economics (dissertation).

Davidsson, P. 1989b. Entrepreneurship – and after? A study of growth willingness in small firms. *Journal of Business Venturing* 4(2): 211–26.

Davidsson, P. and Delmar F. 1997. High-growth firms: characteristics, job contribution and method observations. Paper presented at RENT XI Conference, Mannheim, Germany, November 27–8.

Day, G.S. 1981. The product life cycle: analysis and application issues. *Journal of Marketing* 45(fall): 60–7.

Delmar, F. 1997. Measuring growth: methodological considerations and empirical results. In R. Donckels and A. Miettinen (eds.), *Entrepreneurship and SME Research: On its Way to the Next Millennium*. Brookfield, VA: Aldershot, pp. 190–216

Delmar, F. and Davidsson, P. 1998. A taxonomy of high-growth firms. Paper presented at 1998 Babson Entrepreneurship Research Conference, Ghent, Belgium, May 21–3.

Evans, D.S. 1987. Tests of alternative theories of firm growth. *Journal of Political Economy* 95(4): 657–74.

Flamholtz, E.G. 1986. *Managing the Transition from an Entrepreneurship to a Professionally Managed Firm*. San Francisco: Jossey-Bass.

Foxall, G. 1984. Evidence for attitudinal-behavioural consistency: implications for consumer research paradigms. *Journal of Economic Psychology* 5: 71–92.

Hoy, F., McDougall, P.P., and Dsouza, D.E. 1992. Strategies and environments of high-growth firms. In D.L. Sexton and J.D. Kasarda (eds.), *The State of the Art of Entrepreneurship*. Boston: PWS-Kent Publishing, pp. 341–57.

Kirzner, I.M. 1983. Entrepreneurship and the entrepreneurial function: a commentary. In J. Ronen (ed.), *Entrepreneurship*. Lexington MA: Lexington Books, pp. 281–90.

Muthén, B. 1997. Latent variable modeling of longitudinal and multilevel data. In A. Raftery (ed.), *Sociological Methodology*. Boston: Blackwell, pp. 453–80.

Muthén B. and Curran, P.J. 1997. General longitudinal modeling of individual differences in experimental designs: a latent variable framework for analysis and power estimation. *Psychological Methods* 2(4): 371–402.

Schein, E.H. 1983. Role of the founder in creating organizational culture. *Organizational Dynamics* (summer): 13–28.

Schumpeter, J. 1934. *The Theory of Economic Development*. Cambridge: MA: Harvard University Press.

Seth, A. and Thomas, H. 1994. Theories of the firm: implications for strategy research. *Journal of Management Studies* 3(2): 165–91.

Sexton, D.L. 1997. Entrepreneurship research needs and issues. In D.L. Sexton and R.W. Smilor (eds.), *Entrepreneurship 2000*. Chicago: Upstart.

Storey, D.J. 1997. *Understanding the Small Business Sector*. London: Routledge.

Weinzimmer, L.G., Nystrom, P.C. and Freeman, S.J. (1998). Measuring organizational growth: Issues, consequences and guidelines. *Journal of Management* 24(2): 235–62.

Wiklund, J. 1998 Small firm growth and performance: entrepreneurship and beyond. Jönköping: Jönköping International Business School (dissertation).

Wiklund, J., Davidsson, P., Delmar, F. and Aronsson, M. 1997. Expected consequences of growth and their effect on growth willingness in different samples of small firms. In P. Reynolds, D. Bygrave, N. Carter, P. Davidsson, W. Garnter, C. Mason and P. McDougall (eds.), *Frontiers of Entrepreneurship Research*. Wellesley, MA: Babson College.

3

The Intersection of Entrepreneurship and Strategic Management Research

MICHAEL HITT AND R. DUANE IRELAND

THE ENTREPRENEURSHIP DOMAIN
DOMINANT DOMAINS OF ENTREPRENEURSHIP AND STRATEGIC
MANAGEMENT RESEARCH
RESEARCH METHODS IN ENTREPRENEURSHIP AND STRATEGIC MANAGEMENT
CONCLUSIONS

Strategic management, grounded in the actual practice of management, is at the core of wealth creation in modern industrial societies and, increasingly, in emerging economies as well. Thus, the primary interest of strategic management scholars is to gain the insights required to explain differential firm performances (Dyer and Singh 1998). Increasingly, the same interest is associated with the core of a great deal of entrepreneurship research (Cliff 1998).

From an academic perspective, the discipline known as strategic management emerged in business schools during the 1960s. At that time, the primary course was called business policy; it examined the decisions made by executives and the conditions under which they were reached. Typically, a business policy course was one in which students integrated functional knowledge stocks acquired in other academic courses, such as finance, manufacturing, marketing and economics. The task of the general manager was viewed to be that of learning how to develop and use a multifunctional perspective. Derived from goals that were to be internally consistent, general managers' decisions were judged to be effective when they allowed the firm to become properly aligned with its external environment (Porter 1994). Economic theory, especially as reflected in studies of economic organization and bureaucracy, provided the research base and evidence that influenced the primary content of the business policy course (Rumelt et al. 1994).

A comprehensive development of the strategic management discipline began in earnest in the early 1980s with an increasing amount of theoretical and empirical research. This growth in strategic management research continues. Insights gained through this research stream indicate that how firms achieve and maintain competitive advantage is the central task of those making strategic decisions and remains the key question examined by strategic management scholars (Teece et al. 1997). Evidence suggests that competitive advantage can be created through appropriate positioning within an industry (Porter 1980), by exploiting idiosyncratic, firm-specific core competencies (Barney 1991), and by developing and using unique combinations of interfirm cooperative arrangements, e.g., strategic alliances and joint ventures (Dyer and Singh 1998).

Although both the entrepreneurship and strategic management fields are relatively young compared with their counterparts in management and business, research in the strategic management field is beginning to mature. Nonetheless, fundamental questions remain that require investigation (Rumelt et al. 1994). Answers to an array of interesting questions (including the one of intersections between strategic management and entrepreneurship that is addressed herein) have the potential to contribute significantly to the effective and efficient management of complex, larger organizations, entrepreneurial ventures and bureaucratic firms seeking to learn how to act more entrepreneurially.

In contrast to the timing of growth in strategic management research, research in entrepreneurship actually started its rapid development in the 1980s. However, throughout its history and even currently, the relevance (or applicability) of entrepreneurship research has been questioned. In addition, many of the assumptions that drive the decisions made about how to design and complete entrepreneurship studies have been challenged (Aldrich and Baker 1997; Hoy 1997). In general, though, the prevailing wisdom is that progress is being made in terms of the relevance and rigor of entrepreneurship research. Those supporting this view believe that the challenge now is to continue the emerging research momentum to ensure that increasingly significant and applicable questions are examined (Sexton 1997). Thus, in contrast to the research in strategic management, entrepreneurship research is in its growth stage and its development is likely to become exponential in the early part of the twenty-first century (Dean et al. 1998).

While entrepreneurship and strategic management each has its unique roots and bases, research in these fields also *intersects* in several key topical domains and methodologies. In this regard, research constructs and yet-to-be-answered questions are common to both fields. Consider, for example, the increasing number of researchers studying whether the success of an entrepreneurial venture is influenced significantly by the firm's ability to create a competitive advantage through the development and appropriate use of core competencies (Van Horn and Harvey 1998). Thus, it is likely that entrepreneurial ventures possess resources and capabilities that differ from those owned by larger corporations. In turn, these differences may make the entrepreneurial venture uniquely suited to compete successfully in certain industry contexts while its larger counterpart may be positioned uniquely to compete more effectively in another industry context (Dean et al. 1998). This logic is consistent with the core tenets of the resource-based view of the firm that has resulted in meaningful contributions to the strategic management field (Barney 1991; Oliver 1997; Wernerfelt 1984). Further development and understanding of intersections, such as sources of competitive advantage, should facilitate the continued growth and development of research and knowledge in each of these important fields.

The purpose of this chapter is to examine a set of intersections between entrepreneurship and strategic management. Thus, at one level, through this work, we seek to answer Day's (1992) call for researchers to find additional parallels between the entrepreneurship and strategic management fields. An analysis of intersections between the two fields should highlight opportunities for entrepreneurship and strategic management researchers to integrate the design and execution of their studies in order to investigate phenomena that have parallel foci and meaning. This conviction is consistent with Sandberg's (1992) suggestion that momentum continues to build for additional cross-fertilization between the entrepreneurship and strategic management fields.

The domain intersections examined herein are

- innovation
- organizational networks
- internationalization
- organizational learning
- top management teams and governance
- growth, flexibility and change and research methods.

These six domains were selected because of their potential to yield opportunities for integrating entrepreneurship and strategic management research. Contributing to the likelihood of increases in joint research endeavors, and also supporting the selection of the domains chosen for analysis herein, is the fact that both fields provide important findings on these particular topics. Before examining the six domains as well as the increasing similarity in research methods used by entrepreneurship and strategic management scholars, we begin with a discussion of the entrepreneurship domain itself.

THE ENTREPRENEURSHIP DOMAIN

The entrepreneurship literature is grounded in the tenets of several fields, including sociology, economics and psychology. Because it often disrupts the status quo and the sets of traditional methods that are used commonly to accomplish tasks and objectives, entrepreneurship is sometimes viewed as a subversive activity (Smilor 1997). Contributing to this perception is the fact that successful entrepreneurship occurs through the creation of uncertainty that is brought about by considering a large batch of new ideas and alternatives (West and Meyer 1998). More formally, entrepreneurship has been defined as the pursuit of opportunities that are beyond the resources controlled currently (Stevenson and Gumpert 1985). Consistent with this definition is the perspective that generating variety and leveraging resources are the two core entrepreneurial functions (Thiessen 1997).

Venkatraman's (1997) definition of entrepreneurship captures the essence of the field and best suits the purposes of our work: "a scholarly field that seeks to understand how opportunities to bring into existence future goods and services are discovered, created and exploited by whom and with what consequences." Flowing from this definition is the recognition of an entrepreneur as an innovator, decision-maker and organizational builder (Ramachandran and Ramnarayan 1993). Moreover, Venkatraman (1997) argues that it is important to ensure and communicate the distinctive contribution of entrepreneurship to the broader understanding of business enterprise. He suggests that to the extent that this contribution is unclear, delayed or overlaps with other subfields, the legitimacy and very survival of entrepreneurship as a part of business research and education is threatened seriously.

We argue herein that entrepreneurship does make a distinctive contribution to our understanding of business enterprise. This contribution may be especially clear and important in terms of fast-growth firms. In fact, growth that is facilitated through the exercise of entrepreneurial commitments, orientations and practices is frequently a key differentiator between long-term firm success and failure. Furthermore, we suggest that more academics and business executives (particularly those in larger firms) are recognizing entrepreneurship's distinctive contributions. For example, corporate entrepreneurship (intrapreneurship) is linked increasingly with organizational survival, profitability, growth and renewal in larger firms (Zahra 1996). Effective intrapreneurship practices are ones that result in innovation that creates new businesses and facilitates the core firm's efforts to build the types of new capabilities that permit a strategic renewal of the entire corporation (Guth and Ginsberg 1990).

Entrepreneurship has a unique and important role in business research and education. Consider the growing importance of this role in educational settings. In 1970, only sixteen schools included an entrepreneurship course in their curriculum. By 1995, this number had grown to over four hundred with at least fifty universities or colleges offering a minimum of four entrepreneurship courses (Vesper and Gartner 1997). This educational importance is also suggested by the facts that many graduate business students want to be entrepreneurs and start their own company and in a growing number of schools, entrepreneurship is the most popular major (Authers 1998). The criticality of entrepreneurship's role in business research can be demonstrated in part, we believe, by examining the intersections between entrepreneurship and strategic management research. This criticality is indicated by the fact that research outcomes suggested by the intersections we examine have implications for the successful practice of entrepreneurship.

DOMINANT DOMAINS OF ENTREPRENEURSHIP AND STRATEGIC MANAGEMENT RESEARCH

We propose at least six main content domains in which entrepreneurship and strategic management research intersect, as listed above. In addition, the methodologies and tools used in research in these two fields evidence commonalties. In turn, we examine each of the topic areas where the intersections occur. Innovation is the first domain for which we explore the intersections.

Innovation

Across time, researchers have sought to determine the group of factors that determines innovation in an organizational setting (Goes and Park 1997). A key reason for this interest is that innovation is recognized to play a critical role in the success of firms in both domestic and international arenas, especially for multinational corporations (Menke 1997; Nobel and Birkinshaw 1998). In fact, Birkinshaw (1997) suggests that "the ability of the large multinational corporation (MNC) to leverage the innovative and entrepreneurial potential of its dispersed assets is a fundamental strategic imperative." Some believe that for both large corporations and entrepreneurial ventures, innovation will emerge as the core component of the firm's business strategy in the twenty-first century (Hitt et al. 1999; Kuczmarski 1996).

Innovation has long been an important topic in both the strategic management and entrepreneurship fields. For example, Drucker (1985) suggested, "Innovation is the specific function of entrepreneurship.... It is the means by which the entrepreneur either creates new wealth-producing resources or endows existing resources with enhanced potential for creating wealth." Churchill (1992) noted that a consensus was emerging that entrepreneurship could be viewed as a process of uncovering or developing an opportunity to create value through innovation. Through the strategic management lens, Lengnick-Hall (1992) argued that there is an important link between innovation and a sustainable competitive advantage. A sustainable competitive advantage is one through which the firm can expect to earn above-average returns until competitors are able to duplicate the benefits for customers that are provided by that advantage (Hitt et al. 1999). In Lengnick-Hall's (1992) view, innovations that: (1) are difficult for competitors to understand and imitate, (2) are consistent with market realities, (3) permit the firm to exploit the market timing characteristics of the industry in which it competes and (4) rely on the use of capabilities that are readily appropriable by the firm are linked with a sustainable competitive advantage.

Recently, three researchers described a relationship between entrepreneurship and strategic management in terms of innovation that speaks informatively to the arguments presented herein. Dess et al. (1997) suggested that an entrepreneurial approach to strategy-making processes is vital to organizational success. In their view, this type of process exists in a firm that "engages in product market innovation, undertakes somewhat risky ventures and is *first* to come up with proactive innovations, beating competitors to the punch." Thus, it has been argued that *effective* innovation (that which results in a competitive advantage) is the result of entrepreneurial processes.

All this suggests that considerable research on this topic has been conducted, usually with large organizations as the focal firm. However, innovation cannot occur without entrepreneurial activity. Venkatraman (1997) argues that innovation is one of the three sources of entrepreneurial opportunity. Lumpkin and Dess (1996) propose that innovativeness (which reflects the firm's tendency to engage in and support new ideas, novelty, experimentation and creative processes that may contribute to the development of new products, services or processes) is a vital component of an entrepreneurial orientation. Supporting these arguments, Williamson (1985) suggests that small firms are more effective at producing innovation than large firms. However, he also suggests that large firms are more effective at large-scale production and distribution of new products and services. Therefore, Williamson argues that small firms, without the structural impediments to innovation, and large firms, with the capability to mass produce and market new products, should form alliances whereby the smaller entrepreneurial firms develop new product ideas and large firms produce and distribute them to the market.

Some misinterpret the meaning of innovation. According to Schumpeter (1934), innovation can be defined as "gales of creative destruction." In other words, through the formation and use of new combinations of factors of production, innovation is a creative idea that produces value. In the process of doing so, innovation may destroy the value of previous ideas. As a mindset or a mentality, innovation is a way of thinking that drives the firm's activities (Kuczmarski 1996; Martin 1994). Through such a mindset, innovation can lead to a fundamental reconceptualization of the type of value the firm seeks to create and how to create it (Markides 1998). Combining these arguments suggests that innovation can be defined as the use of new technological and/or market knowledge to offer new products or services. Specifically, innovation is the sum of invention plus the commercialization of that invention (Afuah 1998).

In the strategic management field, new product development and innovation are crucial sources of competitive advantage (Tushman et al. 1997). However, Tushman et al. (1997) suggest that a key question in strategic management is why technology and resource-rich firms often fail to develop and / or sustain a competitive advantage. One answer to this question is probably based in the differentiation of incremental versus radical innovation. Oftentimes, larger firms develop bureaucratic (structural) and control system impediments to innovation (Hitt et al. 1990). These impediments may be created partly by the size of the firm and partly by the strategy employed by the firm (Hoskisson and Hitt 1988). The impediments lead to managerial risk aversion and thus lower managerial commitment to innovation (Hitt et al. 1990). As such, larger firms often produce incremental rather than radical innovation. Firms must be more entrepreneurial to produce radical innovation.

A potentially interesting intersection between strategic management and entrepreneurship innovation-related research is that of *innovation implementation*. Increasingly, firms' failures to meet the expectations associated with innovation (including those of enhancements in organizational productivity and performance) are seen as the result of ineffective innovation implementation rather than of the innovation alone. When the firm lacks a supportive climate and when there is not an appropriate fit between a particular innovation and the users' values, efforts to implement an innovation likely will fail. Compared with their larger and more bureaucratic counterparts, entrepreneurial ventures may have a greater capacity to develop supportive climates and to construct effective links between the demands of an innovation and the values of the venture's personnel. Empirical studies are needed to examine this possibility.

Organizational networks

Organizational networks are becoming increasingly important to both entrepreneurial ventures and large corporations (Meyer et al. 1997; Osborn and Hagedoorn 1997). They are being used for a variety of both strategic and tactical reasons, although long-term strategic success is the firm's dominant concern when committing resources to these arrangements. Moreover, organizational networks are a primary driver of internationalization, which is a domain of intersection discussed later.

The growing popularity of networks is not surprising in that economic theory established long ago that resource owners are able to increase their productivity through specialization (Dyer 1997). Beyond productivity enhancements, networks have the potential to become a source of competitive advantage for the firm and to help it support its strengths while buffering its weaknesses (Simonin 1997). Dyer and Singh (1998), for example, argue that firms able to "combine resources in unique ways may realize an advantage over competing firms who are unable or unwilling to do so. Thus, idiosyncratic interfirm linkages may be a source of relational rents and competitive advantage." In other instances, networks are used to help the firm improve its strategic position, control transaction costs, learn new skills and cope positively with rapid technological changes in domestic, international and emerging markets (Das and Teng 1998; Gulati 1995). Especially for entrepreneurial ventures, networks can contribute positively to gaining organizational legitimacy and to developing a desirable marketplace reputation (Sharman et al. 1991).

Organizational networks take a number of forms including those of strategic alliances, joint ventures, licensing arrangements, subcontracting, joint R&D endeavors and joint marketing activities. Regardless of its exact nature, an organizational network is a voluntary arrangement between two or more firms that involves durable exchange, sharing or codevelopment of new products and technologies (Gulati 1995).

The entrepreneurship literature reports that information and social networks are critical to firm formation, survival and success (Malecki 1997). In other words, few entrepreneurial firms would be able to survive without effective and efficient use of information and social networks. In fact, entrepreneurial firms build social capital through networks (Hitt and Bartkus 1997). Linked with both a venture's successful start-up and its long-term operations, social capital is one of three types of capital – personal financial resources, personal skills or social capital – that entrepreneurs bring to an entrepreneurial venture (Hansen 1995).

In addition to formal organizational networks, informal networks such as personal relationships are also used in the pursuit of desired competitive outcomes. In fact, in certain environmental settings, informal networks play a more important role than formal ones in a firm's establishment and growth. Moreover, informal networks can be vital to the entrepreneurial venture's efforts to develop effective formal relationships such as those with financial institutions (Hoing 1998). Thus, while all firms may participate in both formal and informal networks, large organizations are more likely to form formal long-term cooperation agreements, whereas smaller entrepreneurial firms are likely to engage in personal relationships and mutual agreements. In addition, technological learning (and other types of organizational learning) can occur through the use of informal networks (Malecki 1997) or formal networks (Zahra et al. 1998).

Smaller entrepreneurial firms are forming both formal and informal networks as a means of competing against larger firms (Hitt and Bartkus 1997). These networks also allow the smaller entrepreneurial firm to enter international markets. Of course, larger firms are also participating in formal networks as a means of competing in global markets and/or to maintain their competitiveness in domestic markets (Hitt et al. 1998a). Thus, organizational networks may be critical to the competitiveness of larger firms and to the survival and success of entrepreneurial firms. This places more importance on the understanding and knowledge of these organizational networks and thus emphasizes the need for greater and more in-depth research on entrepreneurial and large firm networks.

An issue requiring examination in the context of the organizational networks' domain is that of control. Importantly, decisions regarding how to design and control a formal organizational network have a strong influence on the performance of the voluntary arrangement as well as the satisfaction of those involved (Garvis et al. 1998; Kumar and Seth 1998). Control decisions are required because networks create the possibility for opportunism. When seeking its own self-interest at the expense of others (Williamson 1985), a network partner may fail to fulfill his or her commitments, might withhold or distort information and/or attempt to expropriate proprietary technology (Deeds and

Hill 1999). To protect against possible opportunistic behaviors, firms may use one or more safeguards or governance structures (Dyer 1997). However, too much control has the potential to stifle or even prevent the creation of value from the network arrangement (Lorange 1997). Thus, control issues challenge firms to balance the need for constraints against the desire for reaching valued objectives.

As we have discussed, organizational networks are becoming increasingly critical for entrepreneurial ventures as well as large corporations. Simultaneously, the matter of control is important for both types of firms. Although an intersection exists, the strategic management and entrepreneurship literatures are largely silent on control as it relates to organizational networks. Because of this, a fruitful area of inquiry would be to determine if governance mechanisms should be used differentially by firms (regardless of size) that are committed to entrepreneurial pursuits (have an entrepreneurial mindset) as compared with companies lacking such a commitment.

Internationalization

Internationalization has been a primary driver of the new competitive landscape (Hitt et al. 1998b). A unique mindset, one in which managers and leaders are committed to the need to learn how to balance competing country, business and functional concerns, is required for the firm to successfully internationalize its operations (Murtha et al. 1998). Internationalization can occur through multiple paths including those of exports, licensing, strategic alliances, acquisitions and foreign direct investments (Barkema and Vermeulen 1998). However, as compared to larger multinational corporations, entrepreneurial ventures do not have as many entry modes available to them (Zacharakis 1998).

Some research has suggested that international diversification can produce higher returns for the firm (Geringer et al. 1989). Some of the reasons for the positive outcomes of international diversification include enhanced organizational learning, greater innovativeness and increased strategic competitiveness. For example, recent research suggests that firms that diversify internationally are more innovative (Hitt et al. 1997). Additionally, research by Barkema and colleagues suggests that international diversification enhances a firm's ability to learn and the quantity of its organizational learning (Barkema et al. 1996; Barkema and Vermeulen 1998).

Entrepreneurial firms are also entering international markets in increasing numbers. McDougall and Oviatt (1997) define international entrepreneurship as "new and innovative activities that have the goal of value creation and growth in business organizations across national borders." Thus, the strategic decision for entrepreneurial ventures to internationalize their operations involves them with efforts to grow through the creation of value in nations outside of their host country's market. The decision to engage in international entrepreneurship is influenced by the need for entrepreneurial ventures to adapt effectively and quickly to the competitive pressures brought about by the dynamic global business environment (Covin and Slevin 1997). Recent data suggest that the percentage of US-based small firms operating in international markets has increased from 20 percent in the early 1990s to over 50 percent in the latter 1990s (Hitt and Bartkus 1997). As such, there has been a growing interest in and a proliferation of international entrepreneurial research (e.g., Brush 1995; McDougall and Oviatt 1994; McDougall et al. 1994; Oviatt and McDougall 1994).

While considerable research in international business has been done, relatively little of it has focused on the involvement of entrepreneurial ventures in international cooperative alliances (McDougall and Oviatt 1997). As such, there is a clear and important need for additional research on international strategies and international entrepreneurship. For example, further analysis of cooperative alliances in international markets that involve both large and small firms is required. Relatedly, additional studies regarding the most effective modes of entry into international markets and the types of international markets firms should enter would add value to the entrepreneurship and strategic management literatures. Such research might discover variance between entrepreneurial ventures and established organizations in terms of the entry mode (and its timing) to use when internationalizing operations.

As noted earlier, cooperative arrangements, in the form of organizational networks, are created when two or more firms agree contractually to pool at least a part of their asset bases or to exchange resources in the pursuit of desired competitive outcomes (Stuart 1998). With increases in the intensity and scope of global competition, cooperative arrangements are becoming a preferred choice for firms seeking to enter new markets, obtain new skills and share risks and resources (Inkpen and Beamish 1997).

Some evidence suggests that the reasons for forming international organizational networks may by affected by geographic location. For example, it has been argued that networks developed among European firms are formed primarily for defensive reasons. In this context, a defensive arrangement is one through which partners desire primarily to gain economies of scale through operation of the agreed-upon organizational network. In contrast, global cooperative arrangements (that is, those with at least one non-European partner) are organized with the intention of leveraging partners' skills in order to enter new markets and acquire new competencies (Garrette and Dussauge 1998). This preliminary evidence requires study by both entrepreneurship and strategic management scholars. For example, are entrepreneurial ventures better suited to global cooperative arrangements than are larger, more established organizations? An answer to this question and to others related to this general topic would inform both the research literature and managerial practice.

Recent research suggests that not all international diversification is positive. For example, Hitt et al. (1997) found that firms first entering international markets may experience negative returns unless they have the internal infrastructure and managerial capabilities to manage the complexities created by entry into these markets. Furthermore, they found that more established firms can overdiversify internationally and thereby overload their managerial capabilities. When this occurs, the firm's returns from international diversification may begin to decrease. Likewise, McDougall and Oviatt (1997) suggest that economic development initiatives, international new ventures, initial public offerings and entrepreneurship in transitioning economies are all topics in need of further research.

Organizational learning

Organizational learning is defined as the development of new knowledge that has the potential to influence behavior and improve firm performance. Organizational learning occurs through the three stages of information acquisition, information dissemination and shared interpretation (Sinkula 1994; Slater and Narver 1995).

New knowledge can be acquired through multiple paths and activities, including international diversification and organizational networks. Recent evidence suggests that in addition to the opportunity to rationalize production, standardize products across country borders and coordinate critical resource functions in order to achieve optimal economic scale and amortize investments in critical functions, international diversification may also increase organizational learning (Hitt et al. 1997). For example, multinational firms may increase their capabilities by tapping new resources and knowledge available through international diversification (Kotabe 1990). Learning alliances, which are an important segment of organizational networks or interfirm collaborations, are formed when partners' primary objective is to gain strategic and/or tactical insights from one another (Khanna et al. 1998). Increasingly, alliances of this type are central to successful implementation of the firm's strategies (Doz and Hamel 1998).

Although a complex phenomenon, organizational learning is vital for both small entrepreneurial ventures as well as large corporations (Cohen 1998). A critical reason for this is that in the complex global economy, intellectual assets (e.g., individual knowledge, brands and organizational knowledge) that are generated, stored and transferred through several processes, including the firm's idiosyncratic organizational learning patterns, often have a greater potential to create value than do tangible assets (Bukowitz and Petrash 1997). The increasing competitive value of intellectual assets has significant managerial implications, perhaps especially for firms that have internationalized their operations (Teece 1998a). Through active and effective management of what the organization has learned, the firm is able to create value by leveraging its know-how, judgment and experience (Ruggles 1998). Effective management of what the firm has learned is facilitated through the establishment and use of appropriate organizational structures and communications technologies (Brown and Duguid 1998).

Organizational learning is considered necessary for continued innovation and sustained entrepreneurial success (Hitt et al. 1998c; Nonaka 1994; Nonaka and Takeuchi 1995); it is also necessary to build firm-specific dynamic capabilities and core competencies (Teece et al. 1997; Lei et al. 1996). Firms must have dynamic capabilities and core competencies in order to sustain a competitive advantage. If their capabilities and core competencies remain static, competitors will develop new and more valuable capabilities and competencies, thereby gaining a competitive advantage.

Thus, the evidence suggests that entrepreneurial firms must learn in order to develop and remain entrepreneurial. Larger more established firms must learn new capabilities in order to sustain a competitive advantage. Increasingly, large firms should strive to develop entrepreneurial capabilities (ones that promote rapid innovations that have the potential to quickly transform markets) rather than administrative capabilities (ones linked primarily with organizational control routines). As suggested above, "a changing kaleidoscope of alliances and joint ventures is . . . likely to characterize firms that elevate the entrepreneurial over the administrative" (Teece 1998b). Without effective organizational learning patterns and outcomes, both entrepreneurial ventures and larger firms will stagnate and fail over time.

Top management teams and governance

Most research on top management teams (TMT) and governance has focused on larger firms. Hambrick and Mason (1984) espoused upper echelon theory that argued the importance of top management teams' actions and their effects on firm behavior and performance. One of these key effects is the significant and critical role the top management team plays in determining the firm's strategy (Boeker 1997). Moreover, Geletkanycz and Hambrick (1997) argue that "the ability of executives to formulate and implement strategic initiatives that capitalize on environmental opportunities, while mitigating external threats, is vital to organizational success." For new entrepreneurial ventures, West and Meyer (1998) found that the influence of the CEO's perspective on the development of consensus about the firm's goals is significant. Thus, for entrepreneurial ventures, as compared to large organizations, the effectiveness of the TMT's influence on important strategic decisions may be more parsimonious.

Flowing from Hambrick and Mason's (1984) early work has been a considerable array of research that has examined the efficacy of upper echelon theory in large corporations (e.g., Hambrick and Abrahamson 1995; Hambrick et al. 1996; Rajagopalan and Datta 1996). However, there has been recent research examining top management team/ executive characteristics in smaller entrepreneurial firms (e.g., Bantel 1997; Lewis et al. 1997; Vyakarnam et al. 1997). Another example is provided by Lumpkin and Dess (1996), who examined the relationship between entrepreneurial orientation and firm performance.

Research is also proliferating on strategic leadership, which has grown out of the notion of upper echelon theory and top management teams. Findings are analyzed and interpreted in a book by Finkelstein and Hambrick (1996) and are related to effective managerial practices in a review article by Ireland and Hitt (1999). Some of the strategic leadership research emphasizes the importance of entrepreneurial actions on the part of strategic leaders (e.g., Ireland and Hitt 1999). Virtually all business start-ups involve management teams, increasing the relevance of agency theory for entrepreneurial firms. Additionally, the concepts of strategic choice, competitive positioning and appropriability regimes are highly relevant in entrepreneurial firms (Covin and Slevin 1997).

Some significant research on top management team cognition has also been published (Barr et al. 1992; Hitt and Tyler 1991; Huff 1990), as well as research on entrepreneur/ entrepreneurial team cognition (Busenitz and Barney 1997). Thus, entrepreneurial researchers are drawing on the traditions developed in strategic management research focused on top management teams and strategic leadership to examine entrepreneurial leadership, governance and cognition. They are also extending this research by focusing on new concepts, such as entrepreneurial orientation (Lumpkin and Dess 1996) and entrepreneurial risks (Busenitz and Barney 1997).

Boards of directors, an important governance mechanism, continue to receive a great deal of attention by scholars. To date, however, findings do not converge around a specific set of appropriate orientations and actions for board members (Johnson et al. 1996). Recently this stream of research has been concerned with the influence of a board on the firm's strategic direction and ultimate performance (Beekun et al. 1998). Interesting findings are being reported as a result of these efforts. For example, it has been found that the boards of venture capital-backed entrepreneurial businesses are more involved in both strategic formulation and implementation processes than the boards with members who hold less significant ownership positions (Fried et al. 1998). Additional research, in which the possibility of variance between appropriate roles for board members in entrepreneurial ventures as compared with those in larger firms, should be conducted.

Growth, flexibility and change

Growth has long been a primary goal of large established organizations. For example, growth in order to gain market power is one of the reasons for the present merger and acquisition frenzy (Hitt et al. 1999; Hitt et al. 1996). Inherently a dynamic measure of change over time, the determination of appropriate growth indices remains a key issue for researchers (Weinzimmer et al. 1998), including both entrepreneurship and strategic management scholars.

Sexton and Smilor (1997) argue that growth is not only an objective for large corporations; in fact, they suggest that growth is the essence of entrepreneurship. Moreover, high-growth entrepreneurial ventures contribute significantly to the wealth of a nation's economy (Sexton et al. 1997). In addition to innovation, Venkatraman (1997) suggests that other entrepreneurial opportunities for growth arise from (1) inefficiencies in existing markets such as information asymmetries or limits to technology, and (2) significant changes in social, political, demographic and/or economic forces.

The growth opportunities that Venkatraman (1997) suggested can arise for either large established firms or smaller entrepreneurial firms, but the management of growth is particularly challenging for entrepreneurial ventures. For example, even when growing through geographic expansion, significant managerial challenges often surface in small entrepreneurial ventures. Effective strategic planning improves the likelihood of successful geographic expansions for smaller, yet growing ventures (Barringer and Greening 1998).

Affecting the growth of entrepreneurial ventures are several additional factors, including the entrepreneur's motivations and intentions. Recent evidence suggests that gender may also affect growth intentions and patterns in entrepreneurial ventures. Cliff (1998) found that both male and female entrepreneurs desire firm growth. However, she also discovered that "female entrepreneurs are more likely to establish maximum business size thresholds beyond which they would prefer not to expand . . . and, these thresholds are smaller than those set by their male counterparts." Research should be conducted to determine if gender has similar effects on male and female intrapreneurs (those pursuing entrepreneurial ventures in large organizations).

Recently, interest has focused on high-growth entrepreneurial firms. For example, research has shown that entrepreneurs in high-growth firms are more ambitious, exhibit higher intensity and have greater vision (Gundry and Welsch 1997). Also, integrating entrepreneurship and strategic management research, Ireland and Hitt (1997) found that high-growth entrepreneurial firms may employ several different strategies to create positive returns. Furthermore, they found that configurations of these strategies exhibit relatively complex effects on the performance of entrepreneurial high-growth firms.

It can be argued that large firms must act more like small entrepreneurial firms in order to be flexible and competitive. In fact, both Jack Welch (CEO of GE) and Herb Kelleher (CEO of Southwest Airlines) have suggested the importance of their larger firms acting like small firms. For example, Herb Kelleher suggested that if Southwest Airlines thinks and acts like a large firm, it will get smaller; but, if it thinks and acts like a small firm, it will grow larger (Hitt et al. 1999).

Flexibility is a critical element in the success of any firm in the new competitive landscape (Bettis and Hitt 1995). Flexibility is important because of the critical need for continuous organizational change to navigate effectively with the increasing turbulence in the competitive landscape. Brown and Eisenhardt (1998) suggest that the key strategic challenge is managing organizational change. Effective management of change is required if that change is risky (Greve 1998). Outcomes from organizational change processes are a product of the firm's motivation, opportunity and capability to change (Miller and Chen 1994). It can be argued that most smaller entrepreneurial firms have the type of flexibility that yields an advantage as compared with many larger firms in initiating and managing organizational change. This advantage may be one factor that accounts for smaller entrepreneurial firms' general ability to be more innovative than their larger counterparts. Research should be conducted to test this expectation.

RESEARCH METHODS IN ENTREPRENEURSHIP AND STRATEGIC MANAGEMENT

A convergence in the type of research being conducted in entrepreneurship and strategic management continues to evolve. In the late 1970s, Schendel and Hofer (1979) called for increasing theory-based empirical research in the strategic management field. Empirical research in strategic management has increased in geometric proportion since that call was expressed. Furthermore, a greater focus on theory-based research with hypotheses generation and model specification is emerging. Likewise, Aldrich and Baker (1997) have called for a "normal science" approach to research in entrepreneurship, and recent publications seem to suggest that entrepreneurship scholars are heeding the call.

Hitt et al. (1998d) argued that strategic management research is beginning to use an increasing amount of longitudinal designs and panel methods, dynamic analytical methods and other analytical tools to assess causal structures. For example, Hitt et al. (1996) used structural equations modeling to assess the relationship among acquisitions and divestitures, firm control systems and externally and internally generated innovation. Alternatively, Kochhar and Hitt (1998) used simultaneous equations analysis to examine the capital structure and corporate strategy actions. While entrepreneurship research has employed these sophisticated analytical tools less often, we predict a growing need for and use of these tools in entrepreneurship research in the coming years.

Likewise, other special research tools currently used in strategic management (and other fields of research) may be useful in entrepreneurship research. For example, cognitive mapping (Huff 1990; Barr et al. 1992) and policy capturing (Hitt and Tyler 1991; Hitt et al. 1998d) have been used in recent strategic management research to examine top management teams and their cognition. These tools may also be useful in research on entrepreneurial teams and their cognition, as exemplified in research by Zacharakis and Meyer (1998).

Similarly, systematic qualitative research approaches may become more common in future entrepreneurship and strategic management research (Hitt et al. 1998d). Early work in both strategic management and entrepreneurship emphasized anecdotal case studies. While these represent a simple form of qualitative research, they are less likely to be accepted in either field in future research. Aldrich and Baker (1997) argue for use of ethnography in entrepreneurship research. Additionally, entrepreneurship researchers may employ case survey methodologies and multicase, multirater designs (Hitt et al.

2000) that have been applied in recent strategic management research. We expect greater convergence of research methodologies in these two fields in the coming years.

CONCLUSIONS

While strategic management research is beginning to mature, entrepreneurship research is in a significant growth stage (Dean et al. 1998). Both fields can develop more by internalizing the knowledge, concepts and methods employed in the other field. Therefore, we call for more integrative entrepreneurship and strategic management research. Until about 2010, we expect both fields to mature and to become prominent research domains in business scholarship and education (Cooper et al. 1997). Contributing to this maturation and ability to make significantly more important contributions will be the fields' commitment to verifying that answers to the right questions are being pursued through use of the most appropriate methodologies (Lowendahl and Revang 1998).

REFERENCES

Afuah, A. 1998. *Innovation Management: Strategies, Implementation, and Profits*. New York: Oxford University Press.

Aldrich, H.E. and Baker, T. 1997. Blinded by the cites? Has there been progress in entrepreneurship research? In D.L. Sexton and R.W. Smilor (eds.), *Entrepreneurship 2000*. Chicago: Upstart, pp. 377–400.

Authers, J. 1998. Getting started in the best of company. *Financial Times*, October 5, VII.

Bantel, K. 1997. Growth and performance for technology-based entrepreneurial firms: the role of top team and board of directors. Paper presented at the Babson Entrepreneurship Research Conference, Wellesley, MA, April 17–19.

Barkema, H.G. and Vermeulen, F. 1998. International expansion through start-up or acquisition: a learning perspective. *Academy of Management Journal* 41: 7–26.

Barkema, H.G., Bell, J.H.J. and Pennings, J.M. 1996. Foreign entry, cultural barriers, and learning. *Strategic Management Journal* 17: 151–66.

Barney, J.B. 1991. Firm resources and sustained competitive advantage. *Journal of Management* 17: 99–120.

Barr, P.S., Stimpert, J.L. and Huff, A.S. 1992. Cognitive change, strategic action and organizational renewal. *Strategic Management Journal* 13 (Special Issue): 15–36.

Barringer, B.R. and Greening, D.W. 1998. Small business growth through geographic expansion: a comparative case study. *Journal of Business Venturing* 13: 476–92.

Beekun, R.I., Stedham, Y. and Young, G.J. 1998. Board characteristics, managerial controls and corporate strategy: a study of US hospitals. *Journal of Management* 24: 3–19.

Bettis, R.A. and Hitt, M.A. 1995. The new competitive landscape. *Strategic Management Journal* 16 (Special Issue): 7–19.

Birkinshaw 1997. Entrepreneurship in multinational corporations: the characteristics of subsidiary initiatives. *Strategic Management Journal* 18: 207–29.

Boeker, W. 1997. Executive migration and strategic change: the effect of top manager movement on product-market entry. *Administrative Science Quarterly* 42: 213–36.

Brown, J.S. and Duguid, P. 1998. Organizing knowledge. *California Management Review* 40: 90–111.

Brown, S.L. and Eisenhardt, K.M. 1998. *Competing on the Edge: Strategy as Structured Chaos.* Boston: Harvard Business School Press.

Brush, C.G. 1995. *International Entrepreneurship: The Effects of Firm Age on Motives of Internationalization.* New York: Garland Publishing.

Bukowitz, W.R. and Petrash G.P. 1997. Visualizing, measuring and managing knowledge. *Research-Technology Management* (July/August): 24–31.

Busenitz, L. and Barney, J.B. 1997. Differences between entrepreneurs and managers in large organizations: biases and heuristics in strategic decision-making. *Journal of Business Venturing* 12: 9–30.

Churchill, N.C. 1992. Research issues in entrepreneurship. In D.L. Sexton and J.D. Kasarda (eds.), *The State of the Art of Entrepreneurship.* Boston: PWS-Kent, pp. 579–96.

Cliff, J.E. 1998. Does one size fit all? Exploring the relationship between attitudes towards growth, gender, and business size. *Journal of Business Venturing* 13: 523–42.

Cohen, D. 1998. Toward a knowledge context: Report on the first annual U.C. Berkeley forum on knowledge and the firm. *California Management Review* 40: 22–39.

Cooper, A., Hornaday, J.A. and Vesper, K.H. 1997. The field of entrepreneurship over time. In P.D. Reynolds, W.D. Bygrave, N.M. Carter, P. Davidsson, W.B. Gartner, C.M. Mason and P.P. McDougall (eds.), *Frontiers of Entrepreneurship Research.* Babson Park, MA: Babson College, pp. 11–17.

Covin, J.G. and Slevin, D.T. 1997. High-growth transitions: theoretical perspectives and suggested directions. In D.L Sexton and R.W. Smilor (eds.), *Entrepreneurship 2000.* Chicago: Upstart, pp. 99–126.

Das, T.K. and Teng, B.S. 1998. Resource and risk management in the strategic alliance making process. *Journal of Management* 24: 21–42.

Day, D.L. 1992. Research linkages between entrepreneurship and strategic management or general management. In D.L. Sexton and J.D. Kasarda (eds.), *The State of the Art of Entrepreneurship.* Boston: PWS-Kent, pp. 117–63.

Dean, T.J., Brown, R.L. and Bamford, C.E. 1998. Differences in large and small firm responses to environmental context: strategic implications from a comparative analysis of business formations. *Strategic Management Journal* 19: 709–28.

Deeds, D.L. and Hill, C.W.L. 1999. An examination of opportunistic action within research alliances: evidence from the biotechnology industry. *Journal of Business Venturing* 14: 141–63.

Dess, G.G., Lumpkin, G.T. and Covin, J.G. 1997. Entrepreneurial strategy making and firm performance: tests of contingency and configurational models. *Strategic Management Journal* 18: 677–95.

Doz, Y.L. and Hamel, G. 1998. *Alliance Advantage.* Boston: Harvard Business School Press.

Drucker, P. 1985. *Entrepreneurship and Innovation: Practice and Principles.* New York: Harper Business.

Dyer, J.H. 1997. Effective interfirm collaboration: how firms minimize transaction costs and maximize transaction value. *Strategic Management Journal* 18: 535–56.

Dyer, J.H. and Singh, H. 1998. The relational view: cooperative strategy and sources of interorganizational competitive advantage. *Academy of Management Review* 23: 660–79.

Finkelstein, S. and Hambrick, D. 1996. *Strategic Leadership.* St. Paul, MN: West Publishing.

Fried, V.H., Bruton, G.D. and Hisrich, R.D. 1998. Strategy and the board of directors in venture capital-backed firms. *Journal of Business Venturing* 13: 493–503.

Garrette, B. and Dussauge, P. 1998. Strategic alliances: why Europe needs to catch up. *Financial Times,* February 27, p 6.

Garvis, D., Zahra, S.A. and Ireland, R.D. 1998. Characteristics and outcomes of entrepreneurial collaborations: the effect of trust. Paper presented at the Strategic Management Society meetings, Orlando, November 1–3.

Geletkanycz, M.A. and Hambrick, D.C. 1997. The external ties of top executives: implications for strategic choice and performance. *Administrative Science Quarterly* 42: 654–81.

Geringer, J.M., Beamish, P.W. and da Costa, R.C. 1989. Diversification strategy and internationalization: implications for MNE performance. *Strategic Management Journal* 10: 109–19

Goes, J.B. and Park, S.H. 1997. Interorganizational links and innovation: the case of hospital services. *Academy of Management Journal* 40: 673–96.

Greve, H.R. 1998. Performance, aspirations, and risky organizational change. *Administrative Science Quarterly* 43: 58–86.

Gulati, R. 1995. Social structure and alliance formation patterns: A longitudinal analysis. *Administrative Science Quarterly* 40: 619–52.

Gundry, L.K. and Welsch, H.P. 1997. The ambitious entrepreneur: attributes of firms exhibiting high-growth strategies. In P.D. Reynolds, W.D. Bygrave, N.M. Carter, P. Davidsson, W.B. Gartner, C.M. Mason and P.B. McDougall (eds.), *Frontiers of Entrepreneurship Research*. Babson Park, MA: Babson College, pp. 68–79.

Guth, W.D. and Ginsberg, A. 1990. Corporate entrepreneurship. *Strategic Management Journal* 11 (Special Issue): 5–16.

Hambrick, D.C. and Abrahamson, E. 1995. Assessing managerial discretion across industries: a multimethod approach. *Academy of Management Journal* 38: 1427–41.

Hambrick, D.C., Cho, T.S. and Chen, M.J. 1996. The influence of top management team heterogeneity on firms' competitive moves. *Administrative Science Quarterly* 41: 659–84.

Hambrick, D.C. and Mason, P.A. 1984. Upper echelons: the organization as a reflection of its top managers. *Academy of Management Review* 9: 193–206.

Hansen, E.L. 1995. Entrepreneurial networks and new organizational growth. *Entrepreneurship: Theory and Practice* 20: 7–19.

Hitt, M.A., Hoskisson, R.E. and Ireland, R.D. 1990. Mergers and acquisitions and managerial commitment to innovation. *Strategic Management Journal* 11 (Special Issue): 29–47.

Hitt, M.A. and Tyler, B.B. 1991. Strategic decision models: integrating different perspectives. *Strategic Management Journal* 12: 327–51.

Hitt, M.A., Hoskisson, R.E., Johnson, R.A. and Moesel. D.D. 1996. The market for corporate control and firm innovation. *Academy of Management Journal* 39: 1084–19.

Hitt, M.A. and Bartkus, B.R. 1997. International entrepreneurship. In J.A. Katz (ed.), *Advances in Entrepreneurship, Firm Emergence and Growth*, vol. 3. Greenwich, CN: JAI Press, pp. 7–30.

Hitt, M.A., Hoskisson, R.E. and Kim, H. 1997. International diversification: effects on innovation and firm performance in product diversified firms. *Academy of Management Journal* 40: 767–98.

Hitt, M.A. , Dacin, M.T. and Levitas, E. 1998a. Strategic orientations and partner selection in international strategic alliances: institutional, country heritage and resource-based perspectives. Paper presented at the Academy of Management meetings, San Diego, August 7–12.

Hitt, M.A., Keats, B.W. and DeMarie, S. 1998b. Navigating in the new competitive landscape: Building strategic flexibility and competitive advantage in the 21st century. *Academy of Management Executive* 13(1): 22–42.

Hitt, M.A., Harrison, J.S., Ireland, R.D. and Best, A. 1998c. Attributes of successful and unsuccessful acquisitions of US firms. *British Journal of Management* 9: 91–114.

Hitt, M.A., Gimeno, J. and Hoskisson, R.E. 1998d. Current and future research methods in strategic management. *Organizational Research Methods* 1: 6–44.

Hitt, M.A., Ireland, R.D. and Hoskisson, R.E. 1999. *Strategic Management: Competitiveness and Globalization*, third edn, St. Paul, MN: West Publishing.

Hitt, M.A., Harrison, J.S. and Ireland, R.D. 2000. *Merger and Acquisition Success: Lessons from the Frontline*. Oxford University Press (forthcoming).

Hoing, B. 1998. What determines success? Examining the human, financial, and social capital of Jamaican microentrepreneurs. *Journal of Business Venturing* 13: 371–94.

Hoskisson, R.E. and Hitt, M.A. 1998. Strategic control systems and relative R&D investment in large multiproduct firms. *Strategic Management Journal* 9: 605–21.

Hoy, F. 1997. Relevance in entrepreneurship research. In D.L. Sexton and R.W. Smilor (eds.), *Entrepreneurship 2000*. Chicago: Upstart, pp. 361–75.

Huff, A.S. 1990. Mapping strategic thought. In A.S. Huff (ed.), *Mapping Strategic Thought*. Chichester, UK: John Wiley and Sons.

Inkpen, A.C. and Beamish, P.W. 1997. Knowledge bargaining power and the instability of international joint ventures. *Academy of Management Review* 22: 177–202.

Ireland, R.D. and Hitt, M.A. 1997. Performance strategies for high-growth entrepreneurial firms. In P.D. Reynolds, W.D. Bygrave, N.M. Carter, P. Davidsson, W.B. Gartner, C.M. Mason and P.P. McDougall (eds.), *Frontiers of Entrepreneurship Research*. Babson Park, MA: Babson College, pp. 90–104.

Ireland, R.D. and Hitt, M.A. 1999. Achieving and maintaining strategic competitiveness in the 21st century: the role of strategic leadership. *Academy of Management Executive* (in press).

Johnson, J.L., Daily, C.M. and Ellstrand, A.E. 1996. Boards of directors: a review and research agenda. *Journal of Management* 22: 409–38.

Khanna, T., Gulati, R. and Nohria, N. 1998. The dynamics of learning alliances: competition, cooperation and relative scope. *Strategic Management Journal* 19: 193–210.

Kochhar, R. and Hitt, M.A. 1998. Linking corporate strategy to capital structure: Diversification strategy, type and source of financing. *Strategic Management Journal* 19: 601–10.

Kotabe, M. 1990. The relationship between offshore sourcing and innovativeness of US multinational firms: An empirical investigation. *Journal of International Business Studies* 21: 623–38.

Kuczmarski, T.D. 1996. Creating an innovative mind-set. *Management Review* (November) 47–51.

Kumar, S. and Seth, A. 1998. The design of coordination and control mechanisms for managing joint venture–parent relationships. *Strategic Management Journal* 19: 579–99.

Lei, D., Hitt, M.A. and Bettis, R.A. 1996. Dynamic core competencies through meta-learning and strategic context. *Journal of Management* 4: 547–67.

Lengnick-Hall, C.A. 1992. Innovation and competitive advantage: what we know and what we need to learn. *Journal of Management* 18: 399–429.

Lewis, P.S., Barringer, B.R., Jones, F.F. and Harrison, J.S. 1997. Growth in entrepreneurial firms: the impact of business practices, founder characteristics and future orientation. Paper presented at the Babson Entrepreneurship Research Conferences, Wellesley, MA, April 17–19.

Lowendahl, B. and Revang, O. 1998. Challenges to existing strategy theory in a post industrial society. *Strategic Management Journal* 19: 755–73.

Lorange, P. 1997. Black-box protection of your core competencies in strategic alliances. In P.W. Beamish and J.P. Killing (eds.), *Cooperative Strategies: European Perspectives*. San Francisco: New Lexington Press, pp. 59–73.

Lumpkin, G.T. and Dess, G.G. 1996. Clarifying the entrepreneurial orientation construct and linking it to performance. *Academy of Management Review* 21: 135–72.

Malecki, E.G. 1997. Entrepreneurs, networks, and economic development: a review of recent research. In J.A. Katz (ed.), *Advances in Entrepreneurship, Firm Emergence and Growth*, vol. 3. Greenwich, CN: JAI Press, pp. 57–118.

Markides, C. 1998. Strategic innovation in established companies. *Sloan Management Review* 40 (spring): 31–42.

Martin, M.J.C. 1994. *Managing Innovation and Entrepreneurship in Technology Based Firms*. New York: John Wiley and Sons.

Menke, M.M. 1997. Managing R&D for competitive advantage. *Research-Technology Management* 4: 40–2.

Meyer, G.D., Alvarez, S.A. and Blasick, J. 1997. Benefits of technology-based strategic alliances: An entrepreneurial perspective. In P.D. Reynolds, W.D. Bygrave, N.M. Carter, P. Davidsson, W.D. Gartner, C.M. Mason and P.P. McDougall (eds.), *Frontiers of Entrepreneurship Research*.

Babson Park, MA: Babson College, pp. 629–42.

McDougall, P.P. and Oviatt, B.M. 1997. International entrepreneurship literature in the 1990s and directions for future research. In D.L. Sexton and R.W. Smilor (eds.), *Entrepreneurship 2000*. Chicago: Upstart, pp. 291–320.

McDougall, P.P., Shane, S. and Oviatt, B.M. 1994. Explaining the formation of international new ventures: the limits of theories from international business research. *Journal of Business Venturing* 9: 469–87.

Miller, D. and Chen, M.J. 1994. Sources and consequences of competitive inertia: a study of the US airline industry. *Administrative Science Quarterly* 39: 1–23.

Murtha, T.P., Lenway, S.A., and Bagozzi, R.P. 1998. Global mind-sets and cognitive shift in a complex multinational corporation. *Strategic Management Journal* 19: 97–114.

Nobel, R. and Birkinshaw, J. 1998. Innovation in multinational corporations: control and communication patterns in international R&D operations. *Strategic Management Journal* 19: 479–96.

Nonaka, I. 1994. A dynamic theory of organizational knowledge. *Organization Science* 5: 14–37.

Nonaka, I. and Takeuchi, H. 1995. *The Knowledge-Creating Company: How Japanese Companies Create the Dynamics of Innovation*. New York: Oxford University Press.

Oliver, C. 1997. Sustainable competitive advantage: combining institutional and resource-based views. *Strategic Management Journal* 18: 697–713.

Osborn, R.M. and Hagedoorn, J. 1997. The institutionalization and evolutionary dynamics of interorganizational alliances and networks. *Academy of Management Journal* 40: 216–78.

Oviatt, B.M. and McDougall, P.P. 1994. Toward a theory of international new ventures. *Journal of International Business Studies* 25: 45–64.

Porter, M.E. 1980. *Competitive Strategy*. New York: The Free Press.

Porter, M.E. 1994. Toward a dynamic theory of strategy. In R.P. Rumelt, D.E. Schendel and D.J. Teece (eds.), *Fundamental Issues in Strategy*. Boston: Harvard Business School Press, pp. 423–61.

Rajagopalan, N. and Datta, D.K. 1996. CEO characteristics: does industry matter? *Academy of Management Journal* 39: 197–215.

Ramachandran, K. and Ramnarayan, S. 1993. Entrepreneurial orientation and networking: some Indian evidence. *Journal of Business Venturing* 8: 513–24.

Ruggles, R. 1998. The state of the nation: knowledge management in practice. *California Management Review* 40: 80–9.

Rumelt, R.P., Schendel, D.E. and Teece, D.J. (eds.) 1994. *Fundamental Issues in Strategy*. Boston: Harvard Business School Press.

Sandberg, W.R. 1992. Strategic management's potential contributions to a theory of entrepreneurship. *Entrepreneurship: Theory and Practice* 16: 73–90.

Schendel, D.E. and Hofer, C.W. (eds.). 1979. *Strategic Management: A New View of Business Policy and Planning*. Boston: Little, Brown.

Schumpeter, J.A. 1934. *The Theory of Economic Development*. Boston: Harvard University Press.

Sexton, D.L. 1997. Entrepreneurship research needs and issues. In D.L. Sexton and R.W. Smilor (eds.), *Entrepreneurship 2000*. Chicago: Upstart, pp. 401–8.

Sexton, D.L. and Smilor, R.W. (eds.). 1997. *Entrepreneurship 2000*. Chicago: Upstart.

Sexton, D.L., Upton, N.B., Wacholtz, L.E. and McDougall, P.P. 1997. Learning needs of growth-oriented entrepreneurs. *Journal of Business Venturing* 12: 1–8.

Sharman, M.P., Gray, B. and Yan, A. 1991. The context of interorganizational collaboration in the garment industry: an institutional perspective. *Journal of Applied Behavioral Science* 27: 181–208.

Simonin, B.L. 1997. The importance of collaborative know-how: an empirical test of the learning organization. *Academy of Management Journal* 40: 1,150–74.

Sinkula, J.M. 1994. Market information processing and organizational learning. *Journal of Marketing* 58: 35–45.

Slater, S.F. and Narver, J.C. 1995. Market orientation and the learning organization. *Journal of*

Marketing 59: 63–74.

Smilor, R.W. 1997. Entrepreneurship: reflections on a subversive activity. *Journal of Business Venturing* 12: 341–6.

Stevenson, H. and Gumpert, D. 1985. The heart of entrepreneurship. *Harvard Business Review* 63(2): 85–94.

Stuart, T.E. 1998. Network positions and propensities to collaborate: an investigation of strategic alliance formation in a high-technology industry. *Administrative Science Quarterly* 43: 668–98.

Teece, D.J. 1998(a). Capturing value from knowledge assets: the new economy, markets for know-how, and intangible assets. *California Management Review* 40: 55–79.

Teece, D.J. 1998(b). Research directions for knowledge management. *California Management Review* 40: 289–92.

Teece, D., Pisano, G. and Shuen, 1997. Dynamic capabilities and strategic management. *Strategic Management Journal* 18: 509–33.

Thiessen, J.H. 1997. Individualism, collectivism, and entrepreneurship: a framework for international comparative research. *Journal of Business Venturing* 12: 367–84.

Tushman, M.L., Anderson, P.C. and O'Reilly, C. 1997. Technology cycles, innovation streams and ambidextrous organizations: organization renewal through innovation streams and strategic change. In M.L. Tushman and P. Anderson (eds.), *Managing Strategic Innovation and Change*. New York: Oxford University Press, pp. 3–23.

Van Horn, R.L. and Harvey, M.G. 1998. The rural entrepreneurial venture: creating the virtual megafirm. *Journal of Business Venturing* 13: 257–74.

Venkatraman, S. 1997. The distinctive domain of entrepreneurship research. In J.A. Katz (ed.), *Advances in Entrepreneurship, Firm Emergence and Growth*, vol. 3. Greenwich, CN: JAI Press, pp. 119–38.

Vesper, K.H. and Gartner, W.B. 1997. Measuring progress in entrepreneurship education. *Journal of Business Venturing* 12: 403–21.

Vyakarnam, S., Jacobs, R.C. and Handelberg, J. 1997. Formation and the development of entrepreneurial teams in rapid-growth businesses. Paper presented at the Babson Entrepreneurship Research Conference, Wellesley, MA, April 17–19.

Weinzimmer, L.G., Nystrom, P.C. and Freeman, S.J. 1998. Measuring organizational growth: issues, consequences and guidelines. *Journal of Management* 24: 235–62.

West, G.P. and Meyer, G.D. 1998. To agree or not to agree? Consensus and performance in new ventures. *Journal of Business Venturing* 13: 395–422.

Wernerfelt, B. 1984. A resource-based view of the firm. *Strategic Management Journal* 5: 171–80.

Williamson, O.E. 1985. *The Economic Institutions of Capitalism: Firms, Markets, Relational Contracting*. New York: The Free Press.

Zacharakis, A.L. 1998. Entrepreneurial exporting strategies: contractual considerations. *Journal of Business Strategies* 15: 73–90.

Zacharakis, A.L. and Meyer, G.D. 1998. A lack of insight: do venture capitalists really understand their own decision process? *Journal of Business Venturing* 13: 57–76.

Zahra, S.A. 1996. Governance, ownership, and corporate entrepreneurship: the moderating impact of industry technological opportunities. *Academy of Management Journal* 39: 1713–35.

Zahra, S., Ireland, R.D. and Hitt, M.A. 1998. *International Diversification, Technological Learning and New Venture Firm Performance*. Working paper, Georgia State University.

4

Research Mimicking Policy: Entrepreneurship/Small Business Policy Research in the United States

WILLIAM DENNIS, JR.

NO POLICY AS POLICY
THE STATE OF E/SB POLICY RESEARCH
AN EXAMPLE: MANDATED EMPLOYEE HEALTH INSURANCE
CONCLUSIONS

An assessment of entrepreneurship/small business (E/SB) policy research in the United States must begin with an extraordinary irony: the current elevated status of and interest in E/SB can be traced to a single piece of research, the *Job Generation Process* (Birch 1979). This report's most influential finding – that new and small businesses generate a vastly disproportionate share of the net new jobs – now laces policy debate and repeatedly emerges in the popular media. Yet, policy research that directly considers a growth (entrepreneurship) or a size (small business) variable appears infrequently in the policy, economics, public finance and management literatures and, outside of Birch's job generation thesis, rarely surfaces in policy debate.

The most obvious consequence of this information shortage is that policymaking is less informed about entrepreneurial and small businesses than it would otherwise be. But a strong case can be made that small business and entrepreneurship have neither suffered from it (on a relative, rather than an optimal, basis) nor is fundamental policy toward them unsound. The supporting evidence lies in the result. American E/SBs seem to be doing as well as E/SBs almost anywhere in the world and have for the past several years. Moreover, if share of employment and GDP are appropriate measures, entrepreneurial and small business are, at worst, competing evenly with their larger counterparts. Direct research may not exist to explain the success, but the United States is doing something right (OECD 1997).

The thesis of this chapter is that E/SB policy research in the United States mimics American policy. Research reacts rather than leads. The limited amount of E/SB policy research contributes little to the direct formulation of policy impacting them. Further, to date it contributes little to our understanding of the externalities associated with entrepreneurship and small business. Policymakers are left to make decisions affecting these businesses from theory and research on competition and specific issues, experientially based frames-of-reference and raw political calculation.

The term "policy research" as used in this chapter refers to the analysis of primary material without prejudice to the methodology(ies) employed. The purpose of the definition is to clearly separate research from the plethora of papers, backgrounders, analyses, testimonies and argument that in legislative centers frequently carries the term "research." Many of the latter are thoughtful pieces, carefully constructed from secondary materials. Others are little more than hastily drafted propaganda lacking any semblance of intellectual detachment or merit. Thus, to make a meaningful and objective division, I have drawn a definitional line between primary and secondary research.

The remainder of this chapter is organized as follows: the second section provides a brief overview of E/SB policy in the United States and its association with E/SB policy research. The third outlines the state of E/SB policy research in the United States and discusses its six principal characteristics. The fourth section provides an extended example of the interface between policy and policy research to illustrate the six characteristics. The final section offers observations from the American experience that may help Americans and non-Americans alike to understand the direction E/SB policy research needs to take.

No Policy as Policy

The United States has no small business or entrepreneurship policy. Instead, it has a competition policy in which small business and entrepreneurship play an important role (Aoyama and Tietz 1996; Dennis 1998). The essential characteristic of that policy is to maintain government neutrality among competitors, regardless of size. Activities and programs do exist to reduce size advantages. However, they are not intended to offset economies of scale derived from markets so much as to offset economies of scale resulting from government demands (interventions). Small business policy is also increasingly mixed with a social policy designed to attain greater equity among social groups (Aoyama and Tietz 1996). Despite such departures from the "neutrality among competitors" model, the focus of E/SB policy in the United States is clear if not always consistent.

Revealing is the declaration of policy found in the first sentences of the Small Business Act of 1953, the law establishing the US Small Business Administration and the closest thing the United States has to a framework for policy governing American entrepreneurial and small business. The exposition of "small business policy" in the United States, begins:

> The essence of the American economic system of private enterprise is free competition. Only through full and free competition can free markets, free entry into business, and opportunities for the expression and growth of personal initiative and individual judgment be assured. The preservation and expansion of such competition is basic not only to the economic well-being but to the security of this Nation. Such security and well-being cannot be realized unless the actual and potential capacity of small business is encouraged and developed (15 USC §631(a)).

Small business is not mentioned in its own policy outline until the eightieth word. Three references to competition precede it. Even security is a forerunner. Competition, and implicitly the consumer, is the overriding concern of the law, not entrepreneurial or small business per se.

The logical extension of the competition policy is that no special treatment should be extended to any competitor or any group of competitors. From this framework, programs favoring (subsidizing) one competitor over another regardless of size, financial condition or other factors are irrational. Public intervention to assist competitors can only be justified when markets are distorted and not functioning efficiently. Manifestation of the competition policy has increasingly centered on entry and de-emphasized control of questionable competitive practices.[1] Visible results included deregulation of the trucking, airlines, telecommunications and financial services industries as well as frequent removal of local impediments to home-based businesses – all to reduce or eliminate entry barriers. At the same time, enforcement of competition regulating measures such as Robinson-Patman has all but disappeared.

Subtle changes in policy direction

A subtle change in the dominant policy began to occur in the late 1970s and early 1980s. Birch's (1979) *The Job Generation Process* empirically demonstrated that entrepreneurial and small business do more than simply enhance competition. They are also uniquely involved in the employment process and local economic development. The perspective on entrepreneurial and small firms shifted as a result. The altered view offered intellectual justification for exploring a wider range of policy impacts on E/SBs and gave policymakers a rationale to intervene in their support.

Meanwhile, research associated with the SBA Office of Advocacy demonstrated that government is an important source of market distortion for E/SBs. Government-imposed burdens disproportionately impact (adversely) smaller firms, thereby artificially upsetting the competitive balance among large and small (Cole and Tegeler 1980; Berney 1981; Faucett et al. 1984; Gaston and Carroll 1984; Arthur Andersen 1979). Government-created advantages and disadvantages are not legitimate, while market created advantages and disadvantages are. The result is an equity argument for small business exemptions, exclusions, phase-ins, alternative sets of rules and so forth for various government burdens. (Another American characteristic is that the grievance should typically be redressed through elimination or minimization of the burden, rather than the offer of a compensating initiative.) These arguments become critical because as economic regulation has declined dramatically since the late 1970s, the increase in social regulation has more than offset it.

The small business lobby began its ascent a few years earlier. It brought demands to the political system, and new influence to the ballot box. Increasingly, the lobby forced policymakers to ask, How does this affect small business?[2] Policymakers posed the question not so much for analytic, as for political purposes. Yet, once this simple question became a common inquiry, a new demand was created for E/SB policy research.

In 1976, the small business lobby pushed through creation of the Office of Advocacy at SBA, not to run programs, but to provide E/SB policy research and to serve as an in-house advocate. On the philosophic premise that government regulations are an artifice that disadvantages small business's competitive position, the small business lobby also led the successful effort to pass the Regulatory Flexibility Act (Reg Flex) in 1980. The law requires federal agencies to produce small business impact statements on any significant rule-making and to provide a different, presumably less burdensome, set of regulations for smaller firms when appropriate. The implication of this legal requirement is that agencies must conduct research to determine small business impacts. Though the agencies have treated this mandate as a pariah, requiring the stronger Small Business Regulatory Enforcement Fairness Act (SBREFA) of 1997, Reg Flex laid the ground for creation of an extensive body of small business policy-oriented research. Finally, the Small Business Economic Policy Act of 1980 required the President to provide the Congress an annual report on the state of small business and *competition*. The Act's declaration of policy incorporates the shift to more direct support of E/SBs, but its most visible result is the annual State of Small Business report.

Policy today

Competition policy still reigns. However, political strength, the externality of job generation and the concept of disproportionate impacts, altered the policy landscape. Small business can now expect to receive a reasonable share of any tax reduction and "carve-outs" from major legislation are increasingly a fact of life.[3] Barbieri (1998) identified over twenty examples of carve-outs at the federal and state levels including paperwork in the Occupational Health and Safety Act (OSHA), exemption from the Family and Medical Leave Act and allowance of the smallest businesses to opt out of the Federal Electronic Payments System. These carve-outs can play a pivotal role in the larger debate, as the process of amending "Superfund" illustrates. Environmentalists want to remove small business from parts of the legislation in fear that without relief for these firms, the toxic clean-up program will be lost in its current form. Big businesses want to keep them in because that is the only way the program will be radically changed.

The Clinton Administration would alter the policy focus further. It is intent on moving from the competition model. It would de-emphasize the existing competition policy and focus on social programs, e.g., micro loans, and providing growing business with affirmative assistance (an industrial policy), e.g., the extension service for manufacturers in the National Institute of Standards and Technology. The Congress has resisted, particularly with regard to the latter. Thus, the 1990s has brought little practical change in policy direction.

Interest in small business impacts continues to grow. The demand for E/SB research increases as a result. Quantitative estimates of impacts are particularly desired. But not even the Department of the Treasury appears capable of or willing to produce relevant E/SB estimates. NFIB in the late-1970s and SBA in the mid-1980s attempted to construct E/SB models. The attempts were not successful, but they identified a need. A prominent tax economist restated the issue arguing for

> a robust model of the formation of small businesses and their contribution to the economy. Only through the development and empirical testing of such a model will it be possible to identify any beneficial externalities arising from the formation and growth of small business, and to isolate the parameters that are both crucial to these processes and amenable to policy influence. (Holtz-Eakin 1995: 393)[4]

The State of E/SB Policy Research

E/SB policy research is a rational extension of the competition policy. If policy does not consider the size or growth variable, why bother to research it? If there is no research on these firms, why is there a need for data containing a size or growth variable? And, why is there a need for financial support to pay for the research? If E/SBs thrive in a competitive atmosphere, what more is needed? It is not coincidental that E/SB policy research to date centers on entry, the centerpiece of a competition policy.

The state of E/SB policy research in the United States can be summarized in the following six propositions:

1 The volume of E/SB policy research is small and inadequate to address the most basic questions.
2 Policy research in the United States has an issue-specific, not group-based, focus, except for women and minorities.
3 The people who produce policy research on issues affecting small business and their publication outlets are not often associated with academic business schools.
4 Funding for E/SB policy research is minimal and on a project-by-project basis.
5 A prime reason for the lack of policy-oriented research is a lack of data.
6 If a policy cycle begins with issue development, proceeds to the legislative process and ends with policy evaluation, most E/SB policy research currently addresses issues in the middle or latter stages.

Now let's examine each proposition in greater detail.

The volume of E/SB policy research is small and inadequate to address the most basic questions. Policy decisions affecting these firms are usually made without the benefit of research findings. While there is reason to believe this condition is changing for the better, the lack of research, enabling the development, analysis and evaluation of policy initiatives, "dumbs down" the public policymaking process.

Many, including the author, have lamented the general lack of policy research with an E/SB focus or at least incorporating E/SB impacts. Brockhaus (1987) attempted to add rigor to the consensus opinion when he compared the topics that delegates to the 1986 White House Conference on Small Business voted of greatest concern to the topics addressed in three academic journals and three E/SB proceedings. He found the two groups of topics were almost totally divorced. Owners found policy issues highly relevant; the academic community did not. Hoy (1997) effectively updated the Brockhaus investigation using policy priorities from 1995 White House Conference as a baseline and found virtually the same thing.

Banks and Taylor (1991) addressed the issue differently. They surveyed samples of E/SB owners and academics to determine perceptions of the most pressing business issues. Four of the top ten issues cited by E/SB owners in the Banks and Taylor survey were policy matters including "regulations and paperwork," which topped the list. Regulations and paperwork did not even make the academic top ten nor did any other policy issue.

These authors selected a narrow range of issues and publication outlets. Expand the ranges and the outlook is not as bleak. Make program evaluation the topic. Chrisman and McMullen (1996), Wood (1994),[5] Moini (1998) and Masten et al. (1995) published traditional program evaluations. Brewer and Genay (1995) explored a potential program modification in recent issues of the *Journal of Small Business Management (JSBM)* as examples. While one can argue with their use of small samples and the sophistication of the analyses, these are truly instances of E/SB policy research published in a small business journal.

Moreover, the contributions found in the *JSBM* represent a small portion of the program evaluation literature. Researchers at ABT Associates authored a three-volume series analyzing experiments in Massachusetts and Washington designed to use the unemployment compensation system to help unemployed people become self-employed (ABT 1992, 1994, 1995). Cadwell (1997) recently provided an evaluation of state export promotion programs for the US Small Business Administration (SBA). Lerner (1996) examined the value of the Small Business Innovation Research (SBIR) program for the National Bureau of Economic Research. The General Accounting Office evaluated problems in SBA's 8(a) program for the United States Congress (GAO 1995). In fact GAO produces eight to ten such reports and testimonies every year on topics ranging from estimates of credit subsidies (GAO 1997) to administration of employment taxes (GAO 1996). The foregoing constitute a few selected examples of program (or possible program) evaluations produced outside E/SB-specific journals.

Beyond evaluation, the Office of Advocacy in the SBA has supported about 750 separate pieces of policy-oriented research over the past two plus decades (Phillips 1998). Since 1982, it has also produced the annual State of Small Business report, which though not directly policy research, provides notable statistical background and descriptive material. No other source can claim an equivalent output. Omitting program evaluation, it is likely that all sources combined do not match Advocacy's production. The largest general E/SB research program run in the private sector belongs to the NFIB Education Foundation and it produces or sponsors an average of six or seven pieces in a typical year as well as a monthly economic report. The smaller, RISEbusiness, a private, unaffiliated small business research foundation has begun to produce a limited number of published monographs.

Research volume is only half of the equation. The breadth and variety of issues, issue areas, programs and initiatives that impact E/SBs makes the existing volume of policy research inadequate for the need. This inadequacy means that participants in the legislative process often cannot respond to reasonable inquiries from policymakers seeking information on relevant questions. For example: the Chairwoman of a House Ways and Means subcommittee asked witnesses representing small business owners to respond in writing to several technical questions that arose from testimony presented in support of a proposal allowing the self-employed to deduct health insurance premiums from their federal income tax (Johnson 1998). The witnesses argued their case primarily on the grounds of equity, i.e., since corporate businesses are allowed the deduction, noncorporate businesses should be allowed the deduction as well. But the Chairwoman was interested in impact, particularly the deduction's impact on the number of people with insurance coverage. Witnesses could answer perhaps one-quarter of her questions without new research, much of it complicated and requiring data collection. In this instance, the legislative process moved forward without the information.

If unsatisfied demand from policymakers is the measure of need, there truly is a shortage of E/SB policy research. But what of research on externalities, i.e., the impacts of E/SBs? Externalities, too, is an area ripe with interesting and influential research questions. This field is particularly appropriate for academics who are squeamish about conducting research directly on policy issues. After all, *The Job Generation Process* (Birch 1979) was a study of E/SB externalities, and the work's influence has been immeasurable.

Business formation is the single area where substantial externality research can be found. The Babson Entrepreneurship Research Conference, despite its changing focus, still constitutes a significant effort to understand the creation and growth of business enterprise. The same is true of the Entrepreneurial Research Consortium and work such as the Wells Fargo/NFIB Starts and Stops series (Dennis 1997).

A number of critical areas badly need exploration. Small business advocates boast of the people employed. But how do small business owners select their employees and how do they train them? And, what is the value of that training? Schiller (1981) demonstrated that small employers provide more training to employees on their first jobs than do larger firms. Subsequent studies on the training issue can be cited, but not a number commensurate with the topic's importance. Critics like Bellman and Groshen (1998) prefer to discuss the wages and benefits in small and emerging businesses. Though E/SBs do not come off as well on this count as on others, the subject can't be ignored. And then there are topics like innovation. The strong research base begun in early 1980s has eroded. The same appears true of regulation – and community. Why have so few examined the E/SB contribution to community? In fact, E/SB externalities beg for investigation.

Policy research in the United States has an issue-specific, not a group-based, focus except for women and minorities. The impacts of policy on entrepreneurial and small business, and vice versa, are customarily subordinate to the larger issue. The problem created by this approach for E/SB policy research is that resources (money and talent) and interest are consumed investigating the broader questions. Little is left to examine impacts on E/SBs.

The primary question posed in most policy debates is the overall impact of a proposal on overreaching issue areas, e.g., the budget, employment and inflation. The interests or wishes of specific groups, including entrepreneurial and small business, are measured against larger needs. This approach demonstrates the American preoccupation with business environment and the rules of the game: Get the fundamentals right and "good things" will happen to individuals and groups. The most powerful opponent of various small business efforts to obtain tax incentives, equity, simplification or just plain reductions, therefore, becomes "revenue neutrality," i.e., maintaining a balance between revenues and expenditures. The first research consideration in a tax bill is its budgetary impact. Analysis of the primary macro impacts – economic growth, employment and inflation – follow. Small business impacts (other than political, which are increasingly common) are calculated only as a residual from the analyses of provisions that exclusively or largely affect small or growing businesses.

A Request for Proposal (RFP) from the National Institute of Disability Rehabilitation Research (NIDRR 1998) illustrates the theme. NIDRR's RFP lists one of its five research priorities as identifying and evaluating effective workplace supports to improve the employment outcomes of disabled persons. The tasks include evaluating the effectiveness of tax credits and Medicare "buydowns," examining employer perspectives, along with other research pieces. There are two points to note: the issue focuses on disabled people and implicitly views small business as one of many potential means to assist them.

Second, the agency sponsoring the research is the agency of the disabled, not the agency of small business.

The body of policy research on issues affecting small business can be substantial, while the body of E/SB policy research on the same issue is negligible. The minimum wage presents an excellent example. The literature on the issue is extensive. Most appears in economics publications. It includes assessments of employment impacts (e.g., Welch et al. 1995), impacts on the poor and poverty (e.g., Neumark and Wascher 1997) and impacts on training received by employees (e.g., Hashimoto 1982). Yet, the literature and policy debate revolve around larger issues, i.e., employment, prices, poverty and the impact on employee groups, such as minority teenagers. The impacts on small businesses are largely ignored, though it is clear that retailers and owners of business in rural areas feel vastly more impacted than others (Dennis 1996). The concerns of these owners apparently are inadequate to stimulate research interest.

The focus on issue-specific E/SB policy research puts an implicit premium on issue-based knowledge, such as, taxes, in contrast to group-based knowledge, e.g., small business. (The discussion of research funding later in this chapter steers the reader in the same direction.) This priority means that the bibliographic search must focus on the topic including associated publication outlets rather than on E/SBs and its research publication outlets. The priority also means that at least on one level, academics in the business school operate at a disadvantage compared with those in the traditional disciplines and participants in the policy process. That observation leads to the third point.

The people who produce policy research on issues affecting small business and their publication outlets are not often associated with academic business schools. As many or more can be found in the traditional disciplines, notably economics, and the publication outlets in those fields. E/SB policy researchers are also as likely to be nonacademic, i.e., from government or the private sector, as academic. Research conducted by the former usually does not appear in the journals, but in government, association or private business reports.

Brockhaus (1987), Hoy (1997) and Banks and Taylor (1991) are all relevant in this context. The first two investigated the E/SB policy research published in E/SB-oriented journals and proceedings. The latter two examined attitudes of researchers in business schools. The researchers' results were largely negative. But even by expanding the scope of issues and publications examined, E/SB policy research from those it is assumed would be most productive and interested in these questions, i.e., the business schools, is minimal.

Later in this chapter the author provides a detailed example of a contentious policy issue and the E/SB research involved. Not one pertinent study in this example was produced by an individual associated with a business school. The useful studies were produced by people in schools of health policy, public health, economics and public finance (or outside academe). In fact, there have been more National Bureau of Economic Research (NBER) working papers published on entrepreneurship, small business and self-employment policy since 1996 than appeared during that same time period in articles in *Journal of Small Business Management (JSBM)*, *Entrepreneurship Theory and Practice (ETP)* and *Journal of Business Venturing (JBV)* combined.

The pertinent product from government, including SBA, is vastly greater in quantity than from business schools.[6] Most of the federal reports are lodged in the National Technical Information Service's archives. Unfortunately, studies and reports from the states, economic development organizations, and private groups have no similar central depository, restricting their accessibility for research and policy purposes.

The implications of the business school's divorce from E/SB policy research are a smaller research volume, one less informed about micro questions and a surrender of the policy agenda. Most critically, the business perspective is suborned to other interests. We will examine later the lack of policy research in the developmental stage, a place where the business school might play a key role.

Funding for E/SB policy research is minimal and on a project-by-project basis. The resources available for E/SB policy research are scattered. Disbursement is usually ad hoc and tied to a specific issue rather than an ongoing program. Government resources for this type of work are often found in project or program evaluation.

The primary exception has been SBA's Office of Advocacy, which has maintained a continuing research program since its inception in the late 1970s. Funding has ranged from a high of $4.5 million in the early 1980s to a low of $500,000. Resources of the office became so limited that it was forced to terminate its competitive research grant program (recently reinstated). However, this program has been the one consistent source of support for E/SB policy research. Other federal agencies, such as the Economic Development Administration (EDA) and the Minority Business Development Administration (MBDA), both in the Department of Commerce, have records of supporting E/SB research with policy implications. (Birch produced *The Job Generation Process* under a grant from EDA.) Still other agencies conduct research in-house and publish it in agency journals, e.g., *Statistics of Income Bulletin* (IRS) and the *Monthly Labor Review* (Bureau of Labor Statistics). But Advocacy has been the public sector's principal supporter of E/SB research, despite hard times.

Private foundations in the United States also finance considerable amounts of policy research. A review of contributors to Washington's think-tank community, e.g., American Enterprise Institute, Brookings Institution, CATO, Heritage Foundation, Urban Institute, makes that clear. However, the foundations that fund policy research generally do not include small business specific projects (or at least generally have not), and the largest grant-making foundations focusing on ESBs are not in the policy research business. The Coleman, Kauffman, Lowe and Price foundations do not include E/SB policy research among their funding priorities.[7]

An exception is the Robert Wood Johnson Foundation's (RWJF) ongoing interest in small business and health.[8] RWJF, one of the nation's largest, may have spent more money on small business policy research than any organization in the country excluding the SBA. Its sponsorships include demonstration projects (with accompanying research) among small employers not providing employee health insurance (e.g., Helms et al. 1992; McLaughlin and Zellers 1992) as well as policy evaluations in its State Initiatives in Health Care Reform program (e.g., Cantor et al. 1995; Acs et al. 1996; Long and Marquis 1996). But RWJF's concern is health, not small business. The motive supporting such research is locating means by which small business can provide more employee health insurance. Other foundations provide smaller amounts on occasion to support E/SB policy-oriented research. The Institute for Justice (1996, 1997), for example, employed a consortium of foundations to sponsor the research and publication of its series on government barriers to entry-level entrepreneurial opportunity in seven cities.

Private businesses and business organizations also support E/SB policy research, often as an adjunct to their marketing activities. The Employee Benefit Research Institute (EBRI), a nonprofit research organization in Washington, for example, marshaled a consortium of thirty-three private businesses and nonprofit groups, many in the financial services industry, to sponsor the 1998 Retirement Confidence Survey. One of the project's three modules focused on small business.

A researcher who intends to pursue an E/SB policy-oriented project has no logical or obvious funding source. This is more true today than previously because of the decline in SBA support. Success can be achieved in the public or private sector, in a nonprofit or for-profit organization, but the sponsor will likely dictate the topic, with small business only an ancillary consideration. Different projects probably will require different sponsors. Most support has been relatively modest, though projects such as RWJF's demonstrations (and evaluations) and the Department of Labor's on transforming unemployed people to self-employed people, can involve significant dollars.

A prime reason for the dearth of policy-oriented research is a lack of data. While this difficulty is not unique to E/SB policy research, the lack of timely, detailed, enterprise-specific numbers remains a significant research liability. This does not suggest that the available data have been exhausted. IRS's public use (research) file, for example, has not been explored to any notable extent for E/SB policy questions. The new Longitudinal Enterprise and Establishment Microdata (LEEM) file allows examination of growth questions that other countries have been able to do for years. However, data limitations cause the research questions posed to be more restricted than they would otherwise be.

The United States has a relatively poor statistical system if one is interested in the business size variable (Phillips and Dennis 1997). It has virtually no system for the growth variable. Enough reasonable assumptions and manipulations can be made so that available data will allow the modeling of economic impacts of significant issues (e.g., CONSAD 1994, 1998). However, that type of policy research requires considerable up-front investment and is not applicable for all relevant questions. Moreover, as the budgets of statistical agencies tighten and resistance to questionnaires from business owners stiffen, the capacity of government statistical agencies to provide more and better data diminishes.

Private-sector databases, e.g., Dun & Bradstreet's New Incorporations and Business Failures series, Wells Fargo/NFIB's Business Stops and Starts and NFIB's Small Business Economic Trends, supplement public data sources to a modest degree. They will probably do so more in the future (Phillips and Dennis 1997). However, private institutions cannot and arguably should not replace the Federal government's role in data collection and dissemination.

E/SB researchers as a group rely on ad hoc surveys to collect much of their data. Aldrich and Baker (1997) calculated that surveys were used to conduct entrepreneurship research published in selected outlets during the 1990s about five times as often as were public databases. There is no reason to believe a similar ratio does not hold for E/SB policy research (except tax-related questions). This massive use of surveys carries its own liabilities. Among the more notable are:

- ◆ inconsistency of sample, definition, and inquiry across surveys,
- ◆ poor survey construction in too many instances; inadequate response rates,
- ◆ public inaccessibility (often), and
- ◆ lack of context on all but the immediate question.

E/SB policy research will never reach complete legitimacy without the development of better and more plentiful data sets.[9] These sets unfortunately can take years to create and are costly. Despite a proposal for significant revision of the American statistical system from then-Council of Economic Advisors Chairman, Michael Boskin, no major change in the nation's data collection system appears imminent. Still, those conducting E/SB policy research would do well to invest more time and energy in locating better data sets before resorting to their own surveys.

If a policy cycle begins with issue development, proceeds to the legislative process and ends with policy evaluation, most E/SB policy research currently addresses issues in the middle or latter stages.[10] The dominant reason is that those interested in entrepreneurial and small firms are more likely to defend the status quo, i.e., the competition policy, than they are to initiate change (even through repeal). There are related considerations – cost and the ability to raise funds for a future shared benefit rather than a "present danger," the lack of planning and lead time, comfort with the traditional arguments based on equity, appeals for sympathy as an underdog and, implicitly, political strength. By default, the demand for E/SB policy research at the early stages of the policy cycle is limited. When advocates and other sponsors do press the initiative, they usually draw on available material. An example is Stuart Butler's (1981) *Enterprise Zones: Greenlining the Inner City*, which argues for enterprise zones, an innovative proposal in which entrepreneurs and their businesses are envisioned as central actors in inner-city revitalization. The book was well-documented, well-written and well-argued. It also drew exclusively on secondary materials.

There are limited instances when research plays a role in the earlier stages. Many appear related to tax policy where revenue estimates have been calculated for years. One example involves estate and gift taxes where proponents of their elimination provided notable developmental research. Wagner (1993) and Beach (1996), among others, conducted econometric studies to quantify economic benefits from the repeal. Wagner's work appeared before the issue was taken up, and Beach appeared during consideration. It should also be noted that these projects centered on the overall issue, with E/SBs just a part of it.

Advocates are most likely to produce research when they are combating an initiative. The health example in the next section illustrates the point – so does *The Economic Impact of Mandated Family Leave on Small Businesses and Their Employees* (Barnett and Musgrave 1991). Both health and family leave studies emerged well after the issues were framed and debate begun. Research on the former appeared early enough to influence the course of events; the latter probably did not.

On the other hand, advocates are unlikely to devote resources to evaluating enacted legislation. The premium for them is passing or defeating the initiative, not maximizing or minimizing its impact once the decision has been made. They usually exhibit minimal interest in evaluation, meaning that their later stages research product is practically nil.

Government focuses on the end of the cycle. Since the agencies administer the policy or program, they have a corollary responsibility to evaluate their actions. These evaluations, almost by definition, involve the analysis of primary data, i.e., research. Several examples of government or government-sponsored evaluations were cited earlier. But government also participates in the E/SB policy formulation stages, e.g., ABT Associates (1992, 1994, 1995). It is the entity most likely to do so. However, government-sponsored early-stage research appears much less important as it relates to E/SB than it does for many other interests because:

♦ E/SBs demand less from government than do most interests, which diminishes the pressure for E/SB-oriented government initiatives.
♦ Basic E/SB policy is not sympathetic to intervention on their behalf.
♦ Government, as others, think in terms of overarching issues and questions rather than group impacts, at least business group impacts.

AN EXAMPLE: MANDATED EMPLOYEE HEALTH INSURANCE

A particularly contentious issue appeared in Washington during the first half of the 1990s that illustrates well the six propositions just discussed. The exception, to a degree, is the volume of research produced. The amount of research published on this issue is atypically large, reflecting both the stakes and the ideological splits involved. However, given the immense implications and multiplicity of important topics within the primary issue, the volume is probably less than might have been expected. With respect to the other five points, the issue is a prototype. The legislative example is The Health Security Act of 1993, President Clinton's unsuccessful attempt in 1993 and 1994 to effectively nationalize health care in the United States.

Health care in the United States is financed through a combination of private and public insurance. Those age 65 years and over are covered by a public system (Medicare) while the poorest are covered by a different public system (Medicaid). The remainder of the public obtains private insurance either through employer-sponsored plans or through individual policies. Most employed people and their families are covered by employer-sponsored and subsidized health insurance.[11] However, employee health insurance is a "benefit," and not all employers provide it, nor do all employees choose to be covered if they must contribute a portion of the premium.

Universal health insurance coverage was high on President Clinton's agenda when he entered office. The new President proposed the Health Security Act of 1993 to achieve that objective as well as to retard the rapidly escalating costs of health care. Central to the President's proposal was mandatory employer-provided employee health insurance. All employers would be required either to provide health insurance or to pay a significant penalty. The President subsequently revised his proposal to provide subsidies for small businesses to help them finance the cost, but the health insurance mandate was fundamental to the program from the onset.

Small business was integral to the President's proposal for two reasons: First, almost half of the 23 million employed uninsured were tied to small workplaces (fewer than twenty-five employees). Fewer than 30 percent of firms with less than five employees provided health insurance coverage, though the percentage increased as firm size rose. Second, the remainder of the President's plan could not be financed without the revenues from mandatory coverage.

The literature on the issue of mandatory provision of employer-paid employee health insurance, particularly the tie between small employers and insurance provision, should have been massive. Not only is the health insurance mandate issue not new in health policy circles, but one assumes that a Presidential initiative the magnitude of Health Security Act would have its central features developed from prior inquiry. Unfortunately, that was not the case. The literature on the mandate was practically nonexistent before the debate and then during and after it.

I reviewed the most prominent journals in health policy to ascertain the extent and nature of E/SB policy research published during the relevant period.[12] The primary debate on the Health Security Act occurred between 1993 and 1994. The review arbitrarily covered the ten-year period, 1989-98. Three themes emerged from the analysis:

1 While all three journals bulged with articles on health care reform, assessments of the Health Security Act or parts thereof, and various health policy ideas, comparatively little focused on small business, entrepreneurship, self-employment or small groups.[13] Only about twenty from hundreds of articles proved applicable.

2 Before the introduction of the Health Security Act (January 1, 1993, for purposes of article classification), just five topical articles appeared that fit the author's working definition of E/SB policy research. Four of the five were published in *Health Affairs* (Helms et al. 1992; McLaughlin and Zellers 1992; Zellers et al. 1992; Edwards et al. 1992) and one in *Inquiry* (Kronick 1991); the *Journal of Health Politics, Policy and Law* published none. An equivalent number of thoughtful pieces, not qualifying under my definition of research, ran in all three. The preponderance of this research discussion appeared after the fact and played no role in the policy debate.

3 The emphasis throughout the literature of this period was not on the health insurance mandate, the principal debate topic involving entrepreneurial and small business. Rather, the main topic proved to be the issue of small group reform, irrelevant if the Health Security Act were enacted. The reasons for this focus are not totally clear; however, it is fair to speculate that research dollars, data, complexity of the issues and timeliness all played a role.

Major actors in the debate, Washington-based think tanks and government, provided most of the policy research surrounding the Health Security Act. Lewin, Data Resources Inc. (DRI), O'Neill and O'Neill (sponsored by American Enterprise Institute [AEI]) and the Congressional Budget Office estimated job impacts, for example. The Heritage Foundation, among others, offered a proposal of its own, and Lewin modeled its impacts. The Employee Benefit Research Institute (EBRI) and SBA offered data from the Current Population Survey (Bureau of the Census) on the incidence of health insurance coverage in smaller firms. However, the National Federation of Independent Business (NFIB), a small business advocacy organization, was the only group to provide policy research specifically on small firms. Its most sophisticated inquiries, conducted by CONSAD Research Corporation, modeled job losses, jobs affected, change in wages, and government subsidies by firm size (measured in employees), industry and state (CONSAD 1994). A second iteration modeled business closures by firm size and employment losses (CONSAD 1995). Variants of the CONSAD model simulated the small business impacts of Senator Kennedy's short-lived proposal, those of Congressmen Gephardt and Gibbons and health insurance mandates in Washington state. Though small business was central to the argument on both sides of the Health Security Act and its variations, only the

NFIB-sponsored CONSAD studies and one considerably more modest NFIB research piece became part of the debate.

The data on smaller businesses was not satisfactory to address many of the primary research questions posed. For example, though controlling costs was a principal objective of the Health Security Act, data on premiums paid by small employers for a particular benefit package was either weak or nonexistent. The critical insurance price/employer purchase elasticity used to model the Health Security Act was not size specific. And perhaps, most egregiously, the number and location of impacted firms had to be drawn from establishment rather than enterprise data. An exception was provision of employee health insurance coverage by firm size.

Since the death of the Health Security Act, the nonacademic research community, excluding the Robert Wood Johnson Foundation, has conducted or sponsored relatively little E/SB policy research on health related matters. An econometric analysis projecting impacts of the Expanded Portability and Health Insurance Coverage Act (CONSAD 1998) is an exception. In contrast, the bulk of the academic literature on small business and health appeared during this time, well after the Health Security Act debate was over.

CONCLUSIONS

The United States lags parts of Europe in E/SB policy research. Americans have nothing like the more than twenty years of policy research conferences the United Kingdom has enjoyed. There are no organizations equivalent to the Swedish Foundation for Small Business Research or the Entrepreneurship and the Small Business Research Institute (also in Sweden). The State of Small Business report was an American invention, but the European Observatory for SMEs is now in the same league as are similar reports from Australia to Poland, from Japan to Canada. Government support for E/SB policy research often found elsewhere does not exist in the United States, particularly in recent years. Yet the United States maintains advantages. Perhaps the most important are private-sector involvement and a large cadre of academics interested in E/SBs, if not particularly interested in the policy aspects.

Does the American experience with E/SB policy-oriented research to date hold any lessons for ourselves or for others? The following are a few observations:

The quality and quantity of E/SB policy-oriented research is not necessarily related to the quality of policy impacting E/SBs. De facto E/SB policy in the United States has proven reasonably successful without it. Perhaps, its absence has allowed (required) policymakers to fall back on fundamental principles, i.e., the value and importance of competition, rather than research results on marginal questions. Researchers working in small business policy would do well to devote resources to investigating the relationship and influence of the growth and size variables on competition and vice versa. However, the competition policy is ebbing, and government demands on E/SBs are rising. A successful policy model is changing, and policymakers have no idea of its consequences. E/SB research is necessary to establish the impacts of these alternate policy models. Are they improvements or do they undermine a relatively successful policy direction?

The Job Generation Process (Birch 1979) has been enormously influential. Some complain, tacitly if not explicitly, that it is too influential, even distorting general policy debate (Brown et al. 1990; Davis et al. 1993; Pierce 1998). Though filled with policy implications, Birch's report is not a policy document per se. It is research exploring E/SB externalities. Externalities research is particularly conducive to the academic setting due to unlimited time lines and its essential neutrality on specific issues. Academe can leave interested parties and government to organize, finance and conduct (or have conducted) research on more immediate and direct policy proposals. Though self-interest is usually the motivation behind such research (government must usually be considered an "interested party"), useful material often emerges.

E/SB policy-oriented research in the United States involves widely varying segments of American interest, both public and private: government, academe, trade groups, business associations, private foundations and for-profit businesses. Those planning to use E/SBs to advance their agendas and E/SB owners promoting their own interests are in the mix, but there is no leadership or organizing entity and no centralized research agenda. Such dispersed activity has all the inherent advantages and disadvantages of a highly decentralized system, though it is probably the only arrangement that will work in the United States. Others may prefer a more centralized system, but private-sector involvement should never be marginalized.

American business schools should encourage greater interest in E/SB policy research. Policy is clearly an essential part of today's environmental equation. It is, therefore, highly relevant and offers significant opportunities in a largely unexplored area.

If there are few small business support programs (or if they consume minimal resources), there is no need to spend limited research resources evaluating them. A negligible body of such research also minimizes the opportunity to confuse what is central with what is peripheral.

Mathematical models measuring impacts must be developed sooner rather than later. Quantification of impacts is central to policymaking in Washington (less so at the state and local levels). Federal agencies and others frequently use models to appraise general impacts. Small business must operate models to appraise small business impacts if it wishes to compete.

International research cooperation and participation is increasingly valuable. E/SB researchers often encounter similar questions even when the specific issues and their contexts are quite different. And, even when the specific issues and their contexts are quite different, they are increasingly traded across national boundaries. Mutual efforts allow researchers to leverage resources (intellectual and financial) and reduce repetitive effort. The best example is the Entrepreneurial Research Consortium, which involves over a hundred researchers from nine countries. Moreover, the ongoing sharing of ideas and experiences among policy organizations regarding such policies as compulsory privatized retirement systems can rapidly move relevant policy from one national context into another.

NOTES

1 I am grateful to Jim Morrison for drawing my attention to this point.
2 *Fortune* magazine recently used a poll of White House staff, Congressmen, Congressional staff, and Washington insiders to produce a ranking of the most powerful lobbies in the nation's capital (Birnbaum 1997). The small business lobby, i.e., the National Federation of Independent Business, ranked fourth. It trailed only the AARP (seniors), American-Israel Public Affairs Committee and the AFL-CIO (organized labor confederation).
3 Opposition to the concept, sometimes referred to as regulatory subsidies, is also rising. See, Pierce (1998) as an example.
4 I am grateful to the NFIB Education Foundation for permission to include this quotation.
5 Technically, the exchange does not fit the working definition of research. However, serious debate on the proper methodology to evaluate a program appears to be a qualifying exception.
6 Some double counting occurs because of the way Advocacy issues research contracts. Advocacy prefers to award its contracts to private businesses. As a result, grantees may appear under the name of their consulting firm rather than their academic institution.
7 The Kauffman Foundation appears increasingly interested in policy matters but has yet to show interest in an ongoing policy research program.
8 The Henry J. Kaiser Family Foundation has a similar interest.
9 This includes restructuring current sets, e.g., the inclusion of small, closely held C corporations in the Bureau of the Census's *Characteristics of Business Owners* set.
10 A considerable amount of research produced by SBA involves externalities and is, therefore, insensitive to a policy cycle. Hopkins (1995), for example, attempted to quantify the cost of federal regulation to small business. These data can be used in a variety of legislative and nonlegislative contexts, not exclusively for a particular proposal(s).
11 The federal government also subsidizes employer-sponsored health insurance by the tax exclusion of premium costs. It does not do the same for health insurance purchases made directly by individuals.
12 A list of journals was developed with the help and advice of Robert B. Helms, Director of Health Policy Studies at the American Enterprise Institute in Washington; Michael A. Morrisey, Professor, Department of Health Care Organization and Policy, Department of Public Health, University of Alabama-Birmingham; and, Wilbur A. Steger, President, CONSAD Research Corporation in Pittsburgh. It includes *Health Affairs, Inquiry* and the *Journal of Health Politics, Policy and Law.*
13 "Small group" is an insurance term. While small firms are not always equivalent to small groups, they approximate one another for all practical purposes.

REFERENCES

ABT Associates, Inc. 1992. *Self-Employment Programs for Unemployed Workers.* Unemployment Insurance Occasional Paper 92–2, Employment and Training Administration, US Department of Labor: Washington, DC.

ABT Associates, Inc. 1994. *Self-Employment as a Reemployment Option: Demonstration Results and National Legislation.* Unemployment Insurance Occasional Paper 94–3, Employment and Training Administration, US Department of Labor: Washington, DC.

ABT Associates, Inc. 1995. *Self-Employment Programs: A New Reemployment Strategy, Final Report on the UI Self-Employment Demonstration.* Unemployment Insurance Occasional Paper 95–4, Employment and Training Administration, US Department of Labor: Washington, DC.

Acs, G., Stephen H., Long, M., Marquis, S. and Farley Short, P. 1996. Self-insured Employer Health Plans: Prevalence, Profile, Provisions, and Premiums. *Health Affairs* 15(2): 266–73.

Aldrich, H.E. and Baker, T. 1997. Blinded by the Cites? Has There Been Progress in Entrepreneurship Research? In D.L. Sexton and R.W. Smilor (eds.), *Entrepreneurship 2000*. Chicago: Upstart, pp. 377–400.

Aoyama, Y. and Tietz, M.B. 1996. *Small Business Policy in Japan and the United States: A Comparative Analysis of Objectives and Outcomes*. Institute for International Studies. Berkeley: University of California.

Arthur Andersen & Co. 1979. *Analysis of Regulatory Cost on Establishment Size for the Small Business Administration*. Office of Advocacy, Small Business Administration, Contract No. SBA-263-OA-79, October.

Banks, M.C. and Taylor S. 1991. Developing an Entrepreneur and Small Business Owner-defined Research Agenda. *Journal of Small Business Management* 29(2): 10–18.

Barbieri, D. 1998. *Legislative Definitions of Small Business*. Washington, DC: NFIB Education Foundation.

Barnett, W.S., and Musgrave, G.L. 1991. *The Economic Impact of Mandated Family Leave on Small Businesses and Their Employees*. Washington, DC: NFIB Education Foundation.

Beach, W.W. 1996. The Case for Repealing the Estate Tax. In A.M. Antonelli and C.L. Shortridge (eds.), *Why America Needs a Tax Cut*. Washington, DC: Heritage Foundation.

Belman, D. and Goshen, E.L. 1998. Is Small Business Beautiful for Workers? *Small Consolation: The Dubious Benefits of Small Business for Job Growth*. Washington, DC: Economic Policy Institute.

Berney, R.E. 1981. *Small Business Policy: Subsidation, Neutrality, or Discrimination*. Working Paper No. 1180-1, Economics Department. Pullman, WA: Washington State University.

Birch, D.L. 1979. *The Job Generation Process*. Cambridge: MIT Program on Neighborhood and Regional Change.

Birnbaum, J. 1997. Washington's Power 25. *Fortune*, December 8, pp. 144–52.

Brewer, E. and Genay, H. 1995. Small Business Investment Companies: Financial Characteristics and Investments. *Journal of Small Business Management* 33(3): 38–56.

Brockhaus, R.H. 1987. Entrepreneurial Research: Are We Playing the Correct Game? *American Journal of Small Business* 11(3): 43–50.

Brown, C., Hamilton, J. and Medoff, J. 1990. *Employers Large and Small*, Cambridge: Harvard University Press.

Butler, S.A. 1981. *Enterprise Zones: Greenlining the Inner City*. New York: Universe Books.

Cadwell, C. 1997. *State Export Promotion and Small Business*, Office of Advocacy, Small Business Administration, Contract No. SBA-5659-ADV-90, August.

Cantor, J.C., Long, S.H. and Marquis. M.S. 1995. Private Employment-based Health Insurance in Ten States. *Health Affairs* 14(2): 199–206.

Chrisman, J.J. and McMullen, W.E. 1996. Static Economic Theory, Empirical Evidence, and the Evaluation of Small Business Assistance Programs: A Reply to Wood. *Journal of Small Business Management* 34(2): 56–66.

Cole, R.J., and Tegeler, P.D. 1980. *Government Requirements of Small Business*. Lexington, MA: Lexington Books.

CONSAD Research Corporation. 1994. *Employment and Related Economic Effects of Health Care Reform*. Prepared for the National Federation of Independent Business, Washington, DC, April.

CONSAD Research Corporation. 1995. *The Impact of Health Care Reform on Business Closures, and Associated Job Losses*. Prepared for the National Federation of Independent Business, Washington, DC, January.

CONSAD Research Corporation. 1998. *The Projected Impacts of the Expanded Portability and Health Insurance Coverage Act on Health Insurance Coverage*. Prepared for the National Federation of Independent Business, Washington, DC, June.

Davis, S.J., Haltiwanger, J. and Schuh, S. 1993. *Small Business and Job Creation: Dissecting the Myth and Reassessing the Facts*. National Bureau of Economic Research, Working Paper No. 4492, Cambridge, MA, October.

Dennis, W.J., Jr. 1996. *Small Business Problems and Priorities*. Washington, DC: NFIB Education Foundation.

Dennis, W.J., Jr. 1997. *Wells Fargo/NFIB Series on Business Starts and Stops*. Washington, DC: NFIB Education Foundation.

Dennis, W.J., Jr. 1998. Small Business Policy in the United States. In A. Lundström, H. Boter, A. Kjellberg and C. Öhman (eds.), *Svensk småföretagspolitik: Struktur, resultat och internationella jämförelser (Small Business Policies in Sweden: Structure, Results and International Comparisons)*. Örebro, Sweden: Swedish Foundation for Small Business Research.

Edwards, J.N., Blendon, R.J., Leitman, R., Morrison, E., Morrison, I. and Taylor, H. 1992. Small Business and the National Health Care Reform Debate. *Health Affairs* 11(1) 164–73.

Employee Benefit Research Institute. 1998. *1998 Retirement Confidence Survey*. Washington, DC: Employee Benefit Research Institute.

Faucett, J. and Associates. 1984. *Economies of Scale in Regulatory Compliance: Evidence of the Differential Impacts of Regulation by Firm Size*. Office of Advocacy, Small Business Administration, Contract No. SBA-7188-OA-83, December.

Gaston, R.J. and Carroll, S.L. (1984). *State and Local Regulatory Restrictions as Fixed Cost Barriers to Small Business Enterprise*. Office of Advocacy, Small Business Administration, Contract No. SBA-7167-AER-83, April.

General Accounting Office (GAO). 1995. *Small Business Administration: Case Studies Illustrate 8(a) Program and Contractor Abuse*, December 13, T-OSI-96-1.

General Accounting Office (GAO). 1996. *Tax Administration: Employment Taxes and Small Business*, November 8, T-GGD-97-21.

General Accounting Office (GAO). 1997. *Small Business Administration: Credit Subsidy Estimates for Sections 7(a) and 504 Business Loan Programs*, July 16, T-RCED-97-197.

Hashimoto, M. 1982. Minimum Wage Effects on Training on the Job. *American Economic Review* 72(5): 1070–84.

Helms, W.D., Gauthier, A.K. and Campion, D.M. 1992. Mending the Flaws in the Small-group Market. *Health Affairs* 11(2): 7–27.

Holtz-Eakin, D. 1995. Should Small Businesses Be Tax-favored? *National Tax Journal* 11(2): 387–95.

Hopkins, T.D. 1995. *A Survey of Regulatory Burdens*. Office of Advocacy, US Small Business Administration, Contract No. 8029-OA-93.

Hoy, F. 1997. Relevance in Entrepreneurship Research. In. D.L. Sexton and R.W. Smilor (eds.), *Entrepreneurship 2000*. Chicago: Upstart, pp. 361–75.

Institute for Justice (1996 and 1997), Washington, D.C., seven monograph series. Berliner, Dana, *How Detroit Drives Out Motor City Entrepreneurs*; ———, *Running Boston's Bureaucratic Marathon*; Bolick, Clint, *Brightening the Beacon: Removing Barriers to Entrepreneurship in San Diego*; ———, *Entrepreneurship in Charlotte: Strong Spirit, Serious Barriers*; Bullock, Scott G., *Baltimore: No Harbor for Entrepreneurs*; Mathias, Donna G., *Entrepreneurship in San Antonio: Much to Celebrate, Much to Fight For*; and, Mellor, William H., *Is New York City Killing Entrepreneurship?*

Johnson, N. 1998. Letter to April 23rd House of Representatives Ways and Means Committee hearing witnesses, regarding follow-up questions on health insurance data, May 1.

Kronick, R. 1991. Health Insurance 1979–1989: The Frayed Connection between Employment and Insurance. *Inquiry* 28(4): 318–32.

Long, S.H. and Marquis, S.M. 1996. Some Pitfalls in Making Cost Estimates of State Health Insurance Coverage Expansions. *Inquiry* 33(1): 85–91.

Lerner, J. 1996. *The Government as Venture Capitalist: The Long-Run Impact of SBIR*. NBER Working Paper No. 5753, Cambridge, MA: National Bureau of Economic Research, September.

Masten, J.G., Hartmann, B. and Safari, A. 1995. Small Business Strategic Planning and Technology Transfer: The Use of Publicly Supported Technology Transfer Agencies. *Journal of Small Business Management* 33(3): 26–37.

McLaughlin, C.G. and Zellers, W.K. 1992. The Shortcomings of Voluntarism in the Small-group Insurance Market. *Health Affairs* 11(2): 28–40.

Moini, A.H. 1998. Small Firms Exporting: How Effective are Government Export Assistance Programs? *Journal of Small Business Management* 36(1): 1–15.

National Institute of Disability Rehabilitation Research. 1998. *Federal Register.* Washington, DC: Government Printing Office, April 14, pp. 18300–6.

Neumark, D. and Wascher, W. 1997 *Do Minimum Wages Fight Poverty?* Cambridge, MA: National Bureau of Economic Research, Working Paper No. 6127.

Organization for Economic Cooperation and Development. 1997. *OECD Economic Surveys: United States, 1996-1997.* Paris: OECD, pp. 151–72.

Phillips, B.D. 1998. Director of the Office of Economic Research, Small Business Administration, conversation with author June 10.

Phillips, B.D. and Dennis, W.J., Jr. 1997. Databases for Small Business Analysis. In D.L. Sexton and R.W. Smilor (eds.), *Entrepreneurship 2000.* Chicago: Upstart, pp. 341–60.

Pierce, R.J., Jr. 1998. Small Is Not Beautiful: The Case Against Special Regulatory Treatment of Small Firms. *Adminstrative Law Review* 50(3): 537–78.

Schiller, B.R. 1981. *Human Capital Transfers From Small to Large Businesses.* Office of Advocacy, US Small Business Administration, Contract No. SB-1A-00067–1.

State of Small Business: A Report of the President (annual). Washington, DC: Office of Advocacy, US Small Business Administration.

United States Code Annotated. 1998. St. Paul, MN: West Publishing.

Wagner, R.F. 1993. *Federal Transfer Taxation: A Study in Social Cost.* Costa Mesa, CA: Center for the Study of Taxation.

Welch, F., Murphy, K. and Deere, D. 1995. Employment and the 1990-91 Minimum Wage Hike. *American Economic Review* 85(2): 232–43.

Wood, W.C. 1994. Primary Benefits, Secondary Benefits and the Evaluation of Small Business Assistance Programs. *Journal of Small Business Management* 32(3): 65–75.

Zellers, W.K., McLaughlin, C.G. and Frick, K.D. 1992. Small-Business Health Insurance: Only the Healthy Need Apply. *Health Affairs* 11(1): 174–80.

Part II

GOVERNMENT IMPACTS ON ENTREPRENEURSHIP

In almost every discussion about entrepreneurial growth, the concept of a level playing field is discussed. At the national level, government policies attempt to provide a level playing field by establishing competitive or economic policies that apply to all businesses. With globalization, differences in national policy may tend to make the playing field uneven as countries take different approaches to public policies. Further, in the European Union, member states made the change to a market economy from different economic conditions and perspectives.

This part provides an overview of the government impacts on entrepreneurship through a review by De of "SME Policy in Europe" in chapter 5; a discussion of "Entrepreneurship in Germany" by Audretsch in chapter 6; an examination of the "Regulatory Policies and Their Impact on SMEs in Europe" by van der Horst, Nijsen, and Gulhan in chapter 7; an analysis of "The Climate for Entrepreneurship in European

Countries in Transition" by Mugler in chapter 8; and a proposed approach to "Evaluating the Impact of Public Policies to Support Small Business in Developed Economies" by Storey in chapter 9.

When the public policies in Europe are compared with public policy in the United States, one can almost reach the conclusion that the only thing growing faster than fast-growth firms is the number and impact of the regulations and administrative burdens of public policy.

The general theme that appears to be consistent across the chapters in this section is that policies in Europe are developed and implemented at two different levels, the member states and the European Union. As a result of the different starting points among the member states in economic development, an uneven playing field exists. Further, there is a feeling that the policymakers have failed to consider the administrative burdens associated with regulations and reporting requirements, that the SME sector is an important, if not the most important, factor in economic development, and that regulations, once developed, do not seem to have a period for review and/or elimination.

De in the opening chapter of this section makes the following observations:

- Policies across the member states in the European Union are considerably different because of size, economic structure and approach to economic policy.
- Policies are driven by the larger European Union members as they attempt to solve various policies simultaneously.
- SME policy has evolved from regional/structural policy, competition policy and labor policy.
- The recession in the late 1980s and the early 1990s underlined the need to stimulate the creation of new businesses.
- The overall objectives of SME policy are to create employment, to improve competitiveness and to enhance regional/structural development.

Audretsch suggests that the economic problems that have arisen since the reunification of Germany have resulted in an increased awareness of the importance of the SME sector. He notes that:

- The "economic miracle" of the 1950s has been associated with remarkable prosperity and stability providing both high employment and wage rates.
- In the late 1980s, the unification opened the door to a global economy. To compete in the arena, large firms downsized and transferred production to countries with lower labor costs.
- The economic crises in the 1990s resulted in the highest unemployment rate since the 1930s.
- Empirical evidence suggests that Germany has not generated a vibrant sector of growing new firms and new industries.

Van der Horst, Nijsen and Gulhan provide insights into the cost and burdens imposed by regulatory policies on the operation of SMEs. Through an examination of the administrative burdens imposed by regulatory policies, they suggest that:

- The ambitious economic and social policies were legitimized by the belief that governments can control the economy while ensuring social justice and equality in the distribution of wealth.

- Regulation of business is a major objective and feature for policy makers.
- Both the number and complexity of policies designed to regulate the market have increased dramatically.
- The European Union and the member states are now reviewing and reformulating policies to create an environment in which SMEs can realize their full potential.

Mugler in an examination of the economic climate for entrepreneurship in the European countries in transition notes that:

- The main task of the European countries in transition is to overcome their centrally planned system and to adopt the market economy.
- Each country had a different starting point, and each has undergone its own individual transition process.
- The transformation can be analyzed by examining the progress related to political, economic and social factors.
- Measuring the economic transition is difficult since aggregated economic data does not yet follow market principles and Eurostat standards.
- Overcoming the decades of communist domination is a very lengthy process.

Storey provides an outline of a methodology for evaluating the impact of public policies to assist the small business sector. He contends that the absence of specified objectives for the policy make it is impossible to conduct an evaluation of the impact, either positively or negatively on small businesses.

In this regard he notes the following shortcomings of the policy evaluation process, if one exists:

- A characteristic of governments in all developed countries seems to be, at best, opaque about the objectives of small business policy.
- Not only is there a conspicuous absence of clear objectives, but implied objectives can often be conflicting.
- In many countries, there is an overtly political element to small business policies. A failure by analysts to consider this element results in an underestimate of the role it plays in politicians' calculations.
- Governments should be required to specify their objectives of SME policy and provide measurable targets with a timetable for their attainment.

Politicians tend to establish policy without concern for their impact on small businesses. As the changes to a free market economy in Europe have been made, it almost seems that regulations are growing more rapidly than new businesses. Earlier Dennis noted that entrepreneurship researchers should be more proactive by conducting research on the expected impact on SMEs before the proposed policy or regulation has been implemented rather than after the fact. Storey's recommendations support the concept.

5

SME Policy in Europe

DENNIS DE

EVOLUTION OF SME POLICY
THE CONCEPT OF SME POLICY IN EUROPE
OBJECTIVES AND SME POLICY FIELDS
OUTLOOK

Small and medium-sized enterprise (SME) policy has gained considerable recognition throughout Europe. This is not only reflected in numerous communications, white papers and programs released by the European Commission[1] but also in day-to-day politics within the member states of the European Union. However, these member states display considerable differences in size, economic structure and their approach toward economic policy that is reflected by the policies applied.

On the other hand, SME policy is a fairly young discipline of research, and it is still unclear what SME policy actually is. According to the general understanding, any policy directed toward SMEs is considered to be a SME policy. Unfortunately, this apparently clear distinction is not as clear as it may seem. Many policies and regulations applied within the context of regional, structural or even environmental policy in some countries could also include competition, minorities or sectorial policy, leaving it open for more policies targeted toward SMEs. Alas, the motivations and overall objectives of respective activities most commonly differ from each other.

This chapter focuses on what SME policy is about, how it is pursued in Europe and the differences between the European countries.

EVOLUTION OF SME POLICY

Looking at Europe as a whole, the shift toward SME policy was mainly driven by the larger EU member states, like Germany or France, attempting to solve various economic problems simultaneously. This was in the middle to late 1970s (De 1994). About a decade later, the European Commission began to direct more attention toward SMEs, eventually setting up DG XXIII,[2] the youngest directorate and in charge of SME-dominated sectors. Together with other DGs, DG XXIII – although not in charge for national measures – has nonetheless been influential for the further development of SME policy in a number of European countries, such as Ireland, Portugal and Luxembourg.

However, SME policy initially evolved from three different policy areas on national levels: regional/structural policy, competition policy and labor policy, all of which, though for different reasons, identify SMEs[3] as a target group.

Regional/structural policy

Regional policy and, often linked to it, structural policy[4] has been and still is an important part of the general economic policy pursued by both member states and the European Commission.[5] Originally focused on large corporations, regional policymakers recognized that they were soon competing with each other for affiliates and production sites of large enterprises (LEs) and multinationals by offering them high subsidies. On the other hand, structural policymakers had to acknowledge that substituting one sector (and thus a given economic structure) with another sector by stimulating the latter's development, does not necessarily change the vulnerability of the respective region to changes in the business cycle.

Given this background, attracting SMEs and stimulating start-ups as well as providing other necessary infrastructures has proven to be a more beneficial strategy (as in France, Ireland, Spain or Germany). It provides for new business and at least partly reduces the ups and downs of the business cycle with the heterogeneous sectorial division of SMEs.

Thus, regional and structural policymakers throughout Europe are paying much more attention to SMEs as a fast track to regional and structural change. SME-oriented programs originating from the EC Structural Funds prove that this view is also shared at the supranational level.

Competition policy

The competition policies pursued by European countries differ. However, they all are market economies that to different extents favor competition as a precondition for growth. The number of competing enterprises in total and in the various sectors is a common measure for the degree of competition. Thus, mergers and acquisitions, often a result of internationalization and globalization aspirations, tend to affect the degree of competition negatively.

Given this background, policymakers throughout Europe have acknowledged the need to guarantee a sufficient number of enterprises in order to safeguard competition. The recession of the late 1980s and early 1990s and the corresponding increase in bankruptcies during that period underlined the need to stimulate the creation of new business throughout Europe. As a consequence, national governments and later the EC began to focus far more attention on the competitive environment of SMEs in general[6] and start-ups in particular.

In this context, the EC adopted a new set of competition rules,[7] which in part reflect the role given to SMEs for safeguarding competition. Under rather broadly defined conditions, the general ban of cartels is exempted for SMEs.[8] This especially holds for the retail trade that is experiencing increasing degrees of concentration throughout Europe. Allowing for SME cartels will help them fight their battle more successfully by guaranteeing a higher degree of competition and variety.

(Un)employment

Creating employment is one of the most prominent, if not major, aims of most European governments. In this context, the focus on LEs as employers of scale has shifted toward SMEs as employers of scope. Economic development and the changed perception of SMEs are mainly responsible for this shift. Today, SMEs are seen to offer more heterogeneous, relatively more stable and relatively more new jobs than large enterprises.[9] This perception was underlined by the inability of LEs to avoid large redundancies during the recession.[10] However, in relative terms LEs account for far more employment than the bulk of SMEs. In absolute terms though, SMEs provide roughly 66 percent of total employment (ENSR 1997) in the private sector in Europe.

The tendency of LEs to export employment outside Europe is a further reason for European governments to address the more "loyal" SMEs in their search for potential – preferably more – employment. In recent years, this has resulted in numerous new employment-oriented programs geared toward SMEs throughout Europe. Indeed, in many European countries including the EC SME policy is close to being a synonym for job creation.

THE CONCEPT OF SME POLICY IN EUROPE

The question whether SME policy is conceptually comparable to other lines of economic policy (e.g., monetary policy) that usually includes more or less clear-cut aims and an institutional setup such as a central bank, is disputable. At least for Europe, comparisons along clear and measurable lines are not possible. The origins and aims of SME policy are too heterogeneous to present a precise picture of SME policy in Europe, that itself is made up of many countries, different in size and economic structure.

However, dominant aims, the political structure and budgetary responsibilities most commonly determine the concept (though this may mean having none at all) and institutional setup of SME policy within the European countries. Despite these differences, SME policy in Europe is nonetheless geared toward overall objectives.

Overall objectives of SME policy

Although meaningful differences between the European countries exist, the overall objectives pursued by means of SME policy most commonly fall together with those pursued in the context of the general economic policy:

- ◆ create employment
- ◆ foster economic growth

- improve competitiveness
- regional/structural development.

This reveals that SME policy is in fact part of a government's general economic policy. However, the major difference between the various European countries is whether SME policy is embedded in a conceptual framework or not. In countries where this is not the case, SME policy, or whatever is labeled as such, tends to be little more than a collection of programs introduced on a piecemeal basis at different times and for different purposes. In contrast, in countries that have conceptually incorporated SME policy into the framework of general economic policy, it can be identified as a policy line of its own, with a concept and defined fields of activity. It then serves the same overall objectives as other lines of economic policy, in a manner comparable to a violinist in an orchestra.

Thus the first line of differentiation is to ask two questions: Has a concept for SME policy been formulated, and if so, has it been incorporated into the framework of general economic policy?

Conceptual framework: or lack thereof

The question whether or not a concept for SME policy has been formulated separates European countries. Although they all entertain programs favoring SMEs to different extents, only a few of them do so on the basis of a concept. Of these, Germany, the Netherlands, Portugal, Belgium, Ireland and France have conceptually incorporated SME policy into their general framework of economic policy. Other countries have refrained from both (Greece, Italy, Spain, Austria, United Kingdom, Switzerland and Denmark) or have at least formulated goals[11] (Sweden, Finland, Norway and Luxembourg) without conceptually incorporating them into the framework of economic policy.

These differences are mainly due to the size class and sectorial structure of the economies and/or the general approach to economic policy. In predominantly SME-structured countries (i.e., where the employment share of LEs is under average), governments tend to see no case in a conceptual differentiation between SMEs and LEs (as in Greece or Iceland). But in other countries (e.g., Finland, Luxembourg, Ireland and Portugal), this structure is said to be one of the reasons for formulating SME-specific goals. A further explanation may be found in the approach to economic policy. Governments following a more neoliberal approach often judge enterprise discrimination (by size or sector) negatively and thus rather avoid developing a conceptual framework for SME policy (e.g., the United Kingdom and Liechtenstein). Apart form these differences, states in federal countries (Germany, Spain, Switzerland or Belgium) enjoy freedoms that enable them to formulate and pursue their own SME policies (to different extents) while at the same time restricting federal action and the scope of an eventual overall concept for SME policy.

The approach to SME policy in selected European countries

The approach of European countries to SME policy is not only influenced by the existence or lack of concept. The enterprise size distribution by sector, the various sector's contribution to GDP, political preferences and the political structure further influence a country's approach to SME policy. The latter has a far stronger influence than might be expected at first sight. The degree of autonomy regions enjoy varies between the countries. This autonomy in some cases like Spain considerably restricts the SME-related room for maneuvering of central governments, but in other countries like Germany, the states (*Länder*) rely much more on federal funding and hence are more vulnerable to federal directives.

Some examples for the various approaches to SME policy are presented below; in all of these countries SMEs account for more than 99 percent of all enterprises.

Germany

In western Germany SMEs account for an employment share of 64 percent. In contrast, the employment share in the *Neue Bundesländer* is estimated at roughly 52 percent. Apart from the *Neue Bundesländer*, federal SME policy has no specific sectorial or regional approach. Only since unification are SME policy instruments being applied in the *Neue Bundesländer*, giving this policy a regional approach in this specific case. SME policy in general aims at supporting SMEs in fields that have a size-induced competitive disadvantage. On the federal level the major responsibility lies with the Ministry for Economic Affairs, although other ministries such as the Chancellor of the Exchequer or the Ministry for Research and Technology and Ministry for Labor also run programs aimed at SMEs. Such measures generally are not carried out by the ministries themselves but by agents, the most prominent of which are the Kreditanstalt für Wiederaufbau (KfW) and the Deutsche Ausgleichsbank (DtA). Both banks can be approached either directly or through commercial banks. The institutional framework of SME policy in Germany combines federal institutions with those of the sixteen states in a complementary manner, leaving the states responsible for the regional impact of a number of programs. Apart from the self-financed programs, that often display a sectorial or regional focus, the states can also influence programs cofunded by the federal government. Responsibility on the state level commonly lies with the Ministries for Economic Affairs, most of which use agents for venture capital, loan guarantee and partnership programs.

Spain

Spanish SMEs account for 83 percent of total employment. The seventeen regions of Spain are autonomous and hence carry out their own policy for SMEs. The policy of each region is characterized by a strong regional approach, commonly focusing on sectorial matters in the region. The framework the regions operate within is similar in the sense that twelve of the seventeen regions founded institutes in charge of carrying out a variety of programs. Because of the regional impact, the measures do differ by sector and/or criteria they are based on. Next to support offered by the regions, additional assistance is also available from the federal government. The central agent for national programs is the Institute for Small and Medium-sized Enterprises (Instituto de la mediana y pequeña empresa industrial, or IMPI), an institution founded and funded by the ministry for industrial affairs. IMPI, mainly provides transfers in kind (services) and is involved in improving horizontal (between the regions) and vertical (regional and federal governments and EC) transparency.

Portugal

SMEs employ 80 percent of Portugal's total employment. Although a number of programs do include favorable conditions for certain sectors or regions, a general sectorial or regional approach is not pursued. The basic objective of SME policy in Portugal is the compensation of size-induced disadvantages. This policy mainly focuses on fields such as information, education, cooperation, technology and innovative start-ups. The main responsibility for this is with the ministry for industrial affairs. Institute for Small and Medium-sized Enterprises and Societies (Instituti des Apoyo às Pequenenas e Médias Empresas e ao Investimento, or IAPMEI), an institute founded by this ministry in 1974, acts as central agent. It generally is in charge of executing national support measures. Next to this, IAPMEI runs its own programs that also favor SMEs.

Italy

Italian SMEs account for 81 percent of total employment. Similar to other European countries, SME policy is carried out from two levels. Twenty areas execute regional programs often tailored to the needs of small and medium-sized enterprises. Depending upon the location, institutes or regional authorities are in charge of these measures. On the national level SME policy has long been a part of the government's regional policy. The shift toward a policy based on size classes is rather new and was "institutionalized" by Act L317/1991 in 1991. This Act actually is the basis of the national policy for SMEs. The institutional framework (i.e., loan guarantee programs are still being handled by the Chancellor of the Exchequer) has not been completed yet. Many programs are thus run directly by various ministries.

The Netherlands

In the Netherlands SME policy is part of the general economic policy. Programs commonly are defined by size class: enterprises with fewer than 100 employees are considered SMEs. As in most countries, the three most prominent ministries in charge are the Ministry for Economic Affairs, the Chancellor of the Exchequer and the Ministry for Labor and Social Affairs. Although in general these ministries can be approached directly by SMEs (commonly for information purposes), the SME policy is carried out by agents such as banks and organizations (commonly public bodies) present in all eleven provinces. The provinces run additional measures that are of relevance to SMEs; their implementation, though, requires the approval by the national ministries.

United Kingdom

The employment share of SMEs in the United Kingdom amounts to 65 percent of total employment. The driving force behind SME policy partly can be seen in the government's attempts to respond to changes in the macroeconomy (Storey 1997) by creating an enterprise culture characterized by dynamic firms. The approach, hence, has a structural bias, aiming at a shift from large "inefficient" enterprises to small dynamic firms. This process has been going on for years. In fact, it has a sectorial dimension in the sense of a resulting shift from the manufacturing to the service an other sectors. On the national level the Secretary of State for Employment originally in charge of this policy has passed this responsibility on to the Department for Trade and Industry (DTI), which is now primarily in charge of SME policy. The Chancellor of the Exchequer is involved to the extent that some of the financial support originates from here. Programs are carried out by ministries on the national level and on the regional level by a network of agents (Training and Enterprise Councils, or TECs) headed by DTI. A network of twenty banks is in charge of loan guarantee programs throughout the United Kingdom.

Denmark

In Denmark, SME policy is closely linked to industrial policy and in fact can be considered as part of it. This is not surprising as 90 percent of all enterprises in the industrial sector can be considered SMEs. The Ministry for Industry, generally responsible for industrial policy, is also in charge of SME policy. The central agents are the Danish Agency for Development Industry and Trade and the Industry and Trade Development Council. They actually execute industrial and SME policy. Headed by the Industry and Trade Development Council, a network of fifteen Technology Information Centres (TICs) offer services to enterprises (free of charge to SMEs). Further, the Danish Technical Institute (DTI), a nonprofit foundation and the largest of its kind, is active in a variety of SME-specific fields. DTI offers consultancy, general services and a technology-oriented hotline for SMEs; recently an Internet network for SME-dominated sectors has been added.

France

Despite working definitions, France actually has no legal definition of SMEs (this also holds true for Germany). The origins of SME policy are to be found in the sectorial approach of France's traditional industrial policy (De 1994). Following this line, responsibility for SME-related programs is spread over several ministries: Agriculture, Employment, Fiscal Affairs and Industry (where the major responsibility lies). For a short period this also included a Ministry for SMEs, which has been abolished for political reasons. The Ministry for Industry entertains a network of affiliates (*directions régionales*) in all of the twenty-two regions. These delegations are in charge of executing the ministry's policy, that basically consists of programs. However, France being a rather large country, the *directions régionales* delegated most of their upfront work to *subdivisions*, present in all of the ninety-five departments. They nonetheless are approachable for entrepreneurs. The regions, although to a far lesser degree, offer SMEs additional assistance. Regional programs are mainly executed by agents that are organizations specially founded for this purpose.

Belgium

Belgium accounts for at least two working definitions for SMEs. The most common feature, however, is that enterprises with less than fifty employees are said to be SMEs.[12] This was also stated in the national economic plan that was introduced in 1992. The policy for SMEs has its origins in the central policy that is dominated by neither a regional nor a sectorial approach but can include both. The major responsibility for central SME policy lies with the administration for SMEs within the Ministry for SMEs and Agriculture. Actions are restricted to the fields of employment, social security, regulation of the professions and fiscal matters. This rather general, more framework-oriented approach of central policy results from a shift of responsibility from the central government to the regions[13] Flanders, Brussels and Walloon in 1988. Since then, the regions are far more in charge of and actually deal with economic matters within their respective boundaries. They are free to formulate and fund their own SME policy (with funds being the bottleneck and backdoor for the central government). For this, responsibility within the regions commonly lies with the ministries for economic affairs. As on the national level, regional ministries also execute their programs directly via their own departments rather than external agents. Departments are the Service for SMEs and the Self-employed in Flanders, Secretary for Economics and Employment (Direction générale de l'Economie et de l'Emploi) in Walloon and Economic Services in Brussels.

OBJECTIVES AND SME POLICY FIELDS

Existing structural differences and the different approaches to SME policy in the European countries discussed only allow for a very general distinction of SME policy fields. In addition, the various activities pursued (programs that often reflect national particularities) by European governments cover a wide range of policy fields.

In this context, relating even general SME policy fields to overall objectives is a useful method to obtain a structured picture of what is done for what. Unfortunately, existing differences and the common lack of concepts render this approach difficult. A common practice to overcome this problem is the target-oriented analysis of existing programs favoring SMEs. This approach reveals that the various programs, most of which can be attributed to policy fields, commonly serve multiple objectives.

Table 5.1 shows that most of the policy fields (where programs belong) are geared toward more than one objective. This explains why instead of only one, several ministries tend to be in charge or at least deal with SME-related policies. These commonly are the ministries for Economic Affairs and/or Industry that tend to be primarily responsible and the ministries of Labour/Employment, R&D, Agriculture and Fiscal Affairs. Shared responsibilities (due to multiple objectives) obviously require a structured institutional setup, in order to be transparent for civil servants and more important still, entrepreneurs and SMEs, the actual target group of this policy.

Institutional setup maze

Conceptual frameworks once formulated and implemented by and large tend to survive changes in governments. This also holds for the institutional setup such frameworks commonly entail.[14] On the other hand, the lack of a conceptual framework especially for SME policy often goes along with ad hoc task forces for SME-related matters and/or an unstructured institutional setup that lacks a ministry heading and/or coordinating the various SME-specific actions. This regularly results in an institutional maze made up of various SME-related authorities on different policy levels that formulate and pursue their own policies. Overlaps of SME-related programs that are hard to avoid anyway in the context of multiple objectives, then, tend to occur rather frequently. This is especially true when relevant authorities act in an uncoordinated manner and/or are not aware of other authorities' activities.

Since only a few European countries have developed a conceptual framework for

TABLE 5.1 Objectives and policy fields

Improve competitiveness	Foster economic growth	Create employment	Regional/structural development
R&D	R&D	Job creation	Job creation
General investments	General investments	Education	General investments
Finance and capital	Finance and capital		Finance and capital
	Start-ups	Start-ups	Start-ups
Internationalization/ exports	Internationalization/ exports		
	Subcontracting	Subcontracting	Subcontracting
Training		Training	
Infrastructure			Infrastructure
New technologies			
Information	Information		Information
Red tape	Red tape	Red tape	

SME policy, SMEs or individual entrepreneurs wanting to apply for support often are confronted with an nontransparent setup to begin with. In fact, SMEs and entrepreneurs often state that even after finding their path through this institutional maze they would not know whether they actually missed a more beneficial program. This lack of awareness and knowledge of existing programs is criticized regularly. However, in most European countries new informational measures are aimed at alleviating this problem.

The institutional structure in table 5.2 is strongly generalized and does not distinguish between structured and unstructured setups. It does however show common features. One of the not so apparent similarities is that the budgets at the various national policy levels for SME-related measures tend to decrease from top to bottom. At the supranational level, where budgets are allotted according to tasks (DGs are then in charge of), these tasks and policy issues commonly materialize in programs of limited duration (and varying relevance for SMEs).

Although descending degrees of budgetary independence are most common for European countries,[15] this cannot be transferred to the *contents* of programs offered at the various policy levels.[16] This especially holds true for federal countries (Germany, Spain, Switzerland Belgium), but it can also be observed to a lesser extent in countries with no conceptual framework for SME policy. Thus, it is very likely that an up-and-coming entrepreneur will be able to choose from several start-up programs offered by the EC, central, regional and/or local authorities.[17] This holds true for most of the fields of SME policy in Europe.

TABLE 5.2 Institutional setup of SME policy in Europe: a simplified presentation

Policy levels	Public	"Semi" public/private
Supranational	EC 23 Directorate Generals + structural funds (various SME related or relevant programs)	
National	National/central government X ministries (joint and separate programs often designed for specific SMEs, i.e., according to region sector, age or size)	Chambers of commerce Public business associations Private business associations
Regional	X Government agencies/institutions (i.e., export bureaus, loan guarantee banks, public–private partnerships etc.) Regional/state authorities	Mutual loan guarantee funds
Local	X departments + public–private partnerships, start-up centers etc. (programs designed for the region/state commonly differentiated by sector and size Local development agencies	Public–private partnerships (all of which commonly offer own programs funded by membership fees or co-funded by public authorities)

Working the fields of SME policy in Europe

The fields of SME policy were at first closely linked to its origins (e.g., start-ups in economically deprived regions or in new sectors like exports or finance) but now address a wide range of topics and areas at which SMEs are assumed to be disadvantaged.[18] This includes the recruitment of qualified staff, R&D, collecting information on foreign markets, punctual payment and women-run businesses and start-ups.

Neglecting overlaps and duplications, the larger European countries like Germany or France account for more than 600 different SME-specific programs, most of which include financial assistance of one kind or the other.

Theoretically, antidiscrimination programs are the example par excellence of an interventionist policy. In this context, using the number of programs as a measure might leave us with Liechtenstein[19] as a paramount of neoliberal economic policy followed by Switzerland and, at some distance, the United Kingdom. However, the number of programs reveals intention but not always action. Many programs are furnished with budgets too small to grant much SMEs support. This especially holds true for local measures, but it is also not uncommon for regional measures in Spain or national programs in Greece. In fact, Italy is known for a fairly large number of programs of which many have not been allotted a budget for years.[20] Institutional structures that make it difficult or at least time-consuming to identify available programs further reduce the number of actual applications.[21]

Fields and instruments

The variation of instruments used in the fields of SME policy is less extensive. Options basically are transfers in cash or transfers in kind or a combination of both. Viewed by fields, a clear distinction of instruments might only be possible for late payment and red tape. In both cases, programs or measures usually are based on regulation rather than transfers in cash or kind. Red tape is tackled by reducing SME burdensome regulations whereas the problem of late payment, if approached at all, is commonly met by fast-track courts or prompt payment rules for public bodies that purchase services or goods from SMEs. The following overview is restricted to fields of SME policy in most European countries

Start-ups

Hardly a field accounts for as many different programs including all kinds of transfers as that of start-ups. Start-ups are supported in all European countries. In most of them (Austria, Belgium, Denmark, France, Germany, Ireland, Italy, Portugal, Spain and the Netherlands), this field has in fact been subdivided, such as start-ups by women, the young, those in economically deprived regions, those in new sectors or the service sector, just to name few. Most countries (especially Austria, Belgium, Germany, Spain, Sweden and Switzerland) offer the relevant programs at all levels of policy. Entrepreneurship courses and training are offered additionally by business associations, chambers of commerce and banks. Sweden provides a telephone hotline for potential start-ups.

The variety of programs and instrumental combinations (i.e., feasibility study plus subsidized loans) only permit a rather general overview of major programs for start-ups (table 5.3). Being one of the first fields that SME policy focused on may explain the variety of existing start-up programs in Europe. In many countries new measures were simply added to existing ones. As a result in most countries the extent and scope of start-up support has increased considerably since the late 1980s. However, new programs most commonly combine transfers in kind (i.e., feasibility studies and courses) with transfers in cash (e.g., subsidized loans).

Finance

Originally, this field was closely linked to start-ups and exports but has since included measures for SMEs in all sectors. The key to financial support of SMEs is government intentions (e.g., to increase exports). Financial support rarely is granted to SMEs just for the sake of them being either small or medium sized. Although the program targets are commonly said to be linked to improving SMEs' financial environment, most programs reveal other intentions with closer inspection. SMEs with financial disadvantages *welcomed* specific business actions aimed to alleviate their problems with financial assistance programs. Such "business actions" or investments might include adjusting the production

TABLE 5.3 Major instruments applied in the field of start-ups

Instrument	Common feature
(Un)returnable grants or subsidies	Linked to specific characteristics of a start-up (i.e., age of the founder(s), sector etc.)
Subsidized loan	Requires founder's equity of min. 15%; linked to start-up capital and equipment
Loan guarantee	Often unsecured, covering up to 80% of the loan sum
Guarantee to providers of venture capital participative loans[a]	Offered to providing agents or individuals
Public venture capital funds	Venture capital for start-ups in new sectors with new technologies
Tax holiday	First 1 to 3 years
Information lines, offices, booklets	Offer general start-up specific information
Feasibility studies	Identify viable projects
Consultancy services	Vouchers or reimbursements on start-up consultancy
Entrepreneurship courses	Business plan, accounting, taxation
Start-up centers or parks	Offer infrastructure (office rooms, joint secretary etc.)

[a] Commonly default guarantees and/or tax exemptions on (venture) capital invested in SMEs. This instrument aims at channeling private capital into SMEs. Effectively introduced, it helps reduce the burden on public budgets.

to environmental standards, expansion (which usually entails more employment), shifting loans from short to long-term (while decreasing financial costs and increasing viability) or investing in new technologies (thus modernizing the standard of the enterprise population). Hence, the actual targets of programs in the field of finance most commonly overlap with targets of measures linked to other fields. In practice, this makes it difficult to identify programs geared toward the field of finance from others that likewise use transfers in cash, but aim at nonfinancial targets (table 5.4).

For obvious reasons, the instruments applied in the field of finance are based on transfers in cash, rather than transfers in kind. However, a fairly new trend in Europe is to move on from improving the financial situation of SMEs that pursue certain aims or plan specific business actions toward improving their financial environment unconditionally. This is the major approach of most programs that include tax redemptions on private venture capital investments[22] and of the so-called secondary markets, which exist in Belgium, France, Germany, Ireland and Italy. These markets are not restricted to specific sectors but are open to all SMEs. The sector or action-specific restriction however, does hold for many public venture capital funds (e.g., in Finland, Germany,

Table 5.4 Major instruments applied in the field of finance

Instrument	Common feature
(Un)returnable grants or subsidies	Linked to specific business issues, i.e., enlargement
Subsidized loan	Linked to specific investments or to start-ups
Loan guarantee	Secure on average some 75% of a loan
Guarantee to providers of venture capital participants loans[a]	Offered to providing agents or individuals
Second markets	Modified publication and/or entry thresholds (low participation rate of SME)

[a] Commonly default guarantees and/or tax exemptions on (venture) capital invested in SMEs. This instrument aims at channeling private capital into SMEs. Effectively introduced, it helps reduce the burden on public budgets.

Ireland and France). They commonly prefer investments in information technology or in innovative (or R&D-active) SMEs, the area for which they were initiated.[23]

Exports and internationalization

Export promotion has a long tradition and is not exclusively linked to SMEs. This is true for most European countries, which nowadays head toward internationalizing their economies. In this context, many of these countries added SME specific provisions (e.g., lower thresholds for export guarantees) to existing export promotion measures. The increasing degree of foreign direct investments (FDI) and cross-border mergers and acquisitions (M&A) of LEs in the context of globalization seemed to widen the gap between SMEs and LEs in

TABLE 5.5 Major instruments applied in the field of export and internationalization

Instrument	Common feature
Information supply	Foreign markets, communion payment modalities, shipment, etc.
Grant	Export projects, feasibility studies, etc.
Wage subsidy	For export-related specialized staff
Training	On export-related issues (duties, technical requirements, forwarding, etc.)
Export guarantee	Issued for the foreign purchaser, commonly covers up to 80%
Subsidized loan	Export channels, related investments (i.e., a branch) abroad

terms of degrees of internationalization. In response to this development, most European governments expanded their portfolio of SME-oriented export promotion measures.[24]

Table 5.5 offers a brief overview of major instruments applied.[25] Export bureaux including affiliates abroad that offer information on foreign markets are a standard in a number of European countries (e.g., Germany, Ireland, France and Italy). Wage subsidies for export-oriented staff – although uncommon – are being favored by a growing number of European countries, including Belgium, Sweden and Finland. Although the Single Market generally facilitates intra-EU trade, European SMEs only account for roughly 40 percent of total exports. This has been identified by the EC, which now stimulates and actively supports cross-border co-optations (for exports, joint R&D, etc.) among SMEs.

Information
Information as a field of SME policy is fairly new in Europe. This originally was linked to exports and some start-ups, but now relates to most areas of the business environment. Within some countries, the approach followed is to offer general information from central sources – commonly local one-stop shops, as in Finland, France and the United Kingdom – that direct customers seeking more specific information to the relevant sources. This approach is also followed by the Euro-Info Centres, EC-coordinated and locally co-funded bureaux set up across Europe (in fact, in every major town) to provide information on EU-related issues and EC-funded programs. Moreover, a number of countries established websites based on the same concept.[26] They tend to be linked with, or actually include, databases on SME-related issues including public support programs. Initiated by the EC, most countries also run sites that provide current information on open tenders and public procurement in general (mostly for the building and construction sector), as shown in table 5.6.

An interesting feature of these sites is that they are case-sensitive, meaning that size or sector-specific information can be obtained at the regional or level. However, despite these attempts to improve the information base of SMEs, the institutional set-up of SME policy still includes numerous hurdles and is commonly perceived to be nontransparent by entrepreneurs.

Research and development
In Europe efforts to foster R&D activities of SMEs has increased considerably. Much of this is due to the pace of new technology development and the corresponding intention

TABLE 5.6 Major instruments applied in the field of information

Instrument	Common feature
Central information sources	Support overviews and booklets, one-stop shops on local level
Fast-track access to information	Website with 'case sensitive' (size, sector, etc.) search engines

TABLE 5.7 Major instruments applied in the field of R&D

Instrument	Common features
Accessible public research and R&D centers	Contracted research at "reduced" fees
Budgets for networking and co-operation	Granted to research centers and universities for building up networks with SME
Wage subsidies	For R&D-related staff
Guarantee[a] to providers of venture capital participative loans	Offered to providing agents or individuals investing in innovative SME and/or start-up
Grants and tax redemption	For costs incurred by innovative projects or the implementation of new technologies

[a] Commonly default guarantees and/or tax exemptions on (venture) capital invested in SMEs. This instrument aims at channeling private capital into SMEs. Effectively introduced, it helps reduce the burden on public budgets.

of governments to have firms at the forefront of these up-and-coming sectors.[27] On the other hand, the speed of the developments in information technologies (IT), and even more influential, their wide dissemination, has increased the degree to which companies rely on such technologies. Thus, next to fostering R&D activities in general, the main target here is to stimulate the usage of new technologies among SMEs (table 5.7).[28]

In this context, the general approach of most instruments is either to reduce the costs incurred by R&D/new technology-related issues or to offer financial assistance. In practice all European countries follow both paths simultaneously. Networks and cooperation with research institutions (e.g., Austria, Denmark, Finland, Germany, Netherlands, Portugal, Sweden and Switzerland) are also meant to reduce the cost of R&D while specialized seed capital and venture capital funds (e.g., in Norway, France, Ireland, Germany and Iceland) should provide the necessary capital for growth.

Labor

Labor is the most prominent area of SME policy and also the most disputed. Does stimulating job creation in SMEs really lower unemployment, or does this prevailing problem of most European countries have other reasons? And if so, why not tackle them first? Do SMEs create more employment, relative to LEs or is it more a problem of SMEs being restricted to national – often rigid – labor markets? The number of new programs implemented in this field during the past five years reveals that most European governments believe the job-creation hypothesis,[29] much to the benefit of SMEs. Measures to stimulate job creation in SMEs are in vogue. They are mainly based on payments in cash rather than in kind and include peculiarities such as a bonus for SMEs with no reduction in employment (e.g., Belgium) or an extra premium for those that actually did hire additional staff (e.g., Belgium and Portugal).

Table 5.8 provides a brief overview of employment-related programs that benefit

TABLE 5.8 Major instruments applied in the field of labor

Instrument	Common feature
Modified labour regulations	Modifications referring to limited contracts, working hours, lower minimum wages for SMEs
Reduced social security contributions	On the employment of disadvantaged, unemployed, the young and/or for small business in general
Wage subsidy	Limited duration, for small business, on hiring the unemployed
Grants and tax redemption	For SMEs employing additional personnel

European SMEs. More structural programs such as the abolishment of minimum wages[30] or freeing the labor market of at least parts of its rigidities,[31] tend to be more difficult and thus, rarely are achieved. This requires that all sides (politicians, the social partners and lobbies) agree, which has happened in only a few countries. Many programs therefore aim at alleviating the difficulties SMEs face when confronted with rigid labor markets and/or high indirect labor costs, rather than at reforming the labor markets as such. Provisions to reduce the social security contributions of employers (as in Belgium France, Germany, Netherlands and Spain) are a common feature of these initiatives, as are grants and tax redemptions on hiring additional staff (as in Belgium, Netherlands, Portugal and Spain).

Red tape

Regulated labor markets, environmental standards, liability legislation, tax statements and other reporting requirements, permits and licensing all form a maze of administrative burdens for SMEs and LEs. In Germany the total cost of red tape was estimated at 10.3 billion euros (about $11.9 billion U.S.) in 1994, with SMEs spending roughly 3 percent and LEs 0.1 percent (Clemens and Kokalj 1996: 62), of turnover. The annual growth rate of the costs of administrative burdens can be estimated at roughly 4 percent. The EC alone produces some six hundred new decrees, recommendations and decisions per year, most of which add to the existing set of rules. With this background, both business associations and scientists (in some cases successfully) have called for reductions in red tape. Most European governments have recognized the problem (and related costs) that red tape presents to SMEs. Some countries (e.g., Greece, Luxembourg, Germany, France, Denmark and Belgium) have started to deal with the problem; others are planning to do so (table 5.9).

Simplifications typically relate to regulations most commonly complained about (e.g., in some regions of the Netherlands, Portugal, Finland and Spain). A more structured approach is only pursued in a few countries, such as the United Kingdom,[32] Austria and Italy, which have, in fact, started to reduce the volume of business-related regulations. Reforming the tax system, in contrast, seems to be far more difficult. Measures in this area therefore commonly focus on simplified tax collection methods (e.g., in Ireland, Luxembourg, Spain, France, Denmark, Sweden or Switzerland) and reduced accounting requirements for SMEs (e.g., in France, Italy, Ireland and the United Kingdom).

TABLE 5.9 Major instruments applied in the field of red tape

Instrument	Common feature
Simply regulatory requirements	Exemptions or "easy tracks" for SMEs (i.e., simplified licensing, permits or reporting requirements)
Reduce regulation	Abolishment of duplications, modification of burdensome requirements
Reform the tax system	Simplified tax collection, statements via e-mail

Best practice and why it can't work

"Mirror, mirror on the wall, which is the fairest program of all?" This quote seems to characterize the most recent approach of the supranational bodies such as the EC or the OECD. The variety of existing programs and measures offered in Europe obviously is rather unstructured and can only be structured in a general manner (i.e., by target or instrument). Supranational bodies wanting to either recommend (OECD) or implement (EC) additional (and hopefully successful) measures therefore seek to identify best practices from the pool of existing initiatives geared toward SMEs.

The difficulties in doing so, however, often become obvious only with hindsight. As is the case with all comparisons, identifying the best from second best requires objective criteria. Against what criteria should success be measured is the first question to answer. Using overall objectives (e.g., the best practice for job creation) is a common approach. The still influential origins of SME policy, however, tend to frustrate this approach altogether. It becomes obvious when looking at a start-up program for young people in an economically deprived region. The likely result of reading the background documentation and questioning policymakers is that the program aims at job creation, increasing the business population, getting young people off the dole and possibly also structural change; thus it is likely to reveal a multitarget design.

Apart from this, having clear and measurable objectives is only the first step to actually comparing measures and eventually identifying best practices. What is needed is a program evaluation that clearly states in what time and at what cost the set goals were achieved. Unfortunately, evaluations that meet this standard hardly exist in Europe. Besides this (and overlapping objectives), national and regional programs often account for country-specific and/or regional circumstances that other countries do not display. Hence, a successful measure in the Mezziogiorno in Italy might not be applicable in the Netherlands and vice versa. These limitations are obvious. However, taking into account the difficulties (if not the impossibility) of identifying best practices, existing evaluations or summaries of best practices, this approach appears to be little more than guesswork.

OUTLOOK

The SME-related policy that most European countries pursue includes a collection of various objectives and fields of economic policy rather than a conceptual framework. Thus an outlook of future SME policy in Europe is not possible without bearing in mind the different general approaches to economic policy and the ups and downs of the business cycle. SME policy is mainly made up of a variety of programs that favor SMEs to different extents and for different reasons. Theoretically, these are interventions that discriminate enterprises according to size, sector or other criteria. Whether this practice is accepted and/or expanded is a matter of a government's general approach to economic policy. With most European governments coming from a Social Democratic tradition, the more interventionist approach seems likely to prevail. However, in many cases this only means continuing what conservative governments started and what the EC basically recommends: increase the degree of competition and stimulate job creation by supporting SMEs and start-ups.[33] With job creation as a campaign winner in most European countries, the job-creation hypothesis is likely to generate further SME-specific programs. Using unemployment rates as an indicator, upturns in the business cycle might have a limiting effect on this development, as do budget constraints that, for example, narrow a government's ability to lower corporate taxation.

The lack of a conceptual framework for SME policy is partly due to its origins. These origins, however, do not belong to history but are acute problems to many European countries. It therefore seems rather likely for European governments to continue their multitarget design of SME-related programs. Hence, sound evaluations – whether these are for best practice summaries or simply to find out if adopted measures are worthwhile to continue – presumably will remain rare exemptions.

As to the programs themselves, recent developments have been influenced by the narrowing financial maneuvering of most European governments. The share of transfers in kind and/or combinations of cash and in kind transfers are thus likely to increase further. This might well entail more benefits than disadvantages for SMEs and start-ups. Their day-to-day life is often characterized by attempts to increase sales, problems accessing timely information and, last but not least, long working hours. Reducing red tape and having better access to information might therefore prove to be a better way to encourage more competitiveness than just adding further transfers in cash to the existing portfolio of financial support.

However, SMEs most likely will continue to benefit from labor-related measures, even though high unemployment rates are not a result of the labor-related measures. In this context it might be far easier to free their job potential with reforms to the labor market than by allowing for further exemptions and deductions applicable to SMEs according to, for example, size, sector, age, ownership or the like.

NOTES

1 See Commission of the European Communities, Recommendation of the Commission, Official Journal of the European Communities, No. L 107/6, 1996

2 DG XXIII is the twenty-third (and youngest) Directorate General of the European Commission. Its premises are in Brussels, as is the case for the other twenty-two DGs.

3 Although the European Commission has meanwhile defined SMEs to be economically independent, enterprises with less than 250 employees and a turnover of less than 40 million euros (see Recommendation of the Commission, *Official Journal of the European Communities*, No. L 107/6, 1996), this definition is a recommendation that only a few member states comply with. National working definitions reach from fifty employees in Ireland to 2,000 in French industrial SMEs.

4 Regional policy is mainly geared toward economically deprived regions, most commonly dominated by single industries like agriculture or rapidly declining industries, such as coal or steel)

5 Numerous programs funded by the Structural Funds and run by the European Commission underline this fact.

6 This includes such areas as finance, exports, R&D, employment, subcontracting and (only recently) problems associated red tape and late payments.

7 They were widely fathered by the German *Gesetz gegen Wettbewerbsbehindernde Maßnahmen* (GWB), which is the equivalent of the UK Fair Trade Act, but GWB is far more extensive and, in fact, identifies a long list of unfair behaviors or practices.

8 The underlying motivation for this basically follows Galbraith's theory of countervailing power, which to many European countries is not new.

9 The job-creation hypothesis, which assumes that SMEs and especially start-ups generate relatively more new jobs than LEs, still lacks sound scientific proof. However, most European governments, including the EC, regard this as a fact.

10 A fact often referred to by European governments in the context of SME policy.

11 Most commonly White Papers referring to SMEs in general (including start-ups) or to SME-dominated sectors, such as crafts, tourism or retail.

12 That is, for bookkeeping further criteria add on: (1) less than fifty employees, (2) turnover less than 4.2 million euros and (3) a balance-sheet total less than 2.1 million euros. Two of three criteria must be fulfilled in order to qualify for reduced bookkeeping requirements.

13 The Belgian regions are also divided by languages: Flanders (Flemish), Brussels (Flemish and French), Walloon (French and German).

14 As is the case in the Netherlands, Portugal, Germany (though only for federal measures) and Belgium.

15 Switzerland is an exception; its regions enjoy rather far-reaching rights of independent taxation.

16 That is, regional measures are often geared toward the same topics or issues as federal ones, with the only difference, that the available budget might be lower and that they are only offered in the relevant region.

17 For this reason, many programs include exclusivity clauses that forbid simultaneous applications for programs covering the same issue.

18 "Disadvantage" actually is a key indicator for potential fields for SME policy. The argument is, that disadvantaged SMEs cannot fully exploit their potentials (i.e., generate further employment), which reduces their contribution to achieving overall economic objectives.

19 Liechtenstein has virtually no discriminating support programs for business, except for the restrictions foreigners wanting to set up business in Liechtenstein face; local businesses are favored.

20 This is due to the political system; programs are implemented by Acts passed by the parliament and thus often include no time limitation.

21 It is estimated that less than 5 percent of all start-ups in Germany actually benefited from public support.

22 This exists in Belgium, France, Spain and Sweden and is planned in Greece; it is also being

discussed in other European countries, e.g., Germany and Luxembourg.

23 The United Kingdom is an exception in this context because its market for venture capital is by far the largest and most sophisticated in Europe; more important still, it is privately funded.

24 The United Kingdom earmarked 33.3 million euros for increasing the number of exporting firms from 100,000 (in 1995) to 130,000 by the year 2000, and Austria announced that it wants to increase its share of exports (especially to Latin America) from 22 to 25 percent of its GDP.

25 Further measures include "peculiarities" such as a "compliance unit" to which new trade barriers can be reported in the Netherlands or an insurance on nonguaranteed debts of foreign customers and exchange rate risks in France.

26 For example, Spain, Germany, United Kingdom, France and Denmark; also DG XXIII of the European Commission.

27 This corresponds to the overall objectives to "foster economic growth" and "create employ-ment."

28 Which corresponds to the goal of "increase the competitiveness of enterprises."

29 The job-creation hypothesis assumes that SMEs, especially start-ups, generate more new jobs than LEs, in relative and absolute terms.

30 Germany never had an official minimum wage; the Netherlands has lowered it and also permits it to be undercut for certain job-related conditions; Italy subsidizes jobs under mini-mum wage.

31 Iceland made provisions for firm level negotiations; Spain reduced the period of notice; Finland prolonged fix-term contracts.

32 The United Kingdom has, in fact, abolished some 1,000 pertinent regulations since 1995.

33 See Commission of the European Communities: Maximising European SMEs' Full Potential for Employment, Growth and Competitiveness, COM, 1996 (98).

REFERENCES

Clemens, R. and Kokalj, L. 1996. *Bürokratie – ein Kostenfaktor (Bureaucracy – A Cost Factor)*. Stuttgart: Poeschel.

Commission of the European Communities. 1996. Recommendation of the Commission, *Official Journal of the European Communities*, No. L 107/6.

Commission of the European communities. 1996. Maximising European SMEs' full potential for employment, growth and competitiveness, COM(96) 98.

De, D. 1994. *Mittelstand und Mittelstandspolitik in den Mitgliedsstaaten der Europäischen Union (SME Policy in the Member States of the European Union)*. Stuttgart: Poeschel.

ENSR (European Network for SME Research). 1997. *The European Observatory for SMEs, Fifth Annual Report*. Zoetermeer.

Storey, D. 1997. *Understanding the Small Business Sector*. London: Routledge.

6

Entrepreneurship in Germany

DAVID AUDRETSCH

HOW ENTREPRENEURIAL IS GERMANY?
ENTREPRENEURIAL CHARACTERISTICS: DOES THE INDIVIDUAL MATTER?
ENVIRONMENTAL CHARACTERISTICS: DOES THE INDUSTRY MATTER?
PUBLIC POLICY: DOES THE GOVERNMENT MATTER?
CONCLUSIONS

As in virtually every developed country, research on entrepreneurship in Germany has exploded since the late 1980s.[1] This research reflects a growing awareness about the importance of entrepreneurship as a source of employment, innovation, growth and global competitiveness. Scholars from disciplines spanning management, finance, strategy, sociology, geography and economics have responded with a wave of new studies that shed new light on the role of entrepreneurship in Germany. The purpose of this chapter is to report on this literature. The second section addresses two broad issues: How entrepreneurial is Germany, and is it entrepreneurial enough? Considerable concern is expressed by the popular press over the current policy debate, and a growing body of research shows that Germany's economic crisis of the 1990s called the *Standortkrise* (competitiveness crisis), which resulted in the highest unemployment rates since the 1930s, is linked to a deficiency of entrepreneurship.[2] In asking the question whether the individual matters, the third section focuses on the links between characteristics specific to individuals and entrepreneurial activity. The fourth section addresses an analogous question for the external environment, both in terms of the industry and region. Finally, the last section examines the impact that the government has on entrepreneurial activity, in terms of finance, start-up programs and regional programs.

How Entrepreneurial Is Germany?

Ever since its famous economic miracle (*Wirtschaftswunder*) of the 1950s, the rest of the world has associated Germany with remarkable prosperity and stability, providing both high employment and wage rates. The German model of a social market economy (*Sozialmarktwirtschaft*) has generated a standard of living (*Wohlstand*) that created not only the material wealth found on the other side of the Atlantic but also the high degree of social services and security found elsewhere in Europe. What has become known as the German economic model demonstrated that not only could capitalism generate a high and equitable standard of living but it could also have a friendly face.

The economic model of the social market economy at the heart of the German economic miracle and the general postwar standard of living have been based on consensus. This consensus consisted of three principal actors: the industry employer associations (*Arbeitgeberverbände*), labor unions (*Gewerkschaften*) and the government. Through a broad spectrum of institutions, such as the work councils (*Betriebsrat*), industry-wide wage agreements and the apprentice system (*Lehrstellen*), these actors provided the basis for unparalleled success in generating high wages and levels of employment. Under this consensus, labor fulfilled its obligation in the social contract by supplying workers with not only the highest skill levels in the world but also the most disciplined. On their part, the employers associations – the leading German industrial firms – provided stable and generous employment, including a rich array of social services. With labor and industry working together under this consensus facilitated by the government, industries such as automobiles and metalworking were more competitive in Germany than anywhere else in the world. The task of the major political parties was to shift the fruits of this enviably productive consensus either more toward labor (the Social Democratic Party), or toward the status quo firms comprising the employer associations (Christian Democratic Union).

In 1989, not only was Germany reunified, but the process of globalization also accelerated, enabling previously excluded countries to participate in the global economy. This globalization combined with the telecommunications revolution has shattered the viability of the social contract inherent in the consensus demanded of the German social market economy. Pressed to maintain competitiveness in traditional industries, where economic activity can be easily transferred across geographic space to access lower production costs, the largest and most prominent German companies have deployed two strategic responses. The first is to offset greater wage differentials between Germany and low-cost locations by increasing productivity through the substitution of technology and capital for labor. The second is to locate new plants and establishments outside of Germany.

What both strategic responses have in common is that the larger German companies have been downsizing in the domestic economy. For example, Siemens increased the amount of employment outside Germany by 50 percent, from 108,000 in 1984–5 to 162,000 in 1994–5. Over the same period it decreased the amount of employment in Germany by 12 percent, from 240,000 to 211,000. Volkswagen increased the amount of employment in foreign countries by 24 percent, from 78,000 in 1984 to 97,000 in 1994. But it also decreased employment in Germany by 10 percent, from 156,000 to 141,000. Similarly, Hoechst increased the number of jobs outside of Germany by 9 percent, from

78,925 in 1984 to 92,333 in 1994. The number of Hoechst employees in Germany fell over that same period by 26 percent, from 99,015 to 73,338. And Badische Anilin- und Sodafabriken (BASF) increased employment in foreign countries by 34 percent, from 29,966 in 1984 to 40,297 in 1994. Domestic employment by BASF fell by 17 percent over that same time period, from 85,850 to 65,969.

These examples are not isolated but rather typical of the wave of downsizing in Germany in the 1990s that has resulted in levels of unemployment – four million – not seen since World War II. The reaction of the German public has been to accuse German firms of not fulfilling their social contract. As one of the leading newspapers, *Die Zeit*, accused German industry in a recent headline, "When profits lead to ruin – more profits and more unemployment: where is the social responsibility of the firms?"

That the bottom would drop out of such a successful economic model responsible for postwar German living standard has sent shock waves both within and beyond the country's borders. Early in 1998 the unemployment rate reached nearly 13 percent at 4.7 million people, which was the highest levels since the pre-Nazi Weimar Republic era. There is no doubt that these persistent record levels of unemployment led to the demise of the Bundeskanzler Helmut Kohl and the Christian Democratic Union (CDU), which had ruled Germany for nearly 18 years.

Germany has not generated a vibrant sector of new firms and new industries (see Berger et al. 1990). An irony is that the small and medium-sized enterprises (SMEs) of Germany – the *Mittelstand* – were the backbone of the industrial structure throughout the postwar prosperity. But these SMEs are typically family-held in traditional industries. New firms in new industries are much rarer. One of the most repeated phrases on the pages of the business news over the last months has been what Helmuth Guembel, who is research director of the Gartner Group in Munich observed, "Put Bill Gates in Europe and it just wouldn't have worked out."[3] A similar sentiment was expressed by Joschka Fischer, parliamentary leader of the Green Party in Germany, who laments, "A company like Microsoft would never have a chance in Germany."[4] Thus, small firms have been a unique strength of postwar German industrial success. Ironically, at the heart of the current German economic crisis is also small firms.

Why has Germany been unable to grow the German equivalent of a Microsoft? *Der Spiegel* observed recently: "Global structural change has had an impact on the German economy that only a short time ago would have been unimaginable: Many of the products, such as automobiles, machinery, chemicals and steel are no longer competitive in global markets. And in the industries of the future, like biotechnology and electronics, the German companies are barely participating."[5]

In fact, the number of businesses in Germany has been declining. Based on data from the Statistical Office of Lower Saxony, Wagner (forthcoming) reports that the number of manufacturing businesses declined considerably between 1978 and 1994.[6] There were 7,584 manufacturing establishments in 1978 and only 6,620 by 1994.

Job creation

While small firms have been identified as the engine of job creation in almost every developed country, this has not been the case for Germany. For example, Wagner (1995b) used a unique longitudinal data set covering all manufacturing establishments between 1978 and 1993 in Lower Saxony and found that while small firms account for most of the gross job creation, they also account for most of the job destruction. This confirms the earlier findings of Michael Fritsch (1993), who uses the Business Census (*Arbeitsstättenzählung*) to examine the long-term trends in the role of German SMEs. Fritsch (1993: 50) concludes, "There is no dramatic job generation by small firms in West Germany."[7] As for other countries, gross job creation and destruction rates tend to decline with firm size. What is different about Germany is that "net job creation rates and firm size are not systematically related."

Similarly, in most developed countries, a turbulent industry structure – a high rate of both firm births and exits – often is associated with greater job creation. However, Audretsch and Fritsch (1993, 1996) find that the opposite is true. Employment growth was not associated with a turbulent environment in Germany during the late 1980s. In fact, their evidence suggests that in both the manufacturing and the service sectors, a high rate of regional turbulence tends to lead to a lower, not a higher, rate of job creation.

Some evidence suggests that in the last several years small firms in Germany are emerging as the engine of job creation, as in other developed countries. For example, Haid and Weigand (1998) find that family-owned firms (typically SMEs) increased employment between 1989 and 1993, while large management-controlled firms decreased employment.

Weigand and Audretsch (1999) use a longitudinal database consisting of 344 firms tracked over a six-year period, 1991 to 1996. They split the sample into high-tech and low-tech industries. As table 6.1 shows, they find that in the high-tech industries the large firms that are listed experienced a decrease in employment by an average of −0.21 percent per year. By contrast, the SMEs (with fewer than 500 employees) experienced an

TABLE 6.1 Employment and sales growth of small and large German firms, 1991–1996 (standard deviation in parentheses)

	Small firms		Large firms	
	Employment (%)	Sales (%)	Employment (%)	Sales (%)
High-tech firms				
Listed	3.57	3.33	−0.21	−0.41
	(28.46)	(20.61)	(14.80)	(17.04)
Non-listed	3.17	1.06	−4.21	−2.40
	(29.46)	(20.53)	(14.39)	(26.78)
Low-tech firms				
Listed	−3.97	−4.60	−1.00	−1.07
	(16.88)	(15.68)	(26.48)	(24.30)
Non-listed	−3.36	−1.26	−4.60	−1.60
	(11.83)	(34.66)	(18.98)	(19.96)

Source: Weigand and Audretsch (1999)

increase in employment by an average of 3.57 percent annually. Similarly, those large firms which are not listed experienced an annual decrease in employment of −4.21 percent, while the SMEs experienced an increase in employment of 3.17 percent.

For low-tech industries, Weigand and Audretsch (1999) found that the listed large firms experienced a decrease in employment of an annual mean rate of −1.00 percent. Similarly, the SMEs also experienced a decrease in employment of an annual mean rate of −3.97 percent. For the nonlisted firms the large firms experienced a decrease in employment of −4.60 percent. The SMEs experienced a decrease in employment of − 1.26 percent. Thus, the empirical evidence strongly suggests that downsizing in Germany results in a decrease in employment in (1) high-tech corporations, (2) large low-tech corporations and (3) small low-tech firms. The most striking finding is that strong job growth is exhibited by the remaining fourth category − high-tech SMEs.

Innovation

During the early 1990s several case studies suggested that German entrepreneurs are faced with barriers impeding innovative activity.[8] For example, a software firm that was founded in Bavaria (FAST) needed more capital to fund product development. But after being continually refused by financial and nonfinancial institutions, the founder, Matthias Zahn, is planning not only an initial public offering on the NASDAC but also to move the company's headquarters from Bavaria to Redwood City, California.[9] This is no isolated example. Scores of entrepreneurs in newly emerging industries, ranging from computer software and hardware to biotechnology and virtual reality have engaged in a kind of emigration (*Auswanderung*) in order to appropriate the expected value of their technological knowledge.

Labor market institutions also may tend to impede the development of new firms pursuing different ideas. For example, SPEA Software is a new start-up based near Munich.[10] This developer of multimedia equipment boosted its sales by 60 percent last year to about 180 million DM and got Germany's biggest-yet injection of venture capital. SPEA has met opposition from German unions because its 130 employees are not unionized, and it does not yet belong to an employer's association. It is thus not part of the centralized system of labor relations to which most of German industry belongs.

Similarly, tax laws force the chief executive officers of new companies to start paying out dividends from earnings almost as soon as they appear, pre-empting high reinvestment policies. And bankruptcy laws in Germany make it clear that to start a new business and to fail is socially unproductive. After two bankruptcies the entrepreneur is legally left only with the option of becoming an employee. He may not legally rely upon his experience from the bankruptcies to start a third new enterprise.[11]

The most important and careful study to date documenting the role of German SMEs in innovative activity was undertaken by a team of researchers at the Zentrum für Europäische Wirtschaftsforschung (ZEW) led by Dietmar Harhoff and Georg Licht (1996; see also Licht et al. 1995). They analyzed the findings made possible by the Mannheim Innovation Database, which measures the extent of innovative activity in German firms between 1990 and 1992. They found that 12 percent of the R&D expenditures in western German firms comes from SMEs (defined as having fewer than 500 employees).

TABLE 6.2 Innovative activity of (West) German manufacturing SMEs, 1990–1992

Total employment	Non-innovating firms	Innovating firms without R&D	Innovating firms with R&D but without in-house R&D	Innovating firms with in-house R&D labs	Total number of firms
5–49	33,301	15,981	8,146	6,117	63,545
50–249	10,067	4,325	3,129	3,225	20,746
250–499	685	344	487	1,875	3,391
500–999	200	95	165	795	1,255
1,000	119	24	90	559	792
Number of firms	44,372	20,769	12,017	12,571	89,729

Source: Translated and adapted from Harhoff and Licht (1996: 27)

Table 6.2 shows that the likelihood of a firm not innovating decreases with firm size. For example, 52 percent of firms with fewer than fifty employees were not innovative. By contrast, only 15 percent of the firms with at least 1,000 employees were not innovative. More striking is that the smallest firms that do innovate have a greater propensity to be innovative without undertaking formal research and development. Although only 3 percent of the largest corporations in Germany are innovative without undertaking formal R&D, one-quarter of the innovative firms with fewer than fifty employees are innovative without formal R&D. The study also shows that even fewer SMEs in the five new German *Länder* are innovative than is the case in western Germany. Over two-thirds of the smallest SMEs in East Germany are not innovative, and they are less than half as likely to undertake R&D as are their Western counterparts.

Systematic evidence also suggests that the German SME is confronted by considerable barriers to innovative activity. Beise and Licht (1996) analyzed the Mannheimer Innovationspanel consisting of 43,300 innovating firms to identify the main barriers to innovative activity confronting German SMEs. The major barrier to innovation listed in both 1992 and 1994 was too long a gestation period. In 1994 nearly 60 percent of German SMEs reported that this long gestation period was a very important barrier to innovative activity. Other major barriers to innovative activity include legal restrictions, restrictive government policies, excessive delays in obtaining government approval for a new product, a shortage of finance capital, a lack of competent employees, and too high a risk.

International entrepreneurship

Germany's SMEs have been particularly strong in international entrepreneurship (see Burgel et al. 1998; Wagner 1995a). Many of these companies, such as Krones, Körber/Hauni, Weinig, Webasto and Terta Werke are virtually unheard of by the public, in contrast to such household names as Mercedes-Benz, Siemens, Bosch and Bayer. At the same time, the global market share of these companies typically far exceeds that of the giant companies of Germany. That is, when calculated in terms of the specialized products they manufacture, these SMEs have global market shares ranging between 70 and 90 percent. And in what ranks among one of the biggest German secrets, these enterprises account for the bulk of the country's trade surplus.

One of the major strategic instruments deployed by these German SMEs is to combine product specialization with geographic diversity. The focus is typically upon a particular market niche, usually one that requires technical expertise. Most of the company resources are then devoted toward maintaining the market leadership in that niche. Diversification is generally considered to be an anathema to focusing upon the core product. Because of their degree of specialization and relatively small size, SMEs are often at a disadvantage in terms of economies of scale. This is where the second part of the strategy comes in – globalization. That is, the product-market specialization is leveraged across broad geographic markets. Such globalization of marketing and sales provides sufficient scale to recover R&D expenses and to maintain costs at a reasonable level for the world market.

Simon (1992) examined thirty-nine "hidden champions" in Germany that accounted for an average of 22.6 percent of the global market share in the relevant product market and 31.7 percent of the European market share. These SMEs had a total of 354 foreign manufacturing subsidiaries (not including agents, importers and other forms of company representation). Each company has, on average, 9.6 foreign subsidiaries – certainly an extraordinarily high number of foreign subsidiaries given the rather modest size of the parent companies. Thus, direct foreign investment plays a central role in these companies' globalization strategy.

The five-year revenue growth of these companies is 16.2 percent, and the five-year employee growth is 9.8 percent. Thus, the strategy of direct foreign investment certainly appears to have contributed considerably to company growth.

In fact, transnational investment is not a recent phenomenon for these companies. They even began to engage in direct foreign investment activities some thirty years ago. For example, Heidenhain, which is more than one century old and manufactures measurement and control instruments, has earned more than half of its revenues in markets outside Germany.

As mentioned above, one of the most important strategic instruments deployed by this group of SMEs is to engage in direct foreign investment. Virtually all of the thirty-nine companies (97 percent) have production facilities in the United States. And more than half of them have production facilities in Japan. These companies generally prefer to maintain full control over foreign production facilities because they view the relationship as being too important to delegate to another enterprise.

One of the keys to the success of German SMEs in direct foreign investment activities has been their strong commitment to global expansion. This commitment generally takes two forms: investment in plant, equipment and technology and investment in people. Even when a high initial investment may not be justified in terms of short-term returns, the SMEs consider it important to undertake such global investments because of the demonstration effect – to show potential customers and business partners that they are committed and intend to participate.

A central element of the transnational strategies deployed by SMEs has been to set the same high standards in the host market as they do in the home market. In particular, this refers to the servicing of the production through the creation of strong and reliable service networks. For example, the service network of Heidelberger, the world leader in offset printing, is as comprehensive in Japan, where there are a number of subsidiary establishments, as it is in the German home market. What the SMEs of Germany have not been able to overcome is the risk inherently associated with a high degree of specialization. The greater the degree to which an enterprise is specialized, the higher is the exposure to risk, especially in terms of its vulnerability to market changes. But sometimes the flexibility associated with SMEs serves as a key buffer against market volatility and shifts in demand.

SMEs pursue a strategy that does not blindly search for the technological frontier. Consequently, they are much more focused on combining technology with customer service. This takes numerous forms, such as extensive customer training. As the complexity of products increases, the customer requires more operating support and maintenance – one of the strengths of the German SME.

Being oriented to a specialized product niche and typically combining both sophisticated technology with careful devotion to consumer needs make a strategy of direct foreign investment so crucial to the German SME. In order to perceive and understand the peculiarities of each host market, the company benefits by producing at the location of the host market. Apparently the knowledge that is transmitted, which involves a large tacit element, can best be obtained through close geographic proximity, but not over a longer geographic distance. And a second reason why presence is important in the foreign market is to provide services, such as customer training. While such services could be contracted out, the asset specificity of the product, combined with the high-tech sophistication, virtually bundles the service component with the manufactured product.

German SMEs have generally found that when the technology dominates the enterprise, the engineers and scientists tend to be the driving force, but customers may suffer and rearrange their loyalties and explore alternative products manufactured by other companies. Conversely, when the marketing department is the driving force behind the enterprise, technological sophistication of the product tends to suffer. While the customers may be satisfied in a static sense, the enterprise is not meeting a need for dynamic product development, which leaves the company vulnerable to competition from enterprises that invest in technological advances. That is, customers actually demand a technological leader that can provide them with unanticipated product innovations and improvements. Balancing static and dynamic customer demand becomes a delicate strategy that only a very flexible enterprise with both technological competencies and customer sensitivity can accomplish.

Nonmarketing employees in German SMEs engage in direct and repeated contacts with customers twice as often as those in the largest German corporations. This reveals the importance of the strategy found among German SMEs that the best way for engineering, manufacturing and financial employees to become acquainted with customer needs is to actually spend time with the customers. Because scientists, engineers and managers interact frequently and repeatedly with the customers, employees throughout the company become increasingly sensitive to what customers really want.

It should be emphasized that the strategy of combining technological sophistication with close monitoring of consumer needs falls more within the domain of SMEs than with their larger counterparts. Large corporations tend to be focused rather single-mindedly upon technological advances or else on being consumer-driven, but generally not a combination of both. This is one of the key ways in which German SMEs are flexible. They are able to combine both of these elements of the pursuit of technological sophistication with the monitoring of customer needs. But because of the importance of proximity in determining customer needs, sometimes referred to as the *monitoring* problem, it is an especially key strategy for such SMEs to engage in production in the foreign market, that is, to engage in direct foreign investment.

One of the key distinctions between the direct foreign investment strategies of large corporations and SMEs is that the larger companies tend to separate the manufacturing, marketing, R&D and service functions from each other. By contrast, SMEs tend not to compartmentalize such strategic functions but rather to integrate them. This means that when customers have some difficulty with the product, employees from manufacturing, marketing and development typically all participate in providing a solution. An advantage of such functional interaction within the enterprise is that when employees charged with different tasks within the firm come together, they return to their regular tasks with new insights and useful information about how the product is actually performing in the marketplace. This diffusion of knowledge about the match between the customer's needs and the company's products is a central strategic advantage of SMEs.

The involvement of workers at all levels and the orientation to wide range of functions within the enterprise in meeting consumer demand and dealing with unanticipated problems underscore yet another strategic reason why the propensity for these successful SMEs to engage in direct foreign investment is particularly high. Such a strategy of linking the technology and product development to customer needs could not be as efficiently attained if only a representative of the enterprise actually had contact with the customers. Rather, an essential component of this strategy is that production workers, managers and engineers all become involved in an integrated effort to best meet the needs of the consumers. For this reason it is crucial that the enterprise actually produce the goods in the host market in which it wishes to sell. Thus, direct foreign investment is a strategic cornerstone at the heart of the German SMEs.

Successful German SMEs clearly tend to be both interdependent and autonomous. That is, they generally pursue a strategy of entering new markets and solving manufacturing and R&D problems on their own. This enables them to maintain control over standards and prevents leakages in terms of technological know-how.

The more general strategy of interdependence and autonomy practiced by German SMEs clearly reflects the core strategy of product specialization and concentration of the enterprise's assets toward developing competencies almost exclusively for its core products. By solving their own problems, undertaking their own research and development and sometimes even providing their own materials and components, the SMEs are better situated to develop the manufacturing capabilities. That is, the strategy of these companies is actually to make the product themselves rather than to purchase it already made.

ENTREPRENEURIAL CHARACTERISTICS: DOES THE INDIVIDUAL MATTER?

The start-up decision

A series of studies (Klandt 1984; Kulicke 1987; Boegenhold 1985) have identified fundamental characteristics possessed by the typical German entrepreneur who starts a new firm (*Gründer*). These studies have consistently identified the start-up decision to be based on these entrepreneurial characteristics. According to these studies, the character profile of German entrepreneurs varies considerably from their countrymen who choose to remain employed by a firm or the government.

Among the most prominent entrepreneurial characteristics is independence. Entrepreneurs generally place a higher value on career independence than those who do not start new firms. Similarly, responsibility and leadership rank very highly in entrepreneurs compared with the general population.

A study by the ADT (1998) found that the number of spin-offs from research institutes has increased dramatically, from 30 in 1990 to 167 in 1997. The study classified scientific workers at the main German scientific research institutes as being either a "potential entrepreneur" or not. The work values for potential entrepreneurs working at scientific research institutes differ considerably from their colleagues who are not classified as such. Potential entrepreneurs place a higher value on being responsible for their own future, having a position of responsibility, working in a less hierarchical organization and having more independence than scientific workers with no entrepreneurial interest. By contrast, potential entrepreneurs place less of an importance on a secure income and pension than do those with no entrepreneurial potential.

Performance

Almus and Nerlinger (1998a, 1998b) examine why entrepreneurial growth varies between what they call new technology-based firms (NTBFs) and noninnovative start-ups (see also Nerlinger 1998). They perform multivariate analyses on the impact of characteristics specific to the entrepreneur as well as the industry on subsequent firm growth, using a database provided by the largest German credit rating agency, Creditreform (analogous to the Dun & Bradstreet database for the United States). Firms enter the Creditreform database for two reasons: (1) a customer or supplier may inquire about the financial situation of the respective firm, or (2) credit rating agencies exploit economies of scale by gathering information proactively, systematically recording publicly available information on new firms (Stahl 1991; Harhoff and Stahl 1997). Creditreform uses a relational database consisting of more than 580,000 firms in western Germany. The authors find that the growth of new-firm start-ups is shaped by characteristics specific to the founder and firm, as well as the industry environment. For example, they find that large and mature firms have lower growth rates than do small and young firms, both innovative and noninnovative. In particular, they find that the greater the degree of human capital of the founder, the greater is the growth rate, especially in innovative industries.

Weigand and Lehmann (1998) find that family-owned businesses generally out-performed large companies with diffuse ownership controlled by managers and subsidiaries of very large conglomerates with widely dispersed ownership. Their findings are based on a sample of 403 firms from mining and manufacturing between 1991 and 1996, whose performance was measured as net profits divided by total assets. Weigand and Lehmann (1998) find that the mean return on total assets is 32.3 percent for family-owned firms, and 23.1 percent for management-controlled firms. They attribute the systematically superior performance of the family-owned firms, which are typically SMEs, to a better management and decision-making structure.

Bruederl and Preisendoerfer (1998) examine a database consisting of 1,700 new-firm start-ups in Germany and find that the subsequent performance, measured in terms of likelihood of survival and growth, is greater for those entrepreneurs who:

1 participate in a network with other entrepreneurs
2 receive active help from their spouse
3 receive emotional support from their spouse.

In addition, they find that entrepreneurial success is positively influenced by ethnic background, educational background, type of work experience and whether the entrepreneur already had entrepreneurial experience. Their most striking finding is that entrepreneurial success is the highest within the context of a network with other entrepreneurs.

Wagner (1994) employed a longitudinal database consisting of 7,000 manufacturing German firms and found the probability that a firm is an exporter increases along with firm size. However, they caution that there are many successful exporters among small firms and nonexporters among larger firms as well.

In a separate study, Wagner (forthcoming) tracked the performance of small (and large) firms before exit, using a longitudinal database that identified the pre-exit performance of cohorts of firms exiting in 1990, 1991 and 1992. One striking result he found was that more than half of the exiting firms (between 53 percent and 61 percent) were founded before 1979, making them over 11 years old. He also found that young firms (less than 5 years old) accounted for about a quarter of all exits, and three-quarters of exiting businesses were from middle-aged firms. At the same time, he found that the likelihood of survival increases with firm size.

Harhoff and Stahl (1995) used a sample of about 11,000 western German firms spanning manufacturing, construction, trade, finance and services to examine the impact of the role of ownership structure and liability statutes on firm survival and growth.

ENVIRONMENTAL CHARACTERISTICS: DOES THE INDUSTRY MATTER?

The industry environment

Wagner (1994) has found that the industry environment plays an important role in shaping the amount of entrepreneurial activity in Germany.[12] Based on a longitudinal database between 1979 and 1989, he finds that the start-up of new small firms tends to be greater in those highly concentrated industries experiencing high growth. He concludes that start-up activity is not significantly influenced by the importance of capital intensity and R&D in the industry. These nonsignificant statistical results are important because they suggest that entrepreneurs are not deterred from starting new firms even in industries which are capital intensive and where R&D plays an important role.

Harhoff and Stahl (1995) use a database of around 11,000 German firms in manufacturing, construction, trade, finance and services to examine how their postentry performance varies across different sectors in terms of the likelihood of survival and growth. In particular, Harhoff and Stahl find evidence that the likelihood of survival is positively related to firm size. In addition, firm growth is negatively related to firm size, but the likelihood of survival and growth rates differ systematically across different sectors of the economy.

The results of Harhoff and Stahl (1995) are not consistent with those found in earlier studies, according to the careful survey by Joachim Wagner (1992). After reviewing the most important studies, Wagner (1995b: 201) concludes, "Studies using German data tend to show that firm size and firm growth are uncorrelated."

Wagner (1997) uses a large database from Lower Saxony to examine the link between firm size and the quality of jobs and found that small firms have the same propensity to offer high-quality jobs as do their larger counterparts, in terms of job duration. This finding holds across different industries, both high-tech and low-tech sectors.

Almus and Nerlinger (1998a, 1998b) also use a large database to examine how the postentry performance of new firms varies across sectors. In particular, they find that the growth rates of new firms tends to be greater in very high-tech industries rather than in high-tech and other manufacturing industries.

The regional environment

The literature linking SMEs to the regional environment focuses on two themes: (1) which type of regional environment best promotes SME activities and (2) how the presence of a vibrant entrepreneurial region influences subsequent growth.

An example of the first theme is Audretsch and Fritsch's (1994) study, which examines the impact that location plays on entrepreneurial activity in western Germany. Using a database derived from social insurance statistics, which covers about 90 percent of employment, they identify the birth rates of new start-ups for seventy-five distinct economic regions. These regions are distinguished on the basis of planning regions (*Raumordnungsregionen*). They find that, for the late 1980s, the birth rates of new firms are higher in regions experiencing low unemployment, which have a dense population with a high growth rate, a large share of skilled workers and a strong presence of small businesses.[13]

Similarly, Pfirrmann (1994) found that the innovative activity of SMEs in western Germany is shaped by regional factors. He uses a database consisting of innovative SMEs and finds that their activity tends to be greater in those regions where there is a strong presence of business–university alliances. However, his results also indicate that factors internal to the firm are more important for the innovation efforts of a small firm than is the regional environment.

An example of the second type of literature, which focuses on the impact of entrepreneurship on subsequent economic growth, is Audretsch and Fritsch's (1996) study. Their database analysis identified new business start-ups and exits from the social insurance statistics in Germany to examine whether a greater degree of turbulence leads to greater economic growth, as suggested by Joseph Schumpeter in his pathbreaking 1911 treatise. These social insurance statistics are collected for individuals. Each record in the database identifies the establishment at which an individual is employed. The start-up of a new firm is recorded when a new establishment identification appears in the database. While there is some evidence for the United States linking a greater degree of turbulence at the regional level to higher rates of growth for regions, Audretsch and Fritsch (1996) find that the opposite is true for Germany during the 1980s. In both the manufacturing and the service sectors, a high rate of turbulence in a region tends to lead to a lower and not a higher rate of growth. They attribute this negative relationship to the fact that the underlying components – the start-up and death rates – are both negatively related to subsequent economic growth. Those areas with higher start-up rates tend to experience lower growth rates in subsequent years. Most strikingly, the same is also true for the death rates. The German regions experiencing higher death rates also tend to experience lower growth rates in subsequent years.[14]

Audretsch and Fritsch (1996) conjecture that one possible explanation for the disparity in results between the United States and Germany may lie in the role that innovative activity, and therefore the ability of new firms to ultimately displace the incumbent enterprises, plays in new-firm start-ups. It may be that innovative activity does not play the same role for SMEs in Germany as it does for those in the United States (Audretsch 1995). To the degree that this is true, regional growth can be said to emanate from SMEs only when they serve as agents of change through innovative activity.

Public Policy: Does the Government Matter?

Financing German SMEs

Audretsch and Elston (1997) argue that something of a paradox has emerged with respect to the system of financing for German SMEs. On the one hand, the development of a finely layered system linking together financial institutions, governments and private firms, would seem to serve as a model for providing funds to SMEs. Not only was the SME the backbone of the German economic miracle and subsequent rise to economic power, but it also appears to have played a more important role in German economic development than in either the United States or the United Kingdom.

On the other hand, while the SME has provided the backbone for Germany's economic success, one aspect has been noticeably lacking in recent years – emerging small high-technology companies in such industries as software, biotechnology and computers. The lack of entrepreneurial activity in high-tech industries is directly attributable to the rigid constraints in providing liquidity and access to finance of new firms in new industries imposed by the very same system of finance in Germany.

Two institutional features of the German financial system sharply contrast to the system in the United States and the United Kingdom, both of which may impact the extent to which SMEs are able to obtain access to finance (Vitols 1998; Deeg 1998). First, companies in Germany typically rely almost exclusively upon banks for external finance. The external capital market remains relatively undeveloped in Germany. Second, not only do the banks represent the major financial intermediary supplying capital to firms, but they are also extensively represented on the supervisory board of companies.

This paradox explains the emergence of a fierce debate revolving around the viability of the system of finance for German SMEs. As the title of an article in *Business Week* observes, "Suddenly, Germans love to hate their banks."[15]

In Audretsch and Elston's (1994) study, the extent of financial constraints is linked to firm investment behavior through the lens of the Q theory, which assumes that in the absence of capital market imperfections (and taxes), the value-maximizing firm will continue to invest as long as the shadow price of a marginal unit of capital (Q) exceeds unity. One of the greatest impediments to measuring the impact of liquidity constraints on investment behavior across firm size in Germany has been the lack of a reliable and comprehensive panel data set. Audretsch and Elston (1994) employ a database consisting of a collection of financial reports of German firms quoted on the German stock exchange over a long period of time. The authors find no evidence that the institutional structure of finance in Germany has been able to avoid the impact of financing constraints. In particular, they find that the impact of financing constraints on investment behavior tends to increase systematically as firm size decreases. Smaller enterprises tend to be more vulnerable to financing constraints than their larger counterparts, even under the German model of finance where the spread between the large- and small-firm lending rates is relatively low. However, Audretsch and Elston (1994) find evidence that the German model of finance was able to avoid financing constraints on German enterprises before the mid-1970s. A particularly striking feature of this era in the former West Germany was a relative abundance of cheap credit. This era, however, seems to coincide with the economic miracle in Germany. Since the mid-1970s there is no evidence that German firms, particularly the smaller enterprises, have been able to avoid finance constraints.

Haid and Weigand (1998) find that family-owned firms in Germany are not liquidity-constrained in that they have sufficient access to finance. Based on a database consisting of 109 reporting firms, they find that German family-owned firms may have better access to finance than do SMEs in the United States.

A different study, undertaken by Egeln et al. (1997) finds that, in fact, small and young firms in high-tech industries in Germany do experience finance constraints. Forty-two percent of firms less than five years old perceive that access to capital is "an important obstacle to innovation activity," while only 35 percent of firms older than twenty years experience a finance constraint. Similarly, only 2.2 percent of firms with fewer than fifty employees received a credit rating of excellent, while 41 percent of firms with more than 1,000 employees received an excellent credit rating.

Weigand (1998) analyzes an important longitudinal database from the Deutsche Bundesbank (1992) consisting of 18,281 firms from 1978 to 1989. She finds that the share of internal finance by the large firms rose from about 26 percent in 1978 to about 28 percent in 1989. By contrast, the share of total finance accounted for by internal finance by small firms decreased from about 22 percent in 1978 to 18 percent in 1989. Similarly, the share of total finance accounted for by internal finance in medium-sized enterprises fell from about 21 percent in 1978 to 18 percent in 1989. Weigand (1998) also shows that (1) smaller firms tend to have longer-term relationships with financial institutions than their larger counterparts, and (2) this has become more important over time.

Pfirrman et al. (1997) undertook an exhaustive study comparing venture capital in Germany with that in the United States. They identified three major differences:

1 the size and rate of growth of venture capital
2 the legal structure of venture capital funds
3 the market structure of venture capital.

They also find that German venture capital managers typically do not specialize in certain high-technology sectors or industries. Instead, they prefer a broad distribution of industries in their portfolios in order to minimize risk. Although this German strategy of diversification serves to reduce risk, it also reduces the ability of fund managers to accumulate expertise in any particular industry.

The amount of venture capital available to new-firm start-ups in high-technology industries is dramatically increasing. Direct investment and venture capital programs sponsored by the Ministries for Education, Science, Research and Technology has increased from about 10 million DM in 1989 to more than 458 million DM in 1997 (BMBF 1996).

Start-up programs

Indirect promotion of new technology-based firms (NTBFs) by the federal government has risen from 45.9 million DM in 1991 to almost 82 million DM in 1993 (BMBF 1996: 97).[16] Similarly, Sternberg (1996) has shown that several government-sponsored technology policies has triggered the start-up of new firms. The majority of the start-up programs are targeted toward eliminating particular bottlenecks in the development and financing of new firms. Sternberg (1990) examined the impact that seventy innovation centers have had on the development of technology-based small firms and found most entrepreneurs experienced several advantages from locating at an innovation center.[17] Becher and Wolff (1995) provide detailed evidence of the role and impact that government programs play in supporting R&D cooperation among German SMEs.

The German Reconstruction Bank (Kreditanstalt für Wiederaufbau, or KfW) has been one of the most important institutions promoting SMEs in Germany. The KfW provides financial support for about 20,000 SMEs each year. Of these firms, 80 percent have sales less than 10 million DM. The support of SMEs by the KfW resulted in the creation of nearly 150,000 jobs in 1992 and 40,000 jobs in 1995. Similarly, the BMBF has had a series of programs to promote German SMEs.

One of the most important conclusions of Feldman and Pfirrmann (1998: 14) is:

> Since biotechnology has only really begun to be competitive in Germany over the last five years, the financial infrastructure lacks the expertise to invest in promising biotech start-ups. Although venture capital exists, there appears to be a bias against investing in early stage ventures. Established German pharmaceuticals are more likely to invest in foreign biotechs, which are seen as more stable or profitable, than domestic biotechs.

Perhaps in a response to bolster the fledgling biotechnology industry, the German government started a national initiative, *Biotechnologie 2000*, to support entrepreneurship in biotechnology. In addition, the BioRegio program was started, in which the German *Länder* compete for investment in local biotechnology firms. To participate, regions were required to develop a plan for research and commercialization of biotechnology, with a special emphasis on cooperation between the universities and private industry. Feldman and Pfirrmann (1998) concluded that, "without doubt the BioRegio competition fostered biotechnology activities not only in the so-called winner regions Aachen, Heidelberg and Munich, but also in other areas like Berlin/Brandenburg that have got no public support."

Conclusions

The German Economic Model, since the change to a free market economy, has provided a better standard of living, a material wealth and a high degree of social services and security. This has been achieved by a consensus of the industry employer associations, labor unions and the government. In addition, the unification of Germany also enabled the acceleration of a global market place, which contributed significantly to its economic growth. However, the world economy suffered during the period, and large firms enacted a number of downsizing strategies to reduce costs and to become more competitive in the global marketplace. As a result, unemployment levels increased to nearly 13 percent in 1998.

Relationships for progress became "finger pointers" for blame as the economy faltered. What has been discovered is that as the number of employees in large firms has been declining, smaller firms are increasing their number of employees.

New firms now complain that innovative activities are hindered by legal restrictions and restrictive government policies, long delays in government approval for new products, a shortage of finance capital and a lack of competent employees. Many German SMEs have developed a policy of moving the production of parts and assemblies from other firms to in-house operations to offset the policy, finance and employee restrictions.

The government has now embarked on a sponsored program of reducing roadblocks of bottlenecks in the start-up, financing and development of new technology-based firms. It appears that these programs are beginning to have an impact.

What happened in the German economy that resulted in such a reversal of the early results? In retrospect, it appears that the early emphasis was based on an opening of the global markets to large firms. When the downsizing for global competitiveness occurred, there was little growth in the SMEs to provide jobs for the displaced workers.

A number of changes have now occurred that are expected to rectify the problem. Most important, however, has been the recognition of the contribution of SMEs to the economy.

Notes

I am grateful to, Claudia Weigand and Jürgen Weigand for their helpful comments and suggestions. Any omissions or errors remain my responsibility.

1 Harhoff (1997) and Harhoff and Steil (1997) contain a number of excellent studies analyzing the role of entrepreneurship in Germany, such as Licht and Nerlinger (1997).

2 For a detailed discussion of the *Standortkrise* in Germany, see Audretsch (1999a).

3 "Where's the Venture Capital?" *Newsweek*, October 31, 1994, p 44.

4 "Those German Banks and their Industrial Treasures," *The Economist*, January 21, 1995, pp. 77–8.

5 *Der Spiegel*, number 5, 1994, pp. 82–3.

6 For a detailed analysis of the share of economic activity accounted for by small firms and how this has evolved over time, see Schwalbach (1989, 1990, 1994), Stockmann and Leicht (1994) and Fritsch (1997).

7 For a similar analysis of the former East Germany, see Bannasch (1990, 1993) and Prantl (1997).

8 For a detailed analysis, see Weigand (1996), Manz (1990), Picot et al. (1989) and the studies contained in Meyer-Krahmer (1993).

9 "German Innovation: No Bubbling Brook," *The Economist*, September 10, 1994, pp. 75–6.

10 "Out of Service," *The Economist*, February 4, 1995, pp. 63–4.

11 Ibid.

12 For an analysis of the five new *Länder*, see Steil (1997).

13 For an extension of this study that controls specifically for the detailed disaggregated industry, see Audretsch and Fritsch (forthcoming).

14 Similar evidence is provided by Fritsch (1997).

15 "Suddenly, Germans Love to Hate their Banks: Anger over Bank Control of Industry May Reshape the Economy," *Business Week*, February 20, 1995, p. 42.

16 The studies contained in Becher and Kuhlman (1995) provide an excellent overview of the specific technology policy programs in Germany and their impact on SMEs. See, in particular, Kuntze and Hornschild (1995).

17 Additional analyses of German innovation centers can be found in Baranowski and Gross (1996). The advantages of locating within close regional proximity of knowledge resources in Germany is analyzed in Berger and Nerlingner (1997).

References

ADT (Arbeitsgemeinschaft Deutscher Technologie- und Gründerzentren e.V., *Berlin*). 1998. *Ausgründungen technologieorientierter Unternehmen aus Hochschulen und ausseruniversiteren Forschungseinrichtungen (Technology Spinoffs from Universities and Research Institutions)*. Report prepared for the Bundesministerium für Bildung, Wissenschaft, Forschung und Technologie, May.

Almus, M. and Nerlinger, E. 1998a. *Beschäftigungsdynamik in jungen innovativen Unternehmen: Ergebnisse für West-Deutschland (Employment Dynamics in Young, Innovative Firms: Evidence for West Germany)*. Discussion Paper No. 98–09, Zentrum für Europäische Wirtschaftsforschung (ZEW), Mannheim, Germany.

Almus, M. and Nerlinger, E. 1998b. Growth determinants of new technology-based firms: Empirical results for West-Germany. Unpublished manuscript, Centre for European Economic Research (ZEW), Mannheim, Germany.

Audretsch, D.B. 1995. *Innovation and Industry Evolution*. Cambridge: MIT Press.

Audretsch, D.B. 1999a. Creating Jobs in Germany, *Wall Street Journal*, January 12.

Audretsch, D.B. 1999b. Mittelstandspolitik, Neugründungen, und der Standortkrise (Policies toward SMEs, New Firms and the Competitiveness Crisis). In P. Welfens (ed.), *Economic Globalization, Innovation Dynamics and Labor Markets*. Heidelberg: Springer Verlag.

Audretsch, D.B. and Elston, J.A. 1994. *Does Firm Size Matter? Evidence on the Impacts of Liquidity Constraints on Investment Behaviour in Germany*. Centre for Economic Policy Research Discussion Paper No. 1072, London.

Audretsch, D.B. and Elston, J.A. 1997. Financing the German Mittlelstand. *Small Business Economics* 9(2): 97–110.

Audretsch, D.B. and Fritsch, M. 1993. *Betriebliche Turbulenz und regionale Beschätigungsdynamik (Business Turbulence and Regional Employment Dynamics)*. Discussion Paper 93/7, Bergakademie Freiberg.

Audretsch, D.B. and Fritsch, M. 1994. The geography of firm births in Germany. *Regional Studies* 28(4): 359–65.

Audretsch, D.B. and Fritsch, M. 1996. Creative destruction: Turbulence and economic growth in Germany. In E. Helmstaedter and M. Perlman (eds.), *Behavioral Norms, Technological Progress, and Economic Dynamics*. Ann Arbor: University of Michigan Press, pp. 137–50.

Audretsch, D.B. and Fritsch, M. (forthcoming). The geographic and industry components of new firm startups in Germany. *Review of Industrial Organization*.

Bannasch, H.G. 1990. The role of small firms in East Germany. *Small Business Economics* 2(4): 307–12.

Bannasch, H.G. 1993 The evolution of small business in East Germany. In Z.J. Acs and D.B. Audretsch (eds.), *Small Firms and Entrepreneurship: An East–West Perspective*. Cambridge: Cambridge University Press, pp. 55–77, 182–9.

Baranowski, G. and Gross, B. (eds.). 1996. *Innovationszentren in Deutschland* (Innovation Centers in German) *1996/97*. Berlin: Weidler.

Becher, G. and Wolff, H. 1995. Evaluation of the promotion of R&D cooperations of small and medium sized enterprises. In G. Becher and S. Kuhlmann (eds.), *Evaluation of Technology Policy Programmes in Germany*. Boston: Kluwer Academic Publishers, pp. 55–80.

Becher, G. and Kuhlmann S. (eds.), 1995. *Evaluation of Technology Policy Programmes in Germany*. Boston: Kluwer Academic Publishers.

Beise, M. and Licht, G. 1996. Innovationsverhalten der deutschen Wirtschaft (Innovation Behavior in the German Economy). Unpublished manuscript, Zentrum für Europäische Wirtschaftsforschung (ZEW), Mannheim, January.

Berger, G. and Nerlinger, E. 1997. Regionale Verteilung von Unternehmensgründungen in der Informationstechnik: Empirische Ergebnisse für Westdeutschland (Regional Distribution of New Firm Startups in Information Technology: Empirical Evidence for Germany). In D. Harhoff (ed.), *Unternehmensgründungen: Empirische Analysen für die alten und neuen Bundesländer (New Firm Startups: Empirical Evidence for the Old and New German States)*. Baden-Baden: Nomos, pp. 151–86.

Berger, J., Domeyer, V. and Funder, M. (eds.). 1990. *Kleinbetriebe im wirtschaftlichen Wandel (Small Business in Economic Transition)*. Berlin: Campus.

BMBF (Bundesministerium für Bildung und Forschung). 1996. *Bundesbericht Forschung 1996 (German Report on Research 1996)*. Bonn.

Boegenhold, D. 1985. *Die Selbstaendigen (The Self-Employed)*. New York: Springer.

Bruderl, J. and Preisendoerfer, P. 1998. Network support and the success of newly founded businesses. *Small Business Economics* 10(3): 213–25.

Burgel, O., Murray, G., Fier, A., Licht, G. and Nerlinger, E. 1998. The internationalisation of British and German start-up companies in high-technology industries. Unpublished manuscript, Zentrum für Europäische Wirtschaftsforschung (ZEW), Mannheim, Germany.

Deeg, R. 1998. What makes German banks different? *Small Business Economics* 10(2): 93–101.

Deutsche Bundesbank. 1992. Langfristige Entwicklung der Finanzierungsstrukturen westdeutscher Unternehmen (Long-Rung Trends in Financial Structures of West German Firms). *Monatsberichte der Deutschen Bundesbank* 10: 25–39.

Egeln, J., Licht, G. and Steil, F. 1997. Firm foundations and the role of financial constraints. *Small Business Economics* 9(2): 137–50.

Felder, J., Fier, A. and Nerlinger, E. 1997. Im Osten nichts Neues? Unternehmensgründungen in High-Tech-Industrien (All Quiet on the Eastern Front). In D. Harhoff (ed.), *Unternehmensgründungen:*

Empirische Analysen für die alten und neuen Bundesländer (*New Firm Startups: Empirical Evidence for the Old and New German States*). Baden-Baden: Nomos, pp. 73–110.

Feldman, M.P. and Pfirrmann, O. 1998. Bio-entrepreneurship in the US and Germany. Unpublished manuscript.

Fritsch, M. 1993 The role of small firms in West Germany. In Z.J. Acs and D.B. Audretsch (eds.), *Small Firms and Entrepreneurship: An East–West Perspective*. Cambridge: Cambridge University Press, pp. 55–77.

Fritsch, M. 1997. New firms and regional employment change. *Small Business Economics* 9(5): 437–48.

Fritsch, M. and Audretsch, D.B. 1995. Betriebliche Turbulenz und regionale Beschäftigungsdynamik (Business Turbulence and Regional Employment Dynamics). In K. Semlinger and B. Frick (eds.), *Betriebliche Modernisierung in personeller Erneuerung* (*Contemporary Business Modernization*). Berlin: Sigma, pp. 59–74.

Haid, A. and Weigand, J. 1998. Corporate governance and the finance of R&D. Paper presented at the 25th European Association for Research in Industrial Economics (EARIE) Conference, Copenhagen.

Harhoff, D. (ed.). 1997. *Unternehmensgründungen: Empirische Analysen für die alten und neuen Bundesländer* (*New Firm Startups: Empirical Evidence for the Old and New German States*). Baden-Baden: Nomos.

Harhoff, D. and Licht, G. 1996. *Innovationsaktivitäten kleiner und mittlerer Unternehmen* (*Innovative Activities of SMEs*). Baden-Baden: Nomos.

Harhoff, D. and Steil, F. 1997. Die ZEW-Gründungspanels: Konzeptionelle Überlegungen und Analysepotential (The ZEW-Startup Panel: conceptual considerations and analytical potential). In D. Harhoff (ed.), *Unternehmensgründungen: Empirische Analysen für die alten und neuen Bundeslaender* (*New Firm Startups: Empirical Evidence for the Old and New German States*). Baden-Baden: Nomos, pp. 11–28.

Harhoff, D. and Stahl, K. 1997. Unternhemens- und Beschäftigungsdynamik in Westdeutschland: Zum Einfluss von Haftungsregeln und Eigentümerstruktur (Firm and employment dynamics in West Germany: the influence of ownership structure). In K.H. Oppenlaender (ed.), *Industrieökonomik und Finanzmärkte* (*Industrial Organization and Financial Markets*) ifo Studien, 41, 17–50.

Klandt, H. 1984. *Aktivität und Erfolg des Unternehmungsgründers* (*Activity and Success of Entrepreneurs*). Bonn: Bergisch Gladbach.

Klandt, H. 1996. Gründerpersönlichkeit und Unternehmenserfolg (Entrepreneurial Personality and Firm Success). In BMWi (ed.), *Chancen und Risiken der Existenzgründung* (*Chance and Risks for New Firm Startups*). BMWi-Dokumentation Nr. 392, Bonn.

Kulicke, M. 1987. *Technologieorienteierte Unternehmen in der Bundesrepublik Deutschland: Eine empirische Untersuchung der Strukturbildungs- und Wachstumsphase von Neugründungen* (*Technology-Oriented Firms in the Federal Republic of Germany*). Frankfurt.

Kuntze, U. and Hornschild, K. 1995. Evaluation of the Promotion of R&D Activities in Small and Medium Sized Enterprises. In G. Becher and S. Kuhlmann (eds.), *Evaluation of Technology Policy Programmes in Germany*. Boston: Kluwer Academic, pp. 33–54.

Licht, G. and Nerlinger,E. 1997. Junge innovative Unternehmen in Europa: Ein internationaler Vergleich (Young Innovative Firms in Europe: An International Comparison). In D. Harhoff (ed.), *Unternehmensgründungen: Empirische Analysen für die alten und neuen Bundesländer* (*New Firm Startups: Empirical Evidence for the Old and New German States*). Baden-Baden: Nomos, pp. 187–208.

Licht, G., Nerlinger, E. and Berger, G. 1995. *Germany: NTBF Literature Review*. Zentrum für Europäische Wirtschaftsforschung (ZEW), Mannheim.

Loveman, G. and Sengenberger, W. 1991. The re-emergence of small-scale production: an international comparison. *Small Business Economics* 3(1): 1–38.

Manz, T. 1990. *Innovationsprozesse in Klein- und Mittelbetrieben* (*Innovation Process in SMEs*). Cologne: Westdeutscher Verlag.

Meyer-Krahmer, F. (ed.). 1993. *Innovationsökonomie und Technologiepolitik* (*Innovation Economics and Technology Policy*). Heidelberg: Physica-Verlag.

Mugler, J. 1995. *Betriebswirtschaftslehre der Klein- und Mittelbetriebe* (*Managing SMEs*), 2nd edn. Vienna: Springer-Verlag.

Nerlinger, E. 1998. *Standorte und Entwicklung junger innovativer Unternehmen: Empirische Ergebnisse für West-Deutschland* (*Location and Development of Young, Innovative Firms: Empirical Evidence for West Germany*). Baden-Baden: Nomos.

Pfirrmann, O. 1994. The geography of innovation in small and medium-sized firms in West Germany. *Small Business Economics* 6(1): 27–41.

Pfirrmann, O., Wupperfeld, U. and Lerner, J.1997. *Venture Capital and New Technology Based Firms: A US-German Comparison*. Berlin: Physica-Verlag.

Picot, A., Laub, U.D. and Scheider, D. 1989. *Innovative Unternehmensgründungen: Eine ökonomisch-empirische Analyse* (*Innovative New Firm Startups: An Empirical Economic Analysis*). Berlin: Springer Verlag.

Prantl, S. 1997. Unternehmsselektion in Ostdeutschland: Eine empirische Analyse von Neugründungen und Transformationsunternehmen (Firm selection in East Germany: an empirical analysis of new firm startups in the transformation firms). In D. Harhoff (ed.), *Unternehmensgründungen: Empirische Analysen für die alten und neuen Bundesländer* (*New Firm Startups: Empirical Evidence for Old and New German States*). Baden-Baden: Nomos, pp. 110–50.

Schumpeter, J.A. 1911. *Theorie der wirtschaftlichen Entwicklung. Eine Untersuchung über Unternehmergewinn, Kapital, Kredit, Zins und den Konjunkturzyklus* (*Theory of Economic Development: An Investigation of Firm Profits, Capital, Loans, Interest and the Business Cycle*). Berlin: Duncker und Humblot.

Schwalbach, J. 1989. Small business in German manufacturing. *Small Business Economics* 1(2): 129–36.

Schwalbach, J. 1990. Small business in German manufacturing. In Z.J. Acs and D.B. Audretsch (eds.), *The Economics of Small Firms: A European Challenge*. Boston: Kluwer Academic, pp. 63–73.

Schwalbach, J. 1994. Small business dynamics in Europe. *Small Business Economics* 6(1): 21–6.

Simon, H. 1992. Lessons from Germany's midsize giants. *Harvard Business Review* March–April, pp. 115–23.

Stahl, K. 1991. Das Mannheimer Unternehmenspanel: Konzept und Entwicklung (The Mannheim Firm Panel: concepts and development). *Mitteilungen aus der Arbeitsmarkt- und Berufungsforschung* 29: 738–58.

Steil, F. 1997. Unternehmensgründungen in Ostdeutschland (New firm startups in East Germany). In D. Harhoff (ed.), *Unternehmensgründungen: Empirische Analysen für die alten und neuen Bundesländer* (*New Firm Startups: Empirical Evidence in the Old and New German States*). Baden-Baden: Nomos, pp. 29–72.

Sternberg, R. 1990. The impact of Innovation Centres on small technology-based firms: the example of the Federal Republic of Germany. *Small Business Economics* 2(2): 105–18.

Sternberg, R. 1996. Technology policies and the growth of regions: evidence from four countries. *Small Business Economics* 8(2): 75–86.

Stockmann, R. and Leicht, R. 1994. The pattern of changes in the long-term development of establishment size. *Small Business Economics* 6(6): 451–64.

Vitols, S. 1998. Are German banks different? *Small Business Economics* 10(2): 79–91.

Wagner, J. 1992. Firm size, firm growth, and persistence of chance: testing Gibrat's law with establishment data from Lower Saxony, 1978-1989. *Small Business Economics* 4(2): 125–31.

Wagner, J. 1994. Small firm entry in manufacturing industries: Lower Saxony, 1979–1989. *Small Business Economics* 6(3): 211–24.

Wagner, J. 1995a. Exports, firm size, and firm dynamics. *Small Business Economics* 7(1): 29–40.

Wagner, J. 1995b, Firm size and job creation in Germany. *Small Business Economics* 7(6): 469–74.

Wagner, J. 1997. Firm size and job quality. A survey of the evidence from Germany. *Small Business*

Economics 9(5): 411–25.

Wagner, J. (forthcoming). The life history of cohorts of exits from German manufacturing. *Small Business Economics*.

Weigand, C. 1998. *Der Einfluss der Bankkreditvergabe auf den Unternehmenswettbewerb (The Influence of Bank Credit on Firm Competition)*. Hamburg: Verlag Dr. Kovac.

Weigand, J. 1996. *Innovationen, Wettbewerb und Konjunktur (Innovation, Competition and Competitiveness)*. Berlin: Duncker & Humblot.

Weigand, J. and Audretsch, D.B. 1999. *Does Science Make a Difference? Investment, Finance and Corporate Governance in German Industries*. Institute for Development Strategies Discussion Paper 99–1. Bloomington: Indiana University.

Weigand, J. and Lehmann, E. 1998. *Does the Governed Corporation Perform Better?* Institute for Development Strategies Discussion Paper 98–2, Indiana University.

7

Regulatory Policies and Their Impact on SMEs in Europe: the Case of Administrative Burdens

ROBERT VAN DER HORST, ANDRE NIJSEN AND SELCUK GULHAN

SMEs IN EUROPE
REGULATORY POLICIES
ADMINISTRATIVE BURDENS
POLICIES REDUCING ADMINISTRATIVE BURDENS ON ENTERPRISES
CONCLUSIONS AND RECOMMENDATIONS

Following World War II, ambitious economic and social policies were legitimized by the widespread belief that governments would be able to control the economy and businesses by manipulating key macroeconomic variables and, at the same time, ensure social justice and equality in the distribution of wealth. As a consequence, the complexity and number of policies aimed to meet this challenge and regulate the market increased considerably. This was accompanied by a rapid increase in the number and scope of legislative policies. Both the quality and the quantity of such policies began to have their effects on the functioning of the economy. In particular, the regulation of business became a major objective and feature for policymakers.

Although most regulatory policies have benefits for both the business sector and society as a whole, they also have financial consequences for the business sector. The subsequent expansion of government's role, especially in economic issues, led to the business community complaining more and more about the adverse effects of having to deal with this intervention in the form of imposing and executing such regulatory policies. These often resulted in heavy financial burdens for enterprises. Toward the end of the 1970s and the early 1980s the governments of industrialized countries became aware of the unanticipated cost of their policies and actions.

European integration, which continues to gain momentum as the European market grows ever closer, adds another important factor to government regulation and its effect on the business environment. The European business sector affected most is that of the small and medium-sized enterprises (SMEs), even though this sector is considered crucial in enhancing Europe's economic strength. To be able to regulate the market and the well-being of society, the authorities involved require individual citizens, groups, institutions and, of course, businesses to collect, analyze, retain and report information about their activities and operations. The government requires a constant flow of data and information to be able to formulate public policies. Consequently, enterprises have to report to the government at regular intervals information about their business, e.g., annual accounts, Value Added Tax (VAT) and statistical data. As the quantity and frequency of governmental regulations have increased, so has the burden placed on enterprises that are obliged to transfer this information to the relevant regulatory agencies. This burden has proved to weigh more heavily on SMEs, for example, because of their size, number of specialized or unskilled employees and turnover, as compared with larger firms operating in the market.[1]

This chapter aims to provide some insights about the costs and burdens imposed by regulatory policies on the functioning and operations of businesses, particularly those in the European market. We attempt to illustrate the administrative burdens that have mainly indirect financial effects or compliance costs – the consequence of the obligatory transfer of information from the enterprises to the European Union (EU) regulatory agencies.

It is no simple matter to present an overview of what the administrative costs are for European SMEs; however, based on very rough calculations and limited research findings, these annual costs were estimated to be between 180 and 230 billion ECU in 1995, or between 3 and 4 percent of Europe's GDP (ENSR 1995).

SMEs in Europe are still experiencing great difficulties in complying with the policies intended to regulate business performance. National authorities, on one hand, and Brussels, on the other, impose significant financial and administrative burdens on SMEs, making their struggle to survive in the market even more difficult.

This fact has led both the EU and its member states to pay special attention to SMEs during their growth and development. This is done either by reviewing and reformulating policies or by taking steps to create a suitable environment in which SMEs can realize their full potential.

SMEs IN EUROPE

In 1997, the number of enterprises in the nonprimary private sector grew to over 19.5 million. Employment, on the other hand, declined to 115.5 million persons. The vast majority of enterprises can be classified as SMEs. Even if all large enterprises are included, a European company on average provides employment for only six workers (ENSR 1997). Employment in the SME sector is about 65.7 percent of the total nonprimary private enterprise employment. The average European enterprise has a turnover of 800,000 ECU. Labor productivity increases with enterprise size, varying between 30,000 ECU in very small enterprises and 55,000 ECU in large enterprises. Table 7.1 shows some main indicators of nonprimary private SMEs in Europe.

SMEs are concentrated in construction, distribution, most service sectors (e.g., banking, tourism, insurance and transport) and also some manufacturing industries. Compared with large enterprises, SMEs have resource constraints of time, money and personnel. In other words, they have a limited amount of available financial means and

TABLE 7.1 Main indicators of nonprimary private enterprise, Europe, 1997

		Micro enterprises	Small enterprises	Medium enterprises	Total
Number of enterprise	EU	17,710	1,125	165	19,000
(1,000)	Non-EU	420	45	10	475
	Total	18,130	1,170	175	19,475
Number of employees	EU	37,200	21,140	15,110	73,450
(1,000)	Non-EU	970	810	760	2,540
	Total	38,170	21,950	15,870	75,990
Average size enterprise	EU	2	20	90	
(million ECU)	Non-EU	2	20	95	
	Total	2	20	90	
Turnover per enterprise	EU	0.2	3.0	16.0	
million (ECU)	Non-EU	0.3	3.0	16.0	
	Total	0.2	3.0	16.0	
Value added per occupied	EU	30	40	50	
person (1,000 ECU)	Non-EU	45	40	45	
	Total	30	40	50	
Share of labor costs in	EU	38	63	60	
value added %	Non-Eu	43	68	66	
	Total	38	63	60	

Because of rounding, no average enterprise size can be devised from the data on employment and the number of enterprises.

Source: Estimated by EIM Small Business Research and Consultancy; adapted from Eurostat/ DG XXIII: Enterprises in Europe, Fifth Report, Brussels/Luxembourg

a small management team. Their enterprise does not include staff functions. Moreover, SME employees have on average a lower educational level compared with larger enterprises. In other words, there tends to be a lack of expertise and expert knowledge. Most of the time, several functions and duties are performed by the same person.

Defining SMEs

Making an all-encompassing definition for SMEs in the EU is difficult because each member state adopts and uses different standards and criteria in defining their SME sector. For example, a particular enterprise may be described as "small" when compared with a "larger" enterprise in another member state and vice versa. The common criteria for defining SMEs are basically the number of employees, the volume of sales, the value of assets, the insurance in force (for insurance companies) and the volume of deposits (for banks). But to avoid a complexity of different definitions for SMEs in different member states, we simply refer to the more general approach used by the EU. The European Commission has adopted a recommendation concerning the definition of SMEs that now provides a clear general framework for all the measures apply to microenterprises and SMEs (*Office Journal of the European Communities* 1996), as shown in table 7.2.

TABLE 7.2 The European Commission's recommendation for defining SMEs

	Micro enterprises	*Small enterprises*	*Medium enterprises*
Number of employees	0–9	10–49	50–249
Max. turnover (million ECU)	40	7	–
Max. balance-sheet total (million ECU)	27	–	–

To be classified as an SME, a business has to satisfy the criteria for the number of employees and one of two financial criteria, i.e., either the turnover total or the balance sheet total. In addition, it must be independent, which means less than 25 percent owned by one enterprise (or jointly by several enterprises) falling outside the definition of an SME. The thresholds for the turnover and the balance sheet total will be adjusted regularly to take account of changing economic circumstances in Europe.

The Single European Act (SEA) has legally created a Union of Western European countries, allowing the free movement of goods, services, capital and labor. One of the major aims of this Union is to develop the economic potential of Europe to allow it to compete as a world power with other economic powers and blocs. SMEs are recognized as an important aspect of this potential. In particular, smaller firms have become a major source of job creation. The SME sector is considered crucial to European competitive development and to its becoming a leading economic power in the world. SMEs are vital to enhancing Europe's competitiveness and its economic growth and strength. It is widely accepted that European SMEs, because of their easier adaptation to changing situations, flexibility, dynamism and innovation, as well as being the main source of employment, will be the driving force if Europe is to keep pace with the challenges of the ever-increasing globalization of the world economy. However, the importance of the entrepreneur and SMEs tended to be underestimated in the postwar growth of industrialized countries.

REGULATORY POLICIES

The postwar era paved the way for governments or state agencies to become the primary force in driving the economy and social institutions. Governments intervened in almost all aspects of society – social, political and economic. Over the years government has come to play an increasingly important role in the socioeconomic sphere. Allocation of resources, distribution of income and stabilization of such macroeconomic aspects as employment, health, safety and housing were all absorbed as the main functions of the state. There were always economic and noneconomic justifications for regulating the market and performing regulatory policies by governments. Governments claim that overcoming possible market failures is the crucial reason or logic behind the regulation of business activities and the market as a whole.

The regulation of economic activity, through regulatory policies, became one of the primary tasks of government. Some policies and programs are focused on particular industries and sectors, others cut across industry and sectors and deal with functional areas, such as collective bargaining, environmental pollution, competitive practices and social welfare. Regulation makes rules while regulatory policies implement and safeguard the rules being applied. These policies have different forms and substance, different implications and aspects. Some are just vague statements; others are narrowly defined in great detail; still others are general and sweeping in scope. Surely it is not to anyone's advantage if the policies are so complicated that nobody can understand them.

Effects of policies on the business environment

The scope of regulatory policies have an important effect on the activities and perform-ances of the businesses and the business environment as a whole. Beginning from the establishment of an enterprise and during its growth and performance, businesses experience the positive and negative effects of regulatory policies. First of all, they have a determining effect on the decision whether to go into business. A license is often required before one can enter a certain business, and the qualifications needed to obtain one, as well as the conditions that are attached to it, are determined by regulatory policies. Secondly, the location of the enterprise is another regulated aspect. Where to locate a business is not a decision that can be made without reference to rules. Environmental issues have come to play a determining role. Regulatory policies on environmental and zoning matters have a significant influence on where businesses are established. Companies whose operations involve a substantial amount of air or water pollution may find it difficult to locate in areas where rules set strict limits on new sources of pollution.

Once the decision to go into business has been made and a location selected, human resource issues and personnel policies must be resolved. What a new business produces and how that product is made are also governed by a multiplicity of rules, some designed to protect workers, others to protect consumers and still others to protect the environ-ment. Industrial operations are mainly constrained by regulatory policies designed to ensure safety in the workplace and to prevent, or at least to minimize, air, water and soil pollution. These policies specify the types of equipment that may or may not be used and how the machinery is to be designed or operated.

Moreover, once the business has a product to sell, regulatory policies determine how it will be sold, how it will be distributed, the price charged for the goods or service and the company obligations after the product is sold. Policies also govern what information is provided on labels and packaging inserts, informing the public about the content, purpose and potential dangers of the product. The result is that SMEs must rely heavily on attorneys, accountants and other compliance professionals and consultants to avoid a heavy administrative burden. Compared with large enterprises, SMEs are more affected by such regulatory policies because they do not have the necessary time, money and expertise to overcome the adverse effects of the regulatory policies.

Generally speaking, we may classify the impact of regulatory policies on the enterprises as having primary or secondary effects (Kellerman and Azzi 1998: 265), as shown in figure 7.1. Primary effects include direct costs like taxes as well as indirect costs for compliance. Secondary effects are influenced by the functioning of markets (e.g., competitiveness) and socioeconomic or macroeconomic changes (e.g., economic growth and employment).

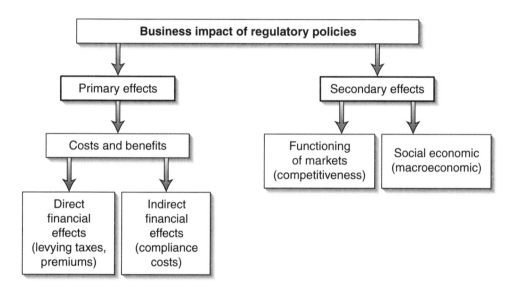

FIGURE 7.1 Types of business impacts of regulatory policies

The European Union case

The EU is a collection of fifteen sovereign nation-states united to cooperate with each other on a voluntary basis for mutual benefit. Member states have voluntarily transferred part of their sovereign rights and means to EU institutions (e.g., the European Council of Ministers, the European Commission and the European Parliament). This results in their business environments being subject to and affected by both national and EU regulations. Eventually, this may lead to many contradictory and overlapping regulations and policies. The influence of European Community regulatory policy in particular is increasingly evident as the European internal market program gathers momentum.

The EU has its own special legal status and extensive powers to make legislation that affects member states, their citizens and businesses. EU legislation primarily involves economic matters, and over the years, the volume of legislation has broadened considerably. For example, environmental issues have considerably expanded. After the Single European Act (SEA) came into force, the EU emerged as a supranational regulatory state. The European Commission is the chief administrative and regulatory body of the EU. As Majone states in the *Journal of Common Market Studies* (34(1): 40), "The costs of regulation are borne directly by the firms and individuals who have to comply with them. Compared with these costs, the resources needed to produce the regulations are negligible."

This simply means that the regulatory framework created by EU institutions creates costs related to rule-making per se – not just to the administration of these rules. But another side must also be considered. Most large firms, especially multinationals, tend to request legislation to avoid the cost of meeting different and often inconsistent national standards and also to avoid the risk of progressively more stringent regulations in other member states. Take, for example, EU Directive 79/831 that amends for the sixth time EU Directive 67/548 on the classification, packaging and labeling of dangerous substances (Grandomenico 1996). The 1979 directive does not prevent member states from including more substances within the scope of national regulations than are required by the European directive itself.

In fact, the British Health and Safety Commission proposed to go further than the directive by bringing intermediate products within the scope of national regulations. This however, was opposed by the chemical industry, which argued that national regulations should not impose greater burdens on British industry than the directive placed on its competitors. Industry's view prevailed, thus ensuring that the European Community regulation would, in fact, set the maximum as well as the minimum standard for national regulation. German firms, concerned about environmentally conscious public opinion at home and wishing to avoid the commercial obstacles that would arise from divergent national regulations, also pressed the European Community for regulation of toxic substances. Environmentalists and consumer-protection groups are also demanding European-wide legislation. But by far the most important source of demand is from the member states themselves for several reasons:

- ◆ to minimize the cost of legal and administrative compliance with new European Community rules and policies,
- ◆ to give a competitive advantage to national industries already familiar with and adjusted to existing regulatory policies, and
- ◆ to reduce the cost advantages of countries with lower levels of protection by forcing all member states to adopt the same regulatory standards and policies.

The aim of greater legal simplicity and fiscal standardization for European SMEs has not yet been achieved. Many of the measures being taken to achieve the single internal market, such as the standardization of business laws, the simplification of border formalities and the harmonization of technical standards, have affected the day-to-day operations of EU enterprises.

Moreover, the new European legislation has created additional administrative burdens on enterprises, even though the aim was to reduce and simplify existing legislation. Adapting to the newly created laws and regulations and their administrative complexity can be seen as the two types of newly created burdens on SMEs in Europe.

ADMINISTRATIVE BURDENS

Administrative burdens on enterprises due to legislation is receiving more and more attention. Both at the EU level and national level, the importance of reducing or minimizing administrative burdens as much as possible has long been recognized. All enterprises have their own administrative procedures when undertaking their activities.

Figure 7.2 illustrates the framework of a theoretical procedure. Administrative burdens arise mainly from the administrative procedures that SMEs are obliged by law to carry out, which no enterprise would perform if no legislation existed (5). Administrative burdens are the outcome of compliance costs and benefits. Those compliance costs and benefits may be distinguished as either costs that are expended as a result of legislation or costs that would be expended even if not required because of regulations.

As for (1) in figure 7.2, administrative burdens of enterprises and the cost of enforcing administration are all costs for information transfer from enterprises to enforcing organizations (e.g., tax authorities) and vice versa, as required by law. Included are start-up costs for new or changing regulations and structural costs (on a yearly basis). Also included are the cost of education, staff training, equipment such as computers and outsourcing of administrative proceedings.

As for (2) in figure 7.2, other compliance costs or benefits are mostly the result of changes in products or production processes.

Perception of administrative burdens by SMEs

In several EU countries entrepreneurs share the opinion that administrative obligations cause problems and are time-consuming and costly. The most common complaints are the complexity of, number of and the frequent changes to the forms and reports they are

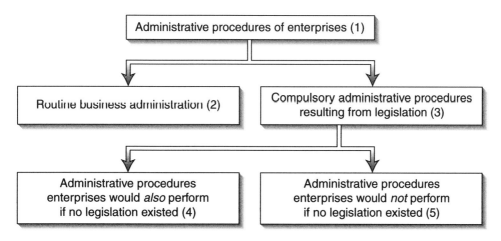

FIGURE 7.2 Theoretical framework of types of administrative procedures for enterprises
Source: ENSR (1995: 277)

required to file. The perception of entrepreneurs of administrative burdens is closely connected to the extent that the companies are informed about the usefulness of the information submitted.

Other criticisms concern the quality of the services provided by administrators and include the long processing times, the delays related to the procedures, the lack of commercial or industrial experience among officials at state agencies, the lack of transparency of administrative procedures and the poor performance of public services. The reporting procedures to the national statistical institutions are considered particularly costly and time-consuming. The penalty system is also criticized, particularly because enterprises are subject to penalties even if they are not familiar with or do not understand the rules and regulations.

Measuring administrative burdens

Administrative burdens can be measured in terms of the time they take, the number of forms that must be completed, the number of obligations that must be met and the financial costs to the enterprise. In terms of financial costs, administrative burdens consist of the labor costs of employees involved in obtaining the information necessary to fulfill the legislative obligations, the costs of training and educating these employees, the labor costs of self-employed who do their own administration, the costs of equipment like computers used to meet the legislative obligations and the cost of external consultants for advice and assistance. Some of these costs are hidden, e.g., the costs of the self-employed who do their own administration or the cost of government and private consultants, both of which are difficult to estimate.

Because of these inherent hidden costs, it is difficult to assess exactly what the administrative burdens are or how many burdens there are. However, it is very useful to know which administrative procedures are carried out by SMEs (see figure 7.2). Administrative procedures that are part of the regular business activities and those that are a result of government-imposed legislation are often intermingled.

The costs of administrative burdens

Based on the information available for the Netherlands, a rough calculation has been made to obtain an indication of the total costs of administrative burdens on enterprises in Europe. This calculation is based on the number of enterprises in Europe by sector and size class as well as the average cost of administrative burdens by firm size and sector in the Netherlands. Because these average costs depend on the time spent on administrative procedures and labor (and other) costs per hour, a correction has been used in averaging costs per firm for the differences in labor costs between the countries. Based on this information, the annual costs of administrative burdens on European enterprises is estimated at between 180 and 230 billion ECU,[2] which is between 3 and 4 percent of Europe's GDP.[3]

In 1993, research was conducted in the Netherlands to determine the administrative burdens on enterprises. The results can be summarized as follows:

◆ The total costs of administrative procedures for enterprises in the Netherlands are estimated at 16.5 billion ECU in 1993.

TABLE 7.3 Estimates of the annual costs of administrative burdens for enterprises in some European countries (in million ECU)

Country	Total cost
Finland (1994)	843
The Netherlands (1993)	6,100
Norway (1991)	838–1,700

Source: ENSR (1995)

- Sixty-three percent of these costs (10.4 billion ECU) resulted from routine business administration. The remainder (37 percent or 6.1 billion ECU) are compulsory and result from legislation.
- Forty-one percent of these administrative burdens (2.5 billion ECU) are associated with procedures that firms would also carry out if no legislation existed. So 59 percent of administrative costs (3.6 billion ECU) are connected to procedures that firms would avoid if no legislation existed.

Table 7.3 provides an overview of the cost of administrative burdens for enterprises in Finland, the Netherlands and Norway, which are estimated to be between 1 and 3 percent of their GDP. Estimating the cost of administrative burdens on enterprises in different countries is difficult because the cost has not been determined in all EU member states, and the findings are often not comparable because of the lack of studies on administrative burdens or similar measurements of them in various countries.

Administrative burdens and types of legislation by policy area
Which legislative or policy areas place administrative burdens on enterprises? Table 7.4 illustrates some of them. Obligations arising from the policy areas are classified in two groups: (1) those associated with being an enterprise and (2) those associated with having employees.

Legislation completely based on EU laws include VAT and excise duties related to imports, exports and transportation. Considerable European legislation exists in five areas: annual accounts, environmental legislation, statistical information, employment contracts and working conditions. Annual accounts are largely based on three European directives:

- environmental legislation, e.g., emission standards and waste processing,
- statistical information for national statistical offices, and
- employment contracts and employee participation.

EU legislation has impacts in the areas of corporate tax, taxes on dividends and revenue taxes. European directives concerning corporation tax, e.g., relate to the fiscal consequences of mergers from different member states. Other taxes include the European tax treaty and legislation dealing with tax on dividends and revenue. European legislation related to income tax and social premiums is almost nonexistent. Attempts are being

TABLE 7.4 The amount of European legislation in various policy areas

Policy area	None	Few	Many	All
Obligations associated with being an enterprise				
Corporate tax, tax dividends revenue tax		X		
VAT and excise duty				X
Annual Accounts		X		
Environmental legislation			X	
Community levies	X			
Operating licenses		X		
Statistical information			X	
Import/export, transport etc.				X
Obligations associated with having employees				
Levying income tax and social premiums		X		
Prevention of absenteeism due to illness	X			
Quota regulations	X			
Employment contract, employee participation			X	
Working condition			X	

Source: ENSR (1995: 282)

made to standardize direct taxes. Taxes on capital have already been standardized and based on European directives. European legislation is only limited in the areas of operating licenses (needed for running a business).

In the remaining three areas – community levies, safety regulations and quotas targeting special groups (such as women, the handicapped and immigrants) – no European legislation exists. Quotas are not dealt with in European directives but through the European Social Fund. Not every member state has collective agreements in the area of employee contracts and employee participation. Some European directives have been adopted, and others are in preparation in relation to employment participation.

Because of the lack of specific research in most European countries, only rough information about the administrative burdens by legislative area in different countries can be determined. The main conclusion can be stated as:

- ◆ Obligations that result from being an enterprise cause more administrative burdens than obligations that result from having employees. Research in Germany shows that the obligations on being an enterprise create about 56 percent of all administrative burdens, while 44 percent are caused by obligations arising out of having employees (Kitterer 1989). In the Netherlands these figures are estimated at 71 and 29 percent, respectively (EIM 1993).

- ◆ Of those administrative burdens applicable to all enterprises (or for being an enterprise), most arise from corporate tax, taxes on dividends, revenue taxes, the annual accounts requirements and VAT and excise levies. Fewer burdens originate from environmental legislation, operating licenses and community levies (local taxes). The order of these may differ by country, size and sector.
- ◆ Of those burdens applicable to enterprises with employees, income taxes and employee benefits cause the greatest administrative burdens. Quota regulations, the targeting of special groups and the prevention of absence through illness cause burdens on enterprises in most member states.

Administrative burdens by size class of enterprises
The administrative burdens on each enterprise and for each employee differ greatly between size classes. Table 7.5 shows the average costs of administrative burdens per size class in the Netherlands. According to the table, the cost of administrative burdens on each enterprise is higher for large enterprises than for smaller ones. The reason for this is that larger enterprises face more administrative obligations than smaller ones. In France, for example, enterprises with no employees receive on average twenty-five forms and compulsory statistical surveys each year, whereas enterprises with one to ten employees receive on average forty-six forms a year. Enterprises with a hundred or more employees receive some 560 forms.[4]

TABLE 7.5 Average costs of administrative burdens per size class, enterprise and employee in the Netherlands, 1993 (in ECU)

Number of employees	Cost per enterprise	Cost per employee
0	2,800	0
1–9	12,100	0
10–19	20,500	1,500
20–29	47,100	1,400
50–99	62,000	900
100 or more	171,000	600
All size classes	9,800	1,800

Source: EIM (1994)

Although the total cost of administrative burdens is, of course, higher in larger enterprises, the relative cost (cost per employee) is higher in small enterprises. Surveys and research carried out in Austria, France, Germany and Greece lead to the same conclusion (ENSR 1995).

Research in several countries (Belgium, Finland, Germany and the Netherlands) also shows that small enterprises make more use of external help to deal with the administrative obligations. Large enterprises usually deal with the administrative obligations within their own organization. In Germany, for example 46 percent of the total cost of administrative burdens in enterprises with fewer than ten employees were external costs. In enterprises with 1,000 to 5,000 employees, this was only 14 percent.[5]

One measure of the size of administrative burdens is the time that enterprises spend complying with their legal obligations. On average, an enterprise needs about 300 hours a year to deal with its administrative obligations.[6] The differences by size class are the same: large enterprises spend more time than small enterprises, but per employee, small enterprises need much more time.

Administrative burdens by sector

The size of the administrative burdens on each enterprise and employee also differ greatly between sectors. Using Germany as an example, table 7.6 shows that the costs per enterprise are highest in industry and lowest in trade and craft activities. It is important to note, however, that the average industrial enterprise is larger than trade and craft businesses. So if one takes the average cost per employee, then administrative burdens are felt most in the trades and crafts.

TABLE 7.6 The average costs of administrative obligations per sector, enterprise and employee in Germany, 1989 (in ECU)

Sector	Costs per enterprise	Costs per employee
Industry	20,900	140
Trade	8,700	350
Craft	9,700	350
Services	12,300	260
All sectors	11,300	250

Source: Kitterer, 1989; (see ENSR 1995: 288)

POLICIES REDUCING ADMINISTRATIVE BURDENS ON ENTERPRISES

Policies and measures at the national level

High unemployment rates and the need to achieve stable and sustainable economic growth have pushed national governments into making new developments in their SME policies. In addition, almost all EU member states have recognized the problem of administrative burdens on SMEs and have introduced measures to improve the administrative and regulatory environment. Most countries concentrate their efforts on the reduction of administrative burdens, the improvement of the financial environment, labor-related issues, internationalization and the enhancement of R&D and innovation. Their main objective is to develop a more favorable business environment for enterprises – an environment in which SMEs receive special attention. Initiatives are being taken to simplify administrative procedures, which includes the modification or abolishment of registering, licensing and merging outlets of authorities to "one-stop stops" (ENSR 1995: 191). In most of the countries improving the business environment also includes reforms of the tax system. Most governments choose to improve the effectiveness of existing measures instead of implementing new ones. Nevertheless, new programs have been established for this purpose (table 7.7). These new measure are implemented only when considered necessary and should be viewed as an extension of the existing SME policy frameworks.

Since there is no unilateral approach to SME policy in the EU, considerable SME-related differences between countries remain. Such differences might reflect specific socioeconomic conditions and/or the variety of approaches employed by individual countries to support, enhance and develop their SME sectors. On the other hand, the impact of administrative burdens on economic development and growth of SMEs obviously differs among the countries.

TABLE 7.7 Implemented and planned national actions by field and country, 1996–1997

	Business environment	Financial environment		Internationalization and information		Labor, training and innovation	
	Administrative burdens	Late payment	Finance	Internation- alization	Infor- mation	Labor	Innovation
Austria	X	—	X	X	—	X	X
Belgium	X	—	X	X	—	X	—
Denmark	X	—	X	X	X	X	X
Finland	X	—	X	X	X	X	X
France	X	X	X	X	X	X	X
Germany	X	—	X	X	X	—	X
Greece	—	—	X	X	X	X	X
Ireland	X	X	X	X	X	X	X
Italy	X	X	X	X	X	X	X
Luxembourg	X	—	X	X	—	X	X
The Netherlands	X	—	X	X	X	—	X
Portugal	X	—	X	X	X	X	X
Spain	X	—	X	X	X	X	X
Sweden	X	—	—	X	X	X	X
United Kingdom	X	X	—	—	X	X	X

Source: ENSR (1997)

Table 7.7 presents programs made by individual member states related to their SME sector. In this chapter the focus is on those designed improve the business environment. In general, the tools applied in almost all countries to improve the business environment for SMEs were (ENSR 1997):

◆ modification of existing regulations, e.g., licensing, reporting, shorter response periods and clearer language for forms,
◆ reduction of such regulatory requirements as licensing, reporting and permits, and
◆ modification of the tax system for more transparency, electronic filing and lower rates.

National policies aimed at improving the business environment consist mainly of simpli-fied administrative procedures, including the modification of existing administrative procedures, such as registering, licensing (Italy, the Netherlands, Portugal, Finland) and merging outlets into one-stop stops or concentrating contacts in one address (Belgium, Denmark, Finland, Portugal, the United Kingdom) or modifying or abolishing regula-tions. In this context, the Belgian government announced the modernization of its establishment law, aimed at setting standards, regrouping related professions with an emphasis on practical experience and new apprenticeship programs leading to an establishment license. The Belgian government is also considering a service to evaluate the impact of regulations and their corresponding costs.

Countries like Austria, Italy, Ireland, the United Kingdom, Sweden and France have been or currently are reducing the volume of regulations for SMEs. In Austria, a framework of business acts (*Gewebeordnung*) was modified in 1997 that reduced the number of trades subject to specific regulation from 153 to 84. In the United Kingdom, more than 1,000 regulations had been abolished by 1997. An additional 150 licensing laws are currently under review, and seventy have been targeted for repeal. Reduced accountancy reporting requirements have also been implemented since March 1997, affecting SMEs with a turnover of less than 490,000 ECU. In Italy and Ireland, similar modification cover SME accounting requirements. Reductions have been legislated in Italy, and Ireland has decided that the statutory audit requirement on private limited companies and cooperatives with an annual turnover of less than 134,000 ECU will be removed entirely. In Sweden, a committee investigating barriers to SME growth hopes to reduce them 25 percent. France is implementing reduced reporting requirement for statistical purpose by about 30 percent.

Furthermore, shortening administrative application and certification periods appears to be a common approach. France, for instance, introduced a three to six-month response deadline, according to which failure to comply automatically means that the application is accepted. In Italy, certain application formalities are now subject to an "automatic interven-tion system," with which under certain conditions, enterprises no longer need to comply. In a similar context, a radical cut has been introduced in the Netherlands where eighty-eight branch-specific licenses have now been replaced by eight (ENSR 1996: 245).

Most national policies discussed so far have aimed at improving the business environ-ment but have also included reforms and modifications of the existing tax system. Although still under current investigation in Germany and Italy, tax rate reductions favoring SMEs have been legislated in Ireland, Luxembourg and Spain. Other measures are geared toward simplifying tax reporting by enabling electronic declaration (Finland, France, Denmark and Sweden), reducing the number of forms (France and Spain) and simplifying their language and details (Ireland).

What has been achieved by these new measures and policies to reduce administrative burdens? Have the strategies and policies been effective? Unfortunately, the answers are not as optimistic as one might believe. This can be illustrated by the very limited research done in the Netherlands regarding the effectiveness of the new policies and attempts to reduce administrative burdens. Since 1993, no known additional wide-ranging research on this subject has been conducted. The research on the total administrative burdens of Dutch enterprises applies only to some specific policy area. However, these are accepted to be basic policy areas in which the enterprises encounter the most administrative burdens:

TABLE 7.8 Estimated total administrative burden arising from three policy areas in the Netherlands

Policy area	Total 1994	Total 1995	Total 1996	Total 1997
Corporate tax, tax dividends, revenue tax	6.83 billion	7.34 billion	7.49 billion	7.78 billion
Annual Accounts; and levying income tax and social premiums	Dutch HLF	Dutch HLF	Dutch HLF	Dutch HLF

These estimates are made using the MISTRAL instrument, developed by EIM Small Business and Research Consultancy in the Netherlands in order to measure administrative burdens
Source: EIM (1998)

corporate tax, tax on dividends, revenue tax, annual accounts, income tax and social premiums. The EIM Small Business Research and Consultancy in the Netherlands estimates the amount (cost) of the administrative burdens emerging from these policy areas in order to evaluate the development whether there was a cost reduction or not (table 7.8).

Policies and measures taken at the EU level

The Single European market (SEM) program was a major act of regulatory reform. It involves the removal, simplification and standardization of legislation in nearly three hundred regulated areas. Although it requires the removal of many regulations at the national level, it also enacts a new set of regulations to ensure that SEM goals will be realized and that the business environment is generally in line with SEM requirements. However, EU legislation has increased the administrative and legal burdens of enterprises in many areas. The efficiency and effectiveness of the European regulatory policies directed toward the business environment in European markets has received a great deal of criticism. Together with individual members' governments, the EU formulated special programs and drew up policies to create a better and more desirable business environment, particularly for SMEs.

The enterprise policy of the European Union
Since the adoption of the Single European Act (SEA) in 1986, the European Community (EC) has embarked on a path of reform that is expected to have a significant impact on the enterprise sector. A serious need existed for an EC-wide enterprise policy. Enterprise policy is wide-ranging and covers a number of areas of EC responsibility established in the Treaty of Rome. It was expanded to include the EC level. Since its inception in the mid-1980s, the enterprise policy has had the objective of administrative and legislative simplification, along with the provision of certain types of direct support.

One of the first measures establishing enterprise policy was the organization in 1983, following a proposal from the European Parliament, of the European year of Small and Medium-Sized Enterprises and Craft Industry. At its meeting in Luxembourg in 1985, the European Council decided to institute an assessment of the impact of EC proposals on SMEs and the preparation of measures to simplify their administrative, tax and regulatory environment. These priority tasks were carried out based on Article 235 of the Treaty of Rome in two stages. The first stage established the SME task force in June 1986. The Council adopted an action program in a resolution on November 3, 1986, that was an important step in the development of an EC enterprise policy. A coherent framework for EC policies in relation to enterprise was for the first time designated. In the Council decision of July 1989 on the improvement of the business environment and the promotion of enterprises in the EC, the enterprise policy was stated as having three broad and basic objectives:[7]

1 to safeguard and improve the business environment during the completion of the single internal market and beyond,
2 to develop policies designed to help new and growing enterprises benefit from the opportunities offered by the internal market, and
3 to ensure that there is a consistent framework of principles and methods for implementing major EC policies by using the enterprise sector to an important degree as an intermediary. The areas in question include the policy for scientific and technological development and the pursuit of economic and social cohesion.

On December 22, 1986, the Council adopted a resolution on an action program for promoting employment. The section of that resolution concerning steps to promote new enterprises and increase employment contained a number of measures designed to assist SMEs.

The second stage began in 1989 when the EC decided to allocate more resources to its enterprise policy in the wake of the new impetus of the Single European Act. A new Directorate General (DG XXIII) was created, that is principally responsible for implementing the enterprise policy. Article 130 of the Treaty on European Union, which was enacted on November 1, 1993, provides a new and more specific legal base for the enterprise policy.

On June 14, 1993, a Decision relating to a multiannual program (from July 1, 1993, to December 31, 1996) of EC measures designed to ensure the continuity and consolidation of the enterprise policy was adopted by the Council (OJEC 1993). The framework of the enterprise policy was enlarged by a Council Resolution of November 22, 1993, on strengthening the competitiveness of enterprises and developing employment in the Union.

The European Commission on May 25, 1994, proposed the implementation of an Integrated Program in Support of SMEs and the Craft Sector. The objective of this program is to bring together the member states and the EU in a concerted manner to allow SMEs to take advantage of the opportunities offered to them. It is intended to carry out the objectives stated in the White Paper on Growth, Competitiveness and Employment. The Integrated Program also aims to harmonize the regulations across the EU, to reduce the administrative and tax implications of transferring a business and to encourage existing owners to prepare for the eventual transfer of their business. SMEs are recognized as not being homogeneous, and the problems and needs of SMEs differ at the various stages of their development and depending on their location. In a Resolution of October 10, 1994, that enhances the dynamism and innovative potential of

SMEs and the craft sector, the Council called on the Commission to propose measure for the implementation of the initiatives announced in the integrated program (OJEC 1994).

EU policies and programs

After the Edinburgh European Council in December 1992, the EU acknowledged the role European SMEs can play in economic recovery, growth and job creation. The importance of the enterprise policy was once again stressed in the multiannual program, which was adopted by a Decision on June 14, 1993. The priority areas of enterprise policy were:

- implementing measures aimed at removing undue administrative, financial and legal constraints on the development and creation of enterprises,
- informing enterprises, particularly SMEs, about EC policies, regulations and activities and those of each member state that concern them, and
- encouraging cooperation and partnership between enterprises from different EC regions.

In addition, when drawing up and implementing policies specific to SMEs, the proposals presented by the Commission to the Council and the Parliament were to be accompanied by an impact assessment describing their likely effects on business (Moussis 1996: 206).

At the Amsterdam European Council on June 16–17, 1997, Europe's political leaders confirmed their "strong commitment to the simplification of existing and new legal and administrative regulations in order to improve the quality of Community legislation and reduce its administrative burden on European business, particularly small and medium-sized businesses" (European Communities 1998). Soon after, the European Commission was invited to establish a task force for reducing the regulations and broadening its own rolling program of simplification.

On July 30, 1997, the Business Environment Simplification Taskforce (BEST) was established. The objective for BEST was to prepare an independent report that would make proposals for concrete measures to be taken by the Commission and the member states to improve the quality of legislation and eliminate the unnecessary burdens that restrain the development of European businesses, particularly SMEs. This taskforce also looked at the issues of financing for SMEs, management, employee training, innovation and technology transfer, as well as all aspects of administration (European Communities 1998). BEST was composed of entrepreneurs and experts on regulation and enterprise policy from each member state. They reported to the Cardiff European Council in June 1998.

Moreover, in recent years, a range of programs to help SMEs has been introduced at the EU level, complementing measures taken at national levels. For instance, the White Paper on the Growth, Competitiveness and Employment of the European Union stressed the need to create an environment as favorable as possible to business (ENSR 1995). The exchange of information among the European Institutions and member states is considered another important factor to at least minimize the problems caused by the extensive and frequent regulations. In line with this purpose, reports, such as those by the European Observatory for SMEs and the European Employment Observatory, which are issued by the EU, have proven to be a good source of information on both the analysis and practice of SME policy across the European Union.

Some of the other important actions and programs of the EU to stimulate the SME sector and to find solutions to the problems of those enterprises are the various networking and innovation centers.

Conclusions and Recommendations

Throughout history, governments in all countries have issued regulations and designed regulatory policies for trade and business. The rationale behind them was usually to overcome market failures. In other words, there is no call for government regulation until specific market failures occur, for example:

- the external effects of market activities, where the social benefits or costs of a given activity differ from private ones,
- imperfect or unfair competition in the market, such as monopolies, or
- the problem of asymmetric information between two parties who enter into a contract.

Depending on time and circumstances, policies have taken different forms and substance. For instance, today regulations mostly apply either to competition and preventing firms from dominating a market to environmental concerns. However, regulatory policies are not only designed to restrict and control business activities; they are also designed to stimulate and support growth and development of businesses. Although government regulations and policies often have a beneficial effect, they are not without drawbacks. The number of advantages and disadvantages vary according to the capacity and the size of the enterprises operating in the market. Generally speaking, the SME sector is the one most seriously affected by government regulatory policies. Complaints are mostly related to the costs and burdens imposed by legislation.

Within this chapter we have tried to bring to the fore the issue of administrative burdens on SMEs operating in the European market as a result of both EU and national legislation. However, leaving aside the rationale for making and performing regulatory policies, the question that should be asked is, Which body – national governments or EU institutions – should make and introduce those policies? And also, should it be through the cooperation of member states without transferring the decision-making process of formulating regulatory policies to the EU as a supranational body?

We suggest that the most suitable way to perform regulatory policies is through EU institutions, especially since the adoption of a single European market program, the amount of regulatory policies and regulations to which the enterprises were subjected have decreased. European regulatory policies took the place of national regulatory policies. In other words, many policies of the member states on regulating the market were amended by European legislation or totally disappeared. However, even though we assert that European legislation should replace national legislation, several important items have to be considered when making and enforcing regulatory policies at the EU level – such as taking into account the principle of subsidiarity while making policies. Policies should be formulated at the most suitable level: European, national or regional. According to this principle, only those policy functions that can be more efficiently discharged at the EU level should be transferred from the national or regional level. When preparing a draft legislation, the European Commission should do so in the light of the principle of subsidiarity and adopt the legislation only if it is in the common interest of the entire Union and the enterprises operating in the European market.

Another important point is the correct application of instruments used by the EU in making regulatory policies, the most common of which are the regulation and the directive. The EU issues, on average 4,000 regulations per year and about 120 directives (Nugent 1994; ENSR 1996). In fact, applying the principle of subsidiarity implies that the legal framework for Europe will arise from directives rather than regulations. We believe that the EC should use directives rather than regulations because directives allow a degree of flexibility in the adoption of regulatory policies and they are more general in nature than regulations. Moreover, directives are not so much concerned with the detailed and uniform application of some specific kind of a policy as with establishing EC principles. Member states are allowed to choose their own means under their own respective administrative structures and legal system. This implies for the regulation of business activities within the EU that the regulatory agencies of member states will become more effective in formulating and making their regulatory policies.

NOTES

1 It is important to note, unfortunately, that the data used in this study to estimate the administrative burdens and to make country-based comparisons are not (very) recent. We have tried to use the best data and research available for any given country.

2 Because the administrative burdens in the Netherlands are probably not the same as the average burdens in Europe, three estimates have been made. The first is with the average costs per enterprise, branch and size class per enterprise in the Netherlands. The second is 90 percent and the third is 110 percent of these average costs, which yields a minimum and maximum range. Estimates were made in 1993.

3 The estimates we made in this manner correspond fairly well with the estimates made in France and Norway. Compared with the estimates of Finland and Luxembourg, our estimates are higher. The estimates refer to all compulsory administrative procedures.

4 These figures are based on an estimate made in 1987 by the French Ministry of Industry.

5 See, for Belgium, Donckels et al. 1983; for Finland, Malinen 1997; for Germany, Kitterer 1989; for the Netherlands, "Administrative lasten bedrijven 1993," EIM Small Business Research and Consultancy, 1994.

6 See, for Finland, Malinen 1993; for Luxembourg, "Etude analytique des obligations et formalités administratives imposés aux chefs de petites et moyennes entreprises," 1987; for Germany, Kitterer 1989.

7 Document of the Commission of the European Communities (1989): An enterprise policy for the Community. Brussels, p. 17.

REFERENCES

COM. 1994. Commission of the European Union. COM (94)20.

Document of the Commission of the European Communities. 1989. *An Enterprise Policy for the Community*. Brussels

Donckels, R., Degadt, J. and Uyttenbrouk, J. 1983. *KMO en administratieve verplichtingen-empirisch onderzoek voor Vlaanderen (SMEs and Administrative Obligations: Empirical Research for Flanders)*. Brussels: Small Business Research Institute.

EIM Small Business Research and Consultancy. 1993. *The European Observatory for SMEs. Second Annual Report*, Zoetermeer.

EIM Small Business Research and Consultancy. 1994. *Administrative Burdens in Enterprises 1993*. Zoetermeer. EIM Small Business Research on Consultancy, 1993.

EIM Small Business Research and Consultancy. 1995. *The European Observatory for SMEs. Third Annual Report*. Zoetermeer.

EIM Small Business Research and Consultancy. 1996. *The European Observatory for SMEs. Fourth Annual Report*. Zoetermeer.

EIM Small Business Research and Consultancy. 1998. *Administrative Burdens in Enterprises 1997*. Zoetermeer.

ENSR (European Network of SME Research). 1995. *The European Observatory for SMEs, Third Annual Report*. Zoetermeer.

ENSR (European Network of SME Research). 1997. *The European Observatory for SMEs, Fifth Annual Report*. Zoetermeer.

European Communities. 1998. *Report of the Business Environment Simplification Task Force* 1: 7.

Grandomenico, M. 1996. *Regulating Europe*. New York: Routledge.

Hulshoff, H.E. 1997. *Administrative Burdens with Hiring Employees (Administrative Lasten in Dienst Nemen Werknemers)*. The Hague: OSA.

JCM. 1996 *Journal of Common Market Studies* 34(1): 40.

Kellerman, A.E. and Azzi, G.C. 1998. *Improving the Quality of Legislation in Europe*. The Hague: T.M.C. Asser Instituut.

Kerwin, M.C. 1994. Rulemaking how government agencies write law and make policy. *Congressional Quarterly*, Washington, DC.

Kitterer, W. 1989. *Kostender Bürokratie über Walzung (Cost of Transferring Bureaucratic Costs)*. Institute für Finanzwissenschaft, Universität Kiel.

Lowi, J.T. 1985. The state in politics: the relation between policy and administration. In R.G. Noll (ed.), *Regulatory Policy and the Social Sciences*. Berkeley: University of California Press, pp. 67–105.

Malinen, Pasi. 1993. *First Annual Report. The European Observatory for SMEs*. Zoetermeer.

Malinen, Pasi. 1994. *PK-yritysten hallintomenettely (Red Tape and Finnish SMEs)*. Turun Kauppakorkeakoulu, Yritystoiminnan tutkimuskeskus (Publications of the Business Research Centre), Discussion Series, Turku School of Economics and Business Administration, Turku, Finland.

Malinen, Pasi. 1997. *Fifth Annual report. The European Observatory for SMEs*. Zoetermeer.

Nader, L. and Nader C. 1985. A wide angle on regulation: an anthropological perspective. In R.G. Noll (ed.), *Regulatory Policy and the Social Sciences*. Berkeley: University of California Press, pp. 141–60.

NTSIKA. 1998. *Basic Conditions of Employment Act-Impact Assessment, Final Report*. Pretoria.

Nugent, N. 1994. *The Government and Politics of the European Union*. London: Macmillan.

OJEC (*Official Journal of the European Communities*), 1993, L161, 02.07.

OJEC (*Official Journal of the European Communities*), 1994, C294, 22.10.

OJEC (*Official Journal of the European Communities*), 1996, L107, 30.4, p. 4.

Van der Burg, B.I. and Nijsen, A.F.M. 1998. How can administrative burdens on enterprises be assessed? Different methods: advantages and disadvantages. In A.E. Kellerman et al. (eds.), *Improving the Quality of European Legislation*. The Hague: T.M.C. Asser Instituut, pp. 263–77.

Welford, R. and Prescott, K. 1996. *European Business*. London: Pitman.

Wilson, J.Q. 1980. *The Politics of Regulation*. New York: Basic Books.

8

The Climate for Entrepreneurship in European Countries in Transition

Josef Mugler

The main task of all European countries in transition is to move away from their centrally planned system and to adopt a market economy. All countries analyzed in this chapter started this process between 1988 and 1992, but each country has its own starting point. According to Dahrendorf (1991) the transformation process in European countries in transition can be analyzed by three different factors: politics, economy and society, which leads to political, economic and social transformation. Since these factors occur at varying speeds, each country has undergone its own transition process. Especially in the larger countries, differences in the transition speed may also vary within the same country.

In contrast to political transformation, economic and social transformation are much slower processes and last for decades. Privatization is but one element of the transition. "Free" markets have only recently been introduced to varying degrees in the European countries in transition (OECD 1998: 99).

Because of the common interest of the international community, considerable research in all three transformation processes has been conducted. A wide range of texts on elections and party formation in connection with the political transformation can be found. However, a tendency toward not wanting to express one's opinion can be observed. There is no doubt that the political development from a communist to a democratic system is essential for the transformation to a market economy. For brevity's sake, political factors are not discussed here.

In studying economic transitions, it must be understood that the quality of aggregated economic data does not follow market principles and Eurostat (the Statistical Office of the European Union) standards. The informal economy is a widespread phenomenon in the European countries in transition, and a large proportion of actual economic activity is not measured by formal indicators.

Complex social transformations can only be seen in context of the other two forms of transformation – political and economic. Thus we cannot strictly distinguish between the different transformation processes. During communist domination, concepts such as private ownership, free and democratic behavior, individual responsibility and entrepreneurial and managerial spirit were eliminated from the system to different degrees. In order to enable a democratic market society, the attitudes formed by communism must now be changed, and this is a very lengthy process. The main prerequisite for success is confidence in the new system. Success encourages people to agree with the process of transformation. However, there is no doubt that success comes after disappointment. Negative experiences can encourage people to return to what they are used to rather than to adopt a new system. The alternation between success and failure is a main reason the process of social transformation lasts such a long time.

As already mentioned, the European countries in transition show different stages of development in their transition toward a market economy. The countries that started negotiations with the European Union (EU) in 1998 can be described as the most advanced ones: the Czech Republic, Estonia, Hungary, Poland and Slovenia.

Bulgaria, Croatia, Romania and Slovakia are in an intermediate stage of transition and form the second group. Slovakia was not nominated to join the first round of negotiations because of the lack of democracy under its former government. Moreover, it increasingly lags behind in reforms. The two Balkan countries (Bulgaria and Romania) have been plagued by prolonged economic and financial instability and periodic crises. These countries have been unable to embark on a solid and balanced growth path because of "much slower and hesitant progress in implementing the necessary market reforms, partly because of inconsistent macroeconomic policies, and partly because of unstable internal politics" (Rosati et al. 1998: 2).

The third group consists of the countries of the former Yugoslav Federation, which have experienced long separatist wars: Bosnia, Yugoslavia (now comprising Montenegro and Serbia) and Macedonia. Albania, a neighboring country, has recently been involved in the Kosovo conflict and suffers from an unstable political situation. This third group of countries can be characterized by an extremely difficult political situation on account of which only scarce or unreliable information is available. Although Croatia has been caught up in the Balkan conflicts, it seems to be appropriate, considering its transformation, to list it now in the second group of countries above.

A fourth group of countries in transition consists of former members of the Soviet Union. Much interest is focused on Russia, of course. Two Baltic countries, Lithuania and Latvia, are oriented toward joining the EU, although they seem to be somewhat behind Estonia. Belarus and Moldavia tend to take their lead from Russia. Ukraine, the second largest country in this group, is somewhat stuck in the middle between an Eastern and Western orientation.

In the traditional geographic sense, the eastern border of Europe is formed by a line connecting the Ural Mountains, the Ural River, the Caspian Sea, the Caucasus Mountains and the Black Sea. This means that, with the exception of the western Ural area of

Russia, a few new independent countries from the former Soviet Union could also be considered as European countries in transition, e.g., Kazakhstan, which in geographical terms, is partly situated on both Europe and Asia, like Russia.

FRAME OF REFERENCE AND STRUCTURE OF ANALYSIS

The framework for this investigation will be based on an advanced configuration approach (Mugler 1998; cf. Gartner 1995; Miller 1987; Snuif and Zwart 1994). The main characteristic of this approach is that variables explaining entrepreneurial perform-ance include the environment, entrepreneur, resources and management methods (figure 8.1). This environment is a set of variables influenced by political economic and social transformation processes. These three main factors will again be divided into further subgroups for our investigation.

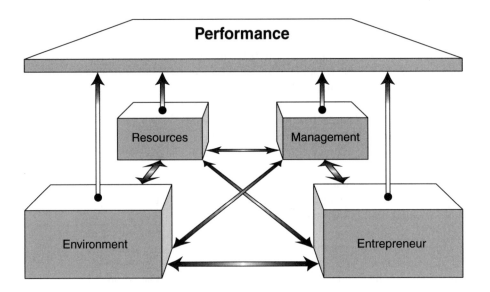

FIGURE 8.1 Structure for analysis

Generally, environmental changes have a strong impact on the three remaining variables. Investigations into the climate for entrepreneurship must consequently concen-trate on the environment of economic units. Because of existing interdependencies between the different variables, impacts of entrepreneurs and firms on their environment must also be taken into account. Increasing entrepreneurship will help to change the economic, social and political situation, which, in turn, changes the environment for entrepreneurship, like an increasingly upward spiral.

Consequently, a workable segmentation of the environment will be the main challenge for our analysis. Though the variables can be illustrated, their effects cannot be analyzed in detail due to interdependencies and the resulting complexity. It is necessary to separate variables within this chapter; however, due to the serial concept of language, it must be recognized that any separation of variables can only be done by artificially eliminating many interdependencies.

My approach will be to provide insights into the social and economic situation in the areas under consideration and will include questions such as:

- How has entrepreneurship research developed in the European countries in transition so far?
- What are the crucial factors that influence the behavior of people and subsequently the development of entrepreneurial activities in the process of transformation?
- Which stages of economic development have already been achieved by the European countries in transition?
- What can we learn from data such as start-up, growth and failure rates about the dynamics of entrepreneurship in countries in transition?

Specific impediments to entrepreneurship in transition economies will be analyzed. Some general impediments can be traced back to the centrally planned economic system; others to the fact that structures of the newly adopted market-oriented system have not yet been fully developed and implemented. Finally, examples will be presented of political measures imposed to improve the framework conditions for entrepreneurship in the countries in transition.

Social and Economic Situation

Entrepreneurship research

Most enterprises created in the European countries in transition are micro, small or medium-sized enterprises (SMEs). Since SMEs are breaking up the large industrial enterprises predominant in centrally planned economies, the creation of SMEs can be considered a synonym for economic transformation. Therefore, intensive research in this new field is underway. However, research results based on official economic data should be interpreted with due care and attention since the economic data do not yet follow Western standards, do not take into account the considerable informal sector and, in many cases, are not up to date. After the collapse of the command economies, data collection was only a secondary task, and research methods used in European countries in transition were heavily influenced by methodologies used in central planning. Usually quantitative data, which are easily obtained, have been used in research instead of qualitative data, which were not required under communism. Hence, researchers have only a little experience with this type of research. Moreover, most surveys are not translated, and those that are often have problems with the different use and interpretation of technical terms.

Many institutions are concerned with investigating the relevance of entrepreneurs and SMEs in macroeconomic terms. The Czech Republic, Hungary, Poland, Slovakia and Slovenia formed Data Base 750, funded by the European Foundation for Entrepreneurship Research (EFER) and the European Venture Capital Association (EVCA). Its major goal is the identification and analysis of fast-growing, job-creating business ventures.

Another area of interest is improving the underdeveloped business and technological infrastructure by means of business incubators, technology transfer centers and promotional networks.

Considerable research has been conducted in the Czech Republic, Hungary, Poland and Slovakia. This might be due to the fact that these countries (except Slovakia) are members of the Organization for Economic Cooperation and Development (OECD) and are all located in western Europe. Until recently, research in the countries of the former Yugoslav Federation and the former Soviet Union was centralized. As a result, hard data is lacking. In some countries, such as Latvia, so-called market-oriented research grants were introduced in order to obtain marketable results (Jaunzems and Elerts 1996).

Entrepreneurship research in European countries in transition has been conducted by both Eastern researchers and visiting researchers from Western countries and presented in many journals and at several conferences, including the International Council for Small Business (ICSB), International Small Business Council (ISBC), Research in Entrepreneurship (RENT), Internationalizing Entrepreneurship Education and Training (INTENT) and European Small Business Seminar (ESBS).

Some additional specialized conferences have contributed substantially to the diffusion of knowledge, e.g., the Management und Entwicklung (MER) Conferences (1994, 1996, 1998) in Portoroz, Slovenia; the conference series organized by the University of Split, Croatia, on Enterprise in Transition (1995, 1997); and international organizations like the OECD. An example of a permanent platform for the exchange of research is the Working Committee on Eastern Europe of the European Council for Small Business (ECSB).

The events and media that publish entrepreneurship research results have grown steadily over the last few years. Hence, an in-depth analysis of the climate for entrepreneurship in European countries in transition is based on a sound body of knowledge. Nevertheless, there is still a lack of information in certain areas, which makes it impossible to maintain the same level of information in all fields. Finally, the dynamics in this area may cause certain information to be obsolete shortly after reporting.

SOCIETAL FACTORS

Attitude toward entrepreneurship in general

A society's business culture plays a crucial role in determining economic progress and prosperity. For an entrepreneurial economy to flourish, a business culture must be receptive to changing demands of a market economy – products, innovations, opportunities and technologies. Enterprises and the business infrastructure provided by the government must be supportive for entrepreneurship, society must value entrepreneurship, and entrepreneurs must have a long-term perspective for future success.

The business culture that developed under the communist system is termed "bureaucratic-administrative" by Bateman (1997a: xv). This business culture did not understand the importance of entrepreneurship and innovation, nor did it favor constructive, efficient entrepreneurial activities. The bureaucratic-administrative business culture generally resisted innovation, flexibility and change. Planning and technical management techniques were ideally suited for rapid industrialization in the early years of communism. However, these methods became redundant in the age of computers and mass communication, which involve rapid product and process change and rising R&D expenditures. Moreover, consumers were demanding constantly updated, better differentiated and higher quality goods. These trends could only be met through more flexible production processes and responsive, entrepreneurial management. Today, the international community is waiting for the displacement of this bureaucratic-administrative business culture by a flourishing entrepreneurial one. Bateman (1997a, 1997b) stresses that in the European countries in transition, business cultures are still at an early stage of transformation.

Within the centrally planned economies, despite all attempts at liberalization, entrepreneurial activities were limited. Under communism, the private sector in Poland and Hungary, for example, remained small and limited to certain areas, but in the former Czechoslovakia private economic activities were totally forbidden. Under this restriction, entrepreneurial-minded people were forced to perform illegal activities in the private economy. Many private entrepreneurs also preferred operating in the black market rather than in the official private sector to avoid being constrained by frequent changes in tax and employment regulations.

It is often argued that in countries undergoing transition the long experience under a planned economic system has shaped the norms, values and social orientation of the citizens, thus impeding entrepreneurial activities. Research conducted more recently (OECD 1996) refutes this claim and underlines the point that entrepreneurial spirit exists in every society. This spirit can be fostered by an appropriate framework. Entrepreneurial attitudes vary widely among European countries in transition, but it cannot be argued that the attitude toward entrepreneurial activities in European countries in transition is generally negative. However, the entrepreneurial culture is widely associated with criminality and corruption. Also, if entrepreneurship is not valued in a culture, government subsidies and other forms of economic encouragement for SME establishment may be ineffective. Empirical studies show that situational factors rather than attitudinal ones contribute to differences in economic behavior of inhabitants of industrialized countries and those of the postcommunist countries. This emphasizes implicitly the relevance of the framework conditions of economic activity (OECD 1996, 1998). Some examples taken from country-specific investigations may illustrate this situation:

♦ In Slovenia, one of the more advanced countries, "the entrepreneurial culture is still weak due to several decades of rupture in entrepreneurial traditions. Entrepreneurship is not yet associated with a positive public image. . . . The negative image of the entrepreneur involved in dubious transactions, trying to evade tax liabilities, has to be replaced by a more positive set of entrepreneurial qualities, highlighting professional skills, organizational and managerial efficiency, readiness to accept challenge, creativity and hard work in order to succeed at home and abroad" (Marot 1997: 61).

♦ In Bulgaria, Romania and Slovakia, a striking and complex situation exists with the re-appearance of SMEs after several years without concepts like private ownership, free and democratic behavior, entrepreneurs and managers. Bureaucratic skills acquired under communism had more harmful than beneficial effects on entrepreneurial activity. Such "skills" encompassed a lack of autonomous decision-making ability and an unwillingness to take risks, focusing only on fostering the best possible relationship with the state administration (Fundatura 1998; OECD 1996; Lynn 1998).

♦ In Russia, the "typical" Soviet mentality encouraged by communism did not foster individuality. Personal interests were dominated by collective interests. The satisfaction of basic needs pleased the typical Soviet. It becomes quite obvious that such a mentality cannot change rapidly and is therefore responsible for difficulties in the transition to a market economy. However, today the majority of the Russian population accepts entrepreneurship and expects increasing welfare from it (Trommsdorff and Schuchardt 1998).

Balance between liberty and order within society

Both liberty and order are required for entrepreneurship. Because entrepreneurship is usually based on innovative action, it needs a climate of tolerance to reduce its liability of newness. On the other hand, entrepreneurship is exposed to framework conditions set up by mighty – legal or illegal – authorities that might cause fair or unfair rules of competition. Thus, a certain level of order is needed to overcome the liability of smallness.

Many researchers report a lack of regulation as well as overregulation, different levels of application of laws, a shadow economy and criminality, as illustrated by the following examples.

The shadow economy is reported to be widespread, e.g., in Hungary, and unfair market behavior is no exception (Papanek 1998). Security problems and criminality have an increasingly negative impact on the Russian economy. The surge in criminal and illegal practices, including racketeering, represent a real barrier to entry in the market, limiting competition and becoming a heavy distortion factor that curtails further expansion (Benini 1997: 30). The substantial unregistered activity in the black market also has to be taken into account. Estimates of the Russian shadow economy suggest that unregistered activities make up between 25 and 50 percent of the GDP. At present, Russian officials are designing a program to collect accurate data on the informal economy and to devise ways in which the state can draw illegal entrepreneurship back into the formal system (OECD 1998).

Technology transfer and innovation

Only a small number of firms are willing to conduct research or to purchase licenses or know-how. This has resulted in a technology gap. "Willingness of enterprises to invest and innovate is not strong. . . . Investment plans to introduce new products or technology are also unjustifiably rare," Papanek (1998) writes, with respect to Hungary.

In Slovenia, links between research and SMEs remain weak (Marot 1997). Since SMEs usually cannot compete in price on the international market, it is important for them to exploit the technological research conducted to promote innovation. For Poland, Gieorgica (1998) reports the government's lack of fostering technology transfer and developing new technologies has hampered growth.

In the countries in an intermediate stage of transition, the motivation for starting a business stem more from the urgent need to have an income and avoid unemployment rather than hopes of becoming wealthy. In Bulgaria and Romania, technological innova-

TABLE 8.1 Survey of general economic data of European countries in transition

	Area in km²	Population (million, mid-1997 estimate)	Labor force (million end of 1997)	Unemployment rate (%, end of 1997)	GDP (per capita in US $)	Inflation rate (annual average %)	Balance of trade (million US$)	Balance payments (million US$)	Budget (balance in % of GDP)
Albania	28,748	3.40	1.60	14.00	655	33.2	-440	-142	-13.0
Belarus	207,595	10.20	*	2.80	1,287	63.0	-1,430	-762	-2.1
Bosnia	51,129	3.30 (4.2)	1.60	65.00	1,212	12.0	-376	*	*
Bulgaria	110,912	8.40	4.70	13.70	1,211	1,082.3	396	446	2.0
Croatia	56,538	4.53	1.60	16.60	4,207	4.1	-5,224	-2,435	-1.0
Czech Republic	78,861	10.30	5.00	5.20	5,042	8.4	-4,590	-3,156	-1.0
Estonia	45,226	1.47	0.80	10.50	3,211	11.2	-1,128	-565	0.4
Hungary	93,033	10.20	4.80	10.40	4,506	18.3	-1,734	-981	-4.5
Latvia	64,589	2.49	1.43	6.70	1,346	8.4	-937	-441	1.2
Lithuania	65,200	3.70	1.80	6.70	2,581	8.9	-1,148	-982	-1.9
Macedonia	25,713	2.00	0.80	31.90	1,900	5.0	-365	-300	-1.5
Moldavia	33,700	4.40	*	1.90	521	12.0	-344	-296	-7.7
Poland	312,683	38.70	17.50	10.50	3,511	14.9	-11,269	-4,268	-1.3
Romania	237,500	22.60	10.70	8.80	1,537	150.7	-2,023	-1,981	-4.5
Russian Republic	17,100,000	147.00	72.20	9.00	2,992	11.0	17,600	3,300	-7.4
Slovakia	49,035	5.40	2.70	12.50	3,632	6.1	-1,472	-1,347	-5.6
Slovenia	20,253	1.98	0.94	14.40	9,074	8.3	-773	37	-1.1
Ukraine	603,700	50.80	*	2.90	977	23.0	-4,205	-1335	-7.1
Yugoslavia	102,173	10.60	5.80	30.00	1,463	22.0	-2,430	*	-10.0

Data from Frankfurter Allgemeine Zeitung (FAZ) 1998a.
* Not available.

tion is hampered by a lack of financial resources (Kelemen and Hristov 1998). In Romania, obstacles to technological innovation are of an organizational, social and managerial nature. However, there is already some awareness of the need for technological advances (Kelemen and Hristov 1998).

The situation in the countries of the former Yugoslav Federation and Soviet Union is quite similar. Constraints to developing new products or services in the Ukraine are reported by Smallbone et al. (1998): 72 percent of all trading firms suffer from a shortage of finance and 25 percent from a lack of suitable production equipment.

General economic data

An overview of the economic situation of the countries in consideration is presented in table 8.1, which includes selected economic data, such as GDP, inflation, unemployment rates, structure and foreign trade. Because of the interest of the international community in the countries in transition, statistics about inflation, unemployment and GDP are readily available. However, aggregated economic indicators, even though improved in quality since the early 1990s, may still be based upon data that do not necessarily follow Western standards. Furthermore, a considerable informal economy in most of these societies means that a large proportion of an individual's actual economic activity is not measured by formal indicators (Wallace and Haerpfer 1998). Although the majority of the European countries in transition have overcome the transitional crisis, "none of them (except for Poland) reached their pretransitional level of development" (Vojnic 1997: 5).

Dynamics of business units

The belief in economies of scale, supply orientation and the complex planing process in centrally planned economies generally left no room for SMEs. After the fall of communism, an enormous growth in the number of registered new private businesses was observed. The substantial increase in small business activity in early stages of transition can be seen as a social and political reaction to the past regime and as a recognition of the new. The new market system put pressure on large state-owned enterprises to restructure. The old state-run enterprise sector had to rationalize and to adjust the production of goods and services to existing and newly emerging consumer demands, thus leading to heavy job losses. A strong SME sector can absorb at least some of the redundant workers and provide an "enormous potential for future employment creation" (OECD 1998: 102).

The shift toward a free market system offered the population access to a whole new range of opportunities, which made private initiative possible, especially in several market niches (OECD 1998). The flexibility of dynamic SMEs was best suited to serve these market niches. However, in the early 1990s, the lack of experience in private entrepreneurship and the unfamiliarity of the market system were responsible for the failure of a high proportion of new businesses. In addition, an ever-changing business, legal and fiscal framework complicated the situation for start-up entrepreneurs.

The first period of extensive growth of the SME sector has ended, as the simple economic reserves have been exhausted. Data on newly registered firms should be treated with caution, as in many countries up to 50 percent have never actually started activities (Liuhto 1996; Matei and Matei 1998; OECD 1998; Raudjarv 1998). Today microenterprises (fewer than ten employees) represent the typical new firm in transitional economies (Lynn 1998). In Estonia, for example, over 80 percent of all enterprises have less than five employees (Liuhto 1996: 324).

Unlike the EU, European countries in transition have no standardized definition of micro, small or medium-sized enterprises yet. Because of the lack of uniform criteria and the fact that available data stem from surveys conducted between 1995 and 1998, it becomes quite obvious that it is impossible to adequately describe and compare the current situation of SMEs in the countries under consideration. Official statistics can only give a rough idea of the overall SME situation (Benini 1997; Raudjarv 1998).

Today, SMEs play a significant role in European countries in transition, but there are large differences among the countries discussed here. In the countries of the former Soviet Union, especially in Belarus, Russia and Ukraine, the role of the SME sector is quite insignificant compared with the counterparts in the most advanced and intermediate transition economies. The contribution of SMEs to the GDP and their job creation effect is still very limited. The share of people employed in small businesses of the total working population amounts only to 5 percent in Belarus as well as in the Ukraine (Balashevich 1996; Kurylyak 1998; Slonimski 1998). In contrast, approximately 75 percent of the total workforce is employed in business ventures with up to fifty employees in Romania (OECD 1996) and 30 percent of the workforce in Bulgaria (OECD 1998).

Considering the performance of SME, Kurylyak (1998) reports that in Russia and in the Ukraine SMEs contribute only 10 percent to the GDP. In Hungary (Institute for Small Business Development 1997) and Poland (Gieorgica 1998) SMEs contributed approximately 50 percent to the GDP in 1995. In Slovakia SMEs contribute almost 65 percent to the GDP (Lesakova 1998a).

Today more than 60 percent of the active Polish workforce is employed by SMEs, which generate approximately half of Poland's GDP. The dynamics of the Polish SME sector becomes even more evident in the fact that one of every seven families runs its own private business. Family firms make up 70 percent of Polish SMEs, showing that self-employment is seen as a way out of unemployment (Gieorgica 1998: 168).

The sectoral distribution of SMEs is distorted in favor of services and trades. Moreover, in each country there are significant regional differences concerning the pace of SME development. This is especially true for large countries such as Russia (Benini 1997). Regional clusters of SMEs develop in dynamic regions thus leading to a gap between the number of SMEs in towns and rural areas. In Estonia, for example, 81.8 percent of all enterprises operating are located in towns and 18.2 percent in the countryside. More than half of both rural and urban enterprises are active in the two major fields: trade and manufacturing. Regionally, the growth of entrepreneurship has been extremely uneven, with a notable concentration on Tallinn, Estonia's capital, and its immediate surroundings.

A distinction must be made between newly created firms that expand and create employment and those that only create one job by self-employment. In an environment of long-term unemployment, self-employment presents a positive alternative and should therefore not be undervalued. According to a Eurostat survey (OECD 1996), one active worker in twenty has tried to become self-employed in recent years. Obviously, nonregistered individual activities also have to be added to this figure. However, most newly created businesses have no salaried employees. Over 80 percent of all enterprises in Bulgaria, and 60 percent in Romania have no salaried employees.

The sharp increase in self-employment in transition economies could be regarded as an expression of particularly problematic developments, such as a breakdown of the social security system, deindustrialization or poverty. By contrast, rise in self-employment could also represent a real entrepreneurial mobilization (OECD 1998). Sole proprietors often operate their businesses in addition to their main source of employment, supplementing the income of their principal job. It should be noted that even in the EU, the self-employed account for close to 50 percent of all enterprises (ENSR 1997).

In most European countries in transition there are few surveys providing failure rates (OECD 1998). However, in Estonia in 1995, 78.8 percent of the enterprises that shut down had operated for less than three years. The main reasons cited for failure were financial difficulties, weaknesses in or lack of business plans, insufficient awareness of the actual economic and market situation and overrating their own abilities and those of their partners. Raudjarv (1998) stresses that all these reasons can be reduced to insufficient education and training of entrepreneurs, whereas Tibor (1998) found out that "failures do not correlate with educational levels."

In summary, the performance of SMEs in the countries of the former Soviet Union is still insignificant. By contrast, in the most advanced countries, those that have already started negotiations with the EU and the ones in an intermediate stage of transition, SMEs represent a dynamic, efficient and very important sector of the economy. However, compared with the SME sector of the EU, these SMEs are less important and less efficient (Fundatura 1998; Gieorgica 1998).

IMPEDIMENTS TO ENTREPRENEURSHIP

Impediments to the development of entrepreneurship in the European countries in transition can be classified as either external or internal factors. External factors refer to the general framework conditions in which enterprises operate and therefore include general macroeconomic development – the legal, financial and administrative infrastructure. Internal constraints include a lack of resources, such as specific knowledge and management techniques in view of market economic needs, not enough innovation and achievement orientation on the part of entrepreneurs and the workforce (Welter 1997). However, according to the theoretical basis of the configuration approach, interrelationships must be taken into account.

Several studies of European countries in transition reveal that entrepreneurs often complain about rigid bureaucratic procedures, nontransparency of accounting procedures and business laws, heavy tax burdens, unstable political and economic conditions, a lack of or difficult access to financing and an underdeveloped infrastructure. Obviously, entrepreneurs only see external impediments as a real threat, thus neglecting the internal constraints they also have to face.

Empirical data from Russia, Romania and Bulgaria show that the unstable economic environment – high inflation, high nominal and real interest rates and exchange rate instability – poses the greatest problem for entrepreneurship (OECD 1998). As most companies in European countries in transition are still in the early period of their life cycle, they are, by nature, unstable and therefore vulnerable to changes in financial and legislative policies (Bobeva 1996). The resulting urgent need for advice and consultancy in fiscal and legal matters cannot be satisfied, as commercial research and consultancy are either not available for SMEs or entrepreneurs cannot afford to pay for them (Jaunzems and Elerts 1996; Kruft and Sofrova 1997; Lynn 1998; Smallbone et al. 1998). Because of a lack of clear market analysis, poor information flows and high transaction costs, SMEs in Russia, for instance, find it difficult to identify niche markets (Benini 1997). This is one of the reasons why many SMEs in European countries in transition are still basically supply-driven.

Another problem that entrepreneurs have to face is that, as a result of meager investments in existing enterprises during communism, production equipment is out of date. This makes it even more difficult for them to compete on world markets. There is definitely a need to stimulate technological renovation with softer loans and tax incentives. New enterprises frequently start with a small capital base. In addition, modern forms of acquiring equipment, like leasing, have not yet been fully established. The fact that products often do not come up to international standards is another reason why these goods are not able to compete on international markets. A Ukraine survey shows that 64 percent of manufacturing firms identified their existing equipment as a major constraint on their ability to increase sales. The main barriers to improving the level of equipment is a shortage of finance (82 percent), although their lack of knowledge about new advances in technology was also mentioned by a significant minority (28 percent) (Smallbone et al. 1998). A shortage of both basic education in economics, management and marketing and limited experience may explain why entrepreneurs in transition economies have difficulties in making sound decisions about their business operation (Marot 1997).

Numerous surveys of the specific impediments to entrepreneurship and to the development of SMEs have been carried out in almost every country. The following areas will now be considered in more detail:

- human capital
- general regulation system
- administration of start-ups
- general infrastructure
- trade unions and employers' associations
- access to capital
- market organization services.

Human capital

The human capital base, comprising the sum of abilities, knowledge and motivation of individuals, is a determining factor in the success of the transformation process. So far, however, it must be seen as a impediment rather than a promoting factor for entrepreneurship and the development of SMEs. Under communism, both vocational training and higher education were fully integrated into and guided by the state socialist structure, taking their orientation from the needs of the predominantly nationalized heavy industry. Key qualifications, such as enterprise management, employee motivation, strategic planning and marketing were restricted to an elite who held high positions in state-owned industries (OECD 1996).

All countries under consideration, even the most advanced ones, suffer from a shortage of entrepreneurial skills (Fundatura 1998; Gortschewa 1998; OECD 1997a, 1997c). According to Gortschewa (1998), the main reasons Czech, Hungarian and Polish enterprises are far from being internationally competitive are a lack of production skills, a lack of marketing know-how and missing channels of distribution.

The same is true for the countries of the former Soviet Union. A study of the structure of qualifications in Latvia reveals that the country suffers from a lack of management skills in productivity, marketing, quality control and project formulation (OECD 1997a). Typically, these qualifications were not demanded under communism and are therefore rare. A 1995 study showed that more than half of the entrepreneurs in Moldavia consider their workforce as insufficiently trained; technical and marketing skills are the most important training need of private firms (Kruft and Sofrova 1997).

General regulation system

Positive framework conditions, crucial for the transformation process include the creation of initial legislation on private economic activities and the establishment of property rights, market-based institutions, a commercial banking system, competition and commercial law, a functioning authority for competition control and business ethics. This framework extends to other prerequisites, such as bankruptcy law and procedures, and the establishment of liberal trade regimes. Elements more specific to entrepreneurship include simple and inexpensive procedures for licensing and registration and a nonprohibitive and transparent system of taxation (OECD 1998, 1996).

Poland, Hungary, the Czech Republic and Slovakia have made the most progress in establishing legal and institutional frameworks appropriate to a market economy. But even in this group, the implementation of certain laws still presents a major problem for the development of entrepreneurship. This can be readily illustrated by Hungary. Although it has a competition law, it cannot prevent unfair competition. Moreover, the lack of assertion of property and contractual rights creates other problems (Papanek 1998). The legal framework in Slovenia is quite favorable for the development of SMEs (Tajnikar 1998), but the application of existing legislation still needs to be simplified (Marot 1997). In the course of eventually gaining EU membership, entrepreneurs expect uniformity, homogenization, qualitative improvement and increased transparency of the regulation system (Grzegorzewska and Koszalka 1998).

The weakness of implementation and enforcement of laws for the establishment of private SMEs is a critical impediment to the emergence of SMEs, as well as a strong disincentive to potential investors. Problems implementing new legislation may be traced back to an inadequate legal infrastructure and a low level of acceptance. In analyzing the reasons for the low acceptance of new laws, it must be considered that they differ fundamentally from the ones of the previous system. The countries in an intermediate stage of transition, along with the countries in the former Yugoslav Federation and the Soviet Union, have to face serious problems in implementing new legislation. For instance, in Romania, due to a highly legalistic tradition, hundreds of laws and regulations have been drafted since the transition started. Their implementation, however, is far from complete (OECD 1998). In Bulgaria, the legal framework for businesses can generally be considered good, although the needs of SMEs are definitely neglected. Relatively long delays in passing bills as a result of frequently changing governments and ineffective employers' organizations has led to a lack of regulations. Moreover, new legislation is frequently outdated or poorly prepared and therefore has negative effects on the start-up rate (Todorov 1996). The legal environment in the Russian Federation is still dominated by uncertainty and is extremely complex, as regional authorities have the ability to impose additional regulations (OECD 1998). Therefore, laws often contradict one another, creating legal confusion. A vacuum still dominates the legal framework. Furthermore, the enforcement of legal rules, especially bankruptcy legislation, is still poor, and there is a lack of rigorous antimonopolistic measures (Benini 1997). SMEs in Latvia suffer from the inconsistent application of regulations combined with poor legal information (Jaunzems and Elerts 1996).

All countries considered, except Romania and Belarus, have adopted the accounting standards of the European Union and have a modern insolvency law. However, it has to be noted that so far this law is of hardly any practical importance in Croatia, Romania, Slovakia and the Ukraine. The slowness of bankruptcy proceedings generally presents a problem (Lynn 1998). The enforcement of bankruptcies in Russia and in Bulgaria is extremely difficult, due to their overloaded court system (Miklos 1997; OECD 1998).

According to a *Frankfurter Allgemeine Zeitung* (FAZ 1998b) study, all the countries under consideration have a working stock exchange. However, there is no working antitrust authority in Slovenia, Bulgaria, Romania, Croatia, Lithuania, Latvia or Belarus. Land registers, and the use of mortgages and loans have been successfully introduced in all countries, except the Ukraine, where the system of land ownership is not reliable enough.

The transformation to a market economy made the complete reorganization of the tax system necessary. All European countries in transition have established new taxation laws and tax administration authorities. "However, there has been a general trend of decreasing government revenues throughout the transition process due to an emerging culture of tax evasion, inability to enforce tax collection and inefficiencies in tax administrations" (OECD 1998: 105).

Administration system for start-ups

Registration procedures for newly created firms are notoriously bureaucratic and lengthy in most European countries in transition. Entrepreneurs experience difficulties in obtaining various permits and licenses for business. It appears that the more advanced transition economies, such as Poland, Hungary and the Czech Republic, have all made efforts to reduce the burden of registration procedures. Countries in an intermediate stage of transition such as those in the former Yugoslav Federation and Soviet Union have not made much progress yet, and bureaucracy presents a major obstacle for start-up enterprises (Fundatura 1998; Leppee 1998; Marot 1997; OECD 1998). Bureaucratic delays and interference have been classified as one of the major problems by Bulgarian entrepreneurs. Similar results emerge from the Russian Federation, where local administrations are not sensitive to the needs of SMEs. In Russia, it is difficult to obtain a business license because there is not yet a well-defined standardized licensing procedure.

Moreover, registration procedures involve difficulties in filing and high application fees (Benini 1997; OECD 1998).

Government employees are as unable to deal with new economic legislation as the owners of private enterprises and potential entrepreneurs. The essential problem is the rather tense relationship between state employees and the commercial sector. Since entrepreneurs often suffered mistreatment by bureaucrats after the fall of communism, it is not difficult for them to recognize that civil servants are supposed to support private initiative. This is illustrated by widespread corruption, an unwillingness to pay taxes and a weakening of central power vis-à-vis local officials. Obviously, even the process of identification with a democratic state requires time for both the population and state employees (OECD 1996).

General infrastructure

The infrastructure for a market economy is still underdeveloped, which creates problems and high transaction costs for new private businesses, especially in the distribution of products. The infrastructure and communication network in European countries in transition is generally quite well developed, yet both need modernization.

During 1997 and 1998, the quality of public transport between Central and Eastern Europe has improved significantly. The fact that large shipping companies are still state-owned is the reason for major drawbacks (as in, e.g., Croatia). The infrastructural progress can be attributed to foreign investment, transfer of know-how, the growing presence of international shipping companies and the emergence of modern logistic centers as a result of direct foreign investment. The high crime rate in the transport sector has been reduced by the use of preventive security measures. However, as this rate still remains high, it is recommended to transport goods by train. In the long run, these problems can be solved by changes in the political and economic environments of the country involved. Another vital problem is sluggish customs clearance due to poor organization, ever-changing regulations and bureaucratic procedures. Major changes will be required in those countries applying for accession to the EU. In Poland, for example, more than two hundred traffic regulations will need to be altered in order to conform with EU provisions.

As one travels away from the EU border, the condition of roads and the quality of equipment of airports and seaports worsens. There is still a strong need for the reconstruction, modernization, improvement and construction of traffic and communication systems. Though international financial aid has been granted, it will take several years for the infrastructure to meet international standards. In the period between 1995 and 2005, the road traffic in European countries in transition is expected to double. A similar increase of traffic is forecast for seaports and airports. Freight traffic in Central and Eastern Europe is dominated by trucks, due to their flexibility and comparative advantages of time and price. A tendency toward introducing toll roads in order to finance highway modernization can be observed. Polish, Estonian, Hungarian and Czech freight transport services have managed to control 35 percent of the East–West freight transport market.

Major improvements in the field of telecommunications have been made, but much remains to be done. Access to internal and external economic information as well as access to efficient transportation routes are important means for a better framework for entrepreneurship (Blawatt 1995; Fundatura 1998).

Trade unions and employers' associations

From an institutionalist point of view, unions and associations form part of the infrastructure of a society. If their organization is efficient, they can offer a platform for self-regulation and management of conflicts between employers and employees by avoiding state intervention. Moreover, unions and associations can also offer services to their members, such as education and training courses and consultancy services. Generally, the state of trade unions and employers' associations in the European countries in transition can be described as a pluralist one.

Since 1990, the old federations of trade unions have been reformed and new unions established as a democratic alternative in almost all countries. Today, the trade unions of the former communist countries need to focus on image-building in order to inspire employees confidence. Most of the poorly paid officials have quit their jobs, the remaining officials have difficulty adapting to market needs. However, these reformed unions cannot afford to employ new, qualified experts. That was one of the reasons for the development of new unions. The acceptance of these newly established unions is generally quite high, although many employees remain members of the old trade unions. The new unions suffer from low membership and must largely depend on dues. This might also be because membership in the communist unions was not based on convictions but on privileges for members or restrictions and disadvantages for nonmembers. With privatization, membership in trade unions has declined. The idea of union solidarity needs to manifest itself within society. In the Czech Republic, for example, about 60 percent of the economically active population is organized in trade unions, but membership continues to decline (FAZ 1998a).

The Western call for the unions to strengthen their bargaining power and improve their efficiency has not yet become popular in Europe's postcommunist countries. The pluralism corresponds with their urge for variety, freedom of choice and voluntary membership. As a consequence, though, the individual influence of these trade unions is relatively weak, for example, in Croatia and Belarus. Czech and Romanian trade unions can be characterized as quite strong compared with unions in the other countries in transition (FAZ 1998a).

Generally, there is a lack of solidarity among employers. In most countries employers are only loosely organized and do not appear united in public. Where voluntary employer organizations exist, they have low membership rates. According to Hisrich and Fulop (1995: 93), the emerging entrepreneurs' associations are "still weak in terms of resources and political clout."

Access to capital

Entrepreneurs in transition countries often identify the lack of capital – both start-up capital and equity – as one of the principal difficulties they face. Venture capital, equity markets and institutional investors are either very underdeveloped or simply not an important source of financing for entrepreneurial projects at this time. Although legislative and institutional frameworks regulate securities exchange and stock markets in most countries, these markets do not yet have a significant role in financing new enterprises (OECD 1998, 1996; Price Waterhouse 1997).

Access to capital is obviously of primary importance to the emergence of entrepreneurship. Conditions for granting credit are extremely unfavorable for SMEs in transition economies. High interest rates and the requirement of substantial credit guarantees for short or medium-term loans make it difficult for small ventures to obtain bank loans. With an interest rate for SMEs in Romania between 60 and 70 percent, for example, there is hardly any activity that merits paying the enormous interest rates demanded by banks (Fundatura 1998).

The access of SMEs to "official" credit facilities of banks and financial support programs is still limited in all European countries in transition. Lengthy application procedures and short credit terms, insufficient for financing a production cycle, are the main factors that encourage SMEs to search for other sources of credit, including informal ones, which contribute to "shadow" turnover, or unreported sales (Eveseyeva and Loupinovitch 1997). In addition, there is an overall lack of risk capital. This situation hinders the creation of enterprises, the privatization process and the operational running of businesses. Suppliers' credits are a quite common form of financing in transition economies (Jaunzems and Elerts 1996; Marot 1997; OECD 1998, 1997a, 1996).

A 1996 survey shows that personal savings were the principal source of start-up capital for 59 percent of small firms in Bulgaria. The situation is similar in Russia, where it is common for entrepreneurs to cover start-up costs with personal savings (OECD 1996). Smallbone et al. (1998) found the most common source of finance (83 percent) for Ukrainian start-ups is self-finance, either from the entrepreneur's own resources or from family members. Obviously, external finance plays a minor role in financing Ukrainian SMEs, both at start-up and in their subsequent development. Only a diminishing percentage of SMEs are able to access bank financing. The reliance on personal equity and retained profits as sources of capital is a clear constraint to their ability to develop (Smallbone et al. 1998).

There are numerous reasons for the financial difficulties faced by SMEs. The existing banking system is responsible for many of their problems. The former monopolistic banking system was successfully transformed into a two-tier structure with central and commercial banks. This process of restructuring was completed rapidly and without major constraints. Today, many of the largest banks are still state-owned, and although new private banks play an important role, they are not yet represented in the entire country. The real problem of the banking reform, however, lies in the microeconomic restructuring of the newly created or privatized commercial banks and in the expansion of the services offered. Generally, the banking system of European countries in transition faces severe liquidity constraints. Because of a lack of expertise and experience with loan applications as well as an unsatisfactory competitive environment, commercial banks are not yet prepared to take the risk of financing SMEs. They favor state-owned ventures for loan approvals because of the secure return of capital, as can be seen from the situation in Poland.

More capital is available in the Polish private market than in other European countries in transition. However, few of these resources are directed at small high-risk enterprises or research-based ventures. Reasons for financing and lending institutions avoiding new enterprises or pre-start-up development proposals include the immaturity of Polish companies, a lack of credibility and transparency in accounting procedures and a lack of sophistication in business planning. The young Polish SME sector has neither developed its management capacity nor has it the experience necessary to attract financing. Gieorgica (1998: 165) states that "relatively few new entrepreneurs understand business well enough to structure acceptable loan applications or equity proposals." In addition to the difficulty in accessing borrowed funds, SMEs face liquidity constraints because of falling sales opportunities in the new market environment. Furthermore, entrepreneurs are only now slowly adapting to the financial discipline demanded by a market economy, which was not necessary in a centrally planned economy. However, these changes are characterized by a slow process of trial-and-error, since entrepreneurs as well as banks are still unfamiliar with business planning and repayment scheduling (Maro 1997; OECD 1996).

Generally, the banking sector in the most advanced countries (those that have already started negotiations with the EU) is relatively developed and efficient, but it has not fully adapted its services to the small business sector. This can be readily illustrated by Slovenia, which neither provides long-term loans for SMEs nor offers financial instruments that meet the needs of small businesses. High interest rates, limited resources of equity capital and prohibitive collateral requirements predominate (Marot 1997).

Insufficient regulations, the image of the European countries in transition and the lack of an effective entrepreneurs' lobby are the main reasons why foreign investments in SMEs are limited (Todorov 1996). Generally, all European countries in transition are interested in foreign investment. Despite a great deal of uncertainty, due to the interdependency of different macroeconomic factors, European transition economies try to present an attractive climate for foreign investors (Trommsdorff and Schuchardt 1998). This is a very important issue for transition economies because direct foreign investment can be a significant player in the field of SME creation and development. Furthermore, it plays a major role in transferring management skills, technological know-how and accessing larger markets (Peitsch 1997).

Market organization services

With regard to the market structure, a significant trend from the primary to the tertiary sector, especially in the more advanced countries, is obvious. In Hungary, for example, two-thirds of the people in the labor market are employed in the service sector (Institute for Small Business Development 1997). However, the service providers' and customers' expectations and perceptions of quality are often disparate. Markets and enterprises definitely need to learn more about service products (Lesakova 1998b). Less advanced countries, like the Ukraine, should probably refrain from the former Soviet policy of supporting the transitional branches of heavy industry and foster the tertiary sector instead (Kurylyak 1998).

Generally, there is almost no market organization for buying, selling or the merger of small firms in European countries in transition. An exception is Hungary, where the Hungarian Investment and Trade Development Agency supports foreign investors in seeking business partners (OECD 1997c).

Promoting Entrepreneurship

The pressure of rising unemployment and the liberalization of economic activity are making transition economies increasingly aware of the importance of the SME sector. The effective implementation of privatization policies, economic and political stability and access to financial resources are key factors for the development and emergence of SMEs. That is why in the early years of a lengthy transition process attention was mostly focused on macroeconomic factors such as price liberalization, the institution of a convertible currency, the privatization process and other market reforms (OECD 1998; Rühl 1998).

Now it is necessary to create appropriate incentives that will turn the existing potential into productive entrepreneurship. The increased political awareness of the importance of the SME sector results in more attention being paid by the governments to setting up and improving structures for a favorable climate for entrepreneurship. Massive international aid was the stumbling block for the establishment of institutions promoting entrepreneurship in the first years of the transition. Today significant government and foreign support are inevitable in this field (OECD 1998; Welter 1997).

Support systems can generally be divided into direct start-up incentives to entrepreneurs by direct financial aid and indirect start-up incentives. The three main categories of indirect start-up incentives in the form of business infrastructure provided by the government are:

1 Business incubators and technology parks,
2 Business advisory services and education and training facilities, and
3 Intermediaries that combine advice and financial assistance to entrepreneurs in the context of a larger development strategy (Welter 1997).

Supporting structures are necessary at three different stages in the development of SMEs:

1 When the idea to set up an enterprise is born, potential entrepreneurs need training on developing business plans and feasibility studies for their activities as well as information on certain procedures.
2 In the start-up stage technology parks, incubators, business advisory and training centers can be effective means to assist the founder.
3 At an early growth stage training and management advisory services are important in order to help entrepreneurs to expand their market (Kruft and Sofrova 1997).

The more advanced countries in transition have created national bodies or ministerial departments for the promotion of SMEs. In the early 1990s, a network of organizations fostering SME development was established in Slovenia. Compared with networks in other postsocialist countries, this network could be described as better conceived and instituted. However, since 1995, the growth of SMEs has been leveling off, so the SME promotion policy is on the decline as well (Tajnikar 1998). Romania has created the National Privatisation Agency (NAP). Bulgaria has established the Agency for SME Development within the Ministry of Industry. The State Committee for Support and Development of Small Enterprise (SCSME), is responsible for SME promotion in the Russian Federation.

Most of these policies have been modeled on the experience of Western economies and have been implemented through various donor assistance programs. For example, the Local Economic and Employment Development (LEED) Program has encouraged entrepreneurship through seminars, associations, business incubators and insistence on the importance of self-employment.

Space does not permit a discussion of all measures adopted for entrepreneurship promotion, but the important ones, such as public start-up incentives, the establishment of start-up and technology transfer centers and the development of a consultancy framework and international cooperation for education and training for entrepreneurs, will be dealt in more detail with in the remainder of this chapter.

Public start-up incentives

One of the most important areas of assistance to small business is the provision of access to financial resources (OECD 1997b). There are three types of direct start-up incentives:

1 the creation of a loan guarantee organization that helps SMEs with no securities to obtain credit,
2 offering nonrefundable finance of investment projects of SMEs, and
3 the creation of venture capital funds (Werner 1996).

Most programs are supported by international institutions, such as the European Investment Bank or the World Bank (Bobeva 1996; OECD 1997b). The Poland and Hungary Aid for Reconstructing of the Economies (PHARE) program of the European Union has been funding the development of SMEs to a great degree.

In Poland, SMEs that are unattractive to commercial banks are provided with loans on special terms by the European Bank for Reconstruction and Development, the European Investment Bank and the World Bank (Lukasik 1998; Gieorgica 1998). Unfortunately, many of the loans granted by international organizations are ending, which will force Poland's SMEs to seek innovative approaches to accessing capital and working with lending institutions. Since the beginning of 1996, the Foundation for Promotion and Development of SMEs has been exclusively focusing on the support and development of SMEs. This organization assists SMEs in obtaining bank financing, by promoting their international competitiveness, by generating data on SMEs and by offering training and commercial information for SMEs (Gieorgica 1998). In Estonia, The Small Business Loan and Guarantee Fund (SBLF) was created in 1995 to provide loans and guarantees exclusively to SMEs (OECD 1997a).

Start-up and technology transfer centers

Start-up and technology transfer centers have been successfully established with the help of international organizations in the more advanced countries (the Czech Republic, Hungary, Poland and Slovenia). Technology parks and business clusters are also becoming more common. Poland, for example, has about sixty incubator centers established by the World Bank and PHARE, which provide various types of assistance to SMEs to help them overcome financial difficulties in the start-up phase (Gieorgica 1998). As technology initiatives are difficult to explain and justify, training courses for redundant workers, job search services and consulting services are offered rather than supporting technology research or development (Gieorgica 1998). Technology transfer centers, business innovation centers and technology parks have also been established in the countries waiting for EU membership, such as Croatia (Svarc 1998).

Consultancy framework for entrepreneurs

SMEs need access to consultancy services and other support targeted at the supply of information. Because the markets for consultancy and business services are weakly developed in the emerging economies, SMEs face many disadvantages resulting from the limited availability and often low quality and high price of these services. Business information and consultancy services have been established in the Czech Republic, Hungary, Poland and Slovenia. Numerous business support organizations have been funded by the PHARE program, but more professional services, including business counseling for SMEs, are needed. The Czech Chamber of Commerce offers counseling for start-up entrepreneurs in the following fields: legal advice, possible types of business organizations, administrative infrastructure, advice in tax issues and the start-up process. They also offer ongoing training in legal, management and communication subjects. However, many founders do not even know about the services offered by the Chamber, which significantly reduces the positive impact of these services on SME development (Gerersdorfer 1997).

The PHARE program has contributed extensively to the progress in the Czech consultancy framework. Regional Consulting and Information Centres (RPIC) have been established to assist entrepreneurs in the start-up and growth of SMEs by using external consultants. PHARE financially backs the establishment of RPICs as well as Business and Innovation Centres (BICs), which offer innovation-oriented services. International consulting firms have been established in the Czech Republic and in many other European countries in transition, but they are very expensive (Werner 1996).

The PHARE program has also established business advisory centers in the second group of countries, which are in an intermediate stage of transition. The Romanian government has established a network of SME support agencies dedicated to collecting data on small businesses in different regions and in supplying hands-on technical and financial assistance to enterprise start-ups (OECD 1998). However, Romania lacks a national organization with governmental and entrepreneurial participation specialized in the problems of SMEs (Fundatura 1998). Among other institutions, the Matej Bel University in Slovakia offers business counseling and advice to business founders with the Faculty of Economics. They offer help in organizational, financial, marketing and technical problems (Lesakova 1998a).

Organizations supporting the development of SMEs have also been established in the countries of the former Yugoslav Federation and the Soviet Union. In Russia, the State Committee for Support and Development of Small Enterprise provides SME support infrastructure projects and limited financing for regionally based lending schemes in cooperation with the Ministry of Economy (OECD 1998). Furthermore, networks of business support agencies throughout the Russian Federation are supported by the OECD and offer business plan advice, counseling, technical assistance and sometimes limited start-up capital. The issue of coordination of federal, regional and international efforts to support entrepreneurs will be critical during the next few years (OECD 1998).

Education and training of entrepreneurs

The education system in western Europe is characterized by independence, in contrast with European countries in transition where hierarchical dependency prevails (Trommsdorff and Schuchardt 1998).

Generally, government-supported facilities for the education and training of entrepreneurs is adapting very slowly to market needs. In most countries in transition, technical classes still dominate the education system. Today, management and marketing courses are found on almost all business administration and economics curricula. However, major obstacles still have to be overcome in order to make education in these fields efficient. Since the professors, teachers and trainers are still predominantly from the communist era, it is difficult for some of them to accept the ideas of market economies and teach them to their students. Obviously, help from the international community is needed. Many Western universities professionally support universities in European countries in transition. However, countries offering special classes for SMEs or entrepreneurship are in existence only where Western universities supported them and only in the more advanced or intermediate transition economies (Kolesnikova and Kolesnikov 1997).

In Poland, the Ministry of Education focuses on independent thinking, entrepreneurship and computer science (Gieorgica 1998). For that reason, there are various schools and colleges offering courses in accounting, controlling, sales and marketing, distribution and finance. Entrepreneurship courses are run by Polish foundations and are usually financed by foreign funds (Sobczyk 1998). The World Bank has established thirty-four Entrepreneurship Support Centers offering intensive training in management and SME-related subjects (Gieorgica 1998). In addition, Polish business schools offer postgraduate courses on management in connection with marketing, industrial information science and business management (Sobczyk 1998). One of the benefits expected as a result of the eventual integration with the European Union is the impetus for permanent training of entrepreneurs and employees (Grzegorzewska and Koszalka 1998).

Similar cooperation on the academic level can be found in most countries, especially at the economic faculties and business schools in Slovenia, Hungary, the Czech Republic and Poland. Unfortunately, organizations such as regional chambers of commerce, regional employment bureaus, employers' associations or regional development agencies do not yet offer any special courses or training for entrepreneurs (Lesakova 1998a).

CONCLUSIONS

The climate for entrepreneurship in European countries in transition shows a wide range of both positive and negative factors. The transition from centrally planned economies to market economies is proceeding at varying speeds, which is caused by unequal starting positions, by continuing ethnic tensions and separatist wars and by different government approaches to improving the framework conditions.

Whereas western Europe has improved its internal economic relations through the concept of the single market, the level of international cooperation with the eastern part of the continent has diminished since the fall of communism, and differences in economic potentials are increasing. Some regions and countries show signs of weakness after initial positive experiences with the transition process, and some countries will probably be advanced enough to join the European Union in a few years. The climates for entrepreneurship in European countries in transition vary greatly, and entrepreneurs must be advised to make a careful analysis of all aspects of the framework conditions of the region where they want to start or to invest in further growth of their businesses.

REFERENCES

Balashevich, M. 1996. Die Rolle der Klein- und Mittelbetriebe in der Entwicklung der Marktwirtshaft in der Republik Belarus. In J. Mugler and M. Nitsche (eds.), *Versicherung, Risiko und Internationalisierung. Herausforderung für Unternehmensführung und Politik.* Vienna: Linde, pp. 457–63.

Bateman, M. 1997a. Introduction: the transitions towards the market economy. In M. Bateman and C. Randlesome (eds.), *Business Cultures in Central and Eastern Europe.* Oxford: Butterworth-Heinemann, pp. xiii–xxii.

Bateman, M. 1997b. Comparative analysis of Eastern European business cultures. In M. Bateman and C. Randlesome (eds.), *Business Cultures in Central and Eastern Europe.* Oxford: Butterworth-Heinemann, pp. 197–231.

Benini, R. 1997. SME development in Russia: main issues and challenges. In *Entrepreneurship and SMEs in Transition Economies.* Paris: OECD 1997, pp. 19–34.

Blawatt, K.R. 1995. Entrepreneurship in Estonia: profile of entrepreneurs. *Journal of Small Business Management* 33(2): 74–9.

Bobeva, D. 1996. Foreign investment and small and medium-sized enterprises in Bulgaria. In *Small Firms as Foreign Investors: Case Studies from Transition Economies.* Paris: OECD, pp. 71–93.

Dahrendorf, R. 1991. *Reflections on the Revolutions in Europe.* London: Chatto and Windus.

ENSR (European Network for SME Research). 1997. *The European Observatory for SMEs. Fifth Annual Report.* Zoetermeer: EIM.

Evsyeva, I. and Loupinovitch E. 1997. How banks cooperate with the small businesses in Russia. In D. Kodonas and M. Argyropoulos (eds.), *Change and Innovation: The Challenge for Small Firms.* Proceedings of the 27th European Small Business Seminar, Rhodes, Greece. European Council for Small Business, pp. 762–9.

FAZ (*Frankfurter Allgemeine Zeitung*). 1998a. *Mittel- und Osteuropa Perspektive. Jahrbuch 1998/99. vol. 1: Politischer Hintergrund und Wirtschaftsentwicklung (Central and East European Perspectives. Yearbook 1998/ 99, vol. 1: Political Background and Economic Development).* Frankfurt: FAZ.

FAZ (Frankfurter Allgemeine Zeitung). 1998b. *Mittel- und Osteuropa Perspektive. Jahrbuch 1998/99. vol. 2: Geschäftspraxis, Investions- und Außehandelsbedingungen (Central and East European Perspectives. Yearbook 1998/99, vol. 2: Business Practice, Framework Conditions for Investments and Foreign Trade).* Frankfurt: FAZ.

Fundatura, D. 1998. The small and medium-sized private enterprises in Romania. Yesterday–today–tomorrow. Paper submitted at the ECSB. Conference, SMEs and SME Policy in the Central and Eastern European Economies, Budapest, Hungary, April 2–4.

Gartner, W.B. 1995. A conceptual framework for describing the phenomenon of new venture creation. *Academy of Management Review* 10: 696–706.

Gerersdorfer, V. 1997. Beratung für Unternehmensgründunger in Österreich, Tschechien und Slowenien (Consultancy for start-ups in Austria, Czech Republic and Slovenia). Seminar paper at the Vienna University of Economics and Business Administration, Department of Small Business Management and Entrepreneurship.

Gieorgica, J.P. 1998. The role of training in developing small and medium enterprises in Poland.

Paper submitted at the 28th European Small Business Seminar. Vienna, Austria, pp. 163–73.

Gortschewa, T. 1998. Internationale Strategien der sich im Transaktionsprozeß befindlichen ost-un mitteleuropäischen Länder (International strategies of East and Central European countries in transition). *Journal for East European Management Studies* 3(3): 227–48.

Grzegorzewska, E. and Koszalka, J. 1998. Expectations of the owners of small and medium-sized businesses in view of Poland's integration in the European Union. Paper submitted at the ECSB-HSBA Conference SMEs and SME Policy in the Central and Eastern European Economies. Budapest, Hungary.

Hisrich, R.D. and Fulop, G. 1995. Hungarian entrepreneurs and their enterprises. *Journal of Small Business Management* 33(3): 88–94.

Institute for Small Business Development. 1997. *State of Small and Medium Sized Business in Hungary 1997.* Annual Report.

Jaunzems, A. and Elerts, M. 1996. Are Latvian SMEs ready for Internationalisation? In *Small Firms as Foreign Investors: Case Studies from Transition Economies.* The Center for Economic Co-operation with the Economies in Transition. Paris: OED, pp. 123–32.

Kelemen, M. and Hristov, L. 1998. From centrally planned culture to entrepreneurial culture: the example of Bulgarian and Romanian Organisations. *Journal of East European Management Studies* 3(3): 216–26.

Kolesnikova, L.A. and Kolesnikov, A.N. 1997. Facing change: marketing strategies of training centres – providers of services for SMEs in Russia. In D. Kodonas and M. Argyropoulos (eds.), *Change and Innovation: The Challenge for Small Firms.* Proceedings of the 27th European Small Business Seminar. Rhodes, Greece, pp. 409–16.

Kruft, A.T. and Sofrova, A. 1997. The need for intermediate support-structures for entrepreneurship in transitional economies. *Journal of Enterprising Culture* 5(1): 13–26.

Kurylyak, V. 1998. Small and middle business in Ukraine and its promotion by the development of an educational infrastructure. Paper submitted at the 28th European Small Business Seminar. Vienna.

Leppee, M. 1998. Program for encouraging the small business. Paper submitted at the 28th European Small Business Seminar. Vienna.

Lesakova, L. 1998a. The role of universities in small and medium businesses. Development in the Slovak Republic. Paper submitted at the 28th European Small Business Seminar. Vienna.

Lesakova, L. 1998b. Service quality as competitive advantage of service firms. Paper submitted at the 28th European Small Business Seminar. Vienna.

Liuhto, K. 1996. The transformation of the enterprise sector in Estonia – a historical approach to a contemporary transition. *Journal of Enterprising Culture* 4(3): 317–29.

Lukasik, G. 1998. Die Finanzierung der Entwicklung von kleinen und mittelständischen Unternehmen in Polen (Financing the development of small and medium-sized enterprises in Poland). Paper submitted at the 28th European Small Business Seminar. Vienna.

Lynn, M.L. 1998. Patterns of micro-enterprise diversification in transitional Eurasian economies. *International Small Business Journal* 16(2): 34–48.

Marot, B. 1997. Small business development strategy in Slovenia. In *Entrepreneurship and SMEs in Transition Economies.* The Visegrad Conference. Paris: OECD, pp. 51–64.

Matei, A. and Matei, L. 1998. Risk of decision-making and entrepreneurial environment. Paper submitted at the 28th European Small Business Seminar. Vienna.

Miklos, I. 1997. Europe's outcast? Slovakia and the European Union. *Economic Reform Today* 3: 26–8.

Miller, D. 1987. The genesis of configuration. *Academy of Management Review* 12: 686–701.

Mugler, J. 1998. *Betriebswirtschaftslehre der Klein- und Mittelbetriebe (Management of Small and Medium-Sized Enterprises)*, 3rd edn. Vienna: Springer.

OECD (Organization for Economic Cooperation and Development). 1996. Small business in transition economies. In *The Development of Entrepreneurship in the Czech Republic, Hungary, Poland and the Slovak Republic.* Paris. OECD.

OECD (Organization for Economic Cooperation and Development). 1997a. Financing: the experience of the economies in transition. In *Best Practice Policies for Small and Medium-Sized Enterprises.* Paris: OECD, pp. 115–34.

OECD (Organization for Economic Cooperation and Development). 1997b. Micro business financing in Hungary: the Start Programme. In *Best Practice Policies for Small and Medium-Sized Enterprises.* Paris: OECD, pp. 31–4.

OECD (Organization for Economic Cooperation and Development). 1997c. The significance of export markets for SMEs in Hungary. In *Best Practice Policies for Small and Medium-Sized Enterprises.* Paris: OECD, pp. 83–8.

OECD (Organization for Economic Cooperation and Development). 1998. *Fostering Entrepreneurship: A Thematic Review.* Paris: OECD.

Papanek, G. 1998. Economic policy and supporting the SMEs in Hungary. Paper submitted at the ECSB-HSBA Conference on SMEs and SME Policy in the Central and Eastern European Economies. Budapest.

Peitsch, B. 1997. The role of foreign direct investment in SME development. In *Entrepreneurship and SMEs in Transition Economies.* The Visegrad Conference. Centre for Co-operation with the Economies in Transition. Paris: OECD, pp. 89–100.

Price Waterhouse. 1997. *Doing Business in Croatia.* Price Waterhouse World Firm Services BV, Inc.

Raudjarv, M. 1998. Some aspects of the policy of small and medium-sized enterprises in the Republic of Estonia. Paper submitted at the ECSB-HSBA Conference on SMEs and SME Policy in the Central and Eastern European Economies. Budapest.

Rosati, D. et al. 1998. *Transition Countries in the First Quarter 1998: Widening Gap Between Fast and Slow Reformers.* Wiener Institut für Internationale Wirtschaftsvergleiche (WIIW).

Rühl, C. 1998. Presentation of EBRD's Transition Report 1997 at the OeNB. In OeNB 1998: *Focus on Transition 1/1998.* Vienna, pp. 118–19.

Slonimski, A. 1998. State support of small business in Republic of Belarus. Paper submitted at the ECSB-HSBA Conference SMEs and SME Policy in the Central and Eastern European Economies. Budapest.

Smallbone, D., Welter, F., Klochko, Y. and Isakova, N. 1998. The support needs of small enterprises in Ukraine. Paper submitted at the ECSB-HSBA Conference SMEs and SME Policy in the Central and Eastern European Economies. Budapest.

Snuif, H.R. and Zwart, P.S. 1994. Modeling new venture development as a path of configurations. In J.J. Obrecht and M. Bayad (eds.), *Small Business and Its Contribution to Regional and International Development.* Proceedings of the 39th ICSB World Conference. Paris: ICSB, pp. 263–74.

Sobczyk, G. 1998. Nichtöffentliches Bildungssystem für Management- und Business-Berufe in Polen (The nonpublic education system for management and business professions in Poland). Paper submitted at the 28th European Small Business Seminar. Vienna.

Svarc, J. 1998. Techno-centers in Croatia. Ministry of Science and Technology. Email of September 10, 1998.

Tajnikar, M. 1998. Failures of successful SME policy in Slovenia. Paper submitted at the ECSB-HSBA Conference SMEs and SME Policy in the Central and Eastern European Economies. Budapest.

Tibor, A. 1998. Why do enterprises fail in Hungary? In H.J. Pleitner (ed.), *Renaissance der KMU in einer globalisierten Wirtschaft (Renaissance of SMEs in a Globalized Economy).* Rencontres de St-Gall 1998. St. Gall: IGW-HSG, pp. 239–48.

Todorov, K. 1996. Between Icarus' flight and heron's boat. the case of Bulgarian SMEs. In *Small Firms as Foreign Investors: Case Studies from Transition Economies.* The Center for Economic Co-operation with the Economies in Transition. Paris: OECD, pp. 95–9.

Trommsdorff, V. and Schuchardt, C.A. 1998. *Transformation osteuropäischer Unternehmen (Transformation of East European Enterprises)*. Wiesbaden: Gabler.

Vojnic, D. 1997. Countries in transition: achievements, problems and prospects. In *Enterprise in Transition*. Second International Conference on Enterprise in Transition. The Faculty of Economics, Split, Croatia, pp. 5–23.

Wallace, C. and Haerpfer, C. 1998. *Three Paths of Transformation in Post-Communist Central Europe*. Vienna: Institute for Advanced Studies.

Welter, F. 1997. *Kleine und mittlere Unternehmen in den mittel- und osteuropäischen Ländern: Trends, Entwicklungshemmnisse und Lösungen (Small and Medium-sized Enterprises in Central and East European Countries: Trends, Impediments to Development and Solutions)*. TWI-Mitteilungen 47: 73–93.

Werner, R. 1996. Die Entwicklung der staatlichen Unterstützung der Klein- und Mittelbetriebe in der Tschechischen Republik (Development of public support of small and medium-sized enterprises in the Czech Republic). *Zeitschrift für Klein- und Mittelunternehmen* 44(1): 55–9.

9

Six Steps to Heaven: Evaluating the Impact of Public Policies to Support Small Businesses in Developed Economies

DAVID STOREY

SPECIFICATION OF OBJECTIVES
THE SIX STEPS
CONCLUSIONS

Virtually all developed economies utilize taxpayers' money to provide either free or subsidized assistance to small business, the self-employed or to potential small business owners. Sometimes this assistance is direct financial payments in the form of subsidies to encourage investment in human or physical capital. In other cases, subsidies are in the form of free or subsidized advisory services in starting or developing small business or in specialized areas, such as exporting or the use of new technology.

Taxpayers' money may also be used to bribe individuals or organizations to behave in a way perceived to benefit both small businesses and the economy as a whole. These bribes often take the form of tax relief. For example, wealthy individuals may be given tax breaks to become equity participants in small or young businesses. Finally, some government procurement programs focus on small businesses, using taxpayers' money to offset any efficiency losses to government by its having to contract with small businesses even if these are not optimal suppliers. The wide range of public support programs to small firms in developed economies and their appraisal is best reviewed in Organization for Economic Cooperation and Development publications (OECD 1995, 1996, 1997).

Given the huge variety of schemes, the diversity of countries in which the schemes are found and the often inflated claims on the part of those administering the schemes for their effectiveness, it is disappointing that the academic community has been rather slow in seeking to address this area. Perhaps more seriously, even when the issues have been addressed by small business academics, the methods of evaluation have rarely been at the intellectual frontier.

This chapter provides an outline methodology for evaluating the impact of public policies to assist the small business sector. It begins, however, by emphasizing the impossibility of conducting an evaluation in the absence of clearly specified objectives for the policy concerned. Ideally, in fact, these objectives should be specified in a quantitative manner in the form of targets.

The chapter then moves on to provide a review of the various methodological approaches to evaluating small business support policies in developed countries. Instead of a comprehensive review, an analytical framework is presented within which a wide variety of types of analyses can be classified. Six approaches are identified, beginning with the most simple and ending with the most sophisticated. These are referred to as the Six Steps with Step 6 being viewed as best practice, or "heaven," in this area. The chapter also makes a distinction between monitoring and evaluation. Monitoring involves Steps 1 to 3, with the more sophisticated approaches being classified as evaluation in Steps 4 to 6.

Specification of Objectives

A fundamental principle of evaluation is that it must first specify the objectives of policy. Unfortunately, a characteristic of governments in all developed countries seems to be, at best, being opaque about the objectives of small business policy. Many phrases characterize this area. Governments talk about "creating an enterprising society" or "maximizing SMEs contribution to economic development" or "enhancing competitiveness" or even "creating jobs." So far as this author is aware, however, no developed country produces a clear set of objectives for each component of small business policy. Analysts therefore are required to infer policy objectives, rather than having these clearly defined. Only then is it possible to determine whether or not the target is achieved and hence able to judge whether or not policy is successful.

Instead, what governments favor are lists of policies: lists of the various measures which have been introduced to help the small business sector, such as taxation exemptions, late payment, administrative burdens, finance and information provision. Typical of these lists are those presented in ENSR (1997) at a European level or DTI (1998) at a national level.

Analysts such as de Koning and Snijders (1992) have made attempts to compare small and medium-sized enterprise (SME) policies in countries. Their work, on European Union (EU) countries, was only able to compare, using such lists, the *number* of policy measures focused upon SMEs in policy fields such as fiscal policies, export policies, information and counseling etc. This is clearly not the same, and indeed is significantly inferior to, specifying objectives.

Not only is there a conspicuous absence of clear objectives for SME policy, but the implied objectives can often be conflicting. The United Kingdom can be taken as illustrative. Table 9.1 reproduces my earlier effort to seek to identify the appropriate objectives for UK small business policy. Note the table only defines the objectives and not the numerical values of the objectives (i.e., targets) themselves.

Table 9.1 distinguishes between intermediate and final objectives. Taking the top line as illustrative, we can identify "increasing employment" as an objective, with a target being where this objective was given a particular measure – such as increasing employment by 5 percent over a five-year period.

TABLE 9.1 Intermediate and final objectives

Intermediate	*Final*
1 Increase Employment	Increase employment
	Reduce unemployment
2 Increase number of start-ups	Increase number of start-ups
	Increase stock of firms
3 Promote use of consultants	Promote use of consultants
	Faster growth of firms
4 Increase competition	Increase competition
	Increase wealth
5 Promote 'efficient' markets	Promote 'efficient' markets
	Increase wealth
6 Promote technology diffusion	Promote technology
	Increase wealth
7 Increase wealth	Votes

Source: Storey (1994)

Taking now the objectives, politicians in most developed countries have SME policies because they believe, rightly or wrongly, that SMEs are both currently a major source of employment and likely to be an increasing source of new jobs in the future (Hughes 1997). Failure to address or encourage the SME sector may lead to slower rates of job creation and hence unemployment being higher than otherwise.

Unfortunately, political leaders frequently couch their rhetoric in terms of employment creation, so their prime concern is, in fact, to seek to reduce unemployment, rather than to increase employment. Increases in employment therefore can be considered as an intermediate objective, with the final objective being that of reducing unemployment.[1] Utilizing SMEs to create jobs can however have a mixed effect upon reducing the numbers of individuals registered as unemployed. From the positive side, SMEs are more likely to employ individuals who are comparatively heavily represented among the unemployed – the unskilled, the very young and the very old (Brown et al. 1990). Yet, in other respects, job creation in SMEs is likely to have only a modest effect upon reducing registered unemployment. This is because SMEs are disproportionately likely to provide part-time work, and these part-time workers (often females) are less likely to be registered as unemployed. There is therefore immediately a question as to whether the real objective of policy in item 1 is the creation of employment or the reduction in unemployment, but this is rarely made explicit in policy pronouncements.

A second area of possible conflict between job creation and reduction in unemployment is that the latter can often be reduced by emigration from a country or region. Policies of job creation, if they are successful, can lead to lower rates of out-migration because workers feel there is a prospect of getting a job in the locality. Success at creating jobs can even, perversely, lead to increased unemployment. Those specifying objectives have to be clear where their priorities lie.

In row 2 of table 9.1 an alternative objective of SME policy is articulated. Many countries have policies to encourage individuals to start businesses. This may be related to aspects of objective 1 (e.g., a view that more people starting businesses leads directly to additional jobs or to reducing the numbers of unemployed). Alternatively, policies to increase the number of start-ups may merely reflect (be a result of) a more dynamic economy, one likely to exhibit prosperity in the longer term. However, it is widely recognized that policies to assist the start-up of new enterprises are most likely to be targeted upon individuals who are unemployed, since these individuals are the most "susceptible." Experience, both in the United Kingdom and the United States (Storey and Strange 1992; Bendick and Egan 1987), shows these individuals often enter trades with low entry barriers – such as vehicle repairers, window cleaners and taxi drivers for which there is a finite and highly localized demand. The net effect of such policies is that public money is used to encourage unemployed individuals to start a business in these sectors but serves primarily to displace other unsubsidized traders in the locality with no obvious benefit either to the local consumer or to the economy in general. The effect then is to increase the number of start-ups, i.e., satisfy intermediate objective 2, but also to increase the number of businesses that cease to trade, with little net change in the number of firms and so not satisfy final objective 2. Even where there is an increase in the number of firms, there may well be a compensating fall in average firm size without any apparent increase in employment (Storey and Strange 1992). A choice therefore has to be made between intermediate objective 1 and intermediate objective 2.

The remainder of table 9.1 identifies several other objectives that are apparent from observing the characteristics of public support for SMEs in the United Kingdom. The interested reader can consult Storey (1994) for a fuller discussion for other potential conflicts. Perhaps the only objective requiring further comment at this point is that in row 7, where the final objective is Votes. This clearly is a fundamentally different objective, since it is explicitly political, rather than being one of the other more economic objectives specified elsewhere. As noted in Storey (1994), there is nothing undesirable in public policies being focused on the achievement of economic objectives and, as a reward for achieving good economic performance, politicians being re-elected. Indeed, such logic is at the cornerstone of democracy. What is more questionable is where policies, using taxpayers' money, are couched in terms of economic objectives but are really a mechanism for persuading a numerically significant group (in this case, small business owners) to vote for the government through the provision of "sweeteners." In many countries there is an overtly political element to small business policies, and failure by analysts to take it into account would be to underestimate the role it plays in politicians' calculations.

Governments, then, should be required to specify their objective in the provision of small business support. Identifying a wide range of sketchy objectives may serve the government's purpose of being able to point to success if there is an improvement in that objective area, but this is clearly unsatisfactory from the viewpoint of the taxpayer. Harrison and Leitch (1996) suggest that it is unsatisfactory for the government to claim that the target is anything it happens to hit. Instead, governments should set objectives, with an indication of which, if there is more than one, takes priority. Once the objectives are set, then numerical targets need to be specified. Only then can evaluation take place.

It is interesting to note that while this chapter was in preparation the issue received some heavyweight support in the United Kingdom from the House of Commons Select Committee (1998):

The Government has yet to state clearly what its policy objectives are with regard to SME policy; how the achievement of these broad objectives can be assessed, or how existing policy measures fit within a broader context. . . . The means by which competitiveness can be measured and the reasons for targeting competitiveness, in terms of its impact on employment, unemployment, GDP and other indicators can only be guessed at. . . . We are not convinced that the Government's SME policy is characterized by sufficient structure and focus. . . . We recommend that, as a matter of urgency, the government define the objectives of SME policy. The objectives chosen must be accompanied by measurable targets, with a timetable for their attainment.

Clearly such a development would be highly desirable and ought to be implemented with all speed.

The Six Steps

This section makes the unrealistic assumption that objectives, either of small business policy as a whole or of the particular program under consideration, are specified. The remainder of the chapter seeks to review how, in practice, appraisal is undertaken. Table 9.2 identifies the six steps, which are ranked in terms of sophistication, with Step 1 being the least sophisticated and Step 6 being the most sophisticated.

TABLE 9.2 The six steps

Monitoring
Step 1: take-up of schemes
Step 2: recipients' opinions
Step 3: recipients' views of the difference made by the assistance

Evaluation
Step 4: comparison of the performance of "assisted" with "typical" firms
Step 5: comparison with match firms
Step 6: taking account of selection bias

Although all six steps are often referred to as evaluations in the literature, Steps 1 to 3 can be considered as merely monitoring, with Steps 4 to 6 being evaluation.[2] The difference between monitoring and evaluation is that the latter are attempts, demonstrating analytical rigor, to determine the impact of the policy initiatives. Monitoring, on the other hand, merely either documents activity under the program or reports participants' perception of the value of the scheme. In short, the difference is that monitoring relies exclusively upon the views of the recipients of the policy, but evaluation seeks to contrast these with nonrecipients in order to present a "counter-factual." The difference between actual changes and the counter-factual is viewed as the impact of the policy (i.e., what is said versus what happens).

Monitoring

Step 1: take-up of schemes

Table 9.3 describes Step 1. This monitoring procedure identifies the characteristics and nature of the take-up of the scheme. For example, it might quantify the number of firms that participated in a particular scheme, their sectoral distribution, the size of such enterprises and possibly their regional distribution. Step 1 reviews also frequently include public expenditure on the schemes so that, for example, expenditure by firm size or the proportion of expenditure consumed by particular regions can be identified. What is much less frequently available is information on the money received by individual firms, since this is thought to contravene a confidentiality relationship between government and the enterprise.

TABLE 9.3 Take-up of schemes

Questions
- How many firms participated?
- What sectors were they in?
- What locations were they in?
- How big were these firms?
- How much money was spent?

Problems
- Tells you almost nothing about policy effectiveness
- Tells you almost nothing about satisfying objectives

Examples

Author	Date	Topic	Country
USA Delegation to OECD	1997	Small Business Investment Co.	USA

The data used in Step 1 are primarily collected by the public sector for accounting purposes. In many instances they appear as appendices to government documents, but because they are collected simply for accounting purposes, they do not even seek to evaluate whether the monies have been effectively spent. Their sole concern is to document expenditure, making it clear that expenditure is compatible with the purpose for which is was intended. In short, Step 1 serves an accounting and legal function but plays no economic role.

The second section of table 9.3 makes it clear that, while Step 1 appraisals are the most frequently conducted, the results obtained provide no insight whatsoever into policy effectiveness. They do not even seek to answer the question, To what extent did the policy achieve the types of objectives outlined in table 9.1?

Despite their ubiquity, Step 1 appraisals can only be considered as the building blocks for evaluation. They provide data on the numbers of firms participating and on expenditures, but these items are not linked.

Step 2: recipients' opinions

In Step 2 those firms who participated in the schemes are asked for their opinions. For example, those participating in subsidized training activities are asked about whether they felt there was value in the training provided; firms in receipt of subsidized loans are asked about whether they thought the loan to be valuable; those who participated in export counseling services are asked whether they felt the advice was helpful and whether it led to new orders. Firms participating in Loan Guarantee Schemes are asked about whether they would have received funding for a project without the availability of the scheme.

Firms are also normally asked about the application procedures to participate in the scheme to determine whether these can be streamlined. For example, firms are asked about how they became aware of the service, about the complexity of the application procedure and whether the application was speedily and fairly handled by the bureaucrat.

Step 1 data is therefore "objective" financial accounting data, whereas Step 2 seeks to obtain the viewpoint of the firms both on the effectiveness of the scheme and on its accessibility.

The Problems section of table 9.4, however, shows that, despite the frequency of such studies, Step 2 information does not help determine whether objectives are achieved. Take, for example, participants in training courses who are often asked to express an opinion about whether they felt the training to be of use to them and whether it was professionally delivered – the so-called happy sheets. It is, however, a considerable leap of faith to believe that satisfaction with the course delivered relates to enhanced firm performance; yet it is only enhanced firm performance which will be related to the objectives of policy.[3] In short, while such assistance may make the recipients happier – and conceivably more likely to vote for the politicians – it does not necessarily relate to the economic objectives of the policy, such as increasing the competitiveness of the firm or job creation.

If the objective of the investigation is, in part, to identify the problems with accessing

TABLE 9.4 Recipients' opinions

Questions
- Course participants: Did they like it?
- Firms: Were there problems in applying? Were procedures too slow? Cumbersome?

Problems
- Even if they like it, it does not tell you if it is effective
- All it can do is offer insights into policy delivery but that is not the key question

Examples

Author	Year	Topic	Country
Moint	1998	Export Assistance	USA
Rogoff and M.S. Lee	1996	Small business support services, in general	USA
Ernst & Young	1996	Business Links	UK

aid, then addressing these questions to only those firms that were successful in overcoming any barriers leads to biases. In particular those who have surmounted the barriers will predictably have a more positive view than those who were discouraged. Questioning only participant firms fails to estimate the extent to which firms are discouraged from participating in a scheme by the real or imagined barriers that exist. Of paramount importance is that the views are sought of all relevant businesses – whether or not they applied. From this, a list of applicants who did not access the aid must also be drawn. Only in this way is it possible to obtain an accurate measure of the extent of any application barriers.

Overall, Step 2 appraisals can offer some insight into policy delivery (especially when combined with the views of nonrecipients), but they remain almost irrelevant to determining the effectiveness of policy. This is because there may be no link between the views of the firm on the value of the policy and the ability of the policy to achieve the objectives specified in table 9.1. For example, the privately rationed firms will prefer public subsidies with high dead-weight elements and might be tempted to speak positively about such policies if they felt this was likely to influence government provision of such subsidies. On the other hand, some firms may be more truthful, yet the evaluator has no means of distinguishing the truthful from the selfish firms.

Step 3: recipients' views of the difference made by the assistance

In Step 3, recipients of the policy are asked not simply whether they liked the policy – the happy sheets – but also whether they thought this made any difference to their firm's performance. Normally quantitative estimates are sought, to determine whether the initiative provided additionality in terms of additional jobs, sales or profits.

Table 9.5 shows that, in the more "sophisticated" Step 3 appraisals, firms may also be asked questions about what would have happened to them if they had not received the policy initiative. Perhaps, most difficult of all, firms may be asked to estimate the extent to which, if there is any enhanced performance on their part, this is at the expense of other firms. Such questions are designed to estimate the extent of any displacement.

TABLE 9.5 Recipients' view of the difference made by the assistance

Questions
- Did firms think it provided "additionality"
- Would firms have done it anyway?
- Does it cause "displacement"?

Problems
- Provide answers they think you want to hear
- No way of checking
- Only snapshot of surviving firms

Examples

Author	Year	Topic	Country
DTI	1989, 1991(a, b)	Subsidized consultancy	United Kingdom

The Problems section of table 9.5 shows there are several fundamental difficulties with this approach in addition to those referred to in Step 2. The most important of these is the extent to which businesses are capable, even if they choose to be truthful, of conducting the mental gymnastics required to answer such questions. To ask small manufacturers to estimate the extent to which the provision of a loan or subsidized advisory service received two or three years previously influenced the subsequent profitability of their firms merely encourages guessing. There are so many influences upon the performance of small enterprises that being able to attribute precisely a number, or even a range, is an unreasonable question.

In many instances it is a perfectly understandable reaction of businesses to provide answers they think the questioner wishes to hear in order to be able to continue untroubled with the running of their business. If they do adopt this response there is, yet again, no way of checking.

Although some entrepreneurs will provide the answer they think the questioner wishes to hear in order to get them out of the door (and by implication therefore overestimate the impact of the initiative), others may adopt the reverse strategy. Many entrepreneurs are fiercely proud of their business and are very reluctant to admit to receiving any assistance whatsoever. Such individuals are therefore likely to underestimate the contribution of policy by claiming that any improvements in their business reflected their entrepreneurial skills, rather than public money. Faced with these extreme groups the analyst has no basis for judging which of the two are numerically dominant in any group.

There is also the issue of when such questions should be asked and of whom. Clearly, they cannot be asked at the time of the loan since any effects (e.g., on profitability or sales) will not have had an effect. On the other hand, a period of more than three years after the loan will mean that too many other influences will have affected firm performance. A balance therefore has to be struck between not waiting long enough for effects to appear and waiting so long that recall deteriorates.

Finally, it is the case for both Step 2 and Step 3 appraisals that interviews can only be conducted for firms that continue to trade. It is very difficult to contact enterprises no longer trading, yet all firms are the target for policy. To have responses only from surviving firms will clearly bias the interpretations placed upon the effectiveness of the policy, serving to make the outcomes more positive than would be the case by the inclusion of both survivors and nonsurvivors.

Overall, therefore, monitoring alone is incapable of offering policy relevant insights into policy effectiveness, where the objective of policy is to enhance the performance of SMEs. This is because the effect of policy cannot be estimated simply by seeking the views of recipient firms, even if these views were honestly provided. It is only capable of soliciting views from operational businesses so, if one objective of policy is to raise survival rates of firms, then this procedure is precluded. To overcome these problems it is necessary to compare the assisted firms with groups of firms not assisted by the policy. This is defined as evaluation. Its challenge is to isolate the appropriate group of firms with which to make the comparison, and to hold constant all other influences.

Evaluation

Step 4: comparison of the performance of assisted and typical firms

The earlier discussion of table 9.2 emphasized that a key distinction between monitoring and evaluation was that monitoring focused exclusively upon firms that have been assisted by policy. Yet to evaluate the impact of the policy it is necessary to decide what would have happened to businesses in the absence of policy – the so-called counterfactual. The effect of policy is therefore defined to be the difference between what actually happened and what would have happened in the absence of policy.

Step 4 estimates this impact by comparing the performance in firms assisted by the policy with those that have not been assisted. The inference is that any difference in the performance of the two groups can be attributed to the impact of the policy.

In table 9.6 assisted firms are compared with typical firms in the population. For example, employment or sales growth in assisted firms is compared with typical firms; alternatively the differences in survival rate of assisted firms may be compared with the survival rates of firms more generally in the economy. The advantage of this approach is that, for the first time, a control group of enterprises is identified. This enables comparisons between the assisted and the control group to be made; it also enables comparisons, in principle, to be made between the survival and nonsurvival of firms in both groups.

Table 9.6 Comparison of the performances of assisted with typical firms

Approach
- Employment/sales growth of assisted firms compared with 'typical' firms
- Survival of assisted firms compared with 'typical' firms

Problems
- Assisted firms are not typical

Examples

Author	Year	Topic	Country
Chrisman et al.	1985	Subsidized consultancy	USA
Deschoolmeester et al.	1998	Management training	Belgium

The problem, as noted in the second half of table 9.6, is that firms in receipt of assistance may not be typical of firms in the economy as a whole. For example, firms in which the entrepreneur seeks training, even when this is subsidized by the state, may be more likely to be growth-oriented than other firms. Those seeking training from a premier university business school are more likely to have graduates in the business than "typical" firms. As Deschoolmeester et al. (1998) show, those seeking training are generally younger and significantly better educated than the population of firms as a whole. Given this, they may also be starting businesses in different sectors. Equally, firms seeking advisory services may be more aware businesses and therefore more likely to be better performing businesses. Thirdly, there may be sectoral or geographical characteristics of recipients, which distinguish them from the population of firms overall. These effects can be either positive or negative.

For example, some SME policies are focused upon the unemployed or at-risk groups. A classic example is Law 44 in Italy, described in detail in OECD (1995, 1997). This scheme targets unemployed young persons in southern Italy and provides financial and mentoring support to these people in start-up and early development of their businesses. It would clearly be inappropriate to compare these businesses with typical Italian small firms for at least two reasons. The first is that these businesses are founded by young people, the survival rate of whose businesses is known to be markedly lower than those of other age groups. The second difference is that the economic and trading environment of southern Italy is significantly more difficult than in other parts of that country, making it more difficult for new businesses to flourish. For these two reasons, to compare Law 44 firms directly with "typical" Italian firms and attribute any difference in performance to the law would be to risk seriously underestimating its impact.

The study by Deschoolmeester et al. (1998), comparing start-ups of businesses from graduates of the Vlerick School, finds marked differences in age, sector and education between the graduates and the number of firms. All these factors will influence the subsequent performance of the firm. To attribute performance differences to the provision of the training requires explicit account to be taken of these factors.

It is therefore necessary to more explicitly take into account the factors likely to influence the performance of the assisted and nonassisted firms and to seek to hold these constant. This process is called matching.

Step 5: comparison of match firms
In Step 5 researchers identify a specific control group with which to compare the assisted businesses. For example, if a policy were implemented to enhance the survival rates of new businesses then it would clearly be inappropriate to compare survival rates of assisted new businesses with that of typical small firms because it has been consistently shown that young businesses have lower survival rates than longer-established businesses and that larger firms have higher survival rates than smaller firms (Storey 1994). Failure to take account of these elements would clearly bias the picture. Equally, if the scheme were focused upon high-tech businesses, then these types of businesses generally have faster growth rates than the SME population as a whole. Hence it would be unreasonable to compare the performance of the two groups of firms and infer that the difference in performance is attributable to the policy.

For these reasons table 9.7 shows that Step 5 appraisals formally identify a control group of firms. These are called match firms, and matching generally takes place on four factors known to influence, to different extents, the performance of firms. In principle, the assisted and the match firms would be expected to be identical on the basis of age, sector, ownership and geography. Given such controls, it is then possible to compare the performance of both groups over the same time period. The inference drawn is that any differences in performance between the two groups are attributable to the policy.

However table 9.7 shows that, even here, there are both technical and inferential problems. The technical problem is that perfect matching upon all four criteria simultaneously can be difficult. Ideally, such matching should take place immediately before the time at which the policy is implemented so that the performance of the two cohorts can

TABLE 9.7 Comparison with match firms

Approach
- Compare assisted with 'match' firms on the basis of: age; sector; ownership; geography
- Compare performance of both groups over same time period

Problems
- Perfect matching on four criteria can be very difficult
- Sample selection bias: more motivated firms apply; attribute differential performance to scheme and not to motivation

Examples

Author	Year	Topic	Country
Westhead and Storey	1994	Science parks evaluation	UK
Lerner	1997	Small business investment companies	USA
Hart and Scott	1994	Financial assistance	UK

be monitored over time. In practice, this rarely happens. Instead information may be available for the assisted firms over a period of time, but then the control group is constructed as part of the evaluation procedure after the policy has been in operation. This means that it can be difficult to accurately estimate the survival/nonsurvival impact of policy – and yet this is a crucial element of SME policy initiatives in most countries.[4]

Although there are technical problems in constructing the sample, there are also major inferential problems. In particular, even if the four matching characteristics are held constant, there may be other factors in which the two groups differ. In the terminology of labor economics, while it is possible to take account of "observables," it is much more difficult to take account of "unobservables" (Lalonde 1986; O'Higgins 1994). The observables can be considered to be age, sector, etc., as discussed above. The key unobservables in this context are the possibly linked issues of motivation and selection.

Taking motivation first; it may be that although firms do not differ in terms of observables, those that seek assistance are more dynamic and growth-oriented. They may be run by individuals who are more aware, better networked and more open to new ideas. If we compare the performance of assisted and nonassisted firms and find the former outperform the latter, it may be tempting to infer the difference is attributable to the policy. But if the two groups also differ in terms of motivation, any performance differences may reflect motivation rather than policy impact. In technical terms the motivated firms are self-selecting, which has to be taken into account. This is subsequently referred to as self-selection.

A second source of selection bias occurs when the scheme providers choose some applicants and not others; which is called administrative selection. Examples include the SBIR program in the United States (Lerner 1997), Law 44 in Italy or the Prince's Youth Business Trust in the United Kingdom. In all three schemes an individual or a business applies to participate. A judgment is made as to whether that individual is suitable (we assume all individuals are eligible but that resources are deemed insufficient to fully satisfy all eligible applicants). Under this selection procedure, it is reasonably assumed that the selectors will seek to identify the "best" cases, or at least seek to avoid the "worst" cases. Otherwise, there would be no value in a selection procedure.

We have to assume the selectors are capable of making informed judgments – otherwise there would be no point in having selectors. In this case the performance of the selected group will, even if the policy yielded no benefits whatever to the firms, be superior to that of the match group since the better cases are being selected. It therefore cannot be inferred that the whole of the observed difference between the assisted group and the nonassisted group in terms of performance is attributable exclusively to the policy.

Two factors are likely to enhance this bias. The first is the extent of competition for the funds. If ninety-nine out of a hundred applicants are successful, sample selection bias is likely to be less than where only ten applicants in every hundred are successful. Secondly, the ability of the selectors to make good decisions is also of considerable importance. Our judgment is that, since so many small business support policies are selective, and substantial resources are devoted to the selection procedure, it must be believed, at least by policymakers, that selection makes a difference. Quite simply, the bigger the difference the selection makes, the more important it is to use control groups, which only take account of observables.

Step 6: taking account of selection bias

How then do we seek to overcome these problems? Table 9.8 shows that Step 6 procedures seek to compare assisted with matched firms, taking account of sample selection. Two procedures can be employed. The first uses statistical techniques to explicitly take into account sample selection bias. These have become standard practice within the labor economics literature dealing with assessing the impact of training upon subsequent employment prospects of individuals (Dolton et al. 1989; O'Higgins 1994). In nontechnical terms the Heckman two-step adjustment procedure formulates a single equation to explain the selection procedure and then, taking account of the selection procedure factors, formulates a second equation to explain performance change, taking account of factors included in the selection equation. The value of the procedure is that the extent, if any, of selection can be taken into account. Thus, the selection equation generates a coefficient (inverse Mills ratio) that is significant where selection is present. Where it is not, then a Stage 5 procedure is perfectly valid.

Where selection is shown to be present, the impact deflation can be considerable. For example, the Wren and Storey (1998) analysis of the impact of the United Kingdom's subsidized consultancy services showed that, taking no account of selection, the policy appeared to raise the survival rate of firms by up to 16 percent over an eight-year period and raised it up to 3 percent over a two-year period. However, when account was taken of selection, these fell to 5 percent over the long term and 2 percent in the short run. Failure to take account of selection can therefore lead to serious overestimates of the impact of policy. Although some policymakers favor this, it clearly is not in the public interest.

Many policymakers, however, are not happy with these statistical methods because the procedures are so complicated and technical that they feel uncomfortable. Their discom-

TABLE 9.8 Compare assisted with match firms taking account of sample selection

Approach
- Use of statistical techniques: Heckman two-step estimator for testing and adjustment
- Use of random panels

Problems
- Policymakers (and some academics) feel uneasy about statistical adjustment
- Use of random panels could mean public money is given to firms and people who will not benefit

Examples

Author	Year	Topic	Country
Wren and Storey	1998	Subsidized marketing consultancy	United Kingdom
		Undergraduate placement program (STEP)	United Kingdom

fort is supported by the findings of LaLonde (1986) who compared the use of random panels with the econometric analysis and found the former to yield superior results. Random panels are particularly valuable if the object is to take account of "committee selection" but they are of only limited value when taking account of self-selection. If we take, as an example, individuals or entrepreneurs who seek to obtain an award of either finance or advice – an example might be SBIR or Law 44 – then it would be appropriate to make a selection in the normal way, but as a control, to allow a random sample of applicants access to the award without selection. The performance of the random access group would then be monitored over the same time as that of the selected applicants. If the selected applicants differ significantly in terms of observables from the random applicants, then this would also have to be taken into account in the analysis. Nevertheless, the prime purpose of the random access group is to seek to take account of the administrative selection influence. The effect of the impact of the policy would be the difference in performance between the assisted and the control group, after also eliminating the influence of selection.

The second part of table 9.8, however, shows problems remain even with these two approaches. Many analysts feel that the fairly complex statistical analysis in the Heckman two-step procedure[5] is difficult to communicate in simple language. Even if they understand it themselves, politicians, faced with having to explain the Heckman two-step to taxpayers and the small business community, would risk being branded as indulging in statistical hocus-pocus.

In principle, the use of random panels is more attractive because it is more easily understood. But if it is known with some degree of certainty that only a small proportion of firms will significantly benefit from the scheme, and it is also known, in advance, the characteristics of those who will benefit – i.e., selection is accurate – then public money is being wasted in providing assistance to businesses unlikely to succeed. The business community itself could therefore justifiably complain that money that otherwise could be usefully used on the scheme is being wasted upon businesses with little prospects in order merely to evaluate the impact of the scheme.

Overall, however, the key message is that selection, both in the form of self-selection and administrative selection, is an important issue. Failure to take it into account seriously risks overestimating the impact of policy. Where administrative selection, in particular, is clearly prevalent, a strong case can be made for the limited use of random panels. If self-selection is likely, more sophisticated statistical analyses have to be conducted – even if explaining the outcome to politicians could be tricky!

CONCLUSIONS

If public money is spent on SME support, then it is vital that evaluation of the impact of these initiatives takes place. Unfortunately, evaluation is not possible unless objectives that are clear and, in principle, measurable are specified. Too often objectives are either not specified or specified in a way that is overly vague and incapable of being used as the basis for deciding whether or not the policies are successful. In my judgment these objectives should be quantified and become explicit targets.

This chapter has also argued that evaluation and monitoring are not identical. We view monitoring as collecting information about the firms in receipt of the scheme, together with financial information of monies expended. We also view monitoring as seeking only the opinions of recipients of the scheme. On the other hand, evaluation seeks to compare performance of recipients with other groups of individuals or enterprises. Unfortunately, most policy initiatives in OECD countries currently are merely monitored, rather than evaluated. In the terminology of this chapter, such appraisals as are conducted rarely pass beyond Step 3, and in many instances do not pass beyond Step 1.

There are problems with all stages in the evaluation procedure, but current best practice is Step 6. In my judgment new SME policies should ensure that, before their implementation, a budget is set aside to ensure that an evaluation plan is established to achieve at least a Stage 5 level of evaluation. Governments are failing in their responsibilities to their taxpayers if they continue to finance evaluations less rigorous than those of Stage 5.

From the viewpoint of the research community, it is important for the most sophisticated analysis possible to be undertaken. Almost all small business policies involve an element of selection – either administrative selection or soft selection. The challenge to researchers is to seek to address the issue of selection. The problem, however, is the payoff to researchers is likely to be negative. This is because the experience chronicled in this chapter suggests that, the more sophisticated and careful the analysis, the weaker the apparent impact of policy. This is because the sophisticated analyst does not attribute to policy effects what are actually attributable to other influences such as selection or firm characteristics.

Unfortunately, the *realpolitik* of the situation is that policymakers generally (but not always) wish to demonstrate the effectiveness of their policies. They are therefore likely to favor sloppy analysts who are capable of "demonstrating" major policy impacts and disfavor careful analysts.

This has potentially serious consequences for the genuine research community; it means we risk exclusion from the policy arena because we do not have access to data. Even when access is granted, the data will almost certainly have not been collected in an ideal way, i.e., data collected after the policy is implemented, no data on control firms included and data on administrative selection not collected.

The challenge then for the research community is to persuade policymakers that it is in their long-term interests to carefully appraise policy and to be involved with that appraisal before policies are introduced. Unfortunately, such ideas may be somewhat naive since policymakers with apparently often very limited budgets prefer "cheap and cheerful" research that yields positive findings rather than accurate and careful research where policy impact is likely to be less. The emphasis that most governments have upon competitive tendering for research contracts only serves to reinforce these competitive advantages of the cheap and cheerful brigade.

NOTES

This paper was first formulated as a result of the authors participation in the evaluation group convened by Anders Lundstrom from the Swedish Foundation for Small Business Research (FSF). The key members of the group were Anders Lundstrom, Dennis De, William Dennis, Lois Stevenson, Jane Wickman, Christer Öhman and Hakan Boter. A major influence on the ideas has also been the author's involvement with the Best Practice Working Party on SMEs at the OECD. Early versions of the chapter were also presented to the I.G. Conference "Processes of Enterprise Creation and Consolidation" in Rome, December 12, 1997, in Mikkeli, Finland on "Growth and Job Creation in SMEs," January 7–9, 1998, and then at the ICSB Conference in Singapore, June 8–10, 1998. Helpful feedback was provided in all instances, particularly from Frank Hoy who pointed me toward US literature of which I was unaware. I also appreciated comments received from Marc Cowling.

1 Here targets are sometimes specified. For example the Swedish government is committed to halving unemployment over a five-year period to the year 2002.
2 "Monitoring has narrower objectives than evaluation. It is limited to observing and recording practical indicators of inputs and outputs. . . . Evaluation has two prime aims: an improving and learning aim [and] a proving aim" (Bridge et al. 1998).
3 Despite this, the link is frequently made. For example, the Barclays 1998 small business review on training reports high levels of satisfaction reported by owner-managers on training courses (91percent felt that quality was good or very good), but no attempt was made to link this to formal performance measures. Despite this Barclays asserted that they believe it to be a critical element to a successful small business. However where such links have been sought through careful work (Hughes 1997) associations are very weak or nonexistent.
4 A classic example of this are the attempts which began to be made in 1997 to evaluate the impact of Business Links in the UK. These seek to provide "soft" assistance to small firms but Business Links had been in operation for three years before any Step 5 type evaluations were contemplated under the Inter-Departmental Working Group on Impact Assessment of Business Support.

5 Despite the fact that Heckman is now a standard procedure in mid-range statistical analysis packages such as STATA or LIMDEP, it is not available on basic packages such as SPSS.

References

Barclays Bank (1998), *Small Business Review*, London.

Bendick, M., Jr. and Egan, M.L. 1987. Transfer payment diversion for small business development: British and French experience. *Industrial and Labour Relations Review* 40: 528–42.

Bridge, S., O'Neill, K. and Cromie, S. 1998. *Understanding Enterprise, Entrepreneurship and Small Business*. London: Macmillan.

Brown C., Hamilton, J. and Medoff, J. 1990. *Employers Large and Small*. Cambridge: Harvard University Press.

Chrisman, J.J., Nelson, R.R., Hoy, F. and Robinson, R.B. 1985. The impact of SBDC consulting activities. *Journal of Small Business Management* (July): 1–11.

Deschoolmeester, D., Schamp, T. and Vandenbroucke, A.M. 1998. *The Influence of Management Training on Entrepreneurial Attitudes and Managerial Techniques of SMEs*. Ghent: Vlerick School of Management.

Dolton, P.J., Makepeace, G.H. and van der Klaaw, W. 1989. Occupational choice and earnings determination: the role of sample selection and non-pecuniary factors. *Oxford Economic Papers* 41: 573–94.

DTI (Department of Trade and Industry). 1989. *Evaluation of the Consultancy Initiatives*. London: HSMO.

DTI (Department of Trade and Industry). 1991a. *Evaluation of the Consultancy Initiatives – Second Stage*. London: HSMO.

DTI (Department of Trade and Industry). 1991b. *Evaluation of the Consultancy Initiatives – Third Stage*. London: HSMO.

DTI (Department of Trade and Industry). 1998. *Small Business Action Update*. Department of Trade and Industry, London, June.

ENSR. 1997. *The European Observatory for SMEs*. Zoetermeer, Netherlands: EIM.

Ernst & Young. 1996. *Evaluation of Business Links*. London: Department of Trade and Industry.

Harrison, R.T. and Leitch, C.M. 1996. Whatever you hit call the target: an alternative approach to small business policy. In M.W. Danson (ed.), *Small Firm Formation and Regional Economic Development*. London: Routledge.

Hart, M. and Scott, R. 1994. Measuring the effectiveness of small firm policy: Some lessons from Northern Ireland. *Regional Studies* 28(8): 849–58.

House of Commons Select Committee. 1998. *Small and Medium Sized Enterprises*, Sixth Report. London: The Stationery Office.

Hughes, A. 1997. *Small Firms and Employment*. ESRC Centre for Business Research WP 71, September, University of Cambridge.

de Koning, A. and Snijders, J. 1992. Policy on small and medium sized enterprises in countries of the European Community. *International Business Journal* 10(3): 25–39.

LaLonde, R.J. 1986. Evaluating the econometric evaluations of training programs with experimental data. *American Economic Review* 76(4): 604–20.

Lerner, J. 1997. *The Government as Venture Capitalist: The Long Run Impact of the SBIR Program*. Cambridge: Harvard Business School.

Moint, A.H. 1998. Small firms exporting: how effective are government export assistance programs. *Journal of Small Business Management* (January): 1–15.

OECD (Organization for Economic Cooperation and Development). 1995, 1996, 1997, *Best Practice Policies for Small and Medium Sized Enterprises*. Paris.

O'Higgins, N. 1994. YTS, employment and sample selection bias. *Oxford Economic Papers* 46: 605–28.

Rogoff, E.G. and Lee, M.S. 1996. Putting government's role in perspective: the impact of government programmes on entrepreneurs and small business owners. *Journal of Developmental Entrepreneurship* 1 (spring): 57–73.

Sardar, J.H., Ghosh, D. and Rosa, P. 1997. The importance of support services to small enterprise in Bangladesh. *Journal of Small Business Management* 35(2): 26–36.

Segal Quince Wicksteed. 1991. *Evaluation of the Consultancy Initiatives – Third Stage*. Department of Trade and Industry. London: HMSO.

Storey, D.J. 1994. *Understanding the Small Business Sector*. London: Routledge.

Storey, D.J. and Strange, A. 1992. *Entrepreneurship in Cleveland 1979–1989: A Study of the Effects of the Enterprise Culture*. Employment Department, Research Series No. 3.

Westhead, P. and Storey, D.J. 1994. *An Assessment of Firms Located on and off Science Parks in the UK*. London: HMSO.

Wren, C. and Storey, D.J. 1998. *Estimating the Impact of Publicly Subsidised Advisory Services upon Small Firm Performance: The Case of the DTI Marketing Initiative*. SME Working Paper No. 58.

Part III

FINANCING GROWTH

If all entrepreneurs were wealthy, the need for financing growth would not be a factor in new firm development and growth. But this is the real world, and new firms typically must secure debt or equity to develop the product or service and to establish the market, the production capacity and the distribution network.

External financing is not only needed at start-up but is required at any time that the growth or the growth plans cannot be funded by internally generated funds. Stevenson and a number of others have suggested that one means of spreading the existing financial resources is to control resources through leasing or renting rather than owning them.

In this part we address the research on financing growth in Europe as well as the importance of informal and formal venture capital as a source of debt and equity for financing growth. Relatively little is known about the performance of the venture capital industry and even less about the informal venture capital market, yet their impact on growth financing is thought to be significant even though most measurements are really only estimates.

This part includes an overview of "Financing Growth: Recent Developments in the European Scene" by Donckels in chapter 10; a review of the research literature related to "Informal Venture Capital and the Financing of Emergent Growth Businesses" by Mason and Harrison in chapter 11; a North American/United Kingdom review of the role of "Venture Capital and Growth" by Manigart and Sapienza in chapter 12; and an analysis of "Venture Capital Financing of Entrepreneurship: Theory, Empirical Evidence, and a Research Agenda" developed by the Canadian research team of Amit, Brander and Zott in chapter 13.

The general theme that transcends the chapters in this section is that one of the most important paradoxes in entrepreneurship research is the mismatch between the significance of both the formal and informal venture capital market in terms of businesses financed and the limited amount of research conducted.

Donckels begins this part of the book by identifying a number of areas that lead to the difficulty in research in financing growth. He notes the following in the current state of the art in research in financing growth:

- The method of measuring growth has a significantly greater influence on the financial growth model than was previously assumed.
- Little attention has been given to the decision-making process of the various stockholders directly or indirectly involved with the financing of growing SMEs.
- More attention must be given to understanding the relationship between the financial structure and the development phase of the company.
- The determining factor in financing is not so much growth per se, but the combination of rapid growth with insufficient access to the capital market.

Mason and Harrison suggest that one of the major differences between informal and formal venture capital investments is that informal investors are investing their own funds. They also make the following observations:

- Establishing the size of the informal venture capital market investments is problematic because of the private and unreported activity and the desire of the investors to preserve their privacy.
- The problem with the informal market for risk capital is not an ability to make contact. It is a scarcity of high-quality opportunities or "investment-ready" entrepreneurs.
- Two encouraging developments in this area include the international diffusion of research on venture capital and attention to the investment process.

Manigart and Sapienza provide a critical evaluation of research on venture capital and growth with the following thoughts:

- Venture capital has been assumed to aid economic development in Europe but evidence is scant.
- Venture capital has been shown to add value to the firm but whether the value is greater than the cost is not known.
- The discipline associated with venture capital investments is both appreciated and resented by entrepreneurs.
- Different risk profiles and timing preferences among investors cause potential conflicts with entrepreneurs.
- Value creation theories are needed to explain the central thrust of venture capital activities.

Amit, Brander and Zott also bemoan the fact that relatively little is known about the venture capital industry and relate this problem to the fact that:

- There is no organized secondary exchange for venture capital investments that provides summary information.
- Direct measurement of the portfolio firm's performances is difficult. Taxes paid and revenues per unit of asset are good proxies.
- Theory-driven research with clearly stated assumptions and formal decision models is relatively scarce.
- Informational asymmetries may offer the premise to a theoretical approach to venture capital financing.

Venture financing either at venture initiation or growth stage is an integral part of entrepreneurship. While considerable information is available and research seems to be well developed in the debt financing area, less is known about venture capital. Even less is known about the informal venture capital market.

The lack of an organized secondary exchange and the desire to protect privacy preclude the availability of summary information. At present, empirical researchers need to follow Amit's lead and join forces with others to develop a large longitudinal database from which a theory of venture capital financing can be developed.

Entrepreneurs seem to complain about insufficient access to risk capital, while the venture capitalists suggest that the problem is a scarcity of high-quality investment opportunities. We suggest that the truth lies somewhere in between the differing assessments.

10

Financing Growth: Recent Developments in the European Scene

RIK DONCKELS

THEORETICAL DEVELOPMENTS AND METHODOLOGICAL APPROACHES
STAKEHOLDERS' ROLE
FOCUS ON THE EUROPEAN SCENE
STRUCTURING THE RESEARCH AGENDA: THE STAR MODEL
CONCLUSIONS

Two publications by Brophy (1997) and Freear et al. (1997) focus on what should be given primary attention when investigating the financing of small and medium-sized enterprises (SMEs). Cressy and Olofsson (1997a), as guest editors of *Small Business Economics* on the theme of European SME financing, present an overview of the current situation in Europe. The conclusions of these three papers are:

1 The specific characteristics of small-scale operations must be given full attention.
2 The decision-making processes of the various stakeholders who are directly or indirectly involved with the financing of growing SMEs must be analyzed.
3 Many recent developments in both theory and research methodology have confirmed the importance of charting the most noteworthy changes.
4 The funding of growth requires a closer examination of the relationship between the financial structure and the development phase of the company.
5 The familial nature of most SMEs is a subject rarely discussed in the literature on financing growth-oriented SMEs.
6 What is currently taking place in Europe with financing growth-oriented SMEs also needs examination.

This chapter first examines recent theoretical and methodological work then provides an overview of the current thinking on the role of the different stakeholders in the financing of SME growth. The third section examines current happenings in Europe and what we can learn from them. Finally, a new research agenda is presented that takes us into the third millennium.

Theoretical Developments and Methodological Approaches

Growth funding is increasingly being studied in a wider context. Models for studying growth finance and statistical techniques for analyzing surveys are presented in this section.

Expanding the scope

Petty and Bygrave (1993) suggested that one cannot say anything sensible about SME financing without considering the heterogeneity of SMEs. Of their four categories (private life-style companies, public non-growth-oriented firms, private entrepreneurial firms and public growth-oriented firms), this chapter focuses on entrepreneurial firms in the private sector.

Given that more and more attention is being focused on the internal and external factors influencing growth, Gibb and Davies (1990) presented four different approaches to the growth phenomenon:

- the role played by the personality of the SME owner,
- the company's organization,
- the business management approach, especially the different resource constraints that hinder company development, and
- growth from an industry-specific and market perspective.

Financing forms part of the business management approach, focusing mainly on the difficulties in obtaining equity finance due to unattractive economies of scale and loan finance. This does not mean that other components do not play a role in growth financing, e.g., the relationship between financial management and turnover growth as a strategic objective (Merikas et al. 1993).

The family character of most SMEs is a further important factor. Although Litz (1995) identifies the need to define the term "family company" with precision, Bopaiah (1998) lists the following positive aspects to conventional family enterprises:

- the ability to find the necessary financial means,
- a more conservative investment policy accompanied by decreased risks,
- the concentration of family ownership that makes hostile take-overs less probable,
- a greater interest in company continuity (often with strong ties to the local community), and
- a greater preparedness to provide personal assets in loan collateral.

Donckels and Frölich (1991) consider the family nature of most SMEs to be a brake on their expansion instead of a stimulus for further growth. Similar conclusions were reached by Corbetta (1995) for Italy, Gallo (1995) for Spain, Cressy and Olofsson (1997b) for Sweden and Smyrnios et al. (1998) for Australia. These studies suggest that isolating a single explanatory factor accords it excessive importance. For example Campbell (1998) charts the export behavior of 101 SMEs in Ontario, noting that resource constraints, indeed, form the main internal obstacle for expanding export. These constraints, however, consist of different types, such as financial resource constraints (mentioned by 30 percent of the respondents) and distribution constraints (by 25 percent).

Obvious, fundamental differences in the financing of SMEs and large companies exist, as emphasized by Welsh and White (1981). Ang (1991) as well as Norton (1990, 1991) continued the search for differences that can be attributed to SMEs' smaller scale. Hughes (1997) summarized the main differences in the United Kingdom as follows:

- a lower ratio of fixed to total assets,
- a higher proportion of trade debts in total assets,
- a much greater reliance on especially short-term bank loans to finance their assets,
- a heavy reliance on retained profits to fund investment flow, though additional funds are mainly obtained from banks (equity being very much less important and financially more risky, e.g., relatively high debt-to-equity ratio).

So far in this chapter, we have been mainly concerned with the internal company situation. However, Gnyawali and Fogel (1994) suggest that growth finance is strongly influenced by the external environment. Their proposed framework comprises government policies and procedures, socioeconomic conditions, entrepreneurial and business skills, financial assistance and nonfinancial assistance. Even though their paper is concerned with business starts, the general framework remains relevant to this chapter. Within the context of growth financing, the capital market plays the most important role as an external factor. Chittenden et al. (1996) investigated the relationship between growth, access to the capital market and financial structure. Similar focus points are found with Petty and Bygrave (1993) and with Van Auken and Holman (1995):

1 The financial structure of SMEs is determined by profitability, asset structure, size, age and access to the capital market.

2 Growth per se does not as significantly affect the financial structure of SMEs as the combination of rapid growth with insufficient access to the capital market.

3 In SMEs, the more difficult access to the capital market often leads to a suboptimal capital structure, which can become a direct cause of bankruptcy.

4 The long-term financing of most SMEs is based on collateral rather than profitability. In fact, the use of collateral is not unrelated to what is suggested by the agency theory: a number of agency problems can be handled thanks to collateral.

5 SME funding lies in the same line as the pecking-order framework proposed by Myers (1984). This theory claims that companies follow a certain hierarchic route in solving their financial needs: first, available internal means are used, debt is utilized and only then does one think of external equity. This hierarchy is a direct consequence of the relative costs connected to the different forms of finance.

6 According to the changing financial environment encountered by the growing company, one also needs to accumulate the necessary skills for handling the new situation.

These findings are mostly based on solid theoretical knowledge and a wide empirical base. For example, Chittenden et al. (1996) tracked no fewer than 3,480 companies for five years. Nonetheless, some authors reach conflicting conclusions. Beaudouin and St. Pierre (1998), for example, conclude from a research project in French:

- SMEs generally do not have difficulties with accessing any source of finance they wish.
- SMEs who make frequent use of short-term loans do so not from necessity but clearly from choice.
- SME funding does not lead to higher risks than financing large companies; nonetheless, SMEs are charged higher interest rates, which only results in higher profits for the banks.
- The claim that insufficient cash flow is a brake on the expansion of SMEs is incorrect.
- The failing of SMEs is unrelated to possible malfunctions of the money markets, which supposedly do not enable SMEs to establish healthy financial structures. Financial management is, by far, the most crucial bottleneck.

Besides the financial sector, governments are also a crucial external factor, which is discussed later.

A breakthrough in modeling

Since Walker's (1989) study, the question of to what extent do current theories and models of capital structures and corporate financing also apply to SMEs has been given more attention. A different and interesting observation is that a number of econometric models of growth financing have also been created in the recent past.

How relevant is the agency theory in explaining SME financing? Earlier we pointed out that collateral makes it possible to handle a number of agency problems. Schnabel (1992), for example, developed a theoretical explanation of the predominance of debt in the capital structure of small businesses using a single-period model of entrepreneurial capital structure choice under conditions of information asymmetry. Basically, the entrepreneur has a clear view of the possibilities of his company and of his personal commitment and efforts while the capital provider, on the other hand, has considerably less information. Schnabel then shows that this situation leads to a clear dichotomy in the financial structure in function of the quality of the overall project: high-quality projects are mainly financed by debt, while less valuable initiatives are continuously searching for equity. Therefore, an external capital provider might see an urgent request for capital as a negative signal regarding the project's quality.

Norton (1995) observed that the capital allocation process is full of potential agency problems. Thus, it appears obvious that agency problems may be relevant to growth financing in general. Several studies support this concept:

- Kirby (1998) notes that franchising is occasionally seen as a formula for decreasing agency costs and for facilitating growth financing. Based on twenty-two in-depth interviews (seventeen operational and five failed initiatives), he concludes that, contrary to what is suggested by the agency theory, substantial problems continue to exist in managing the relationship between franchisers and franchisees.
- McConaughy et al. (1995) concentrate on the operating performance of ninety-nine businesses with an initial public offering (IPO) in 1995. They found that agency costs did not rise after the IPO and also noted that the markets discipline entrepreneurs with incentives to maintain pre-IPO performance.
- Gallo and Vilaseca (1998) note the specific character of family businesses and its

relevance for the agency theory. Since principal and agent are usually one and the same in family businesses, there is less chance of conflicting interests because the increase in costs, which can result from the fact that ownership and control follow different utility curves, is dropped.

Two additional papers shed new light on SME financing. The first, LeCornu et al.'s (1996) analysis of SME funding, relies on the so-called enterprise objective function, which is one of the cornerstones of modern finance theory. The normative goal of wealth maximization of owners is central to it. They are convinced that a different type of utility function must be assumed when analyzing SME financing, namely, the owner-manager utility. According to them, the defining variables are financial return, systematic risk, unsystematic risk and nonfinancial returns. Unsystematic risks include SME-specific factors that both the business and the owner-managers are exposed to: low liquidity, lack of diversification, lack of flexibility, loss of control, accountability and the lack of transferability. Nonfinancial returns mainly related to independence, lifestyle, societal contribution, respect, family security and the need for achievement. Their conclusion is that if one is dealing with a different objective function, it is also logical to assume a different financial management.

The second paper by Pineda et al. (1998) examines the information search activities of small business managers. They consider business financing to be one of eight areas: product or service line, product quality, pricing, employee training, performance evaluation, employee compensation, employee selection and computer systems. They observe that business financing ranks fifth on information search intensity. Employee selection ranks first followed by performance evaluation, product or service line and pricing.

In conclusion, we can assume that research on SME financing in general and of growth financing in particular is increasingly linked to classical financing theory. This does not mean that the specific characteristics of SMEs and their managers should be systematically taken into account.

A number of original econometric models have been developed for growth financing:

- Keasey and McGuinness (1990) determined the extent to which new businesses utilize different finance sources.
- Storey (1994) investigated how banks contribute to growth financing.
- Holtz-Eakin et al. (1994) used econometric techniques to study the role of liquidity constraints in relation to entrepreneurial survival.
- Biks and Ennew (1996) questioned to what extent credit constraints affect the growth of businesses.
- Chittenden et al. (1996) investigated the relationships among company growth, access to the capital markets and the financial structure of the businesses.
- La Porta et al. (1997) examined possible legislative impacts on external financing. Although this study does not focus primarily on SMEs, it is still important in the context of IPOs.
- Bates (1997) used an econometric model to study how the social environment factors affect the finance possibilities of new businesses started by Chinese and Korean immigrants in the United States.
- Egeln et al. (1997) looked at the role of financial constraints in the start-up process of companies in the former West Germany.

- Carter and Allen (1997) test, among other hypotheses, that women business owners who put greater emphasis on financial aspects of their businesses will have larger businesses.

Most models are linear and the most frequently used methods of estimation is Ordinary Least Squares. In the future, more attention will have to be given to the validity of the data used in econometric studies. Many of these studies are based on questionnaires from the persons directly involved. Miettinen (1998) formulates a number of criticisms regarding the accuracy of self-rated business performance. He concludes that we still do not know enough about the factors influencing self-rating (e.g., biodata, individual characteristics, job-relevant experience and cognitive processes). A further caveat concerns the published quantitative data on SMEs: how exactly do they represent business reality? A certain amount of caution is appropriate here.

With the increased interest in modeling studies of growth financing, Bornheim and Herbeck (1998) advocate a theoretical model that assists in providing comprehension of the costs and benefits resulting from relationships between SMEs and banks.

From descriptive statistics to multivariate analysis

Increasingly, advanced statistical techniques are being used to present and analyze surveys. Examples include:

- cluster analysis (Norton 1991; Binks and Ennew 1997),
- discriminant analysis (Chaganti et al. 1995),
- canonic correlation analysis (Van Auken and Holman 1995),
- principal component analysis (Petrakis 1997; Pineda et al. 1998; Smyrnios et al. 1998), and
- multivariate variance analysis (Kotey and Meredith 1997).

This development would have been impossible without a significant growth in sample sizes in the most recent studies. Because of more observations, the database can now be analyzed in far greater depth.

Reid (1996) refers to the application of control theories for the analysis of production processes and financing. McKechnie et al.'s (1998) contribution deserves mention because it combines quantitative and qualitative approaches. They point out the danger of analyses that isolate a single factor. By using the more advanced matched pair technique, they try to compensate for shortcomings they claim to have discovered in other studies. We need to be cognizant of the need for correct data and methodological and definitional problems. Delmar (1997) addressed the methodological problems with measuring growth. Using a double input, namely, a study of fifty-five publications on SME growth and observations of growth-related variables in about four hundred Swedish SMEs, he found that the problems related mainly to:

1 the indicator used to measure growth,
2 how growth was measured (relative or absolute change), and
3 which time period was used.

Delmar concludes that the way in which growth is measured has a significantly greater influence on the final growth model than was assumed previously. He also discusses the validity and reliability of different growth measures and possible divergences between subjective and objective measures (see also Miettinen 1998).

STAKEHOLDERS' ROLE

This section is restricted to three stakeholders: the owners and management, the banking sector and the government.

The role of owners and management

An international comparison of owner profiles (Chell et al. 1997) concluded that the different profiles among entrepreneurs not only are significant for the attitude toward growth but also affect its realization. The role of personal factors was also discussed by Storey (1994), Westhead (1995) and Kotey and Meredith (1997). Moran (1998) also emphasized the importance of personal factors as a function of the dynamics of the entire entrepreneurial process.

Davis and Herrera (1998) examined changes in family shareholders' attitudes. Their conviction is that social psychologists have developed very useful concepts. They emphasize more particularly the role of group cohesiveness, social comparisons, conformance with the majority, diffusion of responsibility, deindividuation and social power. They make clear that a multidisciplinary approach is absolutely necessary in explaining the shareholders' dynamics in family businesses.

With regard to the family aspect of most SMEs, Prasad et al. (1995) asked what is the ideal moment for harvesting. Upton and Heck (1997) link the family nature as an additional dimension to entrepreneurship in general. Wakefield (1997) tested a number of hypotheses regarding the relationship between the financial situation and conflicts in family businesses and concluded that business conflict is inversely related to perceived access to capital but positively correlated with the reported reliance on bank financing and with reported reliance on family funds.

Kimhi (1997) developed a theoretical optimizing model concerning timing of succession in family businesses. He links succession timing to borrowing constraints. Ayres and Carter (1998) leaked the organization of succession and the capital structure. Chrisman et al. (1998) examined the important attributes of successors in family businesses. When about five hundred directors in English-speaking Canada were asked to rank the attributes of successors, financial skills/experience came in fifteenth place!

With regard to financial management, McMahon and Homes (1991) noted that little progress was made during the 1980s. Five years later, Peel and Wilson (1996) pointed out that many bankruptcies could be prevented if financial/working capital management were improved in the SME sector.

Consequently, much still needs to be done regarding the professionalization of financial management. Beaudouin and St. Pierre (1998) have also strongly emphasized this problem. Aronoff (1998) in a study of megatrends in family businesses identified the increasing need of financial sophistication. He points out that a basic knowledge of financial management is necessary not only for executives but also for nonactive stockholders. Also family businesses have to become more and more familiar with concepts like return on investment (ROI), return on assets (ROA) and economic value added (EVA).

The role of the banking sector

The role of the banking sector has been examined extensively in recent years. With regard to the relationship between SME and banks, Bornheim and Herbeck (1998) established a model that defines three functions:

1 the marginal benefit (a representation of the potential benefits of the relationship),
2 the marginal barrier to exit (in which dependence on one bank, decreasing utility of competition and increasing costs of changing banks all play a role), and
3 the marginal net benefits (the difference between the marginal benefit and the marginal barriers to exit).

They found the potential benefits of relationships are:

♦ for the SME, lower cost of capital, greater credit availability, less collateral required, positive market signal and long-term interest of the lender (equity holding),
♦ for the bank, more information and reputation formation, as well as different cost functions. For example, because a long-term relationship can be associated with multiple products, the lender can spread any fixed costs of producing information about the company.

One aspect of this model is that it offers the possibility of incorporating country-specific elements. For instance, the competition between banks can be taken into account. It also emphasizes the relationships between SMEs and banks. The authors follow the same four points as Petersen and Rajan (1994, 1995), Turnbull and Gibbs (1987) as well as Ennew and Binks (1996). Deeg (1998) also studied these relationships and concluded that, as regards the financing of SMEs, German banks are in a special situation with contextual variables of, among others, a complex of legislation, regulations and government financial aid.

To what extent close bank affiliation ultimately has a beneficial effect still remains an unanswered question. Some claim that this is the case, while others disagree. The results obtained by studies in Germany are noteworthy: Elston (1993) concludes that good bank relationships have a positive influence on profit possibilities and liquidity constraints. A later study by Elston and Chirinko (1995) found no significant effects. Perlitz and Seger (1994) found that good banking relationships actually have a negative effect on profitability. Audretsch and Elston (1996) confirm the specific situation of the financial sector in Germany, certainly when compared with the United States and Great Britain. They conclude that there are indications that mainly large companies have access to finance. Thus, they suspect the existence of a size effect. As in most developed countries, German SMEs are also confronted with liquidity constraints. Binks and Ennew (1996, 1997) researched banking relationships in the United Kingdom and concluded that a good relationship can lead to a win-win situation for both parties, but with two reservations: (1) Most SMEs do not need a close relationship because the services they require are mundane and provided in an efficient and orderly manner, and (2) the need to improve the relationship is mainly the result of a growing demand for communication and information. We thus note that successful growth financing is largely based on information and communication.

Banks' attitudes toward risk were examined by Keasey and Watson (1994b), who observed that banks are widely criticized for being too averse to risk-taking. They found that in the United Kingdom the problem is mainly experienced by growing SMEs, those that often have an unhealthy financial structure and poor financial management skills (e.g., insufficient accounting follow-up and use of short-term finance to compensate for lack of owner capital). In the early 1990s the problem became even more urgent due to a general economic depression in the United Kingdom. As a means of therapy they propose that SMEs should realize better what credit actually is. Furthermore, there should be more communication between SMEs and banks.

In his financial analysis of Palestinian industry, Rashid Sabri (1998) concluded that there is a size effect in the SME–bank relation: the opportunities and conditions for borrowing are better for larger firms than for smaller ones. The White Paper on SMEs in Japan (Japan Small Business Research Institute 1998) found that financial institutions, because of the Big Bang (the reform of Japan's financial system), are emphasizing the need to improve risk control and profitability by introducing their own rating systems. The ranking of the rating factors is as follows:

1 customer reliability
2 profitability
3 growth potential
4 security
5 managerial skills
6 business performance
7 contribution to owner profitability
8 number of customers.

So, there is no specific size effect to be expected. But reliability is related to elements such as availability of business and financial management skills, financial position, transparency of general conditions of the firm and the development of management structure. A real challenge for SMEs!

Influence of gender
An issue that has long received attention is whether banks behave differently depending on the gender of the SME person. Riding and Swift (1990), who studied women business owners in Canada, and Koper (1993) in the Netherlands concluded that women are taken less seriously by the financial sector and therefore find it much more difficult to obtain funds.

Koper found that subjective gender-related factors primarily affect the treatment by the contact person in the bank. Palmer and Bejou (1995) focused on gender effects in the relationship between customers and financial advisors. Carter and Allen (1997) identified a correlation in the United States between access of financial resources, on the one hand, and size of the firm, on the other, and stated explicitly that this finding does not imply any causal link.

McKechnie et al. (1998) and Carter and Rose (1998) have provided a good overview of the existing literature by which a number of very pertinent remarks are formulated. McKechnie et al. (1998) suggest that too often the studies are based on perceptions and anecdotes and rely on subjective data; the samples are small, and usually there is no control group of male entrepreneurs for comparison. Their own study examined the effect of gender on interactions between SMEs and banks, based on the terms and conditions on which finance is provided, the quality of service provision and overall banking provisions. The originality of their method resides mainly in the fact that they combine different sources of evidence on the same phenomenon. On the one hand, they use a quantitative study with about six hundred observations; on the other, they use a qualitative survey of twenty matched pairs of male and female entrepreneurs. But this leaves many questions unanswered. One of the main problems is to isolate the impact of gender from other parameters.

Carter and Rose (1998) also used a combined quantitative and qualitative technique. To exclude the effects of other variables, they restricted their study to three sectors: textile manufacturing, business services and hotel and catering. The observations (300 men and 300 women) were made in two regions in the United Kingdom and compared men and women in four areas. Their conclusions can be summarized as follows:

- Starting capital is significantly higher for men than for their female colleagues.
- Women tend to make significantly less use of institutional finance, such as overdrafts, bank loans and supplier credits.
- There are no significant differences among participants in informal financial networks.
- There is no confirmation of the hypothesis that the relationship between female entrepreneurs and bankers suffers because of sexual stereotyping and discrimination.

Familial influences
The nature of family enterprises also have implications for financing and relations with the financial sector. Gallo and Vilaseca (1996, 1998) studied roughly one hundred Spanish family businesses and found that:

- In general, the debt-to-equity ratio is lower in family business, particularly in family businesses that have acquired a leading market position.
- A statistically significant correlation exists between the size of a company and the diversity of its financial practices. Larger family businesses use a larger number of financial institutions and a greater variety of financial products.
- Based on the examined return on sales and return on equity, the performance is weaker in family businesses with a dominant market position.
- Regression analysis shows that the debt–equity ratio is more relevant in explaining variance in performance.

In their 1998 study Gallo and Vilaseca use the agency theory to suggest that the alignment of ownership with control produces advantages for the family business over the organization structures of nonfamily businesses. Concretely, this might mean, e.g., that costs are higher in nonfamily businesses because ownership and control follow different utility curves. A different cost-increasing factor is related to the control over the agent by the principal.

Based on interviews with chief financial officers (CFOs), they observe that family businesses use a small number of banks but that CFOs in nonfamily businesses use a broader range of financial products.

A study by Binks (1991), written on the eve of the creation of the European internal market in 1992, wondered what the relationship would look like in the year 2000. For a desirable SME–bank environment, Brinks suggested that a closer relationship between both parties must exist as a basis for exchanging accurate information and that there must be competition between banks. He also identified several future trends that will determine the SME–bank relationship, including: (1) banks will realize that they should change their attitudes and respond more rapidly to SME needs, (2) competition between banks will continue to grow, and (3) banks will respond to the true needs of the market with appropriate products.

The role of government

In Europe there are at least three levels of hierarchy: regional, federal and European authorities. Hence this discussion relates to more than the government. The following research studies address a number of issues regarding public authorities.

Keasey and Watson (1994a) examined the impact a change in legislation can have on the financing behavior of SMEs. Specifically, they studied the change in the 1986 Insolvency and Company Directs' Disqualification Act in the United Kingdom. This Act made the directors of bankrupt companies personally liable for any form of reckless behavior and incompetent management. With the help of a simple model, they showed that legislation can be counterproductive: owner-managers may have incentives to behave opportunistically with creditor claims, but this legislation reduces these incentives by attempting to ensure that the owner-manager bears the full cost of their decisions.

La Porta et al. (1997) in a comparative study of nine countries concluded that countries with poor investor protection (measured by both the character of legal rules and the quality of law enforcement) have smaller and narrower capital markets.

Pruit (1997) examined the influence of changes in margin levels by the Federal Reserve. Contrary to the finding for large companies, such changes appear to have a significant effect on the security behavior of medium-sized companies.

Bahat (1998) studied the role of loan guarantee schemes in Israel and identified four particular reasons why SMEs find it difficult to access the capital markets: inadequate information, difficulties in raising equity on the stock market and bank perceptions that SMEs entail higher risk and are not capable of providing the required guarantee. Bahat expanded the study to explore what the effect of the state guarantee fund in Israel had on SME affairs by studying 6,619 applications during 1993 and 1997. Of these, 5,046 satisfied the legal requirements and 2,915 were given government support. He concluded that the Israeli guarantee scheme has a positive effect on employment, new economic activities and income levels. Banks, however, still need to respond better to the offered system.

Soeharto (1998) studied the credit schemes for micro and small enterprises in Indonesia. The micro credit programs are designed to assist in eradicating the influence of poverty and to provide self-help groups and technical assistance to ensure the use of credit and credit management. Soeharto identified two major problems: most of the micro enterprises are still not deemed creditworthy by banks (e.g., they still have major problems with submitting acceptable feasibility studies), and the government is no longer capable of funding the system due to the current economic crisis. Evaluation of these credit schemes led to two recommendations: the mechanism should be improved to ensure its efficacy and to enhance skills and competence, and a loan guarantee scheme is needed to cope with the absence of collateral.

Rashid Sabri (1998) suggests the establishment of special funds to give loans to small industrial activities in Palestine. These special funds exist in other Arab countries.

Focus on the European Scene

Cressy and Olofsson (1997a) identified six themes related to European SME financing:

1 differences in the financial structure of small versus large businesses,
2 financial demand and supply constraints,
3 operationalizing the supply and demand constraints,
4 finance constraints and size,
5 real and financial interdependence – the role of policy/product "packages,"
6 the nature of European funding gaps, if they exist.

Landström et al. (1997) in an overview of European research on entrepreneurship and small business identified that finance has certainly not been the most frequently discussed research subject in the past. In preceding sections we referred to European research results. In this section we concentrate on two themes, namely, research that is performed at the initiative of the European Commission and research in central and eastern Europe.

Research at the European Commission's initiative

The original eight countries that became the former European Community proclaimed 1983 as the year of the SME and Craft Sector. This initiative was an external manifestation of the large amount of attention given to SMEs in Europe. Since then, several initiatives were taken to establish a streamlined and scientifically based European SME policy. To obtain a better picture of the SME situation in the member states, the European Network of SME Research (ENSR) was tasked with mapping SMEs in Europe. In each of these countries a specialized research institute was invited to become a member of the network. The first European Observatory for SMEs appeared in 1993 (ENSR 1993). So far, five reports have been completed. Each year the report focuses on one particular facet of finance. Here's an overview:

◆ First Annual Report: Chapter 8: Capital and Finance
◆ Second Annual Report: Chapter 6: Capital and Finance
◆ Third Annual Report: Chapter 9: Capital and Finance
◆ Fourth Annual Report: Chapter 7: Finance
◆ Fifth Annual Report: Chapter 7: Failures and Bankruptcies

Noteworthy is that the attention shifts from a more general treatment of finance to more specific topics. The fourth and fifth reports contain a section on policy issues, which mainly attempts to identify best practices.

Each partner in the ENSR network coordinates one chapter. The input for the chapter is supplied by the different network partners. This method means that the chapters always give a clear picture of the research being carried out in member states.

In 1993, another initiative, the Round Table of Leading Representatives from the Banking Sector, was established. The members were given the task of identifying the main issues concerning the relationship between SMEs and banks. Their report concluded that the SME sector does not function optimally because of:

- insufficient capital to finance the enterprise effectively,
- insufficient cash due to late payment by debtors,
- insufficient access to credit on reasonable terms, and
- inadequate knowledge, experience and capacity to ensure good financial management.

The second Round Table focused on furnishing solutions based on examples of good practice throughout Europe. The conclusion is that the main issues for banks in their relationship with SME clients should be (European Commission 1997):

- Creating a real partnership with clients based on mutual understanding of each other's needs and wishes, mutual respect and above all, equality;
- Shifting the organization's primary forms away from cost reduction toward client service;
- Using high technology within the bank not only for cost-savings and as a replacement for relationship management but also as an instrument for perfecting the personal touch – in other words combining it with more investment in people;
- Offering the benefits of the new information technology, such as extended databases, directly to clients;
- Using their networks of contacts for the benefit of SMEs;
- Searching for cooperation with other organizations that can contribute to SME development by providing added value for clients.

Thus, it is not surprising that in its *Activities in Favor of SMEs and the Craft Sector*, the European Commission (1998) expressly focused on the financial aspects from two angles: improvements in the financial environment and access to finance and credit. In arguing for improvements in the financial environment, the following focus points were discussed:

- *Late payment in commercial transactions.* The Commission in May 1995 established a range of measures to tackle late payment in Europe, but the impact was minimal. The Commission is currently contemplating other initiatives.
- *Preparing SMEs for the introduction of the euro.* SMEs and craft businesses were provided information about the euro, and a 1996 campaign was launched via the Euro-Info Centres to raise awareness.
- Cross-border credit transfer. A Directive was issued to guarantee rapid and more reliable international money transfers.
- *Access to finance for innovation.* In 1996, the Action Plan for Innovation was approved, encouraging the financing of innovation, particularly by venture capital.

The second field of action regarded access to finance and credit via measures promoting access to finance and financial instruments of the European Union. The measures promoting access to finance are mainly recommendations by the Round Table of Leading Representatives of the Banking Sector (see above). The Intensive Trans-European Exchange and Communication of Innovative Financing (ITEC INFO) project will continue studying the support mechanisms created by EU banks to facilitate the financing of innovative projects. The Commission provided financial support for start-up of the European Association of Security Dealers and contributed to the creation of the European Association of Security Dealers Automated Quotation (EASDAQ) stock market. The Commission also closely follows new initiatives on the capital markets, such as the Alternative Investment Market in London, the Nouveau Marché in Paris and other markets trading in Frankfurt, Amsterdam and Brussels. The European Mutual Guarantee Association (EMGA) also supported the mutual guarantee system in Portugal and Greece, which may also work in eastern European countries.

The three financial instruments of the European Union are the European Investment Bank (EIB), the European Investment Fund (EIF) and the Venture Capital pilot schemes. Since 1990, the EIB has indirectly financed SME investments via its global loans and supported nearly 42,000 SMEs with loans totaling more than $14 billion U.S., or nearly 45 percent of the funding granted to industry and services. The EIF provides loan guarantees for projects relating to trans-European networks and SMEs. By June 1997, the sum of the guarantee operations in favor of SMEs amounted to $757 million US (34 percent of the total operation of the EIF). Since mid-1996, the EIF has also participated in the equity of enterprises specialized in financing SME capital. Since 1998, the funds have invested $43 million US in 107 new companies, creating 3,000 jobs. The Eurotech Capital Action also encourages the financing of transnational advanced technology projects by private capital.

Since 1995, a number of actions were also launched with a view to financing innovation. Thus, during 1995 and 1996, seven initiatives were taken that brought 500 innovative SMEs in full expansion seeking funding sources into contact with potential capital providers. In addition, the Eurotech Capital network invested $287 million US in transnational advanced technology projects. The total commitment of the European Union budget is $11.3 million US, resulting in a leverage effect of 1 to 25.

Obviously, the European Commission has taken several initiatives to promote the financing of growth-oriented SMEs. Many of these initiatives are based on the results of research sponsored by it. It is still too early to make any evaluation; but the European Commission certainly intends to evaluate the projects over the long term and correct them when necessary.

Financing challenges for central and eastern European SMEs

The turbulent development in this geographical area also has far-reaching consequences for entrepreneurs. It is promising to note that a number of studies on the financing of growing companies have been completed. These studies include both national studies and studies of multiple countries.

In a study of start-ups in Hungary, Lane (1995) pointed out that the state of financial markets is considered to be one of the greatest hindrances to development in central and eastern Europe. The two crucial financial issues are the availability of capital to support growth and the extent of overdue receivables and the ability to collect them.

Klochko and Isakova (1996) noted that lack of capital is by far the greatest problem for starting and growing companies in the Ukraine. The entrepreneurs do not possess the necessary financial means, and the banks grant loans for no longer than two to three months at prohibitive rates of interest.

In Poland, Arendarski et al. (1994) identified two essential inhibitors to growth: undercapitalization and a lack of sufficient purchasing power.

In Bulgaria, there are serious problems with finance, according to Todorov (1996). Most entrepreneurs state that they rely mostly on their own financing (savings and profit reinvestments). Bank loans are a significant source of financing for just a few. The lack of a genuine capital market is a serious obstacle for the future development of the companies. Bartlett and Rangelove (1997) reach similar conclusions.

Pistrui et al. (1997) observed that Romanian entrepreneurs mostly have very clear plans for financing expansion. They typically obtain financing by using their savings, mortgaging their homes, borrowing on their assets or taking on additional debt.

Besides these national studies, several studies look at multiple countries. Nicolescu (1998) examined 100 observations in Romania and 480 for other countries in the region and concluded that for the sample in general there is a remarkable discrepancy between the rhetoric of the financial sector and actual reality. People talk about improving access to financial markets but do not manage to develop suitable instruments. Financial institutions continue to give number one priority to large companies. Furthermore, SMEs themselves do not always see the importance of sound financial management. Their knowledge of financial management techniques is often insufficient. He also finds that the main problems of Romanian SMEs are a shortage of financial means, high interest rates, excessive guarantees, banks' preference for short-term credit, insufficient comprehension by banks of the specific natures of SMEs, bureaucratic red tape and corruption.

Karsai et al. (1998) reported on the screening and valuing of venture capital investments in Hungary, Poland and Slovakia and observed that venture capital development is very unequal in the three countries. Hungary and Poland have shown a remarkable expansion in venture capital but not Slovakia. In all three countries there are still many infrastructure limitations; they recommend specific legislation to permit venture capital companies, the development of reliable information sources on potential investees and the development of stock and corporate asset markets.

STRUCTURING THE RESEARCH AGENDA: THE STAR MODEL

Future research efforts may be more productive with a more structured agenda. We suggest a model that represents the entrepreneur, his or her business, and the environment in which they operate (figure 10.1). In the future more attention will need to be devoted to the role of the SME owner, particularly because we must consider most emphatically the dynamics of the entire process.

Ten years ago Walker (1989) demonstrated that the financing of an SME varies with the business life phase. The following model shows how the existing factors on the left of the vertical axis impact on the corollary factors on the right of the axis. The horizontal

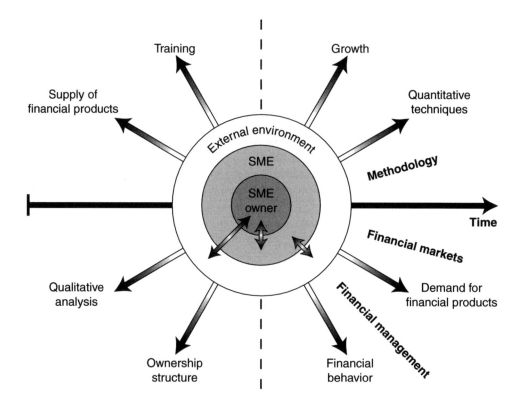

FIGURE 10.1 The star model for structuring research

axis of time shows how these actions affect the factors that impact on the growth of the firm over time. For example, the supply of financial products at any given time may impact on the entrepreneur's demand for additional financial products. Also, the entrepreneur's desire for a specific ownership structure, e.g., total ownership, clearly affects the growth of the firm since only debt financing would meet the owner's requirement. However, if the entrepreneur later accepts others as part owners, then equity financing could be used to achieve the desired growth objectives.

The interaction between the SME owner, the company and the external environment requires further charting. In this regard we suggest particular attention to family SMEs, who in fact form the majority of all SMEs. The specific literature on family businesses can certainly be a source of inspiration because it enlightens financing and financial policy. As regards the companies themselves, we suggest the examination of the heterogeneity of SMEs according to company size and business sector.

The external environment includes the relationship between SMEs and banks as well as SMEs and government. With regard to government, we see an urgent need for serious evaluations of existing programs. Best practices can then be identified allowing any corrections and promoting new initiatives. The role of the intermediaries has not been sufficiently explored. One needs to determine how they can contribute maximally to improving the financial management of SMEs

Besides the fundamental time axis, four other axes have been indicated that represent specific focus points for research:

The objective axis plots growth against ownership structure. Delmar (1997) has shown that the relationship between growth as an objective and the financial model still requires further investigation. This relationship is especially important, for family businesses, which have at least three kinds of objectives – those of the entrepreneur, the company and the family. It is certainly worth the effort to find out to what extent the diverging objectives can be combined with a growth strategy.

The methodology axis (quantitative versus qualitative techniques) is probably the area that has seen the most remarkable changes. Three trends that need to be continued in the future are:

♦ With increasing sample sizes, the empirical foundation becomes strong, but it also becomes possible to compare subsamples. Thus we must consider the increasing diversity of the SME population.

♦ Advanced statistical techniques and econometric models are being used with greater frequency. This is a favorable evolution but should not prevent further development of qualitative research. For example, Steyaert and Bouwen (1997) are performing explorative entrepreneurial studies using narrative-contextual epistemology. Qualitative and quantitative research should not conflict, but instead complement each other. Much more attention will need to be given to the quality of the data and to the influence of measurement methods on the global models.

♦ The SME literature reveals a growing interest in multidisciplinary research. This should definitely be encouraged so that charting the complex financing process in growth-oriented SMEs will eventually succeed.

The financial markets axis (demand and supply of financial products) has already been extensively studied. Nonetheless, much still needs to be done. Three domains should be further investigated:

1 The influence of personal factors on both demand and supply, recognizing that the SME–bank relationship is more often a personal matter than a relationship between companies.

2 Examining how accessible the new banking products are for SMEs (i.e., does financial cutting-edge technology facilitate access to the financial markets for SMEs?).

3 The positioning of government initiatives on the financial markets (the main question is how can the innumerable initiatives at various levels of government be evaluated against their relevance for growth financing?).

The financial management axis (financial behavior and training), specifically inexpert financial management, is the basis of serious and sometimes fatal problems in SMEs. On the other hand, more external accountants or supervising authorities are needed. Whether the knowledge gap can ultimately be bridged remains to be seen.

Conclusions

Growth financing in SMEs is a fascinating subject. It is, however, difficult to determine the best solution – the challenge of obtaining better insights continues and has still not been satisfied. It reminds one of a legend about Pythagoras. One day, the mathematician was approached by a prince, who asked, "I am fascinated by mathematics, but it is a pity that it is so complicated. As a prince of royal blood, is there no easier way of mastering it?" As is fitting for a mathematician, Pythagoras gave a clear and unambiguous answer: "There is no royal road!" Without any doubt, the same applies to growth financing.

References

Ang, J.S. 1991. Small business uniqueness and the theory of financial management. *Journal of Small Business Finance* 1(1): 1–13.

Arendarski, A., Mroczkowski, T. and Sood, J. 1994. A study of the redevelopment of private enterprise in Poland: conditions and policies for continuing growth. *Journal of Small Business Management* 32(3): 40–51.

Aronoff, C.E. 1998. Megatrends in family business. *Family Business Review* 11(3): 181–5.

Audretsch, D.A. and Elston, J.A. 1996. Financing the German Mittelstand. *Small Business Economics* 9(2): 97–110.

Ayres, G.R. and Carter, M. 1998. Approaching succession planning from an ability to pay basis. In J.F. Hair, Jr. (ed.), *Family Business – Progress and Prophecy*. Proceedings of the 1997 Family Firm Institute Conference. Boston: The Family Firm Institute Inc., pp. 62–89.

Bahat, S. 1998. Banks' credit to SME–government policies, banks' interest and employment. In H.J. Pleitner (ed.), *Renaissance of SMEs in a Globalized Economy*. St. Gallen, Switzerland: Swiss Research Institute for Small Business (IGW-HSG), pp. 399–409.

Bartlett, W. and Rangelove, R. 1997. Small firms and economic transformation in Bulgaria. *Small Business Economics* 9(4): 319–33.

Bates, T. 1997. Financing small business creation: the case of Chinese and Korean immigrant entrepreneurs. *Journal of Business Venturing* 12(2): 109–24.

Beaudouin, R. and St. Pierre, J. 1998. The financial problems of small businesses. In P.A. Julien (ed.), *The State of the Art in Small Business and Entrepreneurship*. Aldershot: Ashgate, pp. 276–99.

Binks, M. 1991. Small businesses and their banks in the year 2000. In J. Curran and R.A. Blackburn (eds.), *Paths of Enterprise. The Future of the Small Business*. London: Routledge, pp. 149–62.

Binks, M. and Ennew, C.T. 1996. Growing firms and the credit constraint. *Small Business Economics* 8(1): 17–25.

Binks, M. and Ennew, C.T. 1997. The relationship between UK banks and their small business customers. *Small Business Economics* 9(2): 167–78.

Bopaiah, C. 1998. Availability of credit to family businesses. *Small Business Economics* 11(1): 75–86.

Bornheim, S.P. and Herbeck, T.H. 1998. A research note on the theory of SME–bank relationships. *Small Business Economics* 10(3): 327–31.

Brophy, D.J. 1997. Financing the growth of entrepreneurial firms. In D.L. Sexton and R.W. Smilor (eds.), *Entrepreneurship 2000*. Chicago: Upstart, pp. 5–27.

Campbell, A.J. 1998. The effects of internal firm barriers on the export behavior of small firms in a free trade environment: evidence from NAFTA. *Journal of Small Business Management* 34(3): 50–8.

Carter, N.M. and Allen, K.R. 1997. Size determinants of women-owned businesses: choice or barriers to resources? *Entrepreneurship and Regional Development* 9(3): 211–20.

Carter, S. and Rose, P. 1998. The financing of male- and female-owned businesses. *Entrepreneurship and Regional Development* 10(3): 225–41.

Chaganti, R., DeCarolis, D. and Deeds, D. 1995. Predictors of capital structure in small ventures. *Entrepreneurship. Theory and Practice* 20(2): 7–18.

Chell, E., Hedberg-Jalonen, N. and Miettinen, A. 1997. Are types of business owner-managers universal? A cross country study of the UK, New Zealand and Finland. In R. Donckels and A. Miettinen (eds.), *Entrepreneurship and SME Research: On its Way to the Next Millennium*. Aldershot: Ashgate, pp. 3–18.

Chittenden, F., Hall, G. and Hutchinson, P. 1996. Small firm growth, access to capital markets and financial structure: review of issues and an empirical investigation. *Small Business Economics* 8(1): 59–67.

Chrisman, J.J., Chua, J.H. and Sharma, P. 1998. Important attributes of successors in family businesses: an exploratory study. *Family Business Review* 11(1): 19–34.

Corbetta, G. 1995. Patterns of development of family businesses in Italy. *Family Business Review* 8(4): 255–65.

Cressy, R. and Oloffson, C. 1997a. European SME financing: an overview. *Small Business Economics* 9(2): 87–96.

Cressy, R. and Oloffson, C. 1997b. The financial conditions for Swedish SMEs: survey and research agenda. *Small Business Economics* 9(2): 179–94.

Davis, J.A. and Herrera R.M. 1998. The social psychology of family shareholders dynamics. *Family Business Review* 11(3): 253–60.

Deeg, R. 1998. What makes German banks different. *Small Business Economics* 10(2): 93–101.

Delmar, F. 1997. Measuring growth: methodological considerations and empirical results. In R. Donckels and A. Miettinen (eds.), *Entrepreneurship and SME Research: On Its Way to the Next Millennium*. Aldershot: Ashgate, pp. 199–215.

Donckels, R. and Fröhlich, E. 1991. Are family businesses really different? European experiences from STRATOS. *Family Business Review* 4(2): 149–60.

Egeln, J., Licht, G. and Steil, F. 1997. Firm foundations and the role of financial constraints. *Small Business Economics* 9(2): 137–50.

Elston, J.A. 1993. *Firm Ownership Structure and Investment: Theory and Evidence from German Panel Data*. Wissenschaftszentrum Berlin Discussion Paper, FS IV 93–28.

Elston, J.A. and Chirinko, R. 1995. Finance, control and profitability: an evaluation of German bank influence, mimeo, quoted in Deeg (1998).

Ennew, C.T. and Binks, M.R. 1996. Good and bad customers: the benefit of participation in the banking relationship. *International Journal of Bank Marketing* 14(2): 5–13.

ENSR (European Network for SME Research). 1993–1997. *The European Observatory for SMEs. First to Fifth Annual Reports*. Zoetermeer: EIM Small Business Research and Consultancy.

European Commission. 1997. *The Second Round Table of Bankers and SMEs. Final Report*. Brussels; Directorate general XXIII.

European Commission. 1998. *Activities in Favour of SMEs and the Craft Sector*. Brussels.

Freear, J., Sohl, J.E. and Wetzel, W.E., Jr. 1997. The informal venture capital market: milestones passed and the road ahead. In D.L. Sexton and R.W. Smilor (eds.), *Entrepreneurship 2000*. Chicago: Upstart, pp. 47–69.

Gallo, M.A. 1995. Family businesses in Spain: tracks followed and outcomes reached by those among the largest thousand. *Family Business Review* 8(4): 245–54.

Gallo, M.A. and Vilaseca, A. 1996. Finance in family business. *Family Business Review* 9(4): 387–401.

Gallo, M.A. and Vilaseca, A. 1998. A financial perspective on structure, conduct and performance in the family firm: an empirical study. *Family Business Review* 11(1): 35–47.

Gibb, A. and Davies, L. 1990. In pursuit of frameworks for the development of growth models of the small business. *International Small Business Journal* 9(1): 15–31.

Gnyawali, D.R. and Fogel, D.S. 1994. Environments for entrepreneurship development: key dimensions and research implications. *Entrepreneurship. Theory and Practice* 18(4): 43–62.

Gundry, L.K. and Ben-Yoseph, M. 1998. Women entrepreneurs in Romania, Poland and the United States: cultural and family influences on strategy and growth. *Family Business Review* 11(1): 61–73.

Holtz-Eakin, D., Joulfaian, D. and Rosen, H.S. 1994. Sticking it out: entrepreneurial survival and liquidity constraints. *Journal of Political Economy* 102(1): 53–75.

Hughes, A. 1997. Finance for SMEs: a UK perspective. *Small Business Economics* 9(2): 151–66.

Japan Small Business Research Institute. 1998. *White Paper on Small and Medium Enterprises in Japan – The Need for Small and Medium Enterprises to Change and Display Entrepreneurship*. Tokyo: Japan Small Business Research Institute.

Karsai, J., Wright, M., Dudzinski, Z. and Morovic, J. 1998. Screening and valuing venture capital investments: evidence from Hungary, Poland and Slovakia. *Entrepreneurship and Regional Development* 10(3): 203–24.

Keasey, K. and McGuinness, P. 1990. Small new firms and the return to alternative sources of finance. *Small Business Economics* 6(2): 139–50.

Keasey, K. and Watson, R. 1994a. The 1986 UK insolvency and company directors' disqualification act: an evaluation of their impacts upon small firm financing decisions. *Small Business Economics* 6(4): 257–66.

Keasey, K. and Watson, R. 1994b. The bank financing of small firms in UK: issues and evidence. *Small Business Economics* 6(5): 349–62.

Kimhi, A. 1997. Intergenerational succession in small family businesses: borrowing constraints and optimal timing of succession. *Small Business Economics* 9(4): 309–18.

Kirby, D.A. 1998. Overcoming the financial constraints on small firm growth: the case of franchising. In H.J. Pleitner (ed.), *Renaissance of SMEs in a Globalized Economy*. St. Gallen, Switzerland: Swiss Research Institute for Small Business (IGW-HSG), pp. 411–22.

Klochko, Y. and Isakova, N. 1996. Small business sector in Ukrainian transition economy: achievements to date. *Entrepreneurship and Regional Development* 8(2): 127–40.

Koper, G. 1993. Women entrepreneurs and the granting of business credit. In S. Allen and C. Truman (eds.), *Women in Business: Perspectives on Women Entrepreneurs*. London: Routledge, pp. 57–69.

Kotey, B. and Meredith, G.G. 1997. Relationships among owner/manager personal values and perceptions, business strategies, and enterprise performance. *Journal of Small Business Management* 35(2): 37–64.

Landström, H., Frank, H. and Veciana, J.M. (eds.). 1997. *Entrepreneurship and Small Business Research in Europe: an European Council for Small Business (ECSB) Survey*. Aldershot: Avebury.

Lane, S.J. 1995. Business starts during the transition in Hungary. *Journal of Business Venturing* 10(3): 181–94.

La Porta, R., Lopez-De-Silanes, F., Shleifer, A. and Vishny, R.W. 1997. Legal determinants of external finance. *Journal of Finance* 52(3): 1131–50.

LeCornu, M.R., McMahon, R.G.P., Forsaith, D.M. and Stanger, A.M.J. 1996. The small enterprise financial objective function. *Journal of Small Business Management* 34(3): 1–14.

Litz, R.A. 1995. The family business: toward definitional clarity. *Family Business Review* 8(2): 71–81.

McConaughy, D.L., Dhatt, M.S. and Kim, Y.H. 1995. Agency costs, market discipline and market timing: evidence from post IPO operating performance. *Entrepreneurship. Theory and Practice* 20(2): 43–57.

McKechnie, S.A., Ennew, C.T. and Read, L.H. 1998. The nature of banking relationship: a comparison of the experiences of male and female small business owners. *International Small*

Business Journal 16(3): 39–55.

McMahon, R.G.P. and Holmes, S. 1991. Small business financial management practices in North America: a literature review. *Journal of Small Business Management* 29(2): 19–29.

Merikas, A., Bruton, G.D. and Vozikis, G.S. 1993. The theoretical relationships between the strategic objective of sales growth and the financial policy of the entrepreneurial firm. *International Small Business Journal* 11(3): 59–67.

Miettinen, A. 1998. Accuracy of self-rated business performance and its meaning. In H.J. Pleitner (ed.), *Renaissance of SMEs in a Globalized Economy*. St. Gallen, Switzerland: Swiss Research Institute for Small Business (IGW-HSG), pp. 423–8.

Moran, P. 1998. Personality characteristics and growth-orientation of the small business owner-manager. *International Small Business Journal* 16(3): 17–38.

Myers, S.C. 1984. The capital structure puzzle. *Journal of Finance* 39(3): 575–92.

Nicolescu, O. 1998. Financial problems for Romanian SMEs and the ways to prevent and eliminate them. In H.J. Pleitner (ed.), *Renaissance of SMEs in a Globalized Economy*. St. Gallen, Switzerland: Swiss Research Institute for Small Business (IGW-HSG), pp. 443–8.

Norton, E. 1990. Similarities and differences in small and large corporation beliefs about capital structure policy. *Small Business Economics* 2(3): 229–45.

Norton, E. 1991. Capital structure and small growth firms. *Journal of Small Business Finance* 1(2): 161–77.

Norton, E. 1995. Venture capital as an alternative means to allocate capital: an agency-theoretic view. *Entrepreneurship. Theory and Practice* 20(2): 19–29.

Palmer, A. and Bejou, D. 1995. The effects of gender on the development of relationships between clients and financial advisers. *International Journal of Bank Marketing* 13(3): 8–27.

Peel, M.I. and Wilson, N. 1996. Working capital and financial management practices in the small firm sector. *International Small Business Journal* 14(2): 52–68.

Perlitz, M. and Seger, F. 1994. Regarding the particular role of universal banks in German corporate governance. Unpublished manuscript, University of Mannheim, quoted in Deeg (1998).

Petersen, M.A. and Rajan, R.G. 1994. The benefits of lending relationships: evidence from small business data. *Journal of Finance* 49(1): 3–37.

Petersen, M.A. and Rajan, R.G. 1995. The effect of credit market competition on lending relationships. *Quarterly Journal of Economics* 110(2): 407–43.

Petty, J.W. and Bygrave, W.D. 1993. What does finance have to say to the entrepreneur? *Journal of Small Business Finance* 2(2): 125–37.

Petrakis, P.E. 1997. Entrepreneurship and growth: creative and equilibrating events. *Small Business Economics* 9(5): 383–402.

Pineda, R.C., Lerner, L.D., Miller, M.C. and Philips, S.J. 1998. An investigation of factors affecting the information-search activities of small business managers. *Journal of Small Business Management* 36(1): 60–71.

Pistrui, D., Welsch, H.P. and Roberts, I. 1997. Growth intentions and expansion plans of new entrepreneurs in the former Soviet Bloc. In R. Donckels and A. Miettinen (eds.), *Entrepreneurship and SME Research: On its Way to the Next Millennium*. Aldershot: Ashgate, pp. 93–111.

Prasad, D., Vozikis, G.S., Bruton, G.D. and Merikas, A. 1995. "Harvesting" through initial public offerings (IPOs): the implications of underpricing for the small firm. *Entrepreneurship. Theory and Practice* 20(2): 31–41.

Pruit, S.W. 1997. Further evidence on the firm–size relation and stock market responses to changes in Federal Reserve margin levels. *Small Business Economics* 9(4): 301–7.

Rashid Sabri, N. 1998. Financial analysis of Palestinian industry including small scale industry. *Small Business Economics* 11(3): 293–301.

Reid, G.C. 1996. Financial structure and the growing small firm: theoretical underpinning and current evidence. *Small Business Economics* 8(1): 1–7.

Riding, A.L. and Swift, C.S. 1990. Women business owners and terms of credit: some empirical findings of the Canadian experience. *Journal of Business Venturing* 5(5): 327–40.

Schnabel, J.A. 1992. Small business capital structure choice. *Journal of Small Business Finance* 2(1): 13–21.

Smyrnios, K., Tanewski, G. and Romano, C. 1998. Development of a measure of the characteristics of family business. *Family Business Review* 11(1): 49–60.

Soeharto, P. 1998. Study on the implementation of micro and small business credit schemes in Indonesia. In H.J. Pleitner (ed.), *Renaissance of SMEs in a Globalized Economy*. St. Gallen, Switzerland: Swiss Research Institute for Small Business (IGW-HSG), pp. 449–57.

Steyaert, C. and Bouwen, R. 1997. Telling stories of entrepreneurship: towards a narrative-contextual epistemology for entrepreneurial studies. In R. Donckels and A. Miettinen (eds.), *Entrepreneurship and SME Research: On its Way to the Next Millennium*. Aldershot: Ashgate, pp. 47–62.

Storey, D.J. 1994. New firm growth and bank financing. *Small Business Economics* 6(2): 139–50.

Todorov, K. 1996. The dynamic entrepreneurs: the locomotives of the East European economies in transition. In H.J. Pleitner (ed.), *Significance and Survival of SMEs in a Different Business Environment*. St. Gallen, Switzerland: Swiss Research Institute for Small Business (IGW-HSG), pp. 585–95.

Turnbull, P.W. and Gibbs, M.L. 1987. Marketing bank services to corporate customers: the importance of relationships. *International Journal of Bank Marketing* 5(1): 19–26.

Upton, N.B. and Heck, R.K.Z. 1997. The family business dimension of entrepreneurship. In D.L. Sexton and R.W. Smilor (eds.), *Entrepreneurship 2000*. Chicago: Upstart, pp. 243–66.

Van Auken, H.E. and Holman, T. 1995. Financial strategies of small, public firms: a comparative analysis with small, private firms and large, public firms. *Entrepreneurship. Theory and Practice* 20(1): 29–41.

Wakefield, M.W. 1997. Antecedents of conflict in family firms: an empirical study. In T.G. Habbershon (ed.), *Power Up the Family Business – Proceedings of the 1996 Family Firm Institute Conference*. Boston: The Family Firm Inc., pp. 12–18.

Walker, D.A. 1989. Financing the small firm. *Small Business Economics* 1(4): 285–96.

Welsh, J.A. and White, J.F. 1981 A small business is not a little big business. *Harvard Business Review* (June–August): 18–32.

Westhead, P. 1995. Survival and employment growth contrasts between types of owner-managed high-technology firms. *Entrepreneurship. Theory and Practice* 20(1): 5–27.

11

Informal Venture Capital and the Financing of Emergent Growth Businesses

Colin Mason and Richard Harrison

Informal Venture Capital Research in Retrospect
IVC Research Prospects
Conclusions

Informal venture capital (IVC) – investments and noncollateral forms of lending made by private individuals ("business angels") using their own money directly in unquoted companies in which they have no family connection – plays a key role in the financing of emergent businesses in at least three respects.

First, IVC occupies a critical position in the growth firm financing spectrum, filling the gap between founders, family and friends (which is likely to be used up getting the business through the proof-of-concept stage) and institutional venture capital funds (which because of their high transactions costs, normally do not make investments less than $500,000) (Freear and Wetzel 1990). Indeed, this role is of growing economic significance over time: In an article "No Slacking in Silicon Valley," for example, *Business Week* (August 31, 1998, p. 48) reported that venture capital investors "no longer want to be bothered with small-fry opportunities. The average size of deals has climbed 27%, to $5.3 million, in the past two years. . . . To seed deals too small for venture capitalists, private investors are jumping into the fray. . . . This . . . is helping the Valley refuel itself."

Second, the IVC market is substantially larger than the institutional venture capital market in terms of the amounts invested in businesses at their start-up and early growth stage. Establishing the size of the IVC market is problematic because of the private and unreported nature of investment activity and the desire of most business angels to preserve their privacy (Benjamin and Margulis 1996), and estimates of the market size are therefore highly provisional. In the United States Wetzel (1994) has estimated that there are about 250,000 angels investing $10 to $20 billion every year in over 30,000 ventures, exceeding the investment activity of venture capital funds, which in the early 1990s were investing about $2 billion a year in fewer than 2,000 companies. In the

United Kingdom the annual investment activity by business angels is estimated to be around 3,500 investments, involving an investment of £500 million. This is ten times as many investments and four times the capital invested in early-stage ventures as made by the institutional venture capital (Mason and Harrison 1997a). In the Netherlands business angels have invested in at least 2,500 businesses compared with about 1,500 businesses invested in by venture capital firms (K+V organisatie adviesbureau bv/ Entrepreneurial Holding, Inc. 1996). Moreover, these estimates of the size of the IVC market do not take account of the fact that a majority of business angels have additional funds available but cannot find sufficient investment opportunities (Mason and Harrison 1994a). Furthermore, "virgin angels" – that is, individuals who share the same self-made, high net worth characteristics as active angels but have no venture investment history – might be willing to enter this market with appropriate support and incentives (Mason and Harrison 1993; Freear et al. 1992, 1994), expanding the population of business angels on some estimates by up to 75 percent (Freear et al. 1992).

Third, business angels are hands-on investors, contributing their skills, expertise, knowledge and contacts both formally and informally in the businesses they invest in (Harrison and Mason 1992a; Mason and Harrison 1996a; Lumme et al. 1998). Because of their entrepreneurial background, business angels therefore contribute more to a business than just money. Wetzel (1994: 180) observes that business angels provide the entrepreneur "with the benefits of their know how – most of which they acquired by making their own mistakes in business, the way entrepreneurs learn their most valuable lessons." Harrison and Mason (1992a) report that business angels and venture capital fund managers make contributions in broadly similar areas of the business, with an advisory/sounding board role and with financial advice being the most important. Business angels are more likely to be viewed by entrepreneurs as making a helpful contribution in a number of strategic development and operational areas, whereas venture capitalists typically emphasize more strongly monitoring and control functions. Similar findings are reported by Ehrlich et al. (1994), who identify business angels as playing key roles as sounding boards, in monitoring operating and financial performance and formulating strategy. However, business angels appear less willing (and able) to recommend and effect changes in the management team, which is a key contribution of venture capitalists (Fiet et al. 1997).

One of the most remarkable paradoxes in entrepreneurship research is the mismatch between the significance of IVC, in terms of the number of businesses financed and the limited amount of research it has attracted. The contrast with research on the institutional venture capital industry and on the IPO market is particularly stark. These markets involve a substantially smaller proportion of entrepreneurial businesses (although they are significant in qualitative terms) but have nevertheless attracted many researchers with the result that the knowledge is much more dispersed. This is, of course, in part due to the visibility of the institutional venture capital and IPO markets and the availability of data from published industry sources. The IVC market, by contrast, is largely invisible, and access to data is consequently much more problematic.

In this chapter, therefore, we provide an overview of international research on the IVC market with two primary aims: (1) to provide a comprehensive review of the existing literature and (2) to identify key research themes for future research into the role played by IVC in the emergence and growth of entrepreneurial businesses. The next section reviews what is known about the characteristics and operation of the market in developed economies. This review distinguishes between what we term "first-generation" (or market profile, largely descriptive) and "second-generation" (more analytical and policy-oriented) studies. The following sections go on to consider the unknowns, identifying where further research is required. This discussion also raises methodological issues in researching the IVC market, which future studies need to consider, and highlights the need for future studies to be more theoretically informed.

INFORMAL VENTURE CAPITAL RESEARCH IN RETROSPECT

First-generation studies

Research on the IVC market was pioneered by Wetzel (1981), although he has identified some earlier studies (Wetzel 1986a). The context for this study was the widely held perception that technology-based ventures encountered a "finance gap" when seeking to raise small amounts of early-stage risk capital, although this ran counter to anecdotal evidence that business angels played a key role in filling this gap. However, little was known about their characteristics, the amount of capital available, what they look for in an investment proposal and how entrepreneurs could find them. Wetzel's motivation was therefore to "put some boundaries on our ignorance" (Wetzel 1986b: 132). His study of informal risk capital in New England, undertaken with financial backing from the US Small Business Administration (SBA), provided the first ever detailed profile of business angels, their characteristics, scale of investment activity, investment preferences, risk, return and exit expectations and referral sources (Wetzel 1981, 1983). Emerging directly out of this study was a public policy proposal to mobilize angel money by establishing regional referral networks to enable investors to examine a broader range of investment opportunities. This provided a means of overcoming the absence of efficient channels of communication between entrepreneurs and investors that were impeding the efficient functioning of the market (Wetzel 1981, 1983). Wetzel established such a network – Venture Capital Network – in 1984 (Wetzel and Freear 1996), and this provided the model for similar initiatives elsewhere in the United States (Browne and Stowe 1996) and other countries (Blatt and Riding 1996; Landström and Olofsson 1996; Mason and Harrison 1996d).

Subsequent studies of IVC in other parts of the United States, a number of which were also funded by the SBA, sought to replicate and refine Wetzel's pioneering study (e.g., Tymes and Krasner 1983; Aram 1989; Haar et al. 1988; Sullivan 1996). Here again, the focus of these studies was on description of the attitudes, behavior and characteristics of angels. Gaston's (1989a) publishing of his SBA-funded studies in book form provided an accessible and detailed profile of business angel characteristics, emphasizing their heterogeneity and the types of investments that they make. His objective was to give entrepreneurs insights into the IVC market in order to improve their prospects of successfully raising finance from such investors in a shorter time and at less cost.

The late 1980s and early 1990s saw the international diffusion of research on IVC. Detailed studies of the IVC market have been undertaken in Canada (Riding and Short 1987a, 1987b; Short and Riding 1989), the United Kingdom (Harrison and Mason 1992b; Mason and Harrison 1994a; Coveney and Moore 1998), Sweden (Landström

1993a), the Netherlands (K+V organisatie adviesbureau bv/Entrepreneurial Holding bv 1996), Finland (Lumme et al. 1998), Australia (Hindle and Wenban 1997) and Japan (Tashiro 1999). Work is in progress in a number of other countries, including Denmark, Norway, Germany, Singapore and Saudi Arabia. The main focus of these studies is comparative, replicating earlier US and UK studies, with a similar emphasis on market and investor characteristics. In short, the objective in these first-generation studies continued to be to "put boundaries on our ignorance" but in new geographical contexts. What emerges from these studies is a high degree of similarity in the main characteristics of business angels and their investment activity across countries (Mason and Harrison 1995). Business angels in different countries have many more common features than differences, with only Japanese business angels deviating significantly (Tashiro 1999).

Second-generation studies

Second-generation studies of the IVC market can be grouped into three categories: studies addressing a range of new topics, those focusing on policy issues and research introducing a theoretical perspective. These studies reflect a growing sophistication in the analysis of the IVC market and draw their inspiration more specifically from research in entrepreneurship and institutional venture capital.

Research on new topics

The 1990s has seen research on a growing range of new topics. Four themes in particular have emerged. Analyses of the:

1 investment decision-making process
2 postinvestment relationship
3 angels' risk, return, holding period and exit route expectations
4 private equity finance spectrum.

First, the IVC *investment decision-making process* has been analyzed in terms of a stage model that is similar, although not identical, to that of institutional venture capital funds (Riding et al. 1993). Mason and Rogers (1997) have used verbal protocol analysis to examine the initial screening stage in this process, which is the stage at which angels typically reject more than 90 percent of the investment opportunities that they consider. Feeney et al. (1999) draw upon a large database of information on Canadian business angels to examine both the reasons why investors reject some opportunities and the attributes that encourage them to invest in others. Harrison and Mason (1999a) have examined the approach of "techno-angels" to the initial appraisal of technology-related investment opportunities. These studies suggest that investment opportunities are rejected by investors for a range of reasons and that the credibility of the entrepreneur and the presentation of the opportunity are critical in the initial screening process. Accordingly, the equity gap is not exclusively a supply-side problem. Rather, many entrepreneurs are not "investment ready" (Ernst and Young/Centre for Innovation and Enterprise 1997). Specifically, they do not know how to "audition for money" (Harrison and Mason 1999a). In other words, most entrepreneurs are unaware of how to present their investment proposal in a way that is relevant to potential business angel investors or how to signal their management capabilities.

Although our understanding of the initial screening stage is considerably enhanced, subsequent stages in the investment decision-making process have received much less attention. However, there is some limited evidence on how business angels undertake the due diligence process (Harrison and Mason 1999b). Riding et al. (1993) and Mason and Harrison (1996b) have looked at the entire investment decision-making process, with the latter using a case study of an investor syndicate. These studies reveal, first, that the approach varies between the different stages of the investment decision and, second, that the emphasis given to different investment criteria changes, with financial issues only becoming significant in the later stages of the process.

Second, a number of studies have investigated the *postinvestment relationship*, that is, the nature, extent and impact of the contribution made by IVC investors in the businesses they invest in. For example, Harrison and Mason (1992a) and Ehrlich et al. (1994) have undertaken studies from the entrepreneur's perspective to examine the roles played by business angels in their investee businesses, the entrepreneur's assessment of the value of the contributions made, and to compare business angels with venture capital fund managers. Lumme et al. (1998) have examined the type and effectiveness of contributions made by business angels to the businesses they invest in from the perspective of the investor. Mason and Harrison (1996a) have tracked investors and entrepreneurs to explore some qualitative aspects of the investor–investee relationship. Freear et al. (1995) have presented similar information but only from the perspective of the entrepreneur.

Third, although several early descriptive studies reported on the *angels' risk, return, holding period and exit route expectations* (e.g., Wetzel 1981; Gaston 1989a; Mason and Harrison 1994a), only two studies have presented information on the actual returns achieved, the time to exit and the method of exit (Lumme et al. 1996, 1998; Mason and Harrison 1999a). Although comparison with the investment performance of venture capitalists is problematic, Mason and Harrison's (1999a) study suggests that compared with early stage venture capital funds, business angels have fewer investments which are write-offs and a higher proportion of moderately performing investments. They suggest that the explanation for these differences in return profiles may be related to the fact that business angels generally do not invest on a portfolio basis, hence "it is much more important [for a business angel] to avoid a bad investment than to try to hit a home run" (Benjamin and Margulis 1996: 221). "Unlike a venture capital firm, which makes perhaps 15 investments in a year and can absorb a direct hit, the . . . private investor must take great care with each investment" (Benjamin and Margulis 1996: 82).

Fourth, positioning IVC within the *private equity finance spectrum* represents another emerging research theme (Sohl 1999). To date, this focus has primarily been concerned with establishing the complementarity between informal and formal venture capital. Freear and Wetzel (1990) have demonstrated this complementarity in terms of both size of investment and stage of business development, with private investors dominant in financing rounds of less than $500,000 and at seed and start-up stages in the 35 percent of venture-backed companies who had previously raised business angel capital. Benjamin and Margulis (1996: 71) have likened this situation to a relay race: "angel investment runs the critical first leg of the . . . race, passing the baton to [the] venture capital [fund] only after the company has begun to find its stride." However, replications of this study raises questions concerning the generalizability of this conclusion in different countries and at different points in time. Mason and Harrison (1994b) found no evidence of these complementary relationships in the United Kingdom (albeit using imperfect data), while Freear et al. (1997) concluded that these relationships appeared to be weaker in the 1990s. There are, of course, other forms in which complementarities between venture capital and IVC can take, including co-investing (Lumme et al. 1998) and information exchange. However, these and other complementarities remain to be explored in detail.

Policy issues

Wetzel's pioneering research in the early 1980s made the original case for policy intervention in the IVC market to address market inefficiency issues (Wetzel 1983, 1986b, 1987). The rationale for policy intervention has been elaborated by Wetzel (1987), Mason and Harrison (1995) and Wetzel and Freear (1996). Lumme et al. (1998) have considered a range of policy options to promote IVC activity. Issues in the establishment, operation and effectiveness of business angel networks have been addressed in a number of studies (reviewed in Mason and Harrison 1996d; see also Harrison and Mason 1996a, 1996b).

Most assessments of the effectiveness of business angel networks are favorable, concluding that they have a positive impact on the flow of IVC. An assessment of five local business angel networks in the United Kingdom identified a range of further impacts in terms of induced investment effects (e.g., the effect that business angel investments often have in unlocking further finance from other sources, such as banks). Even wider indirect effects were found, such as:

1 Advisory and signposting functions for businesses and entrepreneurs who approach the network but are inappropriate for equity financing,
2 Feedback received by entrepreneurs as a result of speaking to angels,
3 Education and training services to raise the competence of both investors and entrepreneurs (Harrison and Mason 1996b).

However, Blatt and Riding (1996) provide a much less favorable assessment of Canada Opportunities Investment Network (COIN), a Canadian business angel network. Awareness of COIN was low among the investor community, and the majority of investors who had used COIN reported that it was not an essential, or even important, element in their investment sourcing. Indeed, more than half of the investors stated that, COIN notwithstanding, it was becoming more difficult to find investment opportunities. Half of those investors who had used COIN stated that they would not use it again. These criticisms of COIN are echoed by UK business angels, albeit in less extreme form. Here again, the concern among business angels is the poor quality of investment opportunities that they see, with a significant minority reporting that membership of a business angel network has not enhanced the quality of their deal flow (Mason and Harrison 1999b). Blatt and Riding (1996: 84) are therefore right to conclude that "from the investors' viewpoint . . . the problem with the informal market for risk capital is not an inability to make contact [with entrepreneurs seeking finance]. Rather, the problem . . . is a scarcity of high-quality opportunities." However, efforts by governments in various countries to encourage the development of the IVC market have focused almost entirely on the supply-side, notably through tax incentives for investors who invest in unquoted companies, and on matching initiatives, while largely ignoring the demand-side (Mason and Harrison 1999b).

Theoretical approaches

Theoretical approaches to the analysis of the IVC market are the most recent and least extensive strand of research in the field, and research on IVC has not been characterized to date by a high level of theoretical sophistication (Harrison et al. 1997). Among the exceptions have been attempts to draw on the "pecking-order" hypothesis (Myers and Majluf 1984) to locate the firm's demand for informal investment in context (Harrison and Mason 1991) and Norton's (1990) discussion of applying theoretical models developed in the field of finance (notably efficient capital market assumptions, portfolio management theory, utility theory and decision-making and agency theories of investment risk) to the institutional and informal venture capital markets. However, as a number of commentators point out for both the IVC market (Freear et al. 1997) and the private equity market more generally (Brophy 1997a, 1997b), substantial progress in the application and development of finance theory in this area is hindered by the virtual absence of large-scale data sets.

Landström (1995) and Feeney et al. (1999) have begun to apply elements of decision theory to the informal investor's decision-making processes. Fiet (1995a, 1995b) has examined agency risk and market risk in both the institutional and IVC investment process, concluding that business angels are more concerned with agency risk, relying on the entrepreneur to protect them from market risk. This is supported by Harrison and Mason (1999b), who conclude that informal investors are more interested in backing the jockey (the entrepreneur) than the horse (the business opportunity). Norton (1995: 27) has taken this further to argue that "agency theory may provide the most valuable insights into venture capital practice." However, Landström's (1993b) application of agency theoretic frameworks to explain the interaction between informal and formal venture capitalists and their portfolio firms concludes that the theory fails to provide a satisfactory framework for explaining these relationships in either market.

Given that the relationship between informal investors and entrepreneurs must be based on trust and not control (Landström 1993b), there has been increasing interest in the application of theories of trust to the informal investment domain. Fiet (1995a) has explored trust as part of a wider study of information sources, networks and reliance structures, concluding that the degree of reliance on others was a function of trust, which in turn depended on the amount of network experience. Harrison et al. (1997) have developed a theoretical model of interpersonal trust and cooperation which has been applied to the IVC decision-making process. This draws attention to the importance of the assessment of the investment proposal in terms of perceived risk, utility and importance of the opportunity, competence of the entrepreneur and the role of the coordinator (or intermediary) who introduces the investment opportunity to the investor.

In addition, several attempts to adopt a specifically economic approach to the analysis of the IVC market have been made. For example, Sullivan and Miller (1990) have addressed the issue of IVC as a form of wealth-maximizing behavior (which is not supported in favor of a view of the investor as having multiple objectives and varying individual preferences). In a subsequent paper Sullivan (1994) has applied the economic analysis of altruism to the IVC situation, concluding that, at least in part, a desire for "social return" is important in this market.

IVC RESEARCH PROSPECTS

IVC research remains a relatively small and immature field of academic enquiry. Although the first studies were undertaken in the early 1980s, it was only during the 1990s that researchers outside North America began to focus on it. However, some encouraging signs indicate that interest in the IVC market within academe is growing, particularly in Europe, where a recent European Commission document has emphasized the need to increase the availability of all forms of risk capital in order to encourage greater entrepreneurial activity and to create the jobs that are required to reduce, sustainably and substantially, unemployment levels (Commission 1998). The objective of this final section is therefore to identify where this limited but growing research capacity should be focused in order to expand our understanding of the IVC market and to provide the knowledge base necessary for the design and delivery of effective policies. This research agenda encompasses methodological, analytical, theoretical and policy issues.

Methodological issues

The single most important methodological problem in undertaking research on the IVC market arises from the great difficulty in finding business angels. Benjamin and Margulis (1996: 11) correctly observe that "angels prize their privacy" because of their fear of being deluged not only with unwelcome funding proposals but also other forms of monetary requests (e.g., charitable appeals). Two implications follow. First, they are unwilling to identify themselves, and as a result, there are no directories of business angels (Wetzel 1981, 1987). Second, those business angels who are identified may be unwilling to respond to research surveys (Haar et al. 1988). Nor are there any public records of their transactions (Wetzel 1981, 1987). This, in turn, has two consequence for researchers. First, the size and characteristics of the population of business angels is unknown and unknowable (Wetzel 1983). Second, research on the IVC market has, of necessity, been based on "samples of convenience" whose representativeness can never be verified. Furthermore, a strong probability exists that particular types of samples of convenience (e.g., investors registered with business angel networks) will be particularly unrepresentative, casting doubts on the validity of the findings derived from such sources. Indeed, this is the essence of the debate between Stevenson and Coveney (1996) and Mason and Harrison (1997b) on the size and characteristics of the United Kingdom's IVC market.

Researchers therefore need to give much greater thought to how business angels can be identified. Is it possible to move beyond samples of convenience? Freear et al. (1994) have made an interesting move in this direction by utilizing real estate transaction data as a means of identifying high net worth individuals on the basis of the size of their mortgages, although this data source has its own limitations in terms of its coverage. Is the best approach therefore simply to base research on *several* samples of convenience, so that the effect of individual sample biases is diluted (Mason and Harrison 1997b)? Omnibus surveys have recently been recognized as an effective method of identifying and obtaining information from potential entrepreneurs (Dennis et al. 1995) and are likely to have potential in business angel research. Another potential source of bias is nonresponse rates, which are greatest for noninvestors (Freear et al. 1994), with implications both for estimating the size of the IVC market and also in comparing the characteristics of investors and noninvestors. Thus, another key issue for researchers is how to achieve higher response rates.

Business angel research has tended to be heavily reliant on large-scale postal question-naire surveys. While this methodological approach was appropriate when the emphasis was on research that profiled the characteristics of business angels and their investments, it is less suited to answering questions about how the market actually operates. Thus, further studies of the IVC market need to consider alternative research designs. Kelly and Hay (1996) have demonstrated the value of focusing on particular types of business angel, in this case what they termed "serial" investors. Case studies are also an effective means of exploring particular aspects of the IVC market (Steier and Greenwood 1999). Longitudinal tracking of panels of investors holds promise as means of incorporating the time dimension. Current research has been largely based on snapshots of investor activity. Critical incident analysis (Curran et al. 1993) may be a way of resolving the present impasse in studies that seek to assess the value-added impact of hands-on investors. For the same reason, future research should also experiment with other forms of data capture. Following its use in venture capital studies (e.g., Hall and Hofer 1993) Mason and Rogers (1997) have used verbal protocol analysis to explore the way in which business angels undertake their initial screening of investment opportunities. Conjoint analysis (Landström 1997; Shepherd and Zacharakis 1999) and qualitative approaches such as focus groups may add new perspectives to our understanding of how the IVC market operates.

Analytical issues: extending the boundaries

Wetzel's call for research that can "put boundaries on our ignorance" remains valid. We believe seven issues are priorities for researchers to address:

1 Estimating the size of the IVC market,
2 Developing angel typologies,
3 Determining the organization of the marketplace,
4 Examining geographical perspectives,
5 Analyzing cultural differences,
6 Promoting technology-based firms,
7 Exploring the demand for equity finance.

First, more sophisticated estimates of the *size of the IVC market* are required. Existing estimates – based on extrapolation of fragmentary data – are extremely crude (e.g., Wetzel 1987; Mason and Harrison 1997a). Gaston's (1989b) approach to estimating the size of the IVC market in the United States, which is based on a survey of the financial history of a representative sample of firms, remains the most sophisticated approach but is extremely labor-intensive and was bedeviled by poor response rates. Riding and Short's (1987b) "capture–recapture" approach is ingenious and surely worthy of replica-tion, but it is only appropriate on a local/regional scale. Market size will also be affected by the business angel's investment allocation decision. Business angels are not committing their entire life's savings to the unquoted company sector. They will also have investments in cash, publicly traded shares, real estate and bonds (Benjamin and Margulis 1996) and allocate only a small proportion of their investment portfolio to unquoted companies, typically 5 to 10 percent (Mason and Harrison 1994a). However, the allocation decision-making process remains unresearched. For example, do business angels allocate a certain amount of "play" money in the hope of achieving a significant financial gain and also psychic income, which might have just as well been spent on a racehorse or work of art? Indeed, to what extent do investors trade off financial return for nonfinancial benefits (Sullivan 1994)? Furthermore, there is no evidence on trends in informal investment activity over time, whether cyclical or secular, nor on the macroeconomic influences on the supply of IVC. An exploratory study in the United Kingdom points to the importance of the tax regime (Mason and Harrison 1999b), and the IPO market and trade sale activity (which represent the cashing out of entrepreneurs who, in turn, may become potential business angels) are further influences. However, the macroeconomic effects of diverting investments by high net worth individuals away from alternative purposes into small unquoted companies have not been assessed at all.

Second, it has been recognized from the earliest studies that the business angel population is heterogeneous. However, only a handful of studies have actually developed *angel typologies* (Gaston 1989a; Coveney and Moore 1998; Stevenson and Coveney 1996). The classifications are eclectic, and the methodology used has not been elaborated. Clearly, the lack of studies of angel typologies is related to the difficulties involved in identifying business angels, which makes it extremely difficult to create sufficiently large unbiased samples. Further research therefore needs to build on these initial studies by overcoming the difficulties in creating large samples of business angels and using more sophisticated techniques to develop robust typologies. Complementary studies are also needed that focus on specific types of business angels (Kelly and Hay 1996), such as those who only invest in technology businesses, and particular segments of the high net worth population, such as workers in the financial services industry (Anderson 1998).

Third, *the organization of the marketplace* warrants attention from researchers. Business angels often invest on their own, sometimes with other business angels and, less frequently, alongside other types of investors (e.g., venture capital funds). In fact, the available evidence indicates that "lone wolf" investors account for less than half of all IVC investment activity (Harrison and Mason 1992b). A majority of such investments take the form of business angels investing as part of a syndicate. These can take various forms, including informal groupings of friends and associates, archangel-led syndicates comprising a single lead investor and several passive investors, institutional archangel syndicates that are created and led by financial services firms on behalf of their high net worth clients and "captive" angel funds (Knighton 1996). A high priority for researchers is to map this growing organizational diversity in the informal investment marketplace and explore the differences in the investment behavior and activity of the various segments. This represents a shift from studies of the actors in the market (firms, entrepreneurs and investors) to studies of the market itself, a shift similar to that recommended by Brophy (1997b) for the study of private equity finance more generally.

Fourth, IVC should be examined from a *geographical perspective*. According to Gaston (1989a: 4) "angels live virtually everywhere." If true, this has important implications for regional development on account of the localization of IVC investments, with studies in

a variety of countries consistently reporting that the majority of business angel investments are made locally, typically within 100 miles (one to two hours driving time) of the
investor's home. From a regional development perspective, therefore, the IVC market is
of considerable importance because it fills the regional equity gap in the supply of early
stage risk capital that arises from the spatial concentration of institutional venture capital
investments (Mason and Harrison 1999c) and because it is a mechanism for retaining
and recycling wealth within the regions in which it was created (Mason and Harrison
1995). However, there has been no attempt to identify whether spatial variations in IVC
investment activity exist. In view of their entrepreneurial backgrounds, significant spatial
variations in the density of business angels and perhaps also in their investment activity
might be expected (e.g., preferences, investment frequency and amount invested), with
their distribution reflecting the geography of fast-growth enterprises (Lyons 1995). However, this conclusion is at odds with recent evidence from the economically lagging region
of Cape Breton in Canada, which reveals considerable IVC investment activity (Feeney
et al. 1998; Farrell 1998).

There is considerable debate about the significance of distance in the business angel's
investment decision (Stevenson and Coveney 1996; Mason and Harrison 1997b). Some
long-distance investments do occur, but it is not clear the proportion of total investment
activity that they comprise. The circumstances under which long-distance investments
are made, and the significance of the characteristics and motivation of the investor
relative to the characteristics of the investment opportunity are not clear. Indeed, the role
played by distance in the investment decision-making process is not understood. Mason
and Rogers (1997) suggest that it is an aspect of "investor fit" that business angels
consider in their initial screening of investment opportunities. Do most investors reject
investment opportunities in distant locations because the hands-on nature of their
investments encourages geographical proximity between investor and business? Is this a
factor in risk evaluation? Is it the case that investors and businesses need to be geographically proximate for the investor to be able to add value? Or is the distance between
investor and investment opportunity a compensatory procedure (Riding et al. 1993)? In
other words, would an investor be prepared to invest in a distant business if there were
compensating attractions that increased the rate of return prospects? A further gap in our
knowledge concerns the extent to which business angels invest internationally and under
what circumstances and the barriers to such investments.

Fifth, although the number of *national studies* of IVC has increased, our existing
knowledge remains heavily circumscribed geographically, with much of the existing
research focused on North America and northwest Europe. Although international
comparisons have highlighted surprisingly few differences between countries in the
characteristics of IVC activity, it is nevertheless vital for research to be undertaken in
continental Europe, in major economies such as France, Germany, Italy and Spain, as
well as southeast Asia, where cultural differences might be expected to be reflected in
IVC activities. Tashiro (1999) has made an important contribution with the first study
(published in English) of IVC in Japan.

Another new geographical focus for IVC research should be the transition economies
of central and eastern Europe, where angels have a potentially important role to play in
the development of a thriving SME sector. Latin America represents another type of
transition economy, involving the opening up of formerly protected economies to global

competition during the 1990s. This process has enabled some groups to become quite wealthy, for example, by selling domestic companies to multinational corporations. An important issue for exploration is the extent to which this wealth has been reinvested by these cashed-out entrepreneurs in the SME sector which is now a major focus for industry policy in these countries.

Sixth, the promotion of *technology-based firms* is assuming a more prominent position in the policies of advanced economies. The lack of patient capital is widely believed to be one of the key barriers to the emergence and growth of technology-based firms (Bank of England 1996). So what role do business angels play in financing technology-based firms? Some UK evidence suggests that technology sectors account for up to one-third of investments by business angels (Mason 1998). What is the potential for increasing the volume of IVC that is invested in technology-based firms? Are the investments in technology-based firms restricted to a particular segment of the business angel population – "techno-angels" – who on account of their science or engineering background, are capable of evaluating the risks and merits of such opportunities? In other words, are there specific knowledge-barriers to investing in technology-based firms? If so, could an independent technology evaluation service reduce such barriers (Freear et al. 1996; Mason and Harrison 1998)?

Finally, the *demand for equity finance*, and for IVC in particular, has been largely ignored. Thus, research is needed to explore IVC from an entrepreneur's perspective. It is widely documented that demand for equity finance is confined to a small minority of SMEs. However, some suggest that there may be a latent demand that is only articulated once a supply of finance is available (Mason and Harrison 1996c). This is a particularly important issue for research to address.

Another issue concerns the entrepreneur's decision to seek IVC. To what extent is this decision a negative one, prompted by the failure to raise finance from other sources? How many entrepreneurs are motivated by positive considerations, for example, based on the potential value-added contribution that an angel might make to their business?

A further research priority is the growing evidence that a major constraint on IVC investment activity is that many of the SMEs that seek such financing are not "investment ready" (Ernst and Young/Centre for Innovation and Enterprise 1997). This concept is associated with the "state of mind" of the entrepreneur. It encompasses a number of components, the key ones being the ability of an entrepreneur to articulate the opportunity to potential investors, the preparedness of an entrepreneur to achieve the growth opportunity that has been identified and the willingness of the entrepreneur to trade some ownership and independence in exchange for financing. There is a need to more clearly understand the nature of investment readiness and its significance as a constraint on IVC investment activity and also to identify how best to intervene to raise the level of investment readiness in the SME sector.

Theoretical development

There is a need for further development of theoretically grounded research into the IVC market. Although a number of theoretically grounded studies have been undertaken, they are few in number and have produced conflicting results, which in the case of agency theory, question the extent to which finance theory is relevant to this market. Further tests of the applicability of agency theory frameworks therefore seem warranted. As Brophy (1997b) has argued more generally, with the development of venture capital and private equity finance as major outlets for equity investment by individual, institutional and corporate investors, these mechanisms provide a rich milieu within which to develop and test theories of the firm and of interactions between the entrepreneur and the financier. Of particular relevance are theories of micro-market structure, valuation, structuring and pricing of securities, harvesting through strategic partnering, acquisition and public offering (Brophy 1997b). Contracting relationships between entrepreneurs and informal venture capitalists (Landström et al. 1998) and the application of signaling theory represent additional directions for further research, both to provide a basis for deeper understanding of the investment process in its later stages and to clarify the role and use of information in the investment process (Sapienza and Korsgaard 1996). Gifford (1997) argues that the opportunity costs of the time which venture capitalists devote to supporting the businesses they invest in results in less than optimal allocations in terms of maximizing the profits of those businesses, but it provides an opportunity for application to the informal investor situation. If, as Benjamin and Margulis (1996) and Mason and Harrison (1999a) have argued, informal investors do not invest on a portfolio basis, time rationing may be more readily observed in the search for investments, rather than in the postinvestment relationship. In all cases, the need in developing and applying these theoretical perspectives is not simply to replicate received finance theory but to extend and adapt it to the closely held, privately financed, entrepreneurial, emerging growth company.

The scope for further theoretical development is not restricted to finance and economic theory. As Harrison et al. (1997) and Harrison and Mason (1999a) have demonstrated, developing and applying theories that address the nonfinancial dimensions of the investment process and that draw on other academic disciplines, such as social psychology and sociology, have potential.

Policy issues

Policy development has been the focus for much of the IVC literature. Further policy-oriented research continues to be appropriate, both to assess the need for initiatives to stimulate IVC activity and also to evaluate the initiatives already introduced by policymakers in various countries in response to the recognition that the IVC market plays an important role in underpinning wider initiatives to promote entrepreneurial activity.

Tax incentives are a common way in which governments seek to encourage private individuals to invest either directly or via some pooled investment instrument, in unquoted companies. However, the effectiveness of such schemes – both in terms of targeting and economic impact, taking into account additionality, wastage rates and displacement – is often debated. The most appropriate design of tax incentive schemes is also unresolved. Is it more effective to offer front-end tax rates or relief on capital gains? Are business angels likely to be attracted by tax-based incentives that involve the creation of pooled investment vehicles? Would an equity guarantee scheme encourage business angels to invest more, or to alter their risk-reward calculations, and could such a scheme be operated at little or no cost to the public sector? The available information is based on questionnaire responses (Mason and Harrison 1999b), but this is not a sufficiently rigorous methodological approach to adequately resolve these questions.

Subsidizing the costs of operating business angel networks is an increasingly common way in which governments are trying to encourage the IVC market. However, there is an ongoing debate about the most appropriate format and operation of business angel networks, which in the United Kingdom at least, has revolved around whether the present pattern of independent networks operating predominantly on a local/regional scale should be consolidated into a national business angel network. Blatt and Riding (1996) provide an eloquent argument against national business angel networks. Some commentators have even questioned whether government intervention is necessary, given that a number of privately operated business angel networks are now in existence. Mason and Harrison (1997c) refute this suggestion by demonstrating that private, commercially operated networks and publicly supported networks actually serve different segments of the IVC market.

Meaningful debate on these issues is hampered by the lack of evidence on a number of key issues. First, there is no information on the market penetration of business introduction services. What proportion of business angels are, or have been, members of business introduction services? What is the level of interest among business angels in joining business introduction services? What is their perception of the usefulness of such services? What do they want from such a service, notably in terms of the type of matching service provided? Do different types of investors require different service formats? Is there sufficient variability in their requirements to justify the proliferation of different types of services? Research is also needed to examine how the matching process can be made more effective. Can training of investors and entrepreneurs have a positive effect? What role can new communication technologies play, such as teleconferencing (Bracker et al. 1994), the Internet and multimedia? It is also important that further research is undertaken to examine the economic impact of business angel networks. Both direct and indirect effects must be included (Harrison and Mason 1996b), and an attempt to calculate the cost-per-job created should be made so that the effectiveness of public sector support for the IVC market can be compared with outcomes from spending on alternative initiatives.

Finally, as noted earlier, research that explores ways in which businesses can be helped to become "investment ready" is needed. Various organizations – labeled "venture catalysts" – are emerging in both the United States and United Kingdom to offer assistance to entrepreneurs to turn their business idea into a fully worked up business plan, which they then use as a means of raising finance on behalf of the entrepreneur. However, this generic model has several variations. Research is needed to document these emerging new actors in the IVC market, assess their effectiveness and identify best practices.

CONCLUSIONS

The IVC market is of major and growing significance in the financing of the entrepreneurial start-up and growth business. It has become the increasing focus of policy debates and interventions, both direct and indirect, in a growing number of countries. The growing volume of research on the IVP market has significantly increased our knowledge of the attitudes, behaviors and characteristics of business angels in a number of national and regional contexts, despite the difficulties created by the invisibility of investors. However, much remains that is unknown or inadequately understood about this marketplace, both in terms of empirical research and in terms of the application of theoretical frameworks. Our discussion of the first and second-generation academic studies of IVC represent the ground-clearing phase of this research area. An enormous amount of research remains to be undertaken in order to understand more fully how the IVC market operates as a key element in the emergence and growth of entrepreneurial companies.

REFERENCES

Anderson, M. 1998. *Is the City Angelic?* London: London Business School.

Aram, J. 1989. Attitudes and behaviors of informal investors towards early-stage investments, technology investments and co-investors. *Journal of Business Venturing* 4, 333–47.

Bank of England. 1996. *The Financing of Technology-based Small Firms.* London: Bank of England.

Benjamin, G.A. and Margulis, J. 1996. *Finding Your Wings: How to Locate Private Investors to Fund Your Business.* New York: Wiley.

Blatt, R. and Riding, A. 1996. "Where angels fear to tread": some lessons from the Canada Opportunities Investment Network Experience. In R.T. Harrison and C.M. Mason (eds.), *Informal Venture Capital: Evaluating the Impact of Business Introduction Services.* Hemel Hempstead: Prentice-Hall, pp. 75–88.

Bracker, J., van Clouse, G.H. and Thacker, R.A. 1994. Teleconferencing business forums: an approach to linking entrepreneurs and potential investors. *Entrepreneurship and Regional Development* 6: 259–74.

Brophy, D.J. 1997a. Financing the growth of entrepreneurial firms. In D.L. Sexton and R.W. Smilor (eds.), *Entrepreneurship 2000.* Chicago: Upstart, pp. 5–28.

Brophy, D.J. 1997b. The financing of entrepreneurial ventures: opportunities for research. Paper presented to the Financial Management Association Meetings, Honolulu, Hawaii.

Brown, D.J. and Stowe, C.R.B. 1996. Private venture capital networks in the United States. In R.T. Harrison and C.M. Mason (eds.), *Informal Venture Capital: Evaluating the Impact of Business Introduction Services.* Hemel Hempstead: Prentice-Hall, pp. 101–15.

Commission of the European Communities. 1998. *Risk Capital: A Key to Job Creation in the European Union.* Luxembourg: Office for Official Publications of the European Communities.

Coveney, P. and Moore, K. 1998. *Business Angels: Securing Start-Up Finance.* Chichester: Wiley.

Curran, J., Jarvis, R., Blackburn, R.A. and Black, S. 1993. Networks and small firms: constructs, methodological strategies and some findings. *International Small Business Journal* 11(2): 13–25.

Dennis, W.J., Dunkelberg, W.C. and Dial, T. 1995. Measuring business formations and dissolutions: a new time series. In W.D. Bygrave, B.J. Bird, S. Birley, N.C. Churchill, M. Hay, R.H. Keeley and W.E. Wetzel, Jr. (eds.), *Frontiers of Entrepreneurship Research.* Babson Park, MA, Babson College, pp. 47–59.

Ehrlich, S.B., DeNoble, A.F., Moore, T. and Weaver, R.R. 1994. After the cash arrives: a comparative study of venture capital and private investor involvement in entrepreneurial firms. *Journal of Business Venturing* 9: 67–82.

Ernst and Young/Centre for Innovation and Enterprise. 1997. *Investment Readiness Study.* Canberra: Department of Industry, Science and Tourism.

Farrell, A.E. 1998. *Informal Venture Capital Investment in Atlantic Canada: A Representative View of Angels?* Halifax, Canada: St. Mary's University.

Feeney, L., Haines, G.H. and Riding, A.L. 1999 (in press). Private investors' investment criteria:

insights from qualitative data. *Venture Capital: An International Journal of Entrepreneurial Finance.*

Feeney, L., Johnstone, H. and Riding, A.L. 1998. A profile of informal investors in Canada: a comparison of Canadian and Maritime investors. Paper to the Canadian Council of Small Business and Entrepreneurship 15th Annual Conference, Halifax, Nova Scotia.

Fiet, J.O. 1995a. Reliance upon informants in the venture capital industry. *Journal of Business Venturing* 10: 195–223.

Fiet, J.O. 1995b. Risk avoidance strategies in venture capital markets. *Journal of Management Studies* 32: 551–74.

Fiet, J.O., Busenitz, L.W., Moesel, D.D. and Barney, J.B. 1997. Complementary theoretical perspectives on the dismissal of new venture team members. *Journal of Business Venturing* 12: 347–66.

Freear, J. and Wetzel, W.E. 1990. Who bankrolls high-tech entrepreneurs? *Journal of Business Venturing* 5: 77–89.

Freear, J., Grinde, R. and Sohl, J. 1997. The early stage financing of high-tech entrepreneurs. Paper presented at the 17th Babson College-Kauffman Foundation Entrepreneurship Research Conference, Babson College.

Freear, J., Sohl, J.E. and Wetzel, W.E. 1992. The investment attitudes, behavior and characteristics of high net worth individuals. In N.C. Churchill, S. Birley, W.D. Bygrave, D.F. Muzyka, C. Wahlbin and W.E. Wetzel, Jr. (eds.), *Frontiers of Entrepreneurship Research.* Babson Park, MA: Babson College, pp. 374–87.

Freear, J., Sohl, J. and Wetzel, W.E., Jr. 1994. Angels and non-angels: are there differences? *Journal of Business Venturing* 9: 109–23.

Freear, J., Sohl, J.E. and Wetzel, W.E. 1995. Angels: personal investors in the venture capital market. *Entrepreneurship and Regional Development* 7: 85–94.

Freear, J., Sohl, J.E. and Wetzel, W.E. 1996. Technology due diligence: what angels consider important. Paper to the 16th Babson College-Kauffman Foundation Entrepreneurship Research Conference, University of Washington, Seattle.

Freear, J., Sohl, J.E. and Wetzel, W.E. 1997. The informal venture capital market: milestones passed and the road ahead. In D.L. Sexton and R.W. Smilor (eds.), *Entrepreneurship 2000.* Chicago: Upstart, pp. 47–69.

Gaston, R.J. 1989a. *Finding Private Venture Capital For Your Firm: A Complete Guide.* Wiley: New York.

Gaston, R.J. 1989b. The scale of informal capital markets. *Small Business Economics* 1: 223–30.

Gifford, S. 1997. Limited attention and the role of the venture capitalist. *Journal of Business Venturing* 12: 459–82.

Haar, N.E., Starr, J. and MacMillan, I.C. 1988. Informal risk capital investors: investment patterns on the East Coast of the USA. *Journal of Business Venturing* 3: 11–29.

Hall, J. and Hofer, C.W. 1993. Venture capitalists' decision criteria in new venture evaluation. *Journal of Business Venturing* 8: 25–42

Harrison, R.T. and Mason, C.M. 1991. Informal investment networks: a case study from the United Kingdom. *Entrepreneurship and Regional Development* 3: 269–80.

Harrison, R.T. and Mason, C.M. 1992a. The roles of investors in entrepreneurial companies: a comparison of informal investors venture capitalists. In N.C. Churchill, S. Birley, W.D. Bygrave, D.F. Muzyka, C. Wahlbin and W.E. Wetzel, Jr. (eds.), *Frontiers of Entrepreneurship Research 1992.* Babson Park, MA: Babson College, pp. 388–404.

Harrison, R.T. and Mason, C.M. 1992b. International perspectives on the supply of informal venture capital. *Journal of Business Venturing* 7: 459–75.

Harrison, R.T. and Mason, C.M. (eds.). 1996a. *Informal Venture Capital: Evaluating the Impact of Business Introduction Services.* Hemel Hempstead, Prentice-Hall.

Harrison, R.T. and Mason, C.M. 1996b. Developing the informal venture capital market: a review of DTI's Informal Investment Demonstration Projects. *Regional Studies* 30: 765–71.

Harrison, R.T. and Mason, C.M. 1999a. *Auditioning for Finance: The Entrepreneur's Search for Capital from Informal Investors*. Venture Finance Working Paper No. 17, Southampton: University of Southampton and University of Ulster.

Harrison, R.T. and Mason, C.M. 1999b. *Backing the Horse or the Jockey? Information and the Evaluation of Risk by Business Angels*. Venture Finance Working Paper No. 18, Southampton: University of Southampton and University of Ulster.

Harrison, R.T., Dibben, M. and Mason, C.M. 1997. The role of trust in the business angel's investment decision: an exploratory analysis. *Entrepreneurship Theory and Practice* 21(4): 63–81.

Hindle, K. and Wenban, R. 1997. An exploratory study of Australia's informal venture capitalists: a predicate to theory building in the context of international angel research. Paper to the 17th Babson College-Kauffman Foundation Entrepreneurship Research Conference, Babson College.

K+V organisatie adviesbureau bv. 1996. *The Role of Informal Investors in the Dutch Venture Capital Market*. Arnhem: K+V organisatie adviesbureau bv.

Kelly, P. and Hay, M. 1996. Serial investors and early stage finance. *Journal of Entrepreneurial and Small Business Finance* 5: 159–74.

Knighton, E. 1996. The role and potential of investment syndicates for private investors. In R.T. Harrison and C.M. Mason (eds.), *Informal Venture Capital: Evaluating the Impact of Business Introduction Services*. Hemel Hempstead: Prentice-Hall, pp. 197–208.

Landström, H. 1993a. Informal risk capital in Sweden and some international comparisons. *Journal of Business Venturing* 8: 525–40.

Landström, H. 1993b. Agency theory and its application to small firms: evidence from the Swedish venture capital market. *Journal of Small Business Finance* 2: 203–18

Landström, H. 1995. A pilot study on the investment decision making of informal investors in Sweden. *Journal of Small Business Management* 10(4): 67–76.

Landström, H. 1997. The perception of business opportunities: decision-making criteria used by Swedish informal investors in their assessment of new investment proposals. Paper to the 2nd International Seminar on Risk Behaviour and Risk Management, Stockholm University, Stockholm.

Landström, H., Manigart, S., Mason, C. and Sapienza, H. 1998. Contracts between entrepreneurs and investors: terms and negotiation process. In P. Reynolds, W.D. Bygrave, N. Carter, S. Manigart, C. Mason, D. Meyer, and K. Shaver (eds.), *Frontiers of Entrepreneurship Research*. Babson Park: MA, Babson College.

Landström, H. and Olofsson, C. 1996. Informal venture capital in Sweden. In R.T. Harrison and C.M. Mason (eds.), *Informal Venture Capital: Evaluating the Impact of Business Introduction Services*. Hemel Hempstead: Prentice-Hall, pp. 273–85.

Lumme, A., Mason, C. and Suomi, M. 1996. The returns from informal venture capital investments: an exploratory study. *Journal of Entrepreneurial and Small Business Finance* 5: 139–58.

Lumme, A., Mason, C. and Suomi, M. 1998. *Informal Venture Capital: Investors, Investments and Policy Issues in Finland*. Dordrecht, Netherlands: Kluwer Academic Publishers.

Lyons, D. 1995. Changing business opportunities: the geography of rapidly growing small US private firms, 1982–1992. *Professional Geographer* 47: 388–98.

Mason, C. 1998. *Report on Business Angel Investment Activity 1997/98*. London: British Venture Capital Association.

Mason, C.M. and Harrison, R.T. 1993. Strategies for expanding the informal venture capital market. *International Small Business Journal* 11(4): 23–38.

Mason, C.M. and Harrison, R.T. 1994a. The informal venture capital market in the UK. In A. Hughes and D.J. Storey (eds.), *Financing Small Firms*. London: Routledge, pp. 64–111.

Mason, C.M. and Harrison, R.T. 1994b. The role of informal and formal sources of venture capital in the financing of technology-based SMEs in the United Kingdom. In R. Oakey (ed.), *New Technology-Based Firms in the 1990s*. London: Paul Chapman, pp. 104–24.

Mason, C.M. and Harrison, R.T. 1995. Closing the regional equity gap: the role of informal venture capital. *Small Business Economics* 7: 153–72.

Mason, C.M. and Harrison, R.T. 1996a. Informal venture capital: a study of the investment process and post-investment experience. *Entrepreneurship and Regional Development* 8: 105–26.

Mason, C.M. and Harrison, R.T. 1996b. Why business angels say no: a case study of opportunities rejected by an informal investor syndicate. *International Small Business Journal* 14(2): 35–51.

Mason, C.M. and Harrison, R.T. 1996c. The clearing banks and the informal venture capital market. *International Journal of Bank Marketing* 14(1): 5–14.

Mason, C.M. and Harrison, R.T. 1996d. Informal investment business introduction services: some operational considerations. In R.T. Harrison and C.M. Mason (eds.), *Informal Venture Capital: Evaluating the Impact of Business Introduction Services*. Hemel Hempstead: Prentice-Hall, pp. 27–58.

Mason, C.M. and Harrison, R.T. 1997a. *Supporting the Informal Venture Capital Market: What Still Needs to Be Done?* Venture Finance Working Paper No. 15, Southampton: University of Southampton and University of Ulster.

Mason, C.M. and Harrison, R.T. 1997b. Business angels in the UK: a response to Stevenson and Coveney. *International Small Business Journal* 15(2): 83–90.

Mason, C.M. and Harrison, R.T. 1997c. Business angel networks and the development of the informal venture capital market in the UK: is there still a role for the public sector? *Small Business Economics* 9: 111–23.

Mason, C.M. and Harrison, R.T. 1998. Stimulating investments by business angels in technology-based ventures: the potential of an independent technology appraisal service. In Roakey R. (ed.), *New Technology-Based Firms in the 1990s*, vol. 5. London: Paul Chapman, pp. 81–96.

Mason, C.M. and Harrison, R.T. 1999a. *Is It Worth It? The Rates of Return from Informal Venture Capital Investments*. Venture Finance Working Paper No. 16. Southampton: University of Southampton and University of Ulster.

Mason, C.M. and Harrison, R.T. 1999b (in press). Public policy and the development of the informal venture capital market: UK experience and lessons for Europe. In K. Cowling (ed.), *Industrial Policy in Europe*. Routledge: London.

Mason, C.M. and Harrison, R.T. 1999c (in press). Financing entrepreneurship: Venture capital and regional development. In R.L. Martin (ed.), *Money and the Space Economy*. Chichester: Wiley.

Mason, C. and Rogers, A. 1997. The business angel's investment decision: an exploratory analysis. In D. Deakins, P. Jennings and C. Mason (eds.), *Entrepreneurship in the 1990s*. London: Paul Chapman, pp. 29–46.

Myers, S.C. and Majluf, N. 1984. Corporate financing and investment decisions when firms have information that investors do not have. *Journal of Financial Economics* 13: 187–221.

Norton, E. 1990. *An Overview of Venture Capital Finance*. Working Paper, Fairleigh Dickinson University.

Norton, E. 1995. Venture capital as an alternative means to allocate capital: an agency-theoretic view. *Entrepreneurship Theory and Practice* 20(2): 19–29.

Riding, A. and Short, D. 1987a. Some investor and entrepreneur perspectives on the informal market for risk capital. *Journal of Small Business and Entrepreneurship* 5(2): 19–30.

Riding, A. and Short, D. 1987b. On the estimation of the investment potential of informal investors: a capture–recapture approach. *Journal of Small Business and Entrepreneurship* 5(4): 26–40.

Riding, A., Dal Cin, P., Duxbury, L., Haines, G. and Safrata, R. 1993. *Informal Investors in Canada: The Identification of Salient Characteristics*. Ottawa: Carleton University.

Sapienza, H. and Korsgaard, A.M. 1996. The role of procedural justice in entrepreneur–venture capital relations. *Academy of Management Journal* 39: 544–74.

Shepherd, D.A. and Zacharakis, A. 1999 (in press). Conjoint analysis: a new methodological approach for researching venture capitalists decision policies. *Venture Capital: An International Journal of Entrepreneurial Finance*.

Short, D.M. and Riding, A.L. 1989. Informal investors in the Ottawa-Carleton region: Experiences and expectations. *Entrepreneurship and Regional Development* 1: 99–112.

Sohl, J.E. 1999 (in press). The early stage equity market in the United States. *Venture Capital: An International Journal of Entrepreneurial Finance.*

Steier, L. and Greenwood, R. 1999 (in press). The evolution of "angel" networks. *Venture Capital: An International Journal of Entrepreneurial Finance.*

Stevenson, H. and Coveney, P. 1996. A survey of business angels. In R, Blackburn and P. Jennings (eds.), *Small Firms: Contributions to Economic Regeneration.* London: Paul Chapman, pp. 37–48.

Sullivan, M.K. 1994. Altruism and entrepreneurship. In W.D. Bygrave, S. Birley, N.C. Churchill, E. Gatewood, F. Hoy, R.H. Keeley and W.E. Wetzel, Jr. (eds.), *Frontiers of Entrepreneurship Research.* Babson College: Babson Park, MA, pp. 373–80.

Sullivan, M.K. 1996. Local networks and informal venture capital in Tennessee. In R.T. Harrison and C.M. Mason (eds.), *Informal Venture Capital: Evaluating the Impact of Business Introduction Services.* Hemel Hempstead: Prentice-Hall, pp. 89–100.

Sullivan, M.K. and Miller, A. 1990. Applying theory of finance to informal risk capital research: promise and problems. In N.C. Churchill, W.D. Bygrave, J.A. Hornaday, D.F. Muzyka, K.H. Vesper and W.E. Wetzel, Jr. (eds.), *Frontiers of Entrepreneurship Research.* Babson Park, MA: Babson College, pp. 296–310.

Tashiro, Y. 1999 (in press). Business angels in Japan. *Venture Capital: An International Journal of Entrepreneurial Finance.*

Tymes, E.R. and Krasner, O.J. 1983. Informal risk capital in California. In J.A. Hornaday, J.A. Timmons and K.H. Vesper (eds.), *Frontiers of Entrepreneurship Research 1983.* Babson Park, MA: Babson College, pp. 347–68.

Wetzel, W.E. 1981. Informal risk capital in New England. In K.H. Vesper (ed.), *Frontiers of Entrepreneurship Research 1981.* Wellesley, MA: Babson College, pp. 217–45.

Wetzel, W.E. 1983. Angels and informal risk capital. *Sloan Management Review* 24(4): 23–34.

Wetzel, W.E. 1986a. Informal risk capital: knowns and unknowns. In D.L. Sexton and R.W. Smilor (eds.), *The Art and Science of Entrepreneurship.* Cambridge, MA: Ballinger, pp. 85–108.

Wetzel, W.E. 1986b. Entrepreneurs, angels and economic renaissance. In R.D. Hisrich (ed.), *Entrepreneurship, Intrapreneurship and Venture Capital.* Lexington, MA: Lexington Books, pp. 119–39.

Wetzel, W.E. 1987. The informal risk capital market: aspects of scale and efficiency. *Journal of Business Venturing* 2: 299–313.

Wetzel, W.E. 1994. Venture capital. In W.D. Bygrave (ed.), *The Portable MBA in Entrepreneurship.* New York: Wiley, pp. 172–94.

Wetzel, W.E. and Freear, J. 1996. Promoting informal venture capital in the United States: reflections on the history of the Venture Capital Network. In R.T. Harrison and C.M. Mason (eds.), *Informal Venture Capital: Evaluating the Impact of Business Introduction Services.* Hemel Hempstead: Prentice-Hall, pp. 61–74.

12

Venture Capital and Growth

Sophie Manigart and Harry Sapienza

Venture Capital as a Distinct Industry
Evolution of the Formal Venture Capital Industry
in the 1990s
Government Intervention and Macroeconomic Impact of VC
Role of Venture Capital in Helping Firms Grow
Theoretical Progress and Future Directions

This chapter reviews the literature on the impact of venture capital investments on economic growth, primarily at the firm level. We focus on new insights gained in the 1990s and on North American and European practices.[1] We examine the impact of *formal* venture capitalists (VCs) on growth and thus exclude *informal* or private investors (PIs). It should be noted that although the US venture capital market includes all investment stages and industries typically found in Europe, much of the research on US firms has emphasized the early stage and high-tech aspects of venture capital investing in the United States – what Bygrave and Timmons (1992) term "classic" venture capital. On the other hand, later stage financing and management buy-outs (MBOs) are perhaps the most important areas for venture capital financing in Europe (Ooghe et al. 1991; Wright et al. 1992) and are often central in European studies.

The formal venture capital industry would not exist if it were not for the willingness of many individuals and institutions to face the dangers of betting significant money and effort for the chance of realizing rapid, sustained growth in capital. The perceived risk of financing a new venture with high potential but without collateral or income stream history often deters banks from providing capital. Further, though potentially willing, individual investors often do not have access to the magnitude of capital needed to bring a high potential venture through the critical high-growth phases. While figures on PIs are scant, most believe that VCs invest larger amounts per investment round and invest less frequently in early stage deals than do PIs (Freear and Wetzel 1990; Manigart and Struyf 1997). Thus, a role for formal venture capital has developed in the majority of developed economies.

We begin with an overview of recent explanations for the existence of venture capital. We proceed from there to encapsulate trends in venture capital in the United States and Europe, highlighting the impact of government initiatives on macroeconomic growth. The largest section of the chapter summarizes empirical studies of the impact of VC on the growth of companies. Finally, we focus on theoretical progress made in VC research, and we suggest what may be fruitful routes for future studies.

VENTURE CAPITAL AS A DISTINCT INDUSTRY

Many economic models have examined the distinct role of venture capital firms (VCFs) as intermediaries between entrepreneurs and suppliers of capital. In perfect markets, financing is always available for economically viable investments. In the presence of asymmetric information and potential agency conflicts, however, good projects may be denied financing (Fluck et al. 1998). The role of financial intermediaries in private equity markets is thus essentially one of screening, contracting,[2] and monitoring (Berger and Udell 1998) in order to minimize the costs of delegating decisions to entrepreneurs or inducing them to reveal critical information on their activities. Haubrick (1990), Admati and Pfleiderer (1994) and Reid (1996) stress the role of VCs as inside investors in gaining private information on investment projects, during both preinvestment screening and postinvestment monitoring. Amit et al. (1998) argue that one of the primary reasons for the existence of VCFs is their information processing capacities, which may reduce adverse selection and moral hazard problems and allow VCFs to invest profitably in projects that uninformed outsiders reject.

In order to fulfill their role, VCs have to be more efficient in *selecting* ventures than other investors (Fried and Hisrich 1994; Hirao 1993). Their efficiency arises out of economies of scale (costs decrease as they invest in a large number of ventures), economies of scope (their networks of contacts can be reused), and learning curve effects (specializing allows the application of superior knowledge [Gupta and Sapienza 1992; Hall and Hofer 1993; Norton and Tenenbaum 1993; Sahlman 1990]). VCFs also have to be efficient in *monitoring* the ventures in order to overcome moral hazard problems after the investment is made (Admati and Pfleiderer 1994; Barry et al. 1990; Lerner 1995) and may achieve this by gaining specialist knowledge of specific sectors or industries (Hall and Hofer 1993; Sahlman 1990). Monitoring skills are especially valuable in sectors where assets are largely intangible and growth options and asset specificity are high (Gompers 1995) and, consequently, where informational concerns are important (Amit et al. 1998; Sapienza and Gupta 1994). Finally, Amit et al. (1998) argue that investors who are skilled at providing *value-creating* services to their portfolio companies will undertake certain projects that other, less skilled investors shun. They thus provide an economic rationale for what has long been argued: the time and effort VCs spend in providing value-building services pays off beyond the value of the financing, selecting, and monitoring of ventures. Thus, Gorman and Sahlman's (1989) finding that VCs spend half of their time in postinvestment activities appears well justified.

The three distinct roles of VCs (selecting, monitoring and adding value) make them valuable financial intermediaries to the extent that they finance economically viable projects that might not get financing from outside investors. Based on an extensive case study in the United Kingdom, Reid (1996) emphasizes a fourth role: *risk-sharing*. Because the VCF has greater risk management options than individuals (e.g., portfolio diversification), the entrepreneur and the VCF agree that the VCF will assume a greater proportion of the business risk.

As the above review shows, most theoretical models are based on agency theory. The vast majority view the entrepreneur as the agent of the investor and emphasize that due to information asymmetries in private equity markets, entrepreneurs are able to take actions that harm the investors. They argue that superior information processing capacities, before and after investing, allow VCs to manage information asymmetries more effectively than do other financial intermediaries. Such models could be made more realistic by formally acknowledging that venture capitalists are also agents of entrepreneurs (Cable and Shane 1997; Gifford 1997; Sapienza 1992) and of their fund providers (Robbie et al. 1997). Although suggested in prior work (e.g., Sapienza 1992), Gifford (1997) is the first to develop a formal model examining VCs as agents of investors and entrepreneurs; the model notes the dilemma facing the VCs in allocating their attention between improving current ventures and evaluating possibilities for new investments. Thus, the model acknowledges potential incentives for VCs to take actions that negatively affect the performance of the venture and entrepreneurs' and investors' wealth. As competition for promising deals increases due to the large inflow of funds to the industry (Gompers 1998), this viewpoint takes on increasing importance and should be developed further. Finally, researchers of venture capital are beginning to acknowledge more explicitly that VCs are not primarily in the business of minimizing value loss resulting from agency costs, but rather in the business of maximizing value creation (see Amit et al. 1998; Barney et al. 1996; Landström et al. 1998; Wright and Robbie 1998). Thus, it is incumbent upon theorists and researchers to develop and test theory regarding how successful VCs create value.

EVOLUTION OF THE FORMAL VENTURE CAPITAL INDUSTRY IN THE 1990s

Whereas formal venture capital in the United States experienced explosive growth in the early 1980s and has been revived recently (Bygrave and Timmons 1992; Gompers 1998), such growth has been relatively recent in Europe. Statistics from the EVCA (European Venture Capital Association) indicate that venture capital has grown tremendously in Europe during 1996–7. In the first half of the decade, the total amount of funds *raised* varied between 3.4 and 5 billion ECU per year; this figure rose to 7 billion ECU in 1996 and to 20 billion ECU in 1997. The total amount *invested* in Europe rose steadily during the 1990s, reaching a total of 9.6 billion ECU in 1997. The gap between funds raised and invested shows that the European venture capital market is liquid and ready for investment opportunities.

Referring to similar trends in the United States during the 1990s, Gompers (1998) warned of an "overheating" of the industry, resulting in larger deals, higher prices and lower returns in the long-run. The number of investments has not risen significantly over the last few years, but the average investment is becoming larger. According to the US National Venture Capital Association, about $4.1 billion was invested in 1992 (952 deals), rising to $10 billion in 1996 (1,501 deals). These figures indicate that the average deal size in the United States was about $4 to every ECU in 1996. Even if we take into account the fact that a few supersized deals in the United States inflated the average (e.g., Transition Systems, $115 million, and Renaissance Cosmetics, $115 million), we see that deals tend to be significantly larger in the United States, although fewer deals are consummated.

Differences in deal size are even more startling if one considers that much more of the US money flows to earlier stage investing: whereas 5 to 7 percent of venture capital went to early-stage ventures in Europe over this period (EVCA 1997), 30 to 36 percent of US investments were in early stage ventures (NVCA 1997). Gompers (1998) puts this figure at 17 to 19 percent. Furthermore, venture funding in the United States is increasingly moving toward innovative, high-tech firms in information technology and life sciences. In short, US VCFs appear to take on greater risk in terms of the amount invested per deal, the stage of the venture, and the technological uncertainty facing their portfolio companies.

There is a clear indication in Europe that syndication as a means of risk sharing, access to deal flow and learning (Bygrave 1988; Lerner 1994a) has diminished since 1995. Whereas 60 percent of the European investments were syndicated in 1990, this has dropped to a mere 27 percent in 1997. On the other hand, internationalization has increased to where nearly 20 percent of all funds were invested abroad in 1997. Both findings are consistent with Murray's (1995) forecasts on the evolution of the British venture capital industry. He predicted that prominent players would restrict their syndication activities to a smaller number of co-investors and that continental Europe would further attract considerable investments.

The growth of the venture capital industry mirrors the growth of relevant stock markets (Bygrave and Timmons 1992). In the mid-1990s, secondary or tertiary stock markets have been created all over Europe, e.g., the Alternative Investment Market (AIM) in the UK and Euro-NM (New Market), which links the secondary markets in Amsterdam, Paris, Brussels and Frankfurt. Moreover, Easdaq was established in 1996 as a pan-European counterpart of Nasdaq. Healthy stock markets for small, innovative companies are important exit routes for venture capitalists; the increase in such exit routes has undoubtedly contributed to the growth of European VC activities.

GOVERNMENT INTERVENTION AND MACROECONOMIC IMPACT OF VC

Despite Amit et al.'s (1990) arguments that venture capitalists are excluded from the opportunity to invest in the very best entrepreneurs because of adverse selection problems, it is well accepted that VC is nonetheless available only to a relatively exclusive set – the "happy few." Fenn and Liang (1998) report that slightly over 1 percent of US corporations try to raise private equity from new outside investors per year; half of these are successful. In total, in terms of amount of outside financing thus raised, 10 percent are from formal venture capitalists, 60 percent from angel investors and 30 percent from other sources. Nevertheless, in the 1990s, individual European governments as well as the European Community have enhanced the development of the VC industry both directly, by setting up government-backed VCFs, and indirectly by providing a healthier institutional, fiscal and legal environment.

It is as yet not clear whether *direct* government intervention has driven out the private sector from the VC industry or whether such intervention has filled a gap in the private venture capital market (Surlemont et al. 1998). KPMG (1995) argues that European publicly supported VCFs are complementary to, rather than substitutes for, private VCFs, as countries or regions with the most supportive government funds have the best developed private venture capital industries. Likewise, the US Investment Advisory Council (1992) found that the SBIC program supplemented the venture capital industry by providing financing in smaller sums and to a more geographically and sectorially diverse base than did private VCFs.

The Organization for Economic Cooperation and Development (OECD 1997) distinguishes two types of *indirect* government programs: financial incentives for VC, such as tax credits or guarantee schemes, and investor regulations, such as broadening the types of institutions permitted or encouraged to invest in venture capital. European governments prefer direct intervention; only in Italy and France have there been important investor regulation changes. For example, several European governments have offered front-end tax relief to PIs in unquoted investments; most have established (quasi) tax-neutral investment vehicles for VCFs. The most noteworthy example of a guarantee scheme existed in the Netherlands. Under this scheme, half of the losses of the VCFs were reimbursed by the Dutch government from 1981 to 1995. The scheme was discontinued when the initial goals of developing a private venture capital industry were met. Sofaris, a comparable scheme in France, has realized a rate of return increase to 20 percent (AFIC 1996). Belgium and Italy are the most recent adopters of guarantee schemes.

Governments promote venture capital despite the small number of companies funded through formal venture capital. This practice indicates that governments believe venture capital favorably affects general economic growth. Several studies, commissioned by national venture capital associations and executed by consultant companies (e.g., Coopers and Lybrand in Europe and the US; Arthur Andersen in Australia; Venture Economics Canada in Canada), found that VC-backed companies perform above average on a number of criteria such as job creation, tax payment, growth in sales and export, and R&D expenditures. What is lacking, however, is an analysis of the failures or the low-growth companies.

How much money and effort is "wasted" and is the waste offset by the winners? The overall positive conclusions of the aforementioned studies are not well-reflected in the rates of return reported by EVCA (1998): the median internal rate of return to investors from inception to 1996 was a mere 6.6 percent, including a median of 15.5 percent for specialized buy-out funds. Independent studies may be necessary, therefore, to clarify the macro-economic impact of VC.

ROLE OF VENTURE CAPITAL IN HELPING FIRMS GROW

The largest body of research on the impact of the VC industry on economic growth has been conducted at the firm level, i.e., individual investee companies. Although all phases of the venture capital process from fund generation to portfolio company exit have been studied in the 1990s, the greatest emphasis has been on two phases: VCs' investment selection and postinvestment involvement, with the latter focusing on monitoring and adding value. Very recently additional attention has also been given to the investment deal negotiation phase, but this work is in its infancy.

When well performed, selection, monitoring and value-adding should lead to higher returns for investors and improved performance for the portfolio companies. Effective selection by VCs should result in the funding of the most promising projects. Postinvestment monitoring should enhance information availability for VCs, early problem detection, and effective decision making in the investee companies (Mitchell et al. 1997); value-adding on the part of VCs should lead to more explosive growth and more sustainable advantage for portfolio companies, translating into higher company and shareholder value. One problem, however, in studying VCs' involvement in portfolio companies is that it may be difficult for researchers to distinguish between monitoring and value-adding. This difficulty is not restricted to researchers, needless to say. Entrepreneurs themselves may have trouble reading the purpose of intervention, a fact that may have dramatic effects upon their reading of and receptivity to VC involvement.

Selection

MacMillan et al. (1988) pioneered the studies on selection and decision processes of VCs in the United States; Knight (1994) replicated these in Canada, Europe and the Asian–Pacific region. Recently, by employing data gathering techniques beyond surveys and analysis techniques other than simple linear correlations, many have sought to improve on the initial studies. For example, Muzyka et al. (1996) and Shepherd and Zacharakis (in press) have used conjoint analysis, while Smart (in press) has done in-depth case studies to evaluate the human capital dimension. Despite the variety of new techniques, most studies reach the same conclusions as the earlier ones: the most important decision criterion is human capital, especially the judged quality and character of the entrepreneur and the entrepreneurial team. This criterion is typically followed in rankings by market and product characteristics and expected financial outcomes. Ratings have been remarkably similar in all countries or regions, especially regarding the preeminence of the entrepreneur's personality and experience. Van Osnabrugge's (1998) work in the United Kingdom showed that VCs and PIs had remarkably similar preferences in rating early-stage ventures: VCs rated the entrepreneurs' trustworthiness, experience and enthusiasm as the top three criteria, whereas for PIs the top three were the entrepreneurs' enthusiasm and trustworthiness followed by the sales potential of the venture.

One new twist on the new venture selection research has been a focus on the process VCs go through in evaluating criteria. Hall and Hofer (1993) used a verbal protocol technique whereby VCs stated aloud what they were thinking as they reviewed business plans for potential investments. They, as well as Zacharakis and Meyer (1995), found that VCs attended little to the entrepreneurial character and strategy concerns found in prior studies but instead focused on the growth potential of the opportunity. Grouping selection criteria into business concept, management quality, and return potential criteria, Fried and Hisrich (1994) developed a six-stage screening process model and found that VCs focus attention differentially across these criteria at different phases of their screening. What these studies help to reveal is the dynamic nature of the screening process and its impact on criterion salience.

Studies on selection criteria have often ignored theory development or failed to relate their findings to predictions made by economic models (Wright and Robbie 1998). However, the work of Zacharakis, Shepherd and colleagues on US VCs has challenged rationality assumptions basic to most economic models. The main questions their work explored included: Do VCs understand their own decision process? And do their choices conform consistently to the criteria they espouse? Both Shepherd et al. (1998a) in the United States and Virtanen (1996) in Finland found significant differences between decision policies VCs consciously used and those they apparently used in experimental situations wherein information was condensed and limited. Shepherd et al. (1998b) also found, however, that such discrepancies were lessened with experience of the experimental tasks. It is unclear whether these discrepancies existed because VCs were unable to bring to the conscious level the tacit knowledge inherent in their choices (see Polanyi 1967), because bounded rationality prevented the VCs from applying policies as consistently as they would do if rationally capable or because significant cues available in actual selection situations (e.g., interpersonal discussions with entrepreneurs or details in reports reflecting colleagues' impressions) were not present in the experimental settings.

Postinvestment involvement in portfolio companies

Since Gorman and Sahlman's (1989) observation that US VCs spend about as much time on monitoring and assisting portfolio companies as they do on all other activities combined, a significant stream of literature has examined the level of involvement and its causes, the nature and purposes of involvement and the consequences of greater or lesser involvement (Gorman and Sahlman 1989; MacMillan et al. 1988; Sapienza 1992). The practical issues are clear: Do venture capitalists help grow ventures? If so, *how* do effective ones do it, and is the amount of help worth the price? While many studies look at several aspects of these questions at the same time, we have divided the review into evidence on (1) determinants of the level and type of involvement, (2) VCs' roles in monitoring and advising portfolio companies and (3) the outcomes of the presence, level and type of involvement.

Variations in VC involvement

MacMillan et al. (1988) observed that some US VCs are relatively passive, some moderately involved and some heavily involved with the activities of their portfolio companies. Evidence has been building that wide variations exist in terms of how involved VCs and PIs are in their portfolio companies (Ehrlich et al. 1994). Some VCs or VCFs are very active and some very passive both in the United States (Elango et al. 1995; Fried and Hisrich 1995; Sadtler 1993) and in Europe (Fredriksen et al. 1990, 1991, 1997). Sweeting and Wong (1997), e.g., have shown that some UK VCFs successfully adopt a "hands-off" approach. However, contrary to MacMillan et al.'s (1988) suggestion that variation represents the personal preferences of the VCs, much research has set about trying to uncover systematic variation and theoretical explanations for VC behavior.

Following Barney et al. (1989), most studies have tried to explain greater involvement as VCs' response to greater business and agency risk. Two problems emerge from this: results have been inconsistent, and the relative emphasis such views give to a value-protecting role over a value-creating role appears somewhat inconsistent with the function of venture capital (Wright and Robbie 1998). Elango et al. (1995), Sapienza et al. (1996) and Bruton et al. (1998b) shed a little more light on institutional and country-specific variations in involvement. Elango et al. (1995) showed that significant variation occurred as a function of the VCF itself (in addition to the individual differences between VCs as shown by MacMillan et al. 1988). Sapienza et al. (1996) found not only that variations occur across VCFs, but across countries: US VCs spent the most time involved in portfolio companies, closely followed by UK VCs, but Dutch and French VCs spent about half the time of their US colleagues. This suggests that perhaps frameworks, such as institutional theory or the process theory of internationalization, could be gainfully employed to predict involvement in new contexts (Bruton et al. 1998b).

The evidence on firm-specific factors influencing involvement is scattered but does converge to some degree on several factors. The factors associated with *higher* involvement appear to be:

1 Earlier stage of venture (Bygrave and Timmons 1992; Gorman and Sahlman 1989; Sapienza et al. 1996), though Elango et al. (1995) did not support this finding.
2 Greater technical innovation sought by the venture (Sapienza et al. 1996; Sweeting 1991);
3 Less distance between VCs and the venture (Fiet 1995; Lerner 1995), especially in the United States (Sapienza et al. 1996);
4 Less experience on the part of the parties involved (Lerner 1995; Sapienza 1992);
5 Less personal wealth invested by the entrepreneur and greater ownership (Barney et al. 1989) or greater investment size by the VCF (Sapienza 1992). However, Sapienza (1992) found no ownership relationships, and Hale and Hackbert (1998) found no effects of the amount invested.

Many of these relationships are consistent with Fiet's (1995) speculation that conditions leading to greater agency risk increase involvement. However, the results are as yet open to interpretation, and virtually each one requires some qualifying.

Qualifications of this list depend upon context of studies and the explanatory framework being used. For example, the effects of venture stage may or may not exist in Europe, but so many of the ventures there are later stage that it is difficult to know. Venture stage might relate to involvement because it is a proxy for uncertainty leading to greater information processing needs and assistance from the VC (Fredriksen et al. 1997), or it may represent a state of information asymmetry leading to agency risks (Fiet 1995). Similarly, evidence that VCs are more involved in high-tech firms may be attributed either to task uncertainty or to agency/information asymmetry concerns (Fredriksen et al. 1997; Sweeting 1991). If geographic distance increases agency risks because of the unobservability of entrepreneurial actions (Fiet 1995), why is there a negative relationship between distance and VC board representation (Lerner 1995)? In short, more theoretical and empirical studies are required to advance our understanding of the drivers of involvement.

Besides the amount of involvement, some attention has been given to the type of involvement. Early findings that VCs' key roles are as strategic sounding boards and financial advisors has been largely replicated in most regions. Barney et al. (1996) categorize VC assistance along the lines of business management advice and operational advice and find entrepreneurs' impressions vary systematically with their team experiences. Sapienza et al. (1996) found that in the US as well as in the three European countries in their survey (United Kingdom, France and the Netherlands), both VCs and entrepreneurs rated the importance of VCs' roles in this order: strategic, interpersonal and operational roles.

Monitoring, advising and assisting portfolio companies

Because theories of agency, information processing and value creation depend in part upon understanding the purpose of behaviors, it is important to consider what VCs are seeking to accomplish with their involvement in companies they invest in. In this section we reflect upon what may be concluded about the likely intention of VCs' involvement; in the next, we try to relate such outcomes to behaviors and intentions.

After investment, VCs and entrepreneurs may or may not exchange further capital for further equity. They will certainly exchange information. We could conceive of monitoring, advising and assisting as information flows:

- Flows primarily from the entrepreneur to the VC might be considered monitoring on the part of the VC;
- Flows primarily from the VC to the entrepreneur might be considered advising on the part of the VC;
- Bilateral flows might be considered assisting or value-adding.

Fried et al. (1998) and Rosenstein (1988; Rosenstein et al. 1993) have shown that the board of directors of VC-backed firms is especially active in monitoring such functions as performance and strategy evaluation and is often seen as the primary means by which VCs monitor their portfolio companies (Sapienza and Gupta 1994; Wright and Robbie 1998). However, VCs will also use their board positions to influence or advise (Sapienza et al. 1997) as well as to assist and add value (Barney et al. 1996; Fried and Hisrich 1995). At the same time, informal relationships may be powerful tools to aid in the flow of information (Fried and Hisrich 1995), and there is sufficient evidence to conclude that interpersonal and noneconomic assistance is also provided to entrepreneurs on a routine basis (Fredriksen et al. 1997).

To our knowledge, however, no one has systematically assessed the precursors of information flow direction or the relative emphasis VCs give to monitoring, advising and assisting. Barney et al. (1996) perhaps come closest in examining the determinants of entrepreneurs' receptivity to VCs' advice, but their framework focuses on how new venture team experience moderates their response to advice rather than how the flow itself is affected. Similarly, Sapienza and Korsgaard (1996) studied the effect of entrepreneurs' provision of timely feedback but did not examine the determinants of the feedback itself. In short, most of the studies have *assumed* one or more of monitoring, advising or assisting as the purposes of interaction and have then examined the perceived outcome of generic "involvement" or "interaction."

Outcomes of the presence of venture capital and VC involvement

The explosion of studies on VC presence and involvement in portfolio companies has resulted in a great deal of information about a wide range of outcomes. Those that have focused on trying to quantify VC economic returns have generally compared various types of publicly available accounting or stock market data on firms with and without VC backing. Such studies quantify in a broad fashion how venture capital does in comparison to alternative financing routes. The perception and interaction-based studies, on the other hand, provide a qualitative view of whether or not value is added. Furthermore, studies of this type have begun to investigate other intermediate outcomes of interaction such as fulfillment of expectations, conflict, commitment, trust and learning. Together, these two streams of literature have begun to reveal more fully than ever before the economic and noneconomic implications of venture capital on firm growth.

A number of studies look at the long-term outcome of venture capital investment via objective outcome measures such as accounting data or stock market data of public VC-backed companies. The rationale is that, if VCFs have superior selection, monitoring and value-adding skills, VC-backed companies should in the long term perform better than non-VC-backed companies. If the long-term performance is not better, the economic role of VC is called into question.

Megginson and Mull (1991) and Al-Suwailem (1995) in the United States and Van Hyfte (1998) in Belgium have used accounting data to compare the postinvestment evolution of VC-backed companies with matched samples of non-VC-backed companies. The findings are consistent: VC-backed firms have higher growth rates in terms of assets, sales, revenues and number of employees and invest a larger fraction in R&D. In the United States, they use less debt, while they use more debt in Belgium. The survival rate is comparable for both groups in both countries.

Some American studies compare VC-backed IPOs with non-VC-backed IPOs, thereby focusing solely on successful ventures. At the time of initial offering, VC-backed IPOs are, on average, larger than non-VC-backed companies and experience less underpricing (Lin and Smith 1998; Megginson and Weiss 1991), especially when the VCF is a high-quality company with high-quality monitoring (Barry et al. 1990). High-quality VCFs are found to be those that

1 are older and larger,
2 take the lead investor role,
3 introduce a larger number of investee companies to the stock markets,
4 sit longer on the board of directors of the investee company, and
5 own a larger fraction of the equity.

Moreover, high-quality VCFs are able to time the IPO of investee companies near stock market peaks (Lerner 1994b). Small companies going public are able to attract higher tier underwriters when venture-backed (Barry et al. 1990). After the IPO, VC-backed offerings have more and higher quality analysts following them and have significantly higher returns than non-VC-backed IPOs (Brav and Gompers 1997). These findings indicate a legitimization effect: ventures having a VCF as outside investor are perceived as higher quality. In sum, VCFs appear to enhance value at the time and after IPO, but not all VCFs provide equal value to portfolio companies.

VCFs themselves benefit from the legitimization of the companies they invest in. Evidence is growing that VCFs try to build up their own reputation through IPOs of their portfolio companies, a phenomenon Neck and Meyer (1998) call "certification reciprocity." Gompers (1996) and Neck and Meyer (1998) show that young VCFs take companies public earlier and experience more underpricing than older VCFs. Moreover, young VCFs time IPOs to precede or coincide with raising money for follow-on funds (Lin and Smith 1998). This may create an inverse agency problem, wherein the VCF faces the dilemma of allocating time and effort to "competing" sets of limited partners and entrepreneurs. Of course, entrepreneurs may face other agency problems with regard to the VC, such as, for example, VCs resisting needed follow-on financing that might require a dilution or negative revaluation of the VCs' shares.

Several conclusions may be drawn from these studies of venture capital. First, their great strengths involve their use of objective measures and the power of longitudinal designs. Ultimately, value-adding should be visible in financial outcomes. While such treatments may not be able to tell us whether higher performance is largely an outcome of preinvestment selection ability or postinvestment involvement, it provides the necessary justification for the process-oriented studies that are less able to quantify value-adding. Based on the above empirical findings, we may conclude that high-quality VCFs are able to add value to their investee companies, leading to higher performance and growth. Moreover, recent empirical studies are explicitly acknowledging that VCFs are agents of entrepreneurs and of their investors and that their reputation in the investor community depends largely on the performance of their portfolio companies and the perception of their role in the process (Gompers 1996; Neck and Meyer 1998). This viewpoint, however, has not been incorporated in finance-oriented theoretical models as yet (apart from Gifford 1997).

Most of the studies that directly examine the involvement of VCs in portfolio companies conclude that VCs do add value (Fredriksen et al. 1997). A few, however, reach the opposite conclusion or find no relationship between VC involvement and venture performance. Steier and Greenwood (1995), for example, find in a case study that VCs sometimes hinder the development of the venture, although the presence of venture capital significantly reduces its liability of newness if the relationship is well managed. In a longitudinal study in the United States, Busenitz et al. (1997) found no relationship between performance and degree of involvement. Fredriksen et al. (1997) in Sweden found that more active involvement on the part of VCs was related to better capital acquisition and the development of better control systems but not to other aspects of development. They speculate that Swedish VCs are "fire fighters" who put extra effort into poorly performing firms in order to raise them to the level of other portfolio companies. Ruhnka et al.'s (1992) finding that VCs are able to achieve a successful turnaround in 56 percent of the "living dead" ventures (i.e., ventures that are surviving but are currently unable to produce satisfactory returns to the investors) suggests that putting effort into poor performers might be a viable strategy. However, Sapienza (1992) found a strong positive correlation between US VCs' involvement and perceived performance and argued that VCs may seek to add value to their top performing portfolio companies as a "home run" strategy. As yet, no one has settled the issue of which strategy VCs seek or which one would succeed more fully.

An indirect effect of VC involvement may come in the form of the financial discipline such presence imposes on new firms. An interesting stream of research in Europe investigates the postinvestment information needs of VCs and subsequent changes in accounting and control practices in investee companies (Fredriksen et al. 1997; Mitchell et al. 1995, 1997; Sweeting 1991). These studies indicate that the better the accounting information available in entrepreneurial companies, the better the decision-making and the more likely is firm survival (Mitchell et al. 1997). In most cases, the presence of VCs positively influences the content and frequency of accounting reports, thereby enhancing the control and decision-making functions in the entrepreneurial companies (Fredriksen et al. 1997; Mitchell et al. 1997). This evidence suggests that the monitoring role, often seen by entrepreneurs as a necessary evil, is valuable in itself for the investee company. Such an interpretation is consistent with Sapienza and Amason (1993) who found that while greater involvement of VCs was associated with greater conflict, it was also associated with greater perceptions of value-added.

Researchers have also examined the direct and indirect effects of the intensity of VC involvement on a variety of behaviors and attitudes. Entrepreneurs with active VCs are more likely to have expectations fulfilled than those with passive investors (Fredriksen et al. 1997). Greater involvement is associated with greater satisfaction among VCs (Fredriksen et al. 1997) and greater self-reported value and importance of their roles (Sapienza et al. 1996). VCs who perceive themselves as having more influence on their portfolio companies also have greater commitment to the entrepreneurs' decisions and trust the entrepreneurs more (Sapienza and Korsgaard 1996). These results suggest that, contrary to conventional economic assumptions, there may be some intrinsic rewards associated with involvement in decision-making. Indeed, van Osnabrugge (1998) found that 18 percent of VCs and 35 percent of PIs rated involvement in the venture as a "very important" aspect in investing.

One of the less pleasant aspects of VC presence in entrepreneurial companies in the United States is that their fiduciary responsibilities may put them in the position of having to replace or dismiss the CEO (Bruton et al. 1998a). In contrast, European VCs rarely have the contractual right to dismiss the CEO. Dismissal of an entrepreneurial team member is more likely to occur in poorly performing companies (Fiet et al. 1997); it has a negative impact on long-term venture outcomes (Busenitz et al. 1997). However, following VCs' replacement of a CEO, perceived venture performance improves (Freid et al. 1998).

Our feeling is that this entire area of VCs' roles in venture governance and conflict resolution, especially in light of the dual agency positions of VCs, requires greater scrutiny. Some insights have begun to emerge on conditions inciting conflict and the repercussions. In Canada, postinvestment intensity of conflict is higher than anticipated on issues of strategy, growth planing and financing (Jog et al. 1991), while personnel issues often stir conflict in board meetings in the United States (Sapienza et al. 1997). Conflict, however, need not always be negative. While interpersonal conflict between VCs and entrepreneurs is associated with lower performance in the United Kingdom, cognitive (idea) conflict improves performance (Higashide and Birley 1998).

Finally, several recent studies have begun to apply procedural justice concepts to the building of quality relationships between VCs and entrepreneurs. Whereas Barney et al. (1996) demonstrated that some entrepreneurs may be more or less receptive to different types of managerial and operational advice depending on their team and industry experience, Busenitz et al. (1997) linked entrepreneurial attitudes directly to VC behavior. Using a procedural justice framework, they showed that entrepreneurs respond more negatively to VC influence attempts if they feel they have been treated unfairly. Specifically, a tendency on the part of VCs to invoke contractual covenants undermines trust and reduces receptivity to VC input. Although Cable and Shane (1997) have argued effectively that VCs and entrepreneurs have incentives to cooperate, the reality is that they do not always cooperate. Using a procedural justice framework, Sapienza and Korsgaard (1996) found that when entrepreneurs provided timely feedback on venture activities to VCs, VCs' trust in the entrepreneur, commitment to the entrepreneurs' strategic decisions and inclinations to provide follow-on financing were higher; these effects were stronger the less influence the VC held.

In summary, the above studies suggest that

1 VCs do enhance the growth prospects of their portfolio companies.
2 VCs do monitor, advise and assist, but we know little about how time is split among these activities or which is most effective.
3 Greater involvement may help economically but is not a necessary condition for value adding.
4 Involvement enhances the attitudes of the participants toward the process itself.
5 The cognitive and emotional aspects of the interaction are both important dimensions of the value-adding process.

Theoretical Progress and Future Directions

To date, the majority of theory-driven research on venture capital takes a conventional agency perspective as its overarching framework. It has portrayed entrepreneurs as agents of VCs and the major activities of VCs as seeking protection from information asymmetry, adverse selection and moral hazard problems. Our view is that this perspective is most suitable for explaining the preinvestment selection and contract writing phases and, to some degree, the postinvestment renegotiation phases. Its suitability to explaining postinvestment monitoring, advising and value-adding activities is more open to question. Perhaps if monitoring activities could be unbundled from other activities, they could prove amenable to agency theory predictions. However, involvement may be aimed more at achieving value creation than value protection. Further, VCs are often agents of the entrepreneurs (Cable and Shane 1997). They may take actions against the best interests of the entrepreneurs in venture governance and conflict resolution, in allocating their time and effort (Gifford 1997), in reinvestment decisions (Steier and Greenwood 1995), in taking the investee company public (Gompers 1996; Neck and Meyer 1998) and many other ways. Perhaps researchers should begin to look at how entrepreneurs cope with agency problems!

Further theory development is needed to take these possibilities explicitly into account. Cable and Shane (1997) have offered game theory as an alternative lens. We believe such an approach offers great potential. At the same time, we suspect that realistic predictions may be best attained if strict assumptions of economic gain as the sole motivator are relaxed slightly to take into account principles of relational exchange and governance. As we move toward more fine-grained and realistic models, it is also worth challenging some basic risk assumptions implicit in earlier literature: Are VCs in the business of minimizing agency and/or business risk, or in the business of value creation? It may, in fact, be more economically rewarding for VCs to try to build value by identifying and supporting high-flyers than to protect value through minimizing downside risk. Empirical results often indicate that VC behavior is consistent not with risk avoidance strategies but with maximizing upside return chances (Manigart et al. 1997, 1998). Thus, it may be productive to investigate the risk tolerance of the different economic actors and see who is most risk averse or risk neutral: entrepreneurs, VCs or fund providers?

More theory-driven empirical research into the postinvestment activities of VCs can help to give insight into the dual position of VCs vis-à-vis their investors and the entrepreneurs and in their distinct roles of monitoring and value-adding. Possible theoretical avenues include knowledge-based and learning theories of the firm (e.g., Cohen and Levinthal 1990; Grant 1996) as well as emerging theories of social capital (Nahapiet and Ghoshal 1998). Relational contracting may help to explain part of the interaction during the postinvestment period and some of the renegotiation (e.g., Landström et al. 1998), while social capital and knowledge-based theories may help predict value adding activities.

We still know little about the strategic choices of VCs with respect to their investment policies.

- ◆ Do they select the best available venture regardless of the portfolio?
- ◆ Do they instead try to diversify the portfolio as they go to spread risk?
- ◆ Or do they try to pick ventures most like their existing ones in order to build competencies and enhance the possibility of networking among the investee companies?

These issues have obvious overlap with prior work reviewed on the selection, monitoring, advising and value-adding notions discussed earlier. An intersection of these previous approaches with mainstream strategic management theory may provide insight into both literatures.

Finally, in order to come to a richer understanding of the relationship between VC investing and entrepreneurial firm growth, comparative research of different investor types, of different entrepreneurial firm types and of a multinational and multicultural nature may be required. For example, because PIs are not agents of fund providers they have different incentives than VCs in terms of producing due diligence validation; they may also have different risk preferences and time horizons. Comparisons should allow deeper insights into the roles and determinants of VCs' and PIs' behavior. Comparison across VC activities in different parts of the world may also be helpful in demonstrating how government policies shape and are shaped by the prevailing investment preferences and practices. In short, the opportunities for research in this area is just beginning to be realized. Where in the late 1980s little empirical work existed, now descriptive evidence abounds. More work is to be done building this base and building the theoretical framework to illuminate it.

Notes

We thank Wim Van Hyfte for his excellent research assistance. Part of this research was funded by a research grant of Barones Vlerick.

1 When referring to Europe, the countries of the former Soviet bloc are excluded because the venture capital industry is completely different there due to the different nature of their economies.
2 Although writing adequate contracts is important but not value-enhancing, we will not cover this subject here.

References

Admati, A.R. and Pfleiderer, P. 1994. Robust financial contracting and the role of venture capitalists. *Journal of Finance* 49(2): 371–402.
AFIC 1996. *Mesure de la performance de l'activité du capital investissement en France (1978–1995)*. Paris: AFIC.
Al-Suwailem, S. 1995. Does venture capital financing make a difference? Unpublished doctoral dissertation, University of Washington, St. Louis.
Amit, R., Brander, J. and Zott, C. 1998. Why do venture capital firms exist? Theory and Canadian evidence. *Journal of Business Venturing* 13: 441–66.
Amit, R., Glosten, L. and Muller, E. 1990. Entrepreneurial ability, venture investments, and risk sharing. *Management Science* 36(10): 1232–45.
Barney, J.B., Busenitz, L.W., Fiet, J.O. and Moesel, D.D. 1989. The structure of venture capital governance: an organizational economic analysis of relations between venture capital firms and new ventures. *Academy of Management Proceedings* 10: 64–8.
Barney, J.B., Busenitz, L.W., Fiet, J.O. and Moesel, D.D. 1996. New venture teams' assessment of learning assistance from venture capital firms. *Journal of Business Venturing* 11: 257–72.
Barry, C.B., Muscarella, C.J., Peavy III, J.W. and Vetsuypens, M.R. 1990. The role of venture capital in the creation of public companies: evidence from the going public process. *Journal of Financial Economics* 27: 447–71.
Berger, A.N. and Udell, G.F. 1998. The economics of small business finance: the roles of private equity and debt markets in the financial growth cycle. *Journal of Banking and Finance* 22(6–8): 613–73.
Brav, A. and Gompers, P.A. 1997. Myth or reality? The long-run underperformance of Initial Public Offerings: evidence from venture and nonventure capital-backed companies. *Journal of Finance* 52(5): 1791–821.
Bruton, G. D., Fried, V.H. and Hisrich, R. D. 1998a. Venture capitalists and CEO dismissal. *Entrepreneurship Theory and Practice* 21: 41–54.
Bruton, G., Sapienza, H., Fried, V. and Manigart, S. 1998b. US, European, and Asian venture capitalists' governance: are theories employed in the examination of US entrepreneurship universally applicable? Paper presented at the Academy of Management Meeting, San Diego.
Busenitz, L.W., Moesel, D.D. and Fiet, J.O. 1997. The impact of post-funding involvement by venture capitalists on long-term performance outcomes. In P. Reynolds, W. Bygrave, N. Carter, P. Davidsson, W. Gartner, C. Mason and P. McDougall (eds.), *Frontiers of Entrepreneurship Research*. Wellesley, MA: Babson College, pp. 498–512.
Bygrave, W.D. 1988. The structure of investment networks of venture capital firms. *Journal of Business Venturing* 3: 137–57.

Bygrave, W.D. and Timmons, J.A. 1992. *Venture Capital at the Crossroads*. Boston: Harvard Business School Press.

Cable, D.M. and Shane, S. 1997. A prisoner's dilemma approach to entrepreneur–venture capitalist relationships. *Academy of Management Review* 22(1): 142–76.

Cohen, W. and Levinthal, D. 1990. Absorptive capacity: a new perspective on learning and innovation. *Administrative Science Quarterly* 35: 128–52.

Ehrlich, S.B., De Noble, A.F., Moore, T. and Weaver, R.R. 1994. After the cash arrives: a comparative study of venture capital and private investor involvement in entrepreneurial firms. *Journal of Business Venturing* 9: 67–82.

Elango, B., Fried, V.H., Hisrich, R.D. and Polonchek, A. 1995. How do venture capital firms differ? *Journal of Business Venturing* 10: 157–79.

EVCA (European Venture Capital Association). 1997. *Yearbook 1997: A Survey of Venture Capital and Private Equity in Europe*. Zaventem, EVCA.

EVCA (European Venture Capital Association). 1998. *Yearbook 1998: A Survey of Venture Capital and Private Equity in Europe*. Zaventem: EVCA.

Fenn, G.W. and Liang, N. 1998. New resources and new ideas: private equity for small businesses. *Journal of Banking and Finance* 22(6–8): 1077–84.

Fiet, J.O. 1995. Risk avoidance strategies in venture capital markets. *Journal of Management Studies* 32(4): 551–74.

Fiet, J.O., Busenitz, L.W., Moesel, D.D. and Barney, J.B. 1997. Complementary theoretical perspectives on the dismissal of new venture team members. *Journal of Business Venturing* 12: 347–66.

Fluck, Z., Holtz-Eakin, D. and Rosen, H.S. 1998. *Where Does the Money Come From? The Financing of Small Entrepreneurial Enterprises*. New York University and Leonard N. Stern School of Business, Working Paper Fin 98–038, February 1998.

Fredriksen, O., Klofsten, M., Landström, H., Olofsson, C. and Wahlbin, C. 1990. Entrepreneur–venture capitalist relations: the entrepreneurs' view. In N. Churchill, W. Bygrave, J. Hornaday, D. Muzyka, K. Vesper and W. Wetzel (eds.), *Frontiers of Entrepreneurship Research*. Wellesley, MA: Babson College.

Fredriksen, O., Olofsson, C. and Wahlbin, C. 1991. The role of venture capital in the development of portfolio firms. In N. Churchill, W. Bygrave, J. Covin, D. Sexton, D. Slevin, K. Vesper and W. Wetzel (eds.), *Frontiers of Entrepreneurship Research*. Wellesley, MA: Babson College, pp. 435–44.

Fredriksen, O., Olofsson, C. and Wahlbin, C. 1997. Are venture capitalists firefighters? A study of the influence and impact of venture capital firms. *Technovation* 17(9): 133–50.

Freear, J. and Wetzel, W.E. 1990. Who bankrolls high-tech entrepreneurs? *Journal of Business Venturing* 5: 77–89.

Fried, V.H., Bruton, G.D. and Hisrich, R.D. 1998. Strategy and the board of directors in venture capital-backed firms. *Journal of Business Venturing* 13: 493–503.

Fried, V.H. and Hisrich, R.D. 1994. Toward a model of venture capital investment decision making. *Financial Management* 23(3): 28–37.

Fried, V.H. and Hisrich, R.D. 1995. The venture capitalist: a relationship investor. *California Management Review* 37(2): 101–13.

Gifford, S. 1997. Limited attention and the role of the venture capitalist. *Journal of Business Venturing* 12: 459–82.

Gompers, P.A. 1995. Optimal investment, monitoring, and the staging of venture capital. *Journal of Finance* 50(5): 1461–89.

Gompers, P.A. 1996. Grandstanding in the venture capital industry. *Journal of Financial Economics* 42: 133–56.

Gompers, P.A. 1998. Venture capital growing pains: should the market diet? *Journal of Banking and Finance* 22(6–8): 1089–104.

Gorman, M. and Sahlman, W.A. 1989. What do venture capitalists do? *Journal of Business Venturing* 4: 231–48.

Grant, R. M. 1996. Toward a knowledge-based theory of the firm. *Strategic Management Journal* 17: 109–22.

Gupta, A.K. and Sapienza, H.J. 1991. Determinants of venture capital firms' preferences regarding the industry diversity and geographic scope of their investments. *Journal of Business Venturing* 7: 347–62.

Hale, S. and Hackbert, P.H. 1998. Contribution of formal and informal venture capital investors to value creation by firms in which they invest. Paper presented at the Babson-Kauffman Entrepreneurship Research Conference, Gent, Belgium.

Hall, J. and Hofer, C.W. 1993. Venture capitalists' decision criteria in new venture evaluation. *Journal of Business Venturing* 8: 25–42.

Haubrick, J.G. 1990. *Venture Capital and the Value of Information*. Working Paper, Warton School of the University of Pennsylvania and the Snider Entrepreneurial Center.

Higashide, H. and Birley, S. 1998. Consequences of conflicts in the venture capitalist–entrepreneur team relationship in the United Kingdom. Paper presented at the 1998 Babson-Kauffman Entrepreneurship Research Conference, Ghent, Belgium.

Hirao, Y. 1993. Learning and incentive problems in repeated partnerships. *International Economic Review* 34(1): 101–19.

Investment Advisory Council. 1992. *Entrepreneurial Business: Agenda for Action. An Analysis of the Small Business Investment Company Program Together with Findings and Recommendations Concerning Its Effective Operations*. Report prepared for submission to honorable Patricia Saiki, Administrator, US Small Business Administration.

Jog, V.M., Lawson, W.M. and Riding, A.L. 1991. The venture capitalist/entrepreneur interface: expectations, conflicts, and contracts. *Journal of Small Business & Entrepreneurship* 8(2): 5–20.

Knight, R.M. 1994. Criteria used by venture capitalists: a cross cultural analysis. *International Small Business Journal* 13(1): 26–37.

KPMG (Klynveld Peat Marwick Goerdeler). 1995. *Public Support Systems for the Development of Regional Venture Capital*. Report submitted to the European Commission, DG XVI.

Landström, H., Manigart, S., Mason, C. and Sapienza, H. 1998. Contracts between entrepreneurs and investors: terms and negotiation processes. Paper presented at the Babson-Kauffman Entrepreneurship Research Conference, Ghent, Belgium.

Lerner, J. 1994a. The syndication of venture capital investments. *Financial Management* 23(3): 16–27.

Lerner, J. 1994b. Venture capitalists and the decision to go public. *Journal of Financial Economics* 35: 293–316.

Lerner, J. 1995. Venture capitalists and the oversight of private firms. *Journal of Finance* 50(1): 301–18.

Lin, T.H. and Smith, R.L. 1998. Insider reputation and selling decisions: the unwinding of venture capital investments during equity IPOs. *Journal of Corporate Finance* 4: 241–63.

MacMillan, I.C., Kulow, D.M. and Khoylian, R. 1988. Venture capitalists' involvement in their investments: extent and performance. *Journal of Business Venturing* 4: 27–47.

Manigart, S. and Struyf, C. 1997. Financing high technology startups in Belgium: an explorative study. *Small Business Economics* 9: 125–35.

Manigart, S., Desbrières, P., Robbie, K., Sapienza, H., Beekman A. and De Waele, K. 1998. Venture capitalists, rates of return and valuation: a comparative study, in M. Wright and K. Robbie (eds.), *Management Buy-out and Venture Capital: Into the Next Millennium* (forthcoming). Manchester: Manchester University Press.

Manigart, S., Wright, M., Robbie, K., Desbrières, P. and De Waele, K. 1997. Venture capitalists' appraisal of investment projects: an empirical European study. *Entrepreneurship Theory and Practice* 21(4): 29–43.

Megginson, W.L. and Mull, R.H. 1991. Financial characteristics and financing decisions of venture capital backed firms. Paper presented at the Small Business Finance Conference, Florida, April 1991.

Megginson, W.L. and Weiss, K.A. 1991. Venture capitalist certification in Initial Public Offerings. *Journal of Finance* 46(3): 879–903.

Mitchell, F., Reid, G.C. and Terry, N.G. 1995. The post investment demand for accounting information by venture capital investors. *Accounting and Business Research* 25: 186–96.

Mitchell, F., Reid, G.C. and Terry, N.G. 1997. Venture capital supply and accounting information system development. *Entrepreneurship Theory and Practice* 21(4): 45–62.

Murray, G.C. 1995. Evolution and change: an analysis of the first decade of the UK venture capital industry. *Journal of Business Finance and Accounting* 22(8): 1077–106.

Muzyka, D., Birley, S. and Leleux, B. 1996. Trade-offs in the investment decisions of European venture capitalists. *Journal of Business Venturing* 11: 273–87.

Nahapiet, J. and Ghoshal, S. 1998. Social capital, intellectual capital, and the organizational advantage. *Academy of Management Review* 23(2): 242–66.

NVCA (National Venture Capital Association) 1997 *Annual Report*. VentureOne Corporation.

Neck, H.M. and Meyer, D. 1998. Certification reciprocity: an explanation of added value in the venture capitalist–IPO firm relationship. Paper presented at the Academy of Management Meeting, San Diego.

Norton, E. and Tenenbaum, B.H. 1993. Specialization versus diversification as a venture capital investment strategy. *Journal of Business Venturing* 8: 431–42.

OECD (Organization for Economic Cooperation and Development). 1997. *Government Venture Capital for Technology-based Firms*. OCDE/GD(97)201, Paris.

Ooghe, H., Manigart, S. and Fassin, Y. 1991. Growth patterns of the European venture capital industry. *Journal of Business Venturing* 6: 381–404.

Polanyi, M. 1967. *The Tacit Dimension*. Garden City, NY: Doubleday.

Reid, G.C. 1996. Fast growing small entrepreneurial firms and their venture capital backers: an applied principal–agent analysis. *Small Business Economics* 8(3): 235–48.

Robbie, K., Wright, M. and Chiplin, B. 1997. The monitoring of venture capital firms. *Entrepreneurship Theory and Practice* 21(4): 9–28.

Rosenstein, J. 1988. The board and strategy: venture capital and high technology. *Journal of Business Venturing* 3: 159–70.

Rosenstein, J., Bruno, A.V., Bygrave, W.D. and Taylor, N.T. 1993. The CEO, venture capitalists, and the board. *Journal of Business Venturing* 8: 99–113.

Ruhnka, J.C., Feldman, H.D. and Dean, T.J. 1992. The "Living Dead" phenomenon in venture capital investments. *Journal of Business Venturing* 7: 137–55.

Sadtler, D.R. 1993. How venture capitalists add value. *Journal of General Management* 19(1): 1–16.

Sahlman, W.A. 1990. The structure and governance of venture-capital organizations. *Journal of Financial Economics* 27: 473–521.

Sapienza, H.J. 1992. When do venture capitals add value? *Journal of Business Venturing* 7: 9–27.

Sapienza, H.J. and Amason, A. 1993. Effects of innovativeness and venture stage on venture capitalist–entrepreneur relations. *Interfaces* 23(6): 38–51.

Sapienza, H.J. and Gupta, A.K. 1994. Impact of agency risks and task uncertainty on venture capitalist–CEO interaction. *Academy of Management Journal* 37(6): 1618–32.

Sapienza, H.J. and Korsgaard, M.A. 1996. The role of procedural justice in entrepreneur–venture capital relations. *Academy of Management Journal* 39: 544–74.

Sapienza, H.J., Korsgaard, M.A. and Hoogendam, J. 1997. What do new venture boards do? In W. Bygrave, B. Bird, S. Birley, N. Churchill, M. Hay, R. Keeley and W. Wetzel (eds.), *Frontiers of Entrepreneurship Research*. Wellesley, MA: Babson College, pp. 118–30.

Sapienza, H.J., Manigart, S. and Vermeir, W. 1996. Venture capitalist governance and value added in four countries. *Journal of Business Venturing* 11: 439–69.

Shepherd, D.A., Ettenson, R. and Crouch, A. 1998a. New venture strategy and profitability: a venture capitalist's assessment. *Journal of Business Venturing* 1: 59–82.

Shepherd, D.A. and Zacharakis, A. (In press). Conjoint analysis: a new methodological approach for researching venture capitalists' decision policies. *Venture Capital: An International Journal of Entrepreneurial Finance.*

Shepherd, D.A., Zacharakis, A. and Baron, R. 1998b. Venture capitalists' expertise: real or fallacious? Paper presented at the Babson-Kauffman Entrepreneurship Research Conference, Ghent, Belgium.

Smart, G.H. (In press). Management assessment methods in venture capital: towards a theory of human capital valuation. *Venture Capital: An International Journal of Entrepreneurial Finance.*

Steier, L. and Greenwood, R. 1995. Venture capitalist relationships in the deal structuring and post-investment stages of new firm creation. *Journal of Management Studies* 32(3): 337–57.

Surlemont, B., Wacquier, H. and Leleux, B. 1998. State vs. private venture capital: cross-spawning or crowding out? A pan-European empirical examination. Paper presented at the 1998 Babson-Kauffman Entrepreneurship Research Conference, Ghent, Belgium.

Sweeting, R.C. 1991. Early-stage new technology-based businesses: Interactions with venture capitalists and the development of accounting techniques and procedures. *British Accounting Review* 23(1): 3–22.

Sweeting, R.C. and Wong, C.F. 1997. A UK 'hands-off' venture capital firm and the handling of post-investment investor-investee relationships. *Journal of Management Studies* 34(1): 125–52.

Van Hyfte, W. 1998. Empirische studie naar de toegevoegde waarde van Belgische investeringsmaatschappijen (The added value of Belgian venture capital companies). Unpublished master thesis, University of Ghent, Belgium.

Van Osnabrugge, M.S. 1998. The financing of entrepreneurial firms in the UK: a comparison of business angel and venture capitalist investment procedures. Unpublished doctoral dissertation, Hertford College, Oxford University, England.

Virtanen, M. 1996. Entrepreneurial finance and venture capital advantage. Unpublished doctoral dissertation, Helsinki School of Economics, Finland.

Wright, M. and Robbie, K. 1998. Venture capital and private equity: a review and synthesis. *Journal of Business Finance and Accounting* 25(5–6): 521–70.

Wright, M., Thompson, S. and Robbie, K. 1992. Venture capital and management-led, leveraged buy-outs: a European perspective. *Journal of Business Venturing* 7: 47–71.

Zacharakis, A.L. and Meyer, G.D. 1995. The venture capitalist decision: understanding process versus outcome. In W. Bygrave, B. Bird, S. Birley, N. Churchill, M. Hay, R. Keeley and W. Wetzel (eds.), *Frontiers of Entrepreneurship Research*. Wellesley, MA: Babson College, pp. 465–78.

13

Venture Capital Financing of Entrepreneurship: Theory, Empirical Evidence and a Research Agenda

RAPHAEL AMIT, JAMES BRANDER AND CHRISTOPH ZOTT

LITERATURE REVIEW
A THEORY OF VENTURE CAPITAL FINANCE
THE DATA SET
A STATISTICAL OVERVIEW OF VENTURE CAPITAL BACKED FIRMS
AND INVESTMENTS
CONCLUSIONS AND FUTURE RESEARCH AGENDA

Entrepreneurial activity in North America has steadily increased in the past few decades. For example, the rate of new business registrations in Canada approximately doubled between 1979 and 1989 alone. The entrepreneurial sector is particularly interesting because of its close relationship to innovation and technological progress and the perception that it is the "engine of growth" of the economy in the sense that the entrepreneurial sector is a disproportionate supplier of employment growth. It follows from this perception that modern economies would thrive on a healthy and vibrant entrepreneurial business sector. Despite the observed growth in business initiation, however, only one new firm in five in Canada survives for ten years or more. And of the 80 percent of new ventures that cease operations within a decade, half of those fail within the first two years. Gaps or failures in financing the entrepreneurial sector may account for the observed high failure rates of new businesses.

An important source of financing for the entrepreneurial sector is the venture capital industry. Indeed, venture capital activity is usually defined as the provision of equity and debt financing to young, privately held firms.[1] However, relatively little is known about the performance of the venture capital industry (although Lerner 1994a, 1994b and Gompers 1995 provide sound empirical studies of the US venture capital industry). This is due, in part, to the paucity of information in the public domain regarding venture capital activity. By comparison, a larger body of research is dedicated to the empirical and theoretical analyses of other parts of the financial sector, such as banking, insurance, real estate finance and stock markets. Most of the firms in which venture capitalists invest (referred to as "investees") are privately held and therefore not subject to the same reporting requirements as public companies. There is also no organized secondary exchange for venture capital investments that provides summary information. Furthermore, regulatory scrutiny of venture capital has been modest compared with the level of regulatory scrutiny of banks, insurance and stock exchanges. The information that arises from regulatory proceedings and requirements is thus sparse.

In this chapter, we develop a theoretical approach to venture capital financing based on the premise that informational asymmetries are the key to understanding the venture capital industry. Previous studies have focused on the importance of asymmetric information in venture capital markets, and several authors have suggested that venture capitalists are more active than other financial intermediaries in situations where asymmetric information is significant. In this chapter, we develop a simple, formal model that distinguishes venture capitalists from other potential investors on the basis of their ability to deal with informational asymmetries. We then draw inferences from the model about how venture capital financing would be expected to work. These predictions are compared with the actual pattern of venture capital investment in Canada.

Macdonald & Associates Ltd. uses two surveys to collect the most up-to-date and comprehensive data on the Canadian venture capital industry. We are fortunate to have been granted access, on a confidential basis, to an anonymous version (in which the names of firms have been removed) of their database for this study. Using this unique data source, we report summary statistical information and provide a preliminary econometric analysis of the relationship between venture capitalists' ownership share and firm performance.

The chapter is organized as follows. The next section reviews the relevant literature. The second section summarizes the theoretical structure for interpreting the data and highlights the implications from the framework. The third section describes the database used in the chapter, and the fourth section reports statistical information drawn from the database. The final section is devoted to concluding remarks and suggestions for future research.

LITERATURE REVIEW

The modeling framework in this chapter applies the major aspects of the theory of asymmetric information to a financial-contracting setting in which an entrepreneur may obtain funding from a venture capitalist. By focussing on adverse selection and moral hazard, we seek to capture the essence of the relationship between business founders and outside equity holders.

Akerlof (1970) pioneered the analysis of informational asymmetry. He showed that "hidden information" might lead to a situation in which the market "selects" low-quality items. Such adverse selection is inefficient because potentially efficient (i.e., Pareto-improving) trades will not take place. Hidden information thus causes market failure. Scholars recognized that adverse selection problems can arise in many circumstances, especially in insurance markets, where buyers of insurance know their true risk better than do insurance companies (Pauly 1974), and in labor markets, where workers know their ability better than do their potential employers (Spence 1973). Spence (1973) pointed out that one natural market response to adverse selection is "signaling" quality by mechanisms such as product warranties. Rothschild and Stiglitz (1976), on the other hand, emphasized the role of "screening" in countering the effects of adverse selection. Screening occurs when the uninformed party offers a contract or a set of contracts that cause informed parties to self-select. In general, the efficient response of the seller may be to offer such "screening" or "separating" contracts, but sometimes the efficient response is to offer contracts that do not induce screening, resulting in "pooling" of different quality classes.

The other major informational asymmetry is "hidden action" where one party to a transaction takes an action that is not observed by the other party, and this action affects the returns to both parties. This problem was originally referred to as "moral hazard." Early influential work on moral hazard includes Pauly (1974) and Arrow (1973), who demonstrated that moral hazard causes market failure because it causes failures of Pareto efficiency.

Moral-hazard problems are particularly important in situations where one party acts as an "agent" for another party, such as when a client hires a lawyer, or when the seller of a house hires a sales agent. In these situations, the "principal" cannot perfectly observe the effort (or other actions) of the agent. Jensen and Meckling (1976) argued that agency analysis was the key to understanding the modern firm. Other classic papers on the agency problem include Holmstrom (1979) and Grossman and Hart (1983).

The role of asymmetry of information in financial contracting in venture capital is widely recognized. Sahlman (1990), for example, postulated that contracting practices in the venture capital industry reflect uncertainty about payoffs and information asymmetries between venture capitalists and entrepreneurs. He correctly argued that the lack of operational history aggravates the adverse-selection dilemma.

Amit et al. (1993) suggested that venture capitalists be regarded as financial intermediaries. The authors characterized the relevant informational problems and identified a series of research questions, some of which are addressed in our model. In another review paper on new directions in venture capital research, Barry (1994) emphasized the relevance of the information that only the entrepreneur has prior to contracting regarding his or her own abilities. Overly optimistic and confident entrepreneurs may create a bias toward funding high-risk ventures, as pointed out by Kamien (1994).

A small but growing number of formal models deal with venture capital finance in the context of asymmetric information. In his seminal paper, Chan (1983) emphasized the positive role of venture capitalists in mitigating the adverse selection problem in the market for entrepreneurial capital. He showed that adverse selection derives from the absence of any informed venture capitalists. The result is that only inferior projects are offered to investors. However, the presence of informed investors may alleviate this problem, leading to a Pareto-preferred solution. This analysis highlights the importance of understanding the conditions under which venture capitalists are as well informed about a project's prospects as the entrepreneur.

Chan et al. (1990) presented various "rules of thumb" for contracting practices in venture capital, including the absence of de novo financing, buyout options, performance requirements and earnout arrangements. The central idea is that venture capitalists learn about the entrepreneur's ability as time passes, and then decide whether to fire or retain the entrepreneur to manage the project. In a related paper, Hirao (1993) assumed that the agent's (i.e., the entrepreneur's) unobservable actions affect the learning process. She found that because of the interaction between learning and moral hazard, a long-term contract is not equivalent to a series of short-term contracts. Bergemann and Hege (1998) analyzed a similar situation in which there is a link between moral hazard and gradual learning about project quality. They assumed that an entrepreneur cannot affect the up-side potential of her venture, she can only prevent intrinsically good projects from failing. Withholding effort (moral hazard) not only jeopardizes the success of the venture but also causes the entrepreneur's and the venture capitalist's (initially symmetric) learning about project quality to diverge. Bergemann and Hege (1998) found that the optimal contract in this situation is a time-varying share contract. They also asserted that relationship financing and the adoption of strip financing or convertible securities are consistent with their model.

Amit et al. (1990) presented a principal–agent model in which investors are uncertain about the entrepreneur's type when submitting bids for the company, but the information asymmetry is resolved before actual contracting. The authors related the venture capital financing decision to the entrepreneur's skill level and predicted which entrepreneurs would decide to enter into an agreement with venture capitalists. They also considered moral-hazard problems but treated adverse selection only in the situation where the entrepreneur's type becomes common knowledge between bidding and contracting.

Amit et al. (1994) considered the role of different mechanisms for matching entrepreneurs and venture capitalists in mitigating adverse-selection problems. They extended the work of Rothschild and Stiglitz (1976) by incorporating some assumptions based on empirical regularities in the venture capital finance industry. Specifically, entrepreneurs are assumed to have private information about their types and venture capitalists can participate in the management of investees (at some cost) and thus contribute directly to the venture's success. Entrepreneurs may "shop around" or venture capitalists may actively seek out attractive investment opportunities. With a three-stage game, the authors examined possible pooling and separating equilibria. Although our model ignores the relevance of the matching regime for deriving such equilibria, we regard this as an important potential extension of our model.

In an attempt to characterize the contract that allows optimal continuation decisions with staged finance, Admati and Pfleiderer (1994) found that venture capitalists should prefer a fixed-fraction contract. This contract stipulates that the venture capitalist owns a certain fraction of the final payoffs, and finances that same fraction of any future investment (if continuation of the project is desirable). This result explains why later stages are not fully financed by the lead venture capitalist. It also attributes a positive role to the venture capitalist as a financial intermediary between the entrepreneur and outside investors. The analysis hinges, however, on some very restrictive assumptions.

Following Adamati and Pfleiderer's lead, Hellman (1994) built a multistage model of investment. He explained certain institutional features that he claimed distinguish venture capital from more traditional methods of finance. For example, he explained that only when the venture capitalist has a concentrated stake in investee companies will there be a sufficiently high incentive for active monitoring, which is necessary to avoid the problem of "short-termism" generated by staged finance.

Staged investment, which creates the option to abandon a venture (Sahlman 1990), is an important means for venture capitalists to minimize the present value of agency costs. The active involvement of venture capitalists in the operation of their investee companies may also mitigate the moral-hazard problem.[2] Other suggested solutions engineered by the venture capital industry to overcome problems arising from the asymmetry of information include the use of convertible preferred stock (Barry 1994; Trester 1998), control rights (Hellman 1998), which may include representation on the boards of investee companies (Lerner 1995), and syndication (Lerner 1994b; Brander et al. 1997). Lerner (1994b), for example, argued that syndicating first-round investments leads to better decisions about whether to invest. From the analysis of a sample of investment rounds in biotechnological firms, he found that syndication in early stages often involves experienced and highly reputed venture capitalists, which seemed to corroborate his hypothesis.

The work reviewed thus far is largely "model-based" theory. There is also a substantial descriptive literature on the venture capital industry. Two valuable papers of this type are Tyebjee and Bruno (1984) and Fried and Hisrich (1994), which describe some activities undertaken by venture capitalists to diminish problems arising from the asymmetry of information. Tyebjee and Bruno suggested that venture capital financing involves the following sequential steps: (1) deal origination, (2) deal screening, (3) deal evaluation, (4) deal structuring and (5) post-investment activities.[3] Our model captures steps 3 to 5, which deal with the venture capitalist's choice problem. However, while our model captures some basic (informational) difficulties that arise in the early screening stages, we do not consider the activities described by steps 1 and 2. These issues were addressed analytically by Amit et al. (1994).

Some other useful overviews of the venture capital industry include MacMillan et al. (1985, 1987), and Low and MacMillan (1988). Formal, theory-driven research with clearly stated assumptions, different theoretical perspectives, and formal decision models is still relatively scarce in the literature on new venture financing. In particular, there is a lack of research that links theory with empirical evidence. We hope to fill this gap with the present chapter.

A THEORY OF VENTURE CAPITAL FINANCE

Consider an entrepreneur who has a project and seeks potential investors.[4] To keep the analysis simple, we assume that the project requires fixed financial input (denoted by I) from an investor. The expected cash flow from the project, net of production costs, is denoted R. This expected net operating revenue depends in part on the effort, e, of the entrepreneur and on the underlying project quality, q. The outcome also depends on a random variable, u, with expected value 0. The realized net cash flow is therefore

$$R(e,q) + u \qquad (13.1)$$

where the expected operating revenue is $R(e,q)$. We assume that entrepreneurs and investors are risk-neutral, expected-value maximizers. We therefore ignore u. However, u plays one important role. Given the unobservable random uncertainty represented by u, it is not possible for an investor who knows project quality q to infer effort e from the cash flow realization.

If e cannot be observed by the investor, then it is a "hidden action" and gives rise to a moral hazard (or "agency") problem. If q is known to the entrepreneur, but not to the investor, then it is hidden or private information and gives rise to potential adverse selection. The presence of exogenous uncertainty as represented by the random variable u does not in itself cause market failure. R is taken to be increasing in both e and q. We also assume that there are decreasing marginal returns to effort. The effort effects can be written formally as

$$R_e > 0 \text{ or } R_{ee} < 0 \tag{13.2}$$

where subscripts denote (partial) derivatives.

Let the share of the proceeds that go to the investor (possibly a venture capital firm) be denoted a.[5] The expected return V to the investor is

$$V = aR(e,q) - I \tag{13.3}$$

The expected return to the entrepreneurial firm, denoted Π, is its share of the proceeds, net of the costs of effort e.

$$\Pi = (1 - a)R(e,q) - e \tag{13.4}$$

Variable e is normalized so that providing e units of effort imposes cost e on the entrepreneurial firm.

Moral hazard

To demonstrate the moral hazard problem, assume initially that q is known to both parties. A profit-maximizing entrepreneur will maximize (13.4) with respect to e, leading to the following first-order condition:

$$\Pi_e = (1 - a)R_e - 1 = 0 \text{ or } R_e = 1/(1 - a) \tag{13.5}$$

The second-order condition for a maximum is $(1 - a) R_{ee} < 0$. Noting that the factor $(1 - a)$ is presumed to be strictly positive and using (13.2), this second-order condition must hold.

The efficient or "first-best" level of effort is determined by maximizing the sum of (3) and (4) with respect to e. This sum, denoted S, is

$$S = R(e,q) - I - e \tag{13.6}$$

Maximizing (13.6) with respect to e yields the following first-order condition

$$R_e = 1 \tag{13.7}$$

It follows from (13.5), (13.7) and (13.2) that the entrepreneur will choose less than the efficient level of effort as long as (is strictly positive. This is the moral-hazard problem. It follows from the corresponding algebra that effort is declining in a.

$$de/da < 0 \tag{13.8}$$

The moral-hazard problem might render the project infeasible. The investment is attractive to the investor only if the return equals or exceeds the return that can be obtained by investing I elsewhere. Let this required return or opportunity cost be denoted r. Then feasibility requires

$$(1 + r)I \le aR(e[a],q) \tag{13.9}$$

There may be no value of a for which (13.9) is satisfied. If the expected return to the investor is low, a will have to be high, but then e will fall (from (13.8)), reflecting the idea that the entrepreneur will provide less effort as his stake in the firm falls.

Feasibility for the entrepreneur requires that the expected profit given by (13.4) exceed the return from the entrepreneur's best alternative, which can be normalized to equal 0. It is possible that effort level e^*, the efficient effort level that results when marginal benefit equals marginal cost, would allow feasibility for both investor and entrepreneur, but that the actual effort relationship, $e(a)$, would dictate that the project not be financed. Thus the moral hazard problem may cause the market to fail.

In Amit et al. (1998), we introduced the idea that investors can monitor the entrepreneur and, at cost m, induce the entrepreneur to provide additional effort. We found that projects that are not financed by other investors will be feasible for investors who are good at monitoring (i.e., those for whom the responsiveness of e to m is high). We also explored the possibility that the investor provides valuable (but costly) services, s, to investee companies. These services (e.g., providing strategic and operational advice, helping in fundraising, adding reputation, etc.) are observable by the entrepreneur. We concluded that the provision of s might contribute to the realization of projects that otherwise would have been abandoned, because they did not fulfill the investor's original feasibility constraint (13.9). Considering s, the investor's feasibility constraint becomes

$$(1 + r)I + s \leq aR(e(a),q,s) \tag{13.10}$$

If s is not prohibitively high, then it might relax this constraint through its direct and indirect positive effect on R. Investors who are skilled at providing value-creating services to their portfolio companies will thus undertake certain projects that other, less skilled investors will shun.

Ample evidence shows that venture capitalists provide valuable services to their portfolio companies. Gorman and Sahlman (1989) compiled a list of such services from a survey of venture capital investors. The highest ranked and most frequently used activities they found either directly enhance investee revenues (e.g., providing introductions to potential customers and suppliers or helping obtain additional financing) or enhance the entrepreneur's productivity of effort and thus indirectly boost investee revenues (e.g., through strategic planning, management recruitment or operational planning).

Adverse selection

A similar pattern emerges when adverse selection is considered. Assume that the venture capitalist chooses the optimal amount of services rendered and the optimal amount of monitoring effort, giving rise to associated values of e and s for any given a. Quality level q is now unobservable to the investor. Suppose that the range of q is such that the average quality project does not yield high enough expected returns (for any value of a) to allow the expected return of both the entrepreneur and the venture capitalist to be positive. Thus the average project is not worth funding. Investment in an entrepreneurial firm is a one-period, multistage process as illustrated in figure 13.1.

In the first stage, the investor incurs an up-front cost of d (for "due diligence") in order to assess the quality of a potential investment. With probability $p(d)$ the investor will

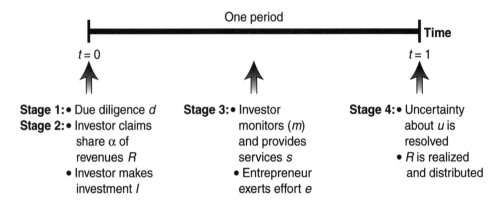

FIGURE 13.1 Venture capital investment process

become informed about q and will therefore find out whether $q > q^0$ or $q < q^0$. Only in the former case will an investment be made. With probability $(1 - p(d))$, however, the investor will remain uninformed about q and will thus refrain from investing (recall that on average he or she would incur a loss). Stage 3, in which the entrepreneur exerts effort and is monitored and supported by the investor, and stage 4, in which the benefits from the investment are reaped and distributed, occur only if q is found to be greater than q^0 in stage 1.

It follows from the model presented in Amit et al. (1998) that investors who are good at doing due diligence are likely to engage in it, select high-quality projects (i.e., projects with positive expected return) and make investments. These are the investors who become venture capitalists.

Implications

The above formulation reflects the idea that venture capitalists are those investors with skills in selecting good projects in environments with hidden information and who are good at monitoring and advising entrepreneurs who might otherwise be vulnerable to moral-hazard problems. The implications of this modeling framework are outlined:

Venture capitalists will operate in environments where their abilities provide an advantage over other investors.

When venture capitalists have an advantage, they will prefer projects where the cost of informational asymmetry is the least severe.

If informational asymmetries are present, the ability of a venture capitalist to exit may be impaired.

The model implies that dR/de $(= Re) > 0$ and $de/da < 0$.

Venture capitalists will operate in environments where their relative efficiency in selecting and monitoring investments and in providing value-enhancing services gives them a comparative advantage over other investors. For example, as we have seen in the "hidden action" case, it may take effective monitoring and specific services to make a project attractive to an investor. In the "hidden information" case, on the other hand, market failure can be avoided if the probability of detecting whether a project is worth supporting is high enough for sufficiently low due diligence costs. This suggests strong industry effects in venture capital investments. We would expect venture capitalists to be active in industries such as biotechnology and computer software where informational concerns are important, rather than in "routine" start-ups such as restaurants or retail outlets.

Within the class of projects where venture capitalists have an advantage, venture capitalists will prefer projects in which selection, monitoring and service costs are lowest, in other words, where the costs of informational asymmetry are the least severe. Thus, within a given industry where venture capitalists would be expected to operate, we would expect venture capitalists to favor firms with some track record over pure start-ups. Note that point 1 compares investment choices across investors while this point considers venture capitalists' choices across investment opportunities. Venture capitalists perceive informational asymmetries as costly, but they perceive them as less problematic to deal with than do other investors.

If informational asymmetries are present, the ability of a venture capitalist to exit may be impaired. Venture capitalists might wish to sell off their share in the venture after it "goes public" on a stock exchange. If, however, these investments are made in situations where informational asymmetries are important, it may be difficult to sell shares in a public market where most investors are relatively uninformed. Many "exits" may thus take place through sales to informed investors, such as other firms in the same industry as the venture, or to the venture's own management or owners. Venture capitalists might also try to acquire reputations for only presenting good-quality ventures in public offerings (but this argument draws on a multiperiod scenario and would therefore require an extension of our model). All this implies that the exits that do occur in initial public offerings are drawn from the better-performing ventures.[6]

The model implies that dR/de $(=R_e a) > 0$ and $de/da < 0$. These two properties together imply that $dR/da < 0$. Other things being equal, we expect entrepreneurial firms in which venture capitalists own a large share to generate lower net returns due to the moral-hazard problem. Higher values of a reduce the incentives of the entrepreneur to provide effort. Nonetheless, it might still be optimal in a given situation for the venture capitalist to take a high ownership share, as this might be the only way to get sufficient financial capital into the firm. However, we would still expect a negative correlation between the venture capital ownership share and firm performance.

The model also suggests a negative relationship between R and a for another reason. Recall that the selection constraint for investors is that $aR \geq (1 + r)I$ or $R \geq (1 + r)I/a$. If the venture capital market were competitive to the degree that investors earned no rents, then this selection constraint would hold with equality and there would be an exact negative relationship between expected net operating revenues and a, whether or not moral hazard was present. Even if venture capitalists expect some rents, this selection constraint will still rule out combinations of low a and low R, which will tend to induce a negative correlation between R and a. For a given investment I, investors will need to be compensated by a large ownership share a if the expected net operating revenues are relatively low.

The Data Set

As indicated in the introduction, the data used for this study were derived from two surveys conducted by Macdonald & Associates. Because of the confidentiality of the data, we do not report or discuss any firm-specific information. The first Macdonald & Associates survey, referred to as the "investment survey," began as an annual survey in 1991 and became quarterly in 1994. It asks approximately 110 Canadian venture capital firms (as of 1997) and other Canadian venture capital providers (such as corporations, institutional investors and even some private individuals) to identify the firms in which they invest (i.e., their investees) and to provide some investment information for each investee. The investment survey asks, for example, about the amount and stage of each investment and about the venture capitalist's ultimate divestiture of its holdings in each investee. An "investment record" refers to information about an investment made by a particular venture capitalist in a particular investee company at a particular point in time. The information from the investment survey covers the period from 1991 through the first quarter of 1998. It comprises 4,280 records on 1,859 investee companies. Macdonald & Associates estimate that 90 to 95 percent of the underlying population of Canadian firms supported by Canadian venture capitalists are captured by the survey. The response rate to the 1997 survey, for example, was 97 percent.

The second survey, referred to as the "economic impact" survey, is an annual survey that began in 1993. This survey asks Canadian venture capital providers for economic impact information (e.g., balance sheet and income statement information, including revenues and taxes paid, information on the structure and amount of employment and information on industry affiliation) about the investees identified in the investment survey that received an investment in or after 1991. Retrospective information was also requested, although in many cases limited retrospective information was provided. The database does, however, contain economic information on a reasonable number of investees going back as far as 1987. The data set thus contains a series of "life histories" for firms backed by venture capital.

The information from the economic impact survey covers the period from 1987 through 1996. A "financial record" refers to information for one particular investee firm for one particular year. There are 825 investee firms in the data available from the economic impact survey, but information on thirty-six firms is significantly incomplete. The remaining 789 firms provide 2,746 reasonably complete financial records. We therefore have an average of just under four financial records for each firm.

The response rate for each year of the economic impact survey over its five-year span has varied between 56 and 74 percent.[7] If the investment survey identifies 90 to 95 percent of the relevant underlying population, then the effective sample coverage of the economic impact survey is between 50 and 70 percent of the underlying population.

This data set targets Canadian investees supported by the Canadian venture capital industry. A Canadian entrepreneurial company that received support from American or Asian-based venture capitalists but no support from Canadian venture capitalists would thus not be included in our data set. It seems unlikely that this omission in the data would bias our analyses.

The coverage by this data set of the target population is comprehensive, partly due to the efforts and reputation of Macdonald & Associates and, for the economic impact survey, partly because of the sponsorship and influence of the Business Development Bank of Canada. The data set has a significant time-series dimension, which allows us to investigate age effects, business cycle effects, and other dynamic considerations of firms over time. It also contains information on revenues, employees, and taxes paid. Thus, the quality of the information used to measure success is unusually high. For an earlier description and analysis of the same data set, see Amit et al. (1997).

A Statistical Overview of Venture Capital Backed Firms and Investments

We next consider general aspects of the data. The summary statements apply to either the subset of the 825 companies in the economic impact database or to the subset of the 1,859 companies in the investment database for whom we have the relevant information. We then provide some descriptive statistics and a preliminary econometric analysis to demonstrate that the data are consistent with our theory.

Table 13.1 provides summary financial information for the economic impact data set. This table shows that the data are skewed; there are a few large investees that make the averages much larger than the medians. It also indicates that, on average, venture capitalists hold a (minority) share of 35 percent ownership in their investee firms. The data in table 13.1 also imply that firms in the data set spend, on average, about 4.5 percent of their revenues on R&D. This is slightly higher than the overall ratio of R&D spending to revenues for the Canadian economy as a whole. Average revenues per

TABLE 13.1 Summary financial data, 1987–1996 (in real C$ 1996)

	Mean ($000s)	Median) ($000s)	Standard deviation	No. of records
Total assets	18,671	5,002	56,859	2,587
Total equity	7,997	1,784	23,710	2,570
VC-share of equity (%)	35	31	28	1,886
Retained earnings	318	56	10,483	2,313
Total fixed assets	10,223	1,853	48,118	1,855
Long-term debt	5,305	826	22,376	2,393
Revenue	21,367	4,852	55,775	2,645
Investments in plant, property and equipment	1,761	253	6,993	2,177
R&D expenditures	954	132	2,373	2,002
Taxes paid	396	10	1,206	2,096
No. of Canadian employees	130	40	292	274

N = 789 firms (some firms fail to report the information for some variables).

Source: Macdonald & Associates Ltd. Economic Impact Database

TABLE 13.2 Employment in venture-backed firms: levels and annual growth

Year	Average employees	Median employees	Aggregate growth of continuing firms (%)	Median growth per firm (%)	No. of firms (total for the year/ continuing from previous years)
1987	176	105	NA	NA	24/NA
1988	120	50	4	1	51/22
1989	148	49	10	4	108/51
1990	163	45	13	4	163/108
1991	150	45	3	0	237/160
1992	146	42	10	5	299/232
1993	150	45	12	14	339/246
1994	141	45	22	14	476/322
1995	106	42	8	12	565/389
1996	94	35	17	4	450/380

Source: Macdonald & Associates Ltd. Economic Impact Database

Canadian employee are about C$164,400, and the average long-term debt-to-equity ratio is a conservative 0.66. This debt–equity ratio may reflect the limited borrowing capacity of entrepreneurial firms. We note also that the average investee is profitable enough to pay nontrivial amounts of tax.

Table 13.2 shows aggregate employment information from the economic impact data set. Average employee numbers were relatively similar from 1989 to 1994. (Data for the years 1987 and 1988 were based on a small and perhaps unrepresentative group of firms, reflecting the fact that only firms that received new venture capital infusions after 1990 are in the data set.) However, average employee levels dropped significantly (by about one-third) in 1995 and 1996 compared with previous years. This was probably due both to the exit of large firms and to the entry of many small ventures. Indeed, the numbers in column 6 point to increased entry and exit activity in 1995 and 1996. Increased exit of large firms may have been induced by favorable capital market conditions in the mid-1990s. On the other hand, an abundance of capital for investment ("too much money chasing too few deals") may have forced venture capitalists to invest in earlier stages, that is, in smaller companies.

Of considerable interest are the indicators of growth provided in table 13.2. Consider, for example, the aggregate annual growth rate of continuing firms in 1994, as shown in column 4. There were 322 firms in the data that were present in both 1993 and 1994 (see column 6). Total employment in this group of 322 firms rose by 22 percent between 1993 and 1994. We might then say that the "representative" venture-backed firm grew by 22 percent over the year. We can also see that – with the exception of 1993 and 1995 – the median growth rate is consistently and significantly less than the aggregate growth rate. This reflects the fact that in any given year, most firms grow modestly, but a few firms grow substantially. This is analogous to the music business or the movie business where a few "hits" account for most of the profits.

Note that omitting exiting firms from growth-rate calculations is unlikely to bias the growth rates upward. Investees may leave the sample because they are unsuccessful (bankrupt), but more commonly they leave because they are successful enough for the venture capitalist to sell out at a profit (following, for example, an initial public offering). In fact, if we considered the employment growth of all investee firms, including those that left the sample, for a particular year, the growth rate might well be higher than that reported in table 13.2.

The next few tables and figures contain information about the structure of venture capital investment. In a given investment "round," an investee may receive money from more than one venture capitalist. This is referred to as "syndication." We refer to an infusion of capital (from one or more venture capitalists) in a given investment round as an investment "package." Between 1991 and the first quarter of 1998, 1,859 investees received 3,075 investment packages in total. Approximately 74 percent were stand-alone investments. Only about 26 percent of investment packages were syndicated across two or more venture capitalists. This contrasts with the United States, where Lerner (1994b) reports that about two-thirds of first-round investments in a sample of biotechnology firms were syndicated. (In our data, 1,219 out of 1,605 first-round investments across all industries were not syndicated.)

Now let us turn to data that we believe support our theory. Table 13.3 shows the industry breakdown of venture capital investment. As can be seen from table 13.3, venture capital is more heavily represented in biomedical areas, computers and communications than would be implied by the overall output shares of these industries in the economy as a whole. Venture capital has a slightly smaller share of manufacturing and industrial equipment than does the economy as a whole and a much lower share of "consumer-related" and "miscellaneous" industries. These categories comprise the retail sector and various services. This picture is even more pronounced when only early-stage venture capital investments are considered. It seems evident that the industries in which venture capitalists concentrate on are those in which informational asymmetries are the most severe. Venture capitalists may invest relatively heavily in high-technology industries for reasons unrelated to information. For example, the high-technology sector may simply have a disproportionately large number of new investment opportunities. It is a growth sector and as such will have high levels of new investment from most financial intermediaries, including venture capitalists. Even so, venture capitalists have a heavier relative investment in high-technology industries than do other financial intermediaries, and informational reasons offer a plausible explanation for this. Table 13.3 is thus consistent with the first of our theoretical implications.

Another noteworthy feature of the data is that the companies in the data set are somewhat older than might be expected. As table 13.4 shows, 9 percent of the 806 companies for whom information on age is available were founded before 1974. As the data set is limited to firms that received at least one infusion of venture capital in 1991 or later, some firms must have obtained venture capital financing long after they were founded. This information may also imply that it takes longer than is commonly perceived, and perhaps more venture capital than originally anticipated, to bring some investee firms to the stage at which exit is feasible. The data also suggest that venture capital focuses on the expansion of existing small companies rather than on the start-up phase of new firms. This is consistent with the second implication of the information-

TABLE 13.3 Industry classification

	Early stage investment[a] (no. of investees)	Total investment (no. of investees)	% of early investment	% of total investment	% of total output 1996
Biotechnology	363 (119)	491.6 (125)	23	10	0
Computer (hardware and software)	210 (203)	979.5 (358)	14	19	3
Medical/health	204.2 (70)	457.5 (97)	13	9	3
Manufacturing and industrial equipment	190.3 (138)	887 (405)	12	18	24
Miscellaneous	192.9 (112)	768.9 (309)	12	15	34
Communications	146.8 (59)	460.1 (121)	9	9	5
Energy/environmental technology	99.1 (61)	206.9 (98)	6	4	4
Consumer-related	74.8 (45)	457.6 (181)	5	9	26
Electrical components and instruments	69.7 (72)	315.3 (142)	4	6	2
Total	1550.8	5024.4	98	99[b]	101[b]

[a] In C$ mill of 1997; [b] Due to rounding

Sources: Macdonald & Associates Ltd. Investment Database. Output shares are based on estimates from Statistics Canada "Gross Domestic Product by Industry," 1996, cat. no. 15–001–XPB.

TABLE 13.4 Age of venture-backed companies

Year founded	Number of companies	% of total
1994–7	171	21
1989–93	255	32
1984–8	164	20
1974–83	142	18
Before 1974	74	9
Total	806	100

Source: Macdonald & Associates Ltd. Economic Impact Database

TABLE 13.5 Number of investments by stage and year

| | Early | | | Late | | | | | |
	SE	ST	ES	EX	AC	TU	WC	OT	Total
1991	3	100	—	86	12	22	—	36	259
1992	15	114	—	66	23	41	2	50	311
1993	5	116	—	126	18	24	25	36	350
1994	3	130	11	206	12	23	—	15	400
1995	11	128	112	242	11	21	2	44	571
1996	31	164	147	397	23	68	—	28	858
1997	29	245	335	559	39	74	—	72	1393
1998(Q1)	17	25	58	26	2	1	2	4	135
TOTAL	114	1,022	663	1,748	140	274	31	285	4,277

SE = seed, ST = start-up, ES = early stage investments, EX = expansion, AC = acquisition, TU = turnaround, WC = working capital, and OT = other.

Source: Macdonald & Associates Ltd. Investment Database

based theory developed in the next section that venture capitalists prefer to invest in firms where the adverse selection and moral-hazard problems are the least severe.

Table 13.5 shows how many investments correspond to each stage in the entrepreneurial firm's life. As already noted, a given investee may obtain financing from multiple venture capitalists and may receive multiple rounds of investment from a given venture capitalist. Each investment is recorded separately. An investment may include debt, equity, or both.

More than half of the "other" investments were management buyouts, in which an investee obtained investments from a venture capitalist to aid in buying out other investors in the company, including (quite possibly) other venture capitalists. As can be seen from this table, about 60 percent (2,578 out of 4,277) of the investments are "late-stage" investments. This is consistent with the implication of table 13.4 that most investees are fairly mature.

Table 13.6 shows investment size by stage. The early-stage average is almost C$900 thousand per investment, while the late-stage average is C$1.4 million. Combining the fact that early-stage investments are both smaller (table 13.6) and less numerous (table 13.5) than late-stage investments, we can again infer that the venture capital industry focuses more on the growth and development of entrepreneurial firms than on start-up activity. Venture capitalists are thus able to focus on firms with a long enough track record to provide significant information about the underlying quality of the venture. Pure start-up activity is probably less attractive to venture capitalists than is later-stage investment because of the adverse selection and moral hazard problems associated with the former.

Putting together information from tables 13.5 and 13.6, we can infer that in 1997 Canadian venture capitalists made 1,393 financings of Canadian firms totaling more than C$1.7 billion.[8] By comparison, US venture capitalists invested U.S.$13.7 billion

TABLE 13.6 Average size of investment by stage and year (in 000s of real C\$ 1997)

	Early			Late					
	SE	*ST*	*ES*	*EX*	*AC*	*TU*	*WC*	*OT*	*Total*
1991	534	741	—	1,271	2,187	1,555	—	1,501	1,156
1992	968	657	—	1,182	1,381	676	517	1,593	989
1993	884	1,164	—	1,799	1,760	1,642	488	1,747	1,464
1994	448	707	901	1,294	2,467	1,605	—	2,454	1,183
1995	356	659	1,037	1,332	2,416	450	1,422	1,614	1,115
1996	467	783	1,078	1,513	2,642	956	—	1,931	1,261
1997	348	1,075	1,069	1,485	1,263	386	—	1,549	1,228
1998(Q1)	237	507	943	648	2,893	126	453	1,911	752
91–8(Q1)	477	846	1,052	1,436	1,869	881	548	1,676	1,198

SE = seed, ST = start-up, ES = early stage investments, EX = expansion, AC = acquisition, TU = turnaround, WC = working capital, and OT = other

Source: Macdonald & Associates Ltd. Investment Database

through 3,279 financings of 2,451 companies (Fineberg 1998). Given the relative size of the two economies, venture capital investment is of similar importance in both countries.

The data afford us the opportunity to explore exits by venture capitalists. An exit occurs when a venture capitalist either sells off or writes off its investment in an investee. Information on exits is available for 1992–7 and for the first quarter of 1998 (439 investee companies with 597 records).

Recall that from our theoretical model, we expect exit to be dominated by "insider" activity rather than by public offerings. Figure 13.2 shows the pattern of exits in the data and indicates that only about 15 percent of exits occur following initial public offerings (IPOs). About 11 percent are third-party acquisitions, often by a firm in the same industry as the venture. The largest category of exits is company buyouts (34 percent), in which the venture capitalist's holding is sold to officers or managers of the investee.

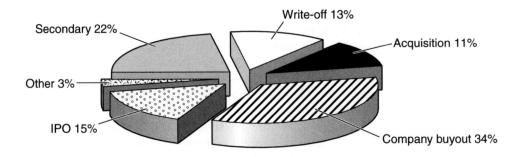

FIGURE 13.2 Distribution of venture capital exits (% of exits)
Source: Macdonald & Associates Ltd. Investment Database

TABLE 13.7 Estimated annual returns by exit type

	% Mean of individual annual returns[a]	% Standard deviation of individual returns	Number of observations	% Annual return of some of investments[b]
IPO	50	79	63	33
Acquisition	48	89	50	16
Secondary purchase	43	86	104	23
Company buyout	10	72	123	4
Write-off	100% loss over holding period	NA	51	100% loss over holding period
Other	8	26	4	7

[a] Individual annual returns are calculated as:
(proceeds from investment/cost of investment)^(1/holding period) − 1
[b] Real annual return of sum of investments is calculated as:
(sum of proceeds from investments/sum of cost of investments)^(1/average holding period) − 1
Source: Macdonald & Associates Ltd. Investment Database

Secondary purchases are purchases of the venture capitalist's holding by a third party in a private transaction that is not an overall acquisition. The "other" category consists of exits for which the exit mode was not identified; we believe that most of these are company buyouts. Approximately 13 percent of exits were in the "write-off" category. If informational asymmetries are important, this distribution is consistent with our theoretical model. (Note, however, that the small share of IPOs may also reflect a minimum scale necessary to sustain a public market in a stock.)

Our theoretical framework also suggests that IPOs would have high returns precisely because venture capitalists seek to reduce the adverse selection problem confronted by buyers of IPOs by "going public" only with relatively strong investee firms. The returns shown in table 13.7 are consistent with our expectations. IPOs are a relatively profitable form of exit. Acquisitions and secondary purchases are similarly profitable in the aggregate.

The final prediction of our model is that the venture capitalist's ownership share is negatively associated with the firm's performance. This derives both from moral hazard and from the venture capitalist's participation constraint that expected returns should at least equal the return from alternative investments. A negative correlation between a venture capitalist's ownership share (and a measure of firm performance could, however, arise from dilution in a multiperiod process (i.e., the possibility that low performance leads to high a). Unfortunately, we do not have adequate data (such as data on a venture capitalist's ownership share in the start-up phase) to correct for dilution.

Firm performance is difficult to measure directly, but taxes paid and revenues per unit asset are good proxies for measures of performance. Although we would like to use profit as a measure of success, this data is not available. However, profit is closely related to

TABLE 13.8 Effect of venture capital share on performance

Dependent variable	Explanatory variable	Coefficient	Standard error	t-statistic	P-value
Taxes paid	VC Share	−8.23	1.65	−4.99	0.000
	Log (age)	500	48.5	10.32	0.000
	Const.	−958	127.6	−7.51	0.000
Taxes paid/ assets (× 10,000)	VC share	−8.76	2.74	−3.2	0.001
	Log (age)	504	80.12	6.29	0.000
	Const.	−1493	211	−7.07	0.000
Revenues/assets	VC share	−2.05	3.54	−0.579	−0.262
	Log (age)	426	104	4.102	0.000
	Const.	899	264	3.45	0.000

Coefficient = estimate returned by the regression, VC share = ownership share of venture capitalist (% owned in a company), Log (age) = logarithm of age of investee firm, Const. = constant in the regression equation.

Source: Macdonald & Associates Ltd. Economic Impact Database

taxes paid, so taxes should be a good proxy for profit. We acknowledge that for emerging companies, taxes paid may be a poor predictor of their value-creation potential. Note that taxes are truncated from below at 0 (i.e., firms do not pay negative taxes no matter how poor their performance). We thus estimate the relationship between performance and ownership share by using a Tobit model rather than by ordinary least squares. Table 13.8 reports the results arising from regressing different measures of firm performance on the venture capital ownership share, correcting for age of the firm.

As can be seen from these regressions, a statistically strong negative relationship exists between the venture capitalist's ownership share and two of our three measures of firm performance. This could be the result of moral hazard or the result of the venture capitalist's self-selection constraint. It is also possible that ventures for which a is high, pay out more earnings to the venture capitalist and therefore have lower future earnings. However, normalizing for asset size should mitigate this concern.

We emphasize that the amount of variation explained by the venture capital share is low. Thus, while the coefficient on the venture capital share is significant in two out of three cases, variations in this share are, at most, a minor determinant of performance. It is also important that these results not be interpreted as suggesting that venture capital is a negative influence on firm performance. The negative correlation tells us only that the best performing companies tend to be those in which the venture capital ownership share is not too high. However, if financial requirements are high and the owner's resources are meager, then a substantial venture capital share might well be the best option, even if there is an associated moral-hazard problem, because the alternative might be outright failure of the company.

CONCLUSIONS AND FUTURE RESEARCH AGENDA

The theoretical framework we offer in this chapter views asymmetric information as the central feature of venture capital investment. Both major forms of asymmetric information, "hidden information" (leading to adverse selection) and "hidden action" (leading to moral hazard) are included in our analysis. While the model abstracts from some important elements of the venture investment process (such as bargaining and syndication),[9] we believe that our focus on informational issues in the venture capital investment process captures the essence of such investments.

The data set used in this study is the most comprehensive and detailed database on Canadian venture capital investments currently in existence. It provides up-to-date financial information about the investee firms and information about the decisions and practices of venture capital firms. Interestingly, the data are consistent with our theoretical structure. Moral hazard and adverse selection create market failures in entrepreneurial financing, which might lead many worthwhile projects to be unfunded or underfunded. Although venture capitalists cannot eliminate these problems, the more skilled they are in reducing these sources of market failures, the more effective this sector will function. Venture capitalists exist because they are better at this function than unspecialized investors. Furthermore, the data set indicates that these problems are more acute for younger firms and most acute for start-up firms. This might explain why venture capitalists tend more to focus on later stage entrepreneurial firms as these firms have a track record that provides information and have enough assets to reduce the problem associated with limited collateral under limited liability. By virtue of their expertise, venture capitalists are better at dealing with informational problems than other investors (on average), but this advantage is better applied to later-stage entrepreneurial firms rather than start-up firms.

This theoretical structure is also consistent with the pattern of exit in our data. If asymmetric information is important, and remains important even at the exit stage, then outside public investors will be in a disadvantaged position in valuing the assets of the entrepreneurial firm. Insiders will be in a better situation to buy out the venture capitalist's position. These insiders might be management or officers of the investee or other firms in a related business. It is thus not surprising that IPOs account for only a modest fraction of exits. In addition, the data corroborate the prediction of our model that there is a negative relationship between the share of venture capital ownership and firm performance.

We recognize that many aspects of venture capital activity have not been captured in our analysis. In particular, we abstract from the matching process of the entrepreneur and the venture capitalist, the process of bargaining between them to determine the price, and the milestone-based staged investment process, all of which are common features in venture capital finance and which can ameliorate problems caused by asymmetric information. It would be worthwhile to extend our model to reflect two-sided moral hazard (i.e., both the venture capitalist and the entrepreneur are faced with the "hidden action" problem) in a multiperiod setting with learning. Future theoretical research might also aim at developing models that simultaneously treat the moral-hazard and adverse-selection problems in multiperiod settings, and models that allow for more sophisticated contracting mechanisms and financial structures that permit both debt and equity.

In this chapter, we have focused exclusively on contracting between venture capitalist firms and entrepreneurs. However, examining situations involving multiple moral-hazard and adverse-selection relationships between investors, fund managers and owner-managers may be crucial for gaining a better understanding of private equity financing of entrepreneurial firms. For example, there may be a moral-hazard problem with a venture capitalist who, as an agent, allocates limited attention between evaluating new ventures and supervising current ventures. A similar problem exists in the relationship between the general partner of a venture capital fund and its limited partners. Gifford (1997) has shown that under such circumstances, the venture capitalist's allocation of time involves moral hazard but is socially efficient.

Relatively little is known about so-called "angel" investors (i.e., investors who use their own funds to provide equity finance to new ventures). The data problems mentioned in the introduction are exacerbated for these private investors. Research in venture capital still has a long way to go in understanding the role and the impact of angel investors. One task, for example, is to explain why they often invest at the seed stage of a venture. The challenge researchers face is to develop theoretical structures that can be subject to empirical validation. Ideally, such theories should also provide normative implications for practice. We hope this chapter is a useful step in this direction.

One of the biggest challenges for researchers of venture capital financing, however, is the development of a valuation model to price venture capital investments.[10] As there is no broadly accepted theoretical tool to price investments, parties often disagree on both the valuation method and the assumptions used in a particular circumstance. This hinders the completion of many potential investments, especially in the early stages of knowledge-based firms before there is any track record, tangible assets or revenues. Research into this important aspect of financing new ventures holds enormous promise.

Notes

We gratefully acknowledge financial support from SSHRC Grant 412–93–0005. We are indebted to Macdonald & Associates Ltd. for providing the data used in this chapter. The data were in anonymous form (i.e., without any company names) to protect the confidentiality of individual investors and investees.

1 Venture capitalists may provide equity, debt or combinations of debt and equity. In addition, they often provide managerial advice to their investees. The other main sources of entrepreneurial finance include bank loans, equity provided personally by the entrepreneur and financing from other firms (including suppliers or customers), government grants and family and friends.

2 This influence is explicitly modeled by Amit et al. (1994).

3 Steier and Greenwood (1995) used case studies to explore deal structuring and post-investment activities of venture capitalists. They found, among other things, that relationships supersede

business plans in securing financial resources. This illustrates the importance of informational issues in venture capital contracting.

4 This section draws on and summarizes Amit et al. (1998), to which the interested reader may refer for more details.

5 The results in this section are based on the assumption of linear contracts. Non-linearities, such as buyback options for entrepreneurs, are not considered here but might be useful in mitigating some of the addressed informational problems.

6 Empirical work by Barry et al. (1990), Megginson and Weiss (1991), Gompers (1995) and Gompers and Lerner (1995) is consistent with the idea that the reputation of venture capitalists is important at the IPO stage.

7 A recent economic impact survey, for example, which was conducted in 1997 (but which asked for 1996 data) had a response rate of 61 percent

8 Macdonald & Associates reports that the total amount invested in 1997 was C$1.82 billion. The discrepancy emerges from the fact that we account for only Canadian investments in Canadian firms, while Macdonald & Associates also reports on some foreign investments in Canadian firms which amounted to about C$100 million in 1997.

9 In particular, the model does not deal with the risk-sharing motive for venture capital investment, nor does it deal with the dynamics or staged structure of venture capital investment. It also does not address the role of gradual learning about project quality.

10 Gompers and Lerner (1997) have provided a first attempt at addressing the question of how private equity investments are valued. They used a hedonic regression approach to show that growth in the money committed to venture capital funds increases the price paid by venture investors.

REFERENCES

Admati, A. and Pfleiderer, P. 1994. Robust Financial Contracting and the Role of Venture Capitalists, *Journal of Finance* 49: 371–402.

Akerlof, G. 1970. The Market for Lemons: Quality Uncertainty and the Market Mechanism, *Quarterly Journal of Economics* 84: 488–500.

Amit, R., Glosten, L. and Muller, E. 1990. Entrepreneurial Ability, Venture Investments, and Risk Sharing, *Management Science* 36: 1232–45.

Amit, R., Glosten, L. and Muller, E. 1993. Challenges to Theory Development in Entrepreneurship Research, *Journal of Management Studies* 30: 815–34.

Amit, R., Glosten, L. and Muller, E. 1994. *Venture Capital Regimes and Entrepreneurial Ability.* University of British Columbia Working Paper.

Amit, R., Brander, J. and Zott, C. 1997. Venture Capital Financing of Entrepreneurship in Canada. In: P. Halpern (ed.), *Capital Market Issues in Canada.* Ottawa: Industry Canada.

Amit R., Brander, J. and Zott, C. 1998. Why Do Venture Capital Firms Exist? Theory and Canadian Evidence, *Journal of Business Venturing* 13: 441–66.

Arrow, K. 1973. *The Limits of Organization.* New York: Norton.

Barry, C. 1994. New Directions in Research on Venture Capital Firms, *Financial Management* 23: 3–15.

Barry, C., Muscarella, C., Peavy, J. and Vetsuypens, M. 1990. The Role of Venture Capital in the Creation of Public Companies, *Journal of Financial Economics* 27: 447–71.

Bergemann, D. and Hege, U. 1998. Venture Capital Financing, Moral Hazard, and Learning, *Journal of Banking and Finance* 22: 703–35.

Brander, J., Amit, R. and Antweiler, W. 1997. *Venture Capital Syndication: Improved Venture Selection versus the Value-Added Hypothesis.* University of British Columbia Working Paper.

Chan, Y. 1983. On the Positive Role of Financial Intermediation in Allocations of Venture Capital in a Market with Imperfect Information, *Journal of Finance* 38: 1543–61.

Chan, Y., Siegel, D. and Thakor, A. 1990. Learning, Corporate Control and Performance Requirements in Venture Capital Contracts, *International Economic Review* 31: 365–81.

Fineberg, S. 1998. Venture Capital Financings Reach Another High, *Venture Capital Journal* 38(7): 37–43.

Fried, V. and Hisrich, R. 1994. Toward a Model of Venture Capital Investment Decision Making, *Financial Management* 23: 28–37.

Gifford, S. 1997. Limited Attention and the Role of the Venture Capitalist, *Journal of Business Venturing* 12: 459–82.

Gompers, P. 1995. Optimal Investment, Monitoring, and the Staging of Venture Capital, *Journal of Finance* 50: 1461–89.

Gompers, P. and Lerner, J. 1995. *Venture Capital Distributions: Short-run and Long-run Reactions.* Harvard Business School Working Paper.

Gompers, P. and Lerner, J. 1997. *The Valuation of Private Equity Investments.* Harvard Business School Working Paper.

Gorman, M. and Sahlman, W.A. 1989. What Do Venture Capitalists Do? *Journal of Business Venturing,* 4(4): 231–48.

Grossman, S. and Hart, O. 1983. An Analysis of the Principal–Agent Problem, *Econometrica* 51: 7–45.

Hellman, T. 1994. Financial Structure and Control in Venture Capital. Stanford University Working Paper.

Hellman, T. 1998. The Allocation of Control Rights in Venture Capital Contracts, *Rand Journal of Economics* 29: 57–76.

Hirao, Y. 1993. Learning and Incentive Problems in Repeated Partnerships, *International Economic Review* 34: 101–19.

Holmstrom, B. 1979. Moral Hazard and Observability, *Bell Journal of Economics* 10: 74–91.

Jensen, M. and Meckling, W. 1976. Theory of the Firm: Managerial Behavior, Agency Costs, and Ownership Structure, *Journal of Financial Economics* 3: 305–60.

Kamien, M. 1994. Entrepreneurship: What Is It? *Business Week: Executive Briefing Service* 7.

Lerner, J. 1994a. Venture Capitalists and the Decision to go Public, *Journal of Financial Economics* 35: 293–316.

Lerner, J. 1994b. The Syndication of Venture Capital Investment, *Financial Management* 23: 16–27.

Lerner, J. 1995. Venture Capital and the Oversight of Private Firms, *Journal of Finance* 50: 301–18.

Low, M. and MacMillan, I. 1988. Entrepreneurship: Past Research and Future Challenges, *Journal of Management* 14: 139–61.

Macdonald & Associates Ltd. 1994–1998 (annual). *Venture Capital in Canada: Annual Statistical Review and Directory.* Toronto: Association of Canadian Venture Capital Companies.

MacMillan, I., Siegel, R. and SubbaNarasimha, P. 1985. Criteria Used by Venture Capitalists to Evaluate New Venture Proposals, *Journal of Business Venturing* 1: 119–28.

MacMillan, I., Zemann, L. and SubbaNarasimha, P. 1987. Criteria Distinguishing Successful from Unsuccessful Ventures in the Venture Screening Process, *Journal of Business Venturing* 2: 123–37.

Megginson, W. and Weise, K. 1991. Venture Capital Certification in Initial Public Offerings, *Journal of Finance* 46(3): 879–903.

Pauly, M. 1974. Overinsurance and Public Provision of Insurance: the Roles of Moral Hazard and Adverse Selection, *Quarterly Journal of Economics* 88: 44–54.

Rothschild, M. and Stiglitz, J. 1976. Equilibrium in Competitive Insurance Markets: an Essay on the Economics of Imperfect Information, *Quarterly Journal of Economics* 90: 629–49.

Sahlman, W. 1990. The Structure and Governance of Venture Capital Organizations, *Journal of Financial Economics* 27: 473–521.

Spence, M. 1973. Job Market Signalling, *Quarterly Journal of Economics* 87: 355–74.

Steier L. and Greenwood, R. 1995. Venture Capitalist Relationships in the Deal Structuring and Post-Investment Stages of New Firm Creation, *Journal of Management Studies* 32: 337–57.

Trester, J. 1998. Venture Capital Contracting under Asymmetric Information, *Journal of Banking and Finance* 22: 675–99.

Tyebjee, T. and Bruno, A. 1984. A Model of Venture Capital Investment Activity, *Management Science* 30: 1051–66.

Part IV

ACHIEVING GROWTH: INTERNAL AND EXTERNAL APPROACHES

Growth can occur as the result of a number of different actions. To many, growth is defined as an increase in the number and dollar amount of sales. To others, it is the result of selling new products to both new and existing customers. For others, it is an expansion of the sales territory from local to regional to national to international areas.

In this part we examine factors that enhance growth from both an internal, within the firm perspective, to external methods of growth. We also discuss methods of joining forces with others as an entry method or for expansion purposes. Davidsson in chapter 2 describes the processes in this section as being "organic" (growth from within the firm) and acquisitional (joining forces with others.)

This part includes an examination of the impact of the top management teams, "Entrepreneurial Teams and Venture Growth" by Birley and Stockley in chapter 14. Arbaugh and Camp in chapter 15 examine the problems and transitions that a firm experiences as it grows in "Managing Growth Transitions: Theoretical Perspectives and Research Directions." Autio in chapter 16 examines the "Growth of Technology-based New Firms" and provides an overview of the research tradition on these firms that seem to outpace many others. In chapter 17, Cooper and Folta also examine high-technology firms and addresses the issues of why they start where they do and how location makes a difference in the growth and success in their chapter entitled "Entrepreneurship and High-technology Clusters." Johannisson examines how an entrepreneurs friends and friends' friends can provide a network of contacts and information about markets, products, etc., in "Networking and Entrepreneurial Growth" in chapter 18. Weaver in "Strategic Alliances as Vehicles for International Growth" shares his experiences in strategic alliances in a number of different countries in chapter 19. Finally, Hoy, Stanworth and Purdy in chapter 20 examine the phenomenon of franchising and franchising research in "An Entrepreneurial Slant to Franchise Research." Finally Landstrom and Sexton identify the remaining issues and suggestions for further research in chapter 21.

Entrepreneurs and small business owners often have different attitudes toward growth. However, for those that are willing to share ownership in the firm to attract a top management team or the financing required for growth, there are a number of options by which they can grow their companies.

Birley and Stockley remind us that the success of an entrepreneurial venture depends not on a single person, but a team of people. They also note:

- The mixed results of research on the impact of management teams on growth is, in part, due to the inconsistent measures of organizational growth being used.
- What constitutes a strategic or entrepreneurial team has not been adequately defined.
- The competencies and behaviors required of the founding team are likely to change and require augmentation as the firm emerges and grows.
- Our knowledge of how entrepreneurial teams impact growth is incomplete, and much of the dialogue is confused and theoretically incoherent.
- The processes through which team composition impacts performance are not fully understood because of the practical obstacles to conducting research of this nature.

Arbaugh and Camp suggest that managing growth transitions still remains a relatively unresearched topic, even though growth is a primary factor in entrepreneurship. They also suggest:

- The resource and knowledge-based views of the firm may be helpful in explaining how and why growth transitions take place.
- Successful transitions occur when the firm simultaneously builds the resource base to manage their present development and prepare for the next one.
- Transitions do not occur in all areas of operations simultaneously. Some areas move faster than others.
- When a firm's growth reaches a transition point, and the transition problem is not addressed, further growth is hindered.
- Often times, day-to-day problems preclude a step aside to look at critical problems of the time.

Autio draws on Schumpeter's new innovation concept as the driving force of economic change and growth. He notes:

- Technology-based firms, by virtue of their technology intensity, tend to inhabit new industry sectors in which rapid growth tends to be common.
- Grouping firms as technology-based poses a problem for researchers.
- The normal emphasis is on the growth of the firm but in the high-tech area the system of firms is the topic.
- Development of a new technology can result in growth for the firm and also in the firms that use the technology.
- Research on high-technology firms is, in reality, research that examines technological systems.

Cooper and Folta also examine issues related to new technically oriented firms. Their emphasis is on why these firms start operations where they do and how location makes a difference. They hypothesize that:

- Concentrations of higher-tech firms in a number of areas suggest that there are benefits from close geographic proximity.
- Location does make a difference, both in influencing the foundation of new firms and in their subsequent performance.
- While the generalities of cluster locations have been established, many research questions need to be addressed to add to the understanding of clusters and their importance.
- It is interesting to note that geography has re-emerged as important at a time when instantaneous global communication is possible.

Johannisson, continuing with the topic of growth, examines the impact of networking on entrepreneurial growth. He concludes:

- Due to the liability of newness, including lacking legitimacy on the market, prospective entrepreneurs need to mobilize social networks in addition to those assets controlled by ownership.
- Networking enforces identify and builds general support, which provides cultural and emotional capital.
- The birth of a venture may be seen as the institutionalization of a part of the entrepreneur's personal network into a venture.
- Networking is used not only to enact the original firm but to recraft it according to changed intentions, business settings or both.

Weaver addresses the concept of cooperative arrangements or strategic alliances for achieving growth. He states:

- Strategic alliances are cooperative interfirm activities that range from informal sharing of information to joint ventures.
- The growth in technology has led to alliances being received as a device for technology leveraging.
- Eastern Europe is a region in which alliances have enhanced growth and increased international expansion.

- Trust, commitment, shared communication and the use of complementary skills are key benefits of alliances.
- Cultural clashes and management conflicts result when managers underestimate the complexities of managing the alliance.

Hoy, Stanworth and Purdy, following Weaver's discussion, suggest that franchising can be explained in the context of strategic alliances. They also note:

- The recent downsizing by large firms has created opportunities for smaller enterprises and left many former qualified employees searching for carrier opportunities.
- Franchising is not a recent phenomenon. The first franchise in the United States was a distribution system created by the Singer Sewing Machine Company shortly after the Civil War. General Motors began franchising in 1898.
- Sales through franchised outlets account for about 35 percent of all retail sales.
- Franchising has been a major factor in growth through international expansion.

Growth occurs in many different forms. It can be internal or external, national or international, and at various levels of involvement. The recent expansion of the globalized market has provided the opportunity for cooperative arrangements for firms throughout the world and provided employment opportunities in areas where few existed.

Growth is the essence of entrepreneurship. It is the recognition and pursuance of opportunities. In this part we examine some of the approaches entrepreneurs have used to prepare their organizations to pursue growth opportunities.

14

Entrepreneurial Teams and Venture Growth

Sue Birley and Simon Stockley

The question of company growth, particularly the impact of the entrepreneurial team on growth, is central to the study of the entrepreneurial phenomenon. One would normally approach this chapter with a discussion of growth and the problems that the entrepreneurial team faces in attempting to take the actions necessary to accomplish its growth objectives, but the theoretical and methodological issues of growth are addressed in chapter 2 in this book. Therefore, we address here the issues related to the actions of the entrepreneurial team in achieving the desired growth. An assumption behind this approach is that if the new business is to grow at the desired rate, the entrepreneur is unlikely to be able to manage the process alone – the team must be in place at the start. This argument is both appealing and intuitively obvious. A question we will explore is how it works. So, what do we know about the impact of the management team upon the process of growth in the entrepreneurial venture?

PENROSIAN GROWTH: A RESOURCE-BASED PERSPECTIVE

A number of growth models have been developed to explain the growth process. However, the theory most applicable to the impact of entrepreneurial teams on venture growth was developed by Penrose (1959) who suggested that growth of the firm is willed by those who make the decisions of the firm, in other words, the entrepreneurial team.

Penrose (1959) proposed that firm growth was constrained by the availability and quality of managerial resources, and in doing so, she laid many of the foundations for the newly popular resource-based view of the firm (Barney 1991; Wernerfelt 1984) She saw the firm as a collection of physical and human resources whose complementary productive services are made cohesive by, and thereby specific to, the firm's "coherent administrative organisation." To Penrose, a theory of growth was essentially an examination of the changing productive opportunities of the firm. These opportunities are expanded by newly added possibilities for growth only to the extent that the firm's administrative organization perceives these opportunities and is motivated to pursue them. That is, each firm's productive opportunity is restricted to those possibilities for productive resource deployment that its entrepreneurs and managers can see and are willing and able to act on (Penrose 1959: 32). Thus, the perception of new opportunities depends on the quality of *entrepreneurial judgment* within the organization.

To Penrose, two factors that most affect a firm's productive opportunity are the quality of inherited resources and the coherency of its administrative organization. Inherited resources include the firm's management team and its stock of capabilities or routines that constrain (or even specify) what the firm is able to do (Goshal et al. 1997). Thus, administrative coherency is essential for the productive deployment of the firm's resource base. As firms grow, the accumulated stock of resources begins to tax the capacity of the firm's existing managerial resources to maintain the coherency of the organization. Thus, in her revised edition Penrose (1995: xvii) notes that with increasing size both the managerial function and the basic administrative structure of firms undergo an administrative reorganization in order to enable them to deal with increasing growth. This administrative re-organization is neither automatic nor assured but is necessary for growth to occur or, indeed, for a firm to retain its size in any dynamic environment. In other words, the nature and composition of the management team may need to change as the needs of the organization change.[1]

PENROSE AND SCHUMPETER THEORY INTEGRATION

Goshal et al. (1997) reconcile Penrose's approach with Langlois's (1995) concept of "Schumpeterian integration," a term used to describe the entrepreneurial process of "carrying out new combinations" in organizations or a substitution of the current organizational context by a new one that accommodates the firm's entrepreneurial judgment to exploit an expanding set of productive possibilities. Thus, Covin and Slevin (1997) argue that the ability of the entrepreneurial team to manage the process of Schumpeterian integration or successive high-growth transitions is central to understanding the impact of teams on growth. They view the organizational problems identified by the stage models as contributing to an increase in complexity as the firm grows. This complexity has to be managed if the firm is to control its operations or, as Penrose might have put it, maintain its administrative coherency. This complexity provides another insight into why entrepreneurial teams may be a necessary, but not sufficient, determinant of growth in high-potential ventures. Fortunately, the field of entrepreneurship need not reinvent the wheel when considering how complexity may be managed. An extensive and mature body of literature on the topic exists in the field of operational research (e.g., Ashby 1956; Espejo and Harnden 1989). Although the need for brevity precludes a discussion of this literature, we would nevertheless draw the reader's attention to Ashby's (1956) law of requisite variety, which states that the variety (complexity) faced by an organization or system can only be controlled by a system (e.g., management within a coherent administrative framework) of at least equivalent variety. Thus, in high-potential ventures, the presence of an entrepreneurial team might be viewed as necessary from the outset to allow the greater complexity inherent in these ventures to be managed.

GROWTH THROUGH NETWORKS AND ALLIANCES

The theories considered thus far largely view growth as a process by which resources are internalized and controlled by the organization's management. In this respect they relate mostly to what Stevenson (1997) refers to as "administrative behaviour" rather than to "entrepreneurial behaviour." To Stevenson, the essence of entrepreneurship is the pursuit of opportunity without regard to resources currently controlled: a concept that reminds us that growth frequently occurs through the coordination of resources neither owned, nor indeed managed, by the firm. Examples of this type of behavior include growth through networks, strategic alliances and constellations (Forrest 1990; Lorenzoni and Ornati 1988; Shepard 1991; Jarillo 1988; Larson 1992) facilitated by the presence of an entrepreneurial team that may expand the organization's network of contacts and provide the balance of expertise required to profit from certain types of cooperative activity (McGee et al. 1995).

DEFINING THE TEAM

The inevitable conclusion from the above review is that the impact of the management team on company growth is a dynamic and highly contingent concept. However, it begs the question of the definition of the team. As Cooper and Daily (1997) note, the question of what constitutes a strategic or entrepreneurial team is far from clear:

- Eisenhardt and Schoonhoven (1990) define top management team members as founders if they worked in full-time executive positions when the firm was founded.
- Kamm et al. (1989, 1993) consider two or more people who are involved in pre-start-up activities and who formally establish and share ownership of their new organization.
- Watson et al. (1995) define venture teams as two or more individuals who jointly found a business and who are still involved in operating it jointly.

- Katzenbach (1997: 84) says, "A *real* team [is] a small number of people with complementary skills who are committed to a common purpose, performance goals, and an approach for which they hold themselves mutually accountable" (italics added).
- Weinzimmer (1997) suggests that the inclusion of the term "strategic teams" broadens the scope to include established firms acting in an entrepreneurial manner in the pursuit of growth.
- Cooper and Daily (1997) report that the question has been dealt with most commonly by asking the president who he or she considers to be the *founders* of the venture.

What is clear from the above sample of definitions is that the base can vary and may include ownership of equity, full and/or part-time managerial involvement, position within the hierarchy or some measure of commitment or purpose. What is also clear is that any of the above may be appropriate, according to the research focus. Unfortunately, this issue is often neglected in published papers, making comparison of results very difficult.

Growth and the Entrepreneurial Team

The above difficulties are confounded by the fact that the competencies and behaviors required of the founding team are likely to change and necessitate augmentation as the firm "emerges" and grows (Gartner et al. 1992). Consequently, at any point in time, there is likely to be a mismatch between the competencies required by the firm and those possessed by the team. Thus, team membership is likely to vary over time (Virany and Tushman 1986).

In any new venture, the managerial team is a repository for a range of entrepreneurial, managerial and technical competencies (Chandler and Jansen 1992) that manifest themselves as behaviors (Herron and Robinson 1993). These competencies, when combined with the other productive resources of the organization, form capabilities and "routines" that effectively define both what the firm is capable of doing (Nelson and Winter 1982; Goshal et al. 1997) and what it actually does – its strategy (Sandberg 1986). The capabilities of the team also affect the extent to which problems or barriers to growth can be avoided or overcome. However, the relative importance of specific capabilities are likely to shift over time but not always in a direction that is easy to predict (Miller and Friesen 1984; Teece et al. 1997). Thus, Penrose (1959) suggests that the extent to which these changing requirements present a problem to the firm depends, in the first instance, on the extent to which management already *possesses* the required competencies, recognizes this fact and has the motivation and capacity to deploy them in a new configuration. Weick (1977: 199) made essentially the same point.

The Impact of the Entrepreneurial Team

So far, we have argued that the team has an important impact on the growth of the firm. We now proceed to examine the exact nature of the impact – those variables that explain why individuals and groups behave as they do (Hambrick and Mason 1984) and that are especially relevant to the emergence and growth of the firm (Gartner et al. 1992). However, let's first consider the current state of the literature.

Although mainstream entrepreneurship journals are far from replete with studies that investigate the impact of teams on growth, very extensive bodies of research in such fields as organizational behavior, strategic management and social psychology have examined relevant issues in some detail. Our experience suggests that the principal difficulties in conducting a coherent analysis of this literature are that:

- It is interdisciplinary in nature and highly fragmented.
- Ostensibly similar concepts are approached from multiple theoretical perspectives.
- The focus, unit and level of analysis vary widely between and within studies.
- Research questions frequently overlap.

Consequently, our knowledge of *how* entrepreneurial teams impact on growth is incomplete and much of the dialogue confused and theoretically incoherent. Thus, a real danger exists that entrepreneurship researchers will unwittingly reinvent the wheel when conducting research in this area.

FRAMEWORK FOR ANALYSIS

If we accept that it is behavior (specific observable actions or what people do) that *directly* affects performance (Weick 1979; Drucker 1985; Sandberg and Hofer 1987; Gartner 1988, 1989; Stevenson and Jarillo 1986), then an investigation of what determines and guides behavior is self-evidently important to our understanding of the relationship between entrepreneurial teams and growth. Here, however, we sound a word of caution in referring to Pfeffer's (1983: 350) argument that it is impossible for researchers to measure the effects of all possible behaviors and intervening process variables. His warning against "an infinite regress of reductionism from which there is no logical escape" appears well-placed.

The numerous difficulties in untangling and identifying the determinants of firm performance (Lenz 1981; Murray 1989) necessitate the adoption of an initial framework for analysis. Several such frameworks exist in the contemporary literature (Gartner 1985; Sandberg 1986; Herron and Robinson 1993; Naffziger et al. 1994) although it should be noted that these were developed primarily to explain the entrepreneurial performance of individuals rather than groups. The absence of agreement on which framework most adequately explains variance in performance (Cooper and Gimeno-Gascon 1992) forces us to make a choice and to make explicit the theoretical perspectives applied at each level of our analysis. The basic framework adopted for our analysis is that proposed by Herron and Robinson (1993: 281), who argue that empirical and theoretical understanding of the influence of the entrepreneur on new venture performance has long been stymied. Demographic studies of entrepreneurial traits or characteristics have also largely failed to demonstrate convincing links with performance (Begley and Boyd 1987). Clearly, in this instance, what can be said of the entrepreneur can also be said of the entrepreneurial team.

Herron and Robinson (1993) begin by discussing the relationship between personality traits and behavior and note that the field of psychology has long studied the predictive link between the two. Although the debate is complex, it does appear that the personality of an individual demonstrates remarkable longitudinal stability (Epstein and O'Brian 1985), and that, over time, it is reasonably predictive of behavior averaged over a sample of situations and/or occasions (Epstein 1979). Personality is not, however, a reliable predictor of single instances of behavior. Herron and Robinson hypothesize that the behaviors responsible for the short-term performance of ventures are insufficiently aggregated to be reliably predicted by personality traits, which may help to explain the failure of studies to demonstrate such links.

Using Hollenbeck and Whitener's (1988) model of job performance (which states that the effects of personality on performance are mediated by motivation and moderated by ability) as their starting point, Herron and Robinson (1993) develop a more detailed formulation that views behavior as a function of ability and personality (mediated by motivation) and states that the relationship between behavior and performance is moderated by the situational context (the organizational environment in which the behaviors take place). In other words, behavior is context-specific. The authors proceed to combine their model with that of new venture performance developed by Sandberg (1986). Sandberg's entrepreneurial characteristics are substituted by Herron and Robinson's new formulation. Once the causal antecedents of motivation and ability are added, the model illustrated in figure 14.1 emerges.

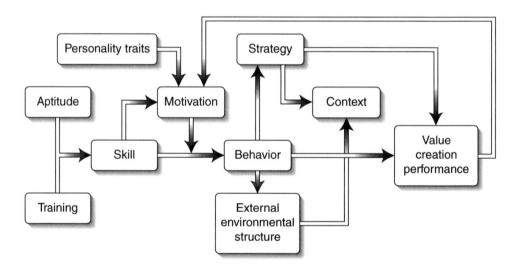

FIGURE 14.1 Behavior and performance as modified by the situational context
Source: Herron and Robinson (1993: 290)

While it would be possible to suggest some enhancements to the model as presented (behavior is surely influenced by context both directly and via motivation), its usefulness in framing a "team-based" research agenda is undoubted. When applied in this manner, the model makes it abundantly clear that an understanding of the relationships between individuals, groups and the environment are required to explain the maximum amount of variance in venture performance. However, as noted by Chandler and Hanks (1994), even relatively simple cross-level theories pose problems for researchers because relationships are often difficult to isolate and measure.

THE DEMOGRAPHIC APPROACH

Figure 14.1 clearly shows that behavior, and thus by implication group behavior, is critical to explaining performance. Unfortunately, our search of the literature failed to identify studies that directly monitored or measured entrepreneurial team behavior, much less its impact on performance. However, a number of studies and, indeed, entrepreneurial classifications have used demographic characteristics as a surrogate for skill. So, for example, an individual's age may be used to indicate experience or maturity; experience in the same industry may imply the presence of a wider range of useful contacts than may otherwise be the case. This focus upon skill is important, for as Herron and Robinson (1993: 291) inform us, "Both skills and behaviours are more proximal to VCP (value creation performance) than are personality traits."

The popularity of the demographic approach in team-based research owes much to development of the "upper-echelons" paradigm by Hambrick and Mason (1984; cf. Gupta 1984). The roots of this theory may be traced directly to Cyert and March's (1963) concept of the dominant coalition. Upper-echelons theory views organizational outcomes (strategies and performance) as a reflection of the values and cognitive bases of powerful actors in the organization (Hambrick and Mason 1984: 193). In doing so, it takes the view that top management has a powerful influence on performance outcomes. The underlying premise of the approach is that the personal experiences, values and likely behaviors of managers or entrepreneurs can be inferred from observable individual characteristics, such as years of experience, age and level of education.[2] The intuitive plausibility of the theory together with the ready availability of quantifiable data no doubt accounts for the popularity of demographic or bio-data studies.

Although upper-echelon theory implicitly acknowledges that behavioral processes form the link between demographic characteristics and performance, it largely treats these processes as a black box (Muzyka 1991; Jackson 1992). The need to open this box and study the underlying processes through which team demography affects organizational performance has been stressed by many scholars (Weick 1979; Sandberg and Hofer 1987; Gartner 1988; Herron and Robinson 1993), but to date, relatively few studies have attempted this (Smith et al. 1994). Consequently, the processes through which top management team[3] composition impacts performance are not yet fully understood, perhaps because of the many practical obstacles to conducting research of this nature (Jackson 1992: 348).[4] What is accepted, however, is that the previous experience of the team is considered an important determinant of performance (Chandler and Hanks 1991) since it demonstrates characteristics such as skill and aptitude (see figure 14.1). The issue for the researcher is, having arrived at some measure of the track record of individual members of the team, how do they combine to impact on performance?

Heterogeneity or homogeneity?

In the majority of studies that investigate the impact of teams on growth, most of which have been conducted in large, established organizations (Cooper and Daily 1997), the primary compositional dimension of interest has been the amount of variance among group members with respect to demographic and psychological characteristics. However, the choice of which aspects of composition to study is not as straightforward as it might first appear for, as Jackson (1992) observes, there is currently too little theory to guide researchers in predicting which particular inputs and outcomes are likely to be associated with each other and under what conditions. This situation may be attributed to the fact that most group or team-based research conducted over the last fifty years[5] has focused on processes and outcomes *within the boundaries of the group*: for example, consensus, conflict, problem-solving and decision-making (Ancona 1987). In entrepreneurship and strategic leadership research, the primary focus is the performance of the organization, a construct that is external to the leadership group and influenced by a wide range of factors outside the group's control. The link between group composition, group behavior and performance is therefore highly contingent and difficult to prove empirically (Smith et al. 1994). Reflecting on these difficulties, Hambrick (1992: 388) observed, "Improving our understanding of how team composition finds its way into strategic and performance outcomes is a research area of the highest priority for students of strategic leadership."

In a later study, Hambrick et al. (1996: 679) examine the influence of top management team heterogeneity on the competitive moves of thirty-two US airlines. Team heterogeneity was operationalized in terms of functional background, educational background and company tenure. They found that heterogeneity was positively related to a tendency to undertake competitive initiatives and to the magnitude of competitive actions. However, heterogeneous teams were slower in their action execution than their homogeneous counterparts, reflecting friction and slowness in decision-making and implementation. Interestingly, homogeneous teams were most likely to respond to their competitor's initiatives. The authors hypothesize that homogeneous teams, by virtue of smoother group processes, are better able to interpret competitors' moves and decide quickly on a countermove. Groups with shared experiences and perspectives, they argue, are the most able to react to clear-cut stimuli.

Intragroup process outcomes

The intragroup process outcomes most often studied with reference to variance in group composition have been cohesiveness and conflict. In turn, these outcomes have implications for downstream processes (e.g., decision speed, decision quality and task implementation) and ultimately performance. Further, conflict and cohesion may have an important bearing on survival factors, such as group stability or team break-up. Jackson (1992: 361) notes that group composition seems to play an important role in determining cohesiveness,[6] but that specifying the nature of that role has proved difficult:

> Whilst no clear conclusions can be drawn about the relationship between personality composition and cohesiveness, research relating group members' attitudes is more easily interpreted. One of the most robust psychological principles is that people are attracted to others with similar attitudes. Group members tend to become more similar in their attitudes

over time – long-standing groups are especially likely to be characterised by attitude homogeneity.

Murray (1989) uses the analogy of clans (Ouchi 1980; Wilkins and Ouchi 1983) to argue that cohesive groups exert more influence on their members, thereby lessening the need for formal communication and bureaucratic control. This reduces internal transaction costs and contributes to organizational efficiency. Similarly, Pfeffer (1983) states that socialization or informal control will be most effective when group members are more homogeneous. In contrast, demographic diversity will necessitate the use of impersonal bureaucratic controls, which can damage performance in high-velocity environments. The broad conclusion from the literature is that homogeneous groups tend to be more cohesive than heterogeneous groups and that cohesion is associated with greater efficiency. The potential dangers associated with group homogeneity are documented in the groupthink literature (Janis 1972) but may be overcome where groups adopt norms of critical appraisal.

The causes and effects of intragroup conflict have been much discussed in the management and social psychology literature. The proposition in much of the research is that conflict is more likely to occur in heterogeneous groups than in homogeneous groups (Wagner et al. 1984; Tsui and O'Reilly 1989) and that conflict, although beneficial in making high-quality decisions (Eisenhardt and Schoonhoven 1990), is damaging to group cohesion (Schweiger et al. 1986). Although this has been cited as a dilemma (Van de Ven and Delbecq 1974), a closer investigation of the conflict literature suggests that this need not always be the case. For example, Amason and Schweiger (1994) and Jehn (1994, 1995, 1997) observe that it is important to distinguish between cognitive conflict, which is task-oriented and arises from differences in judgment, and affective conflict, which involves personalized, individually oriented disagreements. If group norms accept cognitive conflict and such cognitive scrutiny does not escalate into affective conflict, cohesion may be preserved while reaping the benefits of the superior decisions that emerge when opposing views are aired within the group (Eisenhardt and Zbaracki 1992; Priem et al. 1995). Recent evidence (Amason and Sapienza 1997) suggests that teams that display a high degree of mutuality (a shared belief that members are mutually accountable and responsible for the consequences of their strategic decisions) are most able to reduce affective conflict while obtaining the benefits associated with open interaction and cognitive conflict. However, the demographic characteristics associated with mutuality have yet to be established.

The effects of conflict and politics on strategic decision-making in the microcomputer industry are examined in a series of empirical studies by Bourgeois and Eisenhardt (1988; Eisenhardt and Bourgeois 1988; Eisenhardt 1989). Together these studies emphasize the crucial importance of top management teams and the effectiveness of the interaction patterns within them as determinants of organizational outcomes. Specifically they highlight the importance of cognitive conflict and consensus "with qualification" in making fast high-quality decisions. This leads us to the issue of the process through which the group or team arrives at decisions.

Strategic issue processing groups

In her theoretical paper on strategic issue processing groups, Jackson (1992) views the presence of opposing views and diverse capabilities as important determinants of decision quality. Based on a comprehensive review of the literature, she reports that heterogeneous groups are more likely than homogeneous groups to be creative and to reach high-quality decisions and that this finding holds for personal attribute composition, including personality and attitudes, as well as abilities (Jackson 1992: 355). However, the work of Pelz (1956) suggests that diverse perspectives alone may not be the mechanism through which heterogeneous groups achieve their creativity – groups that are more diverse may draw upon a larger social and knowledge network when generating ideas.

The role of social networks, or external ties, in shaping the strategy of the firm has recently been investigated by Geletkanycz and Hambrick (1997).[7] The authors observe that executives operate in a social context that spans organizational boundaries. These external relationships serve as a conduit for information about the environment and possible alternative strategies. In testing the effects of various intra and extra-industry ties on strategic conformity[8] they found only a weak association between intra-industry linkages and conformity.[9] However, extra-industry ties were strongly associated with the adoption of "deviant" strategies. Strategic conformity was found to be associated with high performance in the computer industry while nonconformist strategies were associated with high performance in the more stable food industry.

Based on the available evidence, what are we able to conclude about the relationship between group heterogeneity or homogeneity and firm performance? First, it should not surprise the reader that research to date has produced decidedly mixed results. As reported by Hambrick et al. (1996), team heterogeneity has potential benefits and drawbacks. It is, in effect, a double-edged sword. The extent to which group composition translates into superior performance appears to depend heavily on the competitive environment and the degree to which teams are able to overcome a series of apparent paradoxes (Bourgeois and Eisenhardt 1988). For heterogeneous teams the challenges appear to revolve around the management of conflict, decision speed, timely implementation and issues of longer term group stability and ownership (Virany et al. 1992). Further, as observed by Geletkanycz and Hambrick (1997), heterogeneity can lead to the adoption of nonconformist strategies, which make it harder for new ventures to overcome the liabilities of newness. Homogeneous groups, on the other hand, may lack the ability to innovate (Bantel and Jackson 1989), may lack rigor in decision-making and may be less willing to make changes to group composition as the firm grows.

Prior experience

Central to the above argument is the question of group cohesion. Extending this analysis to new ventures suggests that teams with prior joint work experience should exhibit higher levels of cohesion than those without such experience. Empirical studies support this suggestion and link it to performance (Roure and Maidique 1986; Roure and Keeley 1990). Prior experience in all its conceptualizations is seen as a proxy for the possession of relevant knowledge (Cooper et al. 1994; Chandler 1996). As we have discussed, industry experience suggests knowledge of the task environment and the possession of

TABLE 14.1 Behavior and performance as modified by the situational context

Type of knowledge	Learning process	Example of derived competence
Know-how	Learning by doing	Maintaining control of existing processes for making current products
Know-why	♦ Theoretically directed learning by doing ♦ Importing new theory	♦ Adapting existing products products and processes ♦ Development of new products and processes
Know-what	♦ Learning from changes in state and process theory ♦ Learning by emulation, metaphor or imagination	Identify and define new kinds of products and processes

Source: Herron and Robinson 1993

critical competencies while prior joint experience suggests knowledge of how to work productively with other members of the team. Sanchez (1997) suggests the process through which experience becomes knowledge is learning by doing, and he distinguishes between three types of knowledge, each with a different learning process (table 14.1). He observes that these types of knowledge are likely to have different degrees of strategic significance in different competitive contexts. Thus, in stable environments, "know-how" is likely to be important whereas in high-velocity environments (Eisenhardt 1989) "know-what" is likely to be of greater strategic relevance.

The foregoing begs the question of *which* situation-specific behaviors need to be displayed in order for the entrepreneurial team to grow their business and how these behaviors might be meaningfully categorized. Remembering that the range of required behaviors changes, sometimes dramatically, over time (Virany and Tushman 1986), we propose the following categorization based on formulations by Chandler and Jansen (1992) and Chandler and Hanks (1994). In addition, we propose that the three different kinds of knowledge proposed by Sanchez (1997) will inform and direct these behaviors:

1 Entrepreneurial behavior – *know what*: Includes many of the "strategic issue processing" behaviors identified by Jackson (1992), such as scanning the environment, opportunity recognition and selection, formulating strategies and networking.
2 Managerial behavior – *know why* and *know how*: Self-management and management of relationships inside the team and within the organization. Coordinating and controlling the activities of the organization such as acquiring resources, budgeting, planning and monitoring.
3 Functional or technical behavior – *know how*: Performing specific technical and functional tasks required by the organization such as R&D, production, marketing and financial management. Sanchez's concepts of know-how.

This leads logically to the question of what might affect the ability of the team to display

TABLE 14.2 Barriers to learning

Barriers to behavioral variety	Primary causal antecedents
Not knowing which behaviors are required	Lack of "know what", insufficient knowledge of task and fuctional environments (internal context and external environment)
Not possessing the skills required to apply behavior	Lack of "know how" and "know why"; a function of aptidude, prior training (including experience), team composition, team size
Not knowing that you possess the required skills	Self-knowledge, communication and understanding within the team
Not being motivated to display appropriate behavior	Numerous antecedents of individual and group motivation including personality traits
Being unable to apply appropriate behavior	Lack of capacity, team size, organizational structure, rate of change

growth-promoting behaviors relevant to the context. Taken together, the factors listed in table 14.2 would appear to offer comprehensive coverage and to demonstrate the natural link between demographic characteristics and barriers to behavioral variety. We hypothesize that, in practice, various combinations of these barriers will be present and that these will impact upon entrepreneurial, managerial and functional behaviors. So, as the firm evolves within its environment, the nature and relative significance of these barriers is likely to shift. Further, the impact of these barriers is likely to vary in different environments.

THE ROLE OF EXPERIENCE

Experience is, clearly, multidimensional. In the entrepreneurship literature, the following have been found to be important when studying the track record of the entrepreneur:

- Prior industry experience (Chandler and Hanks 1991; Chandler and Jansen 1992; Siegel et al. 1993; Cooper et al. 1994; Chandler 1996).
- Prior functional/task experience (Murray 1989; Stuart and Abetti 1990; McGee et al. 1995).
- Prior joint working experience (Roure and Keeley 1990; Eisenhardt and Schoonhoven 1990).
- The degree of similarity between prior experience and current (Chandler and Hanks 1991; Chandler and Jansen 1992; Chandler 1996).

For the team, however, only a handful of empirical studies have investigated these dimensions (Chambers et al. 1988; Roure and Keeley 1990; Eisenhardt and Schoonhoven 1990; Stuart and Abetti 1990). Thus, although the significance of team experience has been extensively investigated in relation to the decision criteria used by venture capitalists (e.g., Tyebjee and Bruno 1981; MacMillan et al. 1985, 1987; Timmons et al. 1987), there remain many unanswered questions about the impact of experience on the performance of the entrepreneurial team and on the growth of the firm.

Prior industry experience

Industry-specific expertise and knowledge of the task environment appear to impact particularly heavily on the ability of the team to display appropriate entrepreneurial behavior. They enable, for example, a more accurate evaluation of the environment in terms of customers, suppliers, competitors, technology and the interaction between them (Cooper et al. 1994; Chandler 1996) and inform superior strategic issue processing (Jackson 1992). As pointed out by Cooper et al. (1994), experienced managers may bring with them a network of customers, suppliers and advisers that help to establish the credibility of the venture as it emerges. So, for example, Siegel et al. (1993) examined the characteristics distinguishing high-growth ventures with particular emphasis on those factors that lend themselves to objective evaluation. Of the twenty variables used to characterize the experience and orientation of a company's management team, the only one that discriminated between high and low-growth firms was the amount of experience in a similar industry, which they suggest, embodies other vital subjective criteria.

Prior management, functional and start-up experience

Using a sample of fifty-two new technical ventures, Stuart and Abetti (1990) investigated the impact of entrepreneurial and management experience on early performance. The experience of the management team was measured in terms of the number of year's experience in management, technical, marketing and financial functions together with the total years of experience for the whole group. The experience of the founder was operationalized using a composite measure of entrepreneurial experience, the highest previous level of managerial responsibility, total business experience, age and level of education. Performance was operationalized as a *composite measure* of growth and profit. They found that their composite measure of the founder's entrepreneurial experience (number of previous ventures and role played in them) was the only one correlated with performance. The finding that management expertise, per se, has a weak effect on performance is similar to that reported by Cooper et al. (1994). Thus, they conclude that it is not the *amount* of experience but the *type* of experience that is important.

Chambers et al. (1988) examined the relationship between the previous experience of the founding management team and performance in 100 new ventures. They found only partial support for their hypothesis that high performance will be associated with prior start-up experience in the team. More specifically, they found that prior start up experience was only associated with high performance when only some team members had it. They conclude that the *balance* of experience could be a crucial variable in new firm success.

In their exploratory study of eight team-based new ventures, Roure and Maidique (1986) found that it was the *nature* of the founding teams' prior experience and the characteristics of the organizations in which they gained it that discriminated between the high and low performers. They found that more than two years experience in a similar functional position within a large, high-growth business was a characteristic of the high-performing founders. Further, they had previously experienced successful and fast-rising careers. Specifically, they concluded that the degree of team completeness in terms of functional areas was a principal determinant of success. Similarly, Roure and Keeley (1990) found that overall team completeness was significantly related to success. Interestingly, individual level characteristics, such as prior functional experience and prior experience in a high-growth environment, were not found to discriminate between high and low-performing firms. They observed that most teams scored very highly in these areas, leading them to conclude that above some threshold, additional qualifications may add no value.

McGee et al. (1995) investigate the role of management experience on performance with reference to the use of strategic alliances and cooperative inter-organizational relationships. Their hypothesis, that managers with more functional experience in the area most closely associated with the firms' competitive strategy should be more success-ful in their use of cooperative activities chosen to support that strategy, was supported. The effect was particularly marked in R&D where the pursuit of cooperative relation-ships in the absence of experience was found to be associated with poor performance. They suggest that inexperienced managers "do not know what they do not know" and, hence, what they need to learn − a point entirely consistent with our notion of barriers to behavioral variety. In the pursuit of knowledge, they may only succeed in giving away their technology.

The empirical results reported above need to be interpreted with caution. The studies use differing operationalizations of experience and performance and report apparently contradictory findings. They have also been conducted within different settings. Overall, the picture that emerges is intuitively obvious − the balance and completeness of experience (and hence knowledge and skill) in the team is important.

Prior joint working experience

Roure and Maidique (1986) found that at least six months prior joint work experience among the members of the entrepreneurial team was associated with venture success. Agreeing with Stinchcombe (1965), they state that such experience avoids wasted time and resources on team-building. Roure and Keeley (1990) report similar findings. Eisenhardt and Schoonhoven (1990) hypothesized that past joint experience among the founding team is one factor that might lead to speed in decision-making. Such executives are likely to have learned performance routines for making decisions quickly and are more likely to understand the idiosyncrasies and strengths of their colleagues than are teams formed by strangers. The authors characterized strong teams as those with over 50 percent prior joint experience, at least three founders and at least three years of industry experience variation. Hambrick's (1994) notion of "behavioural integration" suggests that teams with prior joint experience are likely to display higher levels of this phenomenon. Behavioral integration manifests itself as shared information exchange, collaborative behavior and joint decision-making. All things being equal, the degree of prior joint experience is likely to impact upon the team's knowledge of the skills and abilities at its disposal, our third barrier to behavioral variety (see table 14.2).

The gaining of experience

An interesting question, which cuts to the heart of entrepreneurship, is by what processes do individuals and entrepreneurial teams gain "know-what." If such learning really is by imagination and metaphor, then years of experience in a similar industry may not be as critical as hitherto assumed. On a related theme, a further perspective that appears to have been overlooked in the entrepreneurship literature is the presence of economies of learning.[10] Grant observes that the principal source of experienced-based cost reduction is learning by organization members. Citing Nelson and Winter (1982), Grant (1991: 158) argues:

> Learning effects are the result of the establishment and refinement of organizational routines. . . . Efficiency depends critically on the quality of coordination between the people in each routine and between the various routines. The start-up of a new company involves a huge input of conscious planning and management to achieve the co-ordination needed for output to occur at all.

Grant also states that economies of learning tend to increase as the complexity of the operation increases.

This leads us to hypothesize that prior learning within the entrepreneurial team will differentially impact on performance depending on the complexity of the new venture. If experience is regarded as a proxy for learning, then the possession of relevant experience is likely to be a more significant predictor of performance in complex businesses operating in turbulent environments. In addition, prior joint experience may enable the more rapid development of organizational routines.

TEAM SIZE

There is one issue remaining. Throughout the discussion so far, no mention of optimum team size has been made. Empirical evidence suggests that larger new ventures are significantly more likely to have multiple partners than smaller start-ups (Cooper et al. 1989). Further, large teams have been associated with success, particularly in high-technology ventures (Cooper and Bruno 1977; Teach et al. 1986; Roure and Maidique 1986; Roure and Keeley 1990). Other research, however, has failed to demonstrate that team size confers significant early advantages (Doutriaux and Simyar 1987). Indeed, in the few studies that have examined the relationship between team size and performance, causation is not clear (Cooper and Gimeno-Gascon 1992). Equally possible, for example, is that large-scale start-ups require large teams to successfully undertake the enormous job of starting them (Eisenhardt and Schoonhoven 1990) and that large teams will be attracted to high-growth ventures that have the potential to support them (Cooper and Daily 1997). However, the theoretical basis for the "size matters" argument is strong. For example, our earlier discussion of Ashby's (1956) law of requisite variety suggests that larger and more complex new ventures require teams capable of generating sufficient variety to manage them. Team size is one mechanism for generating this variety. Hambrick and D'Aveni (1992) observe that, at a basic level, the resources available on a team result from how many people are on it. Bantel and Jackson (1989) posit that larger teams have greater cognitive resources than smaller teams while other researchers view team size as a proxy for cognitive capability (Halebian and Finkelstein 1993). Eisenhardt and Schoonhoven (1990) propose that larger teams, by virtue of specialization in decision-making, may make faster decisions than their smaller counterparts. Further, they argue that conflict is more likely to be generated and aired in larger groups, thereby improving decision quality.

Although size may confer advantages, large teams also face potential difficulties. For example, Amason and Sapienza (1997) found that large teams produced high levels of both cognitive and affective conflict, which have been shown to have damaging effects on both group cohesion and performance (Jehn 1994). Large groups also have a greater potential for heterogeneity (Wiersema and Bantel 1992), which may slow decision-making and implementation (Hambrick et al. 1996). Here, then, is an apparent paradox. Size may either enable faster decisions or cause friction and reduce decision speed.

A timely insight into this phenomenon is provided by Weinzimmer (1997) who compared the effects of a number of top management team variables, including team size, on sales growth in a sample of 74 small and 114 large firms. In smaller firms (with a mean of 54 employees) a larger top management team was associated with growth. No such relationship was found for larger firms (with a mean of 1,867 employees). Weinzimmer (1997: 6) hypothesizes that the "bureaucratic decision making hierarchies inherent to larger organisations may reduce the potential advantages of top management team size realised by smaller firms." In doing so, he concludes that the relationship between team size and growth is moderated by the size of the organization. Given the focus and level of his study, this is a plausible explanation and one that again highlights the need for us to develop stronger theoretical links between demography, behavior and performance (Hambrick 1992; Smith et al. 1994).

Another word of caution is appropriate here. Perhaps more than any other demographic variable, the impact of team size on growth is highly contingent. For example, the assumption is that larger teams are more heterogeneous, which leads to the assumption of higher levels of conflict, which in turn leads to other assumptions about better decisions or group disharmony. Toward the end of this chain of logic, the links become very weak.

CONCLUSIONS

It is clear that the study of the entrepreneurial team is well overdue. It is also clear that it is complex, rife with methodological problems and able to be explored from a wide variety of theoretical perspectives, all of which can provide a kaleidoscope of images and insights. Nevertheless, one simple truth is obvious. The team is fundamental to the success of the venture. All that we need to do is to discover more about how and why.

NOTES

1 Virany and Tushman (1986) empirically investigated this relationship. An extensive body of work on executive succession may be found in the strategic management and organizational behavior literature.

2 This use of observable demographic characteristics overcomes the difficult problem of gaining access to entrepreneurs to measure psychological or behavioral variables (Smith et al. 1994).

3 The term "top management team" is used frequently in the strategic management literature.

4 Jackson (1992: 349) emphasizes problems of access and methodology. See also Rousseau (1985) for a discussion on the problems associated with cross-level research.

5 The field of social psychology has a long tradition of such research.

6 Cohesiveness refers to the degree of interpersonal attraction and liking among group members (Jackson 1992).

7 See, e.g., Birley (1985) and Aldrich and Zimmer (1986) for a discussion of the role of social networks in the creation of new ventures.

8 Finklestein and Hambrick (1990) refer to strategic conformity as the extent to which a firm's strategy matches the central tendency of strategies within its industry.

9 They note a curvilinear relationship between team tenure and conformity. Short and long tenured teams were associated with conformity. Moderate tenure was associated with "deviant" strategies.

10 Economies of learning are often referred to as economies of experience (Grant 1991).

REFERENCES

Ashby, W.R. 1956. *An Introduction to Cybernetics*. London, Chapman & Hall.

Aldrich, H. and Zimmer, C. 1986. Entrepreneurship through Social Networks. In D.L. Sexton and R.W. Smilor (eds.), *The Art and Science of Entrepreneurship*. Cambridge, MA: Ballinger, pp. 3–23.

Amason, A.C. and Sapienza, H.J. 1997. The effects of top management team size and interaction norms on cognitive and affective conflict. *Journal of Management* 23(4): 495–516.

Amason, A.C. and Schweiger, D.M. 1994. Resolving the paradox of conflict, strategic decision making, and organizational performance. *The International Journal of Conflict Management* 5(3): 239–53.

Ancona, D.G. 1987. Groups in organizations: extending laboratory models. In C. Hendrick (ed.), *Annual Review of Personality and Social Psychology: Group and Intergroup Processes*. Beverley Hills, CA: Sage, pp. 207–31.

Bantel, K. and Jackson, S. 1989. Top management and innovations in banking: does the composition of the top team make a difference? *Strategic Management Journal* 10: 107–24.

Barney, J. 1991. Firm resources and sustained competitive advantage. *Journal of Management* 17: 99–120.

Begley, T.M. and Boyd, D.P. 1987. Psychological characteristics associated with performance in entrepreneurial firms and smaller businesses. *Journal of Business Venturing* 2(1): 79–93.

Birley, S. 1985 The role of networks in the entrepreneurial process. *Journal of Business Venturing* 1(1): 107–18

Bourgeois, L.J. and Eisenhardt, K.M. 1988. Strategic decision processes in high velocity environments: four cases from the microcomputer industry. *Management Science* 34(7): 816–35.

Chambers, B.R., Hart, S.L. and Denison, D.R. 1988. Founding team experience and firm performance. In B.A. Kirchhoff et al. (eds.), *Frontiers of Entrepreneurship Research*. Wellesley, MA: Babson College, pp. 106–18.

Chandler, G.N. 1996. Business similarity as a moderator of the relationship between pre-ownership experience and venture performance. *Entrepreneurship Theory and Practice* 20(3): 51–65.

Chandler, G.N. and Hanks, S.H. 1991. How important is experience in a highly similar industry? In N.C. Churchill et al. (eds.), *Frontiers of Entrepreneurship Research*. Wellesley, MA: Babson College, pp. 1–10.

Chandler, G.N. and Hanks, S.H. 1994. Founder competence, the environment and venture performance. *Entrepreneurship Theory and Practice* 18(3): 77–89.

Chandler, G.N. and Jansen, E. 1992. The founder's self-assessed competence and venture performance. *Journal of Business Venturing* 7: 223–36.

Cooper, A.C. and Bruno, A. 1977. Success among high-technology firms. *Business Horizons* 20: 16–22

Cooper, A.C. and Daily, C.M. 1997. Entrepreneurial Teams. In D.L. Sexton and R.W. Smilor (eds.), *Entrepreneurship 2000*. Chicago: Upstart, pp. 127–50.

Cooper, A.C. and Gimeno-Gascon, F.J. 1992. Entrepreneurs, processes of founding and new firm performance. In D.L. Sexton and J.D. Kasarda (eds.), *The State of the Art of Entrepreneurship*. Boston: PWS-Kent, pp. 301–40.

Cooper, A.C., Gimeno-Gascon, F.J. and Woo, C.Y. 1994. Initial human and financial capital as predictors of new venture performance. *Journal of Business Venturing* 9: 371–95.

Cooper, A.C., Woo, C.Y. and Dunkelberg, W.C. 1989. Entrepreneurship and the initial size of firms. *Journal of Business Venturing* 4(5): 317–32

Covin, J.G. and Slevin, D.P. 1997. High growth transitions: theoretical perspectives and suggested directions. In D.L. Sexton and R.W. Smilor (eds.), *Entrepreneurship 2000*. Chicago: Upstart, pp. 99–126.

Cyert, R.M. and March, J.G. 1963. *A Behavioural Theory of the Firm*. New York: Prentice-Hall.

Doutriaux, J. and Simyar, F. 1987. Duration of the comparative advantage accruing from some start up factors in high-tech entrepreneurial firms. In N.C. Churchill et al. (eds.), *Frontiers of Entrepreneurship Research*. Wellesley, MA: Babson College, pp. 436–51.

Drucker, P.F. 1985. *Innovation and Entrepreneurship*. New York: Harper & Row.

Eisenhardt, K.M. 1989. Making fast strategic decisions in high velocity environments. *Academy of Management Journal* 32: 543–76.

Eisenhardt, K.M. and Bourgeois, L.J. 1988. Politics of strategic decision making: Towards a mid-range theory. *Academy of Management Journal* 31: 737–70.

Eisenhardt, K.M. and Zbaracki, M.J. 1992. Strategic decision making. *Strategic Management Journal* 13: 17–37.

Eisenhardt, K.M. and Schoonhoven, C.B. 1990. Organizational growth: linking founding team, strategy, environment, and growth among US semiconductor ventures, 1978–1988. *Administrative Science Quarterly* 35: 504–29.

Epstein, S. 1979. The stability of behaviour: on predicting most of the people much of the time. *Journal of Personality & Social Psychology* 37(7): 1097–126.

Epstein, S. and O'Brian, E.J. 1985. The person–situation debate in historical and current perspective. *Psychological Bulletin* 98(3): 513–37.

Espejo, R. and Harnden, R. (eds.) 1989. *The Viable System Model*. Chichester: John Wiley & Sons

Finklestein, S. and Hambrick, D.C. 1990. Top management team tenure and organizational outcomes: the moderating role of managerial discretion. *Administrative Science Quarterly* 35: 484–503.

Forrest, J.E. 1990. Strategic alliances and the small technology based firm. *Journal of Small Business Management* 28(3): 37–45.

Gartner, W.B. 1985. A framework for describing the phenomenon of new venture creation. *Academy of Management Review* 10(4): 696–706.

Gartner, W.B. 1988. Who is the entrepreneur? Is the wrong question. *American Journal of Small Business* 12(4): 11–32.

Gartner, W.B. 1989. Some suggestions for research on entrepreneurial traits and characteristics. *Entrepreneurship Theory and Practice* 14(1): 27–37.

Gartner, W.B., Bird, B.J. and Starr, J.A. 1992. Acting as if: differentiating entrepreneurial from organizational behaviour. *Entrepreneurship Theory and Practice* 16(3): 13–31.

Geletkanycz, M.A. and Hambrick, D.C. 1997. The external ties of top executives: implications for strategic choice and performance. *Administrative Science Quarterly* 42: 654–81.

Goshal, S., Hahn, M. and Moran, P. 1997. *An Integrative Theory of Firm Growth: Implications for Corporate Organization and Management.* London Business School Working Paper.

Grant, R.M. 1991. *Contemporary Strategy Analysis*, Cambridge, MA: Basil Blackwell.

Gupta, A.K. 1984. Contingency linkages between strategy and general manager competencies: A conceptual examination. *Academy of Management Review* 9(3): 399–412.

Halebian, J. and Finkelstein, S. 1993. Top management team size, CEO dominance and firm performance: the moderating roles of environmental turbulence and discretion. *Academy of Management Journal* 36: 844–63.

Hambrick, D.C. 1992. Commentary: consequences of group composition for the interpersonal dynamics of strategic issue processing groups (S. Jackson). In P. Shrivastava et al. (eds.), *Advances in Strategic Management*, vol. 8 Greenwich, CT: JAI Press, pp. 383–9.

Hambrick, D.C. 1994. Top management groups: a conceptual integration and reconsideration of the "team" label. *Research in Organizational Behaviour* 16: 171–213.

Hambrick, D.C. and D'Aveni, R.A. 1992. Top team deterioration as part of the downward spiral of large corporate bankruptcies. *Management Science.* 38: 1445–66.

Hambrick, D.C. and Mason, P.A. 1984. Upper echelons: the organization as a reflection of its top managers. *Academy of Management Review* 9: 193–206.

Hambrick, D.C., Cho, T.S. and Chen, M. 1996. The influence of top management team heterogeneity on firms' competitive moves. *Administrative Science Quarterly* 41: 659–84.

Herron, L. and Robinson, R.B. 1993. A structural model of the effects of entrepreneurial characteristics on venture performance. *Journal of Business Venturing* 8: 281–94.

Hollenbeck, J. and Whitener, W. 1988. Reclaiming personality traits for personnel selection. *Journal of Management* 14(1): 81–91.

Jackson, S.E. 1992. Consequences of group composition for the interpersonal dynamics of strategic issue processing groups. In P. Shrivastava et al. (eds.), *Advances in Strategic Management*, vol. 8 Greenwich, CT: JAI Press, pp. 345–82.

Janis, I.L. 1972. *Victims of Groupthink.* Boston, MA: Houghton Mifflin.

Jarillo, J.C. 1988. On strategic networks. *Strategic Management Journal* 9: 31–41.

Jehn, K.A. 1994. Enhancing effectiveness: an investigation of advantages and disadvantages of value-based intra-group conflict. *International Journal of Conflict Management* 5: 223–8.

Jehn, K.A. 1995. A multimethod examination of the benefits and detriments of intra-group conflict. *Administrative Science Quarterly* 40: 256–82.

Jehn, K.A. 1997. A qualitative analysis of conflict types and dimensions in organizational groups. *Administrative Science Quarterly* 42: 530–57.

Kamm, J.B., Shuman, J.C., Seeger, J.A. and Nurick, A.J. 1989. Are well-balanced teams more successful? In R.H. Brockhaus et al. (eds.), *Frontiers of Entrepreneurship Research.* Wellesley, MA: Babson College, pp. 428–9.

Kamm, J.B. and Nurick, A.J. 1993. The stages of team venture formation: a decision making model. *Entrepreneurship Theory and Practice* 17(2): 17–28.

Katzenbach, J.R. 1997. The myth of the top management team. *Harvard Business Review.* 75(6): 83–91.

Langlois, R.N. 1995. Capabilities and coherence in firms and markets. In C.A. Montgomery (ed.), *Resource-based and Evolutionary Theories of the Firm: Towards a Synthesis.* Norwell, MA: Kluwer Academic, pp. 71–100.

Larson, A. 1992. Network dyads in entrepreneurial settings: a study of the governance of exchange relationships *Administrative Science Quarterly* 37: 76–104.

Lenz, R.T. 1981. "Determinants" of organizational performance: an interdisciplinary review. *Strategic Management Journal* 2: 131–54.

Lorenzoni, G. and Ornati, O.A. 1988. Constellations of firms and new ventures. *Journal of Business*

Venturing 3: 41–57.

MacMillan, I.C., Siegel, R.M. and Subba Narasimha, P.N. 1985. Criteria used by venture capitalists to evaluate new ventures. *Journal of Business Venturing* 1(1): 119–28

MacMillan, I.C., Zemann, L. and Subba Narasimha, P.N. 1987. Criteria distinguishing successful from unsuccessful ventures in the venture screening process. *Journal of Business Venturing* 2(2): 123–37.

McGee, J.E., Dowling, M.J. and Meggison, W.L. 1995. Co-operative strategy and new venture performance: the role of business strategy and management experience. *Strategic Management Journal* 16: 565–80.

Miller, D. and Friesen, P.H. 1984. A longitudinal study of the corporate life cycle. *Management Science* 30(10): 1161–83.

Murray, A.I. 1989. Top management group heterogeneity and firm performance. *Strategic Management Journal* 10: 125–41.

Muzyka, D.F. 1991. The nature of entrepreneurial decision making: inside the black-box. In S. Birley and I.C. MacMillan (eds.), *International Perspectives on Entrepreneurship Research*. Amsterdam: Elsevier, pp. 61–75.

Naffziger, D.W., Hornsby, J.S. and Kuratko, D.F. 1994. A proposed research model of entrepreneurial motivation. *Entrepreneurship Theory and Practice* 18 (spring): 29–42.

Nelson, R.R. and Winter, S.G. 1982. *An Evolutionary Theory of Economic Change*. Cambridge, MA: Harvard University Press.

Ouchi, W.G. 1980. Markets, bureaucracies and clans. *Administrative Science Quarterly* 25: 129–41.

Pelz, D.C. 1956. Some social factors related to performance is a research organization. *Administrative Science Quarterly* 1: 310–25.

Penrose, E. 1959. *The Theory of the Growth of the Firm*. Oxford: Blackwell.

Penrose, E. 1995. *The Theory of the Growth of the Firm*, 3rd edn. Oxford: Oxford University Press.

Pfeffer, J. 1983. Organizational demography. In L.L. Cummings and B.M. Staw (eds.), *Research in Organizational Behavior*, vol. 5, Greenwich, CT: JAI Press, pp. 299–357.

Priem, R.L., Harrison, D.A. and Muir, N.K. 1995. Structured conflict and consensus outcomes in group decision making. *Journal of Management* 21(4): 691–710.

Roure, J.B. and Keeley, R.H. 1990. Predictors of success in new technology based ventures. *Journal of Business Venturing* 5: 201–20.

Roure, J.B. and Maidique, M.A. 1986. Linking prefunding factors and high-technology venture success: An exploratory study. *Journal of Business Venturing* 1: 295–306.

Rousseau, D.M. 1985. Issues of level in organizational research: multi-level and cross-level perspectives. In L.L. Cummings and B.M. Staw (eds.), *Research in Organizational Behavior*. vol. 7. Greenwich, CT: JAI Press, pp. 1–37.

Sanchez, R. 1997. Managing articulated knowledge in competence-based competition. In R. Sanchez and A. Heene (eds.), *Strategic Learning and Knowledge Management*. Chichester: John Wiley & Sons, pp. 163–87.

Sandberg, W.R. 1986. *New Venture Performance: The Role of Strategy and Industry Structure*. Lexington, MA: DC Heath.

Sandberg, W.R. and Hofer, C.W. 1987. Improving new venture performance: the role of strategy, industry structure and the entrepreneur. *Journal of Business Venturing* 2(1): 5–28.

Schweiger, D.M., Sandberg, W.R. and Ragan, J.W. 1986. Group approaches for improving strategic decision making: a comparative analysis of dialectical inquiry, devil's advocacy and consensus. *Academy of Management Journal* 28: 51–71.

Shepard, J. 1991. Entrepreneurial growth through constellations. *Journal of Business Venturing* 6(5): 363–73.

Siegel, R., Siegel, E. and MacMillan, I.C. 1993. Characteristics distinguishing high-growth ventures. *Journal of Business Venturing* 8: 169–80.

Smith, K.A., Smith, K.G., Olian, J.D., Sims, H.P., O'Brannon, D.P. and Scully, J.J. 1994. Top management team demography and process: the role of social integration and communication. *Administrative Science Quarterly* 39: 412–38.

Stevenson, H. 1997. The six dimensions of entrepreneurship. In S. Birley and D.F. Muzyka (eds.), *Mastering Enterprise*, London: Pitman, pp. 9–14.

Stevenson, H.H. and Jarillo, J.C. 1986. Preserving entrepreneurship as companies grow. *Journal of Business Strategy* 6(5): 10–23.

Stinchcombe, A.L. 1965. Organizations and social structure. In J.G. March (ed.), *Handbook of Organizations*. Chicago. Rand-McNally, pp. 142–93.

Stuart, R.W. and Abetti, P.A. 1990. Impact of entrepreneurial and management experience on early performance. *Journal of Business Venturing* 5: 151–62.

Teach, R.D., Tarpley, F.A. and Schwartz, R.G. 1986. Software venture teams. In R. Ronstadt et al. (eds.), *Frontiers of Entrepreneurship Research*. Wellesley, MA: Babson College, pp. 546–62.

Teece, D.J., Pisano, G. and Sheen, A. 1997. Dynamic capabilities and strategic management. *Strategic Management Journal* 18(7): 509–33.

Timmons, J.A., Muzyka, D.F., Stevenson, H.H. and Bygrave, W.D. 1987. Opportunity recognition: the core of entrepreneurship. In N.C. Churchill et al. (eds.), *Frontiers of Entrepreneurship Research*. Wellesley, MA: Babson College, pp. 109–23.

Tsui, A. and O'Reilly, C.A. 1989. Beyond simple demographic effects: the importance of relational demography in superior–subordinate dyads. *Academy of Management Journal* 32: 402–23.

Tyjbee, T.T. and Bruno, A.V. 1981. Venture capital decision making: preliminary results from three empirical studies. In N.C. Churchill et al. (eds.), *Frontiers of Entrepreneurship Research*. Wellesley, MA: Babson College, pp. 281–320.

Van de Ven, A.H. and Delbecq, A.L. 1974. The effectiveness of nominal, delphi and interacting group decision making processes. *Academy of Management Journal* 17: 605–21.

Virany, B. and Tushman, M.L. 1986. Top management teams and corporate success in an emerging industry. *Journal of Business Venturing* 1: 261–74.

Virany, B., Tushman, M.L. and Romanelli, E. 1992. Executive succession and organizational outcomes in turbulent environments: an organizational learning approach. *Organization Science* 3: 72–91.

Wagner, W.G., Pfeffer, J. and O'Reilly, C.A. 1984. Organizational demography and turnover in top management groups. *Administrative Science Quarterly* 29: 74–92.

Watson, W.E., Ponthieu, L.D. and Critelli, J.W. 1995. Team interpersonal effectiveness in venture partnerships and its connection to perceived success. *Journal of Business Venturing* 10: 393–411.

Weick, K.E. 1977. Repunctuating the problem. In P.S. Goodman and J.M. Pennings (eds.), *New Perspectives on Organizational Effectiveness*. San Francisco: Jossey Bass.

Weick, K.E. 1979. *The Social Psychology of Organizing*. New York: Random House.

Weinzimmer, L.G. 1997. Top management team correlates of organizational growth in a small business context: a comparative study. *Journal of Small Business Management* 35: 1–10.

Wernerfelt, B. 1984. A resource based view of the firm. *Strategic Management Journal* 5: 171–80.

Wiersema, M.F. and Bantel, K.A. 1992. Top management team demography and corporate strategic change. *Academy of Management Journal* 35(1): 91–121.

Wilkins, A.L. and Ouchi, W.G. 1983. Efficient cultures: Exploring the relationship between culture and organizational performance. *Administrative Science Quarterly* 28: 468–81.

15

Managing Growth Transitions: Theoretical Perspectives and Research Directions

J.B. (Ben) Arbaugh and S. Michael Camp

GROWTH: THE ROLE OF RESOURCES
REVIEW OF THE LITERATURE ON MANAGING GROWTH TRANSITIONS
RESOURCE AND KNOWLEDGE-BASED VIEWS OF THE FIRM
RESOURCE-BASED APPROACH TO MANAGING GROWTH TRANSITIONS
RESEARCH DIRECTIONS
CONCLUSIONS

As we begin the twenty-first century, many organizations are facing ever-increasing levels of complexity both internally and with their external environments (Tushman and O'Reilly 1996). For a comparatively small number of organizations, this complexity is magnified by the challenge and opportunity of rapid growth. At a minimum, rapid growth accelerates the pace of internal complexity as structures and procedures are developed to support a larger organization (Ashmos et al. 1996; Miller 1993). In addition, the organization's external environment also becomes more complex since growth redefines relationships with suppliers, customers and sources of financing, and most firms attract new competitors to their markets (Hambrick and Crozier 1985; Kazanjian 1988; Miller et al. 1996; Sexton and Bowman-Upton 1991). Since these growth-oriented firms are being increasingly relied upon to generate jobs and economic development in the global economy, their founders and managers need to know about successfully managing the combination of increased complexity and rapid growth.

The process of managing this combination has been described in previous literature as growth transitions (Covin and Slevin 1997; Flamholtz 1995). While the challenges of increased complexity and rapid growth have been researched somewhat extensively separately (Child et al. 1991; Dodge et al. 1994; Hambrick and Crozier 1985; Stacey 1995), research that studies them together is somewhat limited. Previous studies have identified various management challenges, environmental conditions and organizational characteristics associated with rapid growth (Eisenhardt and Schoonhoven 1990; Fombrun and Wally 1989; Hambrick and Crozier 1985; Siegel et al. 1993). However, these studies have tended not to look at the types of complexity or transitions that these firms encounter as they grow. Other authors have conceptually described various types of challenges that will emerge as a firm progresses through various stages of growth (Churchill and Lewis 1983; Greiner 1972; Scott and Bruce 1987). Empirical work based on such stage models has tended to focus on changes in organizational structural characteristics rather than examining how organizations develop these characteristics (Hanks and Chandler 1994; Hanks et al. 1993; Olson and Terpstra 1992).

A potentially powerful perspective that may help to explain how rapidly growing organizations develop the ability to manage these transitions may be found in the emerging resource and knowledge-based views of the firm (Barney 1991; Grant 1991, Grant 1996; Nonaka 1994). From this perspective, organizations manage transitions by using tangible and intangible resources to develop organizational routines (Nelson and Winter 1982). These routines, in turn, produce firm-specific knowledge that allows the firm to both manage expanding internal processes (Ashmos et al. 1996; Barnett et al. 1994) and attract additional tangible and intangible resources that they can use to propel future growth (Levinthal and March 1993). Thus, this perspective can help to explain the sources of transitions and complexity as the firm grows and the approach that the firm needs to take to address these challenges.

This chapter seeks to integrate these theoretical perspectives, thereby enhancing our understanding of growth transitions. The chapter is divided into four sections. First, we will review literature on growth and transitions, paying particular attention to recent work. Then, we will extend this review to literature in the resource and knowledge-based views of the firm to develop an enhanced perspective on growth transitions. Next, we will discuss the findings of a series of research studies conducted by the Kauffman Center for Entrepreneurial Leadership on managing transitions in light of this theoretical discussion, which shows how the entrepreneurs manage defining growth transitions and what resources and approaches to managerial complexity were most effective in the transition. Lastly, we will identify several specific areas where further research could improve our understanding of the role of resource configuration in the management of growth transitions.

GROWTH: THE ROLE OF RESOURCES

At its core, entrepreneurship is comprised of unique human behaviors. The challenge for the field has been to identify the behaviors that distinguish entrepreneurship from other general management activity. In this effort, two distinct lines of inquiry have developed. The first concludes that the activity that most uniquely distinguishes entrepreneurial behavior is the creation of new business ventures (Gartner 1985; Gartner et al. 1992; Shaver and Scott 1991; Vanderwerf 1993). This line of inquiry is heavily focused on the entrepreneurial behaviors of individuals engaged in efforts to start new enterprises, though researchers have also successfully used this framework to isolate the entrepreneurial activities of established organizations. The second line of inquiry distinguishes entrepreneurship as the unique behaviors employed in the pursuit and management of growth (Birley and Westhead 1990; Carland et al. 1984; Sexton and Bowman-Upton 1991). This perspective primarily focuses on the entrepreneurial behaviors of the firm in pursuit of market opportunities for long-term gain. Compared with entrepreneurship as the creation of new ventures, studying the unique behaviors associated with the pursuit and management of growth is methodologically demanding (Weinzimmer, 1998). Scholars are attracted to this line of inquiry, however, because while only a small percent of new firms ever grow to any substantial size (Reynolds 1987), growth-oriented firms account for a significant portion of our nation's social and economic gain. Though these competing behavioral perspectives are different in many ways, when examined through the lens of the resource-based theory, they obviously share a common foundation.

Schumpeter (1934) noted that the role of the entrepreneur in the economy is to assemble and deploy resources in new combinations that disrupt the otherwise static nature of the market. Kirzner (1973) suggested that how the resources are actually configured is determined by the entrepreneur's perception of the market opportunity. Kirzner (1973) added that perceived opportunities are contrived from the entrepreneur's assessment of the "waste" in existing (i.e., competitive) resource combinations. Waste is evident in resource combinations that fail to obtain the maximum value from a given market opportunity, particularly an opportunity that has long-term potential. Sexton and Bowman-Upton (1991) followed this approach when they concluded from their detailed review of the literature that entrepreneurship is the process of acquiring, assembling and deploying resources in the pursuit of perceived opportunities for long-term gain.

What is partly intriguing about this definition is that the distinct behaviors in recognizing and pursuing opportunities are present in the creation of new business ventures and in the pursuit and management of growth. Just as new resource combinations are required in each new business startup, so new combinations are employed in each new effort on the part of the existing firm to grow. With growth comes increased complexity. Under the pretense of firm growth and added complexity, the entrepreneur accumulates and combines resources to simultaneously expand the burgeoning firm's internal processes for managing growth (i.e., building capacity) and to provide the means for future growth (i.e., innovation) (Adizes 1996). As noted, the particular configuration is still determined by how the entrepreneur frames the opportunity. As the firm becomes more capable of recognizing and pursuing new opportunities, the process of acquiring and deploying resources to accommodate the growth and to provide for future growth becomes more standardized or routine (Adizes 1996). The study of such routines should provide substantial insight into how entrepreneurs are able to manage the growth process. As such, the resource-based perspective may provide the first true foundational framework from which to understand entrepreneurship.

REVIEW OF THE LITERATURE ON MANAGING GROWTH TRANSITIONS

Researchers generally agree that studying how entrepreneurs manage growth transitions is critical because the ability to manage growth is vital to a firm's continued success (Sexton and Bowman-Upton 1991). Though conceptual models are abundant, the study of managing growth transitions has generally failed to identify and explain the tactical approaches that entrepreneurs utilize. Early studies of growth transitions focused on the founder's ability to attract new people to the organization and to change their managerial style in response to the firm's rapid growth (Clifford 1975; Greiner 1972). A few subsequent research studies identified various tactics successfully used by rapidly growing firms once they attracted new people. Hambrick and Crozier (1985) found that rapidly growing firms were not only able to attract new people but often employed people with senior level experience at large corporations in the early start-up stage and generally gave all employees a financial stake in the firm. They also found that the founders envisioned their firm as a large entity long before it became one, and they were able to reinforce that vision throughout the organization. Lastly, these firms tended to minimize organizational hierarchy and introduced new processes gradually.

More recent empirical work has identified relevant structural and organizational characteristics of growth transitions. As a firm grows, it appears to move from simple to divisional structures with increased specialization and formality. These structures tend to comprise more specialized functions and less centralized decision making (Fombrun and Wally 1989; Hanks and Chandler 1994; Hanks et al. 1993; Olson and Terpstra 1992). As these structures are developed, the firm increasingly seeks talent from outside the firm to manage the changes (Eisenhardt and Schoonhoven 1990; Fombrun and Wally 1989; Hambrick and Crozier 1985; Siegel et al. 1993). The management teams of growing firms also tend to place a higher emphasis on strategy making and planning in the midst of growth and face increased internal and external complexity (Boyd and Reuning-Elliot 1998; Lumpkin and Dess 1995; Miller and Chen 1996; Miller et al. 1996).

Further conceptual development has been done on managing growth transitions. Several authors have suggested that in order to manage growth transitions, organizations must be able to simultaneously manage evolutionary and revolutionary change (Fombrun and Wally 1989; Tushman and O'Reilly 1996). Tushman and O'Reilly (1996) contend that managing evolutionary change is important to maintain organization–environment fit, while revolutionary change is necessary to construct an organization that could survive changes in competitors and technology. Firms successfully approach evolutionary and revolutionary change through the use of autonomous groups, increased size to leverage economies of scale and scope, balance in the overall corporate culture with varying subcultures depending on the type of business and reinforcement in the organization's social control system. Flamholtz (1995) examined organizational growth stages and identified key development areas for each stage that must be emphasized if the firm is to progress to the next stage. For instance, for a firm to advance beyond the new venture stage, they must become proficient at identifying and developing products and markets. To move beyond the expansion stage, the firm must develop its resources and operational systems. This growth process continues until the firm is a diversified corporation that must successfully integrate corporate culture, management and operational systems and organizational resources. More recently, Covin and Slevin (1997) argued that sustained firm growth occurs as the firm develops managerial capability to continually reconfigure the firm to manage the increased organizational and environmental complexity that comes as a result of rapid growth.

While this research has been helpful in identifying transition points and the types of organizational and systemic resources necessary to make them, it has yet to identify how organizations develop the appropriate resource configurations or how they manage them once they are firmly in place. Each of these perspectives is fundamentally dependent on firm resources and how entrepreneurs are capable of recognizing and configuring the appropriate mix of resources so as to effectively approach long-term growth opportunities. Thus, we now turn to an emergent body of literature – resource and knowledge-based views of the firm – for insight into the process of managing growth transitions.

RESOURCE AND KNOWLEDGE-BASED VIEWS OF THE FIRM

Given the central role that resources play in an entrepreneur's pursuit of opportunity (Hambrick and Crozier 1985; Siegel et al. 1993), resource-based theory seems a natural framework against which to consider growth as evidence of entrepreneurial behavior. Resource-based theory holds that all firms are comprised of heterogeneous bundles of resources (Penrose 1959; Conner 1991; Barney 1991) that are uniquely fashioned over time according to administrative intentions (Penrose 1959; Barney 1986). There are two dominant lines of inquiry in the resource-based view of the firm. The first, which focuses on the actual resources within the control of the firm (Wernerfelt 1984; Grant 1991; Hall 1993) has studied two classes of resources: tangible (e.g., new products, information systems and financial capital) and intangible (e.g., knowledge, skills and brand power) (Chandler and Hanks 1994; Dean et al. 1998; Kotha 1995; Miller and Shamsie 1996). The second line of inquiry in resource-based theory is concerned with how the resources controlled are actually used to generate and enhance firm performance in accordance with management's perception of the opportunity (Amit and Schoemaker 1993; Leonard-Barton 1992; Teece et al. 1997; Barney 1986). Knowledge-based theory contends that firms are a collection of both tacit (i.e., firm-specific) and explicit (i.e., available across firms) knowledge (Nelson and Winter 1982; Nonaka 1994; Polanyi 1962) located within the total organization as well as its various components (Matusik and Hill 1998). Successful firms are able to arrange and combine their knowledge and other resources in such a way as to create unique value-adding capabilities that allow them to earn abnormal returns (Amit and Shoemaker 1993; Grant 1991; Grant 1996; Peteraf 1993; Stalk et al. 1992). Much of the research in resource-based theory examines various types and dimensions of specific resources. When the emphasis is on growth, the resources of most interest are the managerial knowledge and skills in administering resources for long-term gain. The knowledge and ability to configure resources in pursuit of opportunity, and then to effectively modify the configuration in light of ever-new growth opportunities, is a new and expanding area of resource-based theory that, to date, has not had adequate attention (Spender and Grant 1996).

If one simply distinguishes growth as increase over time, it becomes important to distinguish the unique entrepreneurial behavior involved in configuring resources to accommodate and insure this continued increase. Under the resource-based framework, what actually grows in organizational growth is the size, complexity and value of the resource bundle over time, where value is measured by the ability of the resources to generate economic rents (Barney 1991; Penrose 1959). These rents take the form of firm profits and are simultaneously a product of the current resource configuration and a new resource to be combined with the existing resources for subsequent configurations. What actually transitions through the growth process are:

1 what resources are utilized,
2 how the resources are configured,
3 the end value or product of the resource combinations.

Previous research in the resource-based perspective has focused on resources and their configurations. The "Penrose Effect," however, suggests that a firm's rate of growth will be dictated by the ability (i.e., resources) of the firm to create capacity to accommodate growth (Penrose 1959). Thus, the key issue is in the administrative decisions that determine what resources are used and how they are configured to produce the desired ends in light of the competitive environment in which the firm operates. Success or failure throughout the venture's life can, thereby, be determined by the quality of the decisions in this regard. Resource-based theory holds that there is an unlimited source of opportunities in the marketplace. What is essential in managing the transition (i.e., the point at which the resources are being reconfigured), however, is that a certain portion of the firm's resources be deployed for identifying and exploiting the next growth opportunity (Adizes 1996). As such, a firm's *pattern of growth* and *rate of growth* are subject to management's ability to continually configure the firm's resources for the pursuit of new opportunities. These "cycles" or "routines" constitute the entrepreneur's approach to managing growth. Entrepreneurs who establish a more routinized approach to resource configuration in light of opportunity are able to sustain higher rates of growth over longer periods of time (i.e., more stable patterns), as figure 15.1 shows.

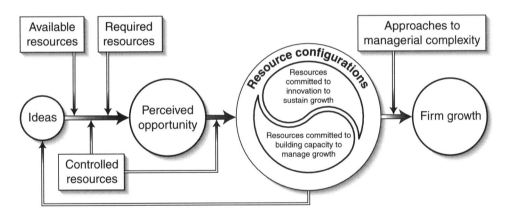

FIGURE 15.1 Resource-based view of entrepreneurship: managing growth transitions

Resource-based view of managing transitions in the life cycle

To date, the most widely used framework for studying growth transitions has been life-cycle analysis. In life-cycle models, firms, like biological organisms, are presumed to grow over time, increasing in size and complexity (Aldrich 1979). However, a great deal of research suggests that this is not the case; that many firms never grow beyond a particular stage in their overall development (Reynolds 1987; Stanworth and Curran

1976). Many of these studies conclude that the extent to which a firm grows is a matter of choice of the lead entrepreneur or entrepreneurial team responsible for the resource configuration and setting the long-term agenda for the resource pool (Covin and Slevin 1991; Covin and Slevin 1997; Sexton and Bowman-Upton 1991). Continued efforts to accumulate resources and increase the economic returns from those resources means that managerial knowledge and competencies are among the most critical of all firm resources. Such knowledge and skill must be applied in determining the most effective way in which to configure the firm's remaining resources in order to properly provide for and sustain growth (Slater and Narver 1995).

There is a definite link between the life-cycle and resource-based perspectives of organizational growth, but can the resource-based perspective explain why firms do not necessarily follow the transitional patterns proposed by the life-cycle analysis? Resource-based theory explains firm development in terms of what resources are controlled and management's ability to access and appropriately configure the resources required for competitive advantage. Posited against the life-cycle theory, resource-based theory contends that it is how the resources are configured at each stage and reconfigured during the transitions between stages that determines successive phases of growth and development.

According to life-cycle models, growth comes in incremental stages. At each phase of development, the firm is able to grow with existing resources until the next measure of growth requires more resources (Adizes 1989). Thus, the skills and knowledge needed in every accumulation and allocation of resources has two components. The first is to account for the growth that has already occurred, and the second is to propel the firm toward the next growth opportunity. However, depending on the speed, growth at some point requires restructuring or periods of reconfiguration. A rapid rate of growth can require relatively frequent restructuring in order to keep up with the pace of growth and to provide adequate means to secure future growth (Schein 1990; Slater and Narver 1995). Some have argued for envisioning a firm as a large entity while it is still small and staffing it accordingly as a means for successfully managing rapid growth (Clifford 1975; Hambrick and Crozier 1985; Reynolds 1993). Firms that successfully manage growth clearly develop resources and knowledge to simultaneously manage their present stage and to transition to the next. Thus, decisions about resources are important at every stage of the firm's development and, thus, are more fundamental to understanding how entrepreneurs manage growth than the stage models of life-cycle analysis. Constant and often unpredictable changes in various market factors create slack in some resources and constraints in others such as financial, human and technological capital (Bruno and Tyebjee 1982; Hannan and Freeman 1984). These ever-changing conditions make it particularly difficult for entrepreneurs to configure resources effectively for long-term gain (Penrose 1959).

As pointed out, growth means an increase in the size and value of the firm's resource pool over time (Weinzimmer et al. 1998). There have been some initial attempts to define the role of resources in fueling strategy and growth in emerging firms (Dean et al. 1998; Greene et al. 1997; Hart et al. 1997; Mosakowski 1993). It is common to hear causes for venture failure, such as lack of adequate supply of capital or not enough good labor or talent (Churchill and Lewis 1983; Flamholtz 1995; Reynolds 1987). These, by definition, represent examples of transition issues associated with growth. We contend that such transitional issues and management's general inability to manage them successfully are why so few firms actually grow. Are there definitive resources that entrepreneurs use to manage growth effectively? Are there stable patterns in how these critical resources are configured in order to sustain high levels of growth over time? Are there unique routines that entrepreneurs use in the resource configuration process that serve to minimize the complexity associated with growth and to enhance the organization's capacity and innovation? In the next section, we briefly review some preliminary findings from several in-depth focus groups with growth-oriented entrepreneurs concerning how they successfully manage growth transitions.

RESOURCE-BASED APPROACH TO MANAGING GROWTH TRANSITIONS

In 1997 and 1998, the Kauffman Center for Entrepreneurial Leadership in Kansas City, MO, conducted a series of in-depth focus groups with CEO/founders of high-growth entrepreneurial firms. The purpose of the gatherings was to discuss the issues and circumstances in high-growth that entrepreneurs recognized as "defining transitions" in the life of their firms. Once identified, each transitional event was discussed in great depth to ascertain how the situation was successfully managed. A total of 173 CEO/entrepreneurs participated in the focus groups in two separate gatherings over the two-year period. To be eligible to participate, an entrepreneur had to be the founder and current CEO of the firm. The firm had to have annual revenues in excess of $3 million. Annual growth rates had to exceed 30 percent per year in revenues for the most recent three years and/or 20 percent per year in the number of full-time employees. According to national statistics, these criteria assured that the participating entrepreneurs were leaders of firms in the top 1 percent of fastest-growing firms in the United States. The participants represented firms in most major industry categories (i.e., manufacturing, services, retail, wholesale, financial/real estate, construction and transportation) and several high-technology sectors. The firms ranged in age from 2 to 48 years old, with a mean of 14 years of age. Average annual revenues were $20 million, and the average number of full-time employees was 80. Approximately 35 percent of the participating entrepreneurs had started more than one business venture, with 10 percent having started more than five separate ventures.

Trained moderators conducted the focus groups around a series of prepared questions that were designed to prompt the entrepreneurs to recall specific transitions in the growth and development of their firm that were particularly defining. Given the open-ended approach to collecting these data, the following review is not intended to represent a scientifically exhaustive list of issues. Rather, the following comments provide a baseline of evidence for the types of issues that define transitional moments for fast-growth entrepreneurial firms and the manner in which entrepreneurial leaders manage those transitions. In addition, the review highlights the importance of the entrepreneur's ability to accurately configure the resources in defining points in the development of the young organization and the way in which those solutions-oriented configurations served to reduce the complexity inherent in the process. As such, the transitions discussed and the solutions the entrepreneurs employed to manage them provide a significant framework from which to study the role that resources and resource configurations play in entrepreneurship, particularly entrepreneurship as the successful pursuit of opportunities for long-term gain (i.e., growth).

Describe key transitions in your firm

When asked to describe defining transitions that significantly shaped the firm's development, the participating entrepreneurs quickly categorized the transitional moments into internal (i.e., events within the firm and within the entrepreneur) or external (i.e., events in the marketplace). When probed for additional reflection, the entrepreneurs also qualified the internal transitions as those under the immediate control of the management team, while external transitions represented those outside of the control of the lead management team. The following is a summary of the transitions the entrepreneurs identified and the resource-based solutions (i.e., configurations) they employed to manage them. After each resource-based solution, the type of resource that the entrepreneur was using in the approach to managing the transitional moment is identified. The resource types were identified from previous research (Chandler and Hanks 1994) and follow the resource typology utilized by Greene et al. (1997): human resources, social resources, technology/physical resources, financial resources and organizational resources.

In addition, after each resource-based solution, we identify how the approach was used in managing the complexity that accompanied the transition itself and the added growth that resulted from the transition. The particular approaches were derived from Covin and Slevin's (1997) proposed typology: (1) diffusion of managerial complexity, (2) reduction of managerial complexity, (3) redefinition of managerial complexity and (4) capability building. *Diffusion* involves distributing the responsibility for managing the challenging issues that create complexity to subunits within the firm that are better capable of handling them. *Reduction* in managerial complexity involves either simplifying the firm's operational structure or redirecting responsibility for certain traditional, in-house functions to outside partners. *Redefinition*, the most reactive of the four proposed approaches to managerial complexity, involves analyzing the growth-derived managerial issues from several vantage points within the firm and utilizing the one perspective that most directly addresses the growth issues from the firm's greatest strengths. Finally, *capability building*, perhaps the most proactive of the four proposed approaches, emphasizes strengthening the firm's skills and creating new competencies within the firm that enhance the firm's capacity for managing complex issues as the firm grows. For each of the following resource-based solutions to managing challenging transitions, we identify which approach(es) to managing complexity is most consistent with that solution.

TRANSITIONS

For review purposes, the transitions identified during the focus groups are separated into six general categories: (1) transitions in personnel, (2) transitions in the underlying business model, (3) transitions in the organizational/management structure, (4) transitions in the lead role of the CEO/entrepreneur, (5) transitions in financial management and (6) transitions in the external environment. Examples of the transition triggers and the implications for resource configurations are reviewed for each category below in the order in which they were identified and discussed in the focus groups.

1 Defining Transitions in Personnel

- Having a valued, long-term senior employee leave the firm for a better opportunity or because they feel restricted by the new structure as the firm grows.
- Outgrowing the need for generalists and requiring the added skills of specialists in key areas as the firm grows.
- Having to fire a long-term, trusted employee because they cannot keep up with the demands of the job as the firm grows.

Resource-based solutions and implications for resource configuration

- ◆ "Don't settle for second best on key positions. Commit the money to hire superstars rather than average performers. If you can't afford the salary, experiment with other creative ways to compensate top players."
- ◆ "Hire specialists before you need them."

Types of resources strategically utilized: human, organizational, financial
- ◆ *Approach to managerial complexity: capability building* – By proactively hiring for future needs, entrepreneurs insure that their firms can continue to create and pursue new growth opportunities, thereby, sustaining a more stable, rapid rate of growth for longer periods.
- ◆ "Secure quality people by selling them on your vision first. Recognize that you are the company and people buy into you and your vision, not the firm."
- ◆ "The entrepreneur should stay involved in the hiring process for key positions."

Types of resources strategically utilized: organizational and financial
- ◆ *Approach to managerial complexity: diffusion and capability building* – The focus on quality people does more than just build capability. The quality emphasis is not directed toward a particular specialization, but also involves those skills and competencies associated with setting direction for the company. Entrepreneurs who are committed to growth choose to hire those who can help define the very nature of the business so as to enable the firm to adequately diffuse complex issues as growth occurs.

2 Transitions in the Underlying Business Model

- When you must question your underlying assumptions about what business you are in and what niche you are serving.

Resource-based solutions and implications for configuration

- ◆ "Implement an official and formal strategic planning process."
- ◆ "We reengineered the business several times in the last few years in order to streamline and automate the process and create commonality among all our lines

of business. We also put a lot of effort into integrating all the different policies
that have evolved as a result of rapid growth."

Type of resources strategically utilized: organizational

♦ *Approach to managerial complexity: redefinition and reduction* – Implementation of a
formal strategic planning process is often viewed as a milestone in the development of the new venture that signals the firm's "coming of age." It is most often
instituted when the entrepreneur realizes that the assumptions on which the firm
was founded are no longer adequate for sustaining the firm's growth rate.
Growth-oriented entrepreneurs are clear in their belief that formal planning
systems provide the means for regularly evaluating the fit between the strategies
and structures within the firm (i.e. reduction) and allow management to view
complex issues in growth from multiple perspectives within the firm (i.e., redefinition).

3 Transitions in Organizational/Management Structure

- Recognizing that your business partner has different goals and values than you.
- Employees begin to lose sight of the original vision.
- Not having the systems in place that you can use to properly assimilate growth as it
  occurs.
- Facing an inability to supply an adequate number of new products, while simulta-
  neously managing increasing demand with a changing management culture.
- Failing in the launch of a major new product line.

Resource-based solutions and implications for configurations

♦ "Establish the infrastructure that will allow you to focus on creating new products
and not dealing with the day-to-day operations of the firm. The infrastructure
should look to automate the process as much as possible."

♦ "Diversify your product/service offering across markets. Carefully balance between launching new product lines and maintaining adequate inventories on old
ones."

♦ "Know your technology needs and employ people that can build the technology
base."

Types of resource strategically utilized: organizational, technology, human

♦ *Approach to managerial complexity: capability building and diffusion* – In each of the
solutions cited above the entrepreneurs sought to expand their firm's capabilities
by configuring the infrastructure, automating various processes, diversifying its
product lines, and managing its technology base. In this case, where the transition
is most felt in the organizational structures, increasing the firm's capabilities is
focused on creating the infrastructure that allows for the diffusion of complexity
as new growth opportunities are pursued.

4 Transitions in the Lead Role of the CEO/ Entrepreneur

■ "Hitting the wall." Experiencing fast growth when some of your key managers are gone and the business is undercapitalized. "This was the first time in my life that I realized I couldn't do it all."

■ Recognizing that you are involved too much in the day-to-day operations and that you have too many people reporting to you.

■ Losing touch with the company as you add layers of management.

■ Feeling burned out and disillusioned with the business and you are no longer having any fun.

Resource-based solutions and implications for configurations

◆ "Delegate responsibility to effective and trustworthy senior managers and learn to live with some failure."

◆ "Build a culture that empowers people to take risks and make mistakes so that you can actually delegate responsibility. Open up lines of communication at all levels within the organization."

◆ "Define your job within the firm as CEO. Identify where you can add value and where you are a drain on the organization and work to make both lists as short as possible."

Types of resource strategically utilized: organizational and human

◆ *Approach to managerial complexity: redefinition* – Scholars have long recognized the changing role of the lead entrepreneur as the firm grows. However, few studies have addressed how entrepreneurs effectively manage these transitions. It is clear from the focus group data that growth-oriented entrepreneurs tend to be slow to recognize the extent to which their changing roles influence the firm's ability to sustain its rapid rate of growth. Also, entrepreneurs are generally reactive in their approaches to how they manage the complexities associated with these transitions. It may be that growth-oriented entrepreneurs opt to redefine the managerial complexity in these critical transitions so as to delay the decisions that determine their role and to make managing the complexity that their incompetence creates the responsibility of another function within the firm.

5 Transitions in Financial Management

■ Borrowing money for the first time or needing your first infusion of growth capital.

■ Realizing that you are able to grow sales but profit growth is slow or non-existent.

■ Experiencing your first significant loss after several years of profitable operations, all as a result of expanding the business too rapidly.

■ Enduring changes in your relationship with your primary lender. "At the time we were losing money and our representative at our bank left. His replacement did not know our company and would not approve our line advances."

■ Starting a second product line or second line of business with the goal of minimizing the cost of capital and maximizing equity.

Resource-based solutions and implications for configurations

◆ "We negotiated with another loan officer and were able to secure the line of credit. To avoid potential losses in the future we did a private placement which gave us enough working capital to support the growth and we switched banks."
◆ "Begin with the business model and build the management team around that model. Go after private equity to start the company because, unlike banks, private investors are able to help build the company, particularly if they are familiar with your industry."

Types of resources strategically utilized: organizational, social, financial
◆ *Approach to managerial complexity: reduction and reduction* – It is perhaps because so many growth-oriented entrepreneurs identify financial management as the area they know the least about that they tend to be most proactive in their approach to managing the complexity associated with defining transitions in this area. These entrepreneurs tend to seek outside advice, pursue an economic model for their businesses that incorporates creative access to the financial capital needed to support growth and simplify the firm's operations so as to minimize the complexity associated with transitions in financial management due to growth.
◆ "Don't underestimate the value of having a great legal/accounting/investment team. Spend plenty of time selecting the team and use them for more than as service providers."
◆ "Know and track your numbers, specifically the five or six key ratios for your business. Also, know how your firm compares to the competitors in your industry on each of these numbers."

Types of resources strategically utilized: organizational, human
◆ *Approach to managerial complexity: diffusion and redefinition* – Having the proper team to manage the complexities in financial management due to growth transitions is a common theme among growth-oriented entrepreneurs. These teams provide a means for diffusing the complexities and assigning the responsibility for managing the transitions to the most capable managers. Also, in financial transitions, knowledge of the key financial ratios that determine the success of the company provides the framework from which to explore the implications of the growth transitions as they occur.

6 Transitions in the External Environment

■ Increasing competition as your market gets smaller and smaller. Losing ground to foreign competition or other global developments.
■ Coming across sudden or unexpected opportunities to: purchase a new product, merge with another company, sell out all together or hire a great employee.

- Being forced to grow the business because a major customer demands more product.
- Developing technology makes your technology obsolete or less effective in meeting the market demands.
- Increasing regulation within the industry and within business in general. It is growing more difficult to just stay abreast of the changing legislation much less comply.

Resource-based solutions and implications for configuration

- "Continually strive to create niche markets to reduce competition and streamline overhead costs. Be willing to give up unprofitable accounts. Don't push growth for growth's sake, but focus on profitable growth."
- "Create a five-year growth plan that leverages your company's core expertise. Don't chase other areas of business that may be "hot" but not consistent with what you do best."

Types of resources strategically utilized: organizational, financial

- *Approach to managerial complexity: reduction* – Part of the approach to complexity here is to reduce complexity by engaging in some level of restructuring and restrategizing as growth opportunities are identified (i.e., reduction). Both suggestions involve the "creation of new markets," once again, revealing a high level of proactivity in dealing with complexity.
- "Stay abreast of changing legislation and recognize it as an 'opportunity.'"
- "Create an information officer within the company to constantly scan the environment and to identify leading trends and opportunities for growth."
- "Involve your key people in strategic planning for the future of the business."

Types of resources strategically utilized: human and organizational

- *Approaches to managerial complexity: diffusion and capacity building* – Most of the efforts to build capability for these transitions was designed around creating knowledge centers within the firm that could identify new opportunities. However, in many instances comments were made about needing the additional capacity within specific areas, functional areas within the firm capable of addressing a relatively high level of complexity and, thereby, supporting a more rapid rate of growth.

Summary

During the focus groups, the high-growth entrepreneurs identified a plethora of transitions that served as defining moments in the life of their entrepreneurial ventures. Such events were discussed as those that, if not properly managed, could mean the difference between the survival or failure of the business. The importance of these transitions suggests that an understanding of the means by which growth-oriented entrepreneurs manage them should be particularly useful for understanding how firms sustain high rates of growth. From the examples cited, clearly the resource and knowledge-based perspectives provide a productive framework from which to consider how the resulting solutions impact the ability of the firm to grow. Generally speaking, the management approaches drew on multiple resources, often required that the resources be deployed in new combinations and required a high level of skill and knowledge on the part of the entrepreneurial leader. In addition, each new resource configuration was designed to address the unique managerial complexity generated in the transition (i.e., complexity that determined the critical nature of the situation) and to enhance the ability of the firm to sustain growth over time. Because of their forward-looking nature, capability-building approaches tended to be the most proactive means for addressing challenging complex issues in growth. Redefinition approaches were the most reactive as the entrepreneur looked for ways to redefine the complexity that had already been incurred through the growth process. In summary, growth-oriented entrepreneurs tend to use a variety of approaches to managing the complexity of growth transitions, with each approach having its own unique obligations on firm resources and how those resources are configured in order to sustain fast growth over time.

RESEARCH DIRECTIONS

Though we have cited several articles in the formulation of these viewpoints, not a lot of literature explores the growth of entrepreneurial ventures or attempts to explain how managers effectively manage the growth process and the complexity that accompanies rapid transitions. This is both surprising and unfortunate: surprising because of the significant contribution that high-growth ventures make to our nation's economic well being and unfortunate because of the relatively small number of companies that do grow fast enough to produce substantial wealth. In light of these considerations, however, there appear to be several opportunities for future research.

One area that needs further attention is *the role of industry context*. Recent debates in strategic management, between industrial organization economists and resource-based theorists, have concluded that one view is not universally better than the other. Rather, it appears that the relative importance of industry-level and firm-level factors are contextual (Eisenhardt and Schoonhoven 1996; Henderson and Mitchell 1997; Mahoney and Pandian 1992; McGrath et al. 1995; Miller and Shamsie 1996). This suggests that the role resources play in managing growth transitions is moderated by the type of industry and the relative strength of industry characteristics, such as size, competitive hostility, growth rate and technological development (Dean et al. 1998; Eisenhardt and Schoonhoven 1990; McDougall et al. 1994). Future research therefore needs to examine growth transitions in a variety of industries to determine which types of resources and resource configurations are most important for managing transitions in certain circumstances (Coff 1997). Industry settings are also important with respect to their effect on the ability of a particular resource configuration (i.e., firm) to generate significantly higher levels of wealth than other configurations. In addition, with assumptions of perfect information and immutable resources, research should explore how multiple configurations can coexist, in fact, flourish, in a single industry.

As is obvious from the results of the Kauffman Center focus groups, the *types of resources* currently recognized in the research literature are inadequate for capturing the core or essence of the role resources play in the entrepreneurial process. As a result, the categorization of resources into types, though methodologically easier to manipulate, can severely limit our understanding of how entrepreneurial leaders successfully manage growth transitions by restructuring or reconfiguring their firm's resources. Additional research could help to identify how entrepreneurs perceive of their resources and what influence their perception has on how they approach the management of growth transitions. Much of the current research into the resource and knowledge-based per-spectives, operationalizes resources by assessing the entrepreneurial leader's perceptions of the importance of certain classes of resources to the growth of the firm. The authors contend that the research has to shift to measuring resources themselves, including critical intangible resources, such as the skill and knowledge of the entrepreneurial decision-maker as part of the resource pool known as the firm.

Throughout this chapter we have explored the role of resource configurations in pursuit of opportunities for long-term gain for two fundamental purposes: (1) to control for and accommodate growth as it occurs, and (2) to provide for future growth through product and process innovation. Consistent with the examples of transitional moments from the Kauffman Center focus groups, the innovation literature has identified the need for entrepreneurs, who desire their firms to grow, to innovate and to create a resource configuration that sustains a high level of growth over time. The rate at which a firm can grow is dictated by the ability of the entrepreneur and the entrepreneurial team to configure the firm's resources to produce a continuous self-sustaining flow of resources. The intent is to maximize the utility of the resources under control with respect to management's long-term intentions toward the opportunity. A key focus for future research, therefore, would be how entrepreneurial leaders strike the appropriate balance within each unique configuration with some resource deployed for control and others deployed for innovation.

Every industry situation requires a unique combination of resources to produce wealth in the face of competitive pressures. Wealth that is produced in relationship to manage-ment's intentions requires that those intentions be imposed on the marketplace. Under such circumstances, the entrepreneurial leader must produce the rents necessary to meet the firm's goals with the resources under his or her control. The question is then, within each unique competitive situation, what is the balance that must be maintained in the resource configurations between resources deployed for innovation to fuel future growth and resources committed to building capacity for sustaining the growth that has and will occur? Not only will each firm's resource pool be unique, but the balance in the configuration between resources committed to these domains may also be unique and, as such, may provide access to the ultimate competitive advantage in growth.

Dougherty and Hardy (1996) found that large, mature firms could not achieve sustained innovation because the champions within the firm responsible for innovation could not overcome the structural issues within the firm which determined when and how innovation got pursued. They argued that the availability of resources, processes and meaning was often happenstance and depended heavily on the individual rather than the organizational system. Thus, if sustaining growth for the long-term requires constant innovation (i.e., constant reconfiguration of firm resources committed to propel-ling future growth), it would be worthwhile to study how entrepreneurial firms develop the commitments, systems and structures that support innovation. The problem with life-cycle models, in this regard, is that they view the growth process in stages without acknowledging that the stages are an artifact of the researcher's explanation of the events and are not indicative of the events themselves. Firm growth does not occur in stages, and thereby, resource configurations are not one-time arrangements. As Greene et al. (1997) found, unique resource configurations do not typically relate to a particular stage of the life cycle.

Learning and sense-making theory might also shed light on the role of resource configurations in the pursuit of opportunities for long-term gain. Many unanswered questions remain about how entrepreneurs make sense of their situations so that they know what resource configurations are appropriate in what circumstances. There are also questions about how they know that a particular configuration will be effective. Likewise, a lot still has to be learned about how the necessary knowledge is acquired and processed since knowledge is required in the ongoing process of managing growth transitions (Greve 1998).

Other issues for further study include regarding the rate or speed at which the firm grows. How is the speed at which a firm grows impacted by the ability to obtain and effectively deploy resources in the pursuit of opportunity? How is the rate of growth impacted over time as the firm grows in size and complexity? How does the rate of change in the external market influence the firm's ability to grow? Chaos theory and the nonlinear dynamic model of firm growth should have a lot to say about how growth firms are able to overcome increasingly difficult change in increasingly turbulent markets. A review of the adaptive characteristics of natural nonlinear and chaotic systems, as applied to organizations, may help to provide a suitable prescription for entrepreneurial firms wishing to match their structures to rapidly changing environments and growth (Neumann 1997).

Another area needing further research is the interaction of resources and knowledge with the stage of organizational development. There have been several life-cycle models represented in the entrepreneurship literature (Churchill and Lewis 1983; Flamholtz 1995; Kazanjian 1988; Scott and Bruce 1987) that have suggested that the types of problems the firm encounters change as it progresses through the representative stages. If the types of problems a firm encounters in each transitional stage differ, then it is likely that the resources and knowledge to address these problems would differ as well. However, work that matches key resources and stage of organizational development is now beginning to appear (Greene et al. 1997; Hart et al. 1997).

It is well-accepted that as firms grow their resource configurations will change from simple at the outset to more complex. As a result, there are also issues over the role and ability of the entrepreneur as he or she attempts to manage the firm toward a particular level of growth. This perspective goes beyond the resource-based view and acknowledges the impact of growth transitions on managerial capabilities. Transitions are said to impact (1) managerial thought processes concerning what types of resource are needed, (2) managerial abilities to coordinate the resource flow and (3) managerial capabilities to support organizational learning and to manage existing knowledge resources effectively (Sanchez and Mahoney 1996). Sanchez and Mahoney (1996) argued that by addressing these three dimensions of transitions, the approach recognizes the future uncertainties inherent in strategic change, the cognitive limitations of entrepreneurs as they attempt to manage within those uncertainties and the added complexity associated with size.

Conclusions

In this chapter we have presented a resource and knowledge-based model of managing growth transitions. We have argued that growth transitions are best managed by identifying and developing the knowledge necessary to make transitions in earlier phases rather than waiting until growth forces them to do so. This perspective provides several advantages to prior perspectives on growth transitions. First, it is proactive rather than reactive in nature. This forces the founders to focus on the firm's future much sooner than they might otherwise and gets them to identify key resources and processes before they are needed. Second, it focuses on intangible resources rather than tangible ones. Many firms may choose not to grow because of the perception that they do not have the adequate physical resources to compete with larger firms in their industry (Dean et al. 1998). The reality, however, may be that specialized knowledge and new organizational routines may allow them the opportunity to use the firm's larger size and more established resource base against it. Third, it makes distinctions in how and what types of knowledge are required to certain types of growth transitions. The flow of knowledge moves from being predominantly founder-based to middle managers to lower levels of the firm as it develops. While the findings from the entrepreneur focus groups provide some support for this perspective, it is clear that there are many more questions than answers about the role of resources and knowledge in the management of growth transitions. Therefore, this topic should provide abundant research opportunities into the twenty-first century.

References

Adizes, I. 1989. *Corporate Lifecycles*. Englewood Cliffs, NJ: Prentice-Hall.

Adizes, I. 1996. *The Pursuit of Prime*. Santa Monica, CA: Knowledge Exchange.

Aldrich, H.A. 1979. *Organizations and Environments*. Englewood Cliffs, NJ: Prentice-Hall.

Amit, R. and Shoemaker, P.J.H. 1993. Strategic assets and organizational rent. *Strategic Management Journal* 14(1): 33–46.

Ashmos, D.P., Duchon, D., Hauge, F.E. and McDaniel, R.R. Jr. 1996. Internal complexity and environmental sensitivity in hospitals. *Hospital and Health Services Administration* 41(4): 535–55.

Barnett, W.P., Greve, H.R. and Park, D.Y. 1994. An evolutionary model of organizational performance. *Strategic Management Journal* 15(1): 11–28.

Barney, J.B. 1986. Strategic factor markets: Expectations, luck, and business strategy. *Management Science* 32(10): 1231–41.

Barney, J.B. 1991. Firm resources and sustained competitive advantage. *Journal of Management* 17(1): 99–120.

Birley, S. and Westhead, M. 1990. Growth and performance measures between "types" of small firms. *Strategic Management Journal* 11(7): 535–57.

Boyd, B.K., and Reuning-Elliott, E. 1998. A measurement model of strategic planning. *Strategic Management Journal* 19(2): 181–92.

Bruno, A. and Tyebjee, T. 1982. The environment for entrepreneurship. In C. Kent, D. Sexton and K. Vesper (eds.), *Encyclopedia of Entrepreneurship*. Englewood Cliffs, NJ: Prentice-Hall, pp. 288–306.

Carland, J.W., Hoy, F., Boulton, W.R. and Carland, J.C. 1984. Differentiating entrepreneurs from small business owners: a conceptualization. *Academy of Management Review* 9(2): 354–9.

Chandler, G.N. and Hanks, S.H. 1994. Resource based capabilities, strategy, and new venture performance. *Journal of Business Venturing* 9(4): 331–49.

Child, P., Diederichs, R., Sanders, F.H. and Wisniowski, S. 1991. SMR Forum: the management of complexity. *Sloan Management Review* 33(1): 73–80.

Churchill, N.C. and Lewis, V.L. 1983. The five stages of small business growth. *Harvard Business Review* 61(3): 30–50.

Clifford, D.K. Jr. 1975. The case of the floundering founder. *Organizational Dynamics* 4(2): 21–54.

Coff, R.W. 1997. Human assets and management dilemmas: coping with hazards on the road to resource-based theory. *Academy of Management Review* 22(2): 374–402.

Conner, K.R. 1991. A historical comparison of resource-based theory and five schools of thought within Industrial Organization economics: do we have a new theory of the firm? *Journal of Management* 17(1): 121–54.

Covin, J.G. and Slevin, D.P. 1991. A conceptual model of entrepreneurship as firm behavior. *Entrepreneurship Theory and Practice* 16(1): 7–25.

Covin, J.G. and Slevin, D.P. 1997. High growth transitions: theoretical perspectives and suggested directions. In D.L. Sexton and R.W. Smilor (eds.), *Entrepreneurship 2000*. Chicago: Upstart Publishing, pp. 99–126.

Dean, T.J., Brown, R.L. and Bamford, C.E. 1998. Differences in large and small firm responses to environmental context: strategic implications from a comparative analysis of business formations. *Strategic Management Journal* 19(8): 709–28.

Dodge, H.R., Fullerton, S. and Robbins, J.E. 1994. Stage of the organizational life cycle and competition as mediators of problem perception for small businesses. *Strategic Management Journal* 15(2): 121–34.

Dougherty, D. and Hardy, C. 1996. Sustained product innovation in large, mature organizations: overcoming innovation-to-organization problems. *Academy of Management Journal* 39(5): 1120–53.

Eisenhardt, K.M. and Schoonhoven, C.B. 1990. Organizational growth: linking founding team, strategy, environment, and growth among US semiconductor ventures 1978–1988. *Administrative Science Quarterly* 35: 504–29.

Eisenhardt, K.M. and Schoonhoven, C.B. 1996. Resource-based view of strategic alliance formation: strategic and social effects in entrepreneurial firms. *Organization Science* 7(2): 136–50.

Flamholtz, E. 1995. Managing organizational transitions: implications for corporate and human resource management. *European Management Journal* 13(1): 39–51.

Fombrun, C.J. and Wally. S. 1989. Structuring small firms for rapid growth. *Journal of Business Venturing* 4: 107–22.

Gartner, W.B. 1985. A conceptual framework for describing the phenomenon of new venture creation. *Academy of Management Review* 10(4): 696–706.

Gartner, W.B., Bird, B.J. and Starr, J.A. 1992. Acting as if: differentiating entrepreneurial from organizational behavior. *Entrepreneurship Theory and Practice* 16(3): 13–31.

Grant, R.M. 1991. The resource-based theory of competitive advantage: Implications for strategy formulation. *California Management Review* (spring): 114–35.

Grant, R.M. 1996. Toward a knowledge-based theory of the firm. *Strategic Management Journal* 17(3): 109–22.

Greene, P.G., Brush, C.G. and Brown, T. 1997. Resources in small firms: an exploratory study. *Journal of Small Business Strategy* 8(2): 25–40.

Greiner, L.E. 1972. Evolution and revolution as organizations grow. *Harvard Business Review* 50(4): 37–46.

Greve, H.R. 1998. Performance, aspirations and risky organizational change. *Administrative Science Quarterly* 43(1): 58–86.

Hall, R. 1993. A framework linking intangible resources and capabilities to sustainable competitive advantage. *Strategic Management Journal* 14(8): 607–18.

Hambrick, DC and Crozier, L.M. 1985. Stumblers and stars in the management of rapid growth. *Journal of Business Venturing* 1(1): 31–45.

Hannan, M. and Freeman, J. 1984. Structural inertia and organizational change. *American Sociological Review* 49: 149–64.

Hanks, S.H. and Chandler, G.N. 1994. Patterns of functional specialization in emerging high tech firms. *Journal of Small Business Management* 32(2): 22–36.

Hanks, S.H., Watson, C.J., Jansen, E. and Chandler, G.N. 1993. Tightening the life-cycle construct: a taxonomic study of growth stage configurations in high-technology organizations. *Entrepreneurship Theory and Practice* 18(2): 5–24.

Hart, M., Greene, P. and Brush, C.G. 1997. Leveraging resources: building an organization on an entrepreneurial resource base. Presented at the Babson/Kauffman Entrepreneurship Research Conference, Wellesley, MA.

Henderson, R. and Mitchell, W. 1997. The interactions of organizational and competitive influences on strategy and performance. *Strategic Management Journal* 18(special issue): 5–14.

Kazanjian, R.K.1988. Relation of dominant problems to stages of growth in technology-based new ventures. *Academy of Management Journal* 31(2): 257–79.

Kirzner, I. M. 1973. *Competition and Entrepreneurship*. Chicago: University of Chicago Press.

Kotha, S. 1995. Mass customization: Implementing the emerging paradigm for competitive advantage. *Strategic Management Journal* 16(1): 21–42.

Leonard-Barton, D. 1992. Core capabilities and core rigidities: a paradox in managing new product development. *Strategic Management Journal* 13(S): 111–25.

Levinthal, D.A. and March, J.G. 1993. The myopia of learning. *Strategic Management Journal* 14(1): 95–112.

Lumpkin, G.T. and Dess, G.G. 1995. Simplicity as a strategy-making process: the effects of stage and organizational development and environment on performance. *Academy of Management Journal* 38(5): 1386–407.

Mahoney, J.T. and Pandian, J.R. 1992. The resource-based view within the conversation of strategic management. *Strategic Management Journal* 13(5): 363–80.

Matusik, S.F. and Hill, C.W.L. 1998. The utilization of contingent work, knowledge creation, and competitive advantage. *Academy of Management Review* 23(4): 680–97.

McDougall, P.P., Covin, J.G., Robinson, R.B. Jr. and Herron, L. 1994. The effects of industry growth and strategic breadth on new venture performance and strategy content. *Strategic Management Journal* 15(7): 537–54.

McGrath, R.G., MacMillan, I.C. and Venkataraman, S. 1995. Defining and developing competence: a strategic process paradigm. *Strategic Management Journal* 16(4): 251–75.

Miller, D. 1993. The architecture of simplicity. *Academy of Management Review* 18(1): 116–38.

Miller, D. and Chen, M.J. 1996. The simplicity of competitive repertoires: an empirical analysis. *Strategic Management Journal* 17(6): 419–39.

Miller, D. and Shamsie, J. 1996. The resource-based view of the firm in two environments: the Hollywood film studios from 1936–1965. *Academy of Management Journal* 39(3): 519–43.

Miller, D., Lant, T., Milliken, F.J. and Korn, H. 1996. The evolution of strategic simplicity: Exploring two models of organizational adaptation. *Journal of Management* 22(6): 863–87.

Mosakowski, E. 1993. A resource-based perspective on the dynamic strategy–performance relationship: an empirical examination of the focus and differentiation strategies in entrepreneurial firms. *Journal of Management* 19(4): 819–39.

Nelson, R.R. and Winter, S.G. 1982. *An Evolutionary Theory of Economic Change*. Cambridge, MA: Belknap.

Neumann, F. Jr. 1997. Organizational structures to match the new information-rich environments: lessons from the study of chaos. *Public Productivity and Management Review* 21(1): 86–100.

Nonaka, I. 1994. A dynamic theory of organizational knowledge creation. *Organization Science* 5(1): 14–37.

Olson, P.D. and Terpstra, D.E. 1992. Organizational structural changes: life cycle structural influences and managers' and interventionists' challenges. *Journal of Organizational Change Management* 5(4): 27–40.

Penrose, E. 1959. *The Theory of the Growth of the Firm*. New York: Wiley.

Peteraf, M.A. 1993. The cornerstones of competitive advantage: a resource-based view. *Strategic Management Journal* 14(3): 179–91.

Polanyi, M. 1962. *Personal Knowledge*. Chicago: University of Chicago Press.

Reynolds, P. 1987. New firms: societal contribution versus survival potential. *Journal of Business Venturing* 2(3): 231–46.

Reynolds, P.D. 1993. High performance entrepreneurship: what makes it different? In N. Churchill et al. (eds.), *Frontiers of Entrepreneurship Research*. Babson Park, MA: Babson College, pp. 88–101.

Sanchez, R. and Mahoney, J.T. 1996. Modularity, flexibility, and knowledge management in product and organization design. *Strategic Management Journal* 17(1): 63–76.

Schein, E.H. 1990. Organizational culture. *American Psychologist* 45(1): 109–19.

Schumpeter, J.A. 1934. *The Theory of Economic Development*. Cambridge, MA: Harvard University Press.

Scott, M. and Bruce, R. 1987. Five stages of growth in small business. *Long Range Planning* 20(3): 45–52.

Sexton, D.L. and Bowman-Upton, N. 1991. *Entrepreneurship: Creativity and Growth*. New York: Macmillan.

Shaver, K. and Scott, L. 1991. Person, process and choice: the psychology of new venture creation. *Entrepreneurship Theory and Practice* 16(2): 23–46.

Siegel, R., Siegel, E. and MacMillan, I. 1993. Characteristics distinguishing high growth ventures. *Journal of Business Venturing* 8(2): 169–80.

Slater, S.F. and Narver, J.C. 1995. Market orientation and the learning organization. *Journal of Marketing* 59(3): 63–74.

Spender, J.C. and Grant, R.M. 1996. Knowledge and the firm: Overview. *Strategic Management Journal* 17(1): 5–9.

Stacey, R.D. 1995. The science of complexity: an alternative perspective for strategic change processes. *Strategic Management Journal* 16(6): 477–95.

Stalk, G., Evans, P. and Shulman, L.E. 1992. Competing on capabilities: the new rules of corporate strategy. *Harvard Business Review* 70(2): 57–69.

Stanworth, M.J.K. and Curran, J. 1976. Growth and the small firm – an alternative view. *Journal of Management Studies* 95–110.

Teece, D.J., Pisano, G. and Shuen, A. 1997. Dynamic capabilities and strategic management. *Strategic Management Journal* 18(7): 509–33.

Tushman, M.L. and O'Reilly, C.A. III 1996. Ambidextrous organizations: managing evolutionary and revolutionary change. *California Management Review* 38(4): 8–30.

Vanderwerf, P.A. 1993. A model of venture creation in new industries. *Entrepreneurship Theory and Practice* 17(2): 39–47.

Weinzimmer, L.G., Nystrom, P.C. and Freeman, S.J. 1998. Measuring organizational growth: issues, consequences, and guidelines. *Journal of Management* 24(2): 235–62.

Wernerfelt, B. 1984. A resource-based view of the firm. *Strategic Management Journal* 5: 171–80.

16

Growth of Technology-based New Firms

Erkko Autio

Streams of Research on Technology-based New Firms
The Strategic Management Stream
Directions for Future Research

This chapter's aim is to provide an overview of the research tradition focusing on technology-based new firms (TBNFs) and to point out directions for potential future research. Another aim is to take a critical look at the foundations of this research. In other words, is there any justification for focusing on TBNFs as a distinct stream of research? Is there anything special about the growth of TBNFs that would differentiate them from other new firms? First, an introduction into the history of research on TBNFs is given. Second, different streams of research on TBNFs are described and their contributions assessed to build a case for a dedicated stream of research on TBNFs. Finally, directions for further research are discussed.

Streams of Research on Technology-based New Firms

TBNFs have always commanded a special place in entrepreneurship research for they are the classic Schumpetarian agents of innovation, which initiated gales of creative destruction in economic systems. Schumpeter (1911) was the first economist to identify technology as the key driving force of economic change and growth. This approach differentiated him from neoclassical and keynesian economists, who relegated technology into the role of residual variable, which explained residual economic change that was unexplained by demand and supply conditions. In his Mark I model of innovation, new firms were assigned the role of offsetting the typical tendency of large firms toward stability and greater productive efficiency, which also meant, for Schumpeter, less innovation.

Later Schumpeter revised his thinking in his Mark II model. In the Mark II model he postulated that the heyday of small firm innovation had passed due to perceived increased economies of scale in R&D, but in fact, the view of TBNFs as agents of innovation has persisted. There are good reasons for this. TBNFs, by virtue of their technology intensity, tend to inhabit new industry sectors, in which rapid growth tends to be more common than in more mature industry sectors. The popular success stories of high-growth firms, such as Apple, Dell, Hewlett-Packard and Microsoft, are almost all examples of TBNFs. The well-known regional success stories, such as the Route 128 around Boston, Silicon Valley in California and the Cambridge region in the United Kingdom, are all spectacular examples of technology-driven regional economic growth. Not surprisingly, TBNFs occupy a prominent place in both the media and research.

Growth is of the essence for entrepreneurship research, and resource-driven growth (as opposed to market-driven growth) represents one of the two fundamental forms of new firm growth (Penrose 1959: 65–6). Technology is one important growth-driving resource, particularly for diversification (Penrose 1959: 109–10). The study of TBNF growth is therefore important for understanding firm growth in general. Distinct streams in research focusing on TBNFs can indeed be identified. The first emerged in the United States in the 1960s and is labeled here as the "spin-off stream" because of its heavy emphasis on spin-off firms emanating from universities and research institutes. The second is labeled the "strategic management stream" because of its theoretical foundation. Note that the above categorization is a simplification of reality, as most categorizations inevitably are.

The spin-off stream

The spin-off stream is so called because of its heavy initial emphasis on spin-off firms. Later, however, this stream has evolved to incorporate studies with a more general focus: for example, on regions or on selected industry sectors. Yet, spin-off studies continue to be carried out even today.

Initially, the driving motivation behind this stream appears to have been the discovery of this "new" breed of entrepreneurial firms. Particularly active in this stream were the research groups of Edward B. Roberts (1968), Roberts and Wainer (1966) and Arnold C. Cooper (1972, 1973). Both groups studied the emergence of technology-based spin-off firms from universities and government research institutes (and sometimes from industry). Roberts focused on MIT-based spin-off firms in the Boston area along Route 128, and Cooper researched mainly what was to be known as Silicon Valley.[1] The work of these groups inspired similar studies elsewhere in North America (e.g., Smilor et al. 1990), Canada (e.g., Doutriaux and Peterman 1982; Doutriaux 1987) and Europe (Watkins 1973; Dickenson and Watkins 1971).

The early spin-off studies were explorative and descriptive in character (Cooper 1973). Roberts's (1968) main emphasis was identifying MIT spin-off firms and studying various aspects of them, including growth. Roberts developed a "snowballing technique" for identifying sample firms, which entailed asking known founders of MIT spin-off firms about any other spin-off firms that they knew about. Regardless of the sample identification methods, the sample selection criteria were quite well established. To qualify as a TBNF, the firm had to be (1) "young," less than 25 years old (Little 1979), (2) based on exploiting a potential invention or a particular technological competence, (3) established by an individual or a group of individuals and (4) if a spin-off firm, have the spin-off relationship controlled by, e.g., previous employment in the incubator organization (Roberts and Wainer 1968) or by the intensity of initial technology transfer from the incubator (Autio et al. 1989).

The interest in this stream focused on four main areas: (1) the technical entrepreneurs, (2) various aspects of their firms, (3) relationships between the firms and their incubating organizations and (4) possible differences between technical and nontechnical firms. In each of these areas, a wealth of empirical data was produced. Technical entrepreneurs, it was learned, tended to be more highly educated than their nontechnical counterparts, were usually in their mid-thirties when starting their firms and often worked in teams. Much effort was invested into understanding the influence of the motivational make-up of the entrepreneur on the growth of new firms (e.g., Smith and Miner 1984), but this research direction never succeeded in establishing definite influences.

A number of studies examined the success of these firms, drawing initially on analyses of the success of technological innovations. A notable model in this regard was provided by the SAPPHO projects carried out by the Science Policy Research Unit (SPRU) of the University of Sussex (Rothwell et al. 1974). These projects produced lists of factors contributing to the success and failure of technological innovations, which were emulated by studies focusing on TBNFs. Recognizing the importance of the entrepreneur for the success of the firm, such studies mostly examined relationships between various characteristics of the founders and firm growth (Maidique 1986). Success was linked, among other things, to the number of members in the start-up team, previous industry experience, complementarity of management team members' skills and previous experience in similar start-ups.

Several studies have examined differences between high-technology and low-technology new firms. Such studies have suffered from a number of methodological points, as illustrated by the Cambridge City Council study (cited in Monck et al. 1988: 46–7). While the study found that high-technology firms (as defined by industry classification) had grown faster than "conventional" manufacturers in the Cambridgeshire area, the comparison was based on relative growth measures that favored small TBNFs. In addition, the selection of "high-tech" or "conventional manufacturing" sectors was based on data availability. Because of such methodological shortcomings, the spin-off stream has not been able to conclusively establish that TBNFs grow more rapidly than conventional new firms do. While it appears clear that new industry sectors, which often are technology-intensive, grow more rapidly than mature industry sectors, the understanding of how exactly technology intensity affects growth remains unclear. In his overview of high-technology entrepreneurship research, Cooper (1986: 163) noted, "the typical young high-technology firm probably grows much more rapidly than its non-technical counterpart." However, little rigorous research existed to back up this assumption at that time.

In Europe, the replications of North-American-type spin-off firm surveys produced largely similar empirical findings with occasional refinements (Watkins 1973; Dickenson and Watkins 1971; Olofsson and Wahlbin 1984; McQueen and Wallmark 1984; Monck et al. 1988; Westhead and Storey 1994). Of these, the studies by Monck et al. (1988) and Westhead and Storey (1994) are perhaps the most interesting. Both looked at the impact of science parks on the growth of TBNFs. Using stratified samples of firms located on and off science parks, the two studies provided some evidence that TBNFs located outside science parks had grown faster. However, the methodologies used did not permit the researchers to establish whether or not these findings were caused by high-growth firms leaving science parks. In any case, toward the mid-1990s, some European research-ers were exasperated by the perceived underperformance of TBNFs in terms of growth. Oakey (1994: 2–6) concluded that "NTBF's [new, technology-based firms] were not a simple panacea for the industrial ills of the United kingdom" and that "it is a gross oversimplification to argue that all (or most) NTBF's have rapid growth potential."

The studies of Monck et al. (1988) and Westhead and Storey (1994) also illustrate the strong regional and economic policy flavor that has always been close to the spin-off stream. Both in Europe and in the United States, the adoption of research parks and science parks as tools of regional economic and technology policy has strengthened this flavor, as the effectiveness of these tools in promoting economic growth has been assessed. While the policy studies tend to sidestep the issue of growth at the firm level (thus outside the scope of this chapter), they added to our insight factors influencing growth at the regional level. Sometimes regional economic studies have implications also for the growth of individual technology-based firms. Particularly illuminating in this regard are Annalee Saxenian's (1994) case studies of Sun in Silicon Valley and Apollo along Route 128, on the one hand, and Hewlett-Packard in Silicon Valley and Digital Equipment Corp. (DEC) along Route 128, on the other, which illustrate the influence of regional culture on firm behavior and growth. In the open and collaborative Silicon Valley environment, Sun and HP were able to increase their flexibility through outsourcing, whereas the more secretive corporate culture of Route 128 pushed Apollo and DEC toward much stronger vertical integration. Where Sun and HP have continued to prosper, DEC and Apollo have ceased to exist as independent companies.

Conclusions about the spin-off stream

The spin-off stream of TBNFs played an important role in raising awareness about this sector and has also produced a wealth of information about these firms, their founders, growth, technology transfer effects and so on. However, as the present and previous overviews of this stream demonstrate (Bollinger et al. 1983; Cooper 1986; Roberts 1991), it has not been very successful in developing a detailed understanding of the growth of TBNFs for the following reasons:

1 The spin-off stream, while producing a wealth of empirical data, was mainly atheoretical, in that it mainly failed to produce coherent theoretical frameworks that might have ensured cumulativeness and guided further research efforts. In the absence of unifying frameworks, success-factor lists easily become idiosyncratic.

2 The study samples were mostly cross-sectional, often paid little or no attention to industry influences and therefore could not generate a very comprehensive under-standing of the growth of TBNFs.

3 Even when comparative research designs were used (e.g., when comparing "techni-cal" entrepreneurs against "nontechnical" entrepreneurs), the rationale for sample selection was often not well established or guided by theory.

4 Focusing on or assuming single-product firms (probably because of the influence of SAPPHO-type role models), the spin-off stream largely rested on an implicit linear

model of technological innovation. The TBNF was treated as a kind of innovation project, which either succeeded or failed with its product.

5 Beyond anecdotal citations of cases of high-growth technology-based firms, the spin-off stream largely failed to establish whether TBNFs indeed grew more rapidly than other new firms and why.

The Strategic Management Stream

In fairness, the primary objective of the spin-off stream was not to provide a detailed understanding of the growth of TBNFs. Such an aspiration finds a more natural home in the strategic management research tradition, of which entrepreneurship is generally considered to constitute a subfield. Like strategy research, entrepreneurship research is interested in explaining performance at the firm level, but it is distinguished from strategy research by the fact that the pursuit of growth is typically pursued without regard to resources currently available to the firm (Stevenson et al. 1989), with the possible exception of technology as a dominant resource in the case of TBNFs.

Further, despite its failure to develop a detailed understanding of technology-based growth, the spin-off stream had a distinctive focus on TBNFs as a distinct group of firms, often defined on the basis of a spin-off and related technology transfer relationship with a public or private sector research institution. In the strategic management stream, a similar distinctive focus is often lacking. For example, different studies have variably focused on single and multiple-industry samples, or they may have controlled the high-technology character of their samples in other ways.

By "strategic management stream" I denote all studies of TBNFs that draw on some established strategy framework. The studies under this heading are quite varied and include both single and multiple-industry studies, using both survey and case methods and on theoretical argumentation and treating technology either both as a firm-level or as an industry-level variable. In addition, the studies have been more or less loosely attached to a variety of strategy frameworks. Although such variety makes it difficult to identify a distinguishable stream of strategic management studies of TBNFs, these studies are important as a group because they improve our understanding of both the growth of TBNFs and of the role of technology in that process.

Of the various strategy frameworks, the following review focuses primarily on those whose unit of analysis is the individual firm. Our primary interest here is on understanding firm-level influences on growth.

Entrepreneurship and strategic management

An important body of research focusing on the growth of new firms, particularly TBNFs, already exists. Yet only few strategy models and frameworks have been developed explicitly for TBNFs. These include the ones proposed by Maidique and Patch (1982) and Kazanjian (1988). Maidique and Patch developed a typology of strategies with particular reference to innovating firms. Kazanjian developed and empirically validated a model of the growth of technology-based new firms.

Maidique and patch typology

Of the different strategy typologies, the Maidique and Patch (1982) model is the one most explicitly developed for innovating firms. Their typology identifies four common strategies in technology-intensive industries, based on timing of entry, competitive scope and source of competitive advantage:

1 *First-mover strategy*, in which the firm attempts to be the first to introduce a new product to the market and exploit the temporary monopoly created by the first entry.

2 *Cost-minimization strategy*, in which the firm attempts to gain advantage through developing a cost-efficient operation.

3 *Fast-follower strategy*, in which the firm relies on rapid imitation of new innovations introduced by competition.

4 *Niche strategy*, in which the firm specializes on servicing narrowly defined customer or application niches.

Note that of the four strategy types, two are defined in terms of timing of market entry, while the remaining two reflect competitive scope. The validity of this typology in the context of technology-intensive firms was examined by Boeker (1989), who found its validity in the context of semiconductor firms to be greater than some alternative typologies (e.g., Porter 1980). Boeker (1989) used this typology to examine the influence of early strategic choices of TBNFs for their later development. He found that early strategy choices tend to become etched in the organization and routines of the TBNF and that the routines and structures developed to support chosen strategies tended to persist and strengthen over time. If the firm adopted, for example, a fast-follower strategy early on, it tended to remain a fast follower later in its life because of the operation of Stinchcombe's (1965) "traditionalizing forces."

Boeker did not find links between strategy types and growth in his study. The Maidique and Patch typology has not been empirically linked with the growth of TBNFs in other studies, either, possibly reflecting the fact that the feasibility of different strategies may vary in different contexts and for different firms. However, looking at the growth of semiconductor ventures, Eisenhardt and Schoonhoven (1990) found evidence of a traditionalizing effect analogous to the one observed by Boeker. In their sample, Eisenhardt and Schoonhoven found that initial performance differences between firms tended to persist, with "success breeding success" and "the poor getting poorer" over time.

Kazanjian's growth model

Since Penrose's (1959) work, in which theory technology and firm-specific knowledge were important drivers of growth, few have attempted to develop theories or models of the growth of technology-based firms. A noteworthy exception is Kazanjian's (1988) model, which identifies four growth stages in technology-based firms, defined in terms of dominant problems characteristic of each stage: (1) conception and development, (2) commercialization, (3) growth and (4) stability. The model was validated using a sample of independent new firms in high-technology industries. While Kazanjian was careful to emphasize that not all firms go through the same sequence of stages and that his model was not a metamorphosis model in which firms go through fundamental, distinct transformations when passing from one stage to another, the model nevertheless received general support in empirical data. Kazanjian found that, as expected, different issues and problems were typical for different self-rated stages of growth. Furthermore, firms in more advanced stages of growth tended to be older than firms in less advanced stages of growth.

Later, Kazanjian and Drazin (1990) used the model to study the influence of fit between a set of relevant organizational design parameters and growth stage. They found that firms that had developed an optimal configuration of decision making centralization, decision-making formalization and functional specialization in different growth stages, had grown faster.

Kazanjian's stated motivation for developing his growth model was that the extant growth models at the time had not been specifically developed for TBNFs. However, apart from incorporating a "conception and development" stage, Kazanjian's model did not incorporate any other elements exclusively for TBNFs. Thus, Kazanjian's model added little to the theoretical and empirical understanding of the relationships between technology intensity and growth in new ventures. His model was developed explicitly for single-product, independent new firms that operated in an existing market. Further, in Kazanjian's model, market acceptance simply happened, but the determinants of market acceptance were never examined. The critical and complex problem of market and industry creation was thus not addressed by his model (Aldrich and Fiol 1994).

Apart from Kazanjian's own work, his growth model has not been widely used in empirical studies. An interesting approximation of growth-stage thinking was employed by Randolph et al. (1991), who examined the effect of fit between technological innovation and organization structure on performance in small firms. In Randolph's study, performance was defined as return on sales (ROS), and sales growth was used as a moderating variable. As hypothesized, they found that the fit between technological innovation and organization structure was a better predictor of performance in mature companies than in young companies. In addition, they found that this fit was a better predictor of ROS in slowly growing firms (in terms of sales growth) than in rapidly growing firms. These findings suggest that during periods of rapid growth, optimizing organizational and internal factors may not be as important as taking advantage of environmental munificence.

Another study focusing on the fit between organizational design parameters and growth was conducted by Naman and Slevin (1993), who developed a normative model of strategic fit for high-technology manufacturing firms. Their model incorporated measures pertaining to environmental turbulence, entrepreneurial style, organization structure (mechanistic versus organic) and mission strategy. Naman and Slevin found a positive relation between their measure of fit and a multi-item operationalization of performance (including sales growth).

Internal and industry influences on firms

Until the mid-1980s, empirical studies on the growth of TBNFs typically produced fairly idiosyncratic lists of internal success factors, such as various aspects of the founder, management team or the product. References to established strategy frameworks were few, due to the absence of such frameworks. In their literature review and hypotheses on TBNFs, Bollinger et al. (1983) examined the known factors contributing to the success of TBNFs. The only empirical findings that they could cite was that the more successful TBNFs (in terms of growth) were started by stronger management teams and that more technology had been transferred from the incubating organization to the more successful new firms. These two influences are probably linked to each other. Of these influences, the important role of the management team in particular has been confirmed in several studies. An example is the study by Roure and Maidique (1986), who analyzed the success factors of eight venture capital-backed high-technology companies. They found that the founders of successful ventures had more joint working experience, that the management teams of the more successful firms were larger and more complete, that the members of the team had more function-specific experience and that the successful teams had more previous experience from high-growth firms in the same industry as the new venture. They also found that successful ventures targeted markets that had a higher buyer concentration.

The consolidation of strategic management research, induced notably by Rumelt's (1974) and Porter's (1980) contributions, was soon reflected in entrepreneurship research. Sandberg and Hofer (1987) were the first to introduce an explicit multilevel framework for analyzing determinants of growth. Most previous studies had focused exclusively on internal factors, such as characteristics of the entrepreneur, the founding team and the initial technology (Bollinger et al. 1983). But by analyzing a multiple-industry group of venture capital-backed firms, Sandberg and Hofer concluded that industry structure and venture strategy constitute more important influences on new venture performance than do bibliographical data describing the entrepreneur. An adaptation of Sandberg and Hofer's contribution is illustrated in figure 16.1.

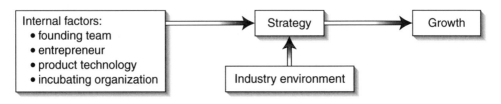

FIGURE 16.1. Sandberg and Hofer's multilevel framework
Source: Adapted from Sandberg and Hofer (1987)

Feeser's (1987) dissertation incorporated elements of a multilevel framework similar to the one used by Sandberg and Hofer. Feeser focused explicitly on the growth of high-technology firms, comparing a sample of thirty-nine high-growth high-technology firms against a sample of thirty-nine low-growth high-technology firms in computing equipment industry (SIC 3573). Feeser found that in high-growth firms, the initial product and market choices had been more stable than in low-growth high-technology firms (Feeser and Willard 1990). In addition, Feeser and Willard (1989) analyzed differences between high and low-growth high-technology firms, focusing particularly on the influence of incubator characteristics on growth. They found that a close association between the technology-bases of the spin-off firm and the incubator was positively associated with growth. They also found that a relatively greater proportion of high-growth firms had incubated from large, publicly held firms.

Reflecting the design of Sandberg and Hofer's framework, Eisenhardt and Schoonhoven (1990) linked characteristics of founding team, strategy and environment to the sales growth of semiconductor firms. Using a carefully compiled and comprehensive sample of US semiconductor firms, they found significant main and interaction effects between founding team characteristics and market stage for growth. On the other hand, they did not find any effect for technological innovation or competition at founding on growth. Even though less innovative firms were found to have an early advantage over more innovative firms, this effect dissipated over time. Eisenhardt and Schoonhoven's (1990: 524) description of the performance of the firms studied illustrates well the conditions that TBNFs face in emergent markets:

> Only a few firms founded in emergent markets reached sales of $20 million. Most languished at low sales levels, waiting for their markets to become established. In some cases, the market never established. In other cases, emergent markets did blossom into growth markets, but the early entrants were often too weak to take advantage.

The above description emphasizes the critical effect of timing of entry on technology-based new venture growth. If the firm manages to catch the market wave and ride it successfully, explosive growth may result. If the timing is not successful, the firm may stagnate and eventually see the rewards of its development work appropriated by others.

Roure and Keeley (1990) studied the success of thirty-six venture capital-backed firms operating in the electronic and information technology industries. They examined the influence of both firm-internal and product-market factors on growth. In their sample, 57 percent of the variance in new venture performance (measured as internal rate of return for shareholders) was explained by founding team completeness, technical superiority of the product, expected time for product development and buyer concentration. Both product development time and buyer concentration were found to depict an inverted U-shaped relationship with performance.

Bantel (1998) identified influences on the performance of "adolescent" firms (5 to 12 years old) in a range of technology-based industries. The industries were selected on the basis of rapid change of their base technologies. Her analysis was based on a framework that identified four strategic archetypes that combined both organizational ecology and strategic choice perspectives along two independent continua: basis of competition (efficiency versus first-to-market) and breadth of competitive domain (narrow versus wide) (Zammuto 1988). She identified six strategy clusters but did not observe great sales differences between clusters.

Bantel identified two characteristic limitations of her study. The first was the use of single respondent measures for analyzing strategies and outcomes. The second was the difficulty of accurately measuring performance for young firms, particularly young technology-intensive firms, for which investments in R&D and market development may take time before coming into fruition. Both are often cited as difficulties in research focusing on TBNFs (e.g., McDougall and Robinson 1990; Eisenhardt and Schoonhoven 1990).

The above studies have operationalized the environment of TBNFs as an industry. But a Standard Industrial Classification (SIC) code-based operationalization of the operating environment is not always the optimal one for new firms because they often suffer from resource scarcity and are dependent on a few key external relationships. Furthermore, the study by Robinson and McDougall (1998) suggests that the application of some widely used operationalizations of various industry characteristics may lead to even conflicting results. They studied different operationalizations of industry concentration, product differentiation and industry life cycle and found that all produced quite different influences on growth, when tested on a sample of "high-potential" manufacturing ventures (defined using the performance of an IPO as a criterion).

A major problem with operationalizing the environment as a product-market combination is that it easily relegates the market to a passive role and treats the new firm simply as a product development project. When the intricacies of market creation and of the achievement of market acceptance for a new technology are not considered, market acceptance is easily treated as something that simply either happens or not. Similarly, markets are treated as something that exist but are not actively created. Further, in such a research setting, industry conditions are easily treated as universally homogeneous and similar to all firms, old and young alike. Such assumptions are, of course, oversimplifying and do not reflect the reality of new firms very well (Aldrich and Fiol 1994; Levinthal 1997).

Studies on resource dependence and network positional influences

An alternative operationalization of the operating environment, and one more compatible with the widely used resource dependence perspective, is to conceive of the operating environment as a set of relationships through which the new firm accesses resources and transacts with other organizations (Aldrich and Pfeffer 1976; Pfeffer and Salancik 1978). In this vein, Venkataraman et al. (1990) analyzed the effects of the liability of newness on the failure of ten software companies and found that the firms used their existing customer relationships to attract other resource providers. This led to the firms being highly dependent on a few key relationships, exposing them to failure in turbulent environments. They proposed that a high growth orientation pushes entrepreneurs toward using such a risky strategy. Later, Venkataraman and Van de Ven (1998) extended their analysis, emphasizing that an industry is most often not the optimal framework for analyzing the operating environment for new firms, due to the stated dependency on a few key relationships.

Particularly in the 1990s, an increasing number of studies have explicitly recognized the importance of external exchange relationships on the early development of TBNFs. In particular, a number of studies have focused on technology outsourcing arrangements and on the creation and exploitation of interorganizational relationships for growth by TBNFs. Zahra (1996), for example, analyzed technological strategies and related differences in the performance of independent and corporate biotechnology ventures. He noted that little is known about how new ventures exploit their technological resources to achieve success. He found several differences in the technology strategies of independent and corporate biotechnology ventures: independent ventures were found to focus more on pioneering products, to emphasize applied R&D more and to rely on internal research and development more than corporate ventures. Interestingly, Zahra found that independent ventures also outperformed corporate ventures in the biotechnology industry in terms of three-year average sales growth, return on equity (ROE) and subjective satisfaction with performance. He speculated that this might be from the greater resource allocation flexibility of independent new ventures, as well as from emphasizing radical innovation at an early stage of industry development.

McGee and Dowling (1994) analyzed relationships between management team experience, R&D cooperative arrangements and sales growth in new high-technology ventures. Their sample consisted of young independent firms (less than eight years old) that had attempted an initial public offering and that operated in a high-technology industry sector, as defined by the National Science Foundation. McGee and Dowling found that the influence of cooperative arrangements was mediated by management's previous industry experience and technical expertise. In the absence of previous industry experience and technical expertise, the association between R&D cooperative arrangements and sales growth was negative. However, if the management team of the biotechnology venture had previous industry experience or if they possessed significant technical expertise, the influence of R&D cooperative arrangements on sales growth was positive, suggesting that experience and expertise is required in order to transform cooperation to growth.

Zhao and Aram (1995) studied networking and growth among young technology-intensive firms in China. They distinguished between "range" and "intensity" of interorganizational relationships and found (in a study of six case firms) that rapidly growing technology-based firms outperformed the slowly growing firms both in terms of range and intensity of network relationships. They refrained from making causal inferences of their findings, however.

Eisenhardt and Schoonhoven (1996) drew on the resource-based view of the firm to look at influences on strategic alliance formation in US semiconductor firms from 1978 to 1985. Their empirical evidence suggests:

1 the number of competitors increases the rate of alliance formation,
2 the rate of alliance formation is higher in younger markets, and
3 the rate of alliance formation increases as a function of the innovativeness of the firm's strategy.

Regarding competition, they argued that alliances can strengthen vulnerable competitive positions and enhance the legitimacy of the new firm. Regarding market stage, they argued that strategic alliances help legitimize a new market and signal that the market will become established. Regarding strategy innovativeness, they argued that strategic alliances help the innovating firm to leverage complementary assets, helping it keep focused on technology development. In addition, they linked the rate of alliance formation to the social capital possessed by the management team of the firm, showing that new firms with a high initial social capital endowment will be better positioned to further increase this capital.

Even though the resource-based view of the firm has been a popular framework for strategic management studies in the 1990s, many of its core constructs have seldom been used in empirical studies. This applies also to research on TBNFs. One reason for this surprising shortcoming is probably the highly qualitative nature of such factors as resource distinctiveness, imperfect resource imitability, resource sustainability and resource rarity (Autio et al. 1998). Only a few studies of these factors could be found.

Conner and Rumelt (1991) and Conner (1995) looked at the role of imitation in market creation. They found that in network externality environments (such as that in many sectors of the software industry), the best strategy for the innovating firm may be to encourage clones, as this helps rapidly expand the user base and thus create positive network externalities. Autio et al. (1998) found that imitability of the core technology is positively related to the international growth of young electronics firms. They speculated that this finding might be due to the market creation effect or imitability, making technology adoption by customers easier. However, they were able to exclude the possibility that higher imitability would have forced the firms to "run faster," as no negative correlation could be found between the timing of international entry and core technology imitability.

Lumme (1998) conducted a study that produced a more fine-grained view of the effects of environmental selection and local adaptation on expectations of entrepreneurial rent and growth among TBNFs. The model combined elements from the resource-based view, evolutionary economics and from the "rugged fitness landscape" literature (Levinthal 1997) to show how internal firm and external environment factors jointly determine the "local fitness" of TBNFs. Her model used a sample of ninety-three independent TBNFs. Of particular interest was her use of the rugged fitness landscape framework to emphasize the importance of the local selection environment, not the industry, for the survival and growth of TBNFs. Levinthal's argument is that the competitive environment of the firm may comprise several local optima and that a new firm's destiny in such a rugged landscape depends on the location at which it enters this landscape at the time of its founding. Different local optima may produce similar performance levels, but it may be very difficult for the new firm to "jump" from one "peak" to another, or even to "see" the entire landscape and thus to locate the highest peaks.

Conclusions about the strategic management stream

The strategic management stream has significantly increased the understanding of the growth of TBNFs, which has become both richer and more varied. The question still remains, however, whether any real progress has been made toward a better understanding of the growth of technology-intensive new firms in particular, or whether one indeed even should expect such progress. Clearly, more theorizing is called for and more application of theory to empirical research is also in demand.

Reflecting on the reality of most TBNFs, most of the studies reviewed focus on single-product firms that operate in a reasonably well-defined product-market environment. The firm either grows or stagnates with its product. This is reflected also in Kazanjian's (1988) growth model, as well as in most of the other extant models of firm growth (for an overview, see Levie 1997). Kazanjian's model discusses only organic growth, without considering other possible growth strategies. Davidsson and Delmar's (1998) empirical study suggests that such an approach may lead to a myopic view of the growth phenomenon. Using corporate demographic data in Sweden, Davidsson and Delmar (1998) found that while over 90 percent of the total growth in firms with less than ten employees was organic growth (as opposed to growth through acquisitions), this percentage fell to 50 percent for firms with 250 or more employees. With a particular reference to TBNFs, McCann (1991) analyzed patterns of growth, financial structure and technology among TBNFs in three broadly defined industry sectors. By means of factor analysis, he identified seven growth strategies among these firms:

1 equity growth (fueling growth through private and public equity placements)
2 acquisitive growth
3 incremental growth (e.g., enhancements and extensions of existing products)
4 breakthrough business venturing (internal venturing via R&D or growth through major innovations)
5 strategic alliances (formal joint ventures and partnering)
6 vertical integration
7 using debt to fuel growth.

While McCann's analysis included both expansion strategies and means for funding them, it illustrates well how limiting the focus on organic growth only can be. In particular, acquisitive growth appears to have been given less attention in empirical studies than its economic importance would appear to justify.

Another interesting aspect of the studies reviewed here is that they all focus on situations in which the market already exists, but the intricacies of market creation have not been given much attention. This situation reflects the well-known practical constraints of the study of new firms. We mostly hear stories about successful companies, but little information is as forthcoming from those who fail to crack the market. Yet the road to successful market creation is littered with the bodies of those who failed to make it. The study of market creation, despite its practical difficulty, would appear to be of particular relevance for TBNFs because of the importance of positive externalities that generate increasing returns to the adoption of new technologies in many industries (Katz and Shapiro 1986; Arthur 1989). When the value of a particular technology to a potential user is a function of the extent of the established user base, such technologies often experience highly nonlinear, almost dichotomous, diffusion curves. The technology may either experience an explosive expansion of user base, or its user base may remain marginal indefinitely (Bettis and Hitt 1995). A good example is provided by the personal computer (PC) operating software industry, where the dominance of Windows appears unassailable (for the moment, at least).

In most of the reviewed studies, technology is primarily embodied in the products of the firm, implying a degree of R&D intensity in the organization. However, in most studies, the role of technology ends here. Causal or correlational influences between aspects of technology and growth have not been empirically tested or theoretically inferred. The main motivation for most studies on the growth of TBNFs appears to be the considerable perceived growth potential of these firms. However, apart from the technology-based label, little in these studies differentiates them from others on the growth of new ventures. In particular, it seems surprising that despite the considerable number of studies focusing on TBNFs, only a few have even attempted to develop and use measures of technological intensity and complexity or other measures that appear to be relevant for the study of technology-based firms. The absence of reliable and robust operationalizations of such constructs has been noted by Singh (1997), for example, who in the absence of absolute measures employed a relative measure of technological complexity in his study on the effect of interfirm cooperation on business survival in the US hospital software industry.

Further, considering that TBNFs have attracted dedicated research interest since the 1960s, it is surprising that no generally agreed measure of technological intensity or sophistication has emerged. Several researchers have commented on the inadequacy of self-reported R&D costs as a measure of technology intensity in the context of new firms, whose R&D may be sporadic and project-based and that may have imported a substantial hidden R&D investment from their incubating organization. New firms often do not have dedicated R&D departments and thus may experience difficulty in assessing the scale of their R&D, and the R&D investment may be heavily loaded with future expectations.

Both single and multiple-industry samples have been analyzed in previous studies. Here, the obvious trade-off is between depth and detail of analysis, on the one hand, and generalizability, on the other. While sampling strategy should be dictated by the research question, many of the multiple-industry samples appear to have been convenience samples. Since solid theoretical justifications for the choice of multiple-industry samples have seldom been put forward, one may even question the justification of restricting the analysis to technology-intensive industry sectors in many cases. Because industry conditions vary considerably and TBNFs face many forms of environmental turbulence, not the least of which are technological factors, controlling variance in external conditions appears to be a generally more recommendable sampling strategy.

Finally, considering how much attention is attached to the protection and exploitation of intellectual property rights (IPR) in technology-intensive industries, the absence of studies examining optimal IPR strategies for TBNFs is baffling. Most often, the only reference to IPR strategies is made by including either the number or the existence of patents in empirical studies. This practice gives an oversimplifyied picture of IPR protection among TBNFs because of the well-known weaknesses of using patents as an indicator of technological competencies, particularly in new and small firms. Furthermore, some studies (e.g., Teece 1986; Conner and Rumelt 1991; Conner 1995; and Garud and Kumarasawamy 1995) suggest that the relationships between IPR protection and growth are far from trivial. On one hand, the firm needs to prevent others from appropriating the economic returns generated by the outcomes of its innovative activity. On the other, because of the operation of network externalities, protecting IPR too tightly may impede technology diffusion and thus thwart market creation. For example, overtly restrictive IPR practices have often been cited as one reason for the failure of Apple to obtain leadership in the PC operating system market despite its clear early technical superiority over the competing Windows system. Clearly, the attention given to IPR issues so far in research on TBNFs seems far from sufficient.

DIRECTIONS FOR FUTURE RESEARCH

Bettis and Hitt (1995) identify four technological trends that shape the competitive environment of firms:

1 the increasing rate of technological change and diffusion
2 the information age, as typified by the Internet
3 increasing knowledge intensity
4 the emergence of positive industry feedback.

All these trends emphasize the importance of the study of TBNFs and highlight the need to develop new approaches. Because of the increasing knowledge intensity of many business transactions, "industry" is becoming less relevant as the operating environment of TBNFs. Competition and growth are increasingly shaped and constrained by the dynamics of technological systems and of technology diffusion, and new approaches must be developed to increase the relevance of studies on TBNFs.

Most of my remarks in previous sections reflect the fact that we still lack a dedicated theory of the relationships between growth and technology in new firms. Most studies to date, true to the entrepreneurship research tradition, focus on the entrepreneur or management team, conventional product and market and industry variables without attempting to develop a theoretical understanding of the influence of technology on new-firm growth. To date, Penrose's (1959) work remains probably the most comprehensive attempt to link technology to firm growth, even though some attempts toward this direction have started to appear. The picture painted by most studies is still overwhelmingly one in which a single-product firm, operating in a passive, existing market, either grows or dies with its product development project (Autio 1997). While this picture is undoubtedly true for most TBNFs, it may fail to accurately reflect some aspects that are intrinsic to them.

In the 1990s, criticizing established theory frameworks for neglecting the social component of business transactions seems to have become fashionable. However, similar criticisms can be extended to extant studies on the growth of TBNFs. The focus on single-product firms and the assumption of a fairly stable product-market combination tend to overlook the fact that technology is essentially a social construct largely created by people (e.g., embodied in the skills and experience of the founding team), and in order to gain commercial success, it needs to be interpreted and put into use by people (Cohen and Levinthal 1990; Liebeskind 1996). The social aspects of technology may have both internal and external implications for the growth of TBNFs. At the internal level, these implications entail, for example, the development of technology and related human and social capital within the firm and applying them to fuel growth. At the external level, the implications pertain to technology diffusion, dominant design selection and lock-in and to the effect technological system architectures have on them.

Future studies focusing on the growth of TBNFs should continue to borrow from other disciplines. For example, many innovation theory models with direct implications for TBNF growth have yet to be implemented, including the competence-enhancing and competence-destroying model of Tushman and Anderson (1986), the model of nonassembled and simple-assembled products, the closed-assembled and open-assembled systems model of Tushman and Rosenkopf (1992), and the model of the evolution of industry product classes by McGrath et al. (1992). Also the emerging knowledge-based view of the firm appears to hold particular promise for the study of the growth dynamics of TBNFs, whose business is largely based on the development and exploitation of technology (Spender 1996; Spender and Grant 1996). This framework reflects many of the ideas originally put forward by Penrose (1959), who defined the "technological base" as comprising all the components of the productive activity of the firm, including machinery, raw materials and related skills and knowledge. As the firm learned to use these more efficiently over time, new knowledge was developed, which in turn created new "productive opportunities." For Penrose, the rate of growth was very much regulated by the growth of the firm's knowledge and of its technology base, or the rate of its learning. Integrative models that link social capital, knowledge, learning and growth appear promising for the development of new insights into the growth of TBNFs.

NOTES

I dedicate this chapter to the memory of my beloved father Seppo, who left this world on December 12, 1998.

1 The name "Silicon Valley" was coined by Don Hoefler, editor of a local electronics newsletter (Larsen and Rogers 1987: 106).

REFERENCES

Aldrich, H.E. and Pfeffer, J. 1976. Environments of organizations. *Annual Review of Sociology* 2: 79–105.

Aldrich, H.E. and Fiol, C.M. 1994. Fools rush in? The institutional context of industry creation. *Academy of Management Review* 19(4): 645–70.

Arthur D. Little. 1979. *New Technology Based Firms in the UK and Federal Republic of Germany*. London: Wilton House.

Arthur, W.B. 1989. Competing technologies, increasing returns, and lick-in by historical events. *Economic Journal* 99(March): 116–31.

Autio, E. 1997. New, technology-based firms in innovation networks: symplectic and generative impacts. *Research Policy* 26(3): 263–81.

Autio, E., Sapienza, H. and Almeida, J. 1998. Effects of internationalization, knowledge intensity and imitability to growth. Presented at the Academy of Management Conference, San Diego, August 8–11.

Autio, E., Kaila, M., Kanerva, R. and Kauranen, I. 1989. *Uudet teknologiayritykset (New, technology-based firms)*, Finnish National Fund for Research and Development, Sitra, B 101.

Bantel, K.A. 1998. Technology-based, "adolescent" firm configurations: Identification, context, and performance. *Journal of Business Venturing* 13: 205–30.

Bettis, R.A. and Hitt, M.A. 1995. The new competitive landscape. *Strategic Management Journal* 16: 7–19.

Bollinger, L., Hope, K., Utterback, J.M. 1983. A review of literature and hypotheses on new technology-based firms. *Research Policy* 12: 1–14.

Boeker, W. 1989. Strategic change: the effects of founding and history. *Academy of Management Journal* 32: 489–515.

Brown, S.L. and Eisenhardt, K.M. 1997. The art of continuous change: linking complexity theory and time-paced evolution in relentlessly shifting organizations. *Administrative Science Quarterly* 42: 1–34.

Cohen, W. and Levinthal, D. 1990. Absorptive capacity: a new perspective on learning and innovation. *Administrative Science Quarterly* 35: 128–52.

Conner, K.R. 1995. Obtaining strategic advantage from being imitated: when can encouraging "clones" pay? *Management Science* 41(2): 209–16.

Conner, K.R. and Rumelt, R.P. 1991. Software piracy: an analysis of protection strategies. *Management Science* 37: 125–39.

Cooper, A.C. 1972. *Spin-off Companies and Technical Entrepreneurship, IEEE Transactions on Engineering Management*, vol. 1, EM-18.

Cooper, A.C. 1973. Technical entrepreneurship: what do we know?, *R&D Management* 3(2): 59–65.

Cooper, A.C. 1986. Entrepreneurship and high technology. In D.L. Sexton and R.W. Smilor (eds.), *The Art and Science of Entrepreneurship*. Cambridge, MA: Ballinger, pp. 153–68.

Cooper, A.C. and Bruno, A.V. 1977. Success among high-technology firms. *Business Horizons* (April): 16–23.

Davidsson, P. and Delmar, F. 1998. Some important observations concerning job creation by firm size and age. Mimeo. Jönköping International Business School, Sweden.

Dickenson, P.J. and Watkins, D.S. 1971. *Initial Report on Some Financing Characteristics of Small, Technologically-based Firms and their Relation to Location*. Manchester Business School.

Doutriaux, J. 1987. Growth pattern of academic entrepreneurial firms. *Journal of Business Venturing* 2: 285–97.

Doutriaux, J. and Peterman, B. 1982. *Technology Transfer and Academic Entrepreneurship at Canadian Universities*. Technological Innovations Studies Program, Ottawa.

Eisenhardt, K.M. and Schoonhoven, C.B. 1990. Oganizational growth: linking founding team, strategy, environment, and growth among US semiconductor ventures 1978–1988. *Administrative Science Quarterly* 35: 506–39.

Eisenhardt, K.M. and Schoonhoven, C.B. 1996. Resource-based view of strategic alliance formation: strategic and social effects in entrepreneurial firms. *Organization Science* 7(2): 136–50.

Feeser, H.F. 1977. Incubators, entrepreneurs, strategy and performance: a comparison of high and low growth high-tech firms. Ph.D. dissertation, Purdue University, West Lafayette, IN.

Feeser, H.R. 1987. Incubators, entrepreneurs, strategy, and performance: a comparison of high and low growth high-tech firms. Ph.D. dissertation. Purdue University, West Lafayette, IN.

Feeser, H.R. and Willard, G.E. 1989. Incubators and performance: a comparison of high- and low-growth high-tech firms. *Journal of Business Venturing* 4: 429–42.

Feeser, H.R. and Willard, G.E. 1990. Founding strategy and performance: a comparison of high and low growth high-technology firms. *Strategic Management Journal* 11(2): 87–99.

Garud, R. and Kumarasawamy, A. 1995. Technological and organizational designs for realizing economies of substitution. *Strategic Management Journal* 16: 93–109.

Katz, M. and Shapiro, C. 1986. Technology adoption in the presence of network externalities. *Journal of Political Economy* 94: 822–41.

Kazanjian, R.K. 1988. Relation of dominant problems to stages of growth in technology-based new ventures. *Academy of Management Journal* 31: 257–79.

Kazanjian, R.K. and Drazin, R. 1990. A stage-contingent model of design and growth for technology-based new ventures. *Journal of Business Venturing* 5: 137–50.

Larsen, J.K and Rogers, E.M. 1987. Silicon Valley: the rise and falling off of entrepreneurial fever. In R.W. Smilor, G. Kozmetsky and D.V. Gibson (eds.), *Creating the Technopolis: Linking Technology Commercialization to Economic Development*. Cambridge, MA: Ballinger, pp. 99–115.

Levie, J. 1997. A review of theories of early corporate growth. Mimeo. Babson Park, MA: Babson College.

Levinthal, D. 1997. Adaptation on rugged landscapes. *Management Science* 43(7): 934–50.

Liebeskind, J.P. 1996. Knowledge, strategy, and the theory of the firm. *Strategic Management Journal* 17: 93–107.

Lumme, A. 1998. Local selection environment nurturativeness in determining the fitness of new, technology-based firms: derivation and validation of a model. Ph.D. Dissertation. Acta Polytecnica

Scandinavica, Mathematics, Computing, and Management in Engineering Series No. 94, Espoo, Finland.

Maidique, M.A. 1986. Key success factors in high-technology ventures. In D.L. Sexton and R.W. Smilor (eds.), *The Art and Science of Entrepreneurship*. Cambridge, MA: Ballinger, pp. 169–80.

Maidique, M. and Patch, P. 1982. Corporate strategy and technological policy. In M. Tushman and W. Moore (eds.), *Readings in the Management of Innovation*. Boston: Pitman, pp. 273–85.

McCann, J.E. 1991. Patterns of growth, competitive technology, and financial strategies in young ventures. *Journal of Business Venturing* 6: 189–208.

McDougall, P. and Robinson, R. 1990. New venture strategies: an empirical identification of eight "archetypes" of competitive strategies for entry. *Strategic Management Journal* 11: 447–67.

McGee, J.E. and Dowling, M.J. 1994. Using R&D cooperative arrangements to leverage managerial experience: a study of technology-intensive new ventures. *Journal of Business Venturing* 9: 33–48.

McGrath, R.G., MacMillan, I.A. and Tushman, M.L. 1992. The role of executive team actions in shaping dominant designs: towards the strategic shaping of technological progress. *Strategic Management Journal* 13: 137–61.

McQueen, D.H, Wallmark, T. 1984. Innovation output and academic performance. In J. Hornaday, F. Tarpley, Jr., J. Timmons, and K. Vesper (eds.), *Frontiers of Entrepreneurship Research*. Babson Park, MA: Babson College, pp. 18–31.

Monck, C.S.B, Porter, R.B., Quintas, P.R., Storey, D.J. and Wynarczyk, P. 1988. *Science Parks and the Growth of High Technology Firms*. London: Croom Helm.

Naman, J.L. and Slevin, D.P. 1993. Entrepreneurship and the concept of fit: a model and empirical tests. *Strategic Management Journal* 14: 137–53.

Oakey, R. 1994. *New, Technology-Based Firms in the 1990's*. London: Paul Chapman.

Olofsson C. and Wahlbin C. 1984. Technology-based new ventures from technical universities: a Swedish case. In J. Hornaday, F. Tarpley, J. Timmons and K. Vesper (eds.), *Frontiers in Entrepreneurship Research*. Wellesley, MA: Babson College.

Penrose, E. 1959. *The Theory of Growth of the Firm*. Oxford: Blackwell.

Pfeffer, J. and Salancik, G.R. 1978. *The External Control of Organizations: A Resource Dependence Perspective*. New York Harper & Row.

Porter, M.E. 1980. *Competitive Strategy*. New York: Free Press.

Randolph, W.A., Sapienza, H.J. and Watson, M.A. 1991. Technology-structure fit and performance in small businesses: an examination of the moderating effects of organizational stages. *Entrepreneurship Theory and Practice* 16(3): 27–41.

Roberts, E.B. 1968. Entrepreneurship and technology: a basic study of innovators. *Research Management* 11(4): 249–66.

Roberts, E.B. 1991. *Entrepreneurs in High Technology*. Cambridge, MA: Oxford University Press.

Roberts, E.B. and Wainer, H., 1966. *Some Characteristics of the Technical Entrepreneur*, Working Paper 195–66, Sloan School of Management, Massachusetts Institute of Technology.

Robinson, K.C. and McDougall, P.P. 1998. The impact of alternative operationalizations of industry structural elements on measures of performance for entrepreneurial manufacturing ventures. *Strategic Management Journal* 19: 1079–100.

Rothwell, R., Freeman, C., Horsley, A., Jervis, V., Robertson, A. and Townsend, J. 1974. SAPPHO updated – Project SAPPHO phase II. *Research Policy* 3: 258–91.

Roure, J.B. and Maidique, M.A. 1986. Linking prefunding factors and high-technology venture success: an exploratory study. *Journal of Business Venturing* 1: 295–307.

Rumelt, R.P. 1974. *Strategy, Structure and Economic Performance*. Cambridge, MA: Harvard Business School.

Roure, J.B. and Keeley, R.H. 1990. Predictors of success in new technology based ventures. *Journal of Business Venturing* 5: 201–20.

Sandberg, W.R. and Hofer, C.W. 1987. Improving new venture performance: the role of strategy, industry structure, and the entrepreneur. *Journal of Business Venturing* 2: 5–28.

Saxenian, A. 1994. *Regional Advantage: Culture and Competition in Silicon Valley and Route 128*. Cambridge, MA: Harvard University Press.

Schumpeter, J. 1911. *Theorie der wirtschaftlichen Entwicklung. Eine Untersuchung über Unternehmer, Kapital, Kredit, Zins und den Konjunkturzyklus*. Berlin: Duncker und Humblot.

Singh, K. 1997. The impact of technological complexity and inter-firm cooperation on business survival. *Academy of Management Journal* 40(2): 339–67.

Smilor, R.W. and Feeser, H.E. 1991. Chaos and the entrepreneurial process: Patterns and policy implications for technology entrepreneurship. *Journal of Business Venturing* 6: 165–72.

Smilor, R.W., Gibson, D.V. and Dietrich, G.B. 1990. University spin-out companies: technology start-ups from UT-Austin. *Journal of Business Venturing* 5: 63–76.

Smith, N.R. and Miner, J.B. 1984. Motivational considerations in the success of technologically innovative entrepreneurs. In J. Hornaday, F. Tarpley, J. Timmons and K. Vesper (eds.), *Frontiers of Entrepreneurship Research*. Babson Park, MA: Babson College, pp. 488–95.

Spender, J.-C. 1996. Making knowledge the basis of a dynamic theory of the firm. *Strategic Management Journal* 17: 45–62.

Spender, J.-C. and Grant, R.M. 1996. Knowledge and the firm: overview. *Strategic Management Journal* 17: 5–9.

Stevenson, H., Roberts, M. and Grousbeck, H. 1989. *New Business Ventures and the Entrepreneur*, 3rd edn. Homewood, IL: Irwin.

Stinchcombe, A.L. 1965. Organizations and social structure. In S.G. Marck (ed.), *Handbook of Organizations*. Chicago: Rand-McNally, pp. 142–93.

Storey, D.J. 1994. *Understanding the Small Business Sector*. London: Routledge.

Teece, D.J. 1986. Profiting from technological innovation. *Research Policy* 15: 285–305.

Tushman, M.L. and Anderson, P. 1986. Technological discontinuities and organizational environments. *Administrative Science Quarterly* 31: 439–65.

Tushman, M. and Rosenkopf, L. 1992. Organizational determinants of technological change: toward a sociology of technological evolution. In B. Staw and L. Cummings (eds.), *Research in Organizational Behavior*. Greenwich, CT: JAI Press, pp. 311–47.

Venkataraman, S. and van de Ven, A.H. 1998. Hostile environmental jolts, transaction set and new business development. *Journal of Business Venturing* 13(3): 231–55.

Venkataraman, S., Van de Ven, A.H., Buckeye, J. and Hudson, R. 1990. Starting up in a turbulent environment: a process model of failure among firms with high customer dependence. *Journal of Business Venturing* 5(5): 277–95.

Watkins, D S. 1973. Technical entrepreneurship: a cis-Atlantic view. *R&D Management* 3(2): 65–70.

Westhead, P. and Storey, D.J. 1994. *An Assessment of Firms Located On and Off Science Parks in the United Kingdom*. London: HMSO.

Zahra, S.A. 1996. Technology strategy and new venture performance: a study of corporate-sponsored and independent biotechnology ventures. *Journal of Business Venturing* 11: 289–321.

Zammuto, R.F. 1988. Organizational adaptation: some implications of organizational ecology for strategic choice. *Journal of Management Studies* 25: 105–20.

Zhao, L. and Aram, J.D. 1995. Networking and growth of young technology-intensive ventures in China. *Journal of Business Venturing* 10: 349–70.

17

Entrepreneurship and High-technology Clusters

Arnold Cooper and Timothy Folta

To What Extent Do Start-ups Occur in Clusters?
What Are the Benefits and Costs of Locating in a Cluster?
What Processes Determine the Location of Start-ups?
What Are the Performance Implications of Clusters?
What Are the Implications for Policymakers and Entrepreneurs?
Conclusions

Why do new technically oriented firms start where they do, and how does location make a difference? New technically oriented companies often seem to start in clusters of related firms. This has led to concentrations of these firms in places such as Silicon Valley, Seattle, Boston and San Diego in the United States; Cambridge in the United Kingdom; Bangalore in India; Tel Aviv in Israel; and Lund in Sweden. Noting the jobs, the wealth and the economic dynamism associated with such clusters, many public policymakers have dreams of establishing Silicon Valleys in their parts of the world. Entrepreneurs, engaged in trying to get ventures started, may wonder how their locations bear upon what they are trying to do.

Clusters can be defined as "groups of firms within one industry based in one geographical area" (Prevezer 1997). They can also be defined as "geographic concentrations of interconnected companies and institutions in a particular field" (Porter 1998). Both definitions suggest a set of related firms in close geographic proximity. It is implied that these firms may draw upon some of the same inputs (including knowledge), that they may have transactions with each other and that some may compete with each other.

Clusters are not purely a high-technology phenomenon. Clustering occurs for many types of industries, including textiles in the Piedmont area of the Carolinas and Georgia in the United States, fashion goods in Milan, Italy, diamond cutting in Belgium and mechanical and scientific pens and pencils in the Nuremberg region of Germany (Krugman 1991; Porter 1990 1998). Nevertheless, the focus of this chapter is on the formation and development of high-technology firms and how they may be distinctive in the ways cluster location affects them.

Although location in a cluster may be important for all firms, it appears to have particular implications for start-ups and small firms (Almeida and Kogut 1997). Start-ups are less likely to have all needed resources in-house, so they must rely upon other organizations. Start-ups suffer from the liability of newness and thus lack credibility. If the key people in a start-up have ties, or can develop relationships, with others in the industry, this increases the likelihood that they can attract key employees, orders, credit and assistance. All of this can be facilitated by location in a cluster.

Several theoretical frameworks suggest that, under some circumstances, similar firms may choose to locate near each other. Staber (1998) notes three relevant theories:

1. Agglomeration theory suggests that cost reductions may result from shared infrastructure, such as communication and transportation facilities, and access to specialized labor and machinery. In addition, reduced consumer search costs and other spillover benefits may occur as companies learn more rapidly about new technologies and market opportunities. There can be increasing returns and positive feedback processes as additional firms join the cluster.

2. Transaction cost theory suggests that under conditions of uncertainty locating near one's trading partners may be most efficient. Spatial proximity facilitates firms' learning and responding quickly to suppliers and customers.

3. Neoinstitutionalism emphasizes the cognitive, regulatory and normative frameworks within which firms are located. Geographic closeness fosters a strong local culture that gives legitimacy and meaning to face-to-face interactions and interfirm resource sharing.

Porter (1998) emphasizes a number of ways in which location in a cluster may allow a firm to operate more efficiently. These include better access to employees and suppliers, access to specialized information, complementarities (such as having nearby organizations that help to attract customers or utilize byproducts), access to institutions and public goods (such as specialized educational programs) and better motivation (from local rivalry).

Almeida and Kogut (1994) argue that clusters may exist to facilitate the transfer of technology across firm boundaries. Emanating from knowledge-based views of the firm (Kogut and Zander 1992), this perspective argues that the transfer of complex and non-codifiable technologies will benefit from repeated formal and informal contact available when firms are in close geographic proximity.

Network theory from sociology emphasizes that entrepreneurs build businesses by interacting with others (Aldrich and Zimmer 1986). If strong ties are developed, there is a basis for trust, which can lead to providing mutual assistance. Geographic proximity may facilitate the development of these social networks.

Obviously, clusters vary along a number of dimensions, such as size, the breadth of technologies utilized and markets served. They may also differ in the life-cycle stage of the industry and of the primary firms in the cluster. The extent to which intracluster transactions occur is likely to be important and varies, as does the amount of diversity in kinds of organizations and in firm strategies. Clusters may also differ in regard to interfirm mobility of people and prevailing attitudes about entrepreneurship. Large clusters may not be uniform, so that benefits to peripheral firms are not the same as for core firms. Different clusters may intersect. For instance, in Phoenix clusters of firms are involved with helicopters, semiconductors and electronic testing labs (Porter 1998). Although previous research has not talked much about these differences across clusters, it seems likely that they bear upon the extent to which location in a cluster affects firm creation and performance.

This chapter considers the following questions:

1 To what extent do new high-technology firms start in clusters?
2 What are the processes that lead high-technology firms to locate in clusters?
3 Are the processes different for start-ups and established firms, and what are the benefits and costs of location in a cluster?
4 Do new firms in clusters do better?
5 What are the implications for policymakers and entrepreneurs?

To What Extent Do Start-ups Occur in Clusters?

Methods for determining clusters are not precise. There is considerable anecdotal evidence about particular clusters, and authors such as Porter (1990, 1998) note a number of areas where there clearly appear to be groups of related firms in particular geographical locations. Krugman (1991) used a technique for particular three-digit (SIC) industries in which he compared state employment with the total national manufacturing employment in that industry. He notes problems with this technique, including that the definition of an industry is problematic and that states are not the most appropriate units of analysis. Much of the recent literature focuses upon a few geographic areas, notably Silicon Valley and the Boston area, and upon only a few industries, primarily electronics, software and biotechnology. Nevertheless, while recognizing these limitations, we can consider the extent to which start-ups seem to be associated with clusters.

First, considering all start-ups, not just high-technology ones, entrepreneurship seems to be concentrated in particular geographical areas. Fritsch (1997) found that over half of all start-ups occurred in highly congested areas. There was a positive relationship between new firm formation and regional population density. Rural areas accounted for only 14 percent of new firms. Phillips et al. (1990: 380) reported that "small firm formation and growth activity has been much greater on average in urban rather than rural environments." Utilizing Dun and Bradstreet data, Birch (1987) found that much of the job creation in the United States was occurring in the "collar counties" around metropolitan areas in firms with fewer than 500 employees. Reynolds et al. (1995) used 382 labor market areas as units of analysis. Considering all industries, they found that entrepreneurship was not uniformly distributed. Higher firm birth rates and death rates tended to go together and were found in regions characterized by greater economic diversity, more population growth, more volatile industries and where greater personal wealth and more mid-career experienced adults were found.

Using clustering algorithms, Prevezer (1997) found that biotechnology firms were clustered into seven main groupings, with 45 percent of the public companies in the San Francisco Bay, New York tri-state region and the Boston area. Other important clusters were in San Diego, Los Angeles, the Washington, D.C., area and the Philadelphia–southern New Jersey region. Almeida and Kogut (1997) found evidence of eighteen main clusters of semiconductor activities, the most important of which were in Silicon Valley and the New York–New Jersey–Pennsylvania area. They reported that "of the 176 semiconductor start-ups founded around the world between 1977 and 1989, 55% were located in Silicon Valley." Data on the geographic location of *Inc.* magazine's top 500 firms suggest the extent to which young high-growth firms may be in particular locations. In considering the 122 manufacturing firms in the 1998 *Inc. 500* list, we found that 85.7 percent of the telecommunications firms and 45.2 percent of the firms in the computer industry were found in just three locations: Silicon Valley, Southern California and the Boston area (*Inc. 500* 1998: 81–118) (see table 17.1).

TABLE 17.1 % of 1998 *Inc. 500* firms in particular locations

	All Mfg. (n = 122)	*Telcomm. (n = 7)*	*Computers (n = 42)*
Silicon Valley	10.7	28.6	16.7
Southern California	11.5	14.3	19.0
Boston area	6.6	42.9	9.5
All three areas	28.8	85.7	45.2

Source: Inc. 500 (1998)

There is also considerable data on the growth of particular clusters of high-technology firms. Saxenian (1994) reported that total high-technology employment for Route 128 around Boston increased from about 60,000 in 1959 to 150,000 in 1990, with the corresponding figures for Silicon Valley being about 20,000 in 1959 and 260,000 in 1990. By 1997, it was estimated that some 7,000 electronics and software companies were located in Silicon Valley (*Business Week* 1997: 66).

Research questions

From the above data, it is clear that entrepreneurship tends to be geographically concentrated, that high-technology employment and high-growth young firms are found particularly in certain regions and that some clusters of high-technology firms have had substantial economic impact. However, few have considered why some clusters may have higher rates of new venture formation than others. Clusters differ in several dimensions, including their size, sociological characteristics, the nature of their dominant industries and the life-cycle stages of those industries. These cluster differences may influence entrepreneurial activity, making some much more fertile seedbeds for the formation and development of new firms. Accordingly, a number of research questions seem worthy of attention:

1 What are ways to identify clusters, to classify them and to measure differences across them?

2 What are the rates of formation of particular kinds of high-technology firms within clusters? How do these rates differ across clusters and over time?
3 How does size of the cluster affect venture formation? Is there some threshold that clusters need to reach before benefits accrue to cluster participants? Do the benefits increase linearly with cluster size or exponentially?
4 What is the role of sociological differences across clusters? Do clusters differ in the extent to which they tolerate interfirm mobility of people and resource sharing? Are there differences in the way in which entrepreneurship (both successful and unsuccessful) is viewed?
5 How do the characteristics of the dominant industry of a cluster affect venture formation? Is new firm formation higher when the industry is in an early life-cycle stage?
6 Do cluster benefits extend to firms that are not in the dominant industry of a cluster? For instance, do biotechnology start-ups benefit from being located in a cluster of electronics firms?
7 What is the influence of technological life cycles and macroeconomic factors? Is the benefit provided particularly important at a certain time in the life of a firm or industry? Do start-up rates within a cluster vary with growth rates of the primary industry?

WHAT ARE THE BENEFITS AND COSTS OF LOCATING IN A CLUSTER?

Much of the literature on facility location provides frameworks for analyzing the economic implications of different locations. Traditionally, there have been three basic components analyzed to determine industrial location (Boyce 1978): (1) procurement costs of raw materials (including transportation costs), (2) on-site or processing costs and (3) distribution costs of bringing the finished product to market.

Recent literature on high-technology clustering has emphasized knowledge spillovers and the benefits of having access to specialized inputs and specialized labor (Almeida and Kogut 1997). Many of the factors important in older industries, associated with transportation costs and with access to raw materials, appear to be of lesser importance for high-technology firms, where specialized knowledge seems to be the critical resource.

Most of the literature examining location decisions implies that firms have considerable mobility, that they will explicitly consider different alternatives and that the decision will be based upon economic attractiveness. This may well be the process by which established high-technology firms make decisions about where to locate plants or laboratories. However, as we shall note, it appears that entrepreneurs are much more constrained as they decide where to start.

We shall examine the influences upon the location decision for both established firms and for start-ups, noting the differences where appropriate. Our framework will consider specialized labor, specialized inputs, access to capital, proximity to customers, psychological support and costs of cluster locations. In the next section, we shall also note the striking patterns of where entrepreneurs tend to locate their ventures and the implications of this for the development of high-technology clusters.

Specialized labor

Table 17.2 lists the top five factors considered in location decisions by 226 established high-technology firms, as reported by Galbraith and DeNoble (1988). Three of the five most emphasized factors relate to availability, productivity and retention of skilled labor. Transportation costs, which are often emphasized in plant location theory, ranked low on the list. (Interestingly, being located near "other high-tech firms in same industry" also was not ranked very high.)

TABLE 17.2 Factors that influenced the location decision (% reporting important or very important)

Availability of technical employees	74
Owner/CEO wanted to live in area	74
Climate	73
Productivity of labor	69
Employee turnover rates	68

Source: Galbraith and DeNobel (1988)

The findings in the Galbraith and DeNoble survey reflect the relatively high skill levels needed for many high-technology ventures. It should be noted that "specialized labor" is a relatively broad term and may encompass many kinds of specific skills and knowledge, including technical expertise possessed by both skilled labor and highly trained professionals. It also can include specialized knowledge about other people and their work (possibly outside the organization) as well as knowledge about how to start and build a business and the kinds of capabilities needed by the founding team. Existing clusters of firms in a particular industry have, by definition, many people with experience in those industries. Depending upon the networks within the cluster and the past history of entrepreneurship, skilled people with all of these kinds of knowledge may be present.

Krugman (1991) argues that several factors related to specialized labor drive the clustering of such firms. A cluster creates a pooled market for workers with specialized skills, benefiting both workers and firms. The interaction of uncertainty and increasing returns from pooling leads to localization. Neither the firm nor the worker is certain of the future. If the firm turns out to have good luck, a larger cluster will be more likely to provide a larger pool of workers (because other firms will likely displace workers of firms having bad luck). If the firm has bad times, then the workers will also have bad times. However, they will benefit if there is another firm nearby because it may be having good times and offer employment opportunities.

Specialized workers who happen to be located within clusters are more likely to be parts of networks whose members are aware of job opportunities. This may decrease search costs for both firms and workers. Of course, all of this may mean that workers within clusters are more mobile. The disadvantage is that turnover may be high and that people with specialized skills (and the knowledge they have) may be lost to a competitor.

The formation of founding teams is so important that it deserves special attention.

New firms must try to attract key technical and management people at a time when their visibility and credibility are low. A promising team can draw upon a broader base of skills, contacts and capital. The team members can divide the work, pool their efforts and capital and provide psychological support to each other. Vesper (1990) notes that if the lead entrepreneur is able and willing to recruit other key team members, this is an indication of that person's ability to attract and manage people, a key requirement for growth. If people who really know the industry are willing to join the team, this serves as an initial check of the venture's promise. Furthermore, from the standpoint of investors, team-based ventures appear much more promising, so they are more likely to attract capital.

Although many teams are formed by partners who first work together in a previous organization, others involve joining up with people from different organizations. Entrepreneurs located within clusters of similar firms may be able to get to know potential cofounders more easily. Physical proximity may lead to more interactions, both professional and social, which provide the opportunity to assess competencies and working styles and to develop trust. For potential cofounders, the switching costs of joining a founding team are less if they do not have to move. In some instances, they can be involved part-time in the beginning, lessening the cash drain on the venture and limiting their personal risks.

The presence of specialized labor and key technical and management people can benefit both established and new firms, but the latter may benefit particularly from location in a cluster. Start-ups are less likely than large firms to be able to afford training programs. In addition, start-ups often hire experienced part-time employees or try to attract part-time partners who are more likely to be available in the organizations within clusters, giving particular benefits to entrepreneurs who start there.

Specialized inputs

High-technology firms often need access to specialized research tools, suppliers or specialized manufacturing facilities. They may also need to have knowledge about current developments in related technologies. Oakley et al. (1988) stressed the technical knowledge embodied in input components. The local availability of suppliers allows personal interaction and two-way exchange of information relating to such components and the way in which they will be used. Pilot production facilities or suppliers that can make up prototypes or small batches of new products are also more likely to be located in clusters. Consultants and specialists in particular technologies may also be found there. Firms located elsewhere can, of course, also deal with specialized suppliers. However, their transaction costs are likely to be higher, particularly for projects with new evolving technologies. In such cases, tacit knowledge must be exchanged, and this is facilitated by geographic proximity.

The specialized research tools, suppliers and manufacturing facilities often found within clusters are even more important for start-ups than for established firms. Entrepreneurs often seek to use assets without owning them. Starr and MacMillan (1990) described how entrepreneurs often rely upon past friendships to persuade others to let them have access to specialized assets. Feldman (1994) found that the presence of specialized business services related to innovative activity of small and large firms.

However, the positive influence is significantly stronger for smaller firms, suggesting that they benefit more from these services.

In areas of active entrepreneurship, professional advisors develop relevant expertise. Stock-option plans and prospectuses can be produced at the touch of a button from the word processors at the leading local law firm. Human resource firms can set up payroll processing or customized benefits plans overnight (*Business Week* 1997: 71).

New firms lack legitimacy. They must persuade other organizations to commit effort and sometimes to incur expenses in working with them, whether that involves extending credit, helping design products, serving as test sites or helping to sell the new company's products. If well-respected, established organizations can be persuaded to work with the new company, this adds legitimacy. Others may then be less reluctant to make similar commitments. These challenges confront all start-ups, regardless of location. However, those located within clusters may be able to draw upon the personal networks of the founders, possibly reflecting past relationships in which trust was established. If a new company and an established organization are in close proximity, then transaction and monitoring costs may be lower for both parties. The established organization may be more willing "to take a chance" with the new company down the street.

Access to capital

Capital is needed both to get started and to enable established young businesses to grow. With early-stage firms, capital often comes from informal investors who are successful professionals or business people. In Silicon Valley, many of these "angel investors" were former founders who had sold their businesses and then had become full or part-time investors in the next generation of high-technology firms (Cooper 1979). Informal investors often provide much more than capital. They can provide advice and utilize their networks to help the venture get access to resources. Research on informal investors shows that they usually invest close to home, often within 50 to 300 miles of where they live. Furthermore, they often expect to be involved in providing advice and in monitoring the progress of the businesses in which they invest (Wetzel 1989).

Clusters of high-technology firms often generate substantial wealth. Many successful start-ups are subsequently acquired, thereby creating wealthy and experienced former founders. There is positive feedback as ex-entrepreneurs, successful professionals and managers then invest individually and collectively in promising local start-ups. In Silicon Valley, one group of 120 industry executives, known as the "Band of Angels," has helped launch sixty start-ups (*Business Week* 1998: 92). Entrepreneurs starting in clusters have lower search costs in finding knowledgeable potential angel investors. From the standpoint of the investors, there are advantages to investing in businesses starting in the same geographic area. They can utilize their existing networks to investigate prospective entrepreneurs they are considering backing. Furthermore, if they invest in a business that is close at hand, their monitoring costs are likely to be lower, and they are more likely to be able to help the new business through utilizing contacts in their networks

Firms with high growth potential are sometimes funded by venture capital firms and, when the firms are more established, through public offerings. The venture capital industry is highly concentrated geographically, with many of the firms located on the coasts. About half of the six hundred venture capital firms in the United States are in

Silicon Valley (*Business Week* 1997: 71). Like angel investors, the professional venture capital firms expect to be involved in monitoring the progress of the firms in which they invest and in providing assistance and advice. When they do invest in a geographically distant firm, they often syndicate with a local venture capital firm that can provide the local presence (Pratt 1989).

One might expect that once a firm has reached a point at which it is ready for an initial public offering, capital would be highly mobile, and because investors would be less actively involved, geographic location might not make much difference. However, Deeds, et al. (1997) found that biotechnology firms located in clusters were able to raise significantly larger amounts of money through public offerings. Those located in clusters did better, possibly because investors perceived that their locations would provide competitive advantages.

Knowledge spillovers

External sources of knowledge are critical to innovation, as evidenced by studies over several decades by Myers and Marquis (1969), Brock (1975), Rosenberg and Steinmuller (1988) and Saxenian (1990). Markusen et al. (1986) suggest that information needs of innovative firms compel potential competitors to locate in close proximity to pioneering firms. Knowledge spillovers leading to interorganizational learning occur both through formal and informal channels of communication. Formal mechanisms include licensing, technology partnerships, strategic alliances and supply contracts. Informal channels include social meetings, trade meetings and interfirm mobility of scientists and engineers.

These information transfers could, of course, occur regardless of firm location. However, Jaffe et al. (1993) found a linkage between the place of a patent and citation of that patent. At three different levels of geographic analysis (country, state and standard metropolitan statistical area [SMSA]), they found evidence that patent citations tend to belong to the same geographic areas as the originating patent. Acs et al. (1992), focusing on the number of innovations in a geographic area rather than patents, found similar support for the localization of knowledge spillovers. Thus, knowledge available in patents appears to be more frequently used by firms within the same locality. Jaffe et al. (1993) argued that geographic regions differ in the sociology of their communities and the structure by which ideas are communicated. Presumably, knowledge spillovers occur more frequently if there are well-developed networks of relationships among people in different organizations and if there is substantial mobility in the workforce. Saxenian (1990) compared Silicon Valley and Boston's Route 128 and concluded that the former has had more long-term success because of the more fully developed network of embedded relationships in Silicon Valley. She pointed to the importance of collective learning and collaborative relationships with customers and suppliers, which were well-established there.

Almeida and Kogut (1994) studied the spatial diffusion of technological knowledge through the analysis of important semiconductor patents and through field interviews with engineers and scientists in the industries. Their findings indicated that knowledge remains localized in the United States, particularly in Silicon Valley. Furthermore, geographic regions differ in the sociology of their communities and the structure by which ideas are communicated. In Silicon Valley, the mobility of the workforce appears to be a primary way by which knowledge is diffused. Thus, they reason, there would be greater diffusion of knowledge within some geographic regions than others.

Diffusion is also affected by the nature of the technology. The more complex and noncodifiable the knowledge to be transferred, the more difficult it is to transfer across firm boundaries. In such situations, firms need to be geographically close to where personal contact is easily achieved. Word-of-mouth communication has been found to be vital in the diffusion and adoption of industrial innovations (Martilla 1971). Other media do not enable the same degree of communication richness (Daft and Lengel 1986). Thus, when networks of firms work together, geographic proximity may be vital if noncodifiable information is being transferred. Adams and Jaffe (1996) also found that knowledge spillovers were a function of the "technological distance" between firms. They noted that knowledge must be transferred not only across geographic boundaries but also across institutional and cultural boundaries. The magnitude of these transaction costs affects knowledge transfers.

In some clusters a great deal of informal communication occurs among organizations. Rogers (1982) reported that engineers at different companies share problem-solving information by discussing failed avenues of exploration. Solutions are also likely to be communicated. Many of these conversations take place at social occasions. Braun and MacDonald (1982) provide an example of a bar located close to Intel, Fairchild, Raytheon and other semiconductor companies that served as a place where engineers "drank, exchanged information and hired employees."

Knowledge spillovers can be of even more benefit to start-ups than to established firms. New firms lack the resources to explore multiple approaches to technical problems. They also lack central R&D organizations that could share information gained through previous research. Larger firms are more self-reliant and have less need to build relationships with other institutions within a region. This is consistent with findings from a study by Acs et al. (1994), who examined spillover benefits separately for large and small firms and concluded that large firm branches often benefited from knowledge flows from corporate R&D, whereas small firms more often gained new knowledge from university research laboratories. They also found that the geographic proximity between university and corporate laboratories within a state serve as a catalyst for innovative activity for firms of all sizes, but the impact of location on innovative output is four times greater for small firms than for large firms. In a similar study based on twenty Italian regions over a period of nine years, Audretsch and Vivarelli (1996) found that the spillovers from university research were apparently more important for small firm innovation than for large firm innovation. Feldman (1994) used Small Business Administration data to ascertain the importance of inputs to innovation for firms of different sizes. She found that, although large firms benefited from local innovation, local university research had twice the impact on the innovative output of small firms.

The technical and managerial teams of start-ups must rely on what they bring with them from prior education and jobs and what they can pick up through trying to access what is being learned in other organizations. Locational proximity reduces the cost and increases the frequency of personal contacts and serves to build social relations. Professional relationships are often embedded in these social networks. Local social and professional networks decrease the uncertainty and costs associated with start-up activity.

The transfer of knowledge from previous organizations is illustrated by the large number of spin-offs of similar firms in many clusters. The start-ups often utilize the same technology or serve the same markets as the organizations they left (Spiegelman 1964; Cooper 1985; Freeman 1982). Saxenian (1994) concluded that the unique nature of Silicon Valley with regard to its sociology (e.g., attitudes toward failure, risk-taking and interfirm mobility) contributed to the high rate of new firm formation. Some organizations have been prolific incubators, spinning off many entrepreneurial ventures. For instance, it is estimated that Fairchild Semiconductor spun off at least fifty high-technology firms between 1959 and 1979 in Santa Clara County alone (Saxenian 1985).

Thus, in well-developed clusters of firms, knowledge can flow both in and out. Firms within clusters may acquire knowledge through the many well-established networks of relationships and from employee mobility; however, they may lose knowledge to other firms in the same ways.

Proximity to customers

Location within a cluster should lead to lower search costs for customers, particularly when sales are made to other firms in the cluster. Location near users may facilitate quick response and make it easier to exchange information between suppliers and customers. When new technology is incorporated into products and services, customers often test the products and serve as test sites. Customers provide feedback and even make suggestions about products to be developed. If information exchange is helped by frequent interaction and by the building of trust, then geographical proximity should facilitate developing such relationships. For high-technology firms, transportation costs associated with shipping goods to customers typically are not very important. However, the building of close relationships with customers is often critical to success.

New firms should realize marketing benefits from location in a cluster in the same ways as established organizations. However, because new firms do not have well-developed reputations, the personal relationships and credibility of the founders are more important. Because they do not have stable relationships with customers, the cost of finding and working with prospective customers is vital. Entrepreneurs within clusters are in a better position to learn of developing market opportunities. If the new firm is based upon technology that is changing and not fully codifiable, then the ability to have sales and engineering people work closely with customers is valuable. All of these considerations suggest that new firms (with their lack of history, limited resources and lack of organizational specialization) may particularly benefit from location in a cluster.

Psychological support

Psychological input, which is a form of specialized input, is probably important in new firm formation. Entrepreneurs start businesses based upon their perceptions of the feasibility and the risks and potential rewards. These, in turn, can be influenced by role models, advisors and the perceptions of friends and family members. Founders located in clusters with a high degree of entrepreneurial activity are surrounded by role models. Investors and others who might contribute resources also are surrounded by examples of successful ventures and of those who have made money by supporting new ventures. In this climate, the perceptions of rewards and risks may be more favorable than in locations where entrepreneurship is relatively rare. An entrepreneurial environment may develop so that potential founders are buoyed and encouraged by the success of others and by the willingness of investors and other suppliers of resources to be supportive (Cooper 1979: 38–9).

Costs of location in a cluster

As clusters grow, demand for workers, land and utilities increases, leading to shortages and increased costs. The infrastructure can become overloaded, leading to traffic jams and a decline in the quality of life. In Silicon Valley, the median cost of a home climbed to $319,000 by 1997. Hourly manufacturing wages are about 25 percent higher there than elsewhere (*Business Week* 1997: 66, 80).

For established organizations considering the location of branch facilities, the benefits of locating in a well-established but expensive cluster must be balanced against the costs. For entrepreneurs with limited resources, the costs must be of even more concern. However, although costs in clusters may seem high, start-ups can take steps to minimize the cash needed. Sometimes, they can utilize subsidized space, as in university or community-sponsored incubators. They do not need large amounts of space and sometimes can get started in basements, garages (e.g., Hewlett-Packard) or old buildings. Employees can be attracted with stock options and hope. (An entrepreneurial environment can contribute to a sense of euphoria, in which every start-up seems to be a potential Microsoft.)

Some owners of high-technology firms have tended to prefer rural or semirural nonagglomerated locations in order to reduce factory and housing land costs and to maximize personal amenities (Saxenian 1985).

Some of the major costs of locating in a cluster may not show up on the income statement. The organizational boundaries of firms in clusters may be permeable, with knowledge flowing out as well as in. Employees may share information with others in the industry so that it is more difficult to keep plans and knowledge proprietary. In an entrepreneurial environment, some of the best employees may lay plans to leave and start their own firms (and take the knowledge and relationships they have developed with them).

Research questions

In summary, supply-side considerations seem to play a very important role, possibly the dominant one, in the formation of clusters in high-technology industries. A number of research questions can be suggested:

1 Are there differences in the processes by which entrepreneurs within clusters and those not in clusters assemble specialized labor, founding team members and specialized inputs?

2 Are there differences in the cost of capital for start-ups across clusters? Are there differences according to geographic proximity to venture capital firms?

3 How does the nature of technology, including the extent to which it is tacit and still developing, bear upon the importance of locating a facility within a cluster?

4 How are knowledge spillover benefits related to the personal networks of key managers, engineers and scientists within the firms?
5 Are there differences in the perceived risks and benefits associated with entrepreneurship according to whether entrepreneurs are located within clusters?
6 How do firm characteristics, including size, strategy and degree of vertical integration, bear upon the relative benefits and costs of locating within a cluster?

What Processes Determine the Location of Start-ups?

It might appear that the benefits of location within a cluster would lead entrepreneurs to move to whatever cluster seems to be most desirable from a cost–benefit standpoint. However, most entrepreneurs do not seem to engage in an explicit search and comparison process when deciding where to locate.

Prior location of the entrepreneur

Technical entrepreneurs tend to start their new firms within commuting distance of where they were previously working and living for several reasons:

1 They can utilize their existing networks to seek partners, employees, suppliers, customers, advisors and investors. Not only does this decrease search costs, but it also permits them to build upon credibility and trust developed in past relationships.
2 They can start on a part-time basis (as can prospective partners and employees) and delay full-time commitment until the venture seems sufficiently promising.
3 A spouse can keep a job so that some income continues to flow to the family; other aspects of a founder's life can remain the same. The full energies of the entrepreneur can then be devoted to the start-up.

Table 17.3 summarizes findings from relevant studies on the percentage of entrepreneurs who moved when starting their firms. In addition to these large-scale studies, a number of researchers have commented upon the location decision of the entrepreneur at the time of starting. For instance, in Sweden, it was reported that "the venture is typically launched where the founder lives" (Johannisson 1996: 256). There may be differences across industries in this aspect of the founding process. One study, based upon firms featured in *Inc.* and *Venture* magazines, reported that biotechnology and medical technology firms were more likely to move, with 47 percent of a subsample of seventeen moving at the time of start-up (Cooper 1985). A broad-based study of 890 (mostly nontechnical) entrepreneurs reported that 25 percent moved when starting (Cooper and Dunkelberg 1981).

Entrepreneurs do not seem to move when starting, regardless of where they are located. The studies reported in Table 17.3 are in some instances limited to particular clusters (Silicon Valley and Austin, Texas). Other studies consider start-ups from industry-wide or national samples. In most instances, the percentage of those moving is very low, regardless of whether it is cluster-specific. Cooper (1985) considered the small number of entrepreneurs moving to see if there were any patterns. For the twenty-one

TABLE 17.3 % of entrepreneurs who moved when starting

Silicon Valley firms	(n = 250)	3	(Cooper 1979)
Growth-oriented firms	(n = 161)	16	(Cooper 1985)
Semiconductor firms	(n = 75)	12	(Almeida and Kogut 1997)
Austin high technology	(n = 31)	10	(Susbauer 1972)

Source: compiled by the authors from the sources indicated

entrepreneurs moving, there was a tendency to move away from larger cities. However, for this small sample, it was difficult to say whether there was much movement toward or away from "quality-of-life" states or "more attractive" economic climates.

All of this suggests that entrepreneurs are relatively constrained as they decide where to locate their start-ups. How then does it happen that they often end up in clusters? It could be argued that those entrepreneurs already within clusters search and then decide that their present locations are the best places to start. However, what about those entrepreneurs coming out of organizations that are not in clusters? Do they move, start where they are or give up because the environment where they are located is unpromising for start-ups?

Start-ups may be more likely to be found in clusters because nascent entrepreneurs (those trying to start firms) are less common outside clusters, in part because of the lack of role models and perceived support. The perceptions of risks and rewards associated with entrepreneurship may vary across geographical locations, and this may influence whether potential entrepreneurs even try. Alternatively, the reason for relatively fewer high-growth ventures outside of clusters may relate to what happens to the new firms after they are started. Those in relatively isolated locations may be smaller to start with or they may be less likely to survive or to grow. These possible explanations have not been the focus of much systematic study to date. In fact, characteristics of clusters and how those bear upon start-up decisions seem to offer many opportunities for research.

Research questions

1 What is the relative presence of nascent entrepreneurs within and outside clusters? What is their relative presence across clusters, and are differences related to cluster characteristics?
2 Are there differences in the percentages of nascent entrepreneurs who proceed to start businesses across clusters or across technologies? Do these percentages change over time, and are they related to economic conditions or the availability of capital?
3 Are there differences in the perceptions of risks and rewards associated with entrepreneurship for potential founders located in clusters and those in other locations?
4 Are there differences in the initial size of new firms started within and outside clusters? Do within-cluster start-ups tend to be larger?

WHAT ARE THE PERFORMANCE IMPLICATIONS OF CLUSTERS?

Are new firms started in clusters more likely to be successful than those located else-where? The factors considered earlier suggest that new (as well as established) high-technology firms located in clusters should enjoy many advantages. However, as noted, clusters also have higher operating costs and risk knowledge leakages. Relatively few empirical studies look at the performance implications of location in a cluster.

It is not clear whether all technically oriented firms benefit from location in clusters. Porter (1998) suggests that certain "home base" activities, such as R&D, strategy devel-opment and a critical mass of production or service activities derive particular benefits from being located near similar firms. However, other activities, such as manufacturing, might be better off in locations where factor costs are lower. Prevezer (1997) found that biotechnology clusters developed only in particular sectors of that industry. Activities associated with therapeutic and diagnostic sectors resulted in clusters, but this was not the case for food processing, chemicals or energy sectors of biotechnology. The benefits of cluster location may also depend upon the nature of a company, including its size, its strategy and the extent to which it has transactions with similar companies.

Almeida and Kogut (1997) argue that only when there is sufficient technological opportunity (relative to the number of firms in a cluster) do the benefits outweigh potential costs. If the opportunity space is densely populated by firms, then firms will have greater rivalry for necessary resources and will cooperate less.

Staber (1998) used event history analysis of failure rates of firms in the knitwear industry in Germany to consider the performance effects of location. He hypothesized that geographic proximity to other firms in the industry reduces the likelihood of business failure and that the benefits are particularly strong for specialized firms and for firms in vertically related industries.

Staber's findings were the exact opposite of what he had hypothesized. The more firms in a ten-kilometer radius, the greater the likelihood of failure. The effect of proximity on business failure was lower for specialized firms and was higher for vertically related firms. In addition, the national sample had lower returns than the cluster for the period studied (1978-81). Although this was not a high-technology industry and the results were counter to what was expected, it did constitute an approach to systematically trying to examine the effect of cluster location upon performance.

Hill and Naroff (1984) examined high-technology firms listed in the *Million Dollar Directory*. A sample of firms in Silicon Valley (21), the Boston area (31) and elsewhere (50) was analyzed to determine whether location within these two clusters had any relation-ship to firm performance. Multivariate analysis disclosed that the high-technology firms within the Silicon Valley and Boston clusters had significantly lower risk (market risk, company-specific risk and total risk). In addition, the national sample (not in these clusters) had lower actual returns for the period studied (1978–81).

Goss and Vozikis (1994) found that value-added per worker was greater for high-technology industries in states with an already high concentration of such firms. This was not the case for other industries. Thus, high-technology firms appear to benefit more from location near similar firms, possibly because of spillover benefits.

Because of the limited empirical research to date, we do not know whether the impact of location in a cluster varies for firms or clusters with different characteristics. Location in a cluster may be most important for firms trying to compete with differentiation strategies that emphasize product or service features rather than low-cost strategies. It may also be most valuable for firms that make a high percentage of their sales to other firms in the cluster, particularly when the technology or market is changing rapidly. Industries experiencing rapid change may be ones for which cluster membership is most important because of the importance of spillover effects and informal communication about tacit knowledge. As noted at a number of points in this paper, cluster membership probably has the most impact on performance of new or small firms and probably also for corporate headquarters or R&D facilities, rather than for manufacturing facilities. All of this suggests that the impact of location upon the performance of technically oriented firms may not be uniform across firms.

When business survival is used as a performance measure, researchers should be sensitive to the impact of different "threshold levels" on the decision to continue to terminate a business (Gimeno et al. 1997). The threshold level is the required level of performance for an entrepreneur or group of entrepreneurs to decide to stay in business, which is affected by switching costs, income available in other employment and relative psychic income from the venture. Whether a venture is located in a cluster should impact switching costs. A member of a founding team who considers leaving a venture may face relatively high personal switching costs if in an isolated location. However, if that person is in a cluster of similar firms, then he or she can often use personal networks to join another similar company. The spouse can keep a job; the family does not have to move, and the switching costs are relatively low. If the location brings the team member into contact with other entrepreneurs who are starting or developing ventures, then other, even more attractive new ventures may beckon. Thus, the perceived income associated with other employment (joining another start-up) may appear to be high. Both of these factors may raise required threshold levels. Thus, members of founding teams or key employees of new ventures located in clusters may be more likely to leave or close down new companies experiencing marginal performance. Their counterparts in more isolated locations may keep going, thereby having longer survival periods.

Research questions

The following research questions seem promising:

1 How does cluster location affect performance for firms with different strategies? Is it relatively more important for firms with strategies emphasizing new products or processes than for those competing through low cost?
2 Does the stage of development of an industry influence the relative desirability of being located in a cluster? When an industry is in an early stage, with rapidly changing technologies and with much tacit knowledge embodied in key employees, is location more important because of spillover effects?
3 Conversely, for firms whose competitive advantages are based upon proprietary tacit knowledge, do they do better in more isolated locations where it is more difficult for competitors to acquire that knowledge through hiring their key employees?

4 How does location influence performance for firms that primarily sell inside a cluster versus those that do not?

5 Does the required threshold level of performance (for entrepreneurs to decide to stay in business) vary according to whether the new business is in a cluster? Is it higher for firms in clusters? Do thresholds differ across clusters or for firms within a cluster?

6 Are there performance benefits for technically oriented firms starting in clusters, even if the firms are in somewhat different industries? For instance, would a biotechnology business starting in a cluster of software firms enjoy some benefits, possibly through accessing such infrastructure resources as venture capital or knowledgeable consultants?

WHAT ARE THE IMPLICATIONS FOR POLICYMAKERS AND ENTREPRENEURS?

As noted earlier, entrepreneurs usually do not move (or even give serious consideration to moving) when they are forming new businesses. Many potential entrepreneurs are already located in clusters (because that is where they work). Furthermore, as noted earlier, a number of factors present in a cluster may make it more likely that a nascent entrepreneur will try to start a venture. However, for entrepreneurs starting elsewhere, there is the question of whether to move. Some early-stage businesses have moved after they have started but before they had had much success. Microsoft, which moved from New Mexico to Seattle, and Netscape, which was based upon work originally conducted at Champagne–Urbana, Illinois, but then moved to Silicon Valley, are two notable examples. For many entrepreneurs, the potential benefits of being located in a cluster are probably hard to assess. However, the personal costs of moving (e.g., giving up jobs or having spouses move) and the implications of leaving one's network behind may be very visible. When there is strong external support for a move (such as investors who want the new venture to be located where they can monitor and assist it), then a move may be considered much more seriously.

Many policymakers are interested in trying to create conditions that lead to clusters of technically oriented firms in their locations. When a cluster begins to form, feedback processes also begin to change the climate, often making it more attractive both for entrepreneurs and for established firms considering locating laboratories or facilities there. Porter (1998) notes that a self-reinforcing cycle can develop, spurred on by active local competition and by supportive local institutions. However, it is less clear whether deliberate policy initiatives can make major differences. Porter (1998) notes that most clusters do not form because of government action – in fact, sometimes it is in spite of it. He argues, though, that governments should ensure high-quality inputs, such as infrastructure and educated workers. They may also play a role in the development of public goods (such as specialized education programs or research centers) that can support a developing cluster.

Many clusters can trace their origins to a handful of entrepreneurial ventures that started there or branch facilities located there. Some clusters appear to have been influenced by external events or by local advisors who played a major role in helping companies get started. Thus, Frederick Terman, the provost at Stanford, advised many prospective entrepreneurs and also assisted in attracting technical organizations to the Bay Area. Porter (1998) notes that clusters may arise from sophisticated or stringent local demand, from prior existence of supplier industries, from one or two innovative firms that stimulated the establishment and growth of others or from chance events.

Research questions

1 To what extent do growth-oriented new firms move after founding? What is the role of investor pressure or quasi-government incentives in such moves?
2 Across clusters, what is the initial "seed organization" of each cluster? How did it come to be located there? Can its location be traced to branch facilities, to local organizations not in the same industry or to an entrepreneur who moved when starting or shortly after?
3 What are the characteristics of organizations more likely to serve as "seed organizations" or incubators from which entrepreneurs then spin off?
4 To what extent are clusters formed where they are because of government incentives or the establishment of supporting public institutions?

CONCLUSIONS

Location does seem to make a difference, both in influencing the formation of new firms and in their subsequent performance. As Feldman (1996) notes, ironically, geography has re-emerged as important at a time when instantaneous global communication is possible. However, as this review makes clear, many important questions remain to be resolved, and many opportunities exist to add to our understanding of clusters and their role in the formation and development of new firms.

REFERENCES

Acs, Z., Audretsch, D.B. and Feldman, M.P. 1992. Real effects of academic research. *American Economic Review* 82: 363–7.

Acs, Z., Audretsch, D.B. and Feldman, M.P. 1994. R&D spillovers and recipient firm size. *Review of Economics and Statistics* 75(4): 336–40.

Adams, J.D. and Jaffe, A.B. 1996. Bounding the effects of R&D: an investigation using matched establishment-firm data. *RAND Journal of Economics* 27(4): 700–21.

Aldrich, H. and Zimmer, C. 1986. Entrepreneurship through social networks. In D.L. Sexton and R.W. Smilor (eds.), *The Art and Science of Entrepreneurship*. Cambridge, MA: Ballinger, pp. 3–23.

Almeida, P. and Kogut, B. 1994. *Technology and Geography: The Localization of Knowledge and the Mobility of Patent Holders*. Philadelphia: Huntsman Center for Global Competition and Innovation.

Almeida, P. and Kogut, B. 1997. The exploration of technology diversity and the geographic localization of innovation. *Small Business Economics* 9: 21–31.

Audretsch, D.B. and Vivarelli, M. 1996. Firm size and R&D spillovers: Evidence from Italy. *Small*

Business Economics 8: 249–58.

Birch, D.L. 1987. *Job Creation in America: How Our Smallest Companies Put the Most People to Work.* New York: Free Press.

Boyce, R.R. 1978. *The Bases of Economic Geography.* New York: Holt, Rinehart and Winston.

Braun, E. and MacDonald, S. 1982. *Revolution in Miniature.* New York: Cambridge University Press.

Brock, G.W. 1975. *The US Computer Industry.* Cambridge, MA: Ballinger.

Business Week. 1998. The hot new tech cities. November 9: 44–56.

Business Week. 1997. Silicon Valley: how it really works. August 18: 64–147.

Cooper, A.C. 1979. *The Founding of Technologically-Based Firms.* Milwaukee: Center for Venture Management.

Cooper, A.C. 1985. The role of incubator organizations in the founding of growth-oriented firms. *Journal of Business Venturing* 1(1): 75–86.

Cooper, A.C. and Dunkelberg, W.C. 1981. A new look at business entry: experiences of 1805 entrepreneurs. In K. Vesper (ed.), *Frontiers of Entrepreneurship Research.* Wellesley, MA: Babson Center for Entrepreneurial Studies.

Daft, R. and Lengel, R. 1986. Organizational information requirements, media richness and structural design. *Management Science* 32 (5): 554–71.

Deeds, D.L., Decarolis, D. and Coombs, J.E. 1997. The impact of firm-specific capabilities on the amount of capital raised in an initial public offering: Evidence from the biotechnology industry. *Journal of Business Venturing* 12(1): 31–46.

Feldman, M. 1994. *The Geography of Innovation.* Boston: Kluwer.

Feldman, M. 1996. Geography and regional economic development: the role of technology-based small and medium sized firms. *Small Business Economics* 8: 71–4.

Freeman, C. 1982. *The Economics of Industrial Innovation.* London: Frances Pinter.

Fritsch, M. 1997. New firms and regional employment change. *Small Business Economics* 9: 437–48.

Galbraith, C. and DeNoble, A. 1988. Location decisions by high-technology firms. *Entrepreneurship Theory and Practice* 13(2): 31–47.

Gimeno, J., Folta, T.B., Cooper, A.C. and Woo, C.Y. 1997. Survival of the fittest? entrepreneurial human capital and the persistence of underperforming firms. *Administrative Science Quarterly* 42(December): 750–83.

Goss, E. and Vozikis, G.S. 1994. High-tech manufacturing: firm size, industry and population density. *Small Business Economics* 6: 291–7.

Hill, J. and Naroff, J.L. 1984. The effect of location on the performance of high-technology firms. *Financial Management* 13(spring): 27–36.

Inc. 500. 1998. October 20: 81–118.

Jaffe, A.B., Trajtenberg, M. and Henderson, R. 1993. Geographic localization of knowledge spillovers as evidenced by patent citations. *Quarterly Journal of Economics* 108(3): 577–98.

Johannisson, B. 1996. The dynamics of entrepreneurial networks. In P.D. Reynolds et al. (eds.), *Frontiers of Entrepreneurship Research.* Wellesley, MA: Babson Center for Entrepreneurial Studies, pp. 253–67.

Kogut, B. and Zander U. 1992. Knowledge of the firm, combinative capabilities, and the replication of technology. *Organizational Science* 3(3): 383–97.

Krugman, P. 1991. *Geography and Trade.* Cambridge, MA: MIT Press.

Markusen, A., Hall, P. and Glasmeier, A. 1986. *High-Tech America.* Boston: Allen and Unwin.

Martilla, J. 1971. Word-of-mouth communication in the industrial adoption process. *Journal of Marketing Research* 8(May): 173–78.

Myers, S. and Marquis, D.G. 1969. *Successful Industrial Innovations: A Study of Factors Underlying Innovation in Selected Firms.* Washington, D.C.: Government Printing Office.

Oakley, R., Rothwell, R. and Cooper, S. 1988. *The Management of Innovation in High-Technology Small Firms.* New York: Quorum.

Phillips, B., Kirchhoff, B. and Brown, H.S. 1990. Formation, growth and mobility of technology-based firms in the US economy. In N. Churchill et al. (eds.), *Frontiers of Entrepreneurship Research*. Wellesley, MA: Babson College, pp. 378–93.

Porter, M. 1990. *The Competitive Advantage of Nations*. New York: Free Press.

Porter, M.E. 1998. Clusters and the new economics of competition. *Harvard Business Review* 76(6): 77–90.

Pratt, S.E. 1989. The organized venture capital community. In J.K. Morris and S. Isenstein (eds.), *Pratt's Guide to Venture Capital Sources*, 13th edn. Needham, MA: Venture Economics, pp. 97–8.

Prevezer, M. 1997. The dynamics of industrial clustering in small and medium-sized firms in West Germany. *Small Business Economics* 9: 255–7.

Reynolds, P.D., Miller, B. and Maki, W.R. 1995. Explaining regional variation in business births and deaths: US 1976–88. *Small Business Economics* 7: 389–407.

Rogers, E. 1982. Information exchange and technological innovation. In D. Sahal (ed.), *The Transfer and Utilization of Technical Knowledge*. Boston: Lexington Books, pp. 105–23.

Rosenberg, N. and Steinmueller, W. 1988. Why are Americans such poor imitators? *American Economic Review* 78(2): 229–34.

Saxenian, A. 1985. The genesis of Silicon Valley. In P. Hall and A. Markusen (eds.), *Silicon Landscapes*. Boston: Allen & Unwin.

Saxenian, A. 1990. Regional networks and the resurgence of Silicon Valley. *California Management Review* 33(fall): 39–112.

Saxenian, A. 1994. *Regional Advantage: Culture and Competition in Silicon Valley and Route 128*. Cambridge, MA: Harvard University Press.

Spiegelman, R.G. 1964. A method of analyzing the location characteristics of footloose industries: a case study of the precision instruments industry. *Land Economics* 40: 79–86.

Staber, U. 1998. Organizational survival in small-firm clusters. *Academy of Management Proceedings*. San Diego, CA: Academy of Management.

Starr, J.A. and MacMillan, I.C. 1990. Resource cooptation via social contracting: Resource acquisition strategies for new ventures. *Strategic Management Journal* 11(summer): 79–92.

Susbauer, Jeffrey. 1972. The technical entrepreneurship process in Austin, Texas. In A. Cooper and J. Komives (eds.), *Technical Entrepreneurship: A Symposium*. Milwaukee: Center for Venture Management, pp. 28–46.

Vesper, K.H. 1990. *New Venture Experience*. Seattle, WA: Vector Books.

Wetzel, W.W. Jr. 1989. Informal investors – when and where to look. In J.K. Morris and S. Isenstein (eds.), *Pratt's Guide to Venture Capital Sources*, 13th edition. Needham, MA: Venture Economics, pp. 101–2.

18

Networking and Entrepreneurial Growth

BENGT JOHANNISSON

NETWORK VOCABULARY: FROM INTERORGANIZATIONAL TIES TO
PERSONAL NETWORKING
THE PERSONAL NETWORK AS THE ORIGIN OF BUSINESS VENTURES
ENTREPRENEURIAL NETWORKING AND VENTURE PERFORMANCE
CREATING SPACE FOR GROWTH: THE ORGANIZING CONTEXT
LESSONS FOR RESEARCHERS AND PRACTITIONERS

In her 1959 seminal work on firm growth, Edith Penrose states that entrepreneurs and managers complement each other. Entrepreneurs innovate and create new markets, usually by starting their own firm, while managers amplify entrepreneurial projects through control and routinization. This image of entrepreneurship and management taking on different roles seems to be very harmonic; the question is whether that harmony remains in times calling for more fluent, network-like structures. Penrose (1995: xx) in the foreword to her third edition states: "The business network is very different from a cartel of independent firms in its structure, organization, and purpose. . . . This may call for a new 'theory of the firm.'" Obviously, there will also be a need for a new image of firm growth and, we argue, a new understanding of the linkages between entrepreneurship and management.

Entrepreneurship as the creation of new business and management as the operation of existing firms differ not only with respect to functional assignments in the business-development process; they also differ in kind. The network metaphor for business organizations in general and small business and entrepreneurial ventures in particular reveals this. Within a management perspective, networks and coalitions, e.g., strategic alliances and joint ventures, represent just another calculated way to intermittently reduce environmental uncertainty. Entrepreneurial networking, in contrast, means expanding the action frame of the venturing process. Entrepreneurs continuously network as they pursue and react to new realities. While management needs structure, certainty and decision rationality, entrepreneurship thrives on process, ambiguity and action rationality.

Networking provides an image of entrepreneurship as the emergence and organizing of new business activity (Gartner et al. 1992). Because of liabilities of size and newness, including the lack of market legitimacy, prospective entrepreneurs have to mobilize "social resources" (Starr and MacMillan 1990) in addition to having resources controlled by ownership. Continuous entrepreneurship calls for perpetual venturing as opportunities arise, which suggests that both entrepreneurship and networking remain crucial over the firm life span. It seems reasonable to assume that external supplementation of the internal growth potential is realized by orchestrating an existing network according to need.

Within a general organizational (Nohria and Eccles 1992b) or managerial (Dyer and Singh 1998) perspective, the network or relational view differs from traditional firm-focused inquiries into market behavior. The argument is that firm conduct, like perform-ance or growth, can only be made intelligible if the firm is recognized as a member of an interorganizational network. Research concerning industrial markets elaborates this per-spective conceptually and empirically (e.g., Ford 1990). Albeit with roots in the Kirznerian notion of market dynamics (Snehota 1990), the industrial-market perspective sees the firm as a rational interacting subject in which individuals have to submit to overarching management structures. With virtual organizations, the network itself is the main actor; member identity, whether individual or firm, dissolves (Barnatt 1995).

Individuals with their irrationalities and intuitions cannot be excluded when research-ing entrepreneurship (Bird 1989). As human beings we are the origin of creative action, and as social creatures we are all bound to interact. This suggests that the entrepreneurs' personal networks may be the origin of their venturing careers. Only a personal network is potent enough to make entrepreneurs enforce their identity, i.e., provide existential satisfaction, support sense-making in ambiguous environments and supply resources in the venturing process. Direct interpersonal exchange is irreplaceable (Nohria and Eccles 1992a) since it provides the needed sensitivity, alertness and drive to identify and exploit new opportunities.

This chapter introduces a network vocabulary and elaborates on the personal network-ing mode that, in my mind, is conducive to entrepreneurship and then shows how entrepreneurial ventures emerge from personal networking. This gives us a basis for a discussion of firm growth in a networking perspective in order to introduce the notion of "organizing context" as condensed personal networks and as a conceptual tool with which to identify the action domain wherein entrepreneurs' contributions to economic growth can be enforced. In the final section we briefly discuss some implications for entrepreneurship and small-business research. Practical lessons for promoting entrepre-neurial networking are outlined as well.

NETWORK VOCABULARY: FROM INTERORGANIZATIONAL TIES TO PERSONAL NETWORKING

It is beyond the scope of this chapter to provide a complete review of the rapidly expanding literature on networking in the context of economic activity. Nohria and Eccles (1992b) provide the basic arguments for a network approach when researching organized endeavors. Excellent overviews are provided by Powell and Smith-Doerr

(1994), who examine different images of networks in action, and Grandori and Soda (1995), who discuss interfirm networks. Araujo and Easton (1996) report an insightful multidimensional analysis of ten different network approaches. Here only some basic definitions are provided.

A *network* consists of interconnected dyadic relationships where the nodes may be roles, individuals or organizations. Although research into networks within a management perspective focuses organizations and/or roles (individuals as representatives of organizations), entrepreneurial networks should be addressed as interacting persons.

With respect to the *contents* of ties, information networks, exchange networks and networks of influence are identified. While the first provides business intelligence, including information on business opportunities, exchange networks furnish organizational endeavors with needed resources. With trust as a basc for individual ties and the network at large, exchange networks appear as a special governance form. Networks of influence create legitimacy for their own activities and barriers for potential competitors.

The three proposed networks are interdependent. Information networks pave the way for exchange and influence. Exchange networks also carry information more or less associated with the transactions themselves, but they also create mutual dependencies and influences. Influence networks invite to exchange and carry both solicited and unsolicited information.

The contents of networks as outlined above are especially difficult to separate within the personal network of entrepreneurs. This is because exchange is based on not only calculated but also social interest, i.e., ideological and affective commitments as well (Sjöstrand 1992; van der Poel 1993; Johannisson 1996). Without this blending of commitments in singular network ties, generally referred to by Granovetter (1985) as "social embeddedness," entrepreneurial networks, and ultimately the venturing process, would not get the energy needed. Committed members of the personal network help the entrepreneur to amplify the initiative and subsequent actions. The same passion that triggers personal involvement in the venturing process energizes personal exchange.

Empirical research into personal networking of prospective and new entrepreneurs in different national contexts confirm that personal networks encompass both social and business relationships (Aldrich et al. 1989; Cromie and Birley 1992; Greve 1995; Johannisson 1996). Informal networking remains important throughout the career of the entrepreneur (Birley 1985; Aldrich and Zimmer 1986). That social and business concerns become intertwined in individual ties means that network members are unique. If the individuals leave, the network will change. This is why the network and its ties are labeled *personal* rather than *social*. The latter connotation is self-evident since human organized activities are by definition social.

With respect to *network structure*, the literature usually differentiates between vertical and horizontal networks, i.e., between networks reflecting the value-added chain and those among competitors. The former often have asymmetric ties; the latter, symmetric ties. These structural features reflect the hierarchy. More realistic structures are "lateral networks," where constellations are built regardless of structural predispositions of the involved parties. This freedom of (inter)action, of networking, is crucial to entrepreneurial venturing. The need for independence is a major motive in business start-ups and the existence of internal and external barriers a major hindrance to intrapreneurship.

The need for boundary-spanning networking was stated as a key attribute of innovative organizations already by Burns and Stalker (1961). Once a network structure has become institutionalized, the need for effective coordination seems to generate centralization, i.e., a hierarchical or hub structure. The need for variability of nonrestricted lateral networking and the efficiency of vertical structuring may be combined as in the case of "heterarchy" where leadership varies according to which network member has the proper competencies to cope with the current mission of the organization.

A *process* perspective on networks includes both images of the creation of ties, their interlinking into a network (structure), and the operation of the ties and the network once established. The network tie itself in the business setting is usually the outcome of repeated interaction and occasional contracting, which over time, emerges into a complex tie. Larson (1992) uses case research on entrepreneurial firms to illustrate how exchange in dyadic relationships in this way becomes institutionalized. Ring and Van de Ven (1994) present the making of interorganizational relationships as coordinating formal/organizational and informal/human processes striving toward both efficiency and equitability. They suggest the coordination process continues to develop after the relationship has been established. The industrial market network literature also emphasizes that ties continue to evolve due to both internal changes and market changes, thereby contributing to technological development (Håkansson 1987) and innovation (Shaw 1991).

Entrepreneurial networking has special features also in a process perspective. Driven by opportunity, entrepreneurs may serendipitously invest in coincidental acquaintances, thereby building trust on intuition and a working personal chemistry. Personal ties included in entrepreneurial networks may originate as often in social as in business contexts and may as often emerge out of random encounters as be the outcome of deliberate search. Despite these "irrationalities," personal networks may be analyzed within a rational-choice framework (van der Poel 1993).

Personal networks are as deliberately constructed by entrepreneurs as the ventures they launch. First, the network reflects the personality of the entrepreneur and is a determinant of his or her identity. Second, the personal network carries the generic sense-making processes that guide the entrepreneur both as a businessperson and as a private person. Third, since personal networks are created by entrepreneurs, they are not perceived as a restricting cage but rather as a tool for realizing the venture. While entrepreneurs reject structures imposed upon them, the personal network at large, as does their venture, appears as an extension of self and is taken for granted.

The personal network supplies the entrepreneur with a universal resource kit. Enforcing identity and building general support, as outlined above, it generates cultural and emotional capital. Besides also providing information about and access to supplementary physical and financial resources (Birley 1985; Aldrich and Zimmer 1986), the personal network contains human and social capital. Human capital, i.e., experiences, skills and formal knowledge, is becoming increasingly crucial in business. Practitioners in general and entrepreneurs in particular rely mainly on tacit knowledge, which is mainly transmitted through metaphors, hands-on demonstrations and mentorship, i.e., social learning (Nonaka and Takeuchi 1995). Elaborate ties, such as those provided by a personal network, are needed to make these learning processes work. The trust embedded in individual ties and the network at large generally represents social capital, which gives

TABLE 18.1 Generic functions of entrepreneurial networking

Aspect of personal networking	The entrepreneur	The firm
Amplifying commitment	Enforcing self-confidence	Building/maintaining legitimacy and trust-worthiness
Resourcing	Refining existing competencies	Providing supplementary resources
Reorienting vision	Developing new competencies	Redefining the dominant business concept

access to all other kinds of resources and capital (Coleman 1989) and also helps overcome institutional barriers (cf. Araujo et al. 1998; Honig 1998).

Table 18.1 summarizes the main aspects of entrepreneur's personal networking from the point of view of the entrepreneur and the venture as a formal/legal unit (although this distinction is abandoned below). Personal networking is needed to confirm the identity of the entrepreneur and enforce his or her self-confidence as new challenges are continuously taken on. Networking provides legitimacy in the domain in which the firm operates, supplying the trustworthiness needed to be invited into trust-building relationships. Such trust-building processes do not rely solely on personal trustworthiness but also on the credibility associated with the firm itself as well as its institutional affiliations (Sanner 1997). However, the more radical and youthful the venturing career, the more important are the personalized ties. Lipparini and Sobrero (1994) find that founders use, for example, personal ties to suppliers when launching ventures.

Resourcing the entrepreneur personally as well as the business is another function of personal networking. In experiential learning the entrepreneur mainly learns by reflecting upon his or her own experience and others' concrete actions; peer entrepreneurs appear to be particularly important in such learning networks. Personal trust between economic actors also means that network control over resources becomes as strong as ownership control and considerably enhances the variety and flexibility of resources.

Considering our concern for entrepreneurship and growth, the third aspect of personal networking as outlined in table 18.1 is especially relevant. Networking is not pursued in order solely to enact the original vision but to recraft it according to either changed intentions or changed business conditions, or both. Thus, personal exchange will facilitate single-loop learning and trigger double-loop learning as well. External impulses remain important in the autocratically run small family business where there are by definition no peers to learn from. Carsrud et al. (1987) also report that solo entrepreneurs are more active networkers than individuals running firms with employees. Personal networking, e.g., contacting influential partners, will also help to redefine, and subsequently enact, the strategic focus of the firm.

Empirical research also confirms that entrepreneurs, when acquiring information or resources, prefer informal personal networking to formal networking, which relies on written information (Birley 1985; Specht 1987; Schafer 1990). The image of the entrepreneur as a moderate risk-taker, but not a gambler, may be elaborated with reference as well to the potential of personal ties and networking. Thereby the entrepreneur's vision can be enacted step-by-step, successively incorporating the knowledge, resources and market, an institutional access that network exchange requires. Furthermore, the personal network helps the entrepreneur to control the emotional forces that trigger action. A rich personal network invites moderate arousal since it makes improvisation feasible, whether to overcome unexpected obstacles or to nurture opportunities in the venturing process (Weick 1995: 46). The network obviously does not only offer a variety of opportunities but also different routes to the exploitation of an opportunity once it has been identified.

A generic reason why informal networks are preferred to formal ties is thus that the former simply are much more potent. Personal ties announce involvement that is beyond obligations associated with formal arrangements. Thus, on one hand, some argue that small firms benefit from having external members on their boards (Borch and Huse 1993). On the other hand, small-business owner-managers may also be unwilling to adopt such an arrangement for a number of reasons, including perceived high costs, unwillingness to disclose business secrets and the need for power and control. Yet another explanation may be that the entrepreneur already has a resourceful personal network that collectively provides all the advice needed under mutually negotiated conditions controlled by the entrepreneur.

The Personal Network as the Origin of Business Ventures

Summarizing the arguments thus far, the entrepreneurial process as unbounded in time and space may very well be presented as *organizing through personal networking*. Similar views have been presented by Bouwen and Steyaert (1990), Gartner et al. (1992), Larson and Starr (1993) and Frank and Lueger (1997). In such a perspective individual ventures appear as condensations of nodes and ties in the personal network, demarcated in space and time. The birth of a venture may then be seen as the institutionalization of a part of the entrepreneur's personal network into a venture, subsequently confirmed as a legal construct. This suggests that ventures are created and dissolved at a faster pace than the personal network at large. In Sweden, for example, a population of new firms is halved in about five years, while the preferred ties in personal networks of prospective and new entrepreneurs are on average well over a decade old (Johannisson 1996).

When organizing a venture into being, all business starters appear to be entrepreneurial, using their network as a generic tool for combining financial, human and social capital into a running firm. What differs among entrepreneurs is whether they are committed to continuous venturing, which implies focusing on networking as a means for new ventures (Johannisson 1992), or rather to the creation of a single organization – a stable, persistent structure feasible for management (Larson and Starr 1993). While personal networks retain their importance for all businesspersons, only those who remain entrepreneurial use them to expand their existing firms and to establish new ones. If a personal network is going to feed such a continuous venturing process, it obviously must be much wider in scope than what is needed to embed a single venture. Continuous entrepreneurship, renewal and growth, calls for nurturing a broad "latent network" (Ramachandran and Ramnaryan 1993). As the network grows, the entrepreneur automatically becomes exposed to an increasing number of interdependencies on the market, which may be traded and organized into new ventures (Snehota 1990; Taylor 1999) or provide a (spatial) setting for such entrepreneurial processes (Storper 1995; Maskell et al. 1998).

Figure 18.1 presents the entrepreneurial career as a set of interlocking ventures embedded in the personal network of the entrepreneur. Serial or habitual entrepreneurship in this way can be perceived as the successive enactment of venture opportunities continuously produced through exchange within the personal network. One venture feeds into the next, and they are all integrated by way of intensified networking, whether simultaneously as in the case of portfolio entrepreneurship or sequentially as in serial entrepreneurship (Scott and Rosa 1996; Westhead and Wright 1998). Each of these ventures or firms can be operated at a size that preserves flexibility and the owner-manager's control.

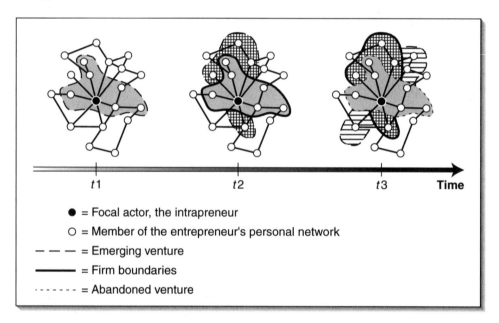

FIGURE 18.1 Organizing the entrepreneurial career by way of personal networking
Source: Adapted from Johannisson (1992: 168)

The entrepreneurial setting can be seen as a collecting area (March and Olsen 1976) where the alert entrepreneur combines random encounters with problems (market needs) and solutions (own or networked resources) into business opportunities. A portfolio of firms may then be just as much an outcome of spontaneous processes in their personal networks as the result of strategic intent in order to spread the commercial risks or exploit calculated synergies. Intuitive and emotional forces in the personal network not under conscious control of the individual entrepreneur may entice him or her into ventures never imagined before.

A network perspective supports the image of entrepreneurial organizations as "operative adhocracies," i.e., project organizations where the formal structure basically appears as a framework for temporary ventures (Peterson 1981). As organizations abandon the idea of position in the value chain as the major determinant of their way of organizing and instead structure according to individual customer need, a networked organization is needed. Generally "temporary organizations" (Lundin and Söderholm 1995) become more frequent since increasingly turbulent business environments call for continuous (re)organizing.

A paradox that challenges both researchers and practitioners is that small firms both grow and do not grow. It is generally accepted that the small-firm sector, both new and established businesses, are major job creators in many industrialized economies, although the statistical picture is unclear (Storey 1997). However, most individual firms rarely grow beyond ten employees, i.e., they remain microfirms. The power to grow as a collective and to create jobs does not seem to call for growth of the individual firm. The dynamics of venturing processes seems rather to be the outcome of linkages between individuals and firms across firm boundaries.

The proposed network approach also invites the image of *entrepreneurship as a collective phenomenon*, i.e., not primarily associated with resourceful individuals or firms. The new venture, as much as any existing organization with its stakeholders, represents a collective effort, possibly orchestrated by a single person. Even though the legal construct may be associated with the entrepreneur, the venturing initiative is in practice conditioned by supportive family members and friends, as well as mentoring colleagues, positive and believing customers, and patient suppliers.

Already the individual tie in the network has a collective core: personal ties are based on mutual consent, trust and reciprocity. More explicit forms of collective entrepreneurship include entrepreneurial teams or partnerships (Cooper and Daily 1997), cooperatives and franchising systems. These all create a potential for growth by synergistically combining each party's internal resources as well as complementary external network resources. Corporate entrepreneurship (Burgelman 1983; Stopford and Baden-Fuller 1994) may be addressed as collective entrepreneurship where internal networking is assumed to vitalize existing structures to the benefit of the corporation at large. The existing structure and the emerging venturing processes appear to be mutually dependent.

Complexity theory has reminded us that any organization in order to stay viable must encourage self-organizing initiatives that can cope with surprises provided by ambiguous environments (Stacey 1996; Morgan 1993). Such sudden and radical changes in business operations are difficult to imagine if individuals and firms are not embedded in already existing networks that provide the requisite variety. As indicated, chance, not just ascribed or achieved competencies and strategic intent, will define the creation and development of the venture (Bouchikhi 1993).

Firms cluster in trade associations because of joint business concerns, and entrepreneurs and owner-managers gather in different organizations because of shared professional interests. With the rise of virtual organizations or similar constructs and the rediscovery of the industrial districts, entrepreneurship as a collective effort has adopted a network image. Strictly defined, collective entrepreneurship means that the entrepreneurial capabilities are not associated with individual members of the collective but rather with the interaction, i.e., networking, between the members. As indicated, with the increasing popularity of the concept almost any system of firms has been addressed as a network. However, these structures, including many virtual organizations, to say nothing of vertical "partnerships" on industrial markets, often appear as hierarchical interorganizational structures where ties are not symmetric as in personal networks. Thus it can be questioned if franchise systems should be addressed as networks; often the franchisor dominates the franchisees in such a way that the hierarchical form seems to be the most adequate one.

There are however a number of other network forms that more genuinely represent collective entrepreneurship as a coalition of peers interconnected by symmetric ties – from the partnering of two or more individuals into a venture to the multifirm region, the industrial district. Between them we may find "team entrepreneurship," as defined by Stewart (1989). Here entrepreneurship is not associated with the individual shopfloor workers or with dyadic ties but with the network itself. Besides the absence of hierarchy, social commitment is mobilized to supplement calculated interest. Stewart talks about workshop employees "running hot," passionate in their ambitions to collectively meet customer expectations.

It seems to be very difficult to construct collective entrepreneurship intentionally. Workers' cooperatives, for example, are based on strong values, but their hierarchical structure (actually it is a double hierarchy since the workers as owners control management) seems to erode their viability. Only if situated in (local) contexts, such as industrial parks that support their organizing form, will cooperatives prosper. The ideal industrial park represents a self-organizing collective of individual firms, embedded in dense socioeconomic networks that include both production networks and personal networks of owner-managers. Collectively the firms and the community demonstrate entrepreneurial capabilities.

Entrepreneurial Networking and Venture Performance

A network approach to entrepreneurship, especially its questioning of ventures as an outcome of unique efforts by especially gifted individuals or single resourceful firms, provides an adequate reason for asking whether it is the individual, the firm, or a collective of firms that represents the growth potential in the economy. Obviously then, that as much as creativity is an outcome of a dialogue between two persons, each with a strong opinion, innovation is often associated with interaction between firms (Lorenzoni and Ornati 1988). Growth is associated neither with resources as such nor with identified opportunities per se. Resources have to be put to use (Penrose 1995), and this calls for interaction with the market. Also opportunities are not like mushrooms waiting to be picked; they have to be interactively realized or "enacted" (Smircich and Stubbart 1985; Gartner et al. 1992).

The above discussion has indicated a number of reasons why it is difficult to identify a definitive relationship between entrepreneurial networking and the success of a particular venture, its performance and growth.

First, networking is not done by entrepreneurs exclusively to promote individual ventures. Personal networking is, rather, a basic, existential activity, natural to and needed by every human being. The continuous organizing of various resources and people, the pleasure it gives, may very well be the main reason why a venturing career is launched in the first place. If a venture is created in order to enhance the position in society, i.e., decrease marginality (Stanworth and Curran 1973), the network exchange needed to achieve that may itself create the respectability strived for, and no further firm growth will be necessary.

Second, networking is done not just in order to cope with contemporary challenges but also for investment in human and social capital for future use or for reciprocating support received earlier in the career. Many entrepreneurs may spend extra time on networking not primarily in order to increase profits but to be able to maintain the venturing career by launching new ventures (Westhead and Wright 1998).

Third, and associated with the second argument, the fact the an individual's personal network invites habitual entrepreneurship, whether serial or portfolio, means that the venture of the unit of analysis in growth models must be questioned. The individual should be focused upon because only by reviewing all the venturing activities of the entrepreneur will the efficiency of his or her personal network be properly evaluated. Alternatively the firm and its "action set" of business partners should be the unit of analysis since the firm and the partners grow synergistically (Lorenzoni and Ornati 1988).

Fourth, the personal network does not solely represent different kinds of capital that are instrumental to growth (cf. Honig 1998). It also creates unforeseeable business opportunities since they are randomly created by unexpected encounters. According to Bygrave (1989), the evolution of entrepreneurial activity is characterized by quantum jumps – i.e., revolution – and not just continuous change and growth. Thus it is not just the richness of the network as regards scope and density or the activity as regards networking that matters but chance and coincidence as well.

Fifth, networking is not only beneficial for economic organizing for growth but may be the cause of failure (Powell and Smith-Doerr 1994). In order to benefit from a relationship, both parties must commit themselves. If a firm overspecializes to such an extent that it does not retain the capability to evaluate the contributions of potential partners, there is a considerable risk of network failure (Miles and Snow 1992). If the firm does not develop its own "absorptive capacity" (Cohen and Levinthal 1990), it will not benefit from networking, whether it engages in general cooperative arrangements (McGee et al. 1995), outsourcing expertise for innovation (MacPherson 1992) or acquiring supplementary competencies by including consultants in the network (Ylinenpää 1997). Once investments have been made in a network and strong ties become dominant, there is a risk for cognitive lock-ins (Grabher 1993) as well as oversocialized relationships to business partners. Both mechanisms create inertia, which may be lethal to the business.

While the above-mentioned five arguments refer to the networking and growth processes per se, there are additional methodological problems associated with inquiring into networking activities. First, the network is, on one hand, taken for granted and therefore not fully appreciated, if at all. On the other hand, the entrepreneur may very well be aware of the importance of the personal network but have the opinion that to confess a dependence on network mates would be to diminish his or her own capabilities. Second, while new entrepreneurs and unsuccessful businesspersons may attribute their attempts and failure to persons in their environment, established entrepreneurs are self-attributing. That is, they refer success to their own competencies, not those of their network mates. Third, the personal network represents a secret strength that must be treated with care (especially in high-tech industries). On one hand, information exchange is necessary for creating needed knowledge; on the other, the same exchange may reveal unique insights. Issues like these may explain why Curren et al. (1993) in their study of small owner-managers in the United Kingdom found arguments that generally depreciated the benefits of personal networking to owner-managers.

Despite these barriers to proper interpretation of empirical findings, many scholars propose a causal relationship between networking and firm performance (Birley 1985; Aldrich and Zimmer 1986; Dubini and Aldrich 1991). However, the empirical support for the proposition that personal networking generally enhances individual firm survival and growth is not indisputable. General features of the personal network, such as time invested and the scope of the network, do not seem to increase venture performance (Johannisson 1996; Reese and Aldrich 1995). Hansen (1995), though, finds that first-year growth of new ventures was strongly related to personal-network properties, such as size and interconnectivity. Using case data in a Chinese context, Zhao and Aram (1995) demonstrate that the range and intensity of networking differs between high and low-growth ventures over all the different phases of the firm-creation process. Brown and Butler (1995) state that networking with competitors rather than upstream and downstream business partners fosters firm growth. In the industrial-district literature, the combination of cooperation and competition is usually referred to as a main source of viability (Johannisson et al. 1994). Watson et al. (1995) conclude that the quality of the internal network between partners influences the success of the joint endeavor. Cooper and Daily (1997) in their review of the entrepreneurial-team literature state that many teams dissolve but conclude that team venturing, if completed, is more successful than single-founder start-ups.

As indicated above, one reason for not seeing the relationship between networking activity and firm growth may be that an inappropriate unit of analysis has been adopted. Some scholars prefer to study the individual founder, not the firm, because some ventures will fail while others succeed over an entrepreneurial career. As suggested, the entrepreneur's coping with these dramas can be made intelligible within a network perspective. The network will give the entrepreneur early warnings about which ventures may fail and give him or her an opportunity to terminate them before they become insolvent. The network then can be used to supplement those resources from the abandoned venture that are recycled in a new venture. In this perspective an elaborate personal network appears to be a necessary, but not a sufficient, condition for entrepreneurial success.

Obviously, networking is pivotal when we address genuinely collective forms of entrepreneurship, such as team entrepreneurship and industrial districts. The networking activities themselves represent the collective entrepreneurial capabilities. Quantitative empirical research into the scope and contents of networks between owner-managers and their companies in small-firm clusters also confirms that the networks are denser than those of a comparable science park and certainly those of a medium-sized corporation professing to promote entrepreneurship (Johannisson et al. 1994). Nevertheless, contexts differ with respect to their ability to exploit personal networking for venturing, which brings us to the next section.

CREATING SPACE FOR GROWTH: THE ORGANIZING CONTEXT

The network view outlined above suggests that firm growth is an outcome of individual and organizational interdependencies, which encompass both economic and social concerns. This suggests that the entrepreneur as an interactive agent creates the conditions for his or her own development and growth: the environment of the venturing process is enacted (Weick 1979; Smircich and Stubbart 1985). What makes a difference between entrepreneurs is their varying ability to scan and select information about the environment and then interactively impose their image of reality, their vision, on the market. Intense networking provides the overview needed to guide this crafting endeavor; its success depends on how "enactable" the environment actually is. Covin and Slevin (1990) conclude that networked or "organically" structured new ventures are more successful in emerging than in mature industries.

While the Schumpetarian entrepreneur is expected to be able to perceive and act upon the global environment, most businesspersons have a limited reach and a restricted action frame. Even entrepreneurs who can intellectually grasp vague opportunities have to restrict their field of action because of limited resources and time to nurture the personal network needed for those who may supply additional resources. Most businesspersons therefore need an "organizing context" that can help them structure exchange with more distant parts of the environment. A favorable organizing context offers a universal instrument for coping with ambiguity, either by providing a shelter against uncertainties or by assisting in turning unexpected changes on the market into business opportunities. An elaborate organizing context can be used to both launch new ventures according to opportunity and to demobilize resources tied to obsolete ventures and to reallocate them to new emerging ventures. The organizing context thus enforces all the functions needed to make a successful venturing career: business intelligence, resourcing ventures and creating legitimacy. Our model of venturing as successively mobilizing resources in the overall personal network announces the notion of organizing context (see figure 18.1).

Similar ideas about an "immediate" environment, which is especially relevant to the firm, have been presented by Dill (1958). However, previous approaches, well-anchored in functionalistic organization theory, perceive this "task" environment mainly as given to the firm. The organizing context, as defined by us, is in contrast jointly created by the entrepreneur and further context members as a platform for proactive entrepreneurial strategies in the global environment. This image of mutual dependence between venture and context reflects Giddens's (1984: 25) notion of "structuration":

> Analyzing the structuration of a social system means studying the modes in which such system, grounded in the knowledgeable activities of situated actors who draw upon the rules and resources in the diversity of action contexts, are produced and reproduced in interaction. . . . Structure is not "external" to individuals: as memory traces, as instantiated in social practices, it is in a certain sense more "internal" than the exterior to their activities in a Durkheimian sense. Structure is not to be equated with constraint but is always both constraining and enabling.

Thus, in the same way the venture itself can appear as a condensed part of the personal network *the organizing context may be perceived as network with a higher density than the rest of the world*. The ideal organizing context appears to be a loosely coupled system where network nodes, firms and individuals are interdependent, albeit autonomous. Such systems are assumed to have self-organizing properties, which means, for example, that need for change as identified by any member may diffuse throughout the system while temporary disturbances are absorbed by some nodes leaving the others unaffected. These self-organizing features can be achieved either by way of a broad set of weak ties or by strong linkages exploiting the variety of commitments that the social dimension of personal network ties offers.

Generally, the organizing context may be functionally or spatially demarcated (Johannisson 1988). Starting with functionally defined organizing contexts, the innovative corporation is assumed to provide a platform for bold initiatives by intrapreneurs. The overall franchising system provides an organizing context for the individual franchisee. Individuals organize in professional associations and firms in trade associations in order to reduce uncertainty and supply competencies. In these cases, the structure is however hierarchical and exchange mainly instrumental. Such features are not necessarily conducive to entrepreneurship. A spatial demarcation of the organizing context is then more appropriate as it mobilizes by way of lateral networking social as well as calculative commitment.

The Marshallian industrial district appears to be the ideal spatially defined organizing context. Here the individual owner-managers have neither the capabilities needed nor the interest to grow, but the district as a whole offers a highly entrepreneurial learning context. There is a vast literature on spatial organizing of economic activity including perspectives from the original notion of the organically created industrial district (Piore and Sabel 1984; Goodman and Bamford 1989; Pyke et al. 1990; Pyke and Sengenberger 1992; Garofoli 1994) to more or less induced spatial settings, such as the "innovative milieu" (Maillat 1998) and clusters of high-tech firms (Saxenian 1994). Malecki (1997) provides an excellent overview of networks and spatial economic activity (cf. Markusen 1996). The literature also includes critical perspectives on localized (collective) entrepreneurship (Massey et al. 1992; Grabher 1993; Storper 1995; Bianchi 1998).

The reason why we especially focus on the spatially demarcated organizing context where traditional owner-managed firms dominate is that such contexts, due to the members' common roots, physical and social proximity and a shared identity, encourages personal encounters and networking. All the commitments conducive to entrepreneurship may be spontaneously activated: calculative due to business orientation, social due to shared history and identity and affective due to kinship and neighborliness. The fact that the economic actors are independent owner-managers guarantees their autonomy and action orientation; the social embeddedness implies interdependence and encourages the creation of local production systems. Such organizing contexts appear to be self-organizing, not least because mutual learning is enforced due to a shared frame of reference (Lane and Lubatkin 1998). Self-organizing includes the following features, all reflecting the pivotal role of networking:

♦ Dense lateral networks which between and within ties combine information processes, business exchange and rule-producing (and reproducing) behavior.
♦ A rich boundary spanning the flow of information feeding into local and social learning processes where knowledge is (re)produced and applied.

- Constant creation of temporary alliances and partnerships according to individual firm needs as well as shared contextual needs.
- Shared understanding that uncertainty and ambiguity can only be dealt with by variety and improvisation.

Elsewhere we have reported an operationalized network model that demonstrates how these self-organizing features are reflected in different clusters of firms (Dandridge and Johannisson 1996), particularly in the industrial district and science park (Johannisson et al. 1994). Using a learning metaphor, Maskell et al. (1998) discuss how socioeconomic ties between actors initiate and maintain localized knowledge-creating processes, which because they are difficult to copy, create global competitiveness (cf. Storper 1995; Courlet and Soulage 1995; Markusen 1996). These lessons suggest a need for strategies where global and local networking combine.

Lessons for Researchers and Practitioners

The strategic-management literature is flooded with models that propose interorganizational cooperation as a generic way to cope with uncertainty (i.e., reduce it) from environmental change and with incomplete resources while pursuing expansionist goals. Entrepreneurs thrive however on environmental ambiguity because it offers unlimited opportunities which by way of personal networking can be enacted. Because of the liabilities of newness and smallness, most founders need active networking capabilities to become established and possibly to grow. Therefore, my notion of "organizing context" as a springboard and shock absorber from the point of view of the individual independent businessperson is important. As a member of such a context, businesspersons may hand over their entrepreneurial ambitions to the context as such and thereby keep their own firm as small as desired.

Our perspective generates a number of interesting issues for further research. Both on a regional level and individual-firm level, it would be interesting to study how *transfer of resources between terminated and new ventures* is carried out. Such recycling of resources, besides being beneficial to entrepreneurs and their own careers, usually means increased efficiency in the economy in general and the local context in particular. Alternatively, individual entrepreneurial careers may be tracked. In both cases a study of the termination of ventures and restructuring of resources within old or new regimes would provide process insights about change and renewal across systems levels.

Throughout this chapter we have argued that personal networks are irreplaceable in the venturing process. Proximity and time are needed to initiate and build personal ties. Since entrepreneurial activity must cross boundaries, certainly physical ones, and time is a scarce resource for the experientially learning owner-manager, *new modes of networking* must be practiced. Obviously then, information technology with its ability to create even virtual organizations, comes to the fore. The challenge is to nurture personal encounters while exploiting modern information technology. Such networking strategies for amplifying information processes are suggested by Van Horn and Harvey (1998). More in-depth research is, however, needed to find out how information technology influences the personal networking of individual entrepreneurs and interaction within organizing contexts, such as industrial districts.

With regard to policymakers, the lessons are that entrepreneurship should not solely be supported in accessing financial capital and investing in human capital but also in building social capital. This implies supporting both local networking and the creation of global ties. In the same way as entrepreneurs amplify spontaneously initiated processes in the market, policymakers should alertly encourage emerging networking between entrepreneurs (and, of course, enhance their own social skills!). These measures include support for mentoring programs among peer entrepreneurs, for subcontracting systems involving large and small firms and for linkages between small firms and universities. In providing such support, both the authorities and the entrepreneurs themselves must be sensitive to the fact that the effects may differ from expectations. That is, formal training programs for owner-managers may very well create a number of unintended side effects: information sharing, social learning and the emergence of new ventures involving course mates. Support for networking between entrepreneurs in a locality may very well inspire individual networking entrepreneurs to launch a new venture with stakeholders outside the supported group or network itself. Any such emerging self-organizing activities should be accepted, at times even encouraged. Entrepreneurship is not just about planning but also spontaneous and experiential learning.

The locality as a framework for supporting entrepreneurial activity seems to remain important for a number of reasons. First, in most countries the support structure is usually spatially organized; even if available public resources may vary dramatically as, for example, between Scandinavia and the United States. Second, personal networking is for practical and emotional reasons spatially concentrated even if far-reaching external professional and business ties have to be kept in mind. This spatial concentration of networking is a promising base for the creation of self-organizing contextual processes. According to the framework proposed here existing entrepreneurs must then be committed to the creation of such an organizing context. This involvement can be encouraged by inviting the entrepreneurs themselves to make proposals for appropriate measures. Their suggestions for supplementary firms, additional public services, educational facilities and so on should be carefully listened to since they signal the emergence of collective, self-energizing entrepreneurial processes that, in turn, can create growth in individual firms or networks of firms.

REFERENCES

Aldrich, H. and Zimmer, C. 1986. Entrepreneurship through Social Networks. In D. Sexton and R. Smilor (eds.), *The Art and Science of Entrepreneurship*. New York: Ballinger, pp. 3–23.
Aldrich, H. and Reece, P.R. and Dubini, P. 1989. Women on the Verge of a Breakthrough?: Networking among Entrepreneurs in the US and Italy. *Entrepreneurship and Regional Development* 1(4): 339–56.

Araujo, L and Easton, G. 1996. Networks in Socioeconomic Systems. A Critical Review. In D. Iacobucci (ed.), *Networks in Marketing*. Thousand Oaks, CA: Sage, pp. 63–109.

Araujo, L., Bowey, J. and Easton, G. 1998. Social Capital, Industrial Networks and Entrepreneurs. In A. Halinen-Kaila and N. Nummerla (eds.), *Interaction, Relationships and Networks: Visions for the Future*. 14th IMP Annual Conference Proceedings, vol. 1. Turku, Finland: Turku School of Economics.

Barnatt, C. 1995. Office Space, Cyberspace and Virtual Organization. *Journal of General Management* 20(4): 78–91.

Bianchi, G. 1998. Requiem of Third Italy? Rise and Fall of a too Successful Concept. *Entrepreneurship and Regional Development* 10(2): 93–116.

Bird, B.J. 1989. *Entrepreneurial Behavior*. Glenview, IL: Scott Foresman.

Birley, S. 1985. The Role of Networks in the Entrepreneurial Process. *Journal of Business Venturing* 1(1): 107–17.

Borch, O.J. and Huse, M. 1993. Informal Strategic Networks and Boards of Directors. *Entrepreneurship Theory and Practice* 18(1): 23–36.

Bouchikhi, H. 1993. A Constructivist Framework for Understanding Entrepreneurship Performance. *Organization Studies* 14(4): 549–70.

Bouwen, R. and Steyaert, C. 1990. Construing Organizational Texture in Young Entrepreneurial Firms. *Journal of Management Studies* 26(6): 637–49.

Brown, B. and Butler, J.E. 1995. Competitors as Allies: A Study of Entrepreneurial Networks in the US Wine Industry. *Journal of Small Business Management* 33(3): 57–66.

Burgelman, R.A. 1983. Corporate Entrepreneurship and Strategic Management: Insights from a Process Study. *Management Science* 29: 1349–64.

Burns, T. and Stalker, G. 1961. *The Management of Innovation*. London: Tavistock.

Bygrave, W.D. 1989. The Entrepreneurship Paradigm (I): A Philosophical Look at Its Research Methodologies. *Entrepreneurship Theory and Practice* 13(5): 7–26.

Carsrud, A.L., Galio, C.M. and Olm, K.W. 1987. Entrepreneurs–Mentors Networks, and Successful New Venture Development: An Exploratory Study. *American Journal of Small Business* 11(fall): 13–18.

Cohen, W.M. and Levinthal, D.A. 1990. Absorptive Capacity: A New Perspective on Learning and Innovation. *Administrative Science Quarterly* 35: 128–52.

Coleman, J.S. 1989. Social Capital in the Creation of Human Capital. *American Journal of Sociology* 94(supplement): 95–120.

Cooper, A.C. and Daily, C.M. 1997. Entrepreneurial Teams. In D.L. Sexton and R.W. Smilor (eds.), *Entrepreneurship 2000*. Chicago: Upstart, pp. 127–50.

Courlet, C. and Soulage, B. 1995. Industrial Dynamics and Territorial Space. *Entrepreneurship and Regional Development* 7(4): 287–307.

Covin, J.G. and Slevin, D.P. 1990. New Venture Strategic Posture, Structure and Performance: An Industry Life Cycle Analysis. *Journal of Business Venturing* 5: 123–35.

Cromie, S. and Birley, S. 1992. Networking by Female Business Owners in Northern Ireland. *Journal of Business Venturing* 7: 237–51.

Curran, J., Jarvis, R., Blackburn, R.A. and Black, S. 1993. Networks and Small Firms: Constructs, Methodological Strategies and Some Findings. *International Small Business Journal* 2(2): 13–22.

Dandridge, T. and Johannisson, B. 1996. Entrepreneurship and Self-Organizing: Personal Networks in Spatial Systems of Small Firms. In M. Zineldin (ed.), *Strategic Relationship Management*. Stockholm: Almqvist and Wiksell, pp. 219–38.

Dill, W.R. 1958. Environment as an Influence on Managerial Autonomy. *Administrative Science Quarterly* 2(March): 409–43.

Dubini, P. and Aldrich, H. 1991. Personal and Extended Networks are Central to the Entrepreneurial Process. *Journal of Business Venturing* 6: 305–13.

Dyer, J.H. and Singh, H. 1998. The Relational View: Cooperative Strategy and Sources of Interorganizational Competitive Advantage. *Academy of Management Review* 23(4): 660–79.

Ford, D. (ed.). 1990. *Understanding Business Markets: Interaction, Relationships, Networks.* London: Academic Press.

Frank, H. and Lueger, M. 1997. Reconstructing Development Processes. Conceptual Basis and Empirical Analysis of Setting up a Business. *International Studies of Management and Organization* 27(3): 34–63.

Garofoli, G. 1994. The Industrial District of Lecco: Innovation and Transformation Processes *Entrepreneurship and Regional Development* 6(4): 371–93.

Gartner, W.B. and Bird, B.J. and Starr, J.A. 1992. Acting "As If": Differentiating Entrepreneurial from Organizational Behavior. *Entrepreneurship Theory and Practice* 16(3): 13–31.

Giddens, A. 1984. *The Constitution of Society.* Oxford: Polity Press.

Goodman, E. and Bamford, J. (eds.). 1989. *Small Firms and Industrial Districts in Italy.* London: Routledge.

Grabher G. (ed.). 1993. *The Embedded Firm. On the Socioeconomics of Industrial Networks.* London: Routledge.

Grandori, A. and Soda, G. 1995. Inter-Firm Networks: Antecedents, Mechanism and Forms. *Organization Studies* 16(2): 183–214.

Granovetter, M. 1985. Economic Action and Social Structure: The Problem of Embeddedness. *American Journal of Sociology* 91(3): 481–509.

Greve, A. 1995. Networks of Entrepreneurship – An Analysis of Social Relations, Occupational Background, and Use of Contacts During the Establishment Process. *Scandinavian Journal of Management* 11(1): 1–24.

Håkansson, H. (ed.). 1987. *Industrial Technological Development – A Network Approach.* London: Croom Helm.

Hansen, E.L. 1995. Entrepreneurial Networks and New Organization Growth. *Entrepreneurship Theory and Practice* 19(4): 7–19.

Honig, B. 1998. What Determines Success? Examining the Human, Financial and Social Capital of Jamaican Microentrepreneurs. *Journal of Business Venturing* 3: 371–94.

Johannisson, B. 1988. Business Formation – Network Approach. *Scandinavian Journal of Management* 4(3/4): 83–99.

Johannisson, B. 1992. Entrepreneurship – the Management of Ambiguity. In T. Polesie and I.L. Johansson (eds.), *Responsibility and Accounting – The Organizational Regulation of Boundary Conditions.* Lund, Sweden: Studentlitteratur, pp. 155–79.

Johannisson, B. 1996. Existential Enterprise and Economic Endeavour. In *Aspects of Women's Entrepreneurship.* Stockholm: Nutek (Swedish National Board for Industrial and Technical Development), pp. 115–41.

Johannisson, B. and Alexanderson, O., Nowicki, K. and Senneseth, K. 1994. Beyond Anarchy and Organization – Entrepreneurs in Contextual Networks. *Entrepreneurship and Regional Development* 6: 329–56.

Lane, P.J. and Lubatkin, M. 1998. Relative Absorptive Capacity and Interorganizational Learning. *Strategic Management Journal* 19: 461–77.

Larson, A. 1992. Network Dyads in Entrepreneurial Settings: A Study of the Governance of Exchange Relationships. *Administrative Science Quarterly* 37: 76–104.

Larson, A. and Starr, J.A. 1993. A Network Model of Organization Formation. *Entrepreneurship Theory and Practice* 17(1): 5–15.

Lipparini, A. and Sobrero, M. 1994. The Glue and the Pieces: Entrepreneurship and Innovation in Small-Firm Networks. *Journal of Business Venturing* 9:125–40.

Lorenzoni, G. and Ornati, O.A. 1988. Constellations of Firms and New Ventures. *Journal of Business Venturing* 3: 41–57.

Lundin, R.A. and Söderholm, A. 1995. A Theory of the Temporary Organization. *Scandinavian Journal of Management* 11(4): 437–55.

MacPherson, A.D. 1992. Innovation, External Technical Linkages and Small Firm Commercial Performance: An Empirical Analysis from Western New York. *Entrepreneurship and Regional Development* 4(2): 165–84.

McGee, J.E., Dowling, M.J. and Migginson, W.L. 1995. Cooperative Strategy and New Venture Performance: the Role of Business Strategy and Management Experience. *Strategic Management Journal* 16: 565–80.

Maillat, D. 1998. Innovative Milieux and New Generations of Regional Policies. *Entrepreneurship and Regional Development* 10(1): 1–16.

Maillat, D. and Lecoq, B. 1992. New Technologies and Transformation of Regional Structures in Europe: the Role of the Milieu. *Entrepreneurship and Regional Development* 4: 1–20.

Malecki, E. 1997. Entrepreneurs, Networks, and Economic Devlopment: A Review of Recent Research. *Advances in Entrepreneurship, Firm Emergence and Growth* 3: 57–118.

March, J. and Olsen, P. (eds.). 1976. *Ambiguity and Choice in Organizations.* Oslo: Universitetsforlaget.

Markusen, A. 1996. Sticky Places and Slippery Space: A Typology of Industrial Districts. *Economic Geography* 72(3): 293–313.

Maskell, P., Eskelinen, H., Hannibalsson, I., Malmberg, A. and Vatne, E. 1998. *Competitiveness, Localised Learning and Regional Development.* London: Routledge.

Massey, D., Quintas, P. and Wield, D. 1992. *High-Tech Fantasies – Science Parks in Society, Science and Space.* London: Routledge.

Miles, R.E. and Snow, C.C. 1992. Causes of Failure in Network Organizations. *California Management Review* 34(4): 53–72.

Morgan, G. 1993. *Imaginization.* London: Sage.

Nohria, N. and Eccles, R.E. 1992a. Face to Face: Making Network Organizations Work. In N. Nohria and R.E. Eccles (eds.), *Networks and Organizations. Structure, Form and Action.* Boston: Harvard Business School, pp. 288–308.

Nohria, N. and Eccles, R.E. (eds.). 1992b. *Networks and Organizations. Structure, Form and Action.* Boston: Harvard Business School.

Nonaka, I. and Takeuchi, H. 1995. *The Knowledge-Creating Company.* Oxford: Oxford University Press.

Penrose, E. 1995. *The Theory of the Growth of the Firm.* Oxford: Oxford University Press.

Peterson, R.A. 1981. Entrepreneurship and Organization. In P.C. Nystrom and W.H. Starbuck (eds.), *Handbook of Organizational Design*, vol. 1. Oxford: Oxford University Press, pp. 65–83.

Piore, M.J. and Sabel, C. 1984. *The Second Industrial Divide: Possibilities for Prosperity.* New York: Basic Books.

Powell, W.W. and Smith-Doerr, L. 1994. Networks and Economic Life. In N.J. Smelser and R. Swedberg (eds.), *Handbook of Economic Sociology.* Princeton, N.J: Princeton University Press, pp. 368–402.

Pyke, F. and Sengenberger, W. (eds.). 1992. *Industrial Districts and Local Economic Regeneration.* Geneva: ILO.

Pyke, F. and Becattini, G. and Sengenberger, W. (eds.). 1990. *Industrial Districts and Inter-Firm Co-operation in Italy.* Geneva: ILO.

Ramachandran, K. and Ramnarayan, S. 1993. Entrepreneurial Orientation and Networking: some Indian Evidence. *Journal of Business Venturing* 8: 513–24.

Reese, P.R. and Aldrich, H.E. 1995. Entrepreneurial Networks and Business Performance. A Panel Study of Small and Medium-Sized Firms in the Research Triangle. In S. Birley and I.C. MacMillan (eds.), *International Entrepreneurship.* London: Routledge, pp. 124–44.

Ring, P.S. and Van de Ven, A. 1994. Developmental Processes of Interorganizational Relationships. *Academy of Management Review* 19(1): 90–118.

Sanner, L. 1997. *Trust between Entrepreneurs and External Actors. Sensemaking in Organising New Business Ventures*. Department of Business Studies. Uppsala: Uppsala University,.

Saxenian, A. 1994. *Regional Advantage. Culture and Competition in Silicon Valley and Route 128*. Cambridge, Mass.: Harvard University Press.

Schafer, D.S. 1990. Level of Entrepreneurship and Scanning Source Usage in Very Small Businesses. *Entrepreneurship Theory and Practice*. 14(1): 19–31.

Scott, M. and Rosa, P. 1996. Has Firm Level Analysis Reached its Limits? Time for a Rethink. *International Small Business Journal* 14(4): 81–9.

Shaw, B. 1991. Developing Technological Innovations within Networks. *Entrepreneurship and Regional Development* 3(2): 111–28.

Sjöstrand, S.E. 1992. On the Rationale behind "Irrational" Institutions. *Journal of Economic Issues* 26(4): 1007–39.

Smircich, L. and Stubbart, C. 1985. Strategic Management in the Enacted World. *Academy of Management Review* 10(4): 724–36.

Snehota, I. 1990. *Notes on a Theory of Business Enterprise*. Department of Business Administration. Uppsala: Uppsala University.

Specht, P.H. 1987. Information Sources Used for Strategic Planning Decisions in Small Firms. *American Journal of Small Business* 11(spring): 21–4.

Stacey, R.D. 1996. *Complexity and Creativity in Organizations*. San Francisco: Berret-Koehler.

Stanworth, M. and Curran, J. 1973. *Management Motivation in the Small Business*. London: Gower.

Starr, J.R. and MacMillan, I.C. 1990. Resource Cooptation Via Social Contracting: Resource Acquisition Strategies for New Ventures. *Strategic Management Journal* 11(summer): 97–2.

Stewart, A. 1989. *Team Entrepreneurship*. London: Sage.

Stopford, R.D. and Baden-Fuller, C.W.F. 1994. Creating Corporate Entrepreneurship. *Strategic Management Journal* 15: 521–36.

Storey, D.J. 1997. *Understanding the Small Business Sector*. London: Thomson.

Storper, M. 1995. The Resurgence of Regional Economies, Ten Years Later: the Region as a Nexus of Untraded Interdependencies. *European Urban and Regional Studies* 3(2): 191–221.

Taylor, M. 1999. Small Firms as Temporary Coalitions. Forthcoming in *Entrepreneurship and Regional Development*.

Van der Poel, M. 1993. Personal Networks. A Rational-Choice Explanations of their Size and Composition. Lisse: Swets and Zeitlinger.

Van Horn, R.L. and Harvey, M.G. 1998. The Rural Entrepreneurial Venture: Creating the Virtual Megafirm. *Journal of Business Venturing* 13: 257–74.

Watson, W.E., Ponthieu, L.D. and Critelli, J.W. 1995. Team Interpersonal Process Effectiveness in Venture Partnerships and Its Connection to Perceived Success. *Journal of Business Venturing* 10: 393–411.

Weick, K.E. 1979. *The Social Psychology of Organizing*. Reading, Mass.: Addison Wesley.

Weick, K E 1995 *Sensemaking in Organizations*. Thousand Oaks, CA: Sage.

Westhead, P. and Wright, M. 1998. Novice, Portfolio, and Serial Founders: Are they Different? *Journal of Business Venturing* 13: 173–204.

Ylinenpää, H. 1997. *Managing Competence Development and Acquisition in Small Manufacturing Firms*. Luleå: Luleå University of Technology.

Zhao, L. and Aram, J.D. 1995. Networking and Growth of Young Technology-Intensive Ventures in China. *Journal of Business Venturing* 10: 349–70.

19

Strategic Alliances as Vehicles for International Growth

Mark Weaver

ALLIANCES AND GROWTH
REGIONAL GROWTH EXAMPLES
PLANNING FOR SUCCESS AND ENHANCING OUTCOMES
FUTURE RESEARCH DIRECTIONS
CONCLUSIONS

Faced with rapidly changing markets, technology, governance and increased risks of independent actions, small and medium-sized firms (SMEs) are adopting alternative organizational models based on cooperation. Cooperative interfirm activities include forms that range from informal sharing of information to joint ventures, and all manner of agreements in between. Terminology such as cooperative strategies, networks and interorganizational cooperation has evolved to describe relations between organizations. Since the late 1980s, this terminology has become common as the frequency and scope of organizational alternatives has expanded. Kim and Maubourgne (1998) provide a "voluntary" notion of alliances as an overlay to the formation of alliance alternatives to explain success.

SMEs are increasingly turning to alliances as vehicles for growth (MacMillan 1983; Birley 1985; Aldrich and Zimmer; 1986, Weaver and Dickson 1998). Some argue that SMEs are more opportunistic and less strategic in their approach to alliances, and therefore, a multilayered approach to alliance analysis that classifies individual firms as a micro level and environmental factors as macro levels should be considered. This multilayered analysis helps us to understand the development of alliances and their link to growth and development (Monsted 1996). The need to look at the European Union, the Asian growth triangle, Italian clusters and regional trade affiliations as examples of macro alliances has also been suggested (Quinn 1992). Organizations can form alliances with firms, governments, universities and even "virtual companies." As a result, they become packages of interdependent knowledge and should focus on factors that contribute to their competitive advantage (Quinn 1992; Davidow and Malone 1992).

The link between growth and individual orientations, key decision leaders' attitudes, environmental factors and public policy has been established by analyzing the Strategic Alliance Research Group (SARG) data sets (Weaver and Dickson 1998; Dickson and Weaver 1997; Weaver et al. 1997). The SARG project is an informal alliance of researchers in several countries, nine of which will be featured in this chapter. The pilot was done in the United States and has continued with expanded questionnaires in other countries.

The uncertainty in the environment includes technological changes, communication advancements, market pressures, internationalization and increased threats and opportunities faster than firms can take advantage individually (Fenn 1997). These findings lead us to probe deeper to help explain why alliances form, how they are structured, what brings success and what outcomes occur.

For purposes of this chapter, strategic alliances are defined as "structured agreements that establish exchange relationships between cooperating firms," and refer to all forms noted above. This definition is one used in previous articles and papers (Weaver and Dickson,1998; Dickson and Weaver 1997). Alliances occur in both large and small firms and between domestic and international firms. A graphic depiction of this "constellation" of alliances is displayed in figure 19.1. Also included in the figure are basic dimensions to consider when examining growth potential.

The purpose of this chapter is to describe the development of alliance research as it relates to successful outcomes and interorganizational growth. A combination of reviews of significant articles and empirical findings from the SARG project on nine countries will be used to look at the current situation and to identify research opportunities.

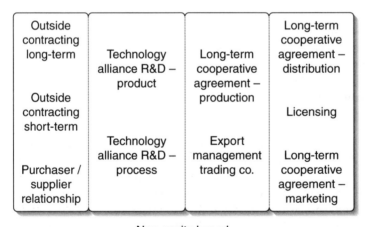

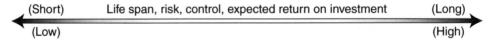

FIGURE 19.1 Constellation of SME-based alliances

Primarily, micro level research will be used, but it is supplemented with a macro level view of industry-wide and regional alliances that facilitate SME growth.

ALLIANCES AND GROWTH

Ticket to Growth (1993) advised readers that alliances were indeed their "ticket to growth." Reporting on a Coopers and Lybrand study, they showed that alliance users had a 20 percent faster growth rate and 11 percent more sales than firms not in alliances. In the early 1990s, *Inc.* reported that "leapfrogging companies" built on constant learning and innovation were setting up alliances (Case 1990). In a more recent edition, *Inc.* noted that "competitor networking" is an alliance form that is increasingly common despite the risks of such organizations (Fenn 1997). Rigby and Buchanan (1994) reported growth rates of 30 percent per year for international alliances. For SMEs, the willingness of large firms like IBM (with over 4,000 alliances) to seek alliances to remain nimble and obtain new technologies is a major growth opportunity.

According to Inkpen (1998), how firms learn will be a strategic necessity to competing in the future. Strategic alliances are viewed as an avenue to provide the knowledge and learning required for growth. Larsson et al. (1998) provide an extensive review of the literature on interorganizational learning and point out the role of alliances in forming a "strategic portfolio" of relationships. Khanna (1998) introduces the idea of concurrent and nonconcurrent learning to explain why and when alliances are terminated. Inkpen (1998) adds to these concepts by looking at how accessible the alliance knowledge is to the partner and how efficient the firms are at learning. This combination of the conceptual and practical questions could add to our understanding of alliances, learning and outcomes. Interpartner learning is critical because going alone may be insufficient in periods of rapid technological and market changes.

In addition to alliances fostering learning, the growth in technology has led to alliances being viewed as devices for "technology leveraging" (Jonash 1996). The form of the alliance is not as important here as is the fact that technology and knowledge change organizations. An Economist Intelligence Unit (1993) reported that a minimum of 50 percent of technology competitiveness will be alliance-based. This limited study shows why alliances are increasing at 25 to 30 percent per year.

A main motivator for alliances is the need for learning alliances that reduce costly individual market entry modes, as suggested by Koza and Lewin (1998). Their idea that alliances should be "imbedded in a firm's strategic portfolio" is a core concept that says firms should consider firm competencies, the environment, and leader preferences. Kasouf and Celuch (1997) also look at how alliances can contribute to the core competency focus needed in times of rapid shifts and globalization. According to Fenn (1997), alliances are not a tidy way to do business and have generated new high-risk growth strategies. Alliances evolve when individual, firm and environmental concerns converge to impact performance of the organization.

Research also suggests that entrepreneurial orientation or the strategic posture of the key decision leader is related to formation of successful alliances. (Lumpkin and Dess 1996; Dickson and Weaver 1997). Alliances are formed that include those with less formal structures to those with more formal structures like joint ventures in a series of

TABLE 19.1 Alliance usage by country

Country	Number of firms responding by country	Number of firms that used alliances	% of firms that used alliances	Average number of alliances for each firm	Number of different types of alliances used by each firm
Eastern Australia	166	126	75.9	10.78	3.05
Sweden	180	167	92.8	16.47	4.72
Costa Rica	87	71	81.6	8.65	3.34
Mexico	363	204	56.2	7.63	2.50
Norway	433	370	85.5	13.44	3.99
Scotland	83	72	86.7	12.42	4.24
Western Australia	147	104	70.7	9.37	2.51
Finland	121	112	92.6	15.42	4.47
Indonesia	285	165	57.9	8.60	2.69

stages (Lorange and Roos 1992; Biemans 1998). SMEs appear to engage in numerous alliances with a high degree of variation in the types used based on the SARG project results. Table 19.1 presents alliance usage by percent of respondents, as well as the average number of current alliances by country and the number of alliance types used by each respondent. The firms were all manufacturers with alliance use reported by 56 to 93 percent of firms. Furthermore, the average number of alliance types suggested multiple approaches to markets, supporting the portfolio idea.

REGIONAL GROWTH EXAMPLES

The use of alliance-based models and techniques for regional or country specific growth is another development in the study of strategic alliances. For countries such as Greece, Makridakis et al. (1997) state that strategic alliances and niche markets are the two most viable strategies for development. Eastern Europe is another region in which alliances have been proposed to enhance economic growth and increase international expansion (Neale and Pass, 1992). Product modifications, overcoming legal hurdles and the use of local talent for marketing and research are strategic advantages partners in eastern Europe can add to alliances. Labbe's (1992) report on Canadian global competitiveness included a 1990 survey showing that 41 percent of Canadian firms participated in alliances. Yu (1996) points to cultural differences in Asia to show why alliances are preferred to hostile takeovers or forced actions. In the United Kingdom, Glaister (1996) has written about the "crucially important" process of partner selection on performance. Others have written of "marriages of convenience" (Weaver et al. 1995), "dangerous liaisons" (Bamford 1994), and "sleeping with the enemy" (Fenn 1997). These marriage or relationship analogies emphasize the mutual benefits and risks inherent to knowledge transfer.

For Irish firms, strategic alliances are reported as options for growth and risk sharing (Wilson 1995). They have also been called "one of the most significant developments in Central and Eastern Europe service sectors" (Wilson 1995). A related study (Cross-border alliances 1993) on 247 cross-border financial alliances in the European Union showed that although susceptible to partner selection errors, they benefited from lower transaction costs if their banks were in multiple markets.

There are numerous other possible benefits for SMEs entering alliances, including uncertainty reduction (Aldrich 1979; Cook 1977; Hirsch 1975; Pennings 1981; Pfeffer and Salancik 1978; Ring and Van de Ven 1992; Stearns et al. 1987), increased organizational power (Pennings 1981; Provan 1982), ensuring a stable flow of critical resources (Oliver 1990; Williamson 1991) and spreading the costs and risks of innovation (Mowery 1988)

Despite all the previously mentioned benefits received from forming alliances, not all alliances result in growth and success. Some studies, including the "Dark Side of Alliances" (Bruner and Spekman 1998), report alliance failure rates of 60 to 70 percent in studies from 1986 to the present (Levine and Byrne 1986; Harrigan 1988; Savona 1992). Their reports on larger firms suggest that break-even results were less than desirable and that alliances can create dependencies that make it difficult to withdraw. However, Bronder and Pritzl (1992) argue that two-thirds of alliances in Europe had difficulties that could have been avoided by developing a set of procedures that consider the decision to enter, configuration, partner selection and management of the alliance. Culture clashes and management conflicts are highlighted by Slowinski (1992), who reports the complexities of managing the alliances were underestimated. Newnab and Chaharbarghi (1996) extend this view and focus on the need to form alliances from the individual firms' strengths to avoid the dependencies suggested earlier. Aside from culture clashes and management conflicts, the possible loss of proprietary information and the threat of partner opportunism were other potential risks attributed to alliances (Hamel 1991; Williamson 1991). Despite these negative reports, authors do suggest that failures may be prevented by considering a selection process, examining cultures, using a proactive rather than reactive approach and understanding that alliances are growth strategies, not survival approaches.

PLANNING FOR SUCCESS AND ENHANCING OUTCOMES

The success or failure of alliances is not well understood despite the popularity and importance of alliances to SMEs and growth (Gulati et al. 1994). Gulati et al. cite failures as high as 80 percent, partly because of opportunistic behaviors. Any alliance needs to determine key success factors and spell out what is required to succeed.

The reports on alliance success factors almost universally point to trust, commitment, shared vision, communication, use of complementary skills and resources, measurement of results, partner selection, forbearance and flexibility, and a knowledge of when to withdraw (Stasiowski 1996; McKee 1994; Dussauge and Garrette 1997; Glaister 1996; Babbio 1996; Weaver et al. 1997). The results of ranking the key success factors in the SARG project are shown in table 19.2. They show a similar pattern to the ones reported here. They showed that six main factors were reported for success in every country, with only minor rank order differences.

TABLE 19.2 Alliance success factors

	Means[a]
1 Support from the chief executive officers of each company	4.14
2 Clear and simple objectives and goals	3.96
3 Common vision for the company	3.88
4 Alliance structures that allow rapid response to problems	3.82
5 Key communicators identified	3.70
6 Adaptive legal agreements between alliance companies	3.66
7 Cooperative cultures	3.55
8 Safeguards against an unfriendly takeover by anyone company in the alliance	3.42
9 Flexible funding and evaluation systems	3.37
10 Free-market environment	3.33
11 Real-time information systems	3.29
12 Separation/Autonomy of alliance partners	3.15
13 Similar decision styles	2.92

[a] All means are based on a 5 point Likert type scale

Support, clear goals, common vision, rapid response, identifying key communicators and adaptive agreements were significantly more likely to be mentioned than the other factors. Cooperation has frequently been cited as a precondition to successful innovation, which is one of the key strategic dimensions of growth in knowledge-based economies (Nooteboom 1994; Groen and Nooteboom 1998; Hakansson 1987). Das and Teng (1997) report high failure rates and attempt to show how a seven-stage process can be used to avoid failures. They cite the need for understanding the benefits from integrating the firms. The cooperation theme that arises from mutual benefits could even work for the weaker firms that have something to offer. This view is counter to the Bleeke and Ernst (1995) view that weak firms should avoid alliances. The Das and Teng (1997) research points to the complexity of alliance management and reviews the stages for success that should be considered before forming new alliances.

Alliances are also increasing in high-growth companies, and it has been suggested that "embedding cooperation" will improve the chances of success (Suarez-Villa 1998). Embedding cooperation refers to the firms' need to tailor their networks to support a strategic focus much like the clear goal and common vision above. The links to commitment and trust are also evident and allow firms to build knowledge networks in order to grow. Beckett-Camarata et al. (1998) study the partnership characteristics that produce success. Especially in uncertain markets, competitors without developed relationships cannot compete with strong alliance-based firms. Similarly, Madhavan et al. (1998) point to the concepts of structure reinforcing events (those that help support the agreements) and structure loosening events (those that help build flexibility and a willingness to compromise) as activities that can influence success. These structure related events could be linked to the forbearance research and investigated for small firms.

Another key success factor is the development of "complementary core competencies"

(Mason 1993). Mason suggests that use of the skills and resources of the partner firms must support and leverage core competencies. A Dutch study of 161 manufacturers (Nagpaul et al. 1998) supports this view and shows perceived success was influenced by the partner contributions to core competencies. Horton and Richey (1997) argue that the closer alliance activities are to the firms' core competencies, the less likely information will be shared or the alliance expanded because of a protective need. Of course, alliances must have some level of trust to succeed.

Kumar and Nti (1998) propose a new theoretical "discrepancy" concept that helps explain why some alliances are perceived to be successful even if financial goals are not met. These firms may have had other goals, such as access to technology, markets or general learning, that would benefit them later, even if short-term financial gains were not achieved. Other authors have also suggested that alliance involvement is beneficial in nonfinancial ways and that costs should not be the overriding concern (Powell 1990; Jarillo 1988; Saxton 1997; Human and Provan 1997). Alliance outcomes should include the traditional profit and performance measures (Smith et al. 1995); however, nonfinancial results must also be considered (Baird et al. 1993; Human and Provan 1997) to determine if alliances are beneficial to SMEs. Human and Provan (1997) identified three nonfinancial categories of outcomes, including: interorganizational exchanges, organizational credibility and access to resources. Another recent approach to measuring outcomes (Saxton 1997) utilized an overall satisfaction measure, expectations and contribution to core competencies to avoid the specific need for financial outcomes. The SARG project modified these and added them to the financial concerns.

Consideration of alliance structures and differing levels and types of outcomes is an area that new research efforts need to consider to expand our knowledge of successful alliance outcomes. For example, Golden and Dollinger (1993) focused on the relationship between alliance use, strategic posture and improved firm performance. One interesting result was a negative impact on net margins that was explained by a "satisficing" (accepting less than optimal performance), rather than maximizing, strategy, which they propose is consistent with game theory. Their findings suggest alliance users had higher sales, profitability and an enhanced ability to survive. These results are consistent with the SARG results and show the need to develop outcome measures.

Another shortcoming of alliance outcome research has been that the reported high failure rates might not have considered multiple outcomes or definitions of success. In the SARG project, overall satisfaction and multiple financial results were considered in the outcome findings. In addition, in later countries the longer-term measures of "additions to core competencies" and "increasing the firm's ability to compete" were collected. Only the Indonesian results are currently available for the added measures, and these are reported with the others in table 19.3. The sample sizes are under the 'N' reported in the table.

Satisfaction ranged from over 73 to 96.5 percent. The financial results show over 90 percent of respondents in each country at least broke even, and two-thirds of the firms in each country reported profitable outcomes. The results are for manufacturers with under 200 employees in random samples from industrial codes representing the majority of GDP in each country. The caution is that these are reports on the overall alliance experience and may hide some severe failures, but the results are consistent across countries and could mean that firms have learned how to form alliances since the late

TABLE 19.3 Company experiences with alliances

At least break even	% Agree	N
Australia	91.7	55
Sweden	96.4	144
Costa Rica	91.5	49
Mexico	97.2	79
Norway	96.3	255
Scotland	92.9	71
Western Australia	94.8	77
Finland	96.1	78
Indonesia	96.0	99
Add to core competencies		
Indonesia	97.0	99
Increase ability to compete		
Indonesia	94.9	99

1980s. Another interpretation of the improvement in results may be that experience with alliances and learning curves has increased success.

Attitudes of alliance users are another way to examine the potential growth of this organizational alternative. Chan and Wong (1994) suggest that alliances are not a way to "learn" if the firm is in a weak position. Eilon (1993) has suggested that in situations with falling demand, alliances can spread costs for key areas such as research and distribution. Converting negatives to positives in the strategic alliance arena is a novel approach that is partially at odds with Chan and Wong. The attitudinal responses from the SARG project did not see alliances as "lifelines" but did respond to the positive impact of alliances on growth.

Table 19.4 summarizes two of the attitudinal statements used in the survey to illustrate the views held by key decision leaders in the firms. The mean responses (based on a Likert 5 scale) for the necessity of alliances exceeded 3.6 in all countries except Australia, where additional research showed a stronger individualistic orientation than in any other country. Although most countries saw a need for alliances, most countries' key firm leaders disagreed with the statement that small would not be enough in the future. Possibly, the firm leaders liked being small and saw their small size as an advantage.

In the future, the question may need to be separated into items to identify and strike the deal dimensions. The highest means in the responses were to the growth-based questions on attractiveness and to alliances as growth mechanisms. It appears as though firms view alliances as growth mechanisms and that investors find alliances attractive.

These attitudinal factors are important because they tell us that SMEs may be ahead of the academic research in understanding the value of alliances. The entrepreneurial notion of "Ready, Aim, Fire" may be in play here. No country in the survey anticipated usage rates nearly as high as were reported, nor did they anticipate the recognition of the need for alliances or the growth potential of alliances. While researchers have been

TABLE 19.4 Average attitudinal responses by country

*In the future, both large and small companies increasingly will be
required to enter into strategic alliances to achieve success*

Australia	3.40
Sweden	3.77
Costa Rica	4.06
Mexico	4.01
Norway	3.66
Scotland	3.73
Western Australia	3.19
Finland	3.88
Indonesia	4.31

*For businesses interested in growth, strategic alliances
offer excellent opportunities.*

Australia	3.86
Sweden	3.88
Costa Rica	4.13
Mexico	4.10
Norway	3.82
Scotland	4.00
Western Australia	3.69
Finland	4.13
Indonesia	4.09

deciding on a model to test or a measure of alliance success, firms are forming alliances.

The SARG project also attempted to measure internationalization and environmental concerns. Earlier citations showed these were primary reasons for the surge in alliance usage. During the project, firms were asked if they sold goods or services outside their home country. Table 19.5 shows alliance users are significantly more likely to be in international markets. Firms that are not involved in alliances are more likely to focus on domestic markets and therefore may be in danger in the future as stronger firms evolve and competition emerges from outside the home market. The percent of exporters in each country and the number of respondents are shown for each country.

A scale adapted from Covin and Slevin (1991) was used to measure environmental uncertainty. Table 19.6 presents the results of mean splits on the scale and shows that firms that perceiving higher levels of uncertainty were more likely to use alliances. Only Australia and Scotland were not significant, which shows that in seven of nine countries, remaining independent was less attractive than forming alliances to spread risks. In Australia, interviews were conducted that indicated that higher uncertainty meant higher perceived returns, and therefore they were willing to go it alone. Since no follow-up was conducted in Scotland because of funding problems, the reason for their low alliance participation in alliances is unknown. Dickson and Weaver (1997) and an unpublished

TABLE 19.5 Export orientation reported by international orientation

Country	Alliance users	Alliance non-users
Australia	12.75 (126)	5.0%(40)
Sweden	59.9% (167)	23.1% (13)
Costa Rica	59.2% (71)	25.0% (16)
Mexico	58.3% (204)	27.7% (157)
Norway	48.4% (370)	36.5% (63)
Scotland	81.9% (72)	63.6% (11)
Western Australia	18.3% (104)	4.7% (43)
Finland	65.2% (112)	66.7% (9)
Indonesia	32.7 (165)	10.0 (120)

paper by Tyler and Steensma (1998) demonstrated a moderating effect of the strategic posture scale (Covin and Slevin 1989, 1991; Lumpkin and Dess 1996) on environmental perceptions and alliance activity. These results support the Palich and Bagby (1995) findings that managers with an entrepreneurial orientation see the world differently. They also support the SARG research that, normally, the higher the entrepreneurial orientation, the more likely firms are to form alliances.

In a related work, Ricks (1993) developed a competitor market entry matrix that shows strong alliances are barriers to entry. For firms involved in alliances in uncertain markets, the alliance could be the difference in keeping another firm from attempting to compete and allow the alliance to grow.

TABLE 19.6 Company experiences with alliances

	Country	%	N
Are you satisfied?	Australia	91.9	55
	Sweden	96.5	144
	Costa Rica	81.6	49
	Mexico	87.3	79
	Norway	93.7	255
	Scotland	91.5	71
	Western Australia	84.4	77
	Finland	79.5	78
	Indonesia	73.7	99
Does it meet your expectations?	Australia	84.9	55
	Sweden	90.6	144
	Costa Rica	84.4	49
	Mexico	90.3	79
	Norway	88.0	255

TABLE 19.6 *contd.*

	Country	%	N
	Scotland	81.4	71
	Western Australia	90.9	77
	Finland	88.3	78
	Indonesia	96.0	99
Is it financially profitable?	Australia	63.0	55
	Sweden	68.6	144
	Costa Rica	89.4	49
	Mexico	94.4	79
	Norway	72.3	255
	Scotland	68.6	71
	Western Australia	63.6	77
	Finland	77.6	78
	Indonesia	76.8	99
At least break even	Australia	91.7	55
	Sweden	96.4	144
	Costa Rica	91.5	49
	Mexico	97.2	79
	Norway	96.3	255
	Scotland	92.9	71
	Western Australia	94.8	77
	Finland	96.1	78
	Indonesia	96.0	99
Add to core competencies	Indonesia	97.0	99
Increase ability to compete	Indonesia	94.9	99

Das and Teng (1998) summarize four types of resources that could be involved in the determination of outcomes: financial, technological, physical and managerial resources. Shamdasani and Sheth (1995) add another layer to the research puzzle by focusing on items like those resources listed above as "outcome" dimensions and then adding "relational" dimensions such as commitment, competence and compatibility. Their view is that the commitment variable is at the heart of any alliance activity. The competence and compatibility variables refer to whether the partner can do what they say and whether they can work with other firms in accomplishing alliance goals. The SARG project and a piece by Blodgett (1991) suggest another possible outcome variable will be an influence-based dimension in developing economics as a partial measure of alliance relationships in global alliances.

The integration of multiple measures of success and outcomes into a broad range of research approaches would help reconcile the vastly different reports on alliance failures. The reviews and reports on the SARG project show a wide range of interests in alliance relationships, widely differing results, numerous research approaches and a lack of comprehensive models to guide future research. The next section will look at articles that can help develop a multifaceted research agenda related to strategic alliances and their growth as alternative organizational models for growth.

FUTURE RESEARCH DIRECTIONS

Several studies have suggested fruitful areas of future research. Van de Ven (1992), who studied the process of innovation, is applicable here because of the similar multidisciplinary nature of the processes. Particularly important is his notion that "messy" research based on theories of change is as necessary as theories of equilibrium if we are to understand a dynamic area like alliances. The paper provides a valuable table adapted from Stevenson and Harmeling (1990) that points to a need for a more "chaotic" theory, which suggests that change is normal, reciprocal causality is normal, small n studies provide insight and key relationships may be nonlinear. This summary appears to characterize the current debates and state of the research in the alliance area.

Churchhill (1992), in discussing the key research needs in the field of entrepreneurship, provides insights that should be considered for the subfield of strategic alliances. For example, the need to consider "internal and external environmental factors" is one area that is being examined in the alliance literature. The key decision leader perspectives, strategic posture, environmental uncertainty and attitudinal variables cited for the SARG project are also examples of factors that can be used for examining alliances.

Churchill (1992) also discusses the development of theoretical and conceptual frameworks. The alliance literature is developing in this area, but the rapid increase in terminology may hinder replication or communication because the same word may have a different meaning in a short period of time. In addition, the "messy" part of the research relates to the direct effects, moderating effects and to the reciprocal influences mentioned previously and needs to be examined. Some of this confusion relates to the differences in mindsets, methods and disciplines noted by Churchill (1992).

A third area discussed by Churchill (1992) is the need to look at the international aspects of our research. The development of multicountry databases, the applicability of concepts in different cultural settings and the macro impacts of such environmental factors as government, education and business associations should all be considered. Overriding all of these topics, however, is the need for longitudinal efforts to track what is happening over time to success, learning in the organization, partner competencies, commitment and growth in the alliance relationships. The extension and expansion of the SARG project in the Netherlands and in Indonesia address these concerns by utilizing multiple reporting over a two-year period, extending the research to include associations and government support units and adding new cultural and partner behavioral measures.

- The motivation to form alliances is the first concern for many researchers.
- Partner selection is critical because of the failures often attributed to mismatches.
- Outcomes of alliances are an ongoing and significant area for research.
- Alternative micro and macro subsets of alliances need to be further explored.
- Cultural and social issues are also ripe for development of research tools.

The motivation to form alliances is the first concern for many researchers. Dyer and Singh (1998) suggest that a desire for rapid growth and "supernatural" profits lead firms to form alliances to achieve a competitive advantage. They suggest alliances can provide a "new lens to examine value creating linkages." Looking at high-growth firms, firms operating in multiple markets and firms in rapidly changing environments could be fruitful areas of research. Databases of the fastest-growing firms published in the popular press and by major accounting firms would be one way to begin. In Indonesia, the financial and political crisis offers a chance to look at whether firms are more or less likely to form alliances as coping mechanisms or to take advantage of opportunities that have been created. Other researchers with interest in cross-border alliances could look at European unity as an external driver of formation, for example. Glaister (1996) offered a look at the strategic motivations of UK firms for alliance formation. Those findings could be used as a basis for an expanded project. They also highlight the need for more research on partner selection.

Partner selection is critical because of the failures often attributed to mismatches. Dickson and Weaver (1997) demonstrated the influence of the strategic orientation of the key decision leader on alliance activity. Mason (1993) offers the view that "fit" increases chemistry, success and operations of the alliance. He also highlights agreement on an exit strategy or termination horizon. Merrified (1992) also adds that success is partially based on a focus on common strategic objectives and an exit strategy. More research on time, depth and exit issues would reduce reliance on the often-used marriage analogy and recognize the sometimes temporary need for alliances.

Another emerging area in partner selection is the issue of whether it is feasible to form alliances with "nonbusiness" partners. Spencer (1996) suggested a need to rethink alliances between industry, universities and government. Fabris (1995), reported on a Coopers and Lybrand study, stating companies forming alliances with universities had productivity rates 59 percent higher than peer companies, which was a key factor in their financial success and growth. Fabris (1995) points out that working with universities is difficult because of culture differences and the speed needed to cope with growth. Similar concerns in private alliances show that partner understanding and compatibility need to be carefully examined. An issue of *Business Mexico* reported on the development of 139 separate agreements between businesses and the Monterrey Institute of Technology based on the firms' need for technology, training and credibility with other companies (Geyer 1992). Similar agreements exist in many countries and are a natural data source for both qualitative fieldwork and more quantitative work.

Associations, government and universities are possible partners to assist in the selection and training partners skills they will need to be successful. An extension of the SARG project is the preliminary development of an internet site that will eventually be a match-making alliance site for countries participating in the project. The use of private partners, government funds, a foundation and the University of Alabama in an alliance mode will make this possible. Development and selection of both traditional and nontraditional sources of alliance partners could form the basis for research conducted on large and small company alliances; racial, ethnic or women groups; regional trading blocks; association member firms, or those firms in incubators or industrial clusters. These subgroups can help define a database, avoid overgeneralization and increase response rates because of their perceived common concerns.

Outcomes of alliances are an ongoing and significant area for research. Kumar and Nti (1998) offer a conceptual approach that looks at success as a function of both unfavorable process actors and discrepancy in outcomes. This discrepancy factor could be one of the reasons that alliances are reportedly "successful" even if financial goals are not met. The article shows that testing is needed to determine what weight can be attributed to both sets of factors. Weaver and Dickson (1998) added several perceptual measures to their logistic regressions and found that they added significantly to the ability to explain alliance use. Factors such as industry, size and financial strength were not significant in defining outcomes (Weaver and Dickson 1998). This result needs to be tested on other samples, especially in other countries, to verify or refute the findings.

Failure can occur even in well-designed alliances as there really is no sustainable market, because of external shocks or changes in management or because the partner fails to deliver (Walters et al. 1994). This research suggests that a tracking and longitudinal look at alliances could be quite different after a change occurs. Revisiting "old" research respondents, even in a small sample, may be a way to reinforce these findings.

New research needs suggested by Das and Teng (1998) include: a two way analysis of partner goals and outcomes, more research on orientations and performance and examination of how firms work out differences as they arise. The links to outcomes and performance are clear, but someone else will need to operationalize these to fit them into a comprehensive model explaining outcomes.

Alternative micro and macro subsets of alliances need to be further explored. Khanna et al. (1998) look at the "learning alliance" as a micro level example of alliance subsets that could be studied. They examine the "private' and "common" benefits that accrue to participants to better understand the alliance. New research in multiple industry segments could be done to examine how firms produce common benefits that extend the life of the alliance. The overall structuring of alliances to produce positive outcomes is supportive of the work by Ring and Van de Ven (1992), Gulati et al. (1994) and Parke (1993) relating to structures and "pay-off" structures that evolve. This evolution in the alliance structure is hypothesized to influence growth in the individual partner firms. The time dimension is again a key factor and must be considered by at least attempting to determine what percent of alliances are relatively new (1 to 2 years), developing (2 to 5 years) and mature (over 5 years). No fixed timetable is intended here, only a suggestion on classification possibilities.

A second approach to studying alliances is to look at the multiple dyadic relationships. Madhavan et al. (1998) suggest that alliances can actually become a strategic resource that influences performance and growth in a firm. They further contend that managerial actions can influence the network and the outcomes of cooperation. The key decision leader concept discussed previously is consistent with their view and suggests that micro level research can help explain macro level results. Dussauge and Garrette (1997) point out that current research may examine the result of the alliance, but seldom considers the impact of collaboration on the various partner firms. Consideration of the long-term impacts on the competitive position of a firm should be evaluated separately from the success determinations.

Rai et al. (1996) examined the information technology sector to determine micro level success factors. This piece serves as a link to external success factors. They discuss the compatibility, cultural, and organizational issues discussed before, but add governmental policies and organizational advocacy that led us to the macro factors.

The role of government policies in emerging markets has a significant impact on success if only by reducing the bureaucratic layers inherent in these markets or opening markets (Rai et al. 1996; Vissi 1997). Vissi also suggested there is a potential downside to alliances in emerging markets because of the emergence of local oligopolies that limit indigenous local firm growth. In Indonesia, for example, there are limits on what sectors are open to new entrants and national oligopolies control distribution of key products that distort the economy based on social and political goals.

Goldstein (1992) has reported on the "growth triangle" of Malaysia, Singapore and Indonesia as an example of environmental uncertainty leading to macro level alliances to foster economic growth. The economic turbulence in the area has made this model difficult to implement, but it is a potential way out of the crisis if protectionism does not take over policymaking.

A CEO report in Baatz (1992) presented numerous recommendations to facilitate alliances. These included: tax incentives for research, infrastructure for communications, protection of intellectual property, currency stability, clear antitrust definitions, a clearinghouse for formation and commercial meetings to find partners. These functions are external to the firm and are not under their control, but they are essential for alliance formation and growth. Research on public policy aspects is needed with the growth of global alliances and knowledge transfers. An example of a crude attempt to examine governmental impacts was done in Indonesia by asking firms to rate how useful nongovernment and quasi-government organizations were in forming their alliances (Weaver 1998). On a scale of 1 to 5, with 5 being no use at all, 8 out of 10 agencies received mean responses of over 4. The organizations were very upset and considered it a biased sample. Additional studies will look at more organizations, what they really provide and the expectations of the firms they assist to determine what can be done to promote growth. A strategy to increase training related to partner selection, negotiations and (often cultural) expectations was proposed (Weaver 1998).

The perceived desirability of a growing, innovative SME sector is well documented, and countries have attempted to push the sector with numerous training, financing and assistance programs. The ability of small firms to identify a broad range of potential partners is typically limited to their personal networks and external assistance could be useful. Research to demonstrate how countries do this would be useful as benchmarks and as prompts to different countries. These macro approaches build on the micro research findings to present a more comprehensive approach to firm and national growth concerns.

Cultural and social issues are also ripe for development of research tools. Weaver and Dickson (1998) showed that the individualism/collectivism dimension was significant in alliance formation. More research on other cultural dimensions to determine both individual and organizational behaviors is needed. Numerous authors have shown an interest in exploring culture (Shane 1992; McGrath et al. 1992; Morris et al. 1994). Of particular interest is the role of partner similarity in forming and managing the alliance. Chen et al. (1998) offer a cultural contingency model of cooperation that needs to be field-tested in comparative settings, despite the inherent difficulties, to determine if a third or "overarching" culture emerges. Another recent model looks at the set of antecedent variables of "social and structural bonding" to determine the establishment and management of alliances (Williams et al. 1998).

Emerging economies, as previously discussed, often have cultural dimensions that need to be considered. For example, in Indonesia a cultural bias to be positive and not to criticize made the research team wonder about inflated responses until the usefulness question was examined. The highly negative responses were one check on inflated responses. In Mexico, the SARG team had to make appointments and hand-deliver the questionnaires because of a basic lack of trust in government organizations. In Costa Rica, the SARG project found there are no addresses on most buildings, and they could only buy a limited supply of stamps per day or the post office would run out! The development of research teams from multiple countries is not an easy task, but using professional organizations and academic groups can be effective.

Additional research questions currently under review include:

- the impacts of information and communication technology on alliance performance
- application of intergroup concepts to alliances
- development portfolio/options theory of alliances
- extension of outcome measures to consider clusters of alliances as opposed to overall experiences
- trust, commitment and competency linkages
- numerous success/failure factor studies
- construct validity analysis of existing instruments and a significant number of case studies on small samples of firms.

More combined qualitative and quantitative methods are needed to examine these issues, such European-style qualitative approaches to focus on improving conceptual bases, testing them empirically and teasing out the why questions from the empirical phase.

CONCLUSIONS

The rapidly growing influence of alliances on firms and economies makes this an area ripe for concerted efforts to explain what has happened, why it has happened, who or what were the driving forces and how we can anticipate what will happen next. The need for operationalizing concepts from the emerging theoretical models, testing them in multiple sectors and multiple environments and using a diverse set of research methods makes a clear and compelling case for more research. Researchers are encouraged to link with their peers and cooperate to increase the development of knowledge that we can use as professionals with both student and practitioner audiences. Sharing research instrumentation, methods and literature through multiple authored articles is the type of alliance-building research activity that needs to be rewarded. The need for databases is a constant worry of younger researchers with a limited network. Cooperation with more senior researchers and links with associations are needed to overcome this problem.

The development of training materials, case studies, checklists and similar products is needed to reduce the learning curve and to improve the chances for success in alliance formation and management. Surely we can train people in alliance formation and management skills to help them grow and be more competitive. The mutual interests of researchers and key decision makers should be made clear to participants in the research to insure cooperation.

The key to change for the next decade will be cooperation. SMEs are embracing the new organizational structures emerging from cooperative relationships out of necessity or as a part of long-range strategic thinking. The impact of alliances on growth has been shown throughout the chapter and new research, applications and development of support mechanisms will enable these alliances to continue. The successful entry of firms into a changing marketplace may be dependent upon the ability of managers to successfully negotiate and manage alliances. The coordination and support role of other organizations in this world of synthesis and cooperation is vital. Universities, foundations, government, nongovernment and professional organizations all have a role to play. The linking of the firm level micro analysis to the macro analysis of economic growth will be needed to influence the operating environments.

NOTE

As the organizer and ad hoc director of the alliance, I am grateful to everyone who has participated in the project. SARG began in the United States and expanded to the nine countries shown here. New data from Denmark, Greece, El Salvador and South Africa is expected. The project has been extended for two years in the Netherlands and Indonesia to enlarge its scope and depth.

REFERENCES

Aldrich, H.E. 1979. *Organizations and Environments.* Englewood Cliffs, NJ: Prentice-Hall.

Aldrich, H. and Zimmer, C. 1986. Entrepreneurship through social networks. In D. Sexton and R.W. Smilor (eds.), *The Art and Science of Entrepreneurship.* Cambridge, MA: Ballinger, pp. 3–23.

Baatz, E.B. 1992. Words from on high. *Electronic Business* 18(6): 145–7.

Babbio, L.T. 1996. Alliances, partnerships: making the marriage work. *America's Network* 100(13): 22.

Baird, I., Lyles, M. and Reger, R. 1993. Evaluation of cooperative alliances: integration and future directions. Paper presented at the annual meeting of the Academy of Management, Atlanta.

Bamford, J. 1994. Not so dangerous liaisons. *Financial World* 163(25): 56–7.

Beamish, P.W., and Killing, J.P., Book Beckett-Camarata, E.J., Camarata, M.R. and Barker, R.T. 1998. Integrating internal and external customer relationships through relationship management: a strategic response to a changing environment. *Journal of Business Research* 41(1): 71–81.

Beckett-Camarata, E.J., Camarata, M.R. and Barker, R.T. 1998. Integrating internal and external customer relationships through relationship management: a strategic response to a changing environment. *Journal of Business Research* 41(1): 71–81.

Biemans, W.G. 1998. The theory and practice of innovative networks. In W.E. During and R. Oakey (eds.), *New Technology-based Firms in the 1990s,* vol. 4. London: Paul Chapman.

Birley, S. 1985. The role of networks in the entrepreneurial process. *Journal of Business Venturing* 1: 107–17.

Bleeke, J. and Ernst, D. 1995. Is your strategic alliance really a sale? *Harvard Business Review* 73(1): 97–105.

Blodgett, L.L. 1991. Partner contributions as predictors of equity share in international joint ventures. *Journal of International Business Studies* 22: 63–78.

Bronder, C. and Pritzl, R. 1992. Developing strategic alliances: a conceptual framework for successful co-operation. *European Management Journal* 10: 412–21.

Bruner, R. and Spekman, R. 1998. The dark side of alliances: lessons from Volvo–Renault. *European Management Journal* 16: 136–50.

Case, J. 1990. Intimate relations. *Inc.* 12(8): 64–72.

Chan, P.S. and Wong, A. 1994. Global strategic alliances and organizational learning. *Leadership and Organization Development Journal* 15(4): 31–6.

Chen, C.C., Chen, X. and Meindl, J.R. 1998. How can cooperation be fostered? The cultural effects of individualism-collectivism. *Academy of Management Review* 23: 285–304.

Churchill, N.C. 1992. Research issues in entrepreneurship. In D.L. Sexton and J.D. Kasarda (eds.), *The State of the Art of Entrepreneurship*. Boston: PWS-Kent, pp. 579–96.

Cook, K. 1977. Exchange and power in networks of interorganizational relations. *Sociological Quarterly* 18: 62–82.

Covin, J.G. and Slevin, D.P. 1989. Strategic management of small firms in hostile and benign environments. *Strategic Management Journal* 10: 75–87.

Covin, J.G. and Slevin, D.P. 1991. A conceptual model of entrepreneurship as firm behavior. *Entrepreneurship Theory and Practice* 16(1): 7–25.

Cross-border alliances in banking and financial services in the single market. 1993. *Bank of England Quarterly Bulletin* 33: 372–8.

Das, T.K. and Teng, B. 1997. Sustaining strategic alliances: options and guidelines. *Journal of General Management* 22(4): 49–63.

Das, T.K. and Teng, B. 1998. Resource and risk management in the strategic alliance making process. *Journal of Management* 24: 21–42.

Davidow, W.H. and Malone, M.S. 1992. *The Virtual Corporation*. New York: HarperCollins.

Dickson, P.H. and Weaver, K.M. 1997. Environmental determinants and individual level moderators of alliance use. *Academy of Management Journal* 40: 404–25.

Dussauge, P. and Garrette, B. 1997. Anticipating the evolutions and outcomes of strategic alliances between rival firms. *International Studies of Management and Organization* 27(4): 104–26.

Dyer, J.H. and Singh, H. 1998. The relational view: cooperative strategy and sources of Inter-organizational competitive advantage. *Academy of Management Review* 23: 660–79.

Economist Intelligence Unit. Research report entitled *Leveraging Technology in the New Global Company* (EIU report No. 1–117 1993).

Eilon, S. 1993. A managerial response to falling demand. *OMEGA* 21: 17–23.

Fabris, P. 1995. Scaling the ivory tower. *CIO* 8(21): 18.

Fenn, D. 1997. Sleeping with the enemy. *Inc. Magazine* 19(16): 78–88.

Geyer, A. 1992. Industry goes to school: companies and educators combine on research and training programs. *Business Mexico* 2(4): 38–41.

Glaister, K.W. 1996. UK–Western Europe strategic alliances: Motives and selection criteria. *Journal of Euromarketing* 5(4): 5–35.

Golden, P.A., and Dollinger, M. 1993. Cooperative alliances and competitive strategies in small manufacturing firms. *Entrepreneurship Theory and Practice* 17(4): 43–56.

Goldstein, H. 1992. Batam and the growth triangle: taking a regional approach to economic development. *East Asian Executive Reports* 14(9): 8–12.

Groen, A.J. and Nooteboom, B. 1998. *Environmental Innovation: Knowledge and Networks*. Maastricht: Egos Colloqium.

Gulati, R., Khanna, T. and Nohria, N. 1994. Unilateral commitments and the importance of process in alliances. *Sloan Management Review* 35(3): 61–9.

Hakansson, H. 1987. *Industrial Technological Development: A Network Approach.* London: Croom Helm.

Hamel, G. 1991. Competition for competence and interpartner learning within international strategic alliances. *Strategic Management Journal* 12 (winter special issue): 83–104.

Harrigan, K.R. 1988. Joint ventures and competitive strategy. *Strategic Management Journal* 9: 141–58.

Hirsch, P.M. 1975. Oraganizational effectiveness and the institutional environment. *Administrative Science Quarterly* 20: 327–44.

Horton, V. and Richey, B. 1997. On developing a contingency model of technology alliance formation. In P.W. Beamish and J.P. Killing (eds.), *Cooperative Strategies: North American Perspectives.* San Francisco: New Lexington Press, pp. 89–110.

Human, S.E. and Provan, K.G. 1997. An emergent theory of structure and outcomes in small-firm strategic manufacturing networks. *Academy of Management Journal* 40: 368–403.

Inkpen, A.C. 1998. Learning and knowledge acquisition through international strategic alliances. *Academy of Management Executive* 12: 69–80.

Jarillo, J.C. 1988. On strategic networks. *Strategic Management Journal* 9: 31–41.

Jonash, R.S. 1996. Strategic technology leveraging: Making outsourcing work for you. *Research-Technology Management* 39(2): 19–25.

Kasouf, C.J. and Celuch, K.G. 1997. Interfirm relationships in the supply chain: the small supplier's view. *Industrial Marketing Management* 26: 475–86.

Khanna, T. 1998. The scope of alliances. *Organization Science* 9: 340–55.

Khanna, T., Gulati, R. and Nohria, N. 1998. The dynamics of learning alliances: Competition, cooperation, and relative scope. *Strategic Management Journal* 19: 193–210.

Kim, W.C. and Mauborgne, R. 1998. Procedural justice, strategic decision making, and the knowledge economy. *Strategic Management Journal* 19: 323–38.

Koza, M.P. and Lewin, A.Y. 1998. The co-evolution of strategic alliances. *Organization Science* 9: 255–64.

Kumar, R. and Nti, K.O. 1998. Differential learning and interaction in alliance dynamics: a process and outcome discrepancy model. *Organization Science* 9(3): 356–67.

Labbe, P. 1992. Tools of the trade: competing in the global market. *Canadian Business Review* 19(3): 38–41.

Larsson, R., Bengtsson, L., Henriksson, K. and Sharks, J. 1998. The interorganizational learning dilemma: collective knowledge development in strategic alliances. *Organizational Science* 9: 285–303.

Levine, J.B. and Byrne, J.A. 1986. Corporate odd couples. *Business Week* July 21, pp. 100–5.

Lorange, P., and Roos, J. 1992. Why some strategic alliances succeed and others fail. *Journal of Business Strategy* 12(1): 25–30.

Lumpkin, G.T. and Dess, G.G. 1996. Clarifying the entrepreneurial orientation construct and linking it to performance. *Academy of Management Review* 21: 135–72.

Macmillan, I.C. 1983. The politics of new venture management. *Harvard Business Review* 61(6): 8–16.

Madhavan, R., Koka, B.R. and Prescott, J.E. 1998. Networks in transition: How industry events (re)shape interfirm relationships. *Strategic Management Journal* 19: 439–59.

Makridakis, S., Caloghirou, Y., Papagiannakis, L. and Trivellas, P. 1997. The dualism of Greek firms and management: present state and future implications. *European Management Journal* 15: 381–402.

Mason, J.C. 1993. Strategic alliances: partnering for success. *Management Review* 82(5): 10–15.

McGrath, R.G., Macmillan, I.C. and Scheinberg, S. 1992. Elitists, risk-takers, and rugged individualist? An exploratory analysis of cultural differences between entrepreneurs and non-entrepreneurs. *Journal of Business Venturing* 7: 115–35.

McKee, D. 1994. Guidelines for strategic development alliance success. *Economic Development Review* 12(1): 90–2.

Merrified, D.B. 1992. Global strategic alliances among firms. *International Journal of Technology Management* 7(1–3) 77–83.

Monsted. 1996. Strategic alliances as an analytical perspective for innovative SMEs. Paper presented at the annual High Technology Small Firms Conferences, Enschede, the Netherlands.

Morris, M.H., Davis, D.L. and Allen, J.W. 1994. Fostering corporate entrepreneurship: cross-cultural comparisons of the importance of individualism versus collectivism. *Journal of International Business Studies* 1: 65–89.

Mowery, D.C. 1988. *International Collaborative Ventures in US Manufacturing*. Cambridge, MA: Ballinger.

Nagpaul, V., During, W.E., Groen, A. and Weaver, K.M. 1998. Use of information and communication technology in small to medium size enterprise-based alliances in the Netherlands manufacturing sector: a key decision leader perspective. Paper presented at the R&D Management Conference, Avila, Spain.

Neale, B. and Pass, C. 1992. Dealing with eastern Europe: countertrade and strategic alliances. *Management Accounting* (London) 70(6): 46–9.

Newman, V. and Chaharbarghi, K. 1996. Strategic alliances in fast-moving markets. *Long Range Planning* 29: 850–6.

Nooteboom, B. 1994. Innovation and diffusion in small firms: theory and evidence. *Small Business Economics* 6: 327–47.

Oliver, C. 1990. Determinants of interorganizational relationships: integration and future directions. *Academy of Management Review* 15: 241–65.

Palich, L.E. and Bagby, D.R. 1995. Using cognitive theory to explain entrepreneurial risk-taking: challenging conventional wisdom. *Journal of Business Venturing* 10: 425–38.

Parke, A. 1993. Strategic alliances structuring: a game theoretic and transaction cost examination of interfirm cooperation. *Academy of Management Journal* 36: 794–829.

Pennings, J.M. 1981. Strategically interdependent organizations. In P. Nystrom and W. Starbuck (eds.), *Handbook of Organizational Design*, vol. 1. New York: Oxford University Press, pp. 433–55.

Pfeffer, J. and Salancik, G.R. 1978. *The External Control of Organizations*. New York: Harper and Row.

Powell, W.W. 1990. Neither market nor hierarchy: Network forms of organization. In L.L. Cummings and B. Staw (eds.), *Research in Organizational Behaviour*. Greenwich, CT: JAI Press, pp. 295–336.

Provan, K. 1982. Interorganizational linkages and influences over decision making. *Academy of Management Journal* 25: 433–51.

Quinn, J.B. 1992. *Intelligent Enterprise*. New York: Free Press.

Rai, A., Borah, S. and Ramaprasad, A. 1996. Critical success factors for strategic alliances in the information technology industry: an empirical study. *Decision Sciences* 27: 141–55.

Ricks, J. 1993. Benefits of domestic vertical and horizontal strategic alliances: To compete with international cartels and the Japanese keiretsu. *Journal of Business and Industrial Marketing* 8: 52–7.

Rigby, D.K. and Buchanan, R.W.T. 1994. Putting more strategy into strategic alliances. *Directors and Boards* 18(2): 14–19.

Ring, P. and Van de Ven, A. 1992. Structuring cooperative relationships between organizations. *Strategic Management Journal* 13: 483–98.

Savona, D. 1992. When companies divorce. *International Business* 5(11): 48–51.

Saxton, T. 1997. The effects of partner and relationship characteristics on alliance outcomes. *Academy of Management Journal* 40: 443–61.

Shamdasani, P.N. and Sheth, J.N. 1995. An experimental approach to investigating satisfaction and continuity in marketing alliances. *European Journal of Marketing* 29(4): 6–23.

Shane, S. 1992. Why do some societies invent more than others? *Journal of Business Venturing* 7: 29–46.

Slowinski, G. 1992. The human touch in successful strategic alliances. *Mergers and Acquisitions* 27(1): 44–7.

Smith, K.G., Caroll, S.J. and Ashford, S.J. 1995. Intra- and interorganizational cooperation: toward a research agenda. *Academy of Management Journal* 38: 7–23.

Spencer, W.J. 1996. R&D at the crossroads. *Electronic Business Today* 22(12): 12.

Stasiowski, F.A. 1996. Here today, here tomorrow. *Facilities Design and Management* 15(11): 44–6.

Stearns, T.M., Hoffman, A.N. and Heide, J.B. 1987. Performance of commercial television stations as an outcome of interorganizational linkages and environmental conditions. *Academy of Management Journal* 30: 71–90.

Stevenson, H. and Harmeling, S. 1990. Entrepreneurial management's need for a more "chaotic" theory. *Journal of Business Venturing* 5: 1–14.

Suarez-Villa, L. 1998. The structures of cooperation: downscaling, outsourcing and the networked alliance. *Small Business Economics* 10: 5–16.

Ticket to Growth. 1993. *Small Business Reports* 18(8): 5.

Tyler, B.B. and Steensma, H.K. (1998). The effects of executives' experiences and perceptions on their assessment of potential technological alliances. *Strategic Management Journal* 19(10): 939–65.

Van de Van, A.H. 1992. Longitudinal methods for studying the process of entrepreneurship. In D.L. Sexton and J.D. Kasarda (eds.), *The State of the Art of Entrepreneurship*. Boston: PWS-Kent Publishing, pp. 579–96.

Vissi, F. 1997. Strategic alliances and global monopolies. *Russian and East European Finance and Trade* 33(2): 73–93.

Walters, B.A. Peters, S. and Dess, G.G. 1994. Strategic alliances and joint ventures: making them work. *Business Horizons* 37(4): 5–10.

Weaver, K.M. 1998. Strategic alliances and SME developments in Indonesia: a public policy perspective. Unpublished report to the Asia Foundation.

Weaver, K.M. and Dickson, P.H. 1998. Outcome quality of small- to medium-sized enterprise-based alliances: the role of perceived partner behaviors. *Journal of Business Venturing* 13: 505–22.

Weaver, K.M., Dickson, P.H. and Davies, L. 1995, SME based strategic alliances: marriages of necessity, convenience, or true love? In the *Proceedings of the Organization for Economic Cooperation and Development: International High-level Workshop on SMEs,* June 1995.

Weaver, K.M., Dickson, P.H. and Gibson, B. 1997. Strategic alliance use, firm size, outcome satisfaction, and partner behaviors. *Small Enterprise Research Journal* 5(1): 3–15.

Williams, J.D., Han, S.L. and Qualls, W.J. 1998. A conceptual model and study of cross-cultural business relationships. *Journal of Business Research* 42: 135–43.

Williamson, O.E. 1991. Comparative economic organization: the analysis of discrete structural alternatives. *Administrative Science Quarterly* 36: 3–37; and in S. Lindberg and H. Schreuder (eds.), *Interdisciplinary Perspectives on Organization Study*. Oxford: Pergamon.

Wilson, L. 1995. Strategic alliances. *Accountancy Ireland* 27(4): 41–2.

Yu, D. 1996. Asia's marriage of convenience. *AsiaMoney* 7(6): 10–12.

20

An Entrepreneurial Slant to Franchise Research

FRANK HOY, JOHN STANWORTH AND DAVID PURDY

ISSUES OF DEFINITIONS
FRANCHISING AS AN ENTREPRENEURIAL ACT
DOMINANT THEMES IN FRANCHISING RESEARCH
PROPOSITIONS FOR FUTURE RESEARCH

Franchising is often considered to be a relatively recent phenomenon, but it can be traced back to preindustrial societies when, for instance, franchised rights were granted for the collection of taxes. In medieval Europe, local Catholic clergy were granted the right to collect tithes from their parishioners on condition of forwarding a portion to Rome. Similarly, feudal nobles in England began enfranchising (literally empowering or granting rights to someone who had none) serfs in exchange for "royal tithes" (i.e., royalties). The thirteen colonies that eventually formed the United States originated as commercial franchises that were granted in exchange for taxes and fees. Izraeli (1972) saw the early nineteenth-century British beer brewers as the real innovators of franchising and labels the relationship existing between the brewers and their licensees as "first-generation franchising."

Another early form of franchising dates to the end of the American Civil War, when the Singer Sewing Machine Company created a distribution system by franchising exclusive territories to affiliated, but financially independent, operators. However, not until 1898, when General Motors used independently owned businesses to increase their own distribution outlets without the need for investment, did the rapid growth of American franchising really begin. Close behind General Motors came Rexall, who franchised drug stores, and then soft drink bottlers, including Coca-Cola, Pepsi-Cola and Seven-Up. Ben Franklin stores pioneered retail franchising in 1920, and Arthur Murray Dance Studios were an early service franchise enterprise in 1938.

These first-generation or "product" franchises were followed by second-generation or "business format" franchises that typically involve a considerable service element and close ongoing relations between franchisor and franchisee. Fast-food restaurants are probably the quintessential example.

Sales through franchised outlets now account for more than a third of all retail volume in the United States and are projected to reach 40 percent early in the twenty-first century. Nearly every product category is represented in franchising. The industry is a huge employer. Countless young people obtain their first jobs in franchising, and more and more college graduates are choosing careers as franchise owners and managers.

Despite the history of franchising as a series of emergent activities and despite the role franchising has played in global wealth creation, the phenomenon has only recently received attention in the entrepreneurship literature.

ISSUES OF DEFINITIONS

Theoretical discussion of a phenomenon first requires a clear definition, so not surprisingly, definitional issues were much discussed when franchising first became a subject for academic research in the 1970s. This debate has now been largely replaced by a taken-for-granted meaning that merely distinguishes between different manifestations of franchising, for instance, business format from product franchising.

Ozanne and Hunt (1971) wrote one of the earliest studies of fast-food franchising in the United States. The following year, Hunt (1972) suggested the following basic characteristics of a franchise relationship:

1 The franchisee operates the business substantially under the trade name and marketing plan of the franchisor.
2 A contract exists that delineates the responsibilities and obligations of both parties.
3 A strong continuing cooperative relationship exists between them.

This definition, he claimed, covered both business format franchising and the quasi-forms found in car and petroleum distribution plus voluntary wholesaler–retailer franchising. However, it was only the first characteristic that really distinguished franchising from other forms of business relationship. The definition, in fact, understated what is involved: the independent franchised outlet is a legally separate business with its own capital base, employees, organizational structure and specific customer relations, so it can be seen as analytically independent of the franchisor's business and marketing strategies.

Rubin (1978) offered another widely cited definition with what are now familiar elements:

> A franchise agreement is a contract between two (legal) firms, the franchisor and the franchisee. The franchisor is a parent company that has developed some product or service for sale; the franchisee is a firm that is set up to market this product or service in a particular location. The franchisee pays a certain sum of money for the right to market this product.

Rubin elaborated by stressing the initial and continuing managerial assistance provided by the franchisor to franchisees, the franchisor's tight control over the operation of franchisee outlets, royalty payments and/or purchase of supplies by franchisees from the franchisor and the right of the franchisor to terminate the contract "almost at will." Rubin (1978) went on to claim much more controversially that: "The definition of the franchisee as a separate firm, rather than as part of the franchisor, is a legal not an economic distinction."

Research in both the United States (Sklar 1977) and the United Kingdom (Stanworth et al. 1983) was already demonstrating that many franchised small businesses were, in a real rather than a nominal sense, independent enterprises, despite close and continuing relations with franchisors. Rubin (and others) often failed to distinguish sufficiently between the formal contractual relations, which emphasize the franchisor's dominance over the franchisee, and the independence experienced by franchisees in everyday operational relations. The latter, the research demonstrated, can depart substantially from the formal contract.

In what became a much cited American analysis of franchising, Vaughn (1979) defined franchising as:

> a form of marketing or distribution in which a parent company customarily grants an individual or a relatively small company the right, or privilege, to do business in a prescribed manner over a certain period of time in a specified place. The parent company is termed the franchisor; the receiver of the privilege the franchisee; and the right or privilege itself, the franchise.

This definition has the merit of carefully distinguishing the franchise from its cooperating agents, the franchisor and the franchisee. But the primary characterization of franchising as a form of marketing or distribution understated the extent to which franchising had evolved into a distinct business form (often referred to now as a total business package), which may be contrasted with other business forms like the conventional independent small enterprise or the vertically integrated large enterprise. Further, Vaughn's definition was linked motivationally only to the franchisor. Any attempted explanation of franchising needs to place equal emphasis on the motivations of the other major party involved, the franchisee. Continuing economic relations cannot be explained adequately by reference to the motivations of the initiator alone.

In an attempt to meet some of the above points, Curran and Stanworth (1983) defined franchising as:

> a business form essentially consisting of an organisation (the franchisor) with a market-tested business package centred on a product or service, entering into a continuing contractual relationship with franchisees, typically self-financed and independently owner-managed small firms, operating under the franchisor's trade name to produce and/or market goods or services according to a format specified by the franchisor.

This definition was seen as covering most modern varieties of franchising. In principle, no barriers appeared to exist to incorporating quasi-forms, but in practice, market-testing may be perfunctory. Franchisee self-financing is often supported significantly by loan finance from banks or other sources, including franchisors. Also, multiunit and corporate franchisees found in such areas as fast food are clearly not always owned by small-firm owner-managers. Indeed, some corporate franchisees, particularly in the United States, may be larger than their franchisors, as measured by value of corporate assets, but in many areas small-scale ownership remains typical.

Also, while the relationship is defined as a continuous one, the actual period covered will, of course, be variable. Some reference ought also to be made to the payment of fees or royalties of various kinds by franchisees to franchisors. Otherwise, the definition embodies a gradually evolved consensus as the study of franchising has developed.

Although the definitional debate occasionally re-emerges (e.g., Spinelli and Birley 1996), it is largely a feature of earlier research.

FRANCHISING AS AN ENTREPRENEURIAL ACT

The *Journal of Business Venturing* recently devoted three special issues to franchising research, an obvious acknowledgment that at least some franchising activities fit within the domain of entrepreneurship. The argument that the formation of franchises excludes creativity and innovation is disputed by Kaufmann and Dant (1999) as they link franchise research to various mainstream definitions of entrepreneurship. Similarly, Hoy (1994) demonstrated how the franchisor–franchisee relationship could be explained using Bull and Willard's (1993) proposed theory of entrepreneurship. Hoy and Shane (1998) introduced a series of articles that presented franchising as an example of organizational entrepreneurship.

Two arguments against franchising as an entrepreneurial act persist. The first raises the question of whether the franchise structure is a permanent and unique form of organization or just a stage in corporate evolution. The second argument relates to the status of the franchisee – an independent venture owner or a quasi-employee of the franchisor?

A permanent organizational form?

An important issue concerns whether franchising is a genuinely stable form of business organization or merely a temporary stage in the development of a business that transmutes into a conventional form. Many scholars have addressed this issue (Oxenfeldt and Kelly 1969; Hunt 1972, 1973, 1977; Lillis et al. 1976; Dant et al. 1992; Lafontaine and Kaufmann 1994), and several offer life-cycle theories which suggest that franchisors ultimately want to own all outlets since this expands their control and profits. Franchising is used to establish the business, but as soon as expansion has been achieved and cheap capital is no longer required, the franchisor will buy out at least the most profitable franchisees. Moreover, the franchisor will also have acquired the experience and time required to train outlet managers and devise an effective means to control their performance. In other words, the franchised business is not a unique organizational form or stable way in which businesses can be federated but merely a possible stage in the development of other types of organization, particularly the hierarchical variety.

If stage or life-cycle theories of the above kind were well supported, it would undermine the need for a developed theory of franchising and the advantages attributed to the franchised business form. For instance, the notion that the franchisee's motivational pattern produces a distinct advantage over the managed outlet would be greatly weakened. In fact, despite well-documented buying back in particular franchises, no trend toward a general increase in franchisor direct ownership appears possible to establish (Dant et al. 1996). Evidence has to be interpreted cautiously here since, at any given point in time, many franchises are relatively new and might be in the early stages of the cycle. On the other hand, the United States has the most developed franchise sector of all industrial societies with many large and long-established franchises and so might be expected to show the stage or life-cycle pattern if it exists. But no such clear pattern is discernible. Franchisor repurchases do occur but apparently for a variety of reasons and are often temporary so that the gross figures do not necessarily represent franchisor decisions to leave franchising. Even where this does occur, the decision may be subsequently reversed. In short, stage or life-cycle patterns seem to be contingent, rather than necessary, forms of organizational change.

The recently fashionable strategy of reducing workforces by subcontracting, downsizing, "right-sizing," business process re-engineering and so forth has both created opportunities for smaller enterprises and left many former employees searching for career alternatives. Franchising is increasingly seen as one alternative, and franchisors often target such individuals, particularly those with capital from severance settlements. Additionally, corporations looking to downsize to a functional in-house "core" operation, distanced from the more "peripheral" elements of their traditional business activity, may utilize the franchise format to ensure the continued supply of needed services. Thus, two allied elements of labor market and economic restructuring appear favorable to the growth of franchising.

Are franchises independent?

Independence from external control has long been regarded as a fundamental characteristic separating small business activity from the corporate activity of the larger enterprise. However, even the independence of the conventional small business is always less than total and often difficult to assess in practice. A small enterprise, whatever its form, is part of a wider network of economic interaction summed up in the economist's notion of the market, and arguably, it is from this source that the main influences on independence are derived.

The problems of assessing the independence of the franchised small business are even more difficult to resolve than those connected with the conventional small business. Mainly, the additional problems arise because of the close links between the franchised small business and another, usually larger business, the franchisor. A good deal of the literature on franchising treats it simply as a marketing strategy, largely avoiding any consideration of the independence of the franchised business, but this is to ignore one of the most important aspects of this increasingly significant form of business activity.

At one extreme, the franchised small business may be viewed as an emerging form of independent business in industrial societies whose distinguishing characteristic is its overt and close relationship with another, usually larger, enterprise. This association, however, might be seen as being little different, except in degree and the explicit form it takes, to that now found between many small businesses and other firms with whom they do business. In an increasingly interdependent economy, such a close association may simply be a reflection of the fact that "no firm is an island entire of itself" in a modern economy.

At the opposite extreme, Rubin (1978) argued that the franchised enterprise is, in reality, a managed outlet in the larger marketing pattern of another truly independent business – the franchisor's. This distribution strategy has certain advantages for the larger enterprise, but just because the manager of the outlet has a capital stake in the business dressed up in the language of entrepreneurship is no reason to confuse a franchise with a genuinely independent small business. The language of independence and entrepreneurship, it might be argued, is being used simply to tempt people into buying a franchise since it exploits the cultural approval given to economic independence in capitalist society, and afterward, the illusion of independence is maintained because it continues to service both parties' interests. This is not to say that the arrangement cannot be highly beneficial to both parties, but illusion should not be substituted for reality in a rigorous analysis of the status of the franchised outlet.

In analyzing franchisee autonomy, the distinction between formal and operational levels of the franchisor–franchisee relationship is useful because franchisee autonomy at either level may vary independently of the other. At the formal level, the franchisor–franchisee contract, which constitutes the basis of this level, is drawn up by the franchisor, offered to franchisees on a take-it-or-leave-it basis and typically favors the franchisor. This is recognized by both parties and largely accepted as a fact of life by franchisees. However, at this level one key point running contrary to the overall weighting should be remembered. That is, legally, the franchise outlet as a business belongs to the franchisee. This is important since the law, with its rather literal approach to social and economic reality, may from time to time give this point overall importance, countering the normal balance of power at the formal level.

This explains the way in which in the United States, for example, state and federal law has often come down on the side of the less powerful franchisee (Nevin et al. 1980). As a legally independent enterprise, the franchised outlet may be treated as the equivalent of the conventional enterprise for interpreting conventions on fair business practices, which has frequently meant bolstering franchisee autonomy.

On the operational level, Stanworth et al. (1983; Stanworth 1984) have shown the franchisor–franchisee relationship is both more complex and more variable than at the formal level. Everyday operational autonomy is much more evenly spread between franchisors and franchisees than suggested by consideration of the formal level alone. More importantly, the formal level usually does not intrude on the operational level to any marked degree except perhaps in times of crisis.

There are clear limits to the control franchisors can exercise physically or normatively at the operational level. In some instances, such as personnel issues in the franchise outlet, the franchisor would not wish to be greatly involved anyway, and in others, the franchisor often finds it convenient not to be too restrictive since oversupervision may produce negative results.

No small business owner, franchisee or otherwise, is entirely independent. Local, national and international (e.g., the European Union) governments, financial institutions (especially banks), other businesses and particularly larger firms all reduce the real level of autonomy of small business owners. In a highly competitive sector of the economy, the squeeze on the small enterprise exerted by some combination of these influences may force a firm out of existence or, at the least, only allow it to operate at the economic margin. Many franchised outlets, on the other hand, are protected small businesses, shielded from many external pressures by their franchisor so that their owners may well enjoy levels of autonomy substantially higher than many nominally independent small enterprises.

The franchise relationship is potentially exploitative, but this should not draw attention away from the fact that, in practice, exploitation by franchisors is not typical and unlikely to be successful except in the short term. This can best be understood in the context of a strategic alliance. The business form at the heart of the franchise relationship changes the character of small business ownership because of the nature of the links between the two organizations. It ceases to resemble the form found in small businesses related solely to other organizations through the classic market relations of the conventional competitive economy. In practice, at the societal level, economies are evolving to produce all kinds of new forms of market and interorganizational relations, of which the franchise relationship is a major example. What patently needs to be avoided are attempts to shoehorn these new forms into theories developed to explain older forms. Patterns of economic self-autonomy, which emerged from nineteenth-century competitive capitalist economy, should not be seen as the only or pure form, compared to which other recent forms are merely debased expressions. For many, the franchised business may, in some ways, realize the cultural values of independence, autonomy, material rewards and even creativity more effectively than older forms.

DOMINANT THEMES IN FRANCHISING RESEARCH

The fact that this is the first chapter on franchise research to appear in the state-of-the-art series since the publication of *The Encyclopedia of Entrepreneurship* in 1982 is indicative of the lack of attention given to franchising in entrepreneurship scholarship. Until the formation of the Society of Franchising in 1986, studies of franchising appeared predominantly in the marketing literature (investigating franchising as a variation of a channel of distribution) or in business law journals (addressing contract or legal and regulatory issues associated with the franchisor–franchisee relationship). The Society of Franchising was created in conjunction with the International Franchise Association. Today, over one hundred researchers in multiple disciplines belong to the Society (Dant and Kaufmann 1999).

The proceedings from annual conferences of the society were used to identify the dominant research themes that have been studied by scholars specializing in franchise research and education in recent years. *Franchising Research: An International Journal*, which grew out of the society, was one of the few outlets devoted to franchise studies, but it did not survive long enough to provide a basis for assessing trends.

Over twenty themes, in which multiple papers could be categorized as overlapping, were extracted from the twelve conference proceedings. Some studies could be grouped together as country-specific, i.e., the status of franchising in a particular country or region. Another group could be labeled industry-specific, e.g., descriptions of fast-food franchises or automobile dealerships. Some studies focused on general management (strategy formulation, performance, measuring) and others on general marketing (pricing, advertising). Six research themes stood out as dominant and are discussed below:

1　Franchising as a channel of distribution
2　Legal, regulatory and contractual issues
3　Growth through international expansion
4　Growth patterns
5　Potential benefits of international expansion
6　Survival/failure rates

Franchising as a channel of distribution

As explained previously, early franchise studies appeared in marketing journals and addressed franchising as a form of distribution channel (cf. Frazier and Summers 1986; Schul et al. 1983; Sibley and Michie 1982). Notice that the recency of these "early" citations demonstrates the neglect of franchising in business research.

Distribution channel studies tend to focus on traditional marketing themes, investigating efficiencies and performance in the wholesale and retail functions of franchise networks. Comparisons are often made with retail chain operations, examining relative profitability.

Some studies more directly address the independence and autonomy of the franchisees. These touch on the opportunities for innovative behaviors by the business owners (Dant and Gundlach 1999), the strategic alliance nature of the franchise relationship (McIntyre et al. 1997) and the conflicts between franchisors and franchisees (Hoy 1994). The last group often overlaps with legal scholarship.

Legal, regulatory and contractual issues

Early academic interest in legal issues concentrated on franchise contracts and the disclosures made when recruiting franchisees (cf. Porter and Renforth 1978; Hunt and Nevin 1976). Over time, scholars observed increasing scrutiny of franchising by government officials and agencies. Serious US government interest in franchising began in the 1950s during a period of rapid economic growth following World War II. Poorly financed, poorly managed and fraudulent franchise operations led to public complaints, business failures and class-action lawsuits. A series of court cases reinforced franchise practices associated with trademark protection and purchase requirements. In the 1960s, the Federal Trade Commission (FTC) responded with opinions that franchisors wielded excessive economic power over franchisees.

The 1970s saw the beginning of state legislation to regulate franchise practices, requiring registration and disclosure. The FTC started conducting fraud investigations in 1975. Also that year, what is now the North American Securities Administrators' Association issued guidelines for a Uniform Franchise Offering Circular, subsequently accepted by the FTC to encourage a uniform format for disclosure documents. In 1979, The FTC introduced the "Disclosure Requirement and Prohibitions Concerning Franchising and Business Opportunities Ventures" (Hoy 1998).

A recent review of the literature shows continuing attention to the concerns of government toward franchising, as displayed in table 20.1. What, if anything does the foregoing have to do with the United Kingdom, the European Union or any country other than the United States? At this point in time, the United States is the world's leader in number of franchisors, franchisees and franchise sales volume. US-based franchisors have globalized to a greater extent than those of other countries. Thus, American government entities at federal, state and local levels have had more experience in grappling with franchise issues than other governments. This has multiple implications:

1 Major areas of concern that governments may have about franchising have been identified.

2 Possible courses of action by government, both in support of and in regulating franchises have already been proposed, enacted, discussed or experimented with.
3 The United States has been a laboratory for actions by franchisors and franchisees to stimulate or prevent government initiatives.
4 The United States has also been a laboratory for observing responses to government initiatives.

TABLE 20.1 Government concerns about franchising

1 Misleading or exaggerated earnings claims by franchisors.
2 Opportunistic behavior by which the franchisor becomes a competitive threat to franchisees.
3 The absence of legal remedies when franchisors engage in harmful, but not illegal, business practices.
4 The lack of specialized professionals who can make franchisees or prospective franchisees aware of risk factors.
5 Intimidation by franchisors of franchisees who attempt to form franchisee associations, seek alternative sources for products or make other efforts to create a more level playing field.
6 Restrictions on franchisees who desire to liquidate their holdings in favour of alternative investment opportunities.
7 One-sided contracts devised by franchisors.
8 Conflicts of interest, such as when a franchisor forces franchisees to be captive outlets for other suppliers owned by the franchisor.
9 Forcing franchisees to purchase products or supplies at higher than market costs.
10 Restrictions on the ability of franchisees to transfer ownership.
11 Encroachment, i.e., locating a new outlet or point of distribution in sufficient proximity to a franchisee to cause a material diversion of sales.
12 The imposition of new restrictions as a requirement of contract renewal.
13 Imposing noncompete clauses on franchisees.
14 Churning, i.e., terminating a successful franchise operation in order to resell it and gain additional franchise fees.

Source: Hoy 1998

Contractual issues were an early research them in the franchising literature and remain important. Not all of the research on the franchisor–franchisee relationship is restricted to the legal environment, however.

Franchisor–franchisee relationships
Much of this research theme examines conflict among parties. Naturally, conflicts can extend into the legal arena. Several studies of franchisor–franchisee relationships seek best practices for conflict resolution, such as mediation, arbitration or the creation of advisory councils (e.g., Dant and Schul 1992).

The research has not exclusively been directed toward conflict. Other topics include the building of consensus (Baucus et al. 1996), cooperative advertising (Dant and Berger 1996), knowledge exchange (Darr et al. 1995), encroachment (Barkoff and Giresi 1996) and joint market research (Justis et al. 1993). Many other subjects can be listed as relationship issues:

- training and development of owners, managers and employees;
- mutual satisfaction measures of franchisors and franchisees;
- financing arrangements between parties; control and reporting mechanisms; and
- site selection practices.

Of course, relationship research overlaps channel of distribution as well as legal and contractual research. The distinction in the studies cited in this theme is the effort made by authors to assess the quality of the relationship and seek normative prescriptions. Studying relationships between franchisors and franchisees extends to international alliances as well as domestic ones.

Growth through international expansion

Where emphasis placed upon economic individualism as a means of initiating or operating economic activity is high, relative to alternative forms of outlet for its expression, franchising may be expected to prosper. Even in the United States, the decline of entrepreneurship and individualism was a significant intellectual theme in the 1950s and 1960s. Mills (1956), for example, discussed the disappearance of entrepreneurs and small business owners. Economic individualism, in his view, was being destroyed by large-scale bureaucracies run by people who were essentially nonentrepreneurial. Riesman (1950) wrote of the displacement of the "inner-directed man," the self-reliant individual who seized opportunities and exploited new situations, by the "other-directed man" perhaps best summed up in the title of Whyte's (1956) book, *The Organization Man*. Yet, as the 1980s and the 1990s showed, economic individualism is difficult to smother. The New Right made the entrepreneur a folk hero and standard-bearer of a rebirth of the enterprise culture to be expressed most potently in small-scale economic enterprise in all its forms (Goss 1991: 8–14).

However, cultural influences do not work alone. The emergence and persistence of the franchised business is also dependent upon economic structure. As societies develop, the proportion of tertiary activities – particularly in the form of services and knowledge-intensive activities in industrialized countries – grow substantially, thereby increasing the likelihood of the franchised business form. Central to many of these activities is the customer–organization interface that frequently occurs through small dispersed outlets remote from the head office. Some argue these changes are so fundamental they warrant a new label for the whole economy, the "post-industrial" or "post-Fordist" economy (Curran and Blackburn 1991).

Large-scale enterprises are, it was argued, ill-suited to the above developments. Decentralization and multiestablishment operations often produced problems of personnel motivation, supervision and quality control. Corporations were forced to seek other means of retaining control over outlying operations or consider abandoning them altogether. Either way, new opportunities for small-scale enterprise arose. One strategy for retaining control of difficult-to-manage outlets was franchising. Here franchising links with trends toward outsourcing or flexible specialization, which allows the core organization to continue unencumbered by the bureaucratic and infrastructural problems of a fully integrated vertical operation.

This does not mean the end of the large corporation, of course. Indeed, alongside the above restructuring, globalization was also occurring. A world market is evolving that includes new, even larger corporations operating globally. But articulating the global level with national, regional and local levels poses considerable problems demanding new kinds of economic arrangements and business forms. Networked organizations, for instance, of which the franchised form is an important example, are critical to this global restructuring (Goffee and Scase 1995). In short, there is a dynamic or contradiction within the emerging global economy that promotes large and small enterprise including the franchised variety. In turn, this provides opportunities for the resurgence of economic individualism.

Certain types of economic activity involve "divergent scale economies" (Caves and Murphy 1976). In other words, the production of the good or service has widely differing economies of scale at different stages. Thus, the manufacture of motor cars is most economically carried out on a large scale but subsequent retailing is most efficiently conducted on the basis of relatively small-scale local outlets. A fast-food franchisor can nationally market the image of a standardized product but servicing consumers is more efficiently achieved on a small localized scale. Wherever highly divergent economies of scale occur in the production of goods or services, therefore, we may expect the organizational form of the franchise relationship to appear. This argument, of course, links with the examination of the macro context of franchising above. The trend toward an economy dominated by tertiary activities produces more and more instances of divergent economies of scale for which the franchised business form may be the preferred organizational solution.

In principle, wherever economic activity involves geographically dispersed outlets servicing small local markets requiring the careful, sensitive meeting of customer needs, the emergence of franchised business forms is likely but only provided the cultural and political contexts are also favorable. Within the political context, a potentially important influence emanates from laws governing economic activities. In the United States, for example, many states regulate franchising for various reasons ranging from promoting competition to ensuring that contracts do not overfavor the franchisor (Hoy 1998). In the United Kingdom, by way of comparison, franchising is subject to few, if any, special laws. But there are indications that franchisors are very sensitive to the possibilities of such legislation. One likely source is the European Union in its regulation of the increasingly unified European Market.

Growth patterns

Figure 20.1 demonstrates that the United States, Japan, Canada, France, Brazil and Britain have the largest franchise sectors, as measured by numbers of franchisees. Franchising is more developed in America than in any other country. Also, research and data-gathering are far more advanced in the United States than elsewhere. Thus, much of what is known about franchising tends to be American in origin, and other countries

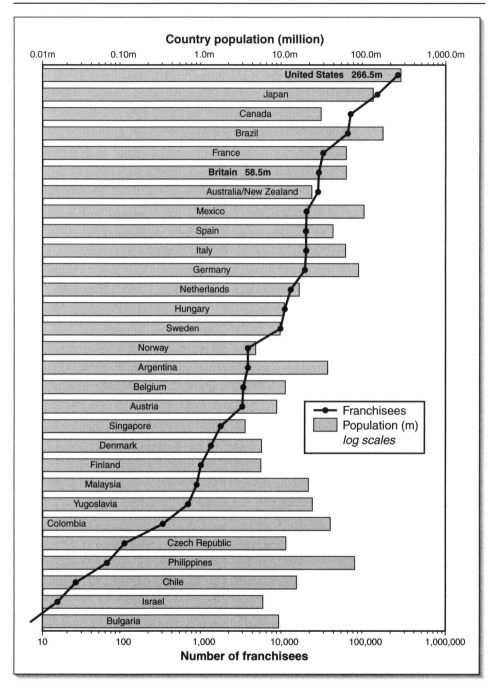

FIGURE 20.1 Country franchisee populations: number of franchisees vs. total population
Source: Stanworth and Purdy (1998)

look toward US experience as heralding the nature and scale of future developments in their own societies.

As a result of its large-scale development of franchising, the United States is the major exporter of franchising on a global scale, and American experience is invariably quoted (or misquoted) in justification of franchising in Britain and elsewhere. Three US statistics are cited above all others:

1 Franchising accounts for approaching 35 percent of all retail sales.
2 Franchising accounts for 10 percent of the GDP.
3 Franchising expanded by around 300 percent between 1975 and 1990.

Allied to these claims is an assumption that franchising is both a low-risk and a largely recession-proof business strategy.

All of the above statistics appear essentially true. However, as figure 20.2 illustrates, inflation-adjusted figures for the growth of franchising in the United States in recent years pull down the overall growth figure for 1975–90 dramatically from 284.6 percent to 58.5 percent, and the average annual growth rate from 9.4 percent to 3.1 percent. Moreover, in 6 years of this 16-year period, franchise growth in the United States was either zero or negative (Trutko et al. 1993). The franchise industry in the United Kingdom appears completely unaware of the existence of the latter adjusted statistics.

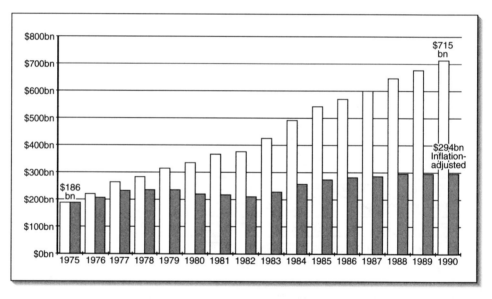

FIGURE 20.2 Trends in total US franchising sales, 1975–1990
Source: Trutko et al. (1993)

Academics, researchers and organizations like the International Franchise Association (America's franchise association) use the terms "franchising" and "business format franchising" almost interchangeably, so for statistical purposes, product and business format franchises are usually grouped together in the United States. In 1990, 48.4

percent of all franchising sales stemmed from the automobile and truck sector and a further 18.0 percent from franchised gasoline service stations. Whereas product franchising grew by only 42.4 percent in inflation-adjusted (constant) dollars between 1975 and 1990, against an overall sector figure of 58.5 percent, business format franchising grew by 115.5 percent, or around 5.1 percent in real terms per annum in the United States.

The expansion and contraction of franchising in America seems to have closely followed general economic trends (Trutko et al. 1993: 3–19). Between 1975 and 1989, the US GNP grew by 52.7 percent in real terms against a comparable growth in franchise sales of 58.5 percent. The decline in franchise sales (in real terms) between 1979 and 1982 again closely reflected the wider economic situation. As the US economy recovered during the mid-1980s, franchise sales reflected the upturn, as they did the subsequent downturn toward the end of the 1980s.

Interestingly, however, while franchise sales performed relatively well between 1975 and 1990, the number of franchise establishments grew by only 13.3 percent compared with a 48.4 percent increase in the number of established units in the United States as a whole. This trend is predicted to continue, with franchisors concentrating on generating higher profits per establishment in the future rather than expansion via increased outlets (Trutko et al. 1993: 9–12). In this sense, franchising could be said to be limiting the number of small business outlets.

Some countries – the United States, most noticeably – have cultivated franchise horizons well beyond domestic boundaries for the following reasons:

> From a balance-of-payments perspective, international franchising is considered [in the United States] as a safe and speedy means of obtaining foreign currency with a relatively small financial investment abroad. It is notable in that it neither replaces [American] exports nor exports [American] jobs, all these reasons making this business arrangement one of the most preferred and government-supported forms of international involvement. (Eroglu 1992)

Potential benefits of international expansion

It would, of course, be problematical to try and translate some speculated level of expansion overseas into a precise economic benefit to other countries. However, we would refer to the following extract from US International Trade Commission's 1995 report on franchising:

> International expansion of US franchisors has led to a substantial trade surplus in franchising fees and royalties. US franchisors enjoy international competitive advantages as a result of the large domestic market, considerable experience with franchise management, and the favorable perception of US products and services around the world. The European Union constitutes the largest single market for US franchisors. . . . Franchising trade data indicate that exports of [US] franchising services [worldwide] amounted to approximately $408 million in 1993, while imports were only $5 million. The resulting trade surplus of $403 million is indicative of the level of US franchisors' international competitiveness. The favorable position of US franchisors reflects [modern] franchising's origin in the United States, the domestic industry's maturity relative to foreign franchise industries, and the high level of demand for "American-style" products and services. As a result of these factors, a very large number of US franchisors have extensive experience in managing expansive franchise systems and implementing ambitious development programs.

TABLE 20.2 US franchisors with international operations, by business category and number of foreign establishments, 1994

	US franchisors with international operations		US franchisors' foreign establishments	
	No.	%	No.	%
Restaurants	41	22.5	4,221	31.3
Business aids/services	17	9.3	302	2.2
Retailing, non-food	15	8.2	392	2.9
Educational products/services	14	7.7	1,837	13.6
Automotive products/services	14	7.7	1,775	13.1
Construction/home improvement	14	7.7	555	4.1
Cleaning services	12	6.6	1,932	14.3
Personal care services	11	6.0	680	5.0
Printing/signs	8	4.4	582	4.3
Auto/truck rental	6	3.3	401	3.0
Postal/shipping	5	2.8	125	0.9
Travel services	4	2.2	346	2.6
Recreation	3	1.7	56	0.4
Laundry/dry cleaning	3	1.7	50	0.4
Retail food, non-convenience	2	1.1	9	0.1
Hotels/motels	1	0.6	2	0.0
Rental equipment	1	0.6	2	0.0
Other	11	6.0	229	1.7
Total	182	100.0	13,506	100.0

Data reflects responses to a survey conducted by the periodical, *Global Franchise*. Totals may not add due to rounding.

Source: Compiled by USITC staff from *Gloval Franchise*, "1994 International Franchise Directory," second quarter 1994, pp. 52–66 [in *Industry & Trade Summary: Franchising*, USITC (1995)]

The volume of US-based franchise activity in foreign markets is indicated by the data in tables 20.2 and 20.3.

Survival/failure rates

At its best, franchising is an avenue to self-employment offered by franchisors (owners of a "tried-and-tested" business format) to franchisees (typically aspiring small business men and women), in exchange for payment of a front-end fee and an on-going royalty. Based on the principle of cloning success, a principal tenet of the franchise community is that franchise failure rates are low. From the viewpoint of small business researchers, franchising has been argued to be of particular importance, since most franchisors still are, or have recently been, small businesses themselves and most of their royalty-paying franchisees

TABLE 20.3 US trade in franchising royalties and fees, by country, 1989–1993
(Exports/imports in $ million)

	1989		1990		1991		1992		1993	
	Exports	Imports	Exports	Imports	Exports	Imports	Exports	Imports	Exports	Imports
Canada	**21**	(ᵃ)	**34**	(ᵃ)	**40**	(ᵃ)	**42**	(ᵃ)	**51**	(ᵃ)
Europe	**107**	**2**	**89**	(ᵃ)	**118**	**1**	**148**	**1**	**155**	**3**
Belgium	3	0	4	0	11	0	9	0	7	0
France	12	0	9	0	8	0	13	0	13	1
Germany	22	(ᵃ)	20	(ᵃ)	34	(ᵃ)	49	(a)	56	1
Italy	3	0	2	0	2	0	3	0	4	0
Netherlands	5	0	4	0	2	0	2	0	4	0
Norway	1	0	1	0	2	0	3	0	1	0
Spain	5	0	4	0	3	0	5	0	6	0
Sweden	8	0	6	0	11	0	12	0	11	0
Switzerland	5	1	3	0	3	0	3	0	3	0
United Kingdom	32	1	19	(ᵃ)	27	(ᵃ)	36	(ᵃ)	31	1
Other	10	0	17	0	15	(ᵃ)	14	(a)	18	0
Latin America and other W. hemisphere	**11**	**0**	**13**	**0**	**29**	**0**	**39**	**0**	**58**	(ᵃ)
South & Central America	9	0	9	0	24	0	33	0	51	(ᵃ)
Argentina	(¹)	0	(¹)	0	1	0	2	0	3	0
Brazil	1	0	1	0	2	0	3	0	5	0
Mexico	4	0	4	0	13	0	16	0	27	(ᵃ)
Venezuela	1	0	1	0	2	0	3	0	4	0
Other	4	0	4	0	6	0	8	0	12	0
Other Western hemisphere	2	0	4	0	6	0	6	0	7	0
Bermuda	(ᵃ)	0	(ᵇ)	0	(ᵇ)	0	(ᵃ)	0	1	0
Other	2	0	(ᵇ)	0	(ᵇ)	0	6	0	6	0
Other Countries	**66**	**0**	**88**	(ᵃ)	**118**	(ᵃ)	**136**	(ᵃ)	**134**	(ᵃ)
Africa	2	0	3	0	3	0	4	0	4	0
South Africa	2	0	2	0	2	0	3	0	3	0
Other	(ᵃ)	0	1	0	1	0	1	0	2	0
Middle East	2	0	4	0	6	0	6	0	10	(ᵃ)
Israel	1	0	2	0	2	0	2	0	4	0
Saudi Arabia	1	0	2	0	3	0	2	0	3	(ᵃ)
Other	1	0	1	0	1	0	2	0	3	0
Asia and Pacific	62	0	81	(ᵃ)	109	(ᵃ)	126	(ᵃ)	120	(ᵃ)
Australia	7	0	9	0	9	0	13	(ᵃ)	13	(ᵃ)
Hong Kong	4	0	8	0	9	0	12	0	13	0
India	(ᵃ)	0	1	0	(ᵃ)	0	(ᵃ)	0	(ᵃ)	0
Indonesia	1	0	1	0	2	0	3	0	4	0
Japan	40	0	48	(ᵃ)	65	(ᵃ)	59	(ᵃ)	44	(ᵃ)
Korea	2	0	3	0	6	0	5	0	7	0
Malaysia	1	0	1	0	2	0	3	0	3	0
New Zealand	1	0	1	0	2	0	3	0	3	0
Philippines	1	0	(ᵃ)	0	1	0	1	0	2	0
Singapore	2	0	2	0	3	0	4	0	5	0
Taiwan	3	0	3	0	4	0	18	0	20	0
Other	1	0	3	0	4	0	5	0	6	0

TABLE 20.3 *contd.*

	1989		1990		1991		1992		1993	
	Exports	*Imports*	*Exports*	*Imports*	*Exports*	*Imports*	*Exports*	*Imports*	*Exports*	*Imports*
International organizations and unallocated	4	([a])	18	2	12	2	10	2	11	1
Addenda										
European Union (12)	87	1	74	([a])	94	1	120	1	127	3
Eastern Europe	0	0	([a])	0	1	([a])	1	([a])	2	0
All countries	**209**	**2**	**242**	**3**	**331**	**3**	**341**	**5**	**408**	**5**

[a] Less than $500,000; [b] Suppressed to avoid disclosure of data of individual companies.

Source: Bureau of Economic Analysis, *Survey of Current Business*, Sept. 1994 [in *Industry & Trade Summary: Franchising*, USITC (1995)]

are also small businesses. Thus, in principle, franchising offers a route to growth for the would-be franchisor and small business opportunities with limited risk for would-be franchisees.

The answer to the question of how many small firms fail is simply that we do not know (Daly and McCann 1992), just as we do not know with precision how many firms there are in any economy. Nonetheless, official statistics, academic research and practical experience all act to foster fairly high failure rate expectations among conventional small firms in their formative years. Though failure rates among young small businesses do appear fairly high, they are probably not as high as is often believed. For instance, US authorities Phillips and Kirchhoff (1989: 69) point out, "Entrepreneurship is clearly an activity involving risk, but the risk of failure is far smaller than popularly believed." They refer to the popular misconception that, "Four out of five new firms fail within the first five years."

After looking at the failure rate levels typical of small businesses, comparing US and UK data, Storey (1994: 109) concludes: "The broad pattern which emerges is that the young are more likely to fail than the old, the very small are more likely to fail than their larger counterparts, and that, for young firms, probably the most powerful influence on their survival is whether or not they grow within a short period after start-up."

Franchise discourse is, by contrast, replete with the message of low risk and high success rates. Indeed, franchising is frequently promoted as a business panacea where the franchisor is almost guaranteed success via access to front-end fees and on-going royalties from franchisees, while the latter are claimed to exhibit a far higher success profile than conventional small businesses due to their access to a "tried-and-tested" or "proven" business formula.

Phillips and Kirchhoff (1989: 74) in their research in small business failures used the US Small Business Administration's 1976–86 Establishment Longitudinal Microdata files and revealed survival rates among start-ups over a 6-year period averaging 40 percent, or better than twice the survival rate suggested by the often quoted adage that four out of five fail in five years. Moreover, for firms that grew, survival rates averaged 66 percent, or two out of three. Growth proved to be a better indicator than sector for failure rate differences. An examination of nine different sector averages showed a sector survival span over 6 years ranging from a low of 35 percent in construction to a high of 47 percent in manufacturing.

The best statistics available in the United Kingdom for practical purposes are those based on VAT (Value Added Tax) registrations and deregistrations, and these reveal a somewhat similar picture to the United States, albeit with slightly higher survival rates in the United Kingdom (Storey 1994: 96). Approximately one-third of all UK small business start-ups fail within 3 years of formation, and about 30 percent survive 10 years (Storey 1994: 104). Rates of failure appear low in the first 12 months of existence, followed by a rapid rise in years 2 and 3. The annual failure rate then falls away to around 7 percent among businesses 10 years old (Daly 1987).

Whereas much of the popular literature on franchising suggests that adoption of the franchise format spells "harvest time" for the entrepreneur, there is a smaller body of expert (though apparently less read) literature that portrays a far different picture. A report commissioned by the US Small Business Administration estimated that initial franchise development costs can exceed $500,000 (Trutko et al. 1993):

> The development of a business from a proven concept through to the sale of its first franchise is typically a long, expensive, and risky process for the franchisor. Even excluding the costs of direct management involvement, the franchisor bears sizeable "upfront" costs for developing a programme before it can be marketed to franchisees.

The *Entrepreneur* Magazine Business Start-Up Guide, *Franchising and Expanding Your Business* (1995: 6), as part of a franchising feasibility questionnaire, poses the question: "Do you have more than $250,000 to invest in the development of your franchise concept?"

Lafontaine and Shaw embarked upon a US franchise system attrition exercise for successive years beginning in 1980. Looking at their most comprehensive data sets, 28.6 percent of 1980 starts survived 12 years and 29.2 percent of 1981 starts survived 11 years. Overall, during the period 1980–92, they identified 2,524 firms entering the franchise industry, of which 1,941 exited during the same period. Lafontaine and Shaw (1997) claim:

> While many firms keep entering into franchising, giving the impression of tremendous growth, many are also exiting, leading to an overall growth rate at best commensurate with that of the economy. . . . From the franchisor's viewpoint, the high rate of exits suggest that many firms fail despite franchising, and many others choose to stop franchising after trying it for a few years. Clearly, these firms have found that franchising is not right for them.

Shane (1996a: 230) tracked 138 US franchise systems with their franchise origins in 1983 and found that only 24.6 percent survived 10 years. He concluded that "the failure rate of new franchise systems approximates that of new organisations." In a follow-up paper, Shane (1996b: 1) commented on the implications of young franchise system failure for would-be franchisees:

> A new franchise system brings with it a high probability that the new franchisor will not be around in future years. . . . Because over half of new franchisors cease to franchise during the first four years, potential franchisees should be very wary of buying into systems that have not yet reached their fourth anniversary.

A similar pattern seems to be evident in the United Kingdom (Stanworth et al. 1997). For instance, Price (1996) constructed a UK franchise database, resulting from a harmonization and conflation of various industry databases, and has calculated the total number of companies offering franchises for sale between 1984 and 1995. A total of 1,658 companies were identified as having been operational; of these, 601 (36 percent) remained in existence at the end of that period. The remaining 1,057 had either failed outright or left franchising by choice, with younger systems displaying higher withdrawal rates than their older counterparts.

The evidence of close similarities between franchise business failure rates and those of conventional small businesses is now strong, certainly if all franchise exits are counted as franchise deaths. However, the evidence points toward franchising being even more risky than conventional small business activity in the first four or five years for both franchisor and franchisee, followed by a period of relatively low failure once break-even has been reached. As Lafontaine points out, franchising does not guarantee success for franchisors or franchisees, and for franchisees investing in less than the very best established franchised businesses, life may well prove even more risky than starting up an independent business. That said, a small minority of leading franchisors account for the majority of franchisees and their chances of continued success appear quite high. Thus, to attempt to quote a single statistic to indicate the probability of success of all franchisors or all franchisees is overly simplistic.

PROPOSITIONS FOR FUTURE RESEARCH

Research to date on franchising has predominantly addressed the themes delineated in this chapter. Of course, several other subjects also receive attention in the literature. The scholarly research is fragmented, typically a function of access to resources or access to data. One effort to provide an integrated approach toward future research is presented in table 20.4 (Stanworth and Curran 1999). The model is based on a set of general propositions that are essentially inferences drawn from the literature on franchising and related subjects relevant to the model. They are *not* offered as laws but as guides for hypothesis generation and testing. Used in this way, the model has the potential to add to theoretical and applied knowledge. As with any model it is incomplete: like other business forms, franchising develops continuously. What, for example, the marriage between franchising and Internet commerce will look like and how the model might need amending to encompass these relations, cannot yet be foreseen.

Franchising at the societal level

Examining franchising at the macro or *societal level* is perhaps the most neglected aspect of franchising and therefore extra attention is given to this here. At this level, *cultural, economic* and *political* contexts may be favorable or unfavorable to franchising and may shift from one to the other. Broadly, in all three there have been changes favorable to the franchised business form in the twentieth century.

In the *cultural realm,* the extent to which economic individualism is a valued

TABLE 20.4 A model of developmental influences on franchising

Franchising at the societal level
Cultural
Economic
Political

Franchising at the organizational level
Rapid market penetration
Capital to finance expansion
Divergent or split economies of scale
Format permanence
Relationship management
Franchise failure rates

Franchising at the individual level
Route into self-employment
Unemployment "push"
Prior self-employment
Complexity of franchisee motivation
System innovation
Contemporary views of autonomy

means of initiating or operating economic activity is of considerable importance. Where such a value is strong, relative to alternative outlets for its expression, franchising may be expected to prosper. Franchisors frequently advertise for new franchisees basing their appeals on values and rewards consistent with economic individualism, i.e., on the psychological and material rewards of self-employment.

In the wider *economic context*, the emergence and persistence of the franchised business will be dependent upon the structure of the economy. To the extent that the economy contains a high proportion of tertiary activities, there is a greater likelihood of the franchised business form. More specifically, where the chain of activities linking producer to consumer become crucially dependent on the final link between the consumer and the distribution outlet, those at the producer end of the chain will find it hard to control the effective meeting of consumer wants. Among solutions to this problem is the formation of joint relationships with independently owned customer servicing outlets. Franchising is a common example of such a relationship.

In the *political context*, the emergence and survival of the franchised business form depends to a large extent on state attitudes to small enterprise. At one extreme, these may take the form of a grudging tolerance as in many former Eastern bloc economies where small independent businesses were only allowed to exist to fill gaps in the provision of goods and services left by large-scale collectively owned producers. In other societies, where small enterprise is seen as highly beneficial to levels of employment and economic activity, as well as symbolizing the positive values of the market-based economic system, the situation is considerably more favorable. The franchised business form will share the benefits to small enterprise of the latter political context. However, the franchised business may also acquire a specific political context in the form of laws governing relations between franchisors and franchisees. These could conceivably operate to restrict the growth of franchising or even bring about its decline, should franchisors find it over-constraining.

Franchising at the organizational level

The *organizational level* of the franchised business form has a relatively well developed, though poorly integrated, literature. It also contains some sharp disagreements. The closest link with the societal level above is with the economic context since it is the implementation of the franchise relationship in organizational terms that provides the focal point of the middle-level concerns of the general theory.

There are six propositions at the organizational level:

1 Franchise organizations, as a variety of business organization, will be common where an initiating organization (which is often relatively small) seeks rapid market penetration through multiple outlets dispersed over a wide geographical area.
2 The above tendency will be reinforced where the initiating organization finds franchisees the most attractive, or only, source of capital to fund rapid expansion.
3 When the linked production and marketing processes associated with the product or service involve strongly divergent or split economies of scale, then again the franchised organizational form may well emerge. Where consumer satisfaction, and hence economic efficiency, is strongly influenced by personnel performance at the point of sale, franchisees who are legally owners and investors in the outlets will usually outperform salaried employees.
4 The franchised business form is relatively permanent and genuine rather than temporary and likely to lapse into the vertically integrated, hierarchical organization. On occasions, particular franchise arrangements may convert to the vertical integrated form but there is no evidence of a widespread trend or cycle of development despite many claims to the contrary.
5 Demonstrating the distinctiveness of the dual organizations, relationships between franchisors and franchisees will, as a matter of operational necessity, contain elements of both agreement and disagreement, harmony and disharmony. Issues ranging from profit levels, fees and contract enforcement, on the one hand, to territorial encroachment, patterns of monitoring and reassignment rights, on the other, will have the potential for conflict. A test of franchisor management will be its facility to contain conflict levels to manageable and nondestructive proportions.
6 Franchise attrition rates, compared to those of independent businesses, will not, in fact, conform to any simplistic and universally applicable ratio, such as sometimes claimed, for example, 8 : 1 or 5 : 1 in favor of franchising. Rather, failure rates will be the result of an interplay between factors such as age of

system, the nature and quality of franchisees' prior experience, sector and niche.

Franchising at the individual level

The third and final level with which the model is concerned is *individual motivation* in franchising, although a narrower usage will be employed than might be first thought appropriate. The individual motivation aspect concerns franchisees who own and run the satellite enterprises associated with the franchisor. Clearly, we might also consider others involved, especially franchisors, but since this was examined at the organizational level, there is no need to pursue it further here. The difference is that franchisor motivation may be usefully treated as a corporate orientation while the franchisee is usually an easily identifiable individual.

The model encompasses six propositions at the individual level:

1 The franchised business form will exist most successfully in societies where there is a supply of individuals positively committed to economic individualism in the form of small business ownership. Compared with other forms of self-employment, franchises may offer a relatively easy way of achieving the transition from employee to self-employed.

2 Franchising may also prove attractive to individuals less fundamentally committed to economic individualism but who find themselves constrained by the wider labor market as a result of economic restructuring and redundancy, life-cycle position or sheer lack of human capital.

3 Franchisees will not necessarily be drawn from risk-averse sections of the population, as distinct from those entering more conventional forms of self-employment. At the very least, a substantial minority (as high as one-third to one-half) will be drawn from those with experience of self-employment.

4 Patterns of franchisee motivation will be more varied and complex than the notions of profit maximization or problems of hierarchical control embedded in agency theory or similar explanations of franchise motivation tend to suggest. For franchisees with no prior experience of self-employment, for instance, notions of independence and autonomy act as strong early motivators. For those with experience of self-employment, although intrinsic goals may yield to extrinsic goals like security and profitability, intrinsic goals are likely to remain significant. Franchisor advertising will typically acknowledge the importance of both kinds of goals.

5 Franchisees can make a substantial contribution to processes of franchise system innovation. As systems grow and become more mature, this contribution will be increasingly formalized.

6 It is wrong to view the patterns of economic self-autonomy that emerged from nineteenth-century capitalist economies as the "pure" institutionalized form compared to which more recent forms are merely debased expressions. For many, the franchised business may, in some ways, realize the cultural values of independence, autonomy, material rewards and even creativity more effectively than older established forms.

The fifteen propositions that form this initial outline of a general theory of franchising in table 20.4 are intended as a skeleton only. Additional propositions will be required at all three levels to flesh out the theory and especially to increase specificity.

As this chapter has demonstrated, and as Shane and Hoy (1996: 326) expressed in their first special issue of the *Journal of Business Venturing*, "Franchising raises important research questions for entrepreneurship scholars."

REFERENCES

Barkoff, R.M. and Giresi, M.A. 1996. Burger King's Collaborative Solution to Encroachment. *Leaders Franchising Business and Law Alert*, 1–4.

Baucus, D., Baucus, M. and Human, S. 1996. Consensus in Franchise Organizations: A Co-operative Arrangement among Entrepreneurs. *Journal of Business Venturing* 11: 359–78.

Bull, I. and Willard, G.E. 1993. Towards a Theory of Entrepreneurship. *Journal of Business Venturing* 8: 183–95.

Caves, R.E. and Murphy, W.F. 1976, Franchising: Firms, Markets and Intangible Assets. *Southern Economic Journal* 42: 572–86.

Curran, J. and Stanworth, J. 1983. Franchising in the Modern Economy – Towards a Theoretical Understanding. *International Small Business Journal* 2(1): 8–26.

Curran, J. and Blackburn R.A. 1991. Changes in the Context of Enterprise: Some Socio-economic and Environmental Factors Facing Small Firms in the 1990s. In: J. Curran and R.A. Blackburn (eds.), *Paths of Enterprise: The Future of the Small Firm*. London: Routledge.

Daly, M. 1987. Lifespan of Businesses Registered for VAT. *British Business* (April 3): 28–9

Daly, M. and McCann, A. 1992. How Many Small Firms? *Employment Gazette* (London) 100(2): 47–52.

Dant, R. and Berger, P. 1996. Modeling Co-operative Advertising Decisions in Franchising. *Journal of the Operations Research Society* 47: 1120–36.

Dant, R.P. and Gundlach, G.T. 1999. The Challenge of Autonomy and Dependence in Franchised Channels of Distribution. *Journal of Business Venturing* 14(1): 35–68.

Dant, R.P. and Kaufmann, P.J. 1999. Preface to the Special Issue on Franchising, *Journal of Business Venturing* 14(1): 1–4.

Dant, R.P. and Schul, P.L. 1992. Conflict Resolution Processes in Contractual Channels of Distribution. *Journal of Marketing* 56: 38–54.

Dant, R.P., Kaufmann, P.J. and Paswan A.K. 1992. Ownership Redirection in Franchised Channels. *Journal of Public Policy and Marketing* 11: 33–44.

Dant, R.P., Paswan, A.K. and Stanworth, J. 1996. Ownership Redirection Trends in Franchising. *International Journal of Entrepreneurial Behavior and Research* 2(3): 48–67.

Darr, E., Argote, L. and Epple, D. 1995. The Acquisition, Transfer and Depreciation of Knowledge in Service Organizations: Productivity in Franchises. *Management Science* 41: 1750–62.

Eroglu, S. 1992. The Internationalisation Process of Franchise Systems: A Conceptual Model. *International Marketing Review* 6(5): 19–30.

Frazier, G.L. and Summers, J.O. 1986. Perceptions of Interfirm Power and its Use Within a Franchise Channel of Distribution. *Journal of Marketing Research* 23: 169–76.

Goffee, R. and Scase, R. 1995. *Corporate Realities: The Dynamics of Large and Small Organisations*. London: Routledge.

Goss, D. 1991. *Small Business and Society*. London: Routledge.

Hoy, F. 1994. The Dark Side of Franchising. *International Small Business Journal* 12(2): 26–38.

Hoy, F. 1998. Franchising and Government Initiatives: The US Experience and International Implications. Paper presented to the 5th Annual Strategy Seminar, International Franchise Research Centre, London, July.

Hoy, F. and Shane, S. 1998. Franchising as an Entrepreneurial Venture Form. *Journal of Business Venturing* 13(2): 91–4.

Hunt, S.D. 1972. The Socioeconomic Consequences of the Franchise System of Distribution. *Journal of Marketing* 36: 32–8.

Hunt, S.D. 1973. The Trend towards Company-Operated Units in Franchise Chains. *Journal of Retailing* 49(2): 3–12.

Hunt, S.D. 1977. Franchising: Promises, Problems, Prospects. *Journal of Retailing* (53): 71–84.

Hunt, S.D. and Nevin, J.R. 1976. Full Disclosure Laws in Franchising: An Empirical Investigation. *Journal of Marketing* 40: 53–62.

Izraeli, D. 1972. *Franchising and the Total Distribution System*. London: Longmans.

Justis, R.T., Olsen, J.E. and Chan, P.S. 1993. Using Market Research to Enhance Franchisee/ Franchisor Relationships. *Journal of Small Business Management* 32(2): 121–7.

Kaufmann, P.J. and Dant, R.P. 1999. Franchising and the Domain of Entrepreneurship Research. *Journal of Business Venturing* 14(1): 5–16.

Lafontaine, F. and Kaufmann, P.J. 1994. The Evolution of Ownership Patterns in Franchise Systems. *Journal of Retailing* 70(2): 97–113.

Lafontaine, F. and Shaw, K. 1997. Franchising Growth in the US Market: Myth and Reality. *Proceedings of the Eleventh Conference of the Society of Franchising*, Orlando, Fla., March 1–2.

Lillis, C.M., Narayana, C.L. and Gilman, J.R. 1976. Competitive Advantage Variation over the Life Cycle of a Franchise. *Journal of Marketing* (October): 77–80.

McIntyre, F.S., Young, J.A. and Gilbert, F.W. 1997. A Strategic Alliance Perspective of Franchise Relationships. *Franchising Research* 2(1): 6–14.

Mills, C.W. 1956. *White Collar*. New York: Galaxy.

Nevin, J.R., Hunt, S.D. and Ruekert, P.W. 1980. The Impact of Fair Practice Laws on a Franchise Channel of Distribution. *MSU Business Topics* 28(3): 27–37.

Oxenfeldt, A.R. and Kelly, A.O. 1969. Will Successful Franchise Systems Become Wholly Owned Chains? *Journal of Retailing* 44(4): 69–83.

Ozanne, U.B. and Hunt, S.D. 1971. *The Economic Effects of Franchising*. Washington, DC: Select Committee on Small Business.

Phillips, B. and Kirchhoff, B. 1989. Formation, Growth and Survival; Small Firm Dynamics in the US Economy. *Small Business Economics* 1: 65–74

Porter, J.L. and Renforth, W. 1978. Franchise Agreements, Spotting the Important Legal Issues. *Journal of Small Business Management* 160(4): 27–31.

Price, S. 1996. *Behind the Veneer of Success: Propensities for UK Franchisor Failure*. Milton Keynes, UK: Small Business Research Trust.

Riesman, D. 1950. *The Lonely Crowd*. New Haven, Conn.: Yale University Press.

Rubin, P.H. 1978. The Theory of the Firm and the Structure of the Franchise Contract. *Journal of Law and Economics* 21: 223–33.

Schul, P.L., Pride, W.M. and Little, T.L. 1983. The Impact of Channel Leadership Behavior on Intrachannel Conflict. *Journal of Marketing* 47: 21–34.

Shane, S. 1996a. Hybrid Organizational Arrangements and Their Implications for Firm Growth and Survival: A Study of New Franchisors. *Academy of Management Journal* 39: 216–34.

Shane, S. 1996b. *Differences between Successful and Unsuccessful Franchisors*. Report produced for the Office of Advocacy, US Small Business Administration, cited in *The Info Franchise Newsletter* (January).

Shane, S.A. and Hoy, F. 1996. Franchising: A Gateway to Cooperative Entrepreneurship. *Journal of Business Venturing* 11(5): 325–8.

Sibley, S.D. and Michie, D.A. 1982. An Exploratory Investigation of Co-operation in a Franchise Channel. *Journal of Retailing* 58(4): 23–45.

Sklar, F. 1977. Franchises and Independence: Interorganisational Power Relations in a Contractual Context. *Urban Life* 6(1): 33–52.

Spinelli, S. and Birley S. 1996. Towards a Theory of Conflict in the Franchise System. *Journal of Business Venturing* 11: 329–42.

Stanworth, J. 1984. *A Study of Power Relationships and Their Consequences in Franchise Organizations.* Report submitted to the Social Science Research Council, London.

Stanworth, J. and Curran, J. 1999 (forthcoming). Colas, Burgers, Shakes and "Shirkers": Towards a Sociological Model of Franchising in the Market Economy. *Journal of Business Venturing.*

Stanworth, J. and Purdy, D. 1998. Introduction to *Breaking Out of the Home Market*, 5th Annual Strategy Seminar, International Franchise Research Centre, London, July.

Stanworth, J., Curran, J. and Hough, J. 1983. The Franchised Small Enterprise: Formal and Operational Dimensions of Independence. In J. Lewis, J. Stanworth and A. Gibb (eds.), *Success and Failure in Small Business.* Aldershot, U.K.: Gower Publishing.

Stanworth, J., Purdy, D. and Price, S. 1997. Franchise Growth and Failure in the US and the UK: A Troubled Dreamworld Revisited. *Franchising Research* 2(2): 75–94.

Storey, D. 1994. *Understanding the Small Business Sector.* London and New York: Routledge.

Trutko, J., Trutko, J. and Kostecka, A. 1993. *Franchising's Growing Role in the US Economy, 1975–2000.* Washington, D.C.: US Small Business Administration

Vaughn, C.L. 1979. *Franchising, Its Nature, Scope, Advantages and Development*, 2nd edn, Lexington, Mass.: Lexington Books.

Whyte, W.H. 1956. *The Organization Man.* New York: Simon and Schuster.

CONCLUSIONS

Remaining Issues and Suggestions for Further Research
HANS LANDSTRÖM AND DONALD L. SEXTON

21

Remaining Issues and Suggestions for Further Research

HANS LANDSTRÖM AND DONALD L. SEXTON

CHANGING RESEARCH THRUSTS
CONTINUING RESEARCH NEEDS
RESEARCH NEEDS AND ISSUES: A BROADER PERSPECTIVE
RESEARCH NEEDS AND ISSUES: PUBLIC POLICY
RESEARCH NEEDS AND ISSUES: FINANCING GROWTH
RESEARCH NEEDS AND ISSUES: GROWTH
CONCLUSIONS

There have been major changes in entrepreneurship, entrepreneurship research, and the importance of entrepreneurship to the economy since the first state-of-the-art in entrepreneurship research book was published in 1982. In response to the changing world economy and research needs, this, the fifth state-of-the-art book and the first international book explores several new areas. In addition, it includes carryover research topics addressed in the earlier volumes that are still in need of additional research to advance our understanding.

Major changes in the political and public policy world include:

1 Recognition of growing businesses as a major component of a country's economic development;
2 Changes from a controlled economy to a free market in eastern Europe;
3 Advancements in research that have moved the field forward and identified new topics;
4 Technological advancements in communications that provide rapid and efficient transfer of information.

CHANGING RESEARCH THRUSTS

Research in entrepreneurship has changed considerably since 1980 and the first state-of-the-art research conference in 1980 and the book in 1982. (Kent et al.1982). At that time, the field was beginning to emerge, and a few serious researchers were turning their attention to entrepreneurship.

By the second conference and book in 1985, the field was beginning to become more structured, and broader concepts started to appear. The implications, process and components of growth replaced studies of the entrepreneur, and distinctions were drawn between entrepreneurs as growth-oriented firms and small businesses (Sexton and Smilor 1986).

The third conference and book occurred in 1990 as the field of entrepreneurship began to be recognized for its enormity and importance. Concurrent with developments in the academic research field of the entrepreneurship studies was the recognition of entrepreneurship as a major contributor to the economy of the United States (Sexton and Kasarda 1992).

At the fourth conference in 1997, many topics changed to reflect the changing issues that confront researchers as the field had emerged. With this conference new topics such as harvesting the firm, family business, and ethnic entrepreneurship were introduced broadening the concept of entrepreneurship (Sexton and Smilor 1997).

The attitude of entrepreneurship researchers toward their field has changed from wonderment in 1980, to excitement in 1985, to an awareness of the magnitude of their tasks in 1990 and in 1997, concern over the changes needed to continue the current momentum into the new century. The current concerns in this book are how can we work together to further our understanding of the globalization of entrepreneurship.

CONTINUING RESEARCH NEEDS

Suggestions of research needs and issues that have been discussed in the past and continue to pose problems include:

1 Databases that can provide larger samples and longitudinal data within specific industries;

2 Theory development and testing to provide direction and research concepts to the field;

3 Quality research from large samples with higher response rates and a definition of the subject of the study to allow replication of the studies to a larger population;

4 Collaborative approach to international entrepreneurship research to allow the discovery of the most powerful rather than the most favorable practices;

5 Recognition that the stakeholders in entrepreneurship go beyond fellow academicians and students to public policymakers and practicing entrepreneurs.

Timmons and Sapienza (1992) called for research that is relevant to the various stakeholders in our efforts. They further iterated that for results to be relevant, researchers must understand "the realities and nuances" of an industry. The consequences of ignorance, they warn, are threefold: (1) we risk alienating the subjects of our inquiries, thus severing our access to data and interviews; (2) we risk ridicule by those who are knowledgeable and informed about the industry, and (3) we risk ridicule by researchers in other fields who might dismiss our work out of hand. These warnings are as important now as they were when the authors made them in 1992.

The chapters in this book were identified via a survey of leading researchers in Europe and North America. After the topics were selected, nominations were made for the person or persons most knowledgeable on the topic. Since this book was designed to be an international approach to entrepreneurship research, approximately 60 percent of the chapters were developed by European authors or authors who have worked in Europe as visiting professors or research associates.

In 1982, when the entrepreneurship field was beginning to emerge, the major topics were financing, economic impact and the psychology and sociology of entrepreneurs. In 1986, the topics began to converge on financing, growth, the process of entrepreneurship and research methodology. By the third book in 1992, the major emphasis was on research methodology, growth and financing. In 1997, the convergence continued with emphasis on financing, growth, research methodology and the process of entrepreneurship. In this book, the major emphasis is on public policy, research, growth and financing. This shows the change in research interests since the late 1970s. The addition of the public policy area was to examine and compare the influences by governments on the free market economy and to compare regulatory and reporting policies in Europe and the United States in order to gain information that might lead to "leveling the field" in international competition.

The purposes of the state-of-the-art research books are to allow faculty in other areas considering involvement in entrepreneurship research to identify current research topics and to evaluate the literature and methodology in the field. A second purpose is to provide research needs and issues for doctoral students writing dissertations in the field. A third area is to provide public policymakers with comparisons of other countries. Finally, a fourth objective is to make entrepreneur researchers aware of the research needs and to encourage their participation in advancing the field.

RESEARCH NEEDS AND ISSUES: A BROADER PERSPECTIVE

The first part of the book is organized to provide an overview of research in research methodology and entrepreneurship/small business public policy in the United States. This part provides a general overview of the parts and topics for the remainder of the book. The second part examines and compares government impacts on entrepreneurship in Europe. Financing growth, the third part, has been a topic in each previous book and is still of major importance. The final part examines a number of papers related to both internal and external approaches to achieving growth.

Aldrich in chapter 1 examines differences in entrepreneurship support and methodology between Europe and North America and suggests the following:

- ◆ Without a single paradigm, the multiple coherent points of view will be of limited topical concern and value to practicing entrepreneurs.

- Researchers on both sides of the Atlantic have a stake in maintaining diversity in the field of entrepreneurship studies.
- Until the private databases under development are available for access, researchers must continue to rely on government data collected for administrative and regulatory purposes.

Davidsson and Wiklund examine the theoretical and conceptual issues in growth in chapter 2 and make the following observations:

- An explicit conceptualization of the firm needs to be developed.
- The firm conceptualization should be matched with the purpose, theories and methods when conducting growth studies.
- Researchers need to develop and evaluate growth models and patterns of firm growth.
- Research will be improved by larger samples, higher response rates and longitudinal studies of industry specific firms.

Hitt and Ireland in chapter 3 assess the research intersections between entrepreneurship and strategic management. They suggest the two areas will complement each other and recommend joint research to resolve the following:

- What are the most effective modes of entry? That is, how do entrepreneurs decide when, what scale and what markets to enter?
- Cooperative arrangements are becoming a preferred choice for entering new markets. When should arrangements be used for defensive purposes rather than offensive or proactive purposes?
- What role has the internationalization of entrepreneurial firms played in the transitioning economies?
- What role has entrepreneurial firms played in economic development initiatives?

Dennis in chapter 4 reviews entrepreneurship/small business policy in the United States and concludes:

- Mathematical models for measuring the impact of policies and regulations on smaller businesses need to be developed.
- International research cooperation and participation in policy areas is increasingly valuable. Researchers often encounter similar questions even when the specific issues and their contexts are quite different.
- Researchers working in the smaller business public policy areas need to devote resources to investigating the relationship and influence of the growth and size variables on competition, and vice versa.
- Research on regulatory impact should be conducted before the regulations are issued.

Research Needs and Issues: Public Policy

This part examines the public policies in different countries and regions in Europe to understand the impact of these policies on entrepreneurship.

De in chapter 5 studies small and medium entrepreneurial (SME) policies throughout Europe and raises some interesting questions:

- What will be the impact of the new trend in Europe that places more emphasis on transfers in kind rather than transfers in cash?
- Does stimulating job creation in SMEs really lower unemployment, or does this prevalent problem in most European countries have other reasons?
- Do SMEs create more employment relative to large enterprises or is it, rather, a problem of SMEs being restricted to national and rigid labor markets?

Audretsch in chapter 6 researches the climate for entrepreneurship in Germany and suggests that researchers address their attention to the following:

- What can be learned from the German economic crisis of the 1990s that resulted in the highest rate of unemployment since the 1930s?
- Why is it that, in Germany, net job creation rates and firm size are not systematically related?
- What is the extent of rigidities and constraints on the impact of entrepreneurial activity in the high-technology area?

Horst, Nijsen and Gulhan in chapter 7 examine the impact of regulatory policies on SMEs in Europe and make the following observations:

- Studies of the costs of administrative burdens have been limited; studies are needed at the national and regional level.
- At what level – European, national or regional – should policies be formulated?
- What would be the impact on SMEs if the European Community utilized directives rather than regulations?

Mugler in chapter 8 researches the climate for entrepreneurship in the European countries in transition and notes:

- What are the main factors that crucially influence the behavior of people and subsequently the development of entrepreneurial activities in the process of transition?
- A standardized definition of micro, small and medium-sized enterprises is necessary to permit replication of previous studies.
- Research is needed to increase the political awareness of the SME sector to encourage a more favorable climate.

Storey in chapter 9 asks and answers the question of why regulatory and reporting requirements never go away. He maintains that:

- If evaluation is a fundamental principle prerequisite in the specification of the objectives of policy, why don't programs include evaluations?
- Almost all small policies involve an element of relation, either administrative selection or "soft selection." The challenge to researchers is to address the issues of selection.
- Studies are needed to persuade policymakers that it is in their long-term interests to carefully appraise policy and to be involved with the appraisal before policies are introduced.

RESEARCH NEEDS AND ISSUES: FINANCING GROWTH

This part explores the area of financing growth, with special emphasis on financing outside of the United States. *Donckels* in chapter 10 suggests:

- The relationship between the financial structure and the development phase of the company needs to be examined closely when studying the funding of growth.
- Attention must be devoted to the decision-making process of the various stakeholders involved with the funding of SMEs.
- Attention needs to be given to the validity of the data and to methodological and definitional problems.
- To what extent can the objectives of the entrepreneur, those of the firm and those of the family be combined with a growth strategy?

Mason and Harrison in chapter 11 examine the difficult state-of-the-art research in the informal venture capital (IVC) area and ask the following questions:

- Does financial theory apply in the IVC market?
- Would the field be enhanced if it moved from studies of the actors in the IVC market to studies of the market itself?
- What role has IVC played in the European countries in transition and in other area such as Latin America and the Pacific Rim?
- What are the investment allocations decisions, and are they affected by the industry, the market and the distance from the firm?

Manigart and Sapienza in chapter 12 provide a joint European and United States background and ask questions and provide observations regarding venture capital and growth:

- There is a need for the development of theories of value creation for venture capital (VC) arrangements.
- What is the role of the venture capitalist as an agent of limited partners, syndicates and entrepreneurs?
- How extensive and how effective is the venture capitalist's post investment involvement? What are the impacts of the differences among monitoring, influencing and assisting?
- What are the effects of the venture capitalist's exit strategies on the entrepreneurial firm?

Amit, Bander and Zott in chapter 13 examine VC financing in Canada and develop a research agenda. They suggest:

- The field needs to develop theoretical structures that can be validated empirically to provide normative implications for practice.
- How much do ownership and capital structures impact on the performance of entrepreneurial firms?
- Do markets for VC sometimes fail? If so, what are the main contributors to the failure?
- What is the appropriate rate of government intervention in the VC market?

RESEARCH NEEDS AND ISSUES: GROWTH

Growth is the essence of entrepreneurship. It is growth that separates status quo or low-growth firms from the fast-growth entrepreneurial firms. Growth can occur either as a result of internal actions of the firm or actions that have utilized external factors in pursuit of growth.

Birley and Stockley in chapter 14 examine the impact of the entrepreneurial team on firm growth. They maintain that growth is more likely to occur when a team of individuals, rather than a single entrepreneur, make the policy decisions of the firm. Some of the concerns they raise include:

- What constitutes a strategic or entrepreneurial team, and what is the impact of the team on the process of growth?
- Studies are needed that provide an empirical and theoretical understanding of the entrepreneurial team on new venture performance.
- Models that consider the relationship between individuals, groups and the environment are needed to explain the variance in venture performance.
- How does the composition of the team affect the strategy and performances of the firm?

Arbaugh and Camp in chapter 15 note that much research is still required in the area of management transitions as the firm grows. They suggest that future researchers examine:

- The role of the industry context in transitions.
- The need for more specific operationalizations of resources.
- Examination of resource deployment decisions related to managing present growth and preparing for future growth.
- The impact of growth transitions on managerial knowledge and capabilities.

Autio in chapter 16 examines the growth in new technology-based firms (NTBF) and suggests:

- A theory needs to be developed that links technology, social capital, market creation and growth.
- Are the growth rate of firms different in high-externality environments?
- Are there concepts in innovation theory that may be applicable to growth in high-technology firms?
- What can we learn from market creation through interorganizational relationships?

Cooper and Folta address the issue of clusters among high-tech firms in chapter 17. They offer a number of research questions:

- What characteristics affect new firm formation within a cluster?
- Are there differences in the perceptions of risks and rewards associated with entrepreneurship for potential founders in and outside of clusters?
- How do firm characteristics including size, strategy and degree of vertical integration bear upon the costs and benefits of cluster location?
- Are there performance benefits for technically oriented firms starting in clusters even if the firms are in different industries?

Johannisson in chapter 18 addresses issues related to expanding our knowledge in the area of networking and entrepreneurial growth. He suggests that future research efforts should address:

- How is the transfer of resources between terminated and new ventures accomplished?
- Is it possible that the dynamics of the venturing process is really the outcome of linkages between individuals and firms across firm boundaries?
- Is the building of social capital as important to entrepreneurs as accessing financial capital and investing in human capital?
- How does information technology influence the personal networking of individual entrepreneurs and interaction within organizing contacts such as industrial districts?

Weaver in chapter 19 continues to examine external vehicles for growth through his consideration of strategic alliances. In addition to stressing the need to develop models of outcome and performance alliances, he also asks the following questions:

- What have been the problems and successes of strategic alliances in more specific focused groups, such as industry or growth rate?
- What are the problems associated with partner selection and maintenance issues in strategic alliances?
- What is the role of and need for external stimuli to foster and facilitate alliances?

Hoy, Stanworth and Purdy in chapter 20 examine a somewhat different approach to cooperative arrangements in their examination of franchising activities. They suggest a number of questions that will enhance our understanding of an entrepreneurial slant to franchising.

- What are the issues of franchisor–franchisee agreements, and how do these issues lead to conflicts?
- How are the problems different between a franchisor that sells franchises and those that sell products and services?
- What are the true failure rates of franchises? How do these failure rates compare with independent businesses?
- How must a franchisee adapt to meet the cultural expectation in different countries and how do these factors affect the ability to compete?

CONCLUSIONS

The field of entrepreneurship and entrepreneurship research has changed, is changing and will continue to change, providing a better understanding of the phenomenon of entrepreneurship. Some aspects of entrepreneurship have developed more rapidly than others. For those that have developed slowly, the problems appear to be the lack of databases, the limited number of researchers addressing the topic and the lack of a coordinated effort in a particular research stream. This book has identified a number of research questions and issues for future researchers to consider – questions and issues that will enhance our understanding of the field.

In closing, it is the hope of the authors and the editors that this book, like the ones that have preceded it, will soon become obsolete as new and more research advances the field of entrepreneurship. As an academic discipline it is our wish that this book will make a difference in the economic development and well-being in Europe and North America.

As we learn more about the field, old questions or issues are resolved and new ones arise. Oliver Wendell Holmes stated "I find the great thing in this world is not so much where we stand, as in what direction we are moving." A comment that reflects the state of entrepreneurship today. Finally, William Harvey in 1628 noted that "all that we know is infinitely less than all that still remains unknown." A thought that will continue to be with us as we continue our efforts to expand our knowledge in the future.

REFERENCES

Kent, C., Sexton, D. and Vesper, K. 1982. *The Encyclopedia of Entrepreneurship*. Englewood Cliffs, NJ: Prentice-Hall.
Sexton, D. and Kasarda, J. 1992. *The State of the Art of Entrepreneurship*. Boston: PWS-Kent.
Sexton, D. and Smilor, R. 1986. *The Art and Science of Entrepreneurship*. Cambridge, MA: Ballinger.
Sexton, D. and Smilor R. 1997. *Entrepreneurship 2000*. Chicago: Upstart.
Timmons, J. and Sapienza, H. 1992. Venture Capital: The Decade Ahead. In D. Sexton and J. Kasarda (eds), *The State of the Art of Entrepreneurship*. Boston, PWS-Kent, 402–37.

Index